This book is dedicated to Bruce Laval—the father of guestology

CONTENTS

Chapter 12: Measuring and Managing Service Delivery

Chapter 13: Fixing Service Failures

Chapter 14: Service Excellence: Leading the Way to Wow!

FOREWORD

Whenever I am in the Orlando area, I try to meet with Bob Ford. He is one of the best scholars of hospitality management. I find that spending an afternoon with Bob fills me with both energy and curiosity. He has an uncanny ability to identify areas of opportunity and to discuss common practices in the hospitality industry and how we can investigate ways to improve them. I value his insights and his ability to recognize the real issues that we need to resolve with service delivery systems, so much so that I have had him come to Houston to spend a day with our faculty.

Through this book, everyone can spend a day with Professor Robert Ford. Bob loves to spend time with hospitality executives, discussing what keeps them up at night. This discussion provides him with not only a real understanding of the industry but also anecdotes he uses to illustrate his text. The examples of best practices presented in this book make it an interesting read. This book is structured as a textbook, but any manager of a hospitality organization will find the time spent reading this book a good investment.

The research suggests that there truly are important differences between managing a service organization and managing a tangible goods producing organization. Yet, there are very few books on the management of services. This book is the only one I know of on the management of hospitality services. When I taught services management, my choice for a text was Bob's *Managing the Guest Experience in Hospitality*. I come from a marketing background. Bob often reminds me that marketers make promises and operators have to deliver those promises. This book explains how to deliver the promise.

This book has been completely updated from *Managing the Guest Experience in Hospitality* with new examples and the latest thought on service management. Although Disney provides great examples of how to deliver great service, the book has been expanded to include examples from a diverse set of hospitality organizations, including international organizations. This inclusion will make it interesting and relevant to students going into any area of the hospitality industry and to students from across the globe. Michael Sturman, the Kenneth and Marjorie Blanchard Professor of Human Resources at Cornell University, joins Bob Ford in this edition. One of Michael's additions is his knowledge of compensation and staffing in the hospitality industry. Michael's research articles have been featured in the top management journals. He is known for his ability to communicate the implications of this research to practitioners and is former editor of and a frequent contributor to the *Cornell Hospitality Quarterly*.

I am delighted that Bob and Mike have created *Managing Quality Service in Hospitality: How Organizations Achieve Excellence in the Guest Experience*, based on *Managing the Guest Experience*. I am delighted not only for myself, but also for my *guests*, the students of hospitality management. I strongly recommend *Managing Quality Service in Hospitality* as a must read for hospitality managers and a text for hospitality management programs.

John Bowen
Dean and Barron Hilton Distinguished Chair
Conrad N. Hilton College
University of Houston

PREFACE

Welcome to *Managing Quality Service in Hospitality*. While this book may look familiar to those who have read *Managing the Guest Experience in Hospitality*, it is so different that we felt it was necessary to change the name. The book continues to be based on the principles of *guestology*, and that means we practice in writing this book what we teach in class. So, we kept some of the positive features of the earlier book while changing those that our readers said needed to be changed.

The book is based on much of what the first author learned when he came to Orlando to head the hospitality program at the University of Central Florida. There, he learned about many different aspects of the hospitality industry from The Walt Disney Company, and specifically about the principles of guestology from its "father," Bruce Laval. Disney was then and still is today a benchmark hospitality organization. People come from all over the world to learn how to use Disney's guestological techniques and apply those principles to their own guest-focused organizations. If there seems to be an abundance of examples in this book from Walt Disney World, there is a reason. This is a visible and familiar service exemplar that most students can relate to easily and which many have visited. Disney also provides an exceptionally wide representation of the hospitality industry. It has successful examples of restaurants from quick-serve to fine dining; lodging from campgrounds to upscale hotels; a transportation system that includes trains, boats, buses, and monorails; catering services, convention and meeting planning services, entertainment and night clubs, retail stores, golf courses, and cruise ships. These organizations include almost every specific job category in the hospitality field. The range of jobs for study on the Disney property—in terms of staffing, training, motivating, and job performance—is very wide. Disney hires and trains thousands of people annually to fill 1,100 different positions.

But there are many other exemplars: companies that use best practices to successfully deliver great service. Aside from Disney, there are many more examples from hotels, restaurants, amusement parks, airlines, and even others that may, at first glance, not appear to be in the service industry. In today's business environment, almost all companies need to know how to provide exceptional service, or their customers will go to their competitors that can. We hope that you will be able to learn from these examples, from firms both familiar and new to you, and see the application of the principles and ideas in the book to whatever hospitality organizations are near you.

We also hope that you will find this book as clearly written and rich in content and real-world examples as its predecessor book. We worked hard to improve the things our student readers and faculty teachers liked while changing what needed to be changed. A lot has happened in the past decade, and this book contains new content to reflect those changes. We hope you like our work and invite you to tell us how well we did or where we could have done better. As practicing guestologists, we sought the input of many former guests and those who were seeking more coverage of managerial topics than is currently available in hospitality texts. We did what we tell you to do as practicing guestologists—ask, ask, ask your guests what they want, need, and expect from an experience. After all, it doesn't matter what we think is a great book if our guests don't see it that way.

We have made two big changes while writing this book. The first involves the changes that have occurred with people. Guests of the late twentieth century are different from today's guests. The current generation of employees now entering the labor force is also different with different expectations, capabilities, and behaviors than the last. The second big change is in the forces impacting the organization. Competitors and the nature of competition have changed. Suppliers are different, technology is very different, and hospitality organizations have discovered that the global nature that all business operates in today impacts them too. We are all hooked together somehow and the result of these global connections is a change in how we manage the guest experience in hospitality.

We have made other changes as well to make the book more relevant in an era where social responsibility, ethics, and environmental concerns are increasingly part of the hospitality manager's world. In each chapter, we have added an ethical dilemma to discuss. Our references have been selected to give the student and instructor further information on each chapter's topics for expanding lectures, opening knowledge doors for papers, more in-depth study of related topics, and offering starting places for further research. We have also included classic references to allow the student to trace the evolution of ideas back to their roots.

Finally, we want to point out that customer service by itself will not save a bad strategy, ineffective staffing, or poorly designed and operated business systems. On the other hand, the research shows that once a business is efficiently run, customer service can give it a sustainable competitive advantage. A big friendly smile won't make up for a ruined meal but a wow service encounter with a well-trained and motivated server can make a routine experience into an unmatchable wow that guests will remember and come back to have again. The exciting thing to us is how great an opportunity this is for gaining a competitive advantage over others in whatever hospitality business you are in. A quick look at the most recent American Customer Satisfaction Index (online) will show that most businesses are at the "C" level in providing customer satisfaction. Where else in the world can you be only a little above average to be seen as "outstanding"? We hope that the lessons learned and the concepts presented here will help you become accomplished guestologists and receive an "outstanding" from your guests.

Purpose of the Book

This book is an attempt to organize, integrate, and present information about managing hospitality organizations, some of which comes from academic studies and some from the school of experience. It has been written to meet the needs of college classes devoted to or including exploration of this exciting, undeveloped area. It should also be of help to executives and managers who want to implement a guest-focused service strategy in any hospitality or service organization that wants to compete successfully in today's customer-driven market.

This book fills a void. Up until now, instructors and students in hospitality management classes have had to use a text that combined services marketing with some services management, with specific applications to restaurants, lodging, and other hospitality areas made by the instructor or by means of handouts and articles on serving guests in hospitality settings. *Managing Quality Service in Hospitality* fills that void. It combines the findings of the most significant research on services and hospitality services in particular with the best practices of leading hospitality organizations such as The Walt Disney Company, Marriott, The Ritz-Carlton, Darden Restaurants, Southwest Airlines, and many others.

In addition to reviews by numerous college and university instructors of hospitality, the material has been reviewed by practicing executives from many successful hospitality organizations, such as The Walt Disney Company, Starwood Hotels, Gaylord Hotels, Hyatt Hotels, Sodexo, Darden Restaurants, and Sheraton Hotels. These academic and practitioner reviews have assured that the text content is supported by sound theoretical underpinnings and real-world findings.

The Hospitality Principles

Managing Quality Service in Hospitality represents theory that has passed the test of relevance. A proven principle of hospitality management keys each chapter of this book. Leading hospitality organizations have found these principles to be important, workable, and useful. They represent the key points to keep in mind when putting the book's material into practice. They can guide hospitality organizations and their managers as they seek to reach the levels of excellence achieved by the benchmark organizations.

Systematic Sequence

To communicate the content of *Managing Quality Service in Hospitality* as clearly as possible, we have used a simple structure for the book so that its organization could be one of this book's major features. One section is devoted to each of hospitality management's three major concerns: *strategy*, *staffing*, and *systems*. Each of the fourteen chapters is keyed to a principle of successful hospitality management.

Section 1, *The Hospitality Service Strategy*, begins by Chapter 1 explaining some of the book's major concepts: some differences between products and services; what is meant by guestology; meeting customer expectations; the three parts of the guest experience; and the definitions of quality, value, and cost in a guest service context. This section then moves to Chapter 2's thorough coverage of the planning processes used to assess and meet guest expectations. Also explained are essential planning topics such as quantitative and qualitative forecasting tools; the importance of demographic trends; and the organization's service strategy origins in its vision, purpose, and mission, which themselves are based on the organization's careful assessment of guest expectations. Chapter 3 describes why the service setting or environment is crucial to service success. We have employed numerous examples to illustrate the principles and best practices of creating an appropriate setting. Section 1 concludes with Chapter 4's discussion of the importance to the hospitality organization of a total service culture and how to achieve it.

Section 2, *The Hospitality Service Staff*, covers how to recruit and hire "persons who love to serve" in Chapter 5, how to train them in Chapter 6, and then how to motivate and empower them to provide outstanding guest service in Chapter 7. A topic that many students and practitioners find particularly important is covered in Chapter 8, how the hospitality organization can, when the conditions are right, encourage and help guests co-produce, or participates in providing, their own experiences!

Section 3, *The Hospitality Service Delivery System*, shows how to glue the different parts of the guest experience together by communicating information to the right person at the right time, described in Chapter 9. Chapter 10 then describes the critically important tasks involved in planning and creating the service delivery system. This includes projecting to meet demand, monitoring the system, and engaging in continuous improvement. Because no organization's server/system combinations can match demand perfectly, Chapter 11 describes techniques for managing the inevitable waits for service. Chapter 12 presents some ways of measuring results in terms of service quality and guest satisfaction so organizations and servers know how well they are meeting guests' expectations. All organizations try to provide perfect experiences, but the leading ones plan for the inevitable failures. Chapter 13 therefore focuses on how to avoid service failures and problems. But because no servers and systems have yet been devised that can provide so complex a service as the guest experience perfectly every time, we have also discussed planning for, finding, and fixing service failures when they occur. Section 3 and the book conclude with Chapter 14, which explains how the organization's people, units, and their efforts must be tied together to provide remarkable guest service that delights guests. That alignment—of strategy, staffing, and systems—is accomplished by outstanding organizational leadership.

Learning Objectives, Key Terms, and Discussion Questions

Every chapter opens with a comprehensive set of learning objectives addressing the chapter's main points. The list of key terms and concepts serves as a brief preview of the subjects and ideas in the chapter to come. These terms and concepts are boldfaced the first time they appear in the chapter. The discussion questions at each chapter's end are designed to provoke thought and classroom interaction about chapter content and to enable students to make self-assessments of how well they have understood the material.

Activities and Case Studies

Each chapter includes at least one hospitality activity to encourage students to visit local hospitality organizations and study them from the perspective of the book's ideas. Some activities suggest that students talk with guests, employees, and managers to obtain a variety of perspectives on the guest experience. Other activities suggest exploration of the Internet to visit sites established by hospitality organizations and to acquire further information on the book's concepts and ideas. Case studies provide an opportunity to discuss hospitality concepts and principles in terms of real (if disguised) and hypothetical hotels, restaurants, and other business types found in the hospitality industry.

Ethical Scenarios

Unethical practices in business are a growing concern. Newspapers commonly report on scandals where someone has embezzled, stolen, forged, misappropriated funds, etc. But even when not dealing with blatantly illegal activities, employees and managers will likely be faced with tough decisions that require uncomfortable choices. The purpose of the "Ethics in Business" section, at the end of each chapter, is to raise such issues that students may need to wrestle with in the services industry. Each chapter presents an issue that students can think about and discuss regarding what is the "right" way to respond. Students are encouraged to consider different perspectives for each scenario, weighing how different individuals may consider the same situation in different ways.

Supplemental Materials

Student Online Companion

Visit www.cengagebrain.com for the student online companion to accompany this text. The student online companion includes learning objectives and key terms with definitions.

Instructor Resources to Accompany Text

The Instructor Resources CD includes the Instructor's Guide, PowerPoint® lecture slides, and an ExamView® computerized test bank. The Instructor's Guide provides answers to the end-of-chapter review questions, answers to the discussion questions following the chapter cases, discussion points regarding the "Ethics in Business" scenarios, true-false and multiple-choice quizzes, and additional material to assist the instructor in preparing course outlines and lesson plans.

To the Student

Managing Quality Service in Hospitality is designed for you. The material has been taught in many classes across the past decade to students with backgrounds similar to yours. The information presented is based on the best available research on services and hospitality services in particular, and on the best practices of leading hospitality organizations. The book should give you a thorough understanding of the principles of managing a hospitality organization. We hope you will want to keep the book if you enter the hospitality field or work in any of the many service organizations that dominate the economy. What we can learn from hospitality leaders is valuable in managing any customer-focused for-profit or nonprofit organization.

Primary Support Staff

Once again and always, we thank our wives, Barbara Ford, Kelly Sturman, and Marieta Barrow Heaton, for unfailing support and for continuing to exceed our expectations; they put the wow! in our lives.

Robert C. Ford
Michael C. Sturman
Cherrill P. Heaton

COMPREHENSIVE TEACHING AND LEARNING PACKAGE

Instructor Resources

The Instructor Resources CD to accompany this text includes the Instructor's Guide, PowerPoint® lecture slides, and an ExamView® computerized test bank. The Instructor's Guide provides answers to the end-of-chapter review questions, answers to the discussion questions following the chapter cases, discussion points regarding the "Ethics in Business" scenarios, true-false and multiple-choice quizzes, and additional material to assist the instructor in preparing course outlines and lesson plans.

Student Online Companion

Visit www.cengagebrain.com for the student online companion to accompany this text. The student online companion includes learning objectives and key terms with definitions.

Special Features

The Hospitality Principles

A proven principle of hospitality management keys each chapter of this book. Leading hospitality organizations have found these principles to be important, workable, and useful. They represent the key points to keep in mind when putting the book's material into practice.

PRINCIPLES OF HOSPITALITY MANAGEMENT

1. Provide the service quality and value that guests expect
2. Focus strategy on the key drivers of guest satisfaction
3. Provide the service setting that guests expect
4. Define and sustain a total service culture
5. Find and hire people who love to serve
6. Train your employees, then train them some more
7. Motivate and empower your employees
8. Empower guests to co-create their experiences
9. Glue the guest experience elements together with information
10. Provide seamless service delivery
11. Manage the guest's wait
12. Pursue perfection relentlessly
13. Don't fail the guest twice
14. Lead others to excel

Ethical Scenarios

Ethical practices in business are a growing concern. Even when not dealing with blatantly illegal activities, employees and managers are often faced with tough decisions that require uncomfortable choices. The **new** "Ethics in Business" section at the end of each chapter encourages students to think about and discuss issues that they may need to wrestle with in the hospitality industry.

Case Studies

Case studies provide an opportunity to discuss hospitality concepts and principles in terms of real (if disguised) and hypothetical hotels, restaurants, and other business types found in the hospitality industry.

Pedagogical Features
Learning Objectives

Every chapter opens with a comprehensive set of learning objectives addressing the chapter's main points.

Key Terms

The list of key terms and concepts serves as a brief preview of the subjects and ideas in the chapter to come. These terms and concepts are boldfaced the first time they appear in the chapter.

KEY TERMS AND CONCEPTS

recruitment
service naturals
selection
human resource planning
KSAs
job analysis

emotional labor
emotional relationship
surface acting
deep acting
hiring from within
succession plans

unstructured interview
structured interviews
behavioral interviews
situational interviews
assessment center
on-boarding

Human Resource Planning

Selecting the best person for the job should begin by first looking not at the applicants but at the job. First, you should engage in **human resource planning**. Human resource planning is the process of analyzing an organization's current human resource capabilities and the organization's human resource needs necessary to meet organizational objectives. Based on your organizational strategy, you must determine what knowledge, skills, and abilities (**KSAs**) employees must possess to accomplish your goals, what levels of KSAs currently exist in your organization, and how you expect both your organization and people to develop over time.

So, who are all the people involved? There was the reservationist who took your reservation, the manager who hired and scheduled the reservationists, the valet who parked your car, the bellperson who took your luggage, the doorman who let you in to the hotel, the front desk agent (whom you did remember), the front desk manager who scheduled

---

REVIEW QUESTIONS

1. Consider the formula presented in the chapter:

   service product + service environment + service delivery system = guest experience

   A. Although all parts are important, do you think these three types of organizations—a hotel, a restaurant, and an airline—would tend to place a different emphasis on the three parts in providing the total guest experience?

   B. If product + environment + delivery system = 100%, how would these organization types rank the three parts of the guest experience in order of emphasis? Or, how would the hotel, restaurant, and airline divide up their emphasis?

2. Imagine that a Rolex watch, a RadioShack watch, an Eagle Mirado #2 pencil, and a Cross fountain pen are sitting on a table in front of you. Which item is highest in quality, and which is lowest in quality?

3. These standard rooms are available in your locality: the Ritz-Carlton Hotel ($450 per night), a Holiday Inn ($150), a YMCA or YWCA ($40), and a No-Tell Motel ($59.95). Which room is highest in quality, and which is lowest in value?

4. Consider the examples in questions 2 and 3 in terms of value. Under what circumstances can quality be high and value low? Value high and quality low?

5. A guest experience is a service, and this chapter explained that services are largely intangible. Think of a somewhat costly guest experience you have had. What tangibles did the organization use to make you feel that your intangible experience was worth the money you paid?

6. Reflect on a recent, enjoyable guest experience and on a disappointing guest experience.

   A. What were the significant events, the moments of truth, during each experience?

   B. How did they contribute to your enjoyment or disappointment?

   C. How do they relate to managing the guest experience in hospitality organizations?

Review Questions

The review questions at each chapter's end are designed to provoke thought and classroom interaction about chapter content and to enable students to make self-assessments of how well they have understood the material.

ACTIVITIES

1. In the chapter appendix, there are four qualitative techniques that can be used for forecasting: brainstorming, the Delphi technique, focus groups, and scenario building. Divide up into groups and, as your instructor directs, come up with a forecasting problem that a local hospitality organization might face and try to arrive at a conclusion about it by using one or more of the techniques. Different groups might use different techniques for the same problem to see if they come up with the same conclusion or problem solution.

2. Find a hospitality organization that uses forecasting techniques. How does the organization use them to predict its staffing and product supply needs, or for other purposes? How does the organization gather data? Does it use prediction models and statistical techniques, or is forecasting done mainly by the seat of someone's pants?

3. This chapter suggests that an organization should focus on its core competencies, not spread itself into areas in which it may not be competent. Some competency pairings are generally accepted, like bar and grill. Others might reflect an organizational intention to operate in unrelated areas, like college and fish camp or blacksmith and nail care. Look for unusual competency pairings in business names you come across and report them back to the class.

4. Go on the Web or across your community and see what the companies you find claim as their mission. What is your estimation of how well this mission helps define strategic decisions they make?

Activities

Each chapter includes at least one hospitality activity to encourage students to visit local hospitality organizations and study them from the perspective of the book's ideas. Some activities suggest that students talk with guests, employees, and managers to obtain a variety of perspectives on the guest experience. Other activities suggest exploration of the Internet to visit sites established by hospitality organizations and to acquire further information on the book's concepts and ideas.

ACKNOWLEDGMENTS

Industry and Practitioner Reviewers

Emily Ellis, Gaylord Hotel Corporation
Mark Havard, Hyatt Corporation
Stephen Howell, US Airways
Rich Jeffers, Darden Restaurants
George Koenig, Sodexo (retired)
Bruce Laval, The Walt Disney Company (retired)
William C. McCreary, Starwood Hotels
Elizabeth McGlasson, Marriott International
John Meunier, Boston Development Group
Michael Sansbury, Over 5 Hospitality
Kent Shoemaker, FreshPoint
Melanie Smith, Six Flags New England

Academic Reviewers

Sherry Andre, Johnson & Wales University, Miami
Paul Bagdan, Johnson & Wales University, Providence
Bill Bennett, Southwest Minnesota State University
Marisa B. Boff, Bradford School
Kathleen Pearl Brewer, University of Nevada, Las Vegas
Duncan Dickson, University of Central Florida
Babu P. George, University of Southern Mississippi
Susan Gregory, Eastern Michigan University
Nan Hua, University of Central Florida
Leonard A. Jackson, University of Central Florida
Miyoung Jeong, University of Massachusetts, Amherst
Richard R. Perdue, Virginia Polytechnic Institute and State University
Peter Ricci, Florida Atlantic University
Theda L. Rudd, The School of Hospitality Business, Michigan State University
Linda Shea, University of Massachusetts

A special thanks to Dr. Linda Shea and her students at the University of Massachusetts for allowing the first author to be part of their class and sharing their helpful feedback on an earlier draft of this book.

ABOUT THE AUTHORS

Robert C. Ford (Ph.D., Arizona State University) is professor of management in the College of Business Administration (COBA) of the University of Central Florida (UCF) where he teaches management of service organizations. He joined UCF as the chairman of its hospitality department. He was also the COBA Associate Dean for Graduate and External Programs.

Bob has authored or coauthored numerous publications in both top research and practitioner journals. He serves on several editorial boards including *Cornell Hospitality Quarterly*, *British Journal of Management*, *Journal of Leadership and Organizational Studies*, *Journal of Convention and Event Tourism*, and *Journal of Service Management*. He has also published several books including *Managing the Guest Experience in Hospitality*, *Achieving Service Excellence: Strategies for Health Care*, *Managing Destination Marketing Organizations*, and *The Fun Minute Manager*.

Bob has been an active participant in many professional organizations. He has served the Academy of Management (AOM) as editor of *The Academy of Management Executive*, Director of Placement, board member of the HRM division, Division Chair for both its Management History and Management Education and Development divisions, a member of its Ethics Adjudication Committee, and a co-founder of the Community of Academy Senior Scholars. Bob has served the Southern Management Association (SMA) in every elective office including president. He was a founding member and Chair of the Accreditation Commission for Programs in Hospitality Administration and currently serves on the Destination Marketing Accreditation Program.

Bob has been recognized for his service by many organizations. He received the Distinguished Service Award from AOM's MED, SMA's Distinguished Service Award, and was elected to SMA Fellows. In recognition of his service to hospitality education, he was given the Paul Brown Award by the Florida Hotel and Lodging Association.

Michael C. Sturman (Ph.D., Cornell University) is the Kenneth and Marjorie Blanchard Professor of Human Resources at Cornell University's School of Hotel Administration. There, he teaches undergraduate, graduate, and executive education courses on human resource management and compensation. His current research focuses on the prediction of individual job performance over time, the influence of compensation systems, and the impact of human resource management on organizational performance. He has published research articles in journals such as the *Journal of Applied Psychology*, *Academy of Management Journal*, *Personnel Psychology*, and *Journal of Management*. He has also published hospitality-focused papers in the *Cornell Hospitality Quarterly*, *International Journal of Hospitality Management*, *Lodging Magazine*, *Lodging HR*, *A.A.H.O.A. Hospitality*, *HR.Com*, and the *American Compensation Association Journal*. Michael holds a Ph.D., M.S., and B.S. from Cornell University's School of Industrial and Labor Relations, and is a Senior Professional of Human Resources as certified by the Society for Human Resource Management.

Cherrill P. Heaton (Ph.D., Florida State University) recently retired as Professor of Organizational Communications from the University of North Florida where he taught organizational and business communications to students in the graduate business programs for thirty years. In addition, he taught short courses in effective business communication in numerous executive education programs. Besides serving as editor of *Management by Objectives in Higher Education*, he is the co-author of several articles on service management and four texts: *Principles of Management: A Decision Making Approach*; *Organizational Theory: An Integrative Approach*; *Achieving Service Excellence: Strategies for Healthcare*; and *Managing the Guest Experience in Hospitality*. He also served as managing editor for the *Academy of Management Executive*.

INTRODUCTION

SERVICE RULES!

The modern economy is dominated by service organizations. The service sector constitutes 75 percent to 80 percent of the U.S. economy and is growing. Even businesses dealing primarily in physical goods now often view themselves primarily as service providers, with the offered good being an important part of the service. These firms have adopted traditional service terms such as customer satisfaction, customer retention, and customer relationships. Some, like IBM, have realized that their future flow of revenues and profits will come from their service businesses.

Yet, surprisingly few articles and books focus on how to manage service organizations, even fewer on how to manage hospitality organizations. The purpose of this book is to provide a comprehensive review of the best that is known about managing hospitality organizations. From the neighborhood restaurant to the resort hotel, from the small convention center to the huge theme park, the principles of managing hospitality organizations are the same. Even more important, they are different from the principles of managing manufacturing organizations taught in most business schools.

HOSPITALITY IS DIFFERENT

Traditional bureaucratic structures and manufacturing management principles get turned on their heads in the hospitality sector. It's one thing to design, organize, and control a work process and motivate a workforce when the product is tangible and the production process takes place in a big closed brick factory with an "Employees Only" sign on the door. A totally different challenge arises when the customer is consuming your "product" while you're producing it. The challenge is often intensified by the product's intangibility: "Hospitality" is intangible, and the hospitality experience may not even physically exist! Designing and producing such an experience is quite different from the design and production of goods.

These "production" problems in the hospitality industry are matched or exceeded by the challenge of managing employees who must be carefully trained to provide a service whose quality and value are defined by each guest. To top it off, employees must be taught to provide this service not behind closed doors but while customers, guests, or clients are watching, asking questions, and changing their minds about what they want. Most even participate jointly with the employees in co-producing the guest experience itself! Manufacturing managers sometimes moan about how hard it is to teach their employees to perform the necessary manufacturing steps accurately. They should talk to their colleagues in the hospitality industry who not only have to teach their employees how to "manufacture" the product but, also, how to do so with the guest watching and co-producing. These managers know that the principles taught in smokestack management courses in traditional business schools don't seem too relevant. Managing in the hospitality industry is a very different world.

STUDY THE BEST

Only recently have researchers and management scholars begun to study this different world as a separate field, and much of what is known is still based on anecdotal information and case-study examples. This makes perfect sense. In the early stages of inquiry into any field of business, the logical approach is to find the best organizations and study them to discover the principles that drive what they do. A review of the service management literature quickly reveals several benchmark organizations. The list includes Darden Restaurants, Four Seasons Hotels and Resorts, JetBlue Airways, Marriott International, Nordstrom's Department Store, The Ritz-Carlton Hotel Company, Southwest Airlines, Starwood Hotels and Resorts Worldwide, and The Walt Disney Company. And there are, of course, many others large and small. These organizations learned long ago the importance of understanding what their customers expect from all parts of their service experience, and they manage their businesses around satisfying those expectations. Because they have studied their guests long and hard, they know what their guests want, what they are willing to pay for it, and how to give it to them. The magic of Disney and the other outstanding hospitality organizations is that they meet guest expectations, of course, and then exceed them in a thousand ways that get guests not only to say "wow!" on the first visit but to return repeatedly and say "wow!" every time. Customers, clients, patrons, and guests return to the great organizations—manufacturing or service—because they get it right and then some.

FOCUS ON YOUR GUEST

Two fundamental concepts, based on the practices of successful hospitality organizations, will appear in one form or another throughout the book. First, everything the organization does should focus on the guest. Most managers think first about their organization, their production requirements, and their employee needs. They are used to starting with themselves or their employees when they design their product, create the setting or environment in which the customer interacts with the organization, and set up the system for delivering the goods or services that their customers buy. They manage from the inside out. This first fundamental that we stress is that you must manage from the outside in! Start with the guests. Study them endlessly; know what they want, need, value, expect, and actually do. Then focus everyone in the organization on figuring out how to do a better job of meeting and exceeding guest expectations in a way that allows the organization to make a profit.

YOUR CUSTOMER IS YOUR GUEST

The second fundamental concept that must be part of the hospitality organization's culture is that you must treat each customer like a guest. If appropriate to the organization (and it probably is appropriate in all hospitality organizations), always use the term *guest* and not *customer*. Create a guest-focused culture. Most important of all, train employees to think of the people in front of them as their guests, whom they are hosting for the organization. This is not a simple change in terminology; it is a big deal. In fact, outstanding companies like Disney think it's such a big deal that they use the term *guest* instead of *customer* for their millions of visitors. They know the importance of constantly reminding their thousands of employees to think of their customers as guests in everything they do. Disney even coined the term *guestology* to refer to the scientific study of guest behavior to learn more about meeting—and exceeding—the expectations of its guests.

Looking at a customer as a guest changes everything the hospitality organization and its employees do. A customer comes to the organization seeking to buy something that the organization sells, and the only obligation of the organization and its employees is to execute a commercial transaction in an effective, businesslike manner. The person comes in the door expecting to be treated like a customer, at best. But if the organization can provide a hospitable experience of which the actual commercial transaction is only a part, the customer will think "wow!" Creating an experience instead of merely selling a product or service is important to turn customers into patrons or guests. Rather than thinking of selling admission tickets or hotel rooms, the truly guest-focused organizations such as The Ritz-Carlton Hotels try to create a memorable event for their customers. They provide the commercial transaction within a warm, friendly experience that makes an emotional connection so memorable that it brings the customer back time after time. The Ritz-Carlton and all other excellent hospitality organizations know that it is cheaper to keep loyal customers than it is to attract new ones, and that repeat business is the key to long-term profitability.

To become a believer in this fundamental concept, think about the business organizations you deal with. To some, you are merely a component in a commercial transaction; others treat you like a guest. The difference is so clear it is unforgettable. Anyone who has been to a Disney theme park or a Hyatt Regency hotel knows the special way they treat their guests. The idea of treating customers like guests is a lesson that any hospitality organization—in fact, any organization that seeks to compete successfully in the modern service-dominated economy—must learn. Customers are increasingly aware of who treats them right and who does not. They know more about what does and does not have value for them, and they expect more from the organizations they deal with. Even more important, the organizations that have discovered and use the principles explained in this book are taking business away from those organizations that still don't understand them. While the best keep raising the bar for each other, they are also making it increasingly difficult for the rest to understand why their customers are never satisfied with their service or product. This book organizes what the best hospitality organizations know and what the rest must learn to compete successfully, over the next millennium, in an increasingly customer-driven marketplace.

Although focusing on customers and treating them like guests sound simple enough, these tasks are actually huge managerial challenges that the exemplars in hospitality services spend enormous amounts of time, money, and energy to meet. They spend countless hours and dollars investing in a service culture that continually reinforces their customer service values.

SOME THEORETICAL UNDERPINNINGS

In addition to studying the best practices of exemplars in the hospitality industry, we have reviewed the services management, marketing, hospitality, and human resource literatures. The concepts and principles contained in this book represent a unique combination of what the academic literature says should work and what the long experience of some of the most successful hospitality organizations in the world have found does work.

STRATEGY, STAFF, AND SYSTEMS

We have organized the best that is known about hospitality management according to the three critical "Ss" of the successful hospitality organization: *s*trategy, *s*taff, and *s*ystems. Each "S" organizes the material in one of the book's three major sections. Each "S" is equally important in providing superior service. First comes strategy and the definition of what plans hospitality organizations must make to be effective in achieving their service mission. Next is the staff. Although every organization wants an effective staff, the hospitality organization depends almost completely upon its personnel to deliver the high-quality guest experience that distinguishes the excellent hospitality organization from the merely good. Finally, the third S represents the systems. The best hospitality staff in the world cannot succeed without an effective array of systems to back them up in delivering the service that the customer comes for. An impressive mission statement and a big server smile can't make up for a burned lasagna, a dirty room, a late flight, unpredictable room service, or a broken air conditioner.

Although the hospitality organization's strategy, staff, and systems are obviously related to one another, they all have one focus—the guest—and exist for one overriding purpose: to provide guest satisfaction.

STRUCTURE AND THE FOURTEEN PRINCIPLES OF HOSPITALITY MANAGEMENT

Within this overall three-section structure, we have framed the information under fourteen principles in fourteen chapters. Here is an overview of how all this fits together.

The Hospitality Service Strategy]

1. Provide the service quality and value that guests expect.]
2. Focus strategy on the key drivers of guest satisfaction.]
3. Provide the service setting that guests expect.]
4. Define and sustain a total service culture.

The Hospitality Service Staff]

5. Find and hire people who love to serve.]
6. Train your employees, then train them some more.]
7. Motivate and empower your employees.]
8. Empower guests to co-create their experiences.

The Hospitality Service Systems]

9. Glue the guest experience elements together with information.]
10. Provide seamless service delivery.]
11. Manage the guest's wait.]
12. Pursue perfection relentlessly.]
13. Don't fail the guest twice.]
14. Lead others to excel.

Within this structure, we think we have captured the important aspects of managing in hospitality organizations. We hope it will be fun for readers to learn more about this fascinating industry and how the best manage to be the best.

PROVIDE THE BETTER CHOICE

Service in the hospitality industry is too often unsatisfactory. Dissatisfied guests can easily switch to competing organizations or even choose alternatives to this industry. Hospitality owners and managers are increasingly aware that if they want guests to keep coming back to their hotel, restaurant, destination, cruise line, or airline instead of going elsewhere, they'd better learn to give good service. If guests feel that they are receiving unsatisfactory service from one organization, they can probably find a similar organization just down the street, and they will go there. Indeed, with the increasing availability of virtual experiences, they can find many alternative ways to spend their money.

Everybody sees the problems with guest service, and many people looking for answers ask; who does it right, and how? This book, which combines the key principles of good hospitality service management research with examples drawn from some of the world's most successful hospitality organizations, should help any hospitality organization or manager who aspires to be a guestologist and provide better service to guests.

PRINCIPLES OF HOSPITALITY MANAGEMENT

1. **Provide the service quality and value that guests expect**

2. **Focus strategy on the key drivers of guest satisfaction**

3. **Provide the service setting that guests expect**

4. **Define and sustain a total service culture**

5. **Find and hire people who love to serve**

6. **Train your employees, then train them some more**

7. **Motivate and empower your employees**

8. **Empower guests to co-create their experiences**

9. **Glue the guest experience elements together with information**

10. **Provide seamless service delivery**

11. **Manage the guest's wait**

12. **Pursue perfection relentlessly**

13. **Don't fail the guest twice**

14. **Lead others to excel**

SECTION 1

The Hospitality Service Strategy

If you don't have a road map, or know where you are, you may be there already.

—Norman Brinker, Former CEO, Chili's Restaurants

Running a business without a plan is like going into the forest, shooting off your rifle and hoping that dinner runs into the bullet.

—Herman Cain, Former Chairman and CEO, Godfather's Pizza

CHAPTER 1

The Basics of Wow! The Guest Knows Best

HOSPITALITY PRINCIPLE: PROVIDE THE SERVICE QUALITY AND VALUE THAT GUESTS EXPECT

The secret to success is to treat all customers as if your world revolves around them.

—Unknown

You don't know what you aren't going to get until you don't get it.

—Theodore Levitt

LEARNING OBJECTIVES

After reading this chapter, you should understand:

- Important differences between making products and serving guests.
- The importance of meeting the hospitality guest's expectations.
- The importance of the guest experience.
- The components of the guest experience.
- The definition of *service quality* and *service value* in the hospitality field.
- The reasons why "it all starts with the guest."

KEY TERMS AND CONCEPTS

hospitality	service environment	service delivery system
service quality	servicescape	service package
service value	service delivery	service encounter
guest experience	expectations	critical incident
moment of truth	guestologist	benchmark organizations
guestology	internal customers	quality
service product	service	value
service setting	KSAs	cost

Serving guests and making products are such different activities that they require different management principles and concepts. Catching a defective tire or a paint blemish on a car's finish at the final inspection stage of an assembly line production process is one thing. Quite another is listening to irate guests telling you in no uncertain terms that your hotel, restaurant, or airline has failed to deliver the service experience they expected. In the first instance, the quality inspector—one of many people between the maker of the product and the final customer—can send the defective product back for rework so that the customer never sees it. In the second situation, there is usually no one to buffer the relationship between the person delivering the unsatisfactory service and the guest dissatisfied with it.

At its most basic level, the **hospitality** industry is made up of organizations that offer guests courteous, professional food, drink, and lodging services, alone or in combination. But the hospitality industry is more than just hotels and restaurants. Beyond these, the industry has been defined in many ways. An expanded definition includes theme parks, airlines, gaming centers, cruise ships, trade shows, fairs, meeting planning and convention organizations. Because we think the principles and practices presented in this book have wide application, we are going to use this more expanded concept of the industry. The challenge for all organizations in this industry is to ensure that their personnel always provide at least the level of service that their guests want and expect—every time, perfectly. This book is designed to show all those working in this industry and those who manage them how to do that.

Even more challenging for those in hospitality organizations is the simple reality that **service quality** and **service value** are defined not by managers, auditors, or rating organizations: They are defined entirely in the mind of the guest. Although there are a few organizations, like J. D. Power, and several Web sites, like TripAdvisor, that rate the service quality of the local Holiday Inn, Friendly Travel Agency, or Olive Garden, individual guests still make their own decisions on whether the quality and value of the service they experienced met their expectations. Even though *BusinessWeek* annually rates the best service companies and the American Customer Satisfaction Index (ACSI) and *Consumer Reports* from time to time offer evaluations of the major airline, hotel, and restaurant companies, in the final analysis, the decision about the quality and value of a hospitality experience is made anew by each individual guest in every transaction with a specific unit of a hospitality organization on a particular date with a certain service staff. If the guest comes on a date or at a time when the organization for whatever reasons fails to meet expectations, for that guest the restaurant is no good, the airline inept, and the hotel a major disappointment. One unfortunate incident can negatively influence the opinion of the guest and anyone the guest talks to both in person and virtually, through a Web site posting, or social media site.

You will find that this text is very different from traditional management texts, because hospitality organizations are very different businesses to run from those discussed in traditional management texts. Most texts emphasize different principles and guidelines for managers seeking to run these organizations well; however, the success or failure of the **guest experience** (to be explained shortly in detail) may depend on how a single **moment of truth** between a hospitality employee and the guest is handled. Management's responsibility is to ensure that each moment of truth has been prepared for—has been managed—as well as humanly possible to yield a satisfying, even outstanding, outcome for the guest.

How to achieve such outcomes is the focus of this book. Once dominated by the manufacturing sector, the economy is now overwhelmingly dominated by the service sector. This shift to a service economy requires that traditional management models and methods be reorganized and redirected if they are to meet the unique challenges and opportunities of hospitality organizations.

GUESTOLOGY: WHAT IS IT?

In this book, we organize the available knowledge about meeting these challenges and opportunities around **guestology**, a term originated by Bruce Laval of The Walt Disney Company.[1] Customer-guests are, to the extent possible, studied scientifically (the *-ology* in *guestology*). Guests' behaviors within the hospitality organization are carefully observed. Their wants, needs, capabilities, and expectations regarding the hospitality guest experience are determined. And ultimately, the service product is tailored to meet their demands and those of future guests. Guestology means simply that all the organization's employees must treat customers like guests and manage the organization from the guest's point of view. All the while, this is a business, and an eye must be kept on the bottom line to ensure that services can continue to be provided in the future. The good news is that guestology makes good business sense. The practice of guestology makes it possible to increase guest satisfaction, which leads to more repeat visits, which in turn drives revenues up. The findings of guestology turn into the organizational practices that provide sustained outstanding services. The organization's strategy, staff, and systems are aligned to meet or exceed the customer's expectations regarding the three aspects of the guest experience: **service product**, **service setting** (also called **service environment** or **servicescape**), and **service delivery**. These aspects or elements are carefully woven together to give guests what they want and expect, plus a little bit more. "It all starts with the guest" is not just an inspirational slogan; in the service-centered hospitality organization, it is the truth and everybody accepts and lives up to it.

Guestology turns traditional management thinking on its head. Instead of focusing on organizational design, managerial hierarchy, and production systems to maximize organizational efficiency, guestology forces the organization to start everything it does by looking systematically at the guest experience from the customer's or guest's point of view. What customers do and want are first systematically studied, modeled, and predicted. Only then can the rest of the organizational issues be addressed. The goal is to create and sustain an organization that can effectively meet the customer's expectations and still make a profit.

Meeting Customer Expectations

Customers come to a service provider with certain **expectations** for themselves, their businesses, and/or their families. First-time guests may have general expectations. For example, a first-time guest of a major hotel may simply expect a nice room, a comfortable mattress, clean surroundings, satisfactory meals, and a reasonable price. A repeat guest may have more specific expectations based on past experience. Olive Garden knows that all guests, new and repeat, have certain expectations that drive their evaluation of the quality and value of the Olive Garden experience. From extensive research of their customers, Olive Garden leaders know that their guests' key drivers are food of good quality, fast and attentive service, cleanliness, and a pleasant atmosphere. Olive Garden not only asks and studies their guests to find their key drivers, they also solicit comments about how well they delivered on those characteristics by gathering customer feedback.

A **guestologist** seeks to understand and plan for the expectations of an organization's targeted customers before they ever enter the service setting, so that everything is ready for each guest to have a successful and enjoyable experience. The road from the Magic Kingdom's Main Street, U.S.A. hub off to the right to Tomorrowland in Orlando's Walt Disney World Resort is wider than the road to Adventureland which is off to the left. This is because Disney carefully studied guest behavior and discovered that when people were otherwise indifferent as to which direction to go, they tended to go in the direction of their handedness. Since there are more right-handed than left-handed guests, Disney made the road to the right wider than the other roads off the main hub anticipating that more people would go in that direction. That is guestology in practice. Here is a second illustration of the concept. Disney knows that one of its greatest assets is its reputation for cleanliness. Keeping a theme park clean is a big job, so the Disney organization encourages its guests to help out by disposing of their own trash. After all, whatever people throw away themselves does not have to be cleaned up by a paid employee. In studying guest behavior, Disney learned two things. First, if cast members (the Disney term for its employees) are visible constantly picking up even the smallest bits of trash, park guests tend to dispose of their own trash. The cast members model the desired behavior of keeping the parks clean to show respect for cleanliness, and guests copy them. Second, people tend to throw their trash away if trash cans are convenient, easily seen, and not far apart. Disney locates the trash cans to match these criteria. For example, visit the Magic Kingdom on a quiet day when the crowds are not distracting; you will notice that Main Street, U.S.A. looks like a forest of trash cans, located 25 to 27 paces apart. Understanding how guests respond to environmental cues and using that knowledge to help maintain a high standard of cleanliness is guestology in practice.

Managers of all hospitality organizations can extend the lessons learned by Disney guestologists and other leading hospitality firms to their own companies. If the organizational goal is to provide an outstanding guest experience, then the organization must understand why its guests come to the hospitality organization, what those guests expect, and what the company can and will actually do in order to meet their guests' expectations. Many people think running a restaurant is simple: Offer good food at a fair price, and everything else takes care of itself. Profitable restaurants know that guests patronize them—or get angry and leave—for a variety of reasons other than food quality and value. Managing the total dining experience is a much bigger job than merely executing a good recipe. Guestology involves systematically determining what those factors are, modeling them for study, measuring their impact on the guest experience, testing various strategies that might improve the quality of that experience, and then providing the combination of factors or elements that attracts guests and keeps them coming back.

Serving Internal Customers

In addition to public consumers, the hospitality organization has within itself many **internal customers**, persons and units that depend on each other and "serve" each other. The principles for providing an outstanding service experience for external customers also apply to these many internal customers. For example, a computer help desk that serves internal customers should understand and fulfill the expectations of these customers just as any organization tries to meet and exceed the expectations of its external customers.

This logic can easily and rightfully be extended to the level of the individual employee. The organization must meet or exceed the expectations of employees about how they will be treated. Smart hospitality organizations know that their employees must get the same care and consideration that they want their employees to extend to their guests. They understand that they can't mistreat their own employees and expect them to then treat the customers well. They know that the way in which the organization treats its own employees will inevitably spill over onto the way their employees treat guests and each other. In these organizations, everyone works hard to avoid employee mistreatment and unfairness. As expressed in the Southwest Airlines mission statement, "Employees will be provided the same concern, respect, and caring attitude within the organization that they are expected to share externally with every Southwest customer." Extending guest treatment to employees is so important to organizational success that much of Chapter 7, on employee motivation and empowerment, will be devoted to it.

Meeting Increased Competition

The competition for guest loyalty and dollars (and euros, rupees, won, yen, yuan, etc.) is intense and will only grow more so in the future. New hospitality organizations spring up every day. Although opening a hospitality organization like a hotel, convention center, travel Web site, or airline costs a lot of money, for thousands of restaurants, travel agencies, sports bars, and convention services organizations, the amount of start-up capital needed is comparatively small. This book is not just for large corporations. These smaller organizations, like the larger ones hoping to survive and prosper in this competitive environment, need to master and practice the principles of guestology. If they don't provide the experience their guests expect, someone else will.

Service

We have frequently spoken of **service**, a word with numerous meanings. A common way to think of service is as the intangible part of a transaction relationship that creates value between a provider organization and its customer, client, or guest.[2] More simply, a service is something that is done for us. Services can be provided directly to the customer (e.g., a spa treatment, a haircut, and medical procedures) or for the customer (e.g., finding and purchasing tickets to a show, lawn care, and car repair). The services can be provided by a person (e.g., by a service associate in a restaurant or by a travel agent) or via technology (e.g., by booking a ticket online or using an ATM). Some of these relationships are depicted graphically in Figure 1-1, later in the chapter. And, of course, services can be provided as a combination of these characteristics.

Most services include a tangible physical product or tangible materials and equipment in the transaction as well: At McDonald's you get a hamburger you can see, touch, eat, or take home in a box; you also get service along with the hamburger. A cruise line will include a ship, a dining experience will provide food, and a teacher's lesson may require chalk, texts, and notes. Other service transactions, like a session with a psychiatrist or Social Security counselor, offer only the customer-provider interaction.

Service Product

Another, perhaps even more common, meaning of service refers to the entire bundle of tangibles and intangibles in a transaction with a significant service component. If you leave town for a month and pay for pet-sitting service, the organization or individual may buy and serve pet food, brush and comb pets, interact with them, bring toys, clean their litter box, and so forth. Some of what you pay for when you purchase the pet-sitting service is tangible (e.g., the cat food); some is intangible. For such tangible-intangible mixtures or bundles, the term *service package* or *service product* is often used. It is used to describe pure services as well, since the pure service provided is the product the organization offers for sale. Although these overlapping meanings can be confusing (*service* sometimes referring to a tangible-intangible mixture, *service product* sometimes referring to a pure service with no tangible product), the way the term is used in context should make clear what we are talking about in this book. In different contexts, sometimes one term will feel appropriate, sometimes the other.

One necessary distinction to realize is that the service product does not refer specifically to the tangible items that may accompany the transaction, though it can include them. That is, if you go to Olive Garden for dinner, the actual meal is not the service product; it is just a tangible part of the service product that Olive Garden delivers to diners within rooms themed to resemble a classic Italian restaurant and a feeling that when you are there "you're family."

A final point about the service product: Both the organization and the guest define it, and the definitions may not be the same. The organization may think its service product is the well-made, tasty hamburger, reliably consistent from location to location. But the guest may be "buying" a more extended service product: a well-made, tasty, consistent hamburger delivered quickly in clean surroundings by a cheerful server. Cleanliness and cheerfulness may be as important as burger taste for many guests. Since it all starts with the guest, a hospitality organization always needs to define its service product not in terms of its own interests but in terms of what its guests want and expect. Charles Revson, founder of Revlon, Inc., long ago drew this important distinction between what his organization makes and what the clientele buys: "In the factory we make cosmetics; in the store we sell hope."[3]

Service Industries

Just as the service product is a mixture of tangible and intangible elements, so are the entire industries that provide these products. Although some industries have traditionally been referred to as service industries, marketing writer Theodore Levitt made an important point about service as early as 1972: "There are no such things as service industries. There are only industries whose service components are greater or less than those of other industries. Everybody is in service."[4]

Goods to Services to Experiences

A characteristic of the contemporary economy that hospitality organizations were the first to understand is that, for many consumers, receiving well-made goods or well-rendered services may no longer be sufficient. If you build a better mousetrap today, the world may or may not beat a path to your door. More and more, today's consumers want their goods and services packaged as part of a memorable experience that has an emotional impact. Of course, today's airlines must fly passengers safely from point to point on schedule; restaurants must serve tasty, safe-to-eat food; hotels must provide clean rooms—all at a price customers are willing to pay. But the most successful hospitality organizations, and an ever-increasing number of organizations of all types, are recognizing the competitive advantage they can gain by providing carefully designed experiences that unfold over a period of time for their customers, clients, and guests.

B. Joseph Pine and James H. Gilmore were among the first to note that just as we had moved from an industrial to a service economy, we have now transitioned to an experience economy.[5] If this is true, thinking in terms of providing customer experiences is important for many organizations in varied industries; in the hospitality industry, such thinking is already considered essential to a successful competitive strategy.

Understanding the Guest

To well-managed hospitality organizations, guests are not statistical entities, vague concepts, or abstractions. They understand that within the heterogeneous mass of people they serve or want to serve, each is an individual, each is unique; some companies use the term *VIP* to remind their employees that they are serving "very individual people." Each guest brings to the guest experience a different bundle of needs, wants, capabilities, and expectations. Some guests will arrive happy and excited about whatever is going to happen to them. Others will arrive unhappy, bored, or even angry. Some guests know how to use the fondue pots. Others need to be taught so they don't burn themselves. Even more challenging is that it is possible that the happy excited guest that came yesterday is the unhappy angry guest coming in the door today. The hospitality organization must not only strive to satisfy each of the guests it seeks to serve in its target market but also adapt what it does to account for the changes in expectations, wants, needs, and capabilities that those guests may have from visit to visit.

The first step in understanding how to manage the guest experience then is to understand the guests that are in their target market, to whatever extent possible. Ideally, this understanding would include (1) the traditional demographic breakdowns of age, race, gender, and guests' home locations; (2) the psychographic breakdowns of how they feel, what their attitudes, beliefs, and values are, and what kind of experience they need, want, and expect the hospitality organization to deliver; and (3) the capabilities (their knowledge, skills, and abilities [**KSAs**]) to coproduce the experience.

Meeting the expectations of a customer who arrives needing but not really wanting the service and angry at the service provider, perhaps even at the world itself, is difficult. In such situations, ensuring the quality of the service experience is even more crucial because of the circumstances leading to the need for the services. For example, those employing the services of a funeral home rarely do so under happy circumstances. Most dental patients coming in for a root canal will neither enter nor leave the dentist's office filled with joy. In hospitality, sometimes people must travel but don't particularly want to, like the overtired business traveler, the reluctant wedding guest, or the child forced to go on the family vacation or out to a family dinner. Fortunately, most guests of hospitality organizations not only are capable of coproducing the experience but also eagerly anticipate the service and have no problems with needing it or wanting it. They are easier to keep happy than the person waiting for the dentist's drill, surgeon's knife, or divorce lawyer's advice, or otherwise forced into circumstances not by their choosing.

Understanding and appreciating that guests, their expectations, and their capabilities are varied motivates the guest-focused organization to design each guest experience from each guest's point of view, to offer a personalized experience insofar as possible.

THE GUEST EXPERIENCE

A term that we have already repeatedly mentioned and will recur many times in the following pages is *guest experience*. It is the sum total of the experiences that the guest has with the service provider on a given occasion or set of occasions. If you tell your friend that last night you had a "wonderful evening at the dinner theater," you are referring to the evening as a whole and are thinking of it that way; the evening of theater was your guest experience. Providing you with the different phases and aspects that made up your wonderful evening, however, took many dinner theater employees, some of whom you saw and some of whom you were not even aware, who produced those different activities and projects flawlessly. For purposes of planning and execution, most hospitality organizations divide the total experience they offer into convenient units or components. For purposes of explaining the total guest experience, we shall do the same, even though such a division is to an extent artificial. W. Neu and S. W. Brown suggest that even traditional manufacturing organizations are increasingly interested in the service component of the manufactured product as they have recognized the value of the total product offering, including the services associated with it.[6]

Product, Setting, and Delivery

In a way, this entire book can be oversimplified into one (fairly long!) sentence: We are going to show how the benchmark hospitality organizations use their strategy, staff, and systems to provide each guest with a seamless three-part guest experience—service product, service setting, and service delivery—each part of which will at least meet the guest's expectations and the sum total of which ideally will make the guest say, or at least think, "wow!" In a simple service situation, the entire guest experience might be delivered by a single person in a single moment, but for the typical guest experience, speaking of a **service delivery system** seems more accurate. That system consists of an inanimate technology part (including organization and information systems and process techniques) and the people part—most importantly, the frontline server who delivers, or presents the service, or co-produces it with the guest.

Here is the basic equation that captures all the components of the customer experience that must be effectively managed by the guestologist:

Guest experience = service product + service setting + service delivery system

All the moments you spent at the theater add up to the guest experience you later describe as a "wonderful evening of theater." But you probably had many, smaller service experiences during the evening. If, for example, at intermission you went to a designated area and received beverage service, that short experience would have its own service, setting, and a delivery system. The next time you go to a vacation resort, take a cruise, fly, or visit a theme park, although you will have numerous separate service experiences, you will end up making a judgment about the quality and value of the *overall* guest experience. If you spend three days or a week at a resort—as many people do—each day's individual guest experiences will add up to the overall day's experience, and the one-day experiences will add up to the overall resort experience.

Unique, Yet Similar

Because incidents and occurrences are never exactly the same for two people—whether at a theater, hotel, vacation resort, restaurant, or on a cruise ship—no two guest experiences are exactly alike. Even if the incidents and occurrences were exactly the same, your experience of them would be unique because the wants, needs, tastes, preferences, capabilities, and expectations you bring to the experience are uniquely yours and may change from day to day. Add in the intangibility of service itself, and the uniqueness of each guest experience cannot be questioned. That uniqueness is what provides the primary challenge to the hospitality service provider. The old saying has it that "you can't please every guest," but the hospitality organization has to try, even though everybody is different.

On the other hand, guests do respond to many experiences in similar if not identical ways. These categories of responses can be sampled, studied, and modeled to produce extremely accurate predictive models of what guests will do and how they will behave. Probabilistic statistics is a major tool in the guestologist's kit for identifying how hospitality organizations can best respond to the needs, wants, and expectations of their targeted guest markets. Successful hospitality organizations spend considerable time, effort, and money studying their guests to ensure that each part of the entire guest experience adds something positive to it. They also expend significant resources finding and fixing the inevitable mistakes as best they can.

Components of the Guest Experience

Though the three elements that the hospitality organization has to work with often blend seamlessly into one experience—and should do so—we can for the purpose of discussion break them out into the service product, setting, and delivery system. Here is a fuller description of each.

The Service Product

The service product, sometimes called the **service package** or service/product mix, is why the customer, client, or guest comes to the organization in the first place. An organization's reason for being is often embodied in the name of the business: Riverside Amusement Park, Omni Convention Center, Sally's Video Arcade, Multiplex Movie Theater, Cheers Bar and Grill. The basic product can be relatively tangible, like a hotel room, or relatively intangible, like a rock concert. Most service products have both tangible and intangible elements and can range from mostly product with little service to mostly service with little if any product.

The Service Setting

The second component of the guest experience is the *setting* or *environment* in which the experience takes place. The term *servicescape*, the landscape within which service is experienced, has been used to describe the physical aspects of the setting that contribute to the guest's overall physical feel of the experience. Las Vegas casinos are famous for using their hotels' designs to make the focus of the service setting on the gambling. Hotel lobbies are lavish, making the customer feel he or she is in a resort. Everything the customer needs— the rooms, bars, fancy restaurants, fast food, shopping, shows—are all conveniently inside the casino. And to get to any service you need—for example, the front desk to check in or out, or to get to any restaurant—you must always pass through the casino. The design of the service setting keeps the customer focused on where the hotel makes its money: from the casino. The servicescape is also extremely important to the themed "eatertainment" restaurants like Bahama Breeze, Hard Rock Cafe, and Rainforest Cafe. They use the distinctive theme of the food-service setting—from the building exterior, to decorations inside the restaurant, to background music choice, to table and menu design—as an important means of making themselves memorable and distinguishing themselves from other restaurants.

The Service Delivery System

The third part of the guest experience is the service delivery system, including the human components (like the restaurant server who places the meal on the table or the sound engineer at the rock concert) and the physical production processes (like the kitchen facilities in the restaurant or the rock concert's sophisticated amplification system) plus the organizational and information systems and techniques that help deliver the service to the customer. Unlike a factory's assembly line system, which is generally distant from and unobservable to consumers, many parts of service delivery systems must necessarily be open to consumers who can avail themselves of the services directly and coproduce the experience. Also, the output products of an assembly line system can be touched,

Bahama Breeze uses its architecture, landscaping, and design to help communicate to the customer the Caribbean theme of the restaurant.

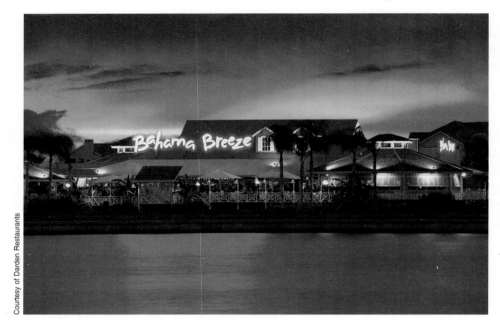

physically owned, and seen; the services produced by the service delivery system are intangible memories of experiences that exist only in guests' minds.

While all aspects of the service delivery system are important, the people interacting with customers or guests are by far the most able to make a difference in how customers feel about the value and quality of the experience. While there is little they can do if the food is ruined or the concert amps fail, customer contact employees make the difference in both how angry the customers are with a failure in the service experience and how happy they are when everything went right. They can be the most important component of the service delivery system—and the most challenging to manage. It is the waitstaff, the cabin crew, the front desk agents, the valet parkers—their attitude, friendliness, genuine concern, and helpfulness in ensuring the success of the guest's coproduction—who largely determine both the value and the quality of the experience for the guest. At the moment or over the series of moments when the service is produced and experienced, that one person, that single employee, is the server's department, the entire organization, perhaps in effect the entire hospitality industry to that guest. The feeling that the guest takes away from the guest experience is largely derived from what happens during the encounters or interactions between the guest and the employee, and the less tangible the service product, the more important the server becomes in defining the quality and value of the guest experience. They make the "wow." No wonder the leading hotels, restaurants, and other hospitality organizations invest substantial time and money finding, training, and supporting their frontline employees. If these folks fail to do it right, the guest and everyone the guest ever tells about the experience may be lost.

Service Encounters and Moments of Truth

The term **service encounter** is often used to refer to the person-to-person interaction or series of interactions between the customer and the person delivering the service. Although both parties are usually people, the many situations or interactions between organization and guest which are now automated—the automatic teller machine, check-in kiosks, and online transactions being familiar examples—may also be considered service encounters. The heart of a service is the encounter between the server and the customer. It is here where emotions meet economics in real time and where most customers judge the quality of service.[7]

An encounter is the period of time during which the organization and the guest interact. The length of a typical service encounter will vary from one service provider or organizational type to another. The purchase of a ticket is a brief service encounter; the interaction between guest and agent at a hotel front desk is usually somewhat longer; and the series of interactions between guest and server comprising a restaurant meal is an even longer encounter. A day in a theme park may involve fifty to a hundred service encounters.

Other service encounters can last for an extended time. For example, at Club Med, where vacationers may spend more than a week at a resort, the guests—called GMs (*Gentil Member*)—regularly interact with Club Med staff—called GOs (*Gentils Organisateurs*)— who play, dance, dine, and drink with the guests every day and night. On cruises, guests may develop a personal relationship with their cabin steward over a multiday voyage. Lindblad Expeditions offers week-long trips to exotic locations which make for extended interactions between service providers and guests on a ship with at most 148 or as few as 12 guests.

Service encounters or interactions, and especially certain critical moments within them, are obviously of crucial importance to the guest's evaluation of service quality; they can make or break the entire guest experience. Jan Carlzon, the former president of Scandinavian Airline Services (SAS), coined a term to refer to the key moments during these interactions, and to some brief encounters or interactions themselves, as *moments of truth*.[8] Obviously, if the airplane wouldn't fly, the meal was bad, or the air conditioning in the hotel room didn't work, you won't care how pleasant the server was or how good that person made you feel. On the other hand, since most plane rides are like other rides, most meals are similar to other meals, and most hotel rooms are like other hotel rooms, the distinguishing characteristic of most guest experiences is how the people providing the service did it! Even if the plane ride, meal, or hotel room is the best of your life, a rude or careless service person can wreck your guest experience in a moment. If that happens, all of the organization's other efforts and expenditures are wasted. It is little wonder that the most effective hospitality organizations spend serious time and money managing those moments.

For example, a potential passenger's first interaction with airline personnel is an obvious moment of truth; it can determine whether the potential passenger leaves your airline and goes to another, or whether a potentially lifetime relationship with the passenger is begun. Carlzon managed the entire airline so as to provide good service at the moment of truth, "the fifteen golden seconds" during which an entire airline is represented to one guest by one server, because the success of the entire organization depends on those first fifteen seconds. The original definition of moment of truth was Carlzon's, but other writers have expanded the term to include any significant or memorable interaction point between server and guest or, if no server is present as at an ATM or a Web site, between organization and guest. In most hospitality organizations, the first fifteen seconds are make-or-break moments as the hospitality organization, like everyone else, gets only one chance to make a first impression.

At the moment of truth, a server or other organizational representative is typically present and attempting to provide service. Some writers include interactions with inanimate objects as potential moments of truth. Opening the door of a hotel room might be such a moment. If the guest's first impression of a room's appearance is negative, or if the organization has slipped up and forgotten to clean the room, for example, a crucial moment has not been properly managed and a guest, possibly an excellent long-term customer, may be lost for good.

The moment-of-truth concept is very important: Each guest may have only a few moments of truth during a single guest experience or many moments in a lifetime relationship with a company, but each one needs to be positive. The best organizations identify when and where these moments of truth occur and ensure they are managed well. Since many involve a customer coproducing an experience with an employee, these organizations make a special commitment to ensuring that their servers know how to deliver on the many make-or-break moments of truth every day by not only delivering a flawless service but by doing so in a way that is memorable to the guest.

Another term often used in the services literature is **critical incident**. Dwayne Gremmler, in his review of the technique for collecting data on critical customer experiences, describes its uses, advantages, and disadvantages. His extensive review of the technique offers a helpful checklist of how to use it and interpret its findings.[9]

Many hospitality organizations have asked their employees to identify such moments of truth or critical incidents and record them in a database. Gaylord Hotels, Hyatt, and Disney, for example, ask their staff members to share stories about critical incidents that they have observed so they can use these stories to help teach employees about their service culture.

The Nature of Services

Services and manufactured products have different characteristics. Manufactured products tend to be tangible; produced, shipped, and purchased now for consumption later; and lacking in much if any interaction between the manufacturer and the consumer. Services tend to be intangible, purchased (if not always paid for) first, then simultaneously produced and consumed, and accompanied by considerable provider-customer interaction.[10] Let's look at these characteristics more closely.

1. Services Are Partly or Wholly Intangible   If the service rendered includes a tangible item (the Mickey Mouse hat, Mardi Gras beads, a good meal), then the total guest experience is the sum of the service-product mix, the environment within which it is delivered, and the service product's delivery. Because all or part of the service product is intangible, it is impossible to assess the product's quality or value accurately or objectively, to inventory it, or to repair it (although we will talk later about correcting service failures). Since the customer decides whether or not the quality is acceptable or value is present, the only way to measure either quality or value is through subjective assessment techniques, the most basic of which is to ask the customer.

A second implication of this intangibility characteristic is that every guest experience is unique. Even though a room at the Ritz-Carlton looks the same to everyone, the overall experience at the Ritz will be different for each guest each time. The less tangible the service provided, the more likely each guest will define the experience differently. The point is simple: Since every guest is unique, every guest experience will also be unique.

Another implication of intangibility is that hospitality organizations cannot keep an inventory of guest experiences. The stockpile of airline seats on today's 10 a.m. flight to New York is gone after the plane leaves. Tonight's unsold hotel rooms cannot be held over until tomorrow night, nor can seats at tonight's rock concert. Once a convention ends, the opportunity to participate in an exciting meeting session is gone. The inability to inventory experiences has important implications for hospitality organizations. One of the more important is the management of capacity. Because capacity is limited and demand for guest experiences varies over periods of time, capacity must be carefully managed to meet demand. If demand exceeds capacity, then guests have to wait or don't get served at all. If capacity exceeds demand, then the hospitality organization's human and physical resources sit idle.

Finally, because services are intangible and therefore difficult to comprehend fully before they are delivered and experienced, organizations wanting guests to try their services rather than those of competitors must find ways to make the intangible tangible—through photographs in advertising, a virtual tour of a hotel interior on the internet, using cloth versus plastic tablecloths at a restaurant, hanging awards on the hotel lobby wall, getting endorsements by famous people, and so forth. Such efforts to give tangible evidence of service quality help the employees as well. After all, the service is as intangible for the organization's employees as it is for guests. Tangibles help organization members form a mental image of what their service should be like and what their organization's quality level should be.

2. Services Are Consumed at the Moment or during the Period of Production or Delivery

Even if the guest takes home the Mickey Mouse hat, or the plastic beads, or the full stomach, or even if the luncheon was prepared an hour before the customer had it, the service as a whole and from the customer's perspective was consumed as delivered. The customer can take home the hat, beads, and the memory of the experience but not the service itself. What are the important implications of this characteristic for hospitality managers? Organizational systems must be carefully designed to ensure that the service is consistently produced so that each guest has a high-quality experience that both meets expectations and is nearly equal to that experienced by every other guest (except for differences supplied by servers in response to each guest's unique needs and coproduction capabilities). In addition, the experience must at least equal that which the same guest had in previous visits. The hospitality organization must think through the service delivery process by *working from the guest backward*.

This working backwards to meet customer desires and expectations is a major difference between hospitality organizations and typical bureaucratic functional organizations, which are often designed for the convenience and efficiency of organizational members. In a well-designed hospitality organization, the focus is on the guest experience and those who coproduce it. All the traditional organizational and managerial concepts that have been classically taught as the best way to manage are turned upside down. Instead of concentrating on top-down managerial control systems to ensure consistency and employee predictability, hospitality organizations must concentrate on *employee empowerment*. They know managers cannot watch every guest-employee interaction. The guest experience cannot be held back until the boss checks it for errors, as would be true of a new book, tractor, or suit. The front-line service provider who cares about the service, the organization, and the guest must be selected in the employment process and then trained and trusted to deliver the guest experience as well as that person knows how. Instead of managers following the traditional model of reviewing employee performance after the fact, in the hospitality organization they must use goal setting skills and create service standards that help the employee know how and why the consistent delivery of a high-quality guest experience is critical to guest satisfaction and organizational success. Instead of tracing information and authority from the top down, the guest-focused organization must trace it from the bottom up.

3. Services Usually Require Interaction between the Service Provider and the Customer, Client, or Guest

This interaction can be as short as the brief encounter between the

FIGURE **1-1** The Different Relationships between Customer/ Guest/Client and Service Provider
© Cengage Learning 2012

	Customer present	Customer not present
Service provider present	Hospitality, medical, professional	Lawn service, jewelry repair
Service provider not present	Electric/gas/phone/internet utilities, ATM, vending machines	On-line stores and travel services, technical help lines, answering services

customer and the order taker at a McDonald's drive thru, or as long as the lifetime relationship between the patient and the family physician. These interactions can be face to face, over the phone, on the Web, or by mail, e-mail, or texting.

When the interaction is face to face, customers and employees must be taught how to coproduce the experience in some systematic way. The Fondue Restaurant trains its servers to train guests on the proper way to cook in a fondue pot, the convention services group stations people to give directions to attendees, and an airline has staff at its check-in counter to help passengers navigate the technology. When the experience happens at the moment of its consumption, then the organization needs to plan on how to ensure that new, untrained, inexperienced, and unknowledgeable customers get the same service experience quality and value that the returning, trained, experienced and knowledgeable ones get. Since each customer is different, the organization cannot expect each customer to consume the same amount of time or resources in the experience. Accommodating the variability in customer differences is how a guestologist can make an important contribution by careful research and thoughtful planning to adjust the service experience provided for each customer.

Figure 1-1 displays four types of relationships between provider and customer, with examples of each type noted inside the respective boxes. Different service situations call for different strategies in systems, personnel, and service environment by the service provider. If the provider is not going to be present in the encounter, the service system must be foolproof for all types of customers who are in the targeted market to use it. In many places throughout the United States, ATMs and automated phone systems, for example, ask customers whether they want to read the instructions on the screen in English or Spanish or even in some other language. Some ATMs at hotels around the world give people the choice of many languages with which to complete their interactions. Web designers spend considerable time testing how people access their Web pages to ensure that they are logical, easily used, and quick to load. On the other hand, if the provider is present, the organization must focus on the customer's interactions with that provider as a major means for adding value to the service product. A full-service hotel or restaurant, for example, relies extensively on its employees to deliver value in the guest experience; the owner of a Web site does not.

Many services are delivered with customers present at some stages but not all. At car dealerships, most car repairs take place out of the customer's sight. Two points of contact occur: at the customer service desk and the payment window. The appearance of both the physical setting and the people at those contact points is quite different from those back in the repair area, beyond the sight of customers. Each type of customer contact may call for a different managerial strategy, environment, and delivery system.

GUEST EXPECTATIONS

Guests arrive with a set of expectations as to what that chosen hotel or restaurant can and should do, how it should do it, how the people providing the service should behave, how the physical setting should appear, what capabilities guests should have to perform their roles or responsibilities in coproducing the experience, how the guest should dress and act, and what the cost and value of the successfully delivered service should be. First-time guests build a mindset of expectations based on advertising, familiar brand names, promotional devices, their previous experiences with other hospitality organizations, their own imaginations, and stories and experiences of people they know who have already been guests. The organizational responsibility for bringing new or infrequent guests to the organization usually lies with the marketing department's ability to make promises about what expectations will be met.

People's past experiences with an organization provide the primary basis for their expectations regarding future experiences. In many instances, this sets a high standard to meet: what may create a "wow" experience for guests upon a first visit may be only "as expected" the next time. The organizational responsibility for getting the repeat business of both new and previous customers rests on the service providers' ability to meet and maybe even exceed both the promises that marketing has made and prior experiences of repeat guests. Depending on what sort of business you are in, you may or may not want to under-promise; but the key to delighting customers is to consistently over-deliver.

Most hospitality organizations try to provide their guests with accurate information ahead of time so these customers come to the experience with expectations that the organization can meet or exceed. If the hospitality organization does not provide that information, guests will obtain or infer it, accurately or inaccurately, from other sources: perhaps the organization's general reputation, ads, experiences that friends have had with the organization, those they themselves have had with similar organizations, or from the Web. People going to Wendy's, for example, have well-defined expectations about the quick-serve experience and soon notice when the food is not up to par, service is slow, the rest rooms are dirty, or something else is different from what they expected.

Meeting Expectations

The major responsibility for fulfilling the expectations created by the marketing department and by the past experiences of repeat guests lies with the operations side of the organization. If what guests experience falls short of what they have been led to expect or have learned to expect, they will be unhappy. They will not remember later a delightful, carefully planned guest experience; they will remember their unmet expectations as poor service and a bad experience. To preserve its reputation and customer base, the hospitality organization must meet or exceed the expectations of its guests. If it cannot or does not, it must either change its marketing strategy and create different guest expectations or change its service product, service setting, and/or service delivery system so that it can meet present guests' expectations. If enough people tell their friends what a terrible experience your restaurant or hotel provided, your reputation will be gone. With easy access to the World Wide Web, happy and unhappy guests are no longer restricted to talking with friends and neighbors over the backyard fence or on the phone. Angry customers can instantly tweet their friends or post their complaints on established Web sites or blogs dedicated to providing a means for customers to convey their experiences with different organizations or products. With such sites easily accessed—and indeed frequently used by individuals when planning trips—customers can convey their opinions about any hospitality organization almost instantly to thousands of strangers all over the world! A visit to TripAdvisor or Eater will provide good examples of the power of individuals to influence others across the world.

The challenge for hospitality organizations is to anticipate guest expectations as accurately as possible and then meet or exceed them. The ones that are consistently ranked as excellent spend extra time and money to ensure that the experience of each guest—first time and repeater—not only matches but exceeds that guest's expectations. This is an especially big challenge when one considers the high expectations with which guests arrive at, say, a fancy cruise ship. First-time customers have probably received travel agency brochures and seen cruise ships in movies and on television for years. They probably know of the cruise line's outstanding reputation and what that brand promises. Repeat passengers arrive with high expectations based on prior cruises. The cruise line wants new and repeat customers to leave the trip wowed and makes a concerted effort to exceed each passenger's expectations.

The same is true throughout the hospitality industry. The Rocky Mountaineer claims that it proudly offers "The Most Spectacular Train Trips in the World" and Planet Earth Adventures claims on its Web page, "At the end of the day, we think you'll treasure the memories of your time with us. We do everything we can to empower you to have the experience of a lifetime. Perhaps that's why many past participants have told us our adventures are the best vacations they've ever had."

If the organization cannot meet certain types of expectations, it should not say it can; it should not promise more than it can deliver. During difficult times for airlines, no-frills Southwest Airlines has continued to do well. One reason is superb service. But another key reason for its real success is that it does not promise more than it can deliver. As one person noted on Yelp, "I really like Southwest Airlines. While not fancy, they do exactly what they are supposed to do—get you where you are going safely and efficiently—with your luggage!"[11] The hospitality organization must assess guest expectations in its target market, assess its own competencies in meeting them, and try to meet or exceed them wholeheartedly.

Do Not Provide More Hospitality Than Guests Want

Organizations must be careful not to over-deliver to the point of making guests feel uncomfortable or unpleasantly surprised. If customers enter Eat 'n' Run, which looks and sounds like a fast-food restaurant, and see white linen tablecloths, they may feel that they are about to experience expensive, leisurely, "fine" dining and incur a bigger cost than they expected. Most restaurant-goers enjoy fine dining, but they want to pick the occasion, not be surprised when it occurs.

Waiters are supposed to be attentive and polite. But consider a dining experience during which the waiter constantly hovers and speaks to the diners. If Mary Jones has taken her boss out for an important business discussion, or Bob Smith has come to the restaurant with his love interest in hopes of finding a quiet moment to propose marriage, the constant presence of an overly attentive waitstaff will be a major annoyance and too much service. When does enough become too much? The excellent hospitality organization will do two things to find out. First, it will spend the time and money to train its employees to be alert to customer cues, signals, and body language so they can fine-tune their interaction with their customers. Second, it will constantly survey or ask its guests what they thought about the experience, to ensure that guests receive more service value than they expect but not so much more as to detract from the experience. As former Chili's Restaurants CEO Norman Brinker said, "Listen to your customers. They'll tell you what to do."[12]

Just What Does the Guest Expect?

Most guests have the same general expectations when they go to a hospitality organization for service. Surveys and interviews are not required to determine that most guests expect cleanliness, courtesy, responsiveness, reliability, and friendliness.

Customers complain when they do not get what they expect or when they have an unpleasant experience. Another way to get at what customers expect is to examine their complaints. Marketing expert Len Berry has listed the ten most common customer complaints. Considering what customers do not want can provide insight into what they do want. A common thread running through the complaints suggests that what bothers customers most is disrespect. Here are Berry's ten complaints[13]; they can help us arrive at a still general but slightly more specific set of guest expectations:

1. *Guest Complaint*: Lying, dishonesty, unfairness.
   Guest Expectation: To be told the truth and treated fairly.
2. *Guest Complaint*: Harsh, disrespectful treatment by employees.
   Guest Expectation: To be treated with respect.
3. *Guest Complaint*: Carelessness, mistakes, broken promises.
   Guest Expectation: To receive mistake free, careful, reliable service.
4. *Guest Complaint*: Employees without the desire or authority to solve problems.
   Guest Expectation: To receive prompt solutions to problems from empowered employees who care.
5. *Guest Complaint*: Waiting in line because some service lanes or counters are closed.
   Guest Expectation: To wait as short a time as possible.
6. *Guest Complaint*: Impersonal service.
   Guest Expectation: To receive personal attention and genuine interest from service employees.
7. *Guest Complaint*: Inadequate communication after problems arise.
   Guest Expectation: To be kept informed about recovery efforts after having or reporting problems or service failures.
8. *Guest Complaint*: Employees unwilling to make extra effort or who seem annoyed by requests for assistance.
   Guest Expectation: To receive assistance rendered willingly by helpful and trained service employees.
9. *Guest Complaint*: Employees who don't know what's happening.
   Guest Expectation: To receive accurate answers from service employees knowledgeable about both service product and organizational procedures.
10. *Guest Complaint*: Employees who put their own interests first, conduct personal business, or chat with each other while the customers wait.
    Guest Expectation: To have customers' interests come first.

Being aware of these common guest concerns and expectations should be part of any hospitality organization's knowledge base and training program. As we shall see later, however, the **benchmark organizations** dig deeper to discover the more specific guest expectations, which allows them to personalize each guest's experience as much as possible. Some organizations keep a record of these specific expectations in their database to be sure of meeting them on the guest's next visit.

QUALITY, VALUE, AND COST DEFINED

In the hospitality industry, the terms *quality*, *value*, and *cost* have specialized meanings to fit the guest-focused orientation of the benchmark firms.

Quality

Two "equations" can help make clear what quality, value, and cost mean to the guestologist and why we say that quality and value are determined not in any absolute sense, as they might be in other situations, but entirely by the guest.[14] The **quality** of the entire guest experience or of any part of it is defined as the difference between the quality that the guest expects and the quality that the guest gets. If the two are the same, then quality in this special sense is average or as expected; you got what you expected and you are satisfied. If you got more than you expected, quality was positive; if you got less than you expected, quality was negative. Let's say that on successive nights you stay at a Hyatt resort hotel and at a Knight's Inn hotel. If the Hyatt hotel did not live up to your high quality expectations and the Knight's Inn exceeded your somewhat lower quality expectations, according to the preceding definition, the Knight's Inn guest experience was of higher quality for you.

The first equation that follows describes these relationships for the quality of the guest experience, Q_e. It is equal to the quality of the experience as delivered, Q_{ed}, minus the quality expected, Q_{ee}. If the delivered and expected quality are about the same, quality is not zero as it would be if these were true mathematical equations but average or normal. If quality is average or above average, the guest can be described as satisfied. If quality is below average, the guest is dissatisfied.

$$Q_e = Q_{ed} - Q_{ee}$$

As reflected on the right side of the equation, quality as perceived by the guest will be affected by changes in either guest expectations or organizational performance. If Q_e is high enough, the guest had an exceptional, memorable, or wow service experience. The quality of any aspect of the service experience could be described in the same way.

Quality is independent of cost or value. Quality can be high and cost also high; quality can be high and cost low, and so forth.

Value

The **value** of the guest experience (V_e) is equal to the quality of the experience (Q_e) as "calculated" using the first equation divided by all the costs incurred by the guest to obtain the experience:

$$V_e = \frac{Q_e}{\text{All costs incurred by guest}}$$

If the quality and cost of the experience are about the same, the value of the experience to the guest would be normal or as expected; the guest would be satisfied by this fair value but not wowed. Low quality and low cost, and high quality and high cost, satisfy the guest about the same, because they match the guest's expectations. Organizations add value to their guests' experiences by providing additional features and amenities without increasing the cost to guests.

Cost

One source of **cost** difference to a guest having lunch today at your restaurant rather than someone else's is, of course, the price of the meal. In addition, experienced restaurant and other hospitality managers appreciate that the guest has also incurred other, less quantifiable costs, including the so-called opportunity costs of missing out on alternative meals at competing restaurants and foregoing experiences or opportunities other than eating a restaurant meal. The cost of the guest's time and the cost of any risks associated with entering into this service transaction must also enter the equation. The guest's time may not be worth an exact dollar figure per minute or hour, but it is certainly worth *something* to the guest, so time expenditures (time spent getting to your restaurant, waiting for a table, waiting for service) are also costly. Finally, the customer at your restaurant runs some risks, slim but real and potentially costly, like the risk that your restaurant cannot meet expectations or the risk that your service staff will embarrass that customer in front of the customer's own special guest today, as in our previous example, her boss.

All these tangible and intangible, financial and nonfinancial costs comprise the "all costs incurred by guest" denominator of the second equation. They make up the total burden on the guest who chooses a given guest experience.

Cost of Quality

An important concept in service organizations is the cost of quality. Interestingly enough, *cost of quality* is often used as a reminder not of how much it costs the organization to provide service quality at a high level but of how little it costs compared to the cost of not providing quality. If the organization thinks about the costs of fixing errors, compensating guests for failures, lost customers, low employee morale, and negative word of mouth that can result from poor service, the cost of quality is low indeed and the cost of not providing quality enormous. That is why benchmark organizations expend whatever resources are necessary to accomplish two complementary goals: exceed expectations to deliver wow to the level of guest delight and prevent failures. Because preventing and recovering from failure are so important, we devote Chapter 13 to these topics.

Who Defines Quality and Value?

Because service is intangible and guest expectations are variable, no objective determination of quality level (and therefore of value) can be made. In some areas of business, a quality inspector might be able to define and determine the quality of a product before a customer ever sees it. In the hospitality field, only the guest can define quality and value. No matter how brilliantly the organization designs the service, the environment, and the delivery system or develops measureable service standards, if the guest is dissatisfied with any of these elements, the organization has failed to meet the guest's expectations; it has not provided a guest experience of acceptable quality and value.

Of course, the hospitality organization may help the guest to perceive quality and value by offering a guarantee or a pledge of satisfaction that can be exercised by the guest when the guest feels that the experience did not meet expectations. Starbucks, for example, promises its customers good value by claiming in its advertising, "More for your money. A value to stay with." Starbucks adds tangibility to this promise by offering a guarantee in its Pledge of Perfection: "Your drink should be perfect every time. If not, let us know and we'll make it right." The customer decides.

Premier Inn in the UK likewise has used a "Good Night Guarantee" that provides its guests with some customer-defined tangibility to its promise of service quality. Its guarantee states, "We know you want your stay with us to be easy and hassle-free; that's why we have our Good Night Guarantee. We believe in our people doing a good job for you—in fact we're so confident, we'll give you your money back if you don't enjoy a good night's sleep—simple!"[15]

To meet or exceed the expectations of all types of guests with their different needs, wants, experiences, capabilities, and moods is the fundamental and most exciting challenge of a hospitality organization. If the hospitality manager does not believe that the guest is always right (at least in the guest's mind), then the manager had better find a new career. Even when guests are wrong by any reasonable standard, the hospitality manager must find ways to let them be wrong with dignity so that their self-esteem and satisfaction with the guest experience and the organization are not negatively affected.

Importance of Guestology

While guestology is obviously most helpful in organizing knowledge about the management of hospitality businesses—like hotels and restaurants, which have traditionally spoken of their clientele as guests—it can be used to study and understand any organization in which people are served in some way. Even manufacturing firms have "guests" or people that they should treat like guests: their customers, their own employees, and their strategic partners. Nevertheless, the traditional management model found in typical texts tends to be oriented toward the manufacturing sector, the making of physical products. Using the manufacturing model to describe how to provide hospitality services and experiences is a questionable approach.

Is hospitality management different from traditional management? Do hospitality organizations face challenges different from those faced by other business organizations? Should they therefore design themselves differently and set different types of goals? Do managers of hospitality organizations face different types of problems and require different training than managers of traditional manufacturing organizations? Do hospitality employees respond best to managerial strategies different from those to which manufacturing employees respond? The growing literature on hospitality management and the experience of successful hospitality organizations indicate that the answer to all these questions is yes.[16] A purpose of this book is to show why.

Why bother to consider the guest part of this guestology material seriously? Why should I think of my subordinate as a guest, the person walking into my travel agency as my guest, or the family coming off I-81 to my tourist attraction as guests? Let's look at the service situation from the other side for a moment. What hospitality organizations do you personally patronize, and what kind of restaurant or hotel would you yourself want to work for? Those that treat you like a special guest, or those that make you feel like an interruption to their organizational procedures and policies?

The answers to all these questions are plain. The hotels and restaurants you return to, the travel agent you call again and again, and the theme park you enjoy and recommend to friends and family are the ones that take the time to figure out what you seek in the guest experience, offer it to you, and then make clear in all they say and do that it was their pleasure that you sought it out from them. If they understand you and give you what you seek in that experience, you will like them, ascribe high value to the guest experience they provide, return when you need that service, and tell your friends and neighbors what a terrific place that hospitality organization is.

1. Treat each customer like a guest, and always start with the guest.

2. Your guest defines the value and the quality of your service, so you had better know what your guest wants.

3. Ask, ask, ask your guests.

4. Provide memorable experiences that exceed guest expectations when possible, but know when enough is enough; deliver more than the guest expects, but not more than the guest wants.

5. Manage all three parts of the guest experience: the service product, the service environment, and the service delivery system (both the processes and the people).

6. The less tangible the guest experience, the more important are the frontline people delivering the service to the guest's perception of quality and value.

7. You may under-promise, but always try to over-deliver.

8. The cost of providing quality is low compared to the potential cost of not providing quality.

9. Service product + service environment + service delivery system = guest experience

10. Experiences that evoke a guest's emotions are more memorable.

1. Consider the formula presented in the chapter:

   service product + service environment + service delivery system = guest experience

   A. Although all parts are important, do you think these three types of organizations—a hotel, a restaurant, and an airline—would tend to place a different emphasis on the three parts in providing the total guest experience?

   B. If product + environment + delivery system = 100%, how would the hotel, restaurant, and airline divide up their emphasis? Or, how would these organization types rank the three parts of the guest experience in order of emphasis?

2. Imagine that a Rolex watch, a RadioShack watch, an Eagle Mirado #2 pencil, and a Cross fountain pen are sitting on a table in front of you. Which item is highest in quality, and which is lowest in quality?

3. These standard rooms are available in your locality: the Ritz-Carlton Hotel ($450 per night), a Holiday Inn ($150), a No-Tell Motel ($59.95), and a YMCA or YWCA. Which room is highest in quality, and which is lowest in quality?

4. Consider the examples in questions 2 and 3 in terms of value. Under what circumstances can quality be high and value low? Value high and quality low?

5. A guest experience is a service, and this chapter explained that services are largely intangible. Think of a somewhat expensive guest experience you have had. What tangibles did the organization use to make you feel that your intangible experience was worth the money you paid?

6. Reflect on a recent, enjoyable guest experience and on a disappointing guest experience.

    A. What were the significant events, the moments of truth, during each experience?

    B. How did they contribute to your enjoyment or disappointment?

    C. How do they relate to managing the guest experience in hospitality organizations?

7. This chapter makes some general statements about how people form their expectations for guest experiences.

    A. How do those statements match up with the way you personally form your expectations for a new upcoming experience?

    B. If you are going for a repeat experience, would your expectations be based totally on previous experiences?

    C. If you were a hospitality manager, what level and type of expectations would you want to create in your guests, and how would you try to create them?

    D. How would you take into account the fact that some guests are new, some are repeaters, and you may not know which are which?

8. You are probably familiar with the expression "too much of a good thing." In the hospitality setting, that would describe over-delivering the service guests have come to receive.

    A. How much service is too much service? Have you ever experienced excessive service?

    B. How does a hospitality manager ensure that guest expectations are met or exceeded without going overboard?

9. From an article in a guest services magazine: "What brings hotel guests back? A fluffy robe hanging on a padded hanger? Creamy chocolate reposing on the pillow? The jungle safari bedroom decor? Or plain vanilla, old-fashioned service?" What do you say?

10. How is service quality related to guest satisfaction?

ACTIVITIES

Many of the chapters in this book will include suggested hospitality field exercises or activities that might involve speaking to customers, employees, and managers of hospitality organizations. Your instructor will guide you on whether to do these assignments and how to go about them. You will also have assignments that ask you to report on a service failure or write a letter of complaint. You are doing these assignments to learn, not to make trouble for hospitality employees, so don't use real names in your reports unless your instructor gives permission. Don't send a fake complaint to an organization to see how they respond; this could get you in real trouble.

Excellent sources for study are your own organization, if you are presently working, and the organizations in which your friends may be working. Ideally, your information will come from hospitality organizations but if your personal situation does not permit that, study some other type of service organization. If you are really at a loss, consider the "service" provided by the instructors of your classes. For some of the requested first-hand information, however, you may have to visit the organization and talk with its people. If so, be a good guest!

For the following three exercises, and all the others in this book, you will write your responses or prepare to discuss them in class, as your instructor directs.

1. Pick two service organizations, in the same service field, you have patronized recently or can visit conveniently. Compare them in terms of the service quality and value you received.

2. Think about the last business establishment of any kind you visited. What were the tangibles of its service product? What were the intangibles?

3. Divide up into groups. On the basis of the group's collective experience, discuss what is good service. Mention some organizations that deliver good service. Compare notes with other groups.

ETHICS IN BUSINESS

This chapter has emphasized the idea of serving the customer's needs, and the general notion that "the guest is always right." Of course, there are times when the guest goes too far, or wants too much. As mentioned earlier in the chapter, in such circumstances, "the hospitality manager must find ways to let them be wrong with dignity so that their self-esteem and satisfaction with the guest experience and the organization are not negatively affected." So, how would you suggest handling the following situations?

- A guest leaves a message that he will be interviewing job candidates in his suite at noon, and so needs the room made up immediately, while he is out for breakfast. The housekeeper sent to the room reports that some illegal drugs were left in the bathroom, and she refuses to make up the room.
- A long-time customer has drunk a bit too much in your hotel bar. He is staying at the hotel that evening, he is not driving, and he insists on one more drink. He says that if the hotel refuses to serve him, he will take his business elsewhere.
- You are working at a fancy restaurant and serving a family. The family orders a 1996 Chateau Margeaux (a bottle of wine that costs roughly $1200). They want you to pour "just a taste" for their child, so that he may share in the experience of trying this exceptional wine. You are unsure what the local laws are, but you think that you are not allowed to serve alcohol to a minor, even with the parents' consent. They, however, insist it is just a taste, and there is no harm.

CASE STUDY

Eastern States Air Environment

Gloria Rooney assumed the presidency of Eastern States Air in the early 2000s, after proving her ability as executive vice president with two other major airlines. Like most other surviving airlines, Eastern States Air weathered rough times during the mid-2000s. But as the year 2011 neared, Rooney was running an airline that was doing well. Naturally, Rooney couldn't be satisfied with simply staying the course; she wanted to do better. And she thought she knew how.

Rooney saw that service in the airline industry had been in a state of steady decline for several years. More and more passengers were flying than ever before, but their level of satisfaction had gone down. Crowded airports, flight delays, overbooking, the occasional disastrous accident, and other factors had combined to raise industry complaints to all-time-high levels just when passenger flight miles were also at an all-time high.

In that atmosphere, Rooney finally had an opportunity to put into practice one of her most deeply held beliefs about running an airline: "It's not what you do; it's how you do it." She told her staff time after time: "The 'what' is the easy part. What we do is take passengers from here to there. The way we can distinguish ourselves favorably from our competitors is in the 'how.'"

Eastern States Air became known as "the airline that put the Frills back into Flying." A small lounge was added to all planes that could accommodate one. For people not wanting to leave their seats, two complimentary drinks per passenger per flight, delivered to the seat, became the standard. An internationally known chef was hired to supervise a food-service system that produced meals as close to the gourmet level as was possible given the state of technology. Just before passengers exited each Eastern States flight, they were surveyed to see how satisfied they had been with the basics of the flight and with the frills that Eastern States had put back into flying. Early results of Rooney's campaign showed that passenger satisfaction levels were off the chart at the top. In one astonishing month, the airline received no complaints about anything. Rooney was overjoyed. "They said zero defects was an impossible standard in airline service. We proved them wrong." The passengers who raved about Eastern States Air and flew the airline as often as they could, sometimes simply for sheer pleasure, understood that there is no free lunch. Eastern States had to raise its fares considerably to provide outstanding service, but some people paid the higher prices happily.

Unfortunately, the number of passengers flying Eastern States Air took a disastrous drop. The ones who stayed loved the airline. They became unpaid spokespeople for Eastern States Air, but there were not enough of them. Rooney realized that she had been somewhat deceived by the excellent survey results. She had been surveying only those who stayed, not those who left.

Surveying a broader cross-section of passengers, former passengers, and passengers of other airlines led Rooney to change her strategy. "When you get right down to it," she said, "this is really a very simple business. Steamships used to be a mode of transportation; now they provide luxury cruises that end up where they started. But in our business, what people want is to get from here to there as inexpensively as possible. In the current market, cheap airfares are what people expect, and that's what we need to give them. But we won't forget the loyal customers who have stayed with us. If we do this right, we can appeal to both groups."

To implement the new strategy, Eastern States Air cut back on the number of seats in first class but increased their size, along with first-class appointments and level of service, to retain the airline guests who had been satisfied to have the frills put back into flying and were willing to pay for them. Throughout the rest of the plane, however, economy became the watchword. More seats were stuffed into each plane, the number of flight attendants was reduced, and "meals" consisted of dry finger food, mainly pretzels. They not only added a fee for luggage, they even charged for carry ons.

Eastern States began to make a financial comeback, but the number of complaints skyrocketed to record levels. The following comments were typical:

"You are putting all your service into the front of the plane. What about those of us stuck in the back?"

"I've seen the animals in cattle cars treated better than this."

"I used to be able to get by a window or on the aisle; now I always seem to get stuck in the middle seat. Why is that?"

"I see that your industry is enjoying record profits. How about using some of that dough to give us a better ride?"

"I'm a little over six feet tall, and I have to twist my legs to fit in that cramped space you give me."

"Seats too narrow, too close together. Flight attendant handed me pretzels just as we were landing."

"I've had better seats and better service on the crosstown bus."

"How can you charge me to stick my own bag under my own feet?"

Some of these disappointed and angry passengers took out their resentment on the flight crews. Morale among the pilots and flight attendants began to drop. Rooney was baffled and disappointed. "You can't win in this business. You give people what they want, and the complaints go through the roof." She was quite concerned about the next board of directors meeting and what the board would have to say about her management of the airline.

1. What is the service product of the airline industry?

2. What were Rooney's mistakes?

3. How could they have been avoided?

4. What now?

Bacon, T. R., & Pugh, D. G. 2004. Ritz-Carlton and EMC: The gold standards in operational behavioral differentiation. *Journal of Organizational Excellence*, 23 (2), 61–76.

Berry, L. L., Wall, E. A., & Carbone, E. A. 2006. Service clues and customer assessment of the service experience: Lessons from marketing. *The Academy of Management Perspectives*, 20 (2), 43–57.

Bowen, John, & Ford, R. C. 2004. What experts say about managing hospitality service delivery systems. *International Journal of Contemporary Hospitality*, 16 (7), 394–401.

Bretthauer, K. M. 2004. Service management. *Decision Sciences*, 35 (3), 325–332.

Brotherton, B. 2005. The nature of hospitality: Customer perceptions and implications. *Tourism and Hospitality Planning & Development*, 2 (3), 139–153.

Capodagli, B., & Jackson, L. 2006. *The Disney Way: Harnessing the Management Secrets of Disney in Your Company*, Revised and fully updated edition. New York: McGraw-Hill.

Chase, R. B., & Dasu, S. 2004. Psychology of the experience: The missing link in service science. *On line Manuscript*, www.almaden.ibm.com/asr/summit/papers/ucscchase.pdf, accessed June 23, 2009.

Davis, T. R. V. 2004. Different service firms, different international strategies. *Business Horizons*, 47 (3), 51–59.

Edvardsson, B., Gustafsson, A., & Roos, I. 2005. Service portraits in service research: A critical review. *International Journal of Service Industry Management*, 16 (1), 107–121.

Ford, R. C., & Heaton, C. P. 2001. Lessons from hospitality that can serve anyone. *Organizational Dynamics*, 30 (1), 30–47.

Ford, R. C., Heaton, C. P., & Brown, S. W. 2001. Delivering excellent service: Lessons from the best firms. *California Management Review*, 44 (1), 39–56.

Gittell, J. H. 2002. *The Southwest Airlines Way: Using the Power of Relationships to Achieve High Performance*. New York: McGraw-Hill.

Hales, D., & Williams, D. 2007. *Wow! That's What I Call Service!* Cornwall, England: Ecademy Press Limited.

Hemmington, N. 2007. From service to experience: Understanding and defining the hospitality business. *The Service Industries Journal*, 27 (6), 747–755.

Hennig-Thurau, T. 2004. Customer orientation of service employees. *International Journal of Service Industry Management*, 15 (5), 460–478.

Heskett, W. E., Sasser, J. L., & Schlesinger, L. A. 1997. *The Service Profit Chain: How Leading Companies Link Profit and Growth to Loyalty, Service and Value*. New York: Free Press.

Johnson, M. D., Olsen, L. L., & Andreassen, T. W. 2009. Joy and disappointment in the hotel experience: Managing relationship segments. *Managing Service Quality*, 19 (1), 4–30.

Kandampully, J. 2006. The new customer-centered business model for the hospitality industry. *International Journal of Contemporary Hospitality Management*, 18 (3), 173–187.

Kandampully, J., & Kandampully, R. 2006. Service system: A strategic approach to innovate and manage service superiority, in B. Prideaux, G. Moscardo, and Eric Laws (eds.), *Managing Tourism and Hospitality Services: Theory and International Applications*. Wallingford, England: CABI, pp. 94–103.

Keillor, B. D., Hult, G. T. M., & Kandemir, D. 2004. A study of the service encounter in eight countries. *Journal of International Marketing*, 12 (1), 9–35.

King, C. A. 1995. What is hospitality? *International Journal of Hospitality Management*, 14 (3/4), 219–234.

Kinni, T., & Eisner, M. D. 2001. *Be Our Guest: Perfecting the Art of Customer Service*. New York: Disney Editions.

Knutson, B. J., Singh, A. J., Yen, H. H., & Bryant, B. E. 2004. Guest satisfaction in the US lodging industry using the ACSI Model as a service quality scoreboard. *Journal of Quality Assurance in Hospitality & Tourism*, 4 (3), 97–118.

Levitt, T. 1981. Marketing intangible products and product intangibles. *Harvard Business Review*, 59 (3), 94–102.

McCaskey, D., & Symes, S. 2004. Travel Inn: Everything you want for a good night's sleep—100 percent satisfaction guarantee or your money back. *International Journal of Contemporary Hospitality Management*, 16 (3), 166–174.

Michelli, J. 2008. Th*e New Gold Standard: 5 Leadership Principles for Creating a Legendary Customer Experience Courtesy of the Ritz-Carlton Hotel Company*. New York: McGraw-Hill.

Oh, H., Fiore, A. M., & Jeoung, M. 2007. Measuring experience economy concepts: Tourism application. *Journal of Travel Research*, 46, 119–132.

Parasuraman, A., Zeithaml, V. A., & Berry, L. L. 1985. A conceptual model of service quality and its implications for future research. *Journal of Marketing*, 49 (4), 41–50.

Petrick, J. F., Tonner, C., & Quinn, C. 2006. The utilization of critical incident technique to examine cruise passengers' repurchase intentions. *Journal of Travel Research*, 44 (3), 273–280.

Rahman, Z. 2004. Developing customer oriented service: A case study. *Managing Service Quality*, 14 (5), 426–435.

Rathmell, J. M. 1966. What is meant by services? *Journal of Marketing*, 30 (4), 32–36.

Rhoades, D. L. 2006. Growth, customer service and profitability Southwest style. *Managing Service Quality*, 16 (5), 538–547.

Schneider, B., & White, S. S. 2004. *Service Quality: Research Perspectives*. Thousand Oaks, CA: Sage Publications.

Scott, N., Laws, E., & Boksberger, P. 2009. The marketing of hospitality and leisure experiences. *Journal of Hospitality Marketing & Management*, 18, 99–110.

Shah, D., Rust, R. T., Parasuraman, A., Staelin, R., & Day, G. S. 2006. The path to customer centricity. *Journal of Service Research*, 9 (2), 113–124.

Sharp, I. 2009. *Four Seasons: The Story of a Business Philosophy*. New York: Penguin Group.

Solnet, D., & Kandampully, J. 2008. How some service firms have become part of "service excellence" folklore. *Managing Service Quality*, 18 (2), 179–193.

Stuart, F. I., & Tax, S. 2004. Toward an integrative approach to designing service experiences: Lessons learned from the theatre. *Journal of Operations Management*, 22, 609–627.

Tajeddini, K. 2010. Effect of customer orientation and entrepreneurial orientation on innovativeness: Evidence from the hotel industry in Switzerland. *Tourism Management*, 31 (2), 221–231.

Tax, S. S., Colgate, M., & Bowen, D. E. 2006. How to prevent your customers from failing. *MIT Sloan Management Review*, 47 (3), 30–38.

Torres, E. N., & Kline, S. 2006. From satisfaction to delight: A model for the hotel industry. *International Journal of Contemporary Hospitality Management*, 18 (4), 290–301.

Treacy, M., & Wiersema, F. 1997. *The Discipline of Market Leaders*. Reading, MA: Addison-Wesley.

Verhoef, P. C., Lemon, K. N., Parasuraman, A., Roggeveen, A., Tsiros, M., & Schlesinger, L. A. 2009. Customer experience creation: Determinants, dynamics and management strategies. *Journal of Retailing*, 85, 31–41.

Wood, R. C., & Brotherton, B. 2008. *The SAGE Handbook of Hospitality Management*. Thousand Oaks, CA: Sage Publications.

NOTES

[1] For an interview with Bruce Laval, the father of guestology, see Ford, R. C., & Dickson, D. D. 2008. Interview with Bruce Laval. *Journal of Applied Management and Entrepreneurship*, 13 (3), 80–99.

[2] For more on the intangibility of services, see Bowen, J. T., & Ford, R. C. 2002. Managing service organizations: Does having a 'thing' make a difference? *Journal of Management*, 28 (3), 447–469.

[3] Quoted in Levitt, T. 1972. Production-line approach to service. *Harvard Business Review*, 50 (5), 50.

[4] Ibid., 41.

[5] Pine, B. J., & Gilmore, J. H. 1988. Welcome to the experience economy. *Harvard Business Review*, 66 (4), 97–105.

[6] Neu, W., & Brown, S. W. 2005. Forming successful business-to-business services in goods-dominant firms. *Journal of Service Research*, 8 (1), 3–17.

[7] Lytle, R. S., Hom, P. W., & Mokwa, M. P. 1998. SERV*OR: A managerial measure of organizational service-orientation. *Journal of Retailing*, 74, 460.

[8] Carlzon, J. 1987. *Moments of Truth*. New York: Ballinger.

[9] Gremler, D. D. 2004. The critical incident technique in service research. *Journal of Service Research*, 7 (1), 65–89.

[10] Ford, R. C., & Bowen, D. 2008. A service dominant logic for management education: It's time. *Academy of Management Education & Learning*, 7 (2), 224–243.

[11] Yelp (a June 16, 2009 blog entry). http://www.yelp.com/biz/southwest-airlines-phoenix-3, accessed December 17, 2009.

[12] Brinker, N., & Phillips, D. T. 1996. *On the Brink: The Life and Leadership of Norman Brinker*. Arlington, TX: The Summit Publishing Group, p. 192.

[13] Berry, L. L. 1999. *Discovering the Soul of Service*. New York: The Free Press, p. 31.

[14] Adapted from Heskett, J. L., Sasser, W. E., Jr., & Hart, C. W. L. 1990. *Service Breakthroughs: Changing the Rules of the Game*. New York: The Free Press, p. 2.

[15]McCaskey, D., & Symes, S. 2004. Travel Inn: Everything you want for a good night's sleep—100 percent satisfaction guarantee or your money back. *International Journal of Contemporary Hospitality Management*, 16 (3), 166–174.

[16]See Dickson, D., Ford, R. C., & Laval, B. 2005. The top ten excuses for bad service (and how to avoid needing them). *Organizational Dynamics*, 34 (2), 168–184.

CHAPTER 2

Meeting Guest Expectations through Planning

HOSPITALITY PRINCIPLE: FOCUS STRATEGY ON THE KEY DRIVERS OF GUEST SATISFACTION

High performing organizations design work processes from the customer backward to ensure a flow that makes sense from a customer's perspective. Internal cross-functional relationships and structures are organized around customer needs. High performing organizations ensure that they are able to respond quickly to customer needs and adapt to changes in the market place. They anticipate trends and get in front of them. Innovations in processes are developed to make it easier for customers to do business. This creates constant innovation in operating practices, market strategies, products, and services.

—Ken Blanchard, Jesse Stoner, and Scott Blanchard, *Serving Customers at a Higher Level*, in Ken Blanchard's *Leading at a Higher Level*

LEARNING OBJECTIVES

After reading this chapter, you should understand:

- The three generic strategies for positioning products and services.

- The organizational planning cycle and how its different elements result in the establishment of the hospitality organization's overall strategic plan and service strategy.

- The basics of how organizations plan and design the guest experience.

- The key external and internal factors that must be examined for successful planning.

- The quantitative and qualitative tools used for forecasting in the hospitality environment—external and internal.

- The process to determine core competencies.

- The importance of including the key drivers of guest satisfaction in the planning process.

- The importance and value of product and service branding.

- A planning model, showing how components are tied together and action plans are developed.

KEY TERMS AND CONCEPTS

forecasting	key drivers	mission statement
low-price provider	quantitative forecasting tools	design day
differentiate, differentiation	qualitative forecasting tools	yield management
market niche	scenario building	revenue management
brand image	Delphi technique	econometric models
brand name	strategic premises	regression analysis
strategic plan	internal audit	time-series and trend analyses
action plans	core competence	brainstorming
environmental assessment	vision statement	focus groups

When guests show up at a hotel, restaurant, or any other hospitality service provider, they have certain expectations of both what will and will not happen. To give guests what they expect requires research to determine exactly what those expectations are. Translating those expectations into a service product that aligns or fits the organization's mission and values takes detailed planning, **forecasting**, and sound intuitive judgment. Managers of excellent hospitality organizations try to mix all three together into a strategy that allows them to give guests exactly what they expect and even a bit more. Guests will return only if their experiences meet, if not exceed, their expectations. The service strategy is the organization's plan for providing the experience that guests expect.

Planning and strategy making are simple to talk about and difficult to do. In theory, all one has to do is to assess the environment within which the organization operates, assess the organization's capabilities, decide where the organization wants to go within that environment and in light of those capabilities, and then make a plan to get there. Unfortunately, the needs, wants, capabilities, and expectations of real customers change; competitors find ways to duplicate the firm's strategic advantage of the moment; governments pass new laws; and advances in technology require the firm to scrap its old delivery system and create a new one. In other words, people change, their needs and expectations change, the competition changes, the environment changes, and so must the hospitality organization. Finding ways to deliver what customers expect in light of the many uncertainties created by such changes is a major challenge.

THREE GENERIC STRATEGIES

A saying in business is, "Price, quality, speed—pick any two." The implication is that no organization can do it all, so no customer should expect it all; the organization must determine the basis on which it hopes to compete. McDonald's gives you speed and price; the Four Seasons Restaurant gives you quality. In addition to price, quality, and speed, the organization could compete on variety, convenience, friendliness, no-frills, uniqueness, helpfulness, or some other basis.

According to strategy scholar Michael Porter, an organization usually employs one or more of three different generic strategies.[1] First, it can aim to be the low-cost producer and **low-price provider** in its industry, area, or market segment. Second, it can **differentiate** its product or service from those of its competitors. Third, it can fill a particular **market niche** or need. Successful hospitality organizations establish a strategy that may include one or more of these generic strategies and stick with it.

A Lower Price

"We will not be undersold!" The low-price provider tries to design and provide pretty much the same service that the competition sells, but at a lower price. Management's focus is on maximizing operational or production efficiencies to minimize the organization's costs. Southwest Airlines focused on reducing the costs of running the airline (turnaround times, loading and unloading, food service, and so forth) to achieve the lowest production cost per mile in the industry. Wal-Mart focused on selling for less by controlling inventory and cutting merchandise costs by mass buying. The low-price provider tries to offer the service at a price so low that competitors cannot offer the same service and value at a lower price without losing money. Red Roof Inn and Motel 6 are competing with Budgetel and Sleep Inn, not with Ritz-Carlton and Hyatt. Of course, all hospitality organizations are cost conscious, but some focus on offering bargain prices to reach a wider market rather than focusing on differentiating their service in a wide market or meeting the special needs of a narrow market.

Companies employing the low-price strategy must recognize that if they reduce prices to customers by reducing their own costs, the deterioration in the guest experience that results may decrease the value of the experience to guests and drive them to competitors. Although some are still able to offer excellent customer service, such as JetBlue and Southwest, it is through the delivery system (e.g., employees, scheduling, and standardization of aircraft) that they add value and not through offering a more expensive service product or employing more staff.

A Differentiated Product

All hospitality organizations practice product **differentiation** to an extent; all want to be perceived as offering a service product—the guest experience itself—that is different in ways their customers find favorable. Many try to attract guests by emphasizing these differences rather than by offering low prices.

Differentiating one's product in the marketplace results from creating in the customer's mind desirable differences, either real or driven by marketing and advertising, between that product and others available at about the same price. In an era when so many hotel rooms of different brands look so similar, the Ice Hotel in Jukkasjärvi, Sweden—a hotel constructed each year out of snow and ice, featuring reindeer skin beds, an ice bar, and magnificent ice sculptures in the lobby—certainly provides a unique experience that differentiates it from every other hotel in the world.

While not all hotels strive to be as unique as the Ice Hotel, hotel companies do try to differentiate themselves in the marketplace by advertising that can create a brand identity that is valued by the targeted customers or offering special amenities ("Free continental breakfast!" "Kids sleep free!") that are attractive to that market segment. They hope that a potential guest looking for a place to spend the night will remember what the brand stands for, want the amenities, and therefore drive into, for example, a Holiday Inn instead of a Ramada Inn, or vice versa, for what is essentially the same service product: a clean room in which to sleep.

For example, the Nickelodeon Suites Resort at Lake Buena Vista, Florida, differentiates itself from most other hotels by focusing on families with children offering suites themed on Nickelodeon's popular children's characters. Besides its unique Kidsuites, it offers a Nick After Dark program, which is an interactive kids-only dinner show with a slime experience, special weekend packages themed on Nickelodeon's characters like SpongeBob SquarePants, gated access to the property and kids' wristbands for parents' peace of mind, and even a kid's spa.

The Ice Hotel, in Jukkas-järvi, Sweden, offers a service product that is clearly differentiated from other hotels.

Image copyright *Elisa Locci, 2010.* Used under license from Shutterstock.com

The Brand Image

A major way to differentiate one's service from those of competitors is through the creation of a strong **brand image**.[2] A brand represents a promise to guests of what the quality and value of experiences associated with that brand will offer them, every time and every place they see the brand. A strong brand promise reduces customer uncertainty about the hospitality experience that the organization offers and, consequently, creates a brand preference and increases customer loyalty. Once a strong brand preference is established, it can provide some protection against cost cutting or other competitive strategies that can get guests to switch to other competing products. The strong **brand name** can also extend the company's reach into new markets. Because services are mostly intangible—with no dress, guitar, or minivan to touch and try out before buying—brands are particularly important in both adding value to the guest experience and differentiating it from competing services. Even producers of mostly tangible products, like detergents and autos, know the value of a brand and work hard to protect its integrity and image. The Golden Arches is a brand worth a great deal as a symbol of quality and value, and it provides McDonald's with a tremendous competitive advantage. The McDonald's brand communicates a certain consistency in quality, price, and type of food served. Although specific menu items may vary worldwide—you can't get beef, but you can get the Maharaja Mac in India; you can get beer in Germany; you can get your Big Mac on a pita in Greece; and you can order Gallo Pinto (rice and beans) in Costa Rica—the mission of each restaurant is the same: to "be our customers' favorite place and way to eat." A McDonald's restaurant is instantly recognizable, and thus any of its restaurants anywhere in the world is immediately differentiated from any other fast-food operation. McDonald's works hard to protect the valuable symbol of its brand logo and maintain the reputation for which it stands.

A high-quality brand image enables a company like McDonald's, Disney, or Marriott to gain acceptance for anything new it brings to the marketplace. Customers will usually be willing to give the new product or service a try on the basis of the brand's reputation.

For example, thousands of people, many of them families that had never before felt comfortable going on a cruise, booked trips on the Disney Magic even before the ship was launched. They knew that Disney would not risk hurting its brand by putting it on something inconsistent with the customer's expectation of what Disney stands for. A brand represents a powerful marketing tool to communicate a promise of quality and value for any experience with that brand. Therefore, companies spend a lot of money to create and protect their brands.

Having a strong brand may sometimes be a disadvantage. When Disney entered the European market by opening Disneyland Paris, it discovered that the Disney brand was not seen favorably by some, who associated the brand with promoting American values. Furthermore, fear of hurting the brand image may unnecessarily inhibit a company from exploring new market opportunities or putting its name on a potentially profitable product or service just because doing so may seem inconsistent with the brand image. However, compared to the advantages of instant and favorable product differentiation, this disadvantage is small, and most companies with strong brands are happy to pay this price.

A Special Niche

Finally, an organization can try to find and fill a particular market niche or gap. It can focus on a specific part of the total market by offering a special appeal—like quality, value, location, or exceptional service—to attract customers in that market segment.

The airline industry is one that is constantly seeking to create and fill niches. For example, JetBlue, WestJet, and Southwest Airlines all elected to pursue a short-haul, low-fare, high-frequency, point-to-point strategy to carve out a specific niche in the airline market. This has been a fairly successful strategy, allowing them to achieve success in comparison to the legacy carriers using a hub-and-spoke, business-class traveler-focused strategy. This strategy has been replicated in Europe as well, with the creation of easyJet and other discount carriers.

Warren Buffet, the legendary chairman of Berkshire Hathaway, has taken the airline niche strategy further by investing in what may become a new type of airline travel: The company is NetJets and the concept is called fractional ownership. NetJets owns its aircraft, flies anywhere in the world, adheres to rigorous safety and maintenance standards, and uses a high-tech operations center to keep an eye on every plane in its fleet. But the resemblances to traditional carriers end there. NetJets' customers travel on their own schedules, avoid check-in and security lines, stretch out in comfort in spacious cabins, and fly with only the passengers they choose.[3]

There are many other examples across the hospitality industry where companies have sought niches that will appeal to specific groups of potential customers. For example, the niche tour industry now includes specialty tours focused on people who want to combine a tour experience with such activities as bicycling; walking; volunteering; golfing; sampling wines, cuisines, pub beers; associating only with a specific group of people, like a university's alumni, families, or gays; or exploring a specific culture, ecology, or heritage. The Society for Accessible Travel & Hospitality reports organizations that have designed special tours for the disabled, such as the walking tour for people with visual impairments offered by Waymark Holidays, a UK walking tour company.[4] Theme parks also have increasingly found niches. Now customers can choose among Christian (Holy Land), kiddie (Wannado City), heritage (Wild West City, Dollywood), water (Aquatica), animal experience (Marineland, Discovery Cove), human bodies (Corpus), and other niche theme parks.

In the fast-food market and budget-hotel market, the competitive positioning of a McDonald's or Day's Inn is to be the low-cost producer in the budget segment of the market. Casual-dining restaurants like Olive Garden and Chili's have tried to position themselves in the dining-out market by offering price and food values at a point above fast-food and below fine-dining restaurants. By focusing on one particular part of the total market, they hope to distinguish themselves from other types of eating places. Other market niches that have been identified and used as a focus for organizational strategies are the healthy-eating niche in restaurants, convention hotels in lodging, and water parks in parks and attractions. In these instances, the market niche is carefully defined demographically, psychographically, or geographically. The organization seeks to build a top-of-mind awareness within customers in its targeted market as to how unique the experience provided is and how, by focusing on that one market segment, it uniquely meets their particular needs. The distinction between *differentiation* and *finding a niche* is not clear cut. One way to think of it is that the organization determines the market at which it wants to aim, the niche it hopes to fill, and then uses strategies to differentiate itself from other organizations in that same market or niche. The most common strategy is to try to differentiate its product or service from similar products or services.

The organization that concentrates on filling niches is often a market innovator seeking to meet an unfulfilled customer need, perhaps a need that customers don't recognize until they see the product that will fulfill it: a high-priced luxury airline for rich people, a sandwich wrap for drivers eating dashboard cuisine, the W hotel for contemporary luxury travelers, or any other of the thousands of innovative products and services brought to the marketplace each year. This unfulfilled need might be identified by careful market research, serious study of population and demographic trends, a lucky guess, or an intuitive combination of these approaches. Some researchers argue that this combination is the most likely way for managers to develop a **strategic plan**, especially those that make a real difference in an organization's success.[5]

The differences between these three competitive strategies—lower cost, product differentiation, and defined market scope (niche vs. broad market reach)—are illustrated in these three restaurant examples. The fast-food, limited-menu restaurants like McDonald's compete on price, Red Lobster differentiates itself from other full-service restaurants by specializing in seafood, and Dave and Buster's fits into a niche, the "eatertainment" restaurant. The differences between the three strategies, however, are not always clear and many authors use a fivefold classification that combines them in their various ways.[6] Consider the Hyatt hotel company. Does it seek to compete on a niche (high-end business and convention traveler) or on price (the best price in its market segment)? Marriott has developed several brands to fit the various market niches it seeks to reach as well as the price points within those segments. It differentiates its brands on the basis of both price and targeted market niche. The point is that a number of strategic opportunities exist for hospitality organizations to consider. Each of these opportunities has advantages and disadvantages that an in-depth review of strategic planning will reveal.[7]

Combining Strategies

The strategies just discussed are not mutually exclusive. An organization can seek to differentiate its product from all others in the market (Strategy 2) by positioning the product in people's minds as the best value for the lowest cost (Strategy 1). This combination of strategies requires the organization to use both effective marketing techniques that reach this best-value, lowest-cost market segment and operating efficiencies that allow it to make money at the low price. Successful theme parks seek to apply this combination by

The Hard Rock Cafe is a themed restaurant, aimed at filling a particular niche in the restaurant industry.

Image copyright Dariusz Majgier, 2010. Used under license from Shutterstock.com

advertising a park visit as a high-value, low-cost, family-entertainment experience while keeping their costs, especially labor costs, low. JetBlue and Southwest Airlines follow the strategy of offering both low prices and excellent service to provide a high-value, low-cost experience in the airline industry to the broadest array of customers possible.

Reinventing the Industry

Picking and following a strategy is an important decision for any hospitality manager seeking to find the best match of the company's mission with present and emerging uncertainties.

If drastic change is forecast, the organization might even have to reinvent itself and learn new core competencies. A strategy might be to get cheaper, or better, or faster. These are all reactive operational strategies that most organizations could adopt as circumstances change.

Most companies listen to their customers and then respond to their articulated needs. But some rare, highly creative organizations can actually create the future for themselves and their industries. Organizational strategists Gary Hamel and C. K. Prahalad note in their book *Competing for the Future* that the organization might even need to "lead customers where they want to go but don't know it yet."[8] They "do more than satisfy customers, they constantly amaze them."[9] In other words, they will need to be capable of reinventing their industry through constant innovation.

The creation of Disneyland Park is a great example of a visionary leader reinventing an industry by leading customers to a place they didn't know they wanted to go. Disneyland was an attempt to move beyond the Coney Island amusement park concept to something new, cleaner, more organized, and safer. Instead of a disjointed array of amusement rides, barkers, and arcades, Walt Disney created within a single setting the feel of being actual participants in a motion picture. The traditional amusement park was embellished in creative ways with new technology and the introduction of theming to become an experience: The theme park didn't exist until Disney and his creative team imagined it and built it.

Providing Superior Service Quality and Value

These three generic strategies—competing on price, finding a niche, and differentiating—may each work for a while, but they also have potential shortcomings. If you compete on price, somebody is eventually going to undercut your price. Also, the costs associated with establishing a close and lasting relationship with guests are difficult to cover if you stress your low price. If you find a niche and succeed there, an imitator eventually will join you in the niche, and soon it will be just another market segment. If you differentiate successfully, somebody will copy your differentiation feature. Many successful service organizations have found that the best way to succeed in the long term is to differentiate on the basis of superlative service quality and value. Provide better service and value than the competition does, and they can't beat you. As Chris Fraser, managing director of multiple award winner HotelConnect, said after winning a customer service award, "Excellence in Customer Service is our competitive advantage within the market; it is at the core of our culture, and affects every area of our business."[10] The well-known management writer, Tom Peters, echoes this idea. He writes, "You can knock off everything … except awesome service."[11]

THE HOSPITALITY PLANNING CYCLE

Leading guests to where they want to go but don't know it yet is how the truly outstanding hospitality organizations become and stay outstanding. The focus of this chapter is to help readers appreciate how service organizations find a way to give guests what they want, when they want it, even if they don't know yet exactly what they want. The organization gathers as much information as it can on what its present customers want, need, and do, tries to imagine what kinds of experiences their future guests will find satisfying, and then plans ways to deliver them. For example, Walt Disney planned out a theme park that he knew would wow park visitors long before they knew what a theme park was. As a more recent example, bank customers didn't know they needed debit cards (on which expenditures are deducted directly from the customer's checking account) until banks offered them. Similarly, phone customers didn't recognize their need for a single telephone number that can be used anywhere and includes texting, picture taking, e-mail, GPS, and Internet capabilities until wireless companies made them aware of how convenient such services could be. Hospitality organizations did not know they needed a Web site until the idea was introduced.

The way to reach these outcomes is through the strategic planning process. The process has two basic steps: assessment (external and internal) and figuring out what to do on the basis of that assessment. The external assessment of environmental opportunities and threats leads to the generation of strategic premises about the future environment. The internal assessment of organizational strengths and weaknesses leads to a redefinition or reaffirmation of organizational core competencies.

As seen in Figure 2-1, hospitality planning follows an ongoing cycle that begins at the big-picture level and ends in specific **action plans**, departmental or project budgets, and individual yearly objectives that can be tested against performance metrics. Typically, such planning is done annually and begins with management's simultaneous consideration of three elements: the external environment with its opportunities and threats, the internal organization with its strengths and weaknesses, and the relationship of these elements to the statements of organizational vision and mission.

Looking Around

The **environmental assessment**, or the long look around for opportunities and threats, in turn defines the strategic premises. These premises are the beliefs of the managers assessing all long-term aspects of the external environment and trying to use them to discover what forces will impact their business in the future and especially what customers

FIGURE **2-1** The Hospitality Planning Process
© Cengage Learning 2012

will want in that future environment. They seek to identify what the **key drivers** or value drivers of guest satisfaction will be in the intermediate-term and longer-term future. Although guests will not always know what the key drivers of their future satisfaction will be, the guestologist will try to find the critical aspects of experiences that guests think will satisfy them in the future.

For example, in response to its recognition of growing concerns over the public health issues with obesity and public interest in calories found in restaurant meals that led to a number of local laws, Darden Restaurants led a restaurant industry proposal for legislation requiring nutrition information to be posted somewhere in chain establishments. It sensed its customers were increasingly interested in having access to that information and, as one of the largest restaurant chains in the United States, it knew the importance of listening to what its customers were asking it to do. Although the entire industry initially opposed any federal regulation, it proposed the Labeling Education and Nutrition (LEAN) Act in 2009. Darden chose to show its support for this act by immediately posting online the nutritional values and calories for each of its menu items. As reported in the Orlando newspaper, "The outcry among consumers demanding to know what, exactly, they are eating in the face of an obesity epidemic became too loud for Orlando-based Darden to ignore any longer."[12]

Looking Within

The internal assessment, or the searching look within for strengths and weaknesses, defines the organization's core competencies and considers the organization's strong and weak points in terms of its ability to compete in the future. It is here that the organization determines what it does well, what it does not do well, and how its strengths and weaknesses pair with what it wants to accomplish.

On the basis of its own internal assessment, for example, Gaylord Hotels realized that it needed to develop a stronger guest focus among its employees. Gaylord Hotels wanted to compete by providing exceptional service; yet, it did not feel it had a corporate culture that helped to direct all employee efforts to fulfill this goal. Using a strategic approach to creating a guest-focused culture, it was able to overcome this internal weakness, develop a strong service culture among its employees, and transform it into an area of strength.

The Necessity for Planning

The process described in Figure 2-1 seems to many like an attempt to apply rationality to an irrational world and to predict an unpredictable future. It will, therefore, lead to errors, wasted time, and frustration. Nevertheless, the planning process is worthwhile. There is an old saying that those who fail to plan, plan to fail. Every hospitality organization needs a road map to unite and focus the efforts of the organization's members and get them prepared for the future that the organizational planners predict. Everyone makes decisions today that they must live with in the future, and most managers want to make those decisions as rationally as possible. Even though no one, including planners, knows what the future will bring, only by creating and implementing plans can we communicate to those both inside and outside the organization where we want to go, what criteria we should use to allocate our scarce resources, and which activities we should pursue or avoid.

This is the kind of thinking that encouraged Warren Buffet to invest in NetJets, the gaming industry to invest in new hotels and casinos in Macau, and China to invest in theme parks. No organization can instantly create such magnificent facilities and   equipment.

The Grand Lisboa, whose casino opened in 2007, was part of a new wave of casinos that were developed in Macau during the 2000s.

The only way it can get to the future it envisions is to invest today. Although no one's foresight as to what customers of tomorrow will want can be perfect, everyone must make decisions today that anticipate the future they expect to see. Creating and following a careful strategic plan is the best known way to do so.

Once the hospitality planning process is complete, the cycle should begin again in some predefined time frame. The planning process should never stop because the world in which any organization operates never stops changing. Moreover, the assessment of the performance metrics associated with each action plan will offer valuable feedback to the organization's leadership as it reviews its strengths, weaknesses, opportunities, and threats in the next cycle of the planning process.

ASSESSING THE ENVIRONMENT

As shown in Figure 2-1, the hospitality planning process begins with a long look around the environment. Here, the organization carefully studies the opportunities and threats the future holds for both it and its industry. Figure 2-2 presents the three categories of factors that should be included in an environmental assessment: those in the overall environment, the industry environment, and the company's operating environment.

Assessing the future depends on a chosen forecasting process. Forecasting techniques range from the heavily quantitative tools, which are objective, to the highly qualitative tools, which are subjective. The **quantitative forecasting tools** include the powerful tools of statistical forecasting. The **qualitative forecasting tools** include **scenario building**, the **Delphi technique**, and pure creative guesswork. Most forecasting techniques are based on the idea that the future is somehow related to the past, that what has already happened has some predictable relationship to what will happen.[13] If a restaurant's customer growth rate has been about 10 percent per year for thirty years, then forecasting that this growth rate will continue next year seems reasonable. If records show that by 10 A.M. on an average day 20 percent of all visitors who will come into a zoo for that

FIGURE **2-2** Environmental Assessment Factors

The Overall Environment

The Economy. What do we project for economic growth, inflation, interest rates, capital and credit availability, consumer confidence, consumer purchasing power? How will changes in the global market affect our business?

Society and Demographics. How will shifts in social attitudes/values regarding child-bearing, marriage, family-work balance, lifestyle, racial equality, retirement, pollution, etc., affect us? How will shifts in population characteristics, language, age distribution, educational backgrounds, health, ethnic mix, cultural values, etc., affect us?

Ecology. Are there foreseeable natural or man-made caused disasters ahead? Environmental legislation?

Politics. What sort of government policy changes regarding antitrust activities, regulation, foreign trade, health care, taxation, depreciation, environmental protection, and foreign trade barriers can we expect? What political factors or legal constraints will affect international business?

Technology. Where is it going? What new products, services, or breakthroughs might we anticipate?

The Industry Environment

New Entrants. Who will our new competitors be? Will technological advances enable them to offset our present competitive advantages (economies of scale, brand-name differentiation, market niche, availability of capital)?

Bargaining Power of Suppliers. How stable, big, and reliable are our current suppliers? Might any become potential competitors? Are substitute suppliers available? Can we supply ourselves?

Substitute Products or Services. Are alternatives to our service product likely? Can we compete with price, brand loyalty, new product offerings, and/or advertising?

Rivalry Among Existing Firms. Is market growth slowing or is competition becoming fiercer? Is there excess capacity in the industry? Can our competitors withstand intensified price competition? Can we better exploit/protect core competencies?

Bargaining Power of Buyers. How big are buyers? Any who might become competitors? Are there intermediaries between us and our ultimate customer and how do they impact the way the industry does business?

The Operating Environment

Competitive Position. What moves are competitors expected to make, inside and outside of our existing markets? How do we compare in customer awareness/preferences on key drivers? Is the competitive behavior of our competitors predictable?

Customer Profiles and Market Changes. Which customer needs are not being met by our or competitors' existing products? Are R&D efforts underway to fill these needs? What marketing and distribution channels should we use? How will demographic and population changes affect our markets? Any new market segments? What technologies are customers using to experience hospitality products in our competitive market domain?

Supplier Relationships. Should we expect cost increases because of dwindling supplies? Will sources of supply, especially of energy, be reliable? Do we anticipate major changes in cost or availability of needed suppliers? Which alternative suppliers in which country might be desirable to use? How can we help our critical suppliers?

Creditors. Will we have enough credit to finance growth? Will we stay worthy of credit? Do we have enough cash if we need it?

Labor Market. Will we have enough employees, with the right skills, when and where we need them? What are the skill sets of new entrants to the labor market? When are people retiring? What changes are ahead for unions?

Source: Adapted from Pearce, J. A. II & Robinson, R. B. Jr. 2009. *Strategic Management: Formulation, Implementation, and Control.* New York: McGraw-Hill, pp. 121–122. With permission of The McGraw-Hill Companies.

day are already on the grounds, then the day's total attendance can be reliably forecasted by 10:15 A.M. On a grander scale, if the growth rate of tourists coming to a Caribbean island paradise has been 10 percent per year for the past decade, then predicting that this growth rate will continue for at least a few more years seems reasonable.

The problem with assuming that the past can be used to predict the future is that all too frequently the assumption does not hold true. In the early days of the telephone, the ratio of phones to operators was very small. If only population trends and that ratio had been used to predict the number of telephone operators to be needed in the distant future, the prediction might well have been that half the people in the United States would now be working as telephone operators. Major improvements in technology and work productivity have greatly increased the ratio of telephones to operators. As the bursting of the housing bubble and the subsequent financial meltdown of 2008 showed to the dismay of many investors and retirees, any forecast based only on the past can be thrown off by unexpected technological, economic, societal, or political changes.

Forecasting techniques are useful to capture the impact of current trends on future business. However, they are only one source of input into the creative process by which thoughtful hospitality managers develop strategic plans. The appendix at the end of this chapter offers a review of the more popular quantitative and qualitative tools such as **econometric models, regression analysis, time-series and trend analyses, brainstorming, and focus groups;** the reader is encouraged to review them.

WHAT THE FUTURE MAY HOLD

Among the many factors that the hospitality organization must forecast for the uncertain future, it must try to predict potential changes in demographics, technology, social expectations, economic forces, competitors, other relevant groups (suppliers of resources, capital, and labor), and surprise factors.

Changing Demographics

Assessing future demographic trends and their effects may require both qualitative and quantitative forecasts. Hospitality organizations already know a lot about their future guests since so many of them are already here. As of 2010, there are more than 300 million people in the United States.[14] Of these, 59 million (approximately 20% of the population) are older than age sixty-three. Add this to the 77 million baby boomers (those born between 1945 and 1964, representing another 26% of the U.S. population) who are nearing or at retirement age. This large group of aging people has had and will continue to have a major impact on the hospitality industry as customers, investors, and employees. As of 2008, the fifty-plus age group had a combined annual income of more than $900 billion and accounted for 80 percent of the nation's savings. Baby boomers and older Americans outnumbered teenagers in 2008, and most will continue to be active twenty to thirty years more than seniors a generation or two ago. The aging baby boomers retiring early with a substantial sum of money available for discretionary use will continue to be a prime target of the hospitality industry. Although many will have at least some child care responsibility for their single-parent children's children, they have the time, money, and physical ability to travel and participate in many guest experiences unimaginable to their parents at comparable times in their lives.

This group of seniors now either in retirement or nearing it will continue to change the workforce and the marketplace for hospitality organizations. They are healthier, financially better off, more willing to travel, are more used to having things "their way," and generally have higher expectations than their parents had. They have the money, time, energy, and inclination to do what they want to do. The hospitality industry will benefit from this large group of potential customers. Moreover, if they follow the trends set by the generation before them, many will work longer in order to enjoy the social benefits of working, delay the consequences of their unwillingness to set aside enough wealth to live as comfortably as they wish in retirement, and fill jobs that require their expertise and experience. Others will use their retirement to seek new and higher-quality experiences (e.g., voluntourism, adventure tourism, ecotourism).

In other words, many of these seniors not only will stay in the workforce longer compared to their predecessors but also may change jobs to pursue an encore career in an entirely different profession, set up entrepreneurial ventures to do something they always wanted to do, or take jobs like teaching and in not-for-profits that their family financial commitments would not have allowed them to take earlier in their lives. There are stories told of people who retired and moved to Orlando to work for Disney because they had always wanted to work in a "magical" place. Likewise, there are people who have always wanted to run a restaurant, open a bed and breakfast, become a full-time meeting or event planner, or cruise line lecturer. Hospitality organizations may find it desirable to look closely at this labor pool.

In contrast, the generations succeeding the boomers (Generations X and Y) have few defined benefit retirement plans. Instead, they must worry about the future of social security, must depend on their own investment successes (or luck) to fund their retirement years, are in the middle of a public health crises with obesity, must prepare for a world that has fewer domestic industrial jobs, and face the prospect of funding one of the largest government debts in American history, incurred as a result of the 2008 financial meltdown, spending on the Iraq and Afghanistan conflicts, and investments in health care and infrastructure. These generations face the possibility of having a lower standard of living than their parents, working more years before retiring, and paying more for the large number of boomers in social security and Medicare, the national debt, and the health care fallout of obesity.

Generation X, Generation Y or the Millenniums, and the Next-Gens

Many future market opportunities can be identified by reviewing information already known about baby boomers and the Generation X and Generation Y segments of the population. The 46 million Americans born in the years 1965–1976 make up Generation X. Generation Y Americans are those born in the years 1977–1997, and Generation

Next (Next-Gens) are those born after 1997. In 2008, these segments represented 15, 27, and 13 percent respectively of the population of the United States. The roughly 81 million Americans of Generation Y, also called the Millennium Generation, between the ages 13 and 33, represent a significant demographic category and constitute the current entry-level workforce. What education and training these people have had or are having will determine the entry-level employee competence and the emerging customer expectations for hospitality experiences. Looking at the demographics, the relatively larger-sized bulges in the postwar baby boom and Generation Y will continue to translate into important trends in both employment and marketing strategies for the hospitality industry. While Generation Y has become an important force of its own, Generation Next will be even more interesting as it evolves. This generation will be different because the world it has to deal with is quite different from the one its parents faced.

Hospitality organizations are making attempts to attract these groups of people. For example, hotels seeking to appeal to a Generation Y group will offer different amenities and features than those targeting boomers. Choice Hotels created a new chain, Cambria Suites, to appeal to this demographic. Its theme is, "Where style, form and function meet." It offers all suite rooms, high-speed Internet, posh gyms, and retail shops that emphasize health foods. To make sure their emphasis is missed by no one, they call their exercise rooms "Refresh," their restaurants "Reflect," and their shops "Renew."[15] Similarly, W Hotels, one of Starwood Hotels' brands, targets the Generation Y market. It attempts to appeal to a younger demographic by making its hotels "unique and individual expressions of modern living, reflected in the brand's sensibility to a holistic lifestyle experience with cutting-edge design, contemporary restaurant concepts, glamorous nightlife experiences, and signature spas."[16] Hotel companies realize that not all generations of guests want the same experience, and so they market different products to appeal to different groups.

Demographic Implications

These statistics have several implications for all organizations serving the public; some of them will have special impact on the labor-intensive hospitality industry. As aging baby boomers press for allocation of more government dollars to their growing health care and retirement needs, funding for education has come under pressure. In this scenario, agile hospitality companies can define themselves as white knights to schools and their students by finding innovative ways to promote their products and services while helping schools achieve their educational mission. The production of support lesson plans, videos, edutainment, and electronic media will represent prime opportunities for companies to do good things for school systems and for themselves. Organizations that have a fundamental appeal to children, like those running theme parks or makers of children's products, can seize these opportunities in education as a cost-efficient and focused marketing strategy for reaching this market estimated to be worth $100 billion per year.

Managerial Implications of Generation Y in the Workforce

Generation Ys are young people who have been called the "most praised generation," as their entire young lives have been filled with positive feedback from parents, teachers, coaches, and others. They won soccer trophies as children just for showing up, ribbons for participating in school events, and were routinely told they were special. Now as members of the labor force, they require different strategies to manage; as customers, they require different strategies to satisfy.[17]

The characteristics of Generation Y have other important implications for managing the workforce of hospitality organizations. The divergence between the haves and the have-nots in this Information Age is already wide among today's school children and tomorrow's workers, and will likely grow wider. It can be seen even at the elementary-school level, where those children who have access to computers are educationally outpacing those who don't.[18] Today's children will be the eighteen- to twenty-one-year-old workers of 2018 and 2020. Those who enter the workforce without the requisite basic skills will represent a major training and development challenge for the many hospitality organizations that depend upon young, eager, capable employees to provide and ensure guest satisfaction. The challenge for managers will be to keep this new group of employees, especially the have-nots, competitive with the rapidly emerging, highly educated workforce of the Asian rim countries, who are now investing heavily in education and training. The labor pool that companies can hire from is rapidly becoming global, and workers from many nations are competing for the same jobs. Advances in technology and communication make where a person is located less important than what the person can do.

These new workers will be different in other ways as well. As the first generation to have easy access to instant and almost constant worldwide communication through the Internet, social media, texting, and twittering, Generation Ys define their friends and their interests globally instead of restricting themselves to the neighborhood. This trend will be both bad and good: The power of neighborhood and community over individual beliefs, values, and behavior will decline while these people will be more inclined to have a global perspective and the diversity of thinking that such a perspective creates. Finally, and more importantly, Generation Ys have grown up expecting to find anything they need—products, knowledge, and services—on the Web. Google and Wikipedia provide a means to access information instantly. Web sites like eBay and craigslist sell everything imaginable and other sites provide instant hotel, restaurant, or conference reservations. They learn online from educational institutions, news sources, and blogs, they entertain themselves online through music and video access, they create online content through YouTube, and they connect online. This is truly a digital generation and the next generation will be more so.

A Different Way of Thinking

In school and preparing to enter the workforce are the Next-Gens. Here, a child's waking moments are carefully scheduled and planned by "helicopter parents," who hope that by packing their kids' days with soccer practice, tennis lessons, foreign language lessons, extra math tutoring, and judo, they can ensure their children's future success. Moreover, today's students spend more time doing homework than previous generations, despite a large body of research that shows that homework not only robs children of precious free time but also fails to accomplish the goals it purports to achieve, namely, promoting higher achievement, reinforcing learning, and teaching both study skills and responsibility.[19]

Grandparents remember how they used to play outside with neighborhood friends, and parents remember how they spent time in front of the television. Today's children pick up their Wii for play in the little time left to them after their working parents pick them up from after-school day care. The impact of such trends on both the future customer and on employee creativity and ability to develop new ideas may be profound. The real question is, how do these generational differences in the amount of free time children have—and in how they use what free time they have—affect what kinds of knowledge, skills, and abilities they will bring into the workplace?

Conventional wisdom would have us believe that when a child has a handheld game console or computer with fantastic games and graphics, the motivation to stretch and grow one's own imagination and creativity is limited. However, numerous studies conducted by cognitive scientists, psychologists, and neurologists point to just the opposite conclusion: Time spent watching TV and playing computer games actually enhances creativity, patience, social competence, cognitive abilities, including pattern recognition, strategic thinking, priority setting, interpretive analysis, plan formulation and execution, and the ability to adapt rapidly to change.[20] While many may assume this generation will have difficulty moving from a virtual entertainment world to the real world of work, there are reasons to predict that this generation of workers will actually be quite well prepared.

For example, cognitive scientists have found that video games exploit the "regime of competence" principle, carefully balancing reward and frustration, demanding that players work at the very limit of their levels of competence. One study showed that gamers consistently outperformed nongamers on standard tests that measure attention span and information-processing time.[21] Other research has revealed gamers to be significantly more confident, more socially capable, and more creative in problem solving than nongamers.[22]

What kind of cognitive skills should we expect to find in Next-Gens? James Paul Gee, an expert in linguistics, literacy, and learning, says, "They're going to think well about systems; they're going to be good at exploring; they're going to be good at reconceptualizing their goals based on their experience; they're not going to judge people's intelligence just by how fast and efficient they are; and they're going to think nonlaterally. In our current world with its complex systems that are quite dangerous, those are damn good ways to think."[23]

Changing Technology

Several developments other than the population trends that are changing the workforce and customer base will affect the strategies of hospitality organizations. Dramatic changes in technology will continue to have a major influence on both organizations and the industry. While many demographic trends shift slowly, changes in technology, especially information technology, occur rapidly, and so they and their impact are difficult to forecast.

The communications and computing power now found in a notebook computer were unthinkable only ten years ago. Today, anyone with a smartphone can search for the lowest airfare to a destination, make a plane reservation, book a hotel room, reserve a rental car, get recommendations on a destination from other travelers, or even take a virtual tour of a hotel, theme park, or destination, all at the same time they are talking. Yesterday's comic-strip fantasy was Dick Tracy's two-way wrist radio. Today, anyone with an iPhone, iPad, or numerous other competing products can download or send text and pictures to others over the Internet, book hotel rooms, or even video conference, over Skype. The implications of fourth-generation technology capabilities for travel agents, hotels controlling their room inventory, and other existing—and yet to be created—parts of the travel, tourism, and other hospitality markets are enormous.[24] The growth of cloud computing, which relies entirely on the Internet to access both programs and data files, will allow unforeseen opportunities for information sharing, collaboration, and networking by people across the globe.

Other aspects of technological change will be equally important to managing the hospitality organization. The need to blend innovative high-tech solutions into high-touch service situations will be increasingly recognized as a competitive strategy and, when done successfully, rewarded in the marketplace. Hotels, restaurants, and other guest service organizations will find new ways to substitute technology for people, to reduce their dependence on this expensive and increasingly scarce resource. At the same time, these same organizations will need to find ways to maintain the high level of personal contact that defines a positive guest experience. The challenge is to substitute technology for labor in

It is difficult, if not impossible, to predict how technology will shape the future of the hospitality industry.

ways that the guest perceives as either a positive increase in service quality and value or does not perceive at all.

Self check-in at hotels or airports is an example of technology with which guests feel increasingly comfortable. While most luxury hotels still check in guests wanting this personal service, they also offer the technology for those who prefer the convenience of checking in themselves. Self check-in is more convenient for those comfortable with the technology, usually takes less time, and is considerably cheaper for the hotel than staffing up to check in guests manually. For some people, the substitution with technology can increase their perception of service quality and value. In contrast, others may want to have a person to talk to and check them in. For these guests, technology decreases their perception of service quality and value rendered by the organization. The point is that some guests like technology and some do not. It is the task of the guestologist to find ways to use technology when it meets guests' needs and not use it when it does not.

Changing Social Expectations

Another factor in an organization's long look around is society's changing expectations for all its institutions, including those in the hospitality industry, as well as emerging social trends and institutional changes. "Dashboard cuisine" with its use of wraps did not exist as a food-service category until recently. Changing social trends led to this new category as very busy families sought a way to find food that they could eat in their cars without making a mess. Similarly, a recent concept is the weekly family meal preparation facilities, where people can go and make a week's worth of nutritious meals at one time. These stores provide the raw materials, necessary utensils, and expert supervision while the customer does all the preparation and packaging work. This enables a busy parent to feed a family for an entire week with meals "like mom used to make" at one time.

Some changing expectations are expressed through trade associations that monitor social trends and their impacts on the industry. Others wind up in the political process and result in new laws, rules, or regulations. An example is the Sarbanes-Oxley Act of 2002, as a response to citizens' lack of trust in the way corporations were governed. Under this act, CEOs and CFOs are required to certify their financial statements as well as the internal controls of their company quarterly. This means they must take much greater responsibility than before to ensure that the company's annual and interim financial statements are fairly represented. Beyond increasing management accountability, Sarbanes-Oxley also requires companies to define, document, and test their internal control structure.[25]

Legislation impacts the way in which hospitality organizations operate, and so do nongovernment organizations (NGOs) and interest groups. Because they are so dependent on maintaining a good relationship with the public, hospitality organizations are especially vulnerable to protests or demonstrations by interest groups that object to management policies or business decisions. If a hospitality organization has any thoughts of building a major facility in a historically significant area, it can expect that groups wanting to preserve the area in its present state will generate negative publicity. Even if constructing the facility is a good business decision, public opposition may make it a bad customer-relations decision. Any hospitality organization dependent on a broad customer base has a real challenge when every action it takes is so visible to its guests.

Perhaps no movement has received more attention recently than the green movement. Not only has it become a national priority, but it has been the subject of industry initiatives across hospitality. The American Hotel and Lodging Association (AH&LA) has established a Green Resources Center that tells hoteliers how to employ best practices in environment and sets Green Guidelines (see Figure 2-3). Some states, for example, Florida, offer green certification for hotels that implement environmentally friendly practices. Other organizations across the globe have developed green certification programs, such as GreenGlobe, Europe's Green Tourism, and the USA's Green Seal. There is even a Green Hotel Association, which includes many members of the leading hotel chains and has a Web site (environmentallyfriendlyhotels) where customers can find lodging that matches their commitment to environmental actions. Being green not only includes the obvious practices like those detailed in the AH&LA guidelines. One hotel offers a bar of Waste Reducing Exfoliating Body Cleanser that has a hole in the middle as its green replacement for the traditional soap bar. Its box proclaims, "This innovative ergonomically shaped 'waste reducing' soap has been designed to eliminate the unused center of traditional soap bars. This soap is cruelty free and contains no animal fat or byproducts. The carton is made from recycled packaging and printed with soy based inks." The degree to which this is a cost-saving move versus an attempt to protect the environment is immaterial to our discussion.[26] Most "green" programs seek to do both to encourage hotels to engage in environmentally beneficial activities. Their requirements are attempts to have hotels do well while doing good.[27] Thus, when a Hyatt or Marriott saves one shift of laundry workers plus the soap, water, and electricity by not cleaning sheets and towels for those guests in stay-over rooms, it is doing both. Likewise, when resorts offer

FIGURE **2-3** American Hotel and Lodging Association Environmental Guidelines

Reproduced with permission of the American Hotel and Lodging Association

1. Each hotel should form an **Environmental Committee** that is responsible for developing an Environmental Green Plan for energy, water, and solid waste use.
2. Manage your hotel's **environmental performance** by monitoring the electric, gas, water, and waste usage information on a monthly and annual basis.
3. Replace **incandescent lamps** with compact fluorescent lamps wherever possible.
4. Install **digital thermostats** in guestrooms and throughout the hotel.
5. Implement a **towel and/or linen reuse** program.
6. Install **2.5-gallons per minute showerheads** or less in all guestroom baths and any employee shower areas.
7. Install **1.6-gallon toilets** in all guestrooms.
8. Implement a **recycling program** – including public spaces – to the full extent available in your municipality; document your efforts.
9. Implement a **recycling program for hazardous materials** found in fluorescent bulbs, batteries, and lighting ballasts through licensed service providers.
10. Purchase **Energy Star** labeled appliances and equipment.
11. All **office paper products** should have 20% or more post-consumer recycled content

carbon-neutral vacations, they are trying to appeal to customers who are increasingly demanding this increased level of environmental sensitivity while still making a profit. The expensive King Pacific Lodge in British Columbia, for example, refused to give a corporate customer three separate boats for his seven guests on a fishing trip as it would waste fuel and contribute to global warming. The Lodge states that its goal is to halve its emissions of carbon dioxide in the next decade.[28]

Hotels are not the only segment of the hospitality industry interested in the environment. The National Restaurant Association has developed an environment program called Conserve/EPA Energy Star Challenge, and the Destination Marketing Association International has included it in their accreditation process. Greening of hospitality is a big issue today and will only become more so in the future as more stakeholders and customers show their concern for the devastation of the rain forest, the melting of the glaciers, and the changes in the earth's environment.

At a minimum, those engaged in strategic planning should try to stay aware of shifting social expectations. Including input from social groups can sometimes enhance the strategic planning process greatly. When planning began for Disney's Animal Kingdom theme park, the organization invited representatives of environmental and animal-rights groups to help in the development process. By working with them, Disney was able to develop a park consistent with the environmentalist's ideals. Similarly, as noted earlier, because of increased attention to health issues and particular concerns about obesity, Darden Restaurants posts nutrition information for its restaurants (e.g., Olive Garden, Red Lobster, Bahama Breeze) online. Although laws are being passed in various states to require this action, Darden took the lead in making this information available to its consumers and even helped lobby for the passage of such legislation. Restaurants need to keep pace with more than just changing customers' preferences for food. They must also monitor broader trends that influence consumer behaviors.

Changing Economic Forces

Many environmental factors already covered have an economic aspect. Economics is such an important issue, however, that it deserves special discussion. The organization must consider the effects of governmental economic policies on its suppliers of capital, the ability of its customers to buy the service, its own cost structure, and direct and indirect competitors' ability to compete. The economic meltdown of 2008 had a major impact on the hospitality industry. Not only did it lead to a virtual halt on new construction but also directly influenced consumer confidence and willingness to spend on vacations, time shares, second homes, and other hospitality and tourism services. Likewise, the resulting governmental intervention and financial subsidies given to the financial and industrial sectors led to public outrage over any business spending viewed as excessive or wasteful, such as resort hotel golfing retreats, meetings in Las Vegas, first class travel, luxury boxes, and premium entertaining. Hospitality organizations serving these governmentally subsidized businesses increasingly found themselves on the defensive justifying to a skeptical public why these expenditures made good business sense.

Perhaps one of the most interesting aspects of the financial market crisis in 2008–2009 was to cause many in the hospitality industry to reevaluate their organizational goals and priorities. The emphasis on investing in real estate and increased debt financing caused many organizations to become distracted from their core competence of managing hospitality operations and instead to focus on the financial aspects of the business, especially real estate. During the middle of the first decade of the twenty-first century, articles appeared in the *Wall Street Journal* that reflected the impact that soaring real estate prices had on the hospitality industry. Articles such as those that wondered where the dude ranches had gone[29] or what happened to bed and breakfasts[30] or what the future of ski resorts might be[31] keyed on the cost of the land. The expectation of ever increasing real estate value and other financial strategies like marketing hotel rooms or housing communities to consumers as time shares offered developers a chance to cash in on the cheap money-fueled market demand for any real estate. A *Wall Street Journal* article in 2006 talked about the rising number of condo-hotels that made up approximately 11 percent of the new hotel market. It noted that condo-hotels were popular among developers because having individual owners not only changed the financing strategy for building new hotels but also cut the costs of maintenance and utilities.[32]

When the real estate markets collapsed and the financial industry stopped loaning money, the wisdom of the financially driven strategies was called into question. In the gaming industry, for example, Harrah's and MGM Mirage nearly collapsed under their debt burdens.[33] Sysco had to initiate various support strategies to help keep its restaurant customers afloat.[34] Financially strapped customers stopped eating out, causing layoffs and closures across the restaurant industry, from the upscale Ruth's Chris to casual-dining Chili's to coffee bar Starbucks.[35] Golf and country clubs scrambled to adapt in the face of membership loss.[36] Conventions attracted significantly fewer attendees, especially in destinations like Las Vegas and Orlando, which might be perceived as places where attendees might be playing instead of taking care of business. Airlines flew empty seats, busses got busier,[37] and barge tours in Europe went on two-for-one sales. In other words, the lack of clear forecasting of the downside of the business cycle and overreliance on a continuing upside caused many financial challenges and employee hardships for all parts of the hospitality industry across the world.

Organizations in the hospitality industry must also consider, besides the influences from the financial environment, numerous other economic factors in their strategic planning process. For example, one important consideration is the future direction of the local, regional, national, and even international economies and how these directions will influence the demand for hospitality services. Consider foreign currency exchange rates. If China's currency is less valuable in foreign exchange than the U.S. dollar, foreign tourists will consider going to China rather than coming to the United States. In the labor-intensive service sector, the influence of inflation on competitiveness is especially important. If inflation rates move up or down, the organization's cost of capital—its ability to expand the business, buy new equipment, and keep up with rising wage expectations—will be affected. Other economic factors would include productivity growth, income distribution, and stage in the business cycle. Most hospitality organizations are more sensitive to variations in general economic health than organizations making and selling necessities. When the economy is in a downward cycle, so too is the travel and tourism industry. People must buy groceries and clothing; they don't have to take vacations, go to meetings and conferences, or go out to eat.

Changing Competitors

An organization has existing competitors, potential competitors, and indirect competitors that offer customers a substitute or alternative service. These competitors can be local, national, or even international.

Existing competitors have an established position in your market niche. If you are a small corner restaurant, your competitors are all those other restaurants in the same market area. Since most people go to restaurants within a short drive from their home, these competitors are easy to identify. Potential competitors are those who are likely to enter your market area. The sign may be up, the building begun, and the "buy one, get one free" coupons distributed to mark the existence of a potential competitor to your restaurant. The alternative or substitute providers include anyone who sells food. They can range from Weight Watchers, which provides its own branded food products to dieters, to the local grocery store, to a food-delivery service. Anyone who can fill the same basic need with an alternative product is a competitor.

In the theme park industry, a competitor is not only anyone that can offer a more attractive use for a guest's funds in the destination but is also anyone who can encourage customers to spend their leisure dollars at some destination besides yours. Because Orlando visitors and locals can spend money in a wide variety of alternative ways, Orlando theme parks are especially sensitive to this competitive market reality. And, of course, people can choose not to come to or stay in Orlando at all; the over 64 million annual visitors that the parks depend on can go to competitive attractions at other destinations, like Las Vegas, Spain, or Branson, Missouri. The in-market competition includes other theme parks, dinner theaters, civic museums, art galleries, factory-outlet stores, or even a trip to the beach. It even includes noncustomers who stay away from parks entirely and watch videos at home or in a motel room. The guestologist tries to find out how guests in the organization's target market—those that come, those that don't come, and those who don't come back—want to spend their time and money, and if possible provide them desired options rather than letting customers go to competitors.

Changes in Other Relevant Groups

In addition to the various factors and groups we have already discussed, several other groups in the organization's external environment must be included in any environmental forecast: the suppliers of resources and raw material, capital, and labor.

Resource Suppliers

When Red Lobster adds a new seafood item to its menu, it must first check to be sure that demand for it doesn't exhaust the world's supply of that item. Because Red Lobster has so many restaurants, adding or removing a menu item can have a major impact on the supply of that product. If a certain type of shrimp now retails for $9.99 per pound, how much will the price change if Red Lobster buys up half of the world's supply next year? Obviously, the planning process needs to take such supply-related issues into consideration.

Capital Suppliers

A second major interested group is the suppliers of capital. As the capital market has become more global and the availability of electronic transfers makes movement of capital easier and quicker, the organization may need to spend more time forecasting the availability of capital for its business and industry. If capital availability is driven by the next quarter's financial report, the impact on the organization's decision-making and planning horizon will be considerable. If Wall Street demands a certain short-run return on investment, finding the extra resources to develop a new service or to take a chance on a new concept or location may be difficult. The airline industry undergoes a periodic

With more than 680 restaurants in the United States and Canada, Red Lobster must carefully forecast the potential supply of any seafood item it might want to add to its menu.

Photo courtesy of Darden Restaurants.

devaluation of its stock prices as the capital market expresses its opinion about the industry's overcapacity problems and how much it will cost to fix them. No matter how good a strategy an organization has, if it can't convince the capital market or if the capital market is unwilling to take the risk, the strategy may be worthless.

The Labor Supply

A third supplier of a crucial resource is the labor market. It is so important that we devote Chapter 5, on staffing, to it.

Surprises

The final external issue to address in this long look around at the environment is the potential for surprise. While one cannot often predict real estate or financial market crashes, terrorist attacks, wars, volcanic eruptions, earthquakes, tsunamis, or other natural disasters, thoughtful planners consider these possibilities. Preparing for such events means having a plan to deal with the immediate consequences (such as on the day of the disaster) and the longer-term implications.

Many "unique" disasters have certain commonalities: loss of power, inability of guests to leave while new guests are arriving, failure of communication networks, fear on the part of both guests and staff, and so forth. Although specific events cannot be predicted, the better companies are well prepared when some sort of disaster occurs.[38] This involves having a plan for where guests will go or stay, what to do with food in the refrigerators without power or knowing how long the generators will last, what circuits are connected to them, and so forth. A well thought out disaster preparedness plan can help make sure that employees know how to respond should some unforeseen event occur. The disruption of air travel across the world resulting from the volcano eruption in Iceland's Eyjafjallajökull made it clear that no one had planned on how volcanic ash would shut down air travel, strand passengers across the world, and generate unexpected economic impacts on hospitality organizations, travelers, and countries alike.

As for longer-term implications, hospitality organizations should consider how surprises can affect overall demand for their service product. If most customers have to drive long distances to get to your service setting, your planners should keep in mind the gas supply problems that intensifying instability in the chief oil-producing nations might create. If your airline serves or your hotel chain is located in an area that seems liable to be a target for terrorist attacks, you need to have a contingency plan. While the terrorist attack of 9/11 may seem like a distant historical event now, its impact has left a lasting impression across the hospitality industry. Conventions still struggle with attendees' reluctance to fly in the face of terror threats and the time-consuming ordeal the Transportation Security Administration (TSA) has introduced to flying. Cruise lines face the additional inconvenience of enforcing new passport requirements, and destinations dependent upon international travelers suffer from the latter's unwillingness to endure the new security procedures for entering the United States. While hoping and planning for the best, strategic planners must realize that any number of unpredictable future events can have a severe impact on how many customers want or need the service the organization offers and plan for them.

The Impact of Change on Strategic Premises

All the changes described above will have varying effects on the organization. But not all factors are equal in either their impact on the organization or in terms of our ability to forecast them fully. Some are predictable and simple, such as the estimated number of teenagers available for work in ten years. Since they have all been born already, predicting the number available in ten years is a straightforward calculation. Some other factors are simple but unpredictable. Using demographics again, estimating the number of skilled and trained employees who will be available in Pocatello, Idaho, in twenty years is a simple number to calculate, but the calculations rest on unpredictable information such as unknown changes in family formation, net migration into southwestern Idaho, local economic changes, and other factors.

As was true of simple future elements, complex future elements are either predictable or unpredictable. Once a certain number of people are in a destination market, a relatively predictable percentage will come to any given tourist attraction on any given day. Calculating the number of people who will be in the market, however, is a complex process; it depends on airline routes and fares, propensity to travel by people all over the world, the price of gasoline, foreign exchange rates, the threat of terrorism, the level of economic activity, consumer confidence, availability of and cost involved in other more attractive destinations, and a variety of other factors.

The complex and unpredictable outcomes are, of course, the hardest to forecast. An example would be changes in technology. If technology develops to the point that the experience of going to a major attraction or a conference can be duplicated through virtual reality, then people won't have to go through the trouble and expense of coming to the site of the attraction or conference to rent cars, stay in hotels, and buy admissions. If this happens, the entire area surrounding the attraction or destination will suffer a severe economic decline. The impact of the financial bailout following the meltdown in 2008 on conference destinations was enormous, with meeting planners switching locations from the ones that were previously desirable because of the extras available, for example, Las Vegas and Orlando, to those that were instead viewed as places to stay focused on strictly business. Predicting what economic impact an event can have is a major challenge for both hospitality and civic forecasters.

Some forecasts are easy, because the elements comprising them (which are themselves forecasts) are predictable and the calculations simple, and others are difficult. Guestologists must try to make the forecasts relevant to their organization's future, regardless of ease or difficulty, and include them in their strategic planning processes. Since things that can be counted are often more comfortable to deal with than those that can't, managers are sometimes tempted to emphasize those factors that are numerical while ignoring those that cannot be easily measured. Unfortunately for those managers, in real life the crucial factors are usually those to which we can't apply numbers.

Strategic Premises

The hospitality organization draws conclusions about the future of its industry and market from its environmental assessment, and then uses this information to make the assumptions, called **strategic premises**, on which its service strategy is based. Strategic premises are educated guesses. The organization's planners may guess wrong; even if they guess right, they may devise the wrong strategy. But not to guess at all means reacting day to day to whatever seems to be going on, without a plan or a focus for organizational activities.

Dave Thomas, founder of Wendy's, told how his environmental assessment led to certain premises on which Wendy's corporate strategy was based. When creating his new restaurant in 1969, he identified five trends[39] he thought offered him a market opportunity that he had the competence to meet:

1. *People wanted choices.* They were tired of living in a prepackaged world; they wanted some influence over the products they were buying in the marketplace, and they wanted something new.
2. *People were fed up with poor quality.* He saw a big interest in things that were fresh and natural.
3. *People were trying to adjust to a newer, more complicated way of life.* Older people were looking for relief from the many social and political changes occurring during the 1960s, and young people were looking for changes that they could handle. Thomas notes, "In a funny way, the old fashioned decor and the Tiffany lamps provided a novelty for the young adults and nostalgia for the older generation at the same time."
4. *People were on the move.* Any business had to accommodate this restless mobility.
5. *People were ready for an upscale hamburger place.* He felt that many people had grown up loving hamburgers but were not satisfied with the product generally available at fast-food outlets.

Thomas wrote, "Knowing these five trends allowed Wendy's to focus on the right market. My bet is that if you looked at any successful business, you would find factors very much like these behind that business's success. If you're going to bet your bankroll on a business concept, you had better be able to understand those forces. If you can't describe them, you had better feel them so clearly in your gut that you know you're right."[40]

ASSESSING THE ORGANIZATION ITSELF: THE INTERNAL AUDIT

On the right side of our planning model shown in Figure 2-1, opposite the long look around, is internal assessment, or **internal audit**, the searching look within. The hospitality organization cannot plan with any confidence until it admits its weaknesses and identifies its central strengths, frequently termed its core competencies.

Core Competencies

The definition given by management strategists Hamel and Prahalad is helpful: An organization's **core competence** is the bundle of skills and technologies that gives the organization an important difference in providing customer benefits and perceived value.[41] Ford's core competence is the ability to make cars. The core competence of the Marriott is the ability to manage excellent lodging facilities. Southwest's core competence is to have efficient operations while maintaining superior customer service. Knowing its areas of competence will enable an organization to make a key strategic decision: What shall we not do?

If a company has proven it has the ability and technology to combine the merchandising of consumer goods, entertainment, and an eating experience in a striking setting, then it can do what Rainforest Cafe and most other theme restaurants have done: Seek to expand the variety of consumer goods it sells alongside its restaurant operations. In contrast, while Darden's core competencies have to deal with its supply chain and restaurant operations, it does not have a core competency in the area of information technology. As a result, Darden outsources its IT system maintenance, because it decided that IT was not part of its core competence and it did not believe that pursuing IT should be its mission. The point is that every successful organization has developed a core competence, an ability to do something very well. As long as it sticks to activities appropriate to that core competence, it will probably continue to succeed. When it strays from its core competence, it may find itself pitting its weaknesses against the strengths of other organizations.

This is why many organizations seek to outsource activities and functions that they believe are not their core competence to another organization that has a core competence in those activities and functions. Forming strategic alliances with these organizations allows that outsourcing organization to gain the competence of another organization instead of trying to do everything itself. An airline, for example, will outsource its fueling function to another organization so that it can retain its focus on those things that are core to its business and let others handle those things that are not core. Schools and universities outsource their food service to Aramark or Sodexo so that they can focus on the academic issues that are core to their mission.

Successful managers must have two skills or qualities: management ability and expertise in a specific industry or functional area. They know, just as successful organizations know, that they should focus on developing their management ability and industry or functional expertise, which as a bundle comprises their core competence. A factory manager and a hotel manager may have many of the same managerial skills, but the successful factory manager may fail as a hotel manager. The core competence leading to success, for managers and for organizations, will be different in the two industries.

The internal audit tells the hospitality organization where it stands now, what new strengths it must develop, and what weaknesses it must eliminate to build the core competence it will need to succeed in the future industry it foresees. If an organization accurately perceives itself to be the dominant force in entertainment and foresees the future of entertainment in electronic media, then that company should probably set its sights on dominating any electronic medium that develops and delivers entertainment. Such reasoning is, of course, what made Wall Street applaud Disney when it bought Pixar. For Disney, the fit with its core competence and industry vision was perfect. Pixar had successfully used computers to replace hand-drawn animation, which most, including Disney, had not thought possible. The purchase of Pixar represented a capitulation of Disney's commitment to hand-drawn animation as the future of entertainment in this electronic medium. The success of *Toy Story*, *Finding Nemo*, and *Up* proved the value of digital animation. Rarely do the internal and external audits lead to such dramatic decisions.

Internal Assets

An internal audit includes an assessment of all the organization's internal assets. Each organization has a reputation, a pool of human capital (its employees), managerial capabilities, material resources, and competitive advantages based on its technology. It also possesses patents, brand names, copyrights, and customer loyalty, all of which help define its core competencies.

The Ritz-Carlton, for example, is generally considered to be one of the world's most able lodging organizations. It knows what it should do to sustain its core competence of providing service excellence in the lodging field. It has a unique, well-established, loyal customer base, a committed pool of employees, strong culture, well-trained management, a strong brand image, and a well-maintained capital base. In an assessment of its own internal strengths and weaknesses, The Ritz-Carlton builds upon its core abilities—by not only acknowledging them as an organizational strength but also incorporating its gold standard into its business plan as a marketable product, to be shared with others through seminars offered at the Ritz-Carlton Leadership Center on how to manage for service excellence.[42]

Likewise, Darden Restaurants understands that one role of planning based on a knowledge of core competencies is to seek business areas that the organization should be in and avoid or exit those it should not. When a company perceives it has reached a critical point in penetrating a market segment, it seeks new segments to satisfy customers or new ways to expand its reach or penetration of its current market segment. If a company achieves great success and finds itself with a lot of cash on its hands, as Darden did with the success of Olive Garden and Red Lobster, it is tempted to try new lines of business because it can afford to and its shareholders expect it to grow. What Darden did was to open Bahama Breeze, Smokey Bones, and Seasons 52 and buy The Capital Grille to expand its penetration of its existing markets. On the other hand, it exited Smokey Bones when its planners determined that a sports bar did not fit its core competence of running casual-dining restaurants.

Alternatively, Marriott provides an example of an organization that reached a critical point in its airline catering and restaurant businesses, which it had operated successfully for sixty years. Marriott's forecasts for future growth in those areas were not promising, so Marriott sold these businesses in spite of their central importance in the early development of the company. At about the same time, the organization realized that the market for its core competence—running large, full-service Marriott hotels—was limited. The company decided to capitalize on its name and core abilities by moving into other segments of the lodging market: small-sized, medium-priced Courtyard by Marriott, economy-priced Fairfield Inn by Marriott, and extended-stay Marriott Residence Inn,

Springhill, and TownePlace Suites. It also acquired the Renaissance and Ritz-Carlton chains and created the JW Marriott for more upscale travelers and conventions. Finally, it added the Execustay and Executive Apartments for the transferred or longer-staying executive and Vacation Club International for the time share market.

An unsatisfactory bottom line will motivate a company to take a searching look within. For years, McDonald's focused on selling hamburgers. Falling sales and the public's obvious desire for healthier foods convinced the company that it had to change the way it executed its core competence: making and selling hamburgers quickly. The company added salads. Executives were aware of the risk but took a chance on capturing that part of its market that it felt it had lost to the more upscale Panera and Cozi, both of which had got the baby boomers eating salads and chicken. After posting losses in 2003, McDonald's offered a $4.50 California Cobb salad with grilled chicken and a new $3.89 grilled chicken club sandwich. Given the historical price points of its product, this seemed to be a risky strategy. It worked: The average check value grew in 2005 by 5 percent to $5. The strategy fueled three years of growth, with salads accounting for between 15 and 20 percent of same-store sales growth.[43] More recently, McDonald's set its sights on Starbucks, by opening up a McCafe in all its 14,000 stores. McCafe's target is the Starbucks customer who felt the pinch of the 2008 economic downturn but still liked good coffee. After beating out Starbucks in a *Consumer Reports* review of coffee in March 2007, McDonald's added specialty coffee drinks to compete on both quality and price for the cappuccino, latte, and mocha drinkers. Starbucks, attacked by this competitive effort and hit by the economic downturn in late 2008, closed 900 of its stores worldwide. Its response has been to seek ways to reinvent the "Starbucks experience." Among other changes, its baristas now grind coffee each time a new pot is brewed because, according to its chairman, Howard Schultz, "preground coffee had taken the 'romance and theatre' out of a trip to Starbucks."[44]

Vision and Mission Statements

Figure 2-1 shows that a vision statement and mission statement are key parts of the hospitality planning process. Most organizations spend a great deal of time trying to articulate these concepts, and the reason is clear: If you don't know what you want to do, how can you decide how to do it? Most companies wind up writing mission and vision statements—and other statements such as credos, beliefs, and values—but not all need to; often, smaller organizations have leaders who know what they are doing and where they are heading without writing it down. Vision and mission statements vary from the simple to the complex, but in general, the simpler the better.

The Vision Statement

A **vision statement** articulates what the organization hopes to look like and be like in the future. Rather than presenting specific principles, goals, and objectives, the vision presents hopes and dreams; it creates a picture toward which the organization aspires; it provides inspiration for the journey ahead. It depicts what the organization hopes to become, not what the organization needs to do to get there. The vision statement is used to unite and inspire employees to achieve the common ideal and to define for external stakeholders what the organization is all about. For example, "McDonald's vision is to be the world's best quick service restaurant experience. Being the best means providing outstanding quality, service, cleanliness, and value, so that we make every customer in every restaurant smile."

Though mission and vision are to an extent overlapping terms, the corporate vision is the really big picture of hopes for the future. Hamel and Prahalad call this vision definition the "quest for industry foresight," as the organization defines what its future could be and works backward to what it must do today to make that future happen. The creative imagination of management and the entire organization needs to be focused on articulating the vision and how to achieve it. Hamel and Prahalad describe the difficulties involved in getting from here to there, from today to tomorrow:

> *Although potentially useful, technology forecasting, market research, scenario planning, and competitor analysis won't necessarily yield industry foresight. None of these tools compels senior management to preconceive the corporation and the industries in which it competes. Only by changing the lens through which the corporation is viewed (looking at core competencies versus focusing on only strategic business units), only by changing the lens through which markets are viewed (functionalities versus products), only by broadening the angle of the lens (becoming more inquisitive), only by cleaning off the accumulated grime on the lens (seeing with a child's eyes), and only by occasionally disbelieving what one sees (challenging price-performance conventions, thinking like a contrarian) can the future be anticipated. The quest for industry foresight is the quest to visceralize what doesn't yet exist. ... Having imagined the future, a company must find a path that leads from today to tomorrow.*[45]

This ability to imagine a future market opportunity that is currently unpopulated with competitors is the focus of a term called blue ocean strategy.[46] This is the idea that the truly innovative organizations seek new market spaces that allow them to operate in a wide open ocean of opportunity because there is no existing competition or there is nothing like it in the marketplace. An example should make this strategy clear. Cirque du Soleil is neither a circus nor a theatrical show but is instead a combination of the two that is unlike anything that has ever been seen before. By eliminating the costs of a circus and embracing the entertainment focus of a themed theatrical show, Cirque du Soleil made something entirely new. It found a blue ocean opportunity that has been very successful.

Sometimes an organization is created to fulfill a personal vision. Walt Disney wanted to build his theme park, Disneyland, so badly that he was willing to borrow against his insurance policy to begin it. He had a vision to fulfill. Selling others on the same vision was a difficult challenge. After all, who else could imagine a theme park built on 182 acres of citrus grove in the middle of then-undeveloped Anaheim, California? The park would wind up costing $17 million to build, far exceeding the original estimates. While Disneyland was a visionary project, it pales in comparison with the vision required to conceive a Walt Disney World Resort and bring the park into being. Disney bought nearly 28,000 acres, mostly citrus groves, near the quiet town of Orlando, Florida, on which to build his dream. It included not only an expanded version of his Disneyland theme park but also hotels, restaurants, and even Epcot, the city of the future. Epcot was originally envisioned as a complete, self-contained city with its own schools, apartments, and shopping facilities. The development of the Celebration community brought to fruition this final part of Walt Disney's grand vision.[47]

The Mission Statement

An organization's **mission statement** articulates the organization's purpose, the reason for which it was founded and for which it continues to exist. The mission statement defines the path to the vision, given the strategic premises and the organization's core competencies. The mission statement is a guide to defining the how, what, who, and where for the organization's overall service strategy that in turn drives the design of the service product, service environment, and service delivery system. These definitions form the basis of action plans and lead to the other steps and decisions that put resources in place to fulfill those plans.

The mission statement should guide managers as they allocate resources, focuses organizational marketing efforts, and defines for all employees how they should deal with guests and customers. A typical mission statement will include at a minimum the following three elements: (1) What you do (What is the product or service you are providing to the customer?), (2) Who you do it for (Who is the targeted customer?), (3) How or where you do it (Where is the product or service going to be provided to the targeted customers? Place, niche or market segment?)

An example would be the simple but elegant motto statement of The Ritz-Carlton Hotel Company, L.L.C., a two-time winner of the Malcolm Baldrige Quality Award: "We are Ladies and Gentlemen serving Ladies and Gentlemen."[48] Every day, employees go over one of the company's twenty basic service standards; the same one is discussed again twenty days later. The purpose of this ritual is to keep Ritz-Carlton's philosophy—its gold standards—in the forefront of employees' minds.

The Ritz-Carlton Credo.

Reprinted with permission of The Ritz-Carlton Hotel Company, L.L.C.

Three Steps Of Service

1
A warm and sincere greeting.
Use the guest name, if and when possible.

2
Anticipation and compliance with guest needs

3
Fond farewell. Give them a warm good-bye and use their names, if and when possible.

"We Are Ladies and Gentlemen Serving Ladies and Gentlemen"

The Ritz-Carlton®

Credo

The Ritz-Carlton Hotel is a place where the genuine care and comfort of our guests is our highest mission.
We pledge to provide the finest personal service and facilities for our guests who will always enjoy a warm, relaxed yet refined ambience.
The Ritz-Carlton experience enlivens the senses, instills well-being, and fulfills even the unexpressed wishes and needs of our guests.

The Ritz-Carlton® Basics

1 The Credo will be known, owned and energized by all employees.

2 Our motto is: "We are Ladies and Gentlemen serving Ladies and Gentlemen." Practice teamwork and "lateral" service" to create a positive work environment.

3 The three steps of service shall be practiced by all employees.

4 All employees will successfully complete Training Certification to ensure they understand how to perform to The Ritz-Carlton standards in their position.

5 Each employee will understand their work area and Hotel goals as established in each strategic plan.

6 All employees will know the needs of their internal and external customers (guests and employees) so that we may deliver the products and services they expect. Use guest preference pads to record specific needs.

7 Each employee will continuously identify defects (Mr. BIV) throughout the Hotel.

8 Any employee who receives a customer complaint "owns" the complaint.

9 React quickly to correct the problem immediately. Follow up with a telephone call within twenty minutes to verify the problem has been resolved to the customer's satisfaction. Do everything you possibly can to never lose a guest.

10 Guest incident action forms are used to record and communicate every incident of guest dissatisfaction. Every employee is empowered to resolve the problem and to prevent a repeat occurrence.

11 Uncompromising levels of cleanliness are the responsibility of every employee.

12 "Smile--We are on stage." Always maintain positive eye contact. Use the proper vocabulary with our guests. (Use words like--"Good Morning," "Certainly," "I'll be happy to," and "My pleasure").

13 Be an ambassador of your Hotel in and outside of the work place. Always talk positively. No negative comments.

14 Escort guests rather than pointing out directions to another area of the Hotel.

15 Be knowledgeable of Hotel information (hours of operation, etc.) to answer guest inquiries. Always recommend the Hotel's retail and food and beverage outlets prior to outside facilities.

16 Use proper telephone etiquette. Answer within three rings and with a "smile." When necessary, ask the caller, "May I place you on hold?" Do not screen calls. Eliminate call transfers when possible.

17 Uniforms are to be immaculate. Wear proper and safe footware (clean and polished), and your correct name tag. Take pride and care in your personal appearance (adhering to all grooming standards).

18 Ensure all employees know their roles during emergency situations and are aware of fire and life safety response processes.

19 Notify your supervisor immediately of hazards, injuries, equipment or assistance that you need. Practice energy conservation and proper maintenance and repair of Hotel property and equipment.

20 Protecting the assets of a Ritz-Carlton Hotel is the responsibility of every employee.

Red Lobster, part of Darden Restaurants, couches its vision and mission in terms of its passion, dream, and goals: "Our passion is hospitality, over-the-top performance, and creating a legacy of greatness that endures and prospers for generations to come. Our dream is to be a world-class company of restaurants that our stakeholders—customers and guests, crew, suppliers, communities, and Darden Restaurants—are proud of. Our goals are to earn a sterling reputation for measured excellence in everything that we do and to retain the loyalty of our stakeholders for life."[49] These somewhat general statements are made specific in the eight principles tied to them under these headings: hospitality, fairness, caring, respect, fun, quality, zip, and balance.

The Olive Garden restaurants (another Darden organization) have a seven-point vision statement and also a simple five-point statement that provides guidance for employees:

1. Hot food hot
2. Cold food cold
3. Know your product
4. Clean rest rooms
5. Money in our bank

These points provide focused and clear guides to employee decisions.

The organization's statement of mission often includes its core values. Wal-Mart founder Sam Walton combined mission and values when he said, "We put the customer ahead of everything else.... If you're not serving the customer, or supporting the folks who do, we don't need you."[50] All these organizations recognize the importance of providing straightforward guidance to all employees as to how the organization expects them to act in their jobs.

Southwest Airlines started out in 1971 with this mission: "Get your passengers to their destinations when they want to get there, on time, at the lowest possible fares, and make darn sure they have a good time doing it."[51] Here is the Southwest mission statement of today[52]:

The mission of Southwest Airlines is dedication to the highest quality of Customer Service delivered with a sense of warmth, friendliness, individual pride, and Company Spirit.

To Our Employees
We are committed to provide our Employees a stable work environment with equal opportunity for learning and personal growth. Creativity and innovation are encouraged for improving the effectiveness of Southwest Airlines. Above all, Employees will be provided the same concern, respect, and caring attitude within the organization that they are expected to share externally with every Southwest Customer.

DEVELOPING THE SERVICE STRATEGY

Once the external and internal assessment factors have been examined in light of the corporate vision and mission, the hospitality organization is ready to define its service strategy. This strategy is critical to any service organization's success because it provides guidance in how to make every organizational decision, from capital budgeting to handling a customer complaint. Defining and creating the service strategy are as much art as science and should involve the voice, ideas, and enthusiasm of its many stakeholders. The organization must now define its market's key drivers, craft its service product to meet that market's needs, create the appropriate service environment, and design the service systems to reach the target market. In Chapter 1 we discussed these key components of the hospitality organization, and this is when the strategy must be translated into specific actions. If the company mission is to deliver a service product to an upscale, educated, retired socioeconomic group, then the service delivery system should be high touch, and the service environment should be elegant and congruent with what an upscale market wants. Knowing what any market wants takes us back to an important point from the first chapter: Ask the customer.

Asking Customers What They Want

Usually, the best way to know what your customers want or expect is to ask them. The organization should not only look inside to evaluate its core competencies but must also ask its customers to determine the key drivers of customer satisfaction. Customers can tell the organization what they really value, and these values should drive the decision process on resource allocations. The customers will tell the organization if its core competencies are important to providing customer value and satisfaction, and excellent hospitality organizations measure these key drivers carefully and frequently.

As a true believer in identifying key drivers, Disney surveys its guests constantly. On one such survey, Walt Disney World Resort guests were asked a variety of questions about their experiences and how those experiences related to both their intention to return to the parks and their overall satisfaction with Walt Disney World Resort. Fast food in the parks received relatively low ratings. However, analysis of the data revealed only a weak statistical relationship between these low ratings and both intention to return and overall satisfaction with Walt Disney World Resort. The quality of the fast food did not seem to matter all that much. On the other hand, ratings of attractions, entertainment, and fireworks were strongly related to both the return intention and the satisfaction measure.

Guided by the survey results, Disney decided to invest available funds in new attractions, entertainment, and expanded fireworks displays. Although the organization felt competent to improve fast food, it allocated scarce resources to improving areas of key importance to guests. The strategic planning process did not just involve managers introspectively looking at organizational core competencies. It incorporated the wishes and expectations of guests into these decisions. Most other guest-focused organizations do the same. They find out what key factors drive the experiences of guests, and they work hard to ensure that the organization has or develops the core competencies to provide and enhance those key drivers.

The Excellent Service Strategy

Berry's Four Components of Excellent Service

Service expert Len Berry suggests that an excellent service strategy has four characteristics.[53]

First, the excellent strategy emphasizes quality. Without a commitment to *quality*, nothing else matters. Any hospitality organization can write a mission statement, but those truly committed to excellence start by committing the organization to providing the customer with a guest experience of high quality.

Second, an excellent service strategy emphasizes *value*. It commits the organization to providing customers with more benefits from the guest experience than their costs. Recall that value and cost cannot be defined solely in monetary terms. If "time is money," organizations can provide value by saving time for customers. Organizations doing so fill a significant market niche. The many people who pay extra for personal shoppers in retail stores believe they receive good value in time saved for the money they spend on having someone shop for them. Home-delivered pizza is even a better value; you save time, and you pay no more than if you had gone to the restaurant. Organizations must budget funds for measuring the perceived value of their services to customers. No matter what the service costs, customers must believe that they are getting significant value for their money.

The third characteristic of an excellent service strategy is that it focuses the entire organizational effort on *service*. This strategy commits the organization to hiring people who believe in service, employee training programs emphasize the commitment to service quality, resources are allocated to serving the customer, the performance and reward systems carefully reinforce the entire workforce's commitment to service, and all action plans support the service mission. The service strategy should ensure that everyone in the organization walks the service-quality walk by constantly reflecting total commitment to service excellence.

Finally, the service strategy should foster among employees a sense of genuine achievement. It should stretch and push every employee to grow and develop so that the employee group stretches and develops the entire organization to do things no one thought were possible. Taco Bell found a way to stretch its employees so that it could operate 90 percent of its company-owned restaurants without a full-time manager. According to Berry, "These locations are team managed by their mostly younger person crews who order inventory, schedule work hours, and recruit and train, among other functions."[54]

Supporting Strategies: Service Product, Environment, and Delivery System

Once the service strategy has been defined, it provides the basis for ensuring that the customers' key drivers are addressed, by determining what the organization's service product should be, what the service environment in which the service product is provided or delivered should look and feel like, and how the service delivery system makes the service product available to the guest.

If the organizational mission, for example, is to create and sustain a low-cost airline to serve the budget market in the western United States, the service product must be designed to meet that market's expectations, the service environment must be designed to fit the product and match or exceed the guest's expectation of how this type of airline experience should look and feel, and the service delivery system must be designed to ensure that the service product is provided to the guest in a way that is congruent with how the guest expects to experience that service. The joint consideration of these three guest-experience components leads to the short-run action plans that can support and implement the components and thereby achieve the organization's mission.

ACTION PLANS

Once this point in the hospitality planning process is reached, action plans can be developed because the organization now has a clear idea of who it wants to serve, what it wants to serve, where the market for that service is, where the company wants to go, and how it intends to get there. The action plans along with appropriate measurement metrics represent the leadership's decisions on how to best implement the service strategy in specific terms that will motivate and guide the rest of the organization's members toward accomplishing the overall service strategy and organizational mission. These plans lay out the specifics of how the organization will operate, what everyone needs to do in the next time period, usually a year, and, through the metrics, how valuable feedback will be elicited on progress in achieving the plan.

Key Action-Plan Areas

The bottom tier of Figure 2-1 indicates the five key areas in which action plans should be established: management, staffing, capacity utilization, finance, and marketing. Benchmark organizations not only develop plans in each of these areas but also make sure each area has an appropriate means for measuring the degree to which those plans were achieved. Not only must employees understand the direction in which everyone is supposed to go but also everyone must know what getting there looks like. The measures ensure that the right actions are taken, the right goals are achieved, and the employees can see how well they're doing as they work toward achieving the goals of the action plans. Good plans are accompanied by good measures of achievement so that everyone knows how the plans are working.

Types of Capacity Utilization Action Plans

The Design Day

A basic problem for many hospitality organizations is that demand is uncertain and capacity is fixed. An important concept in capacity planning for hospitality organizations is the **design day**.[55] Whenever a new restaurant, hotel, theme park, cruise ship, or other service facility is created, management must determine how big to build it. How many people should the new physical facility be able to handle at one time? It should not be designed to accommodate demand on the busiest day of the year, because for the other 364 days, its capacity will exceed demand. On the other hand, if the facility is designed to meet demand on the slowest day, capacity will not be able to meet demand for the rest of the year. The idea of a design day is to decide which day of the year to consider when determining the design capacity of an attraction or facility.

As an example, a theme park could use past and predicted attendance figures to set the design day at the 50th percentile, so that overall park demand (and demand for particular rides and attractions) would exceed capacity on about half the days, and about half the time capacity would exceed demand. But a successful park does not want guests to experience excessive wait times for half the days of the year. The park designers must decide what percentile level they want to establish for their design day. The higher the percentile level chosen, the lower the number of days the organization will exceed its design-day standards for guest wait times. However, higher demand days cost more—greater capacity must be built—but yield greater guest satisfaction. For example, if they choose a 75 percentile design day, the park will exceed wait-time standards on about 90 days of the year; if they choose a 90 percentile design day, they will exceed their wait-time standards on only about 36 days per year.

The design-day percentile is a critical management decision for any hospitality organization. A higher percentile day means increasing capital investment to increase park, restaurant, cruise ship, convention center, or hotel capacity. Building physical capacity based on selecting a lower percentile day will cost less to build and sustain during the nonpeak times, but guest dissatisfaction will likely be higher during peak times. Once the design-day capacity is exceeded, the quality of the experience will be diluted for guests. They will be forced to wait a greater length of time or abandon the idea of experiencing what the organization offers. In either case, customers may be dissatisfied. This dissatisfaction will have a negative impact on repeat visitation, long-term attendance growth, and revenue. Management must balance carefully the trade-off between the increased costs of investment in capacity and dissatisfied guests.

Every hospitality organization uses some method to plan its capacity and decide how big to build its physical facility. The design-day concept is one way to find the best balance between investing in and carrying the costs of excess capacity and ensuring the quality and value of each guest's experience. Costs are associated with buildings, grounds, staff, and inventory. But customers expect the service to be available to them when they want it; otherwise they are dissatisfied with the quality and value of their experience. Finding the best balance between economic realities and the guest satisfaction strategy and mission is what guestologists do.

Consider a theme park with numerous rides and other attractions. Once the design-day decision has been made that is consistent with its mission, the park management can calculate how many demand units (people per time period per attraction) will be in the park to consume or enjoy the capacity available. Thus, if the park attendance on a design day is 18,000 people and a new ride or attraction that takes thirty minutes is expected to capture 3 percent of this capacity per hour, the capacity of the ride has to equal 270. With this capacity and assuming a continuous flow of people coming to enjoy an attraction, no one will have to wait more than thirty minutes. As the ride or attraction begins, the first of the next 270 people wanting to enjoy it will start forming a new waiting line. As soon as the ride gets back to its starting point or the show ends, the 270 people who have been waiting for varying lengths of time will enter the ride or show, and a new waiting line will start to form. If the design-day decision includes allowing guests to wait for a fixed amount of time (e.g., an average of 15 minutes across all park attractions), the actual capacity of the new attraction can be less than 270 because the capacity will assume a certain acceptable number of people waiting in line. The point is that this important capital-allocation decision—how big to build a new ride or other attraction—can be based on straightforward calculations that are themselves based on design-day decisions made long ago, which are in turn based on the organization's estimates of what quality and value customers expect.

For any hospitality organization, the original design-day decision is based on forecasts of guest demand, information derived from organizational past experience, and perhaps from knowledge of similar facilities. Once real information can be gathered through real experience with real people or some other change occurs, the design-day decision can be refined. Because most hospitality organizations would rather add capacity than tear down existing capacity or let it stand idle, the original design-day decision for a new facility should probably use conservative estimates.

Yield Management

A capacity-management concept that has gained substantial favor in the airline, lodging, restaurant, spa, cruise line, and convention industries is **yield management** (YM)—managing the sale of units of capacity to maximize the profitability of that capacity. Also called **revenue management**, yield management involves selling the right capacity to the right customer at the most advantageous price, to maximize both capacity use and revenue. This concept is based on the idea that guest demand patterns can be predicted to some extent and those predictions can be used to allow the hospitality organization to charge different rates to different people (or groups) based on (1) when reservations are made and (2) the capacity projected to be available at any given time. Early reservations with restrictions (e.g., airline passengers staying over Saturday or paying a high financial penalty for schedule changes) might receive the lowest prices. Guests who wait until later to make reservations, with fewer restrictions and more flexibility, can expect and are usually willing to pay more. Balancing capacity, demand, and price is primarily the task of job revenue managers, often with the aid of (and sometimes substituted by) a computerized yield-management system.

For example, a sophisticated YM system will predict the demand pattern for reservations on a specific flight from Los Angeles to New York four months from now, and then price each seat in a way that exactly meets the forecasted demand for travel on that flight. That is, the airline will know how many seats it should set aside on that flight for full-fare guests (who will book their reservations late and will expect to pay more) and how many it must sell at lower prices. Using historical data, for example, the YM program may estimate that 20 percent of the flight's capacity should be reserved for full-fare guests who book late. It may also forecast or calculate a pick-up rate indicating how additional passengers will book reservations from now until the plane flies four months from now. This rate, also based on historical experience, can be a smooth curve or any other distribution that describes how guests make reservations.

The airline's goal is to sell as many seats as possible at the highest rate possible. It will start by setting aside the expected full-fare capacity and then calculate the capacities to be set aside at each successively lower rate. As every traveler knows, the farther out from the flight date the reservation is made, generally the lower the ticket price. The closer to the actual date of the flight, generally the higher the ticket price. The yield-management process is designed to set aside seats at each price level in such a way as to sell each seat at the highest possible price. The airline might set aside the 20 percent mentioned earlier at full fare, 30 percent at a 10 percent discount, 40 percent at a 20 percent discount, and 10 percent at half price. If the airline's predictions are accurate, the bargain hunters will make their reservations early and fill up the half-price seats, followed by the later bargain hunters who were not willing or able to commit to the flight soon enough to fly at half price. They will be disappointed that they can't get the 50 percent off fares but are happy with a 20 percent discount anyway. The guests who commit even later can't get the 20 percent discount but are still relieved not to pay full price. People paying full price are those who have no choice but to travel on that particular day or business travelers who must book their flights close to the actual departure date.

The reservation process is dynamic, and an effective yield-management system will continuously compare the actual reservation rate to the forecasted rate. The number of seats set aside in each price category or the price of seats in each category can be modified based on the actual, evolving relationships between the supply of that flight's seats and the demand for those seats. If the pick-up rate prediction is incorrect, the airline can always advertise the empty remaining seats on its Web page at a substantial discount that still covers its direct costs and contributes to the flight's total revenue, or it can sell the seats to a consolidator.

A good yield-management model can maximize the revenue on every flight by filling up every seat at a price that perfectly balances seat supply and passenger demand. Yield management is an important capacity-planning device not only for airlines but also for other organizations that have both capacity limitations and a perishable commodity, like a room for the night or a cruise date. Because the organization's salespeople must have accurate and timely information about guest demand and available capacity, yield management can hardly be accomplished without the power of computer analysis but still relies in many instances on a person's judgment. In the hotel industry, for example, it is usually one person at a resort hotel who makes the decision as to how many rooms to assign to Hotels.com or to Priceline.com for a given night. While the statistics from data mining the historical demand patterns are a critical starting point, that person will have the responsibility of assessing the usefulness of the predictions based on real-time judgment.

Action Plans as an Integrated Whole

All action plans need to be considered as a whole and individually. No marketing plan or capacity utilization plan, for example, should be set without also taking into account the financial budgeting plan. Similarly, no managerial performance plan can be set without carefully planning for the necessary resources that will allow managers to reach their targeted goals. Just as it makes no sense to put a lot of resources into a marketing plan that will draw many customers without considering the capacity decisions, it also makes little sense to develop performance targets for managers without also considering what physical, financial, marketing, and human resources they will need to reach their targets. This process defines hospitality service planning. The plan lays out the necessary steps and identifies the mileposts along the path that the organization must follow to fulfill its mission, to achieve its vision. If the organization foresees a wrong future, misdiagnoses its core competencies, poorly defines its mission, or chooses the wrong service strategy, it will soon lose its competitive stature.

THE UNCERTAIN FUTURE

Of course, unforeseen developments may disrupt or overturn even the best laid plans. Good plans attempt to bring rationality and stability to the organization's operations and efforts, but organizations seldom operate in purely rational or stable situations. Indeed, the very plans that made a firm competitive under one set of circumstances may make it uncompetitive if managers get so wedded to the plans that they ignore or don't see changes in the marketplace.

The strategic planning model in Figure 2-1 is neat and orderly. But the world is not a neat and orderly place. The cycle of planning may be deftly tied to a yearly calendar and duly placed on everyone's time management screen. But the plans laid out in August may be turned totally upside down in September by such external events as competitors' innovations; terrorist attacks; financial meltdowns; technological developments; or an organizational disaster such as the illness or death of a CEO, a prolonged strike, or an unfavorable judgment in a lawsuit. If such events occur, the organization cannot wait until next August to revise its plan.

Plans are designed to be flexible guides along the path between today and tomorrow, not the final word on everything. Effective hospitality organizations stay nimble in responding to the many uncertainties that can affect their operations and the services they provide. Many create contingency plans, which offer alternative strategies to meet changed circumstances. But since no one can anticipate everything that may happen to an organization, contingency planning can go only so far.

INVOLVING EMPLOYEES IN PLANNING

In February 2007, JetBlue created a major customer service failure when it was forced to cancel 250 flights in the wake of a major ice storm that closed down New York City. The next day was even worse, as the disruptions of the storm were compounded when the airline was unable to fully recover in the days that followed. JetBlue, which books 80 percent of its tickets online, did not have enough reservations agents on its toll-free line to handle all the rescheduling. At Kennedy Airport, there was not enough trained staff to work on rebooking. And the unit in charge of locating pilots and flight attendants and assigning them to their next flight was overwhelmed. In effect, the airline had to shut down and restart the entire airline. One plane that sat for 10 hours on the New York tarmac became a symbol of the whole mess. Across the system, there were numerous customer complaints, national news (and late night comedian) coverage and the recognition that its then President and CEO, David Neeleman, should issue a public apology. The carefully built reputation for excellence in customer service that was the pride of the employees and a competitive advantage was severely damaged in a few hours. The customer relations fallout as well as the employee morale impact of this mistake led the company to undertake a top-to-bottom review of how it ran the airline. One of JetBlue University's leaders was tasked with organizing and interviewing groups of employees at several of the major destinations JetBlue served. The question he asked was, "What are we doing wrong and how do we fix it?"

Over the course of four months, the employees generated about 25 action items that were then presented to management for implementation. These included relatively simple things such as reorganizing the crew scheduling organization, creating a new division to manage transportation and accommodations for flight crews away from home base, redesigning training programs for crew scheduling and operations, and more complex things like whether to upgrade or replace the information systems used to track airplanes and crews. JetBlue's leadership reviewed these items, recognized their worth, and put most of them in place. Things immediately improved, as seen in both employee morale and customer satisfaction scores.

The JetBlue example reinforces the need to plan for the probable and to be nimble enough to react quickly and appropriately if the improbable occurs. Increasingly, hospitality organizations are including their employees in the planning processes. They have learned that good things come from widespread employee participation. First, the frontline employees know more about guests than anyone else does. They understand what makes guests happy and what doesn't. They also have ideas about what products or services the organization could add, redesign, or delete to add value to the guest's experience or to reduce costs. Second, to implement any strategic plan requires that everyone understands it and be committed to its logic. What better way to gain understanding and obtain employee buy-in than to have the employees help develop the plan? After all, if they understand the need to plan and how the plan will help the organization solve problems and reach the future, why wouldn't they support it and try to implement it? Most managers have learned the hard way that the best plan in the world is worthless unless those who have to make it work want to make it work.

A Wal-Mart store in Louisiana had a shoplifting problem, so the manager stationed an elderly man at the door to "greet" customers as they entered and left. Potential shoplifters learned that someone would be observing them directly as they left, but even more significantly, honest customers were impressed by this friendly touch. The idea spread to other stores, and Wal-Mart became known for its friendly greeters.

Was this company success the product of strategic planning, or any planning? A Wal-Mart executive of that time said, "We live by the motto, 'Do it. Fix it. Try it.' If you try something and it works, you keep it. If it doesn't work, you fix it or try something else."[56] The Louisiana manager tried it, and it worked far better than the manager thought it would, so the whole company kept it.

That's one way to run an organization, and Sam Walton built a hugely successful company. Hospitality organizations can learn from Wal-Mart's use of employee ideas. When everyone is responsible for thinking strategically about how to fulfill the organization's mission, the power of individual creativity can be unleashed in very positive ways. A planning process should include the people who must make the plans become reality or the effort will be at least partly wasted. The best plan in the world is worthless without implementation, and the benchmark organizations have learned the power of employee participation in planning to achieve implementation more smoothly and efficiently.

LESSONS LEARNED

1. Strategy starts with the guest. Know what key factors drive the guest's determination of quality and value.

2. Try to understand the future environment and what it might do to you and your future guests.

3. Use appropriate, powerful forecasting tools, but don't let them replace managerial judgment.

4. Know your core competencies, why they are your core, and why you are competent in them.

5. Know which core competencies you need to build for the future.

6. Use the organization's vision to define your mission.

7. Prepare for the unexpected.

8. Involve employees in planning.

9. Compete on value, not on price.

10. Your employees represent the one competitive advantage that your competitors can't easily duplicate.

REVIEW QUESTIONS

1. You are about to start your own restaurant and need to articulate a strategic plan. Think of five key decisions you need to make, and tell how you will make them.

2. List a few necessary core competencies for successfully operating a fast-food restaurant versus a fine-dining restaurant versus a casual-dining restaurant.

   A. Why are these competencies core?

   B. Why do they differ from one type of restaurant to another?

3. How does knowing key drivers help a manager meet guest expectations in a guest experience?

4. Think about kids in junior high school today; they will be part of tomorrow's workforce and customer base. What management and guest-service changes will hospitality organizations have to make if they want to succeed with these future employees and customers?

5. Think of a hospitality organization that you are familiar with.

   A. What seem to be the key drivers of the guests in its target market?

   B. How do these key drivers influence how the organization operates?

   C. How should they influence how that organization operates?

6. Think of a product, service, or brand to which you are loyal. Why are you loyal to that product, service, or brand? What did the organization do to acquire your loyalty, and what has it done to maintain it? Based on the reasons for your loyalty, what one piece of advice would you give to future hospitality managers?

7. How do you define *service*? What are the components of good and bad service? Which components of bad service are due to not getting something that you expected or wanted but don't get? Getting something that you don't expect or want?

8. If an organization like an airline uses yield-management techniques, guests end up paying different prices for what is essentially the same service. What are the implications of that difference, if any, for guest expectations, service quality, value, and guest satisfaction?

9. Consider the expression "Price, quality, speed—pick any two." Do you think a company strategic planner said it, or a customer? Is the expression fair and accurate in today's business world?

ACTIVITIES

1. In the chapter appendix, there are four qualitative techniques that can be used for forecasting: brainstorming, the Delphi technique, focus groups, and scenario building. Divide up into groups and, as your instructor directs, come up with a forecasting problem that a local hospitality organization might face and try to arrive at a conclusion about it by using one or more of the techniques. Different groups might use different techniques for the same problem to see if they come up with the same conclusion or problem solution.

2. Find a hospitality organization that uses forecasting techniques. How does the organization use them to predict its staffing and product supply needs, or for other purposes? How does the organization gather data? Does it use prediction models and statistical techniques, or is forecasting done mainly by the seat of someone's pants?

3. This chapter suggests that an organization should focus on its core competencies, not spread itself into areas in which it may not be competent. Some competency pairings are generally accepted, like bar and grill. Others might reflect an organizational intention to operate in unrelated areas, like college and fish camp or blacksmith and nail care. Look for unusual competency pairings in business names you come across and report them back to the class.

4. Go on the Web or across your community and see what the companies you find claim as their mission. What is your estimation of how well this mission helps define strategic decisions they make?

ETHICS IN BUSINESS

The Kelilah Hotel, an independent four-star property, like most of its competitors, advertises on the Web. It knows from asking its guests that most customers compare prices on distribution Web sites like Orbitz, Travelocity, and Hotels.com to find the best rates for a hotel at their desired destination. While customers do check out online ratings of prospective hotels, they largely select the cheapest listing in the desired hotel category. The Kelilah Hotel has taken a page out of the airlines' pricing strategy in the face of their customers' changing behavior with the new technology and now lists the lowest price they can. What they do when the customer checks in is to add fees to make up the difference in their revenue stream from lowering prices. Thus, they now charge a wireless fee, a parking fee, a health club fee, a fee for a view room, and a few other fees that they have added to increase revenue on the low-priced rooms. When asked why they use all these fees, they respond that it is a competitive necessity. Web sites advertising room rates do not specify when additional fees are charged, so customers are making their purchase decisions without knowing that these additional fees are present. It is unclear what fees, if any, The Kelilah Hotel's competitors are charging. What are the ethics of charging all these additional fees?

CASE STUDIES

Profit? Growth? Survival? Service? Customers? Environment?

Six hospitality management students were having a discussion at the Student Center about the primary goal of hospitality organizations.

Jim said emphatically, "Large hospitality corporations are in business to make as much money as they can. No matter if it's food, lodging, or gaming, profit maximization is their primary goal, and everything else is secondary. Businesses exist to make a profit."

Will agreed, up to a point: "If the hospitality organization is a public corporation, profits are a necessity, but the primary goal of any business is to grow. No business wants to stay small and unimportant. Company officials and stockholders want growth, for the feeling of progress and accomplishment it brings and for the profits that will eventually accompany growth."

Jane said, "There's something to what you both say. Any company needs profits, and any company would like to grow. But survival is the primary goal, because without it you can't have profit or growth."

Sally said, "Any hospitality organization's goal had better be to give good guest service. If the organization achieves that goal, all the rest will fall into place. If they don't, they have no chance anyway."

Spiro said, "My dad owns a restaurant, and he agrees with my professor who said that the main goal of any business is to get and keep customers. No customers, no nothing. I agree with my dad."

Betty said, "No matter what you learned in class, you are all kidding yourselves. Primary goals are just for looks anyway. No matter how specific an organization's goals, no matter how carefully it plans, no matter how hard it works to meet those goals, the environment within which the organization markets its product or service will determine the organization's destiny. Organizations react to environmental forces, regardless of goals. To succeed, a business organization doesn't need to establish goals; it needs to be lucky enough to be in the right place at the right time and take advantage of the opportunities presented to it."

1. With whose position would the company's stockholders most likely agree?

2. What do you think the CEO would say? The employees? The guests?

3. Where do you stand on the issue? (Or do you have an even different view?)

Economy Airlines

Minor Hamblin had a humanistic dream: to found a company in which every employee would be an owner/ manager, a company in which people really would work together. Hamblin started the revolutionary low-fare, no-frills Economy Airlines. Within a few years, Economy was the fifth-largest U.S. passenger carrier. The company had no unions. New employees had to buy and hold 100 shares of Economy common stock, offered at a 70 percent discount. Profit sharing regularly added substantial amounts to their paychecks. Hamblin believed that participatory management was the style that best suited contemporary employees. One university professor wrote that Economy Airlines was "the most comprehensive and self-conscious effort to fit a business to the capabilities and attitudes of today's workforce. Economy Airlines is doing everything right."

Economy had a flat structure with only three management levels. In terms of the organization chart, pilots and flight attendants were on the same level and had the same clout. The company had no secretaries; managers did their own typing and answered their own phones.

The company rapidly expanded its routes and schedules. Unfortunately, traffic growth failed to keep up with expansion. Other airlines adopted the low-fare, no-frills approach and even attacked Economy directly in their advertising campaigns. Economy's stock plunged from over 100 to 8. One employee observed, "When stock prices were high, profit sharing and stock ownership were great. Now they aren't so great." The Air Line Pilots Association began a drive to unionize Economy's pilots. New government regulations made Minor

Hamblin wonder if he could even keep Economy's flying certificate.

Hamblin had a renewed realization that a company can't always control its own destiny. "That professor said I was doing everything right. Now I'm in danger of going belly-up." He wondered if he should convert Economy over to a more traditional structure, with more management layers, a clearly defined chain of command, and specialized employee tasks. Or perhaps he should sell out.

1. What caused Economy's problems?

2. Do you see any way that Economy could have avoided those problems?

3. What steps should Economy Airlines take now?

The Diamondback Plaza Hotel

Dwight Robinson owns The Diamondback Plaza, a large hotel in a popular vacation area. Robinson tries to maintain a reputation of casual elegance for his hotel and is known among local hoteliers for his dignified advertising and for sticking to the "rack rate." He feels that to do otherwise is not fair to guests paying full price. Robinson is happy about all aspects of his hotel operation except his average nightly occupancy rate of 68 percent. The average for his geographic area is 78 percent.

In an attempt to improve his results, Robinson has hired a consultant who, after studying the situation, has presented the following recommendation:

Mr. Robinson, your rooms are not yielding the income that they might because you establish one price for your rooms and then sit back hoping people will stay with you. In today's market that strategy won't work; you have to manage your situation to improve your yield per room.

You need to use all available means to lure travelers into your hotel. When you see at a certain time in the evening that your hotel is not going to be full, you have to cut prices until you sell out. You may not be able to sell every room every night, but don't be satisfied until your occupancy rate is over 95 percent. Follow this principle: Don't go to sleep yourself until you get people to sleep in all your rooms.

Your debt relative to your property value is low; you don't have high interest charges to cover. So you can offer lower room prices than your competitors and still make a profit.

Put a big flashing sign outside your hotel. If people aren't checking in and you foresee vacancies, start that sign flashing at $59.95. If you can't fill up at that figure, drop it to $39.95 or even $29.95. Anything is better than nothing.

First thing every morning, check the previous night's records. If the Diamondback wasn't sold out, ask your night manager why! She'll soon get the message.

Sure, your average daily room rate will drop, but so what? That's just a prestige number to brag about when you get together with other local hotel owners. By managing the yield on each unit, you'll maximize your profits, and isn't that why you're in business?

Should Dwight Robinson take the consultant's advice?

APPENDIX

QUANTITATIVE AND QUALITATIVE TOOLS TO PLAN FOR THE FUTURE

Figure A2-1 presents and briefly describes some popular quantitative and qualitative forecasting techniques and indicates their cost/complexity. We shall discuss some of the more important techniques.

Quantitative Forecasting Tools

Statistical techniques used for forecasting are of several types: econometric, regression, time series analysis, and trend analysis. Each is based on the idea that definable and reliable relationships exist between what the organization wishes to forecast and some other variable.

FIGURE **A2-1** Popular Approaches to Forecasting the Future.

TECHNIQUE	SHORT DESCRIPTION	COST/COMPLEXITY
Quantitative-Causal Models		
Econometric models	Simultaneous systems of multiple regression equations	High
Regression analysis: Single & multiple	Variations in dependent variables are explained by variations in one or more independent variables	Medium/high
Time series models	Linear, exponential, S-curve, or other types of projections	Medium
Trend analysis	Forecasts obtained by linear or exponential smoothing or averaging of past actual values	Medium
Qualitative or Judgmental Models		
Brainstorming	Idea generation in a noncritical group situation	Medium
Delphi technique	Experts guided toward consensus	Medium
Focus groups, customer surveys, market research	Learning about intentions of potential customers or plans of businesses	Medium/high
Scenario building	Impacts of anticipated conditions imagined by forecasters	Medium

Source: Pearce, J. A. II & Robinson, R. B. Jr. 2009. *Strategic Management: Formulation, Implementation, and Control.* New York: McGraw-Hill, pp. 121–122. With permission of The McGraw-Hill Companies.

Econometric Models

Econometric models are elaborate mathematical descriptions of multiple and complex relationships that are statistically assembled as systems of multiple regression equations. If a chain of movie theaters in New England wishes to predict the relationship between theater attendance and the level of economic activity in New England, the chain would use a complex econometric model built to describe how New England's level of economic activity and the amount of personal discretionary income allocated to entertainment purchases relate to movie theater admissions.

Regression Analysis

In **regression analysis**, the relationship between variables of interest is studied so that they can be statistically associated. If statistical studies of a theme park's visitors show that in July and August visitors consumed an average of 1.5 Cokes per visit, determining how many Cokes, cups, servers, and how much ice will be needed on a particular day in those two months is a straightforward calculation. Using regression analysis, we can further predict sales on the basis of other known numbers (probable park visitors) and the known relationships between these numbers and the variable of interest (in this case, Coke sales). If we know that a convention is bringing 15,000 visitors to a city in a certain month, we can predict through regression analysis the number of rooms a hotel is likely to sell, the number of meals that will be consumed at a restaurant, and the number of taxi rides that will be taken in that time period.

Time-Series and Trend Analyses

Time-series and trend analyses are other ways to extrapolate the past into the future. If we know how much our market has grown every year for the last ten years, a time-series forecast will project that rate of growth into the future to tell us what our park attendance, hotel occupancy rate, or covers (the number of meals served at a restaurant) will be in a given future year. These numbers can be adjusted for changes in the economy, seasonal fluctuations, revised assumptions about tourism and population growth rates, or what the competition is doing.

The opening of Walt Disney World Resort's fourth park, Animal Kingdom, changed the historical visitor's patterns in the Orlando area in a major way, so the historical time-series and trend-analysis statistical formulae also had to change. If, for example, visitors to Orlando spend their average five-day visit on Disney property (or connect to Disney Cruise Lines), the number who have extra days to go to Universal Studios, Sea World, or Gatorland drops significantly, unless the number of tourists or average length of stay rises. These other attractions have had to create new strategies to market themselves and all of Orlando as a destination separate from Walt Disney World Resort. If they can convince travelers that there are good ways to enjoy a wonderful family vacation in Orlando besides visiting Walt Disney World, they can attract a new market of visitors who are not planning to visit Walt Disney World Resort or who have been there and done that and are looking for something new to do. The creation of the Universal Studios/Islands of Adventure/Sea World/Aquatica/Wet'n Wild combination ticket (Orlando Flex Ticket) that offers both Universal Orlando Resort's second theme park, Islands of Adventure, and Sea World's water park, Aquatica, are strategic responses to the important changes in visitor patterns created by the opening of Disney's Animal Kingdom. These other theme parks had to define and attract a new market segment by opening up new facilities that would redefine how visitors saw Orlando as a destination that was more than just Disney World.

Qualitative Forecasting Tools

While objective forecasting tools offer many advantages, they require a sufficient quantity of relevant data. Sometimes, particularly when trying to forecast demand for new products and services, relevant data simply do not exist. Here, other forecasting tools can be used to make more qualitative or subjective forecasts. Among them are brainstorming, the Delphi technique, focus groups, and scenario building or war gaming.

Brainstorming

Brainstorming is a well-known strategy of asking a group of people to ponder the future and what it may mean, based on what they already know. Brainstorming can be formal and structured, requiring participation from everyone, or very informal and unstructured. As a forecasting tool, it assumes that everyone has some degree of creativity, that people will voluntarily contribute their ideas in an open group discussion, that the sharing of those ideas will spark others to generate even more new ideas, and that the sum total of those ideas will be a more comprehensive forecast than that of any one person. Although these sessions often yield good new ideas, these assumptions do not always hold up. Many participants forced to brainstorm often view the time spent as wasted in aimless discussions dominated by a few who loudly express their ideas and convince others to keep their ideas to themselves.[57]

The Delphi Technique

The Delphi technique is a more structured process for tapping into the knowledge of experts to create a forecast of future events that are unknown or unknowable. For example, if one wanted to know the market potential of tourism in Botswana, one could empanel a group of experts on the most probable scenario for the future of the tourism and hospitality industry in that country.[58] Likewise, if a convention center wants to know what percent of its center capacity will be filled at this time five years from now, the Delphi technique offers a good tool to use. A group of industry experts would be asked to make individual estimates for five years from now, and the estimates would be combined or averaged. That average estimate would then be communicated back to the experts, along with the thinking that went into the estimates above and below that average. The experts would then be asked to consider this new information and invited to offer a second round of estimates. After several iterations of this procedure, the typical Delphi process tends to yield a fairly tight estimate of the future—in this example, the capacity utilization of the convention center five years from now.

Even though this process cannot guarantee a forecast of such future unknowables as precisely how many Kiwanis Club members will attend a national convention or exactly how many meals will be eaten away from home next year, combining expert estimates can yield the best estimate possible.

Focus Groups

Focus groups are asked to concentrate on an issue and discuss their thoughts about it with a trained group-discussion leader. Focus groups, which will be discussed in more detail in a later chapter, are perhaps most frequently used in assessing the quality of service already rendered and identifying customer key drivers. They can also be helpful in forecasting what innovations people are apt to like and not like about a service experience. If an organization has an innovation in mind, it can form a focus group that is demographically and psychographically representative of its target market and see how the group reacts to the innovation. For example, groups of young teens living in trend-setting areas are frequently used to predict clothing fashion trends that retailers use to order clothing inventories.

Scenarios

Scenario building, or war gaming, has become a fairly popular subjective forecasting technique. We assume a certain future situation or scenario, and then try to assess its implications for our organization. If a hospitality organization has a major investment in Florida and California theme parks, a future scenario of concern might be the rapid developments that are occurring in virtual-reality technology.[59] If this scenario occurs, making quick and easy access to virtual theme parks possible for millions of people, what will its impact be on the willingness of people to travel to distant, fixed-site locations for actual theme park experiences?

Convention centers might try to forecast their future by creating scenarios that embody the new technological advances in teleconferencing. If people can sit in their own offices and experience the feel of being in a crowded meeting at a distant location, will demand for convention centers and planners continue to exist on the present scale?[60]

Scenario builders often need to act quickly. All one has to do is to look at Wii and the other computer games and virtual worlds (e.g., Second Life) that are increasingly available on the Web, inexpensive, and comfortably used by the Millennium Generation to see the potential threat and opportunity they represent for the hospitality industry. Scenario builders are in danger of looking up from their industry scenarios or service simulations to find that the scenario is already here, online, and free.

ADDITIONAL READINGS

Ayon, B., & Moreo, P. 2008. Does national culture affect hotel managers' approach to business strategy? *International Journal of Contemporary Hospitality Management*, 20 (1), 7–18.

Bender, B., Partlow, C., & Roth, M. 2008. An examination of strategic drivers impacting US multinational lodging corporations. *International Journal of Hospitality & Tourism*, 9 (3), 219–243.

Breen, H., & Innes, K. 2006. Strategic management of external change in NSW registered clubs. *International Journal of Hospitality & Tourism Administration*, 7 (2/3), 155–175.

Chung, L. H., & Parker, L. D. 2008. Integrating hotel environmental strategies with management control: A structuration approach. *Business Strategy and the Environment*, 17 (4), 272–286.

Claver-Cortes, E., Molina-Azorin, J. F., & Pereira-Molina, J. 2007. The impact of strategic behaviors on hotel performance. *International Journal of Contemporary Hospitality Management*, 19 (1), 6–20.

Crook, T. R., Ketchen, D. J., & Snow, C. C. 2003. Competitive edge: A strategic management model. *Cornell Hotel and Restaurant Administration Quarterly*, 44 (3), 44–53.

Gursoy, D., & Swanger, N. 2007. Performance-enhancing internal strategic factors and competencies: Impacts on financial success. *International Journal of Hospitality Management*, 26 (1), 213–227.

Harrington, R. J. 2005. The how and who of strategy making: Models and appropriateness for firms in hospitality and tourism industries. *Journal of Hospitality & Tourism Research*, 29 (3), 372–395.

Harrington, R. J., & Kendall, K. W. 2007. Uncovering the interrelationships among firm size, organizational involvement, environmental uncertainty, and implementation success. *International Journal of Hospitality & Tourism Administration*, 8 (2), 1–23.

Harrington, R. J., & Kendall, K. W. 2006. Strategy implementation success: The moderating effects of size and environmental complexity and the mediating effects of involvement. *Journal of Hospitality & Tourism Research*, 30 (2), 207–230.

Harrison, J. S. 2003. Strategic analysis for the hospitality industry. *Cornell Hotel and Restaurant Administration Quarterly*, 44 (2), 139–152.

Heracleous, L., Wirtz, J., & Pangarkar, N. 2006. *Flying High in a Competitive Industry*. New York: McGraw-Hill.

Ireland, R. D., Hoskisson, R. E., & Hitt, M. A. 2008. *Understanding Business Strategy: Concepts and Cases*, 2nd edition. Cincinnati, OH: South-Western College Publications.

Jogaratnam, G., & Law, R. 2006. Environmental scanning and information source utilization: Exploring the behavior of Hong Kong hotel and tourism executives. *Journal of Hospitality & Tourism Research*, 30 (2), 170–190.

Kim, B. Y., & Oh, H. 2003. An integrated approach to strategic management for the lodging industry. *International Journal of Hospitality & Tourism Administration*, 4 (2), 1–16.

Kim, B. Y., & Oh, H. 2004. How do hotel firms obtain a competitive advantage? *International Journal of Contemporary Hospitality Management*, 16 (1), 65–71.

Kim, W. C., & Mauborgne, R. 2005. *Blue Ocean Strategy*. Boston, MA: Harvard Business School Press.

Kimes, S. E. 2002. Perceived fairness of yield management. *Cornell Hotel and Restaurant Administration Quarterly*, 43 (1), 21–30.

Marnberg, E. 2008. Editorial: Strategy in hospitality management. *Scandinavian Journal of Hospitality and Tourism*, 8 (3), 189–194.

Mintzberg, H. 1992. Five Ps for strategy, in H. Mintzberg and J. B. Quinn (eds.), *The Strategy Process: Concepts and Contexts*. London: Prentice Hall, pp. 12–19.

Okumus, F. 2004. Potential challenges of employing a formal environmental scanning approach in hospitality organizations. *International Journal of Hospitality Management*, 23 (2), 123–143.

Okumus, F., & Wong, K. K. F. 2007. A content analysis of strategic management syllabi in tourism and hospitality schools. *Journal of Teaching in Travel & Tourism*, 7 (1), 77–97.

Olsen, M. D. 2004. Literature in strategic planning in the hospitality industry. *International Journal of Hospitality Management*, 23 (5), 411–424.

Olsen, M. D., & Zhao, J. 2004. Industry change, environmental scanning and firm strategy: How is the hospitality industry doing? *Tourism and Hospitality Planning & Development*, 1 (1), 13–18.

O'Neill, J. W., Beauvais, L. L., & Scholl, R. W. 2004. Strategic issues and determinant factors of an interorganizational macroculture in the lodging industry. *Journal of Hospitality & Tourism Research*, 28 (4), 483–506.

Shostack, G. L. 1987. Service positioning through structural change. *Journal of Marketing*, 51 (1), 34–43.

Withiam, G. 2001. Yield management. *CHR Reports*.

NOTES

[1]Porter, M. E. 1980. *Competitive Strategy: Techniques for Analyzing Industries and Competitors*. New York: The Free Press, pp. 40–41.

[2]See, for example, Kim, W. G. 2008. Branding, brand equity, and brand extensions, in H. Oh and A. Pizam (eds.), *Handbook of Hospitality Marketing Management*. Butterworth-Heinemann, pp. 87–119; Graf, N. S. 2008. Industry critical success factors and their importance in strategy, in M. Olsen and J. Zhao (eds.), *Handbook of Hospitality Strategic Management*. Butterworth-Heinemann, pp. 71–90.

[3]Schulze, M. 2008. Best of the best 2008: Flight services: NetJets. *Robb Report*, June 1, http://www.robbreport.com/Best-of-the-Best-2008-Flight-Services-NetJets.aspx, accessed January 5, 2010. Also see http://www.netjets.com/ for company history.

[4]http://www.sath.org/, accessed June 25, 2009.

[5]Mintzberg, H. 1994. *The Rise and Fall of Strategic Planning*. New York: The Free Press, pp. 324–331.

[6]Porter, M. E. 1980.

[7]For thorough discussions on strategic planning, see Thompson, A. A., & Strickland, A. J. 2008. *Strategic Management*, 14th edition. New York: McGraw-Hill; Olsen, M. D., West, J. J., & Tse, E. C. Y. 2007. *Strategic Management in the Hospitality Industry*, 3rd edition. Upper Saddle River, NJ: Prentice Hall; Enz, C. A. 2009. *Hospitality Strategic Management: Concepts and*

Cases, 2nd edition. Hobeken, NJ: Wiley; Thompson, A. A., Strickland, A. J., & Gamble, J. 2005. *Crafting and Executing Strategy: The Quest for Competitive Advantage: Concepts and Cases*, 16th edition. New York: McGraw-Hill; Schoemaker, S., Lewis, R. C., & Yesawich, P. C. 2007. *Marketing Leadership in Hospitality and Tourism: Strategies and Tactics for Competitive Advantage*, 4th edition. Upper Saddle River, NJ: Prentice Hall.

[8]Hamel, G., & Prahalad, C. K. 1994. *Competing for the Future*. Boston: Harvard Business School Press, p. 16.

[9]Ibid., 109.

[10]Quoted from http://www.hotelconnect.co.uk/, accessed June 25, 2009.

[11]Peters, T. 1997. *The Circle of Innovation*. New York: Alfred A. Knopf, p. 457.

[12]Kassab, B. 2009. *Orlando Sentinel*, June 17, p. B-4.

[13]See for a more detailed discussion, Cranage, D. 2003. Practical time series forecasting for the hospitality manager. *International Journal of Contemporary Hospitality Management*, 15 (2), 86–93; Song, H. 2008. Tourism demand modeling and forecasting—A review of recent research. *Tourism Management*, 29, 203–220.

[14]Following discussion is based on information found in Tapscott, D. 2009. *Grown Up Digital*. New York: McGraw Hill.

[15]Kang, S. 2006. Chasing Generation. *Wall Street Journal*, September 1, pp. A11, A12; Tapscott, D. 2009.

[16]http://www.starwoodhotels.com/whotels/about/index.html, accessed August 5, 2009.

[17]Zaslow, J. 2007. The most praised generation goes to work. *Wall Street Journal*, April 20, pp. W1, W7.

[18]Mindlin, S. (2008, August 25). Drilling down—Preferring the web over watching TV. *The New York Times*, p. C3.

[19]Kohn, A. 2006. *The Homework Myth: Why Our Kids Get Too Much of a Bad Thing*. New York: De Capo Books.

[20]Gee, J. P. 2003. *What Video Games Have to Teach Us About Learning and Literacy*. New York: Palgrave Macmillan; Green, C. S., & Bavelier, D. 2003. Action video game modifies visual attention. *Nature*, 423, 534–537.

[21]Dye, M. W. G., Green, C. S., & Bavelier, D. 2009. The development of attention skills in action video game players. *Neuropsychologia*, 47, 1780–1789.

[22]Beck, J. C., & Wade, M. 2006. *The Kids are Alright: How the Gamer Generation is Changing the Workplace*. Boston, MA: Harvard Business School Publishing.

[23]Gee, 2003.

[24]For examples of how the virtual world impacts hospitality, visit following Web sites. Virtual meetings: http://www.mpiweb.org/CMS/MPIWeb/mpicontent.aspx?id=16898; virtual hotel tour: http://www.oberoihotels.com/; telepresence: http://www.hvs.com/Jump/?aid=2971. For an example, see http://www.youtube.com/watch?v=ODjjyf7mrcQ, accessed September 10, 2009.

[25]http://www.hotel-online.com/News/PR2005_1st/Feb05_SarbanesOxley.html

[26]Ambec, S., & Lanoie, P. 2008. Does it pay to be green? *Academy of Management Perspectives*, 22 (4), 45–62.

[27]Audi, T. 2007. Hotel chains grapple with meaning of green. *Wall Street Journal*, September 11, p. B1, B2.

[28]Ball, J. 2007. The carbon neutral vacation. *Wall Street Journal*, July 28–29, pp. P1, P4.

[29]Dougherty, C. 2006. The disappearing dude ranch. *Wall Street Journal*, July 7, pp. W1, W10.

[30]Dougherty, C. 2006. The endangered B&B. *Wall Street Journal*, August 11, pp. W1, W6.

[31]Dougherty, C. 2006. Ski resort deals hit brisk pace, and high prices. *Wall Street Journal*, December 2–3, p. B1.

[32]Corkery, M. 2006. New twist in vacation homes. *Wall Street Journal*, February 25–26, pp. B1, B4.

[33]McCracken, J., & Audi, T. 2009. MGM Mirage facing breakup. *Wall Street Journal*, March 14–15, p. B5.

[34]Palmeri, C. 2009. Sysco hustles to keep restaurants cooking. *BusinessWeek*, May 18, pp. 52–53.

[35]Adamy, J. 2008. Squeezed restaurants shed jobs. *Wall Street Journal*, December, 10, p. A3.

[36]Newport, J. P. 2009. How clubs are surviving now. *Wall Street Journal*, May 9–10, p. W4; Newport, J. P. 2008. Country clubs fight an exodus. *Wall Street Journal*, November 29–30, p. W2.

[37]Chaker, A. M. 2009. Planes, trains ... and buses? *Wall Street Journal*, June 18, pp. D1, D4.

[38]Kwortnik, R. J. 2005. Preparing for disaster: Recommendations based on the blackout of '03. *Cornell Hotel and Restaurant Administration Quarterly*, 46 (1), 47–51.

[39]Thomas, D. 1992. *Dave's Way*. New York: Berkeley Books, p. 94.

[40]Ibid.

[41]Hamel & Prahalad, 1994, pp. 221–222.

[42]Micelli, J. 2008. *The New Gold Standard: 5 Leadership Principles for Creating a Legendary Customer Experience Courtesy of the Ritz-Carlton Hotel Company*. New York: McGraw-Hill.

[43]Gray, S. 2006. McDonald's menu upgrade boosts meal prices and results. *Wall Street Journal*, February 18–19, pp. A1, A7.

[44]Jargon, J. 2009. At Starbucks, it's back to the grind. *Wall Street Journal*, June 17, p. B1.

[45]Hamel & Prahalad, 1994, pp. 114–115.

[46]Kim, W. C., & Mauborgne, R. 2005. *Blue Ocean Strategy: How to Create Uncontested Market Space and Make Competition Irrelevant*. Boston, MA: Harvard Business School Press.

[47]Grover, R. 1991. *The Disney Touch: How a Daring Management Team Revived an Entertainment Empire*. Homewood, IL: Richard D. Irwin, pp. 8–9.

[48]http://corporate.ritzcarlton.com/en/About/GoldStandards.htm, accessed July 27, 2009.

[49]Our compass, Darden Restaurants, company publication, n.d.

[50]Collins, J. C., & Porras, J. I. 1994. *Built to Last: Successful Habits of Visionary Companies*. New York: Harper-Collins, p. 74.

[51]http://www.iflyswa.com/info/airborne.html, accessed May 12, 1999.

[52]http://www.southwest.com/about_swa/mission.html, accessed September 24, 2010.

[53]Berry, L. 1984. The employee as customer, in C. H. Lovelock (ed.), *Services Marketing*. Englewood Cliffs, NJ: Prentice Hall, pp. 65–68.

[54]Ibid., 67.

[55]Dickson, D. D., Ford, R. C., & Laval, B. 2005. Managing real and virtual waits in hospitality and service organizations. *Cornell Hotel and Restaurant Quarterly*, 46 (1), 52–68.

[56]Quoted in Collins & Porras, 1994, p. 98.

[57]Formica, S., & Kothari, T. H. 2008. Strategic destination planning: Analyzing the future of tourism. *Journal of Travel Research*, 46 (4), 355–367.

[58]Erdener, K., & Marandu, E. E. 2006. Tourism market potential analysis in Botswana: A Delphi study. *Journal of Travel Research*, 45 (2), 227–236.

[59]Yeoma, I., & McMahon-Beattie, U. 2005. Developing a scenario planning process using a blank piece of paper. *Tourism and Hospitality Research*, 5, 273–285.

[60]Kim, D. Y., & Park, O. 2009. A study on American meeting planners' attitudes toward and adoption of technology in the workplace. *Tourism and Hospitality Research*, 9 (3), 209–223.

CHAPTER 3

Setting the Scene for the Guest Experience

HOSPITALITY PRINCIPLE: PROVIDE THE SERVICE SETTING THAT GUESTS EXPECT

I don't want the public to see the world they live in while they're in the Park. I want them to feel they're in another world.

—Walt Disney

LEARNING OBJECTIVES

After reading this chapter, you should understand:

- Why the service setting or service environment is important.

- How the service environment affects guests and employees.

- Which elements of the service environment need to be managed.

- How service environment factors moderate or affect the responses of guests, according to the Bitner model.

- Why providing a service environment in which guests feel safe and secure is critical.

- How theming the service setting pays off.

KEY TERMS AND CONCEPTS

| eatertainment | theming | information-rich environment |
| Disney's "the show" | information-lean environment | |

In Chapter 1, we defined the guest experience as consisting of three component elements: the service itself, the service environment, and the service delivery system (the people and the processes that provide the service to the guest). This chapter focuses on the service environment or setting in which the guest experience takes place. For a restaurant, the environment can be a Rainforest Café or Margaritaville, where the physical structure is an integral part of the guest experience, or it can be a Denny's with simple booths. The difference between these two types of restaurants is something more than just the food. An **eatertainment** restaurant, such as House of Blues, ESPN Zone, and Hard Rock Café, create environments that enhance the eating experience well beyond the meals they serve. They deliver a high-quality meal, but they also offer an elaborate themed décor to add a show-like experience for their guests and uniquely differentiate their restaurants from competitors. Although all service organizations give some thought to the service setting, its importance to the customer experience has been most thoroughly understood by those who view and treat their customers as guests—the hospitality industry.

Some in the hospitality industry have embraced the idea of guestology, and have developed service environments to meet or exceed the customers' expectations. Truly amazing examples can be found in amusement parks, hotels, and restaurants, where the entire service setting is crafted to create a specific look and feel for the guest. This service setting is an important part of the service experience being delivered. This chapter will focus on why managing the setting for the hospitality experience is so important, and what major components need to be considered to do it well.

CREATING THE "SHOW"

A term coined by Walt Disney, "**the show**" refers to everyone and everything that interfaces with guests. It reflects his belief that a theme park should make guests feel like they are immersed in a living motion picture, where everything the guest sees, feels, and senses is part of the story being told. Although employees and other customers are also part of any guest service organization's "show" or service environment, the physical aspects of the service setting are equally important.

This chapter focuses on the physical aspects of the service setting. Without question, the setting can have a major influence on the guest's determination of the quality and value of a guest experience. For some experiences offered to guests, the environment is in effect the setting for a dramatic production or play in which the guest is a participant.[1] Occasionally, the environment is so significant to the enjoyment of the fantasy that it should perhaps be considered as a part of the service itself.

Perhaps more than any other organization, Disney understands that its guests have extraordinary experiences largely because of the attention Disney pays to creating the show. Walt Disney originated the idea that a guest experience can be unified and enhanced if it is based on a theme. Disney spends endless time and effort ensuring that the environment and the cast members/employees within it—the show—are as consistently and accurately themed as possible.

Many companies use a theme to create a feeling that guests are somehow immersed in another place and time to provide guests with extraordinary experiences. The lesson that Disney has taught everyone is that by paying attention to the details of creating a themed show, they can add quality and value to the guest experience. Successful hospitality organizations have learned that a great show is well worth spending considerable time and effort.

Much of Walt Disney's early success with Disneyland resulted from his insight that many guests would enjoy feeling like active participants in a drama or movie rather than simply being passive observers. In making movies, Walt had learned to present stories that offered viewers the opportunity to experience fantasy vicariously. Why not set up parks and rides with characters and fantastic settings within which guests could move and participate as if they were immersed in a movie? For an organization offering such an intangible feeling as its "product," the service setting is critical to success.

Themes Create Fantasy

When a company uses the physical environment and other visual cues to create a show as part of its service experience, it is trying to transport its guests into a fantasy world. This strategy can be used for an amusement park, a restaurant, a hotel, a cruise ship, or any place where the hospitality experience would be enhanced by adding some fantasy. Many hospitality organizations have used the environment to create a sense of fantasy through **theming**, as they have learned the value of creating a unique and memorable setting that enhances and contributes to the total guest experience. For example, when the environment serves as an important part of the dining experience, the theme of the setting within which the meal is presented needs to be consistent with the food served.

Walt Disney's genius was to take guests out of the real world and transport them into a world of make-believe, which he accomplished by carefully integrating all the components of the guest experience in his themed parks. Seeing the success of Disney, others adopted this idea. The Medieval Times restaurant created a theme that transports guests to an eleventh century feast and tournament, where knights joust on horseback and dinner is eaten without any utensils. The listings in the "By Experience" section on the Web site Unusual Hotels of the World show an amazing variety of themed hotels available for customers.[2] The Web site lists a variety of themed hotels: an igloo, cave dwellings, 200 meters underground, a train car, and even one where each room is themed after a philosopher (Would you like to stay in the Zen room, the Nietzsche room, or the room themed after Karl Marx, or would perhaps the Aristotle room be more your style?). Regardless of the type of hospitality experience or the specific theme, to visit one of these business establishments is to experience a fantasy. That's what guests want and expect. The details of the environment and employees are carefully themed—organized and presented around a unifying idea, often a fantasy idea—to create the feeling within the guest that every part of the environment is an accurate representation of what the guest might reasonably expect to see if the fantasy were true.

In historic Colonial Williamsburg, for example, not only are employees dressed in authentic eighteenth century attire; each of the working craftsmen uses methods appropriate to that time period to create tools, parts, or other items needed by other parts of the historic community. You can watch the blacksmith make nails, which will be used to restore a new barn, which will eventually house sheep, whose wool will be used to create new period clothing to be worn by future employees.

To Theme or Not to Theme?

Theming can effectively tie all the elements of the service experience together. Yet, by its very nature, a themed service may limit the appeal of the service offering to some people, and theming also limits the sort of new ventures of service products that such a company can provide, because any new elements must remain consistent with that theme. Therefore, the decision whether to theme or not must be considered very carefully.

On the positive side, theming is a way to add value to the guest experience, if used effectively by enhancing it. For a Rainforest Cafe, some Las Vegas hotels, Medieval Times castle, or Disney theme park, the theming contributes to maintenance of the fantasy, enhances visual stimulation, and helps to find one's way around with the visual cues it provides. It gives guests something to talk about after they've gone home, it reinforces their remembrance of what they've done, it can create an emotional connection with the experience, and it provides additional confirmation of the experience's value. Theming is an opportunity for the organization to add wow to the experience, by providing more than guests expect.

Consider a five-star restaurant. It is a kind of fantasyland. It takes guests out of the real world and serves them a memorable meal in a memorable environment. The setting is designed to send signals or cues to its guests that this is a place of consistently high quality, and it enhances and contributes to the total guest experience. While the memorable part is intended to be the world-class meal and the way it is served, it is the first impression created by the physical environment that sets up the guest's expectations for the great meal that follows.

Contrast the fantasy created by the five-star restaurant with the fantasy created by a Rainforest Cafe, Margaritaville, Bahama Breeze restaurant, or any good ethnic restaurant you can name. These restaurants and many other organizations within and outside the hospitality industry have created a service setting through theming. They realize that blending the sights, sounds, and even the tastes and smells of the service setting to fit in with an overall theme can enhance the guest's experience and make it more memorable. The themes can appeal to all the senses. Restaurants have been themed for many years, but at such totally themed restaurants as Medieval Times, Murder Mystery Dinner Theatre, and House of Blues, the food may become a secondary aspect of the overall guest experience. A walk down the Las Vegas strip offers several illustrations of how hotels have added theming to enhance the guest experience. There, one can find structures that remind guests of New York, Venice, Paris, and a circus. Likewise, the cruise industry has added theming to its cruises and ships to make them immediately recognizable and different for guests. Theming makes a trip on a ship like the *Disney Magic* memorable. The theming begins with the ship's outward appearance, and continues with the hallways, food, and activities, all of which carefully and consistently reinforce the fantasy. Today's guests have become accustomed to enriched environments in their homes, offices, entertainment sites, and automobiles. Organizing the experience around a theme is one way for hospitality organizations to meet guest expectations of an enriched service setting, especially when the setting tells a story.

The health care industry has also recognized the value of theming. For example, at High Point Women's Center in High Point, North Carolina, the themed design is a spa.[3] The waiting room has Asian-style furniture, screens, lamps, and simple flower arrangements. A spa-themed postpartum room carries the same minimal, clean design with screen-like lighting and hidden storage for medical equipment and supplies. The spa theme works with clinical requirements and the existing space, but it "alleviates the boredom while waiting, the stress of the medical environment, and the confusion of medical procedures."[4] Similarly, The Windsor of Lakewood Ranch, an assisted living facility in Bradenton, Florida, has a West Indies theme, complete with water-resistant fabrics in bold colors and patterns.[5] These varied service businesses provide themed settings because guests want them. We have become accustomed to richer environments in all aspects of life.

On the negative side, a themed environment is not always appropriate, and theming has its risks. By definition, theming places limits on what the organization can offer in terms of service, setting, and delivery system. Compared to an all-purpose non-themed restaurant, a themed restaurant will generally have a narrower range of menu offerings. Patrons of Lone Star Steakhouse and Saloon want and expect to find steak, ribs, chicken, barbecue, and chili on the menu, and a hot sauce on the table. Only if the market for those offerings continues to be strong, despite a more health-conscious dining public, will Lone Star continue to succeed.

Few organizations are fortunate or insightful enough to develop themes with universal appeal. Hooters, a Florida-based limited-menu restaurant chain, whose waitresses dress in tight orange shorts and skimpy, figure-hugging t-shirts, attracts primarily young white males and not older customers or other ethnic groups. The more specialized the theme, the more it will appeal to customers who already liked that theme anyway, but the narrower the market will be. This appeal to a relatively narrow market niche, however, can succeed. No hospitality organization can be all things to all guests. Hard Rock Cafe does not try to appeal to small children, and rock fans are not the key customers whose expectations Chuck E. Cheese is trying to meet. Even organizations whose themes appeal to a broad audience—like ESPN and its sport stars—must find ways to sustain their novelty by changing their exhibits and improving menu items to keep the experience fresh for returning guests.[6] Otherwise, guests will come once, or perhaps a few times for the novelty, and then seek other experiences. People even become tired of superstars and sports memorabilia.

The organization must provide a service setting consistent with the guest's expectations for the overall guest experience. Theming is one approach toward achieving that goal. All aspects of the physical setting—building design, layout of physical objects, lighting, colors, equipment, signs, employee uniforms, smells, sounds, materials—must complement and support each other and give a feeling of integrated design.

Control and Focus

To maintain the illusion of fantasy in a themed service setting, the experience, as is true of any good story, must be controlled and focused. The guests should see what the storyteller wants them to see. This can be accomplished in a variety of ways. In a theme park, most attractions are designed to control the experience. Rides are designed to give guests the feeling of moving through a story. Guests are positioned to see the right visual cues and not the wrong ones. In a Pirates of the Caribbean or a Haunted Mansion, the positioning of the cars on the ride, the use of light and dark, smells, the pace of the ride, and other elements of the environment create the experience that the storyteller envisioned. Hospitality organizations can also limit where the guests can actually go or what they can see. Bushes are planted to block guest movement to where they are not supposed to go and pathways are paved to promote movement to where they should go. Support functions are carefully hidden from the guest. You never see an un-costumed cast member at Disney, you never see the modern kitchen at Medieval Times, and the lawn is mowed with power lawnmowers at Colonial Williamsburg early in the morning before any guests arrive. Guest flow through a themed setting is carefully planned so the guests experience only what the company intends them to experience.

The Architecture

The same idea, of having the attention of guests engaged in specific things that will reinforce the experience or a story, is carried forward in the architectural theming of the hospitality organization. For example, the Klaus K hotel in Finland was created with a theme based on the Finnish national epic *Kalevala*. The designers studied the story and Finnish history to realize that the country and *Kalevala* are about strong contrasts: life and death, light and dark, pride and humility. Their task was to weave these contrasts into a theme in a way to evoke the story. As scholar Lena Mossberg describes it, "We created an interior design that partly reflects the Finnish nature, temperament, and the country's modern history. The hotel rooms were sectioned into categories like 'passion,' 'jealousy,' 'desire,' and 'mysticism.'" Mossberg continues, "As in all good dramaturgy, the most important ingredients of Kalevala are the contrasts between good and evil, and light and dark. We therefore split the hotel into a light part and a dark part and the dividing line runs through the bar. On one side it's completely white where they serve clear spirits and on the other side, where the bar is black they serve just dark spirits." Mossberg goes on to offer other details in the design but concludes by saying that the Americans didn't get it and the Finns loved it.[7]

Architect Michael Graves designed the Walt Disney World Swan and Dolphin Resort to create in guests a feeling of movement toward a central dreamscape: the huge and spectacular Rotunda Lobby. At the main entrance (Portico) to the Dolphin, one enters the Starlight Foyer with a waterfall cascading down its walls. Above, in the ceiling of the Starlight Foyer, fiber-optic stars twinkle. The various abstract visual motifs—the stars, squiggles, banana leaves—that are first seen on the outside walls of the building are carried forward in a variety of designs as one moves inside the building, to give the guest the sensation of moving through a continuous experience. As the guest moves through the Starlight Foyer, the relaxing and peaceful sound of the waterfall diminishes, to blend in—as the guest continues on—with the sound of the large fountain in the Rotunda Lobby. Visual sensations complement the sounds. Along the way to the Rotunda Lobby, the sound of the waterfall on the hotel's exterior carries the water theme forward. The water sounds in the entry area focus our attention on the sound so we pick it up again as we enter the Rotunda Lobby, and it focuses us on the central fountain. Falling water is a relaxing and peaceful sound and is often used to relax people. It is less pronounced as one approaches the lobby's large fountain so that the interior and exterior sounds will not be

The Klaus K hotel in Helsinki, Finland, was designed so that the architecture reflected Finnish nature, temperament, and the country's modern history.

in competition. While the activity in which the guest is engaged is walking, the environmental setting turns the walk into a fantasy experience in a relaxing tropical forest.

Similarly extensive uses of architecture to reinforce a theme can be found throughout the world of hospitality, such as The Forum Shops connected to Caesar's Palace in Las Vegas, Nevada. The use of simulated ancient Roman architecture, streets, fountains, statues, and facades help complete an image that the hotel is trying to portray.

Some settings can be experienced from a single location. Most architectural structures—environments that often cost millions of dollars to create—can best be experienced by moving through them to perceive the intersecting planes, spaces, and shapes of which architecture is made. Colonial Williamsburg allows guests to experience life in an eighteenth century town, around the time of the American Revolutionary War. You can explore the town, tour the governor's mansion and numerous other buildings, observe (and sometimes assist) craftsmen using authentic eighteenth century methods in their shops, watch historical reenactments outside the courthouse or capitol building, dine in period restaurants, and otherwise fully immerse yourself in this time period. The mission of the Colonial Williamsburg Foundation is to operate the world's largest living history museum, and in doing so, seeks to replicate with as much authenticity as possible the original architecture of this historic location. The architecture is just one part of the overall theme that situates the guests and develops the narrative story as the guest moves through it and becomes immersed in the illusion.

The creation of a movie-type of experience in Disney's Orlando Resort is most evident in the rides, but it is also an important element in the overall architecture of the park. A walk down Main Street, U.S.A., in the Magic Kingdom, for instance, opens up carefully planned and themed vistas, with Cinderella Castle always looming in the distance. The Cinderella Castle appears at first to be far away, as if this symbol of childhood fantasy is only a distant memory, a part of a small middle-American town's collective memory.

The fountain in the lobby of the Dolphin Hotel serves as part of the service experience to help create a relaxing and peaceful environment.

The Governor's mansion in Colonial Williamsburg has been restored to help visitors experience life in an eighteenth century colonial city.

As guests move toward the castle, they see it more distinctly, and they can eventually reexperience the fantasy by entering the castle.

The Casting Center building used for interviewing and hiring staff is themed in a way that introduces potential employees into the Disney culture. Applicants walk up a long incline to a reception desk. The art and architecture along the way portray important Disney images and symbols. The intent of the design is to communicate to prospective cast members some of the Disney culture and a feeling of an open invitation to join the Disney family. In the reception lobby are statues of fifteen famous Disney characters. Even the knobs on the building's front door are designed to replicate the doorknobs from the classic animated feature *Alice in Wonderland* to send the subtle message to potential hires that they are entering a place unlike any other.

Walt Disney World's Casting Center Doorknobs: "One Good Turn Deserves Another."

© Disney Enterprises, Inc. Used by permission from Disney Enterprises, Inc.

Sights and Sounds

Sound is often an important service-setting element. Music is a particularly potent environmental factor.[8] A convenience store that was plagued by some teenagers hanging out at the store and bothering patrons began playing elevator music through its sound system. Unable to fit the classic music to their hip self-image, the troublemakers moved on.

The basic principle, of course, is that environmental sounds should serve a purpose. In general, the sounds (most often music) should complement the experience that the organization is trying to provide to its target guests. Again, in general, but with many exceptions, louder, faster music in the service setting appeals to younger guests; softer, slower music appeals to older guests. The sounds of music can also affect guest behavior. Studies have shown that bar patrons finish their drinks faster or slower depending on the tempo and subject matter of the music being played. People tend to eat faster and drink more (and leave sooner, meaning that more tables are typically turned) if the music is fast and loud. Slow music encourages people to dine in a leisurely fashion. A study of diners at an Italian restaurant in Scotland found that both music tempo and preference were related to time spent by guests in the restaurant. A more detailed analysis indicated that the target guests' music preference was the best explanation of the relationship between music and guest behavior.[9] Similarly, a study in a wine store showed that French wine sold more when French music was playing, while German wine sold more when German music was playing.[10] Clearly, the sights and sounds in the background affect the way consumers behave—and spend their money.

Lighting can be used to create very different moods, as shown here in the Klaus K's nightclub and wine club (facing page).

Photos courtesy of the Klaus K Hotel.

Lighting is an important feature of most service settings. Some guest experiences are best delivered in bright lights, some in dim. Glare and lights at eye level are unpleasant in any setting. If you enter a service setting and don't notice the lighting, it is probably well done. Lighting can focus the eye toward visual cues that emphasize the theme of the experience and away from things that detract from the theme. In a Rainforest Cafe, you see not the lighting but what is lit. Lights should be selected, turned on, and directed not just to avoid darkness. Like every other aspect of the setting, the lighting should be an element of a greater design with the purpose of enhancing the guest experience.

At Walt Disney's Magic Kingdom, careful attention is paid to the meshing of visual and auditory effects to enhance the guest's experience. Music and spoken words are carefully integrated into the design of individual rides so that the guest has a continuing, seamless experience while moving on the ride or through a park area. As the guest moves away from one room or segment area to another of the Haunted Mansion, Pirates of the Caribbean, or It's A Small World, the sounds and visual effects merge, with no sense of overlap, to provide a smooth transition from one phase of the fantasy that makes the experience to the next.[11]

The Entertainment Control System

The entertainment control system (ECS) at the Magic Kingdom is designed to maximize each guest's experience by managing the visual and auditory aspects of the setting. For parades covering the wide geographic area of the Magic Kingdom, the visual and musical effects could easily clash. Since the floats move and the guests stand still, Disney has found a way to accompany each float with appropriate lighting and music as it moves through the 24 zones of the parade route. Disney uses two technological solutions. The first is a series of remote interface cabinets linked together through fiber-optic cable to the ECS. As the parade floats pass by the buried antennae, the ECS reads the code associated with each float and then creates appropriate lights and music, from hidden loudspeakers, near the float. Each float carries an FM wireless receiver, audio amplifier, and speaker system. Each float is designed to carry one channel of the audio signal sent by

Photos courtesy of the Klaus K Hotel.

the ECS and play it through its own sound system. The result is that guests experience the same light-and-sound show, part of which emanates from the float and another part from the hidden light-and-sound sources in each zone, all these media synchronized by the ECS.

WHY IS THE ENVIRONMENT IMPORTANT?

Hospitality managers must pay attention to the environment for several major reasons. It influences guest expectations, creates and maintains the mood, and has positive effects on employees. Finally, the environment serves several functional purposes as part of the service itself. While every hospitality organization has a service environment, the best, such as the memorable ones in theme restaurants, hotels, cruise ships, and parks, know how important they are in creating value and quality for their guests' experiences. They know that their environments are key parts of the service product and carefully plan their service settings to ensure that each component adds to the theme that ties the whole experience together.

Guest Expectations

First, the environment influences the guest's expectations, even before the service is delivered. If the outside of the restaurant is dirty, guests will enter with negative expectations, if they enter at all. Objectively, the number of cigarette butts on the ground next to the restaurant's front door has nothing to do with the chef's ability to prepare a high-quality meal and the staff's ability to present it, but guests do not view the environment objectively. If the restaurant does not care enough to clean up outside its building, the guest may conclude that it does not clean up its kitchen either and probably does not care about how it prepares the meal. Many guests evaluate a restaurant by using the rest room test, to see how much the restaurant cares about cleanliness. Good restaurant managers make sure that procedures are in place to keep the rest rooms clean.

Guest Mood

Second, the environment sets and maintains the mood after the guest begins the guest experience. Once the guest enters the Magic Kingdom, the entire focus is on establishing the fantasy and maintaining the "magic." One way to do so is to maintain the consistency between what the guest expects to see and what the guest actually sees. Guests expect the cast members in Disney costumes to stay in character, and they do. They are not allowed to speak because if they did, Mickey would probably not sound the way he does in the cartoons. Better to make guests wonder than to disappoint them. If the characters were allowed to take off their heads or any other part of their costumes while in public view, they might destroy the magic of the illusion. A Disney rule requires that character costumes must be transported in black bags to ensure that no child will accidentally see a lifeless Mickey or other beloved character being hauled in the back of a van.

In a similar effort, to use the environment to set the mood, Disney spends considerable money on ensuring that the park grounds are clean, the lawns carefully manicured, and the flowers always in bloom. The company has learned through studies of guests that people associate *clean and orderly* with *safe and high in quality*. They know that everyone has been to a typical amusement park and seen the dirt and debris scattered all over the grounds. Walt Disney wanted to differentiate his parks from traditional amusement parks, and cleanliness is one way to do so. The real world is not always a clean place, so providing a sparkling-clean park is yet another way to enable guests to leave the outside world behind and feel safe in the fantasy environment that Disney has created.

Main Street, U.S.A.

As the example of the Walt Disney World Swan and Dolphin Resort suggested, even the architecture should be used to enhance the mood that the hospitality organization strives to create and maintain. Every guest at the Disneyland Park or Walt Disney World's Magic Kingdom must pass through Main Street, U.S.A., and at Tokyo Disney they pass through its World Bazaar as they enter the park. The Main Street buildings are constructed to enhance the feeling of being not in a huge and spectacular park but in a cozy, friendly place. The architectural technique called forced perspective led to designing the first floors of the buildings along Main Street, U.S.A. in Disneyland Park at 9/10th scale, the second floors at 7/8 and the third floors at 5/8 scale. According to David Koenig in *Mouse Tales*,

> *The decreasing heights make the shops appear taller than they are, yet still cozy. The Sleeping Beauty Castle uses the same effect, its stones large at the base and increasingly smaller up high. On the Matterhorn, trees and shrubs halfway up are smaller than those at the base. The Mark Twain [steamboat], Disneyland Railroad, and Main Street vehicles are all 5/8 scale and other structures were built in various scales based on what looked most effective to the designers.*[12]

While this old production technique saves space and costs in building movie sets, it is also an effective means for creating an environment that reinforces the feeling that Disneyland Park seeks to create. Disney consciously conceives and creates all aspects of the service environment, from building architecture to doorknobs, to set and maintain whatever mood is appropriate to each fantasy in the series of fantasies comprising the overall guest experience of a Disney theme park. This attention to detail also creates a competitive advantage. Other organizations use their physical structures and settings to do the same. A doctor hangs her diplomas on the wall to reassure patients that she has the training necessary to provide high-quality medical care. Carrabba's uses an open grille concept to allow its guests to easily see the cleanliness of its food-preparation people and their cooking areas. A checklist of how often the bathrooms have been cleaned is posted on the bathroom door for all McDonald's customers to see. Good hoteliers are constantly stopping to pick up pieces of paper and other debris in their hallways and other hotel spaces, to serve as a role model for others to emulate and to keep the hotel spotless. They know the degree to which guests associate cleanliness with overall quality.

Employee Satisfaction

A third contribution of the service setting to the guest experience is its effect on a group of people who do not even use the service: the employees who coproduce it. Although the environment is designed primarily to enhance the guest's experience, insofar as possible it should be supportive of and compatible with the employee's experience as well. Nobody wants to work in a dangerous or dirty environment. Employees spend a lot more time in the service setting than guests do, and a well-designed environment can promote employee satisfaction, which some argue is highly correlated with guest satisfaction.[13] Hyatt Hotels believes in this philosophy so strongly that it improved its employee entry-way so that it looks as nice as the one used by its guests. They believe that if their employees are happy with the physical environment that impacts their working conditions in the back of the house, that happiness will carry over into the way they serve their guests in the front of the house.

Care and attention to environmental details show employees that the organization is committed to guest satisfaction and service quality. Hyatt employees know that any company that spends the amount of time and energy Hyatt does on the details of the hotel, even on those details that most guests will never notice, must really care about the quality of the guest experience. The impact of this caring on the employees is immeasurable; in ways large and small, it shows employees the commitment that the company expects from itself and from them.

Gaylord Hotels discovered that several of its initiatives to enhance the service environment spill over to its employee satisfaction. At Opryland there is an employee named Davine. She is a woman, dressed as a tree, and standing on stilts. Her job is to position herself at various points in the atrium. She entertains people by making slight movements that catch people by surprise as they think of her as part of the background scenery and not as an animate object. Because the employees know she is there surprising guests, they too are entertained. One of the byproducts of the hospitality industry is utilized fully by Gaylord as it knows that by creating a fun setting for its customers it also creates a fun work setting for its employees.

Setting as a Part of Service

The environment may serve merely as a neutral backdrop for some guest experiences. But for many organizations, the environment is so significant to the success of its guest experience that it represents a fourth important component to manage for hospitality managers: The setting for such guest experiences should be considered as part of the service itself. The guest coproducing the experience is, in effect, inside the "service production factory." Unlike the typical manufacturing production facility, the service production factory has the guest inside it on the production floor and often in the middle of the production process. When the guest is present and coproducing the experience in the hospitality "service factory," the setting represents a major part of what the guest is paying for and seeking from the guest experience. No one wants to go to a fine-dining restaurant and sit on plastic seats, to eat a gourmet meal served on disposable china by a waiter dressed in blue jeans and t-shirt who is trying to turn the table in forty-five minutes. No matter how good the meal, the quality of the food, or the presentation on the paper plates, the guest will be dissatisfied with the fine-dining experience in such an environment. Not only must the meal be good; the decor, ambience, tablecloth, attire of the servers, number and appearance of other guests, and place setting must all be consistent with what the guest expects in a fine-dining experience.

The quality of the environmental context within which the guest's experience occurs affects the quality of the experience itself and also the guest's opinion of the hospitality organization's overall quality. In a fascinating experiment broadcast on Food Network's *Food Detectives*,[14] two groups of individuals were invited to have a meal at what they were told was a possible new restaurant. Both groups received the same food. The first group, however, was served on plastic plates, on tables with plastic tablecloths, and the food was given boring names (like seafood filet and chocolate cake). The second group, however, was served on tables with linen tablecloths, and the food had names like Succulent Italian Seafood Filet and Belgian Black Forest Double Chocolate Cake. Although the food was identically prepared, the group in the fancier environment reported it tasting better, and also reported being willing to spend more money for it. Clearly, one's environment affects the way the guest experience is perceived, and even valued.

The Functional Value of the Setting

Finally, the environment is important for several pragmatic, functional reasons. The guest relies on the hospitality organization to create an environment that is safe and easy to use and understand. Environmental features must be such that the guest can easily and safely enter, experience, and then leave without getting lost, hurt, or disoriented.

For the modern hospitality organization, the issue of safety and security has become more important than ever before. People worry increasingly about whether they will be safe from harm or injury when they go to a restaurant, hotel, or convention or travel. Guests must believe that service settings have a high level of safety and security, and hospitality organizations should find ways to communicate that they are safe places to be. Light, open space, smiling employees making eye contact with guests, and cleanliness make guests feel secure. Such environmental elements as well-lit parking lots and pathways, low-cut hedges behind which no one can hide, and the presence of uniformed employees are appropriate and reassuring in just about any service situation. Many hotels post security guards at entry points to give their customers a feeling of security as they enter and leave the property; hotels also train their employees to emphasize their presence by looking at guests, making eye contact, and speaking to them; and theme parks have vehicles cruising the well-lit parking lots to reassure guests that they are about to enter a crime-free world.

Most hospitality organizations want guests to relax and enjoy the guest experience. Because guests cannot relax if they fear for their safety, managers must provide a safe and secure environment. It's as simple as that.

A second functional aspect of the setting is making it easy for guests to find their way to do whatever it is they seek in the experience. If what guests seek is a specific location, like a meeting room in a hotel or Jaws in Universal Studios, clear, simple signage or strategically located employees can help them find their way. If it is a Web page or a self-service technology, like making an online restaurant reservation or a hotel self-check-out, it is important not only to make sure it works properly but also that clear, easy-to-follow directions on how to navigate the Web page or use the self-service technology are provided to avoid guest frustration. The point is that guests who feel lost or confused are generally unhappy and dissatisfied with their experience and the hospitality organization. All organizations that want their guests to successfully operate their self-service technology or find their way in a physical setting must carefully study guest behavior to ensure that their directions and wayfinding guides are accurate, clear, and easy to find and use and, most importantly, that they work.

A MODEL: HOW THE SERVICE ENVIRONMENT AFFECTS THE GUEST

As we know, the hospitality manager seeking to provide an excellent and memorable experience should give as much attention to managing the setting as to the service product itself and the service delivery system. The rest of this chapter will be based on Figure 3-1. This figure is based on a broader model proposed by Bitner for understanding the environment–user relationship in service organizations.[15] Our figure here focuses on how environmental influences operate on the guest to determine the guest's reaction to the service setting. The combination of elements can cause the guest (and employees as well) to want to approach the setting and remain in it or to leave the setting and avoid it in the

FIGURE **3-1** Guest Responses to Environmental Influences

© Cengage Learning 2012

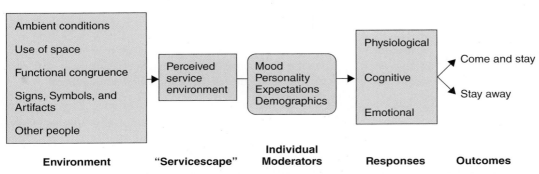

Source: Reprinted with permission from *Journal of Marketing,* published by the American Marketing Association. Adapted from Servicescapes: Impact of Physical Surroundings on Customers and Employees, Mary Jo Bitner, April 1992, Vol. 56, p. 60.

future. Even though our model focuses on guests, it should be noted that it is equally important in seeing the relationship between the environment and employee behavior.[16]

As seen in Figure 3-1, which is to be read from left to right, five environmental components (first block) comprise the service setting as perceived by guests: ambient conditions; use of space; functional congruence; signs, symbols, and artifacts; and other people, comprising employees and other guests. No guest is likely to be aware (at least consciously) of all environmental elements. Consciously and subconsciously, each guest selects the combination of elements that comprises, for that guest, the perceived service landscape, or servicescape, as a whole. Each guest will respond differently to the individual elements of that servicescape, depending on the guest's individual characteristics. The responses will not only be different, but they may be different within any or a combination of three general response types: physiological, cognitive, or emotional. Finally, the guest's overall response to the setting will cause the guest to want to come and stay (or make a purchase, or use the service, etc.) or to avoid it.

Each element in the setting is capable of infinite variation. These variable elements also can be combined in an infinite variety of ways. Thus, each guest's experience of the setting is unique to that guest and more than likely unique to that particular time and place. People change from one service encounter to another and the way they perceive the experience at one time may also change.

Now, let's look at the Servicescape model in Figure 3-1 in more detail.

Environment

Ambient Conditions

Ambient conditions in the environment—the ergonomic factors such as temperature, humidity, air quality, smells, sounds, physical comfort, and light—affect the nature of the guest experience. The effect on a guest of a dark, humid, quiet tunnel with intermittent noises and cool air blowing is different from the effect of a light, airy, music-filled shopping mall. The first setting feels ominous and scary, the second warm and positive. The whole category of "dark" theme park rides and attractions, like Disney's Haunted Mansion, Pirates of the Caribbean, and The Twilight Zone Tower of Terror, is designed around the concept that darkness has an element of suspense, surprise, and potential terror that light does not have. On the other hand, the romantic feel of dimly lit restaurants with soft music, comfortable chairs, and tempting smells is due to the careful management of ambient conditions.

Use of Space

The second environmental category is the use of space. It refers to how the equipment and furnishings are arranged in the hospitality service setting, the size and shape of those objects, their accessibility to the customers, and the spatial relationships among them.

The organization's use of space affects the nature of the guest experience. Depending on how the waiting space is designed, waiting lines can feel open and friendly or they can make a customer feel closed in and alone. How paths are laid out to get from one part of a park, whether a zoo or a community park, to another also influences the feeling of openness or closedness that the guest experiences. Closed spaces evoke different feelings than areas with a lot of open space or green. The basic decision about space is how to use it to lay out the service setting so as to complement and enhance the guest's experience.

Space, however, is expensive and must be used wisely. A restaurant with too many tables and seats or a hotel with too many rooms within its available space may be both unattractive to guests and a poor investment. An organization that attempts to increase the revenue-producing space within which it provides guest experiences at the expense of essential but non-revenue-producing space (e.g., for public areas, offices, kitchens, supplies, and utilities) may have a memorable service setting, but its delivery system will be unable to reliably provide the service product required for a memorable guest experience.

The space layout should also help guests to know where they are and how to find their way to where they want to go. People do not like being lost or confused as to where they are and the benchmark hospitality organizations spend considerable time and effort in making guest wayfinding easy by the way they design their space. As Disney said, "Have a single entrance through which all the traffic would flow, then a hub off which the various areas were situated. That gives people a sense of orientation—they know where they are at all times. And it saves a lot of walking."[17] This commitment to orientation can be seen in each park at Walt Disney World Resort. Logical, easy-to-follow pathways lead people in the Magic Kingdom from one attraction to another. The big circular path around the World Showcase in Epcot makes it easy for guests to go from one attraction to another in an orderly way, and the lake in the middle of everything provides a superb orientation for the guest at any point around the circle. Cinderella Castle in the Magic Kingdom, The Twilight Zone Tower of Terror in Disney's Hollywood Studios, the Tree of Life in Disney's Animal Kingdom, and Spaceship Earth or Epcot Lagoon in Epcot are other landmarks that provide constant points of orientation. Guests know by looking where they are in each of the parks and can see how to get to other locations.

Within specific Walt Disney World Resort areas, many visual and audio aids are provided to help orient the guest. The cast members in each location are costumed consistently within that location. Key structures help identify where one is in the Magic Kingdom. The Cinderella's Golden Carrousel in Fantasyland, the Liberty Belle riverboat in Frontierland, and Space Mountain in Tomorrowland are examples of key attractions that by location, size, and sounds help guests identify where they are. When there are multiple cues, it is even easier to stay oriented. Adventureland, for example, not only has the Jungle Cruise but also clearly displays The Enchanted Tiki Room—Under New Management in Adventureland to help people know where they are. The challenge is to ensure that the physical environment consistently reinforces the feeling of being in a particular section of the park by blocking out the sight of other areas, while providing landmarks that let guests know how to get to other park areas. The need to prevent guests from seeing anything that would make them think that they are anywhere else but in Frontierland, for example, is carefully balanced against the need to provide clear and easy guidance to other park locations.

Hospitality managers must maintain the environmental feel of the setting while also providing orientation devices to help guests locate rest rooms, public phones, meeting rooms, and exits. All service settings face this challenge. Circus legend P. T. Barnum set up his exhibits and signage to guide customers from start to finish. It is said that he used signs guiding guests along, stating, "This way to the egress." Circus patrons (many not knowing *egress* was another word for exit) found themselves passing smoothly, effortlessly, and efficiently through the exhibit through the final door into the alley outside the building.

Hospitality settings should be designed to ensure smooth flow for both guest and employee. Guests must feel they are moving effortlessly through the service setting. Employees must have sufficient space, traffic routes, and sufficiently short distances to travel to provide timely service to guests. In a restaurant, if waiters entering and leaving the kitchen use the same door, collisions and dropped trays—which, of course, do not enhance the

The Enchanted Tiki
Room Under New
Management at Walt
Disney World.

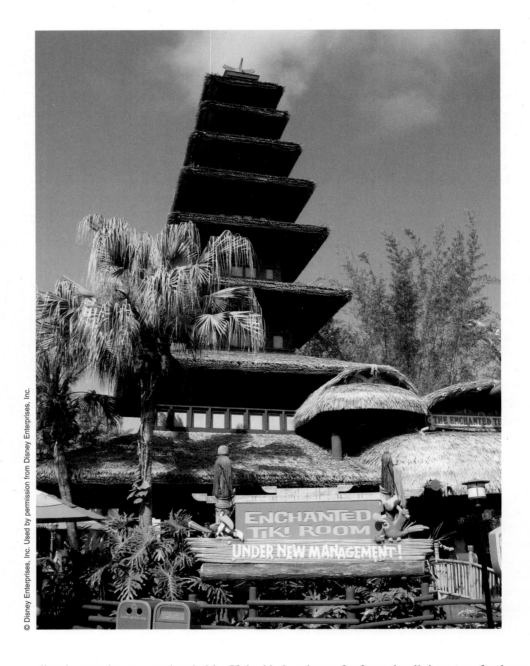

© Disney Enterprises, Inc. Used by permission from Disney Enterprises, Inc.

diner's experience—are inevitable. If the kitchen is too far from the dining area, food temperatures will suffer. If tables are too close together, servers cannot move smoothly across the room, and the guest experience suffers.

Restaurants offer a classic example of how the placement of facilities within a space is related to the level and character of the guest experience provided. In a casual-dining restaurant, guests accept a distance of only two to three feet between tables (plus their chairs). In an upscale restaurant, tables must be at least four feet apart. If they are closer together, guests may not be able to put a finger on just what is wrong, but the service environment will not suit their expectations.

The map of Walt Disney World Epcot shows the careful attention to guest orientation.

Functional Congruence

Functional congruence refers to how well something with a functional purpose fits into the environment in which it serves that purpose. The functioning of the equipment, layout of the physical landscape, design of the building, and the design of the service environment must be congruent with what the guest expects to find in that environment. Entrances should be where guests would logically expect them, rooms should be large enough to house the expected meetings, and rest rooms should be large enough to accommodate expected demand at a convention break. In a self-service environment, items and equipment necessary to the experience must be easy to use, or someone had better be available to help guests figure out how to "serve themselves." If customers must perform complicated or unfamiliar tasks, like figure out how to operate a self-service kiosk at an airport or hotel or a virtual reality experience on a computer, the instructions had better be clear and easily located. Self-service technology, as in pumps at self-service gas stations, airport check-in kiosks, and self-service restaurants, requires more focus on spatial design clarity and layout than would service experiences accompanied by a gas attendant, airline counter personnel, or server.[18]

In an effort to obtain a competitive advantage based on differentiating a functional component of any hotel, Westin Hotels introduced its Heavenly Bed in 1999. Since a bed is the essential functional part of any hotel room, Westin wanted to focus its guests' attention on the comfort of its bed, turning the bed into a nonverbal cue that would signal how Westin's bed would provide a good night's sleep. Westin essentially began a competition among hotels in terms of whose bed could offer the best night's sleep. The Heavenly Bed was so successful that every major hotel brand eventually followed suit with the development of signature beds. Through its Heavenly products, Westin also began the hotel-retail phenomenon, as so many of its guests wanted to purchase the beds, pillow cases, and sheets provided by the hotels.[19]

The functional congruence of environmental elements is given great consideration in a well-designed service environment, so that whatever physical or environmental element the guest requires for maximum enjoyment of the experience is provided when needed. As the Magic

Kingdom guest enters Main Street, U.S.A., stores on the right-hand side sell items useful inside the park, like film, sun screen, and snacks. Disney carefully places theme park eating places where guests can find them, often just after a ride or attraction. Retail shops are located at the exit points of rides for guests wanting a souvenir of the experience they have just enjoyed. As guests leave the park, retail outlets on the right side sell souvenirs. Disney knows that most guests will be looking and walking on the right-hand side of the street, so they make sure that shops on the right sell those things that guests will be looking for at that stage of their park visit.

Signs, Symbols, and Artifacts

The fourth component of the environment is the signs, symbols, and artifacts that communicate information to the guest. Carl Sewell, author of the classic *Customers for Life,* states that signs serve one or more of only three purposes: to name the business (e.g., Nordstrom's Department Store, Ramada Inn, Shula's Steak House), to describe the product or service (e.g., Rooms for Rent, Hot Dogs, Rest Rooms), and to give direction (e.g., Entrance, Do Not Enter, Pay Here, No Smoking, Employees Only, Wrong Way, You Are Here).[20]

Signs are explicit physical representations of information that the organization thinks guests might want, need, or expect to find. Signs must be easy to read, clear, and located in obvious places where they can direct and teach people how to use the service easily. Tourist cities wanting international visitors to come back know that, to encourage returns, they must stimulate positive emotional and cognitive responses within visitors from many countries. Taking guests' national origins and cultural backgrounds (demographics is one of the individual moderators [see Figure 3-1]) into account, they go to great effort and expense to create not small signs in English (which would cause negative cognitive and emotional responses in non-English-speaking visitors) but large, easy-to-see street and directional signs with universal symbols on them to make it easy for all tourists to find their way. Even such an apparently small and easy a job as making a sign must be done from the guest's point of view, rather than the organization's. For example, hotels, airports, and other tourist locations often use "You Are Here" signs to help orient guests within the service environment. If these signs are not done carefully, and from the perspective of a total stranger to the environment, they can cause more confusion than if there was no sign in the first place. Poorly designed signs leave the customer not only lost or disoriented but also feeling stupid, and customers do not continue to patronize organizations that make them feel stupid. Signs are so important that Miami's airport hired a person to specifically audit the naming logic and consistency of its signage when it realized that its existing signage was confusing its visitors trying to find flights, services, or exits. Wayfinding signage is especially important for airports as they deal with so many hurried, tired, global travelers who may be unfamiliar with an airport or the language.[21]

Signs are used to convey messages through the use of symbols, often language itself. Some signs contain not words but other symbols, such as representational icons that can replace any specific language. These signs, of course, are especially important in travel and tourism settings, to which guests come from many nations, cultures, and linguistic backgrounds. If the customer must remember the information on the sign, a symbol often works best. Universal Studios uses its famous movies to represent sections in the parking lot. When parking their cars, the sign is combined with ambient signals such as music from *Jaws*, colors, and sounds to increase the likelihood that people will remember where their cars are. At the end of the day, people should be able to more easily remember that the car is in the Jaws section than in Section 17A or Section 31D.

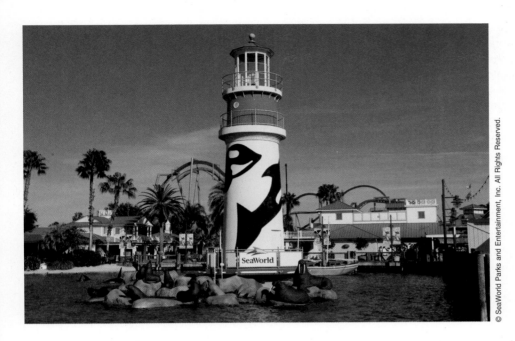

The entrance to SeaWorld in Orlando, Florida, helps to both situate the guest and clearly convey the theme of the establishment.

Artifacts are physical objects that represent something beyond their functional use. As such, they are a type of symbol. Themed restaurants use artifacts extensively to help convey the theme. What would Margaritaville be without an erupting volcano to support the Jimmy Buffet theme?

Other People

The last component of the environment is the other people in it: employees, other guests, or perhaps even audio-animatronics creations that guests come to think of as real people. Guests often want to see other guests. If they are alone, they wonder why; are they foolish to be where no one else is? No one likes to eat in an empty restaurant; you can eat alone at home. A positive eating experience generally requires the presence of other diners enjoying their meals. Guests of many hospitality organizations expect to see other people also enjoying the experience. Happiness and satisfaction are contagious. Many service settings would feel depressing and lonely without other guests.

Employees are environmentally important even before they deliver the anticipated service. A restaurant that employs well-dressed, well-groomed people will have an atmosphere very different from that of a place where everyone wears torn and dirty uniforms. Most guest-service activities have standards of dress and personal appearance codes for employees and guests that can be very structured and specific. Employees must look like what guests expect to see when they enter the organization. If the guests being served view clean, neat, appropriate attire as a mark of respect for them and congruent with the type of place they want to be, then employees need to meet those expectations. Although there are some hospitality organizations that seek to cater to guests who want and expect unshaven, overly made-up, or haphazardly attired employees with multicolored spiked hair and visible body decorations, this is a specific market segment. Though society's standards of dress and appearance are more casual than they once were, that market niche is still fairly small.

Guests also arrive in some service settings with expectations for each other. Although patrons of a fancy restaurant may not expect other guests to dress up to employee standards (who may be wearing tuxedos), most people are less enthusiastic about paying fine-dining prices when some guests are sitting around in cut-off shorts and halter tops. On the other hand, patrons at an open-air fish camp restaurant or at the Phantom Ranch at the bottom of the Grand Canyon would expect a more relaxed dress code for both employees and guests. Some restaurants seeking to serve both types of guests have devised ways to divide their restaurant into separated spaces so that similarly attired guests sit together and apart from dissimilarly attired guests.

Although Figure 3-1 includes other people as part of the environment, and clearly they often are, they sometimes seem almost like part of the service itself. If you go to a baseball camp, dude ranch, a conference, or on an Outward Bound team-building trip through the wilderness, other people are not just wallflowers or scenery; they are necessary to the experience, and you may even participate in or coproduce it with them. However, although the other customers may be an important or even a necessary part of a guest experience, and can even sometimes make it or break it, their presence is only rarely the reason why you sought out the experience. They are usually best thought of as part of the environment within which the service is delivered, which has to be carefully managed so that these other people are congruent with the guest expectations, rather than as part of the service itself, though the distinction is not always clear.

The Servicescape

Temperature, smells, sounds, lights, signs, physical structures, furnishings, green space, open space, other people—although no guest ever singles out or even notices all the elements within the environment, they do combine to create an overall, unified impression of that environment. In the model seen in Figure 3-1, we use the term *perceived service environment* for the general perception or whole picture that the guest draws from the countless individual environmental factors. Bitner calls this overall perception the *servicescape*; it is what the individual environmental factors add up to for each guest.

Because each guest perceives different environmental elements, each guest's servicescape is a little bit different. Making even more difficult what might have seemed an easy task—providing a setting within which to deliver the service—the hospitality service provider must realize that each guest's reaction to the perceived servicescape is affected or "moderated" by the guest's mood, personality, expectations, and demographic characteristics. Even if they perceive the servicescape similarly, a shy seventy-year-old female entering a wild-night club by mistake is going to have a reaction different from that of a twenty-four-year-old male accustomed to spending most evenings there. Not only that, but both the seventy-year-old and the twenty-four-year-old may be in different moods and have different expectations of the night club experience. Service experience designers and hospitality managers must realize that the guest whose perception of the servicescape has been moderated by that guest's individual differences from all other guests is going to respond to the servicescape in one, or perhaps more likely in some combination, of three ways: physiologically, emotionally, and cognitively. We shall discuss each of these below.

Factors That Moderate Individual Responses

Not only do different guests respond differently to the same environment, but even the same guest may respond differently from day to day or even hour to hour. Although the hospitality organization usually provides the same servicescape elements for everyone, it should always remember the uniqueness of guests.

We label as moderators the individual, personal factors that cause guests to respond to the service setting in different ways. Guests bring a particular day's moods, purposes, demographic characteristics, and personality traits to a particular day's guest experience. These factors affect or moderate each guest's response to the servicescape.

Some people like to be alone and object to standing in long, crowded lines. Other people love to be around crowds and view rubbing elbows and sharing harmless gripes with people in line as part of the fun. Some customers arrive in a happy mood while others are angry or upset. Some older people have a hard time walking longer distances while most young adults don't mind and may prefer it. Some parents don't like to get wet on a ride while most teens think it's great. Some people have been there and done that before and have certain expectations of what the environment should be like while others are first timers and find everything fascinating.

Cultural values and beliefs also influence how guests respond to the servicescape. Some cultures find red a happy color, and others find it threatening; some find handshakes a positive gesture, and others are offended. Some cultures believe in waiting in line and others do not. Each culture produces a multitude of cultural nuances, and hospitality managers can only do their best to recognize the individual variations that these differences create and design an environment that will offer a guest experience of high quality and value to most people.

Moderators also include the individual moods that people bring to the servicescape. When people are upset or angry, they may not be able to perceive any environment as positive or fun. Every restaurant server dreads the arrival of an unhappy diner. Regardless of how good the service, fine the dinner, or exciting and pleasant the environment, the diner is likely to leave as unhappy (and unlikely to leave a generous tip) as when that person arrived.

People arriving either in a neutral mood or unfamiliar with the experience awaiting them will be most influenced by environmental cues. The wonderful smell of freshly popped popcorn or baking cinnamon buns will influence the neutral guest to consider purchasing the food product. Smart retailers make sure these familiar odors are fanned out into the wandering crowd to encourage product awareness and interest. Cinnabon does its best to ensure that everyone walking by its retail stores smells the tempting aroma of cinnamon. Among other smells it can produce, the Disney Smellitzer machine reproduces and projects the aroma of freshly baking chocolate-chip cookies to tempt the crowds walking by the bakery on Main Street, U.S.A., in the Magic Kingdom.

Responding to the Servicescape

A guest can respond to a service setting in one or more of three ways: physiologically, emotionally, and cognitively. The moderating factors discussed in the previous section will affect the nature of the response.

Physiological Responses

The Senses   A physiological response results primarily from the servicescape's effects on the guest's senses. As seen in Figure 3-1, most physiological responses to the environment are responses to such ambient conditions as temperature, humidity, air quality, smells, sounds, and light.

Information Processing   A second type of physiological response to the environment is the information-processing capabilities of the brain. A well-known study of how much unfamiliar information a human brain could process at any one time found that the capacity was seven (plus or minus two) random pieces of information, such as random numbers. The study was done for the phone company, which wanted to know how long a telephone number people could remember. The study results led to using combinations of words and numbers (like REpublic-45914) to help people overcome their physiological limitations by combining a familiar word with five unfamiliar numbers. We can see variations on this method today in the word-based phone numbers used by organizations competing for our business with easy-to-remember numbers, such as 1-800-I-FLY-SWA, 1-800-HOLIDAY, 1-800-HILTONS.

The importance of this concept to those managing the service environment is to recognize that random information will quickly overtax the capacity of the human mind to comprehend the environment and enjoy the service experience. It doesn't take much unconnected information—a lengthy menu in an unfamiliar restaurant, for example, or a vast assortment of machines in a self-serve photocopy center—to confuse a customer, and many service experiences are unfamiliar territory to their customers. Guests become frustrated when confused, lost, or overwhelmed with too much information or too many options for their minds to comprehend. Organizations must respect the information-processing limitations that all people share and devise ways to make random information nonrandom and familiar.

Rich and Lean Environments   Environments can be made information rich or information lean. Obviously, an **information-lean environment** will help when guests are expected to be unfamiliar with the setting, or when they have to process a lot of information, whereas an **information-rich environment** can be used when guests are familiar with the setting or have few choices or decisions to make. The directional or instructional parts of the environment must be kept lean enough to make sure that guests can figure out what they are supposed to do or where they are supposed to go; the richer or more elaborate environments can be used when guests have no responsibility for figuring anything out. Thus, a themed restaurant can be rich in detail and content because the guest only has to sit, observe, and eat. If customers must make decisions about where they are or what to do next, as in a major convention hotel complex, the setting should be kept relatively simple and familiar. This point ties in well with the cognitive aspects of the environmental experience.

Cognitive Responses

Expectations and the Servicescape   The cognitive impact of an experience depends on the knowledge the guest brings to the experience. Guests enter every experience with a set of expectations based on what they have seen, heard about, and done before. The human tendency is to seek points of similarity between what we have done, seen, or experienced before and what we encounter in the new situation. These prior experiences build expectations as to what ought to be seen, which obviously influences what is perceived. For example, whn readng sentences, what we expct to read infuenses what we thnk the wrds say. As an example, just consider that last sentence. Likewise, if we enter a cafeteria similar to one we have visited before, we have our behavior scripted to perform the tasks necessary to eat by the familiar cues in the environment (the arrow pointing to the beginning of the line, the arrangement of the trays, the rack for the silverware, and the bars upon which our tray should slide as we review the food items available).

Indeed, one advantage of chain or branded restaurants is that we know what to expect because we have been there before. We know that the environment in one McDonald's is pretty much like the environment in another, and so we know immediately how to get our food selections after a quick scan of the physical facility to confirm that it is set up the same as every other McDonald's. Imagine, in contrast, the customer who has never seen a McDonald's before and has had no similar experience. Or worse, what if McDonald's managers were authorized to lay out the restaurants however they wished, as a cafeteria, a typical restaurant, or otherwise? Without any previously scripted behavior patterns to rely on, customers new to each location would be quite confused and would require employee time and assistance to navigate through this unfamiliar experience.

The point is that hospitality organizations should recognize the information-processing limitations of their guests and seek to introduce the environmental cues necessary to ensure that the present experience ties into some previously built and familiar guest mental map. As noted earlier, theming is used extensively to simplify the ability of guests to orient themselves to a location. If you are in the Magic Kingdom's Frontierland, all the streets, decorations, cast-member costumes, and even the trash cans are themed to provide the multiple cues that help guests quickly determine where in the park they are. The more familiar the organization can make the experience to the guest, the less confusion, frustration, and unhappiness the guest will have. Of course, sometimes guests are seeking a unique experience, and so will purposely seek out an unfamiliar restaurant, perhaps to have an experience unlike ones they have had anywhere else.

Nonverbal Cues and Communication   Those aspects of the environmental setting that evoke a cognitive response can be viewed as a form of nonverbal communication whereby the designers of the guest experience communicate what the experience is and teach the guest how to enjoy it. If patrons see an array of cues such as white linen tablecloth in a restaurant, they link that information back to what they have learned previously about the relationship of white linen to restaurant type and price range.[22] In other words, servicescape layout and content tell the guest something about what to expect from the experience. These informational cues tap into previous knowledge and form the expectations about what the experience should be like. If diners find that the white-linen-tablecloth restaurant also has inexpensive menu prices and excellent food, they will be wowed about what a great deal the experience represents because they have been cued to expect a big bill. Conversely, if the same diners see disposable china on plastic tables and are then handed menus filled with forty-dollar entrees, they will be upset. Guests bring a lifetime of their own experiences and expectations that influences what they expect to find. Whether or not their expectations are met obviously bears on their satisfaction with the experience, so physical cues—like all other aspects of the experience—must be carefully constructed and managed to be consistent with the expected experience.

Emotional Responses

Finally, the customer may react emotionally to the servicescape. Old graduates get choked up when they return for reunions at their college campuses. Children and adults alike are emotionally touched by holiday decorations. The flags flying, the breeze blowing, the dramatic music, and the majesty of the distinguished speakers have strong emotional impact on many American visitors to Epcot's American Adventure. Young children have the same emotional reaction when Sponge Bob SquarePants walks by. It not only represents an individual physical act but also builds an emotional tie to the entire park experience that many children never forget.

Emotional responses have two distinct elements of interest to the hospitality organization. The first is the degree of arousal, and the second is the amount or degree of pleasure/displeasure that the experience represents. The emotional response that the hospitality organization seeks to create should have elements of arousal and pleasure to gain the emotional interest of its guests. People want to spend time and money in pleasurable environments; they avoid unpleasant environments; those that create high levels of arousal are viewed positively unless the arousal is unpleasurable. A sudden explosion that creates loud noise, confusion, and overstimulation would be high on arousal but low on pleasure, except on national holidays like the Fourth of July or during an expected fireworks display. Most people avoid explosive settings.

On the other hand, some people seek out high levels of arousal and pleasure in such activities as sky diving, ultra-light plane flying, playing or watching extreme sports, stock car racing, or rock climbing. A trip on a roller coaster is a scary but not terrifying ride, which yields high levels of pleasant experience combined with high levels of arousal. In such activities, a little fear stimulates a positive experience for the customer. Arousal can also be obtained in other ways, such as the appeal to patriotism in Fourth of July celebrations or Irish music at a St. Patrick's Day parade.

Good hospitality managers have learned to use arousal cues effectively. For example, in the morning when guests are flooding into a theme park, they might hear upbeat, up-tempo music; employees would greet guests in strong, enthusiastic voices to sustain the positive feelings and high level of energy with which guests come into the park. When guests are leaving at the end of the day, both the music and the final comments of employees should probably be sedate and restrained, to be consonant with the lower arousal level of the tired guests.

The Bottom Line: Come and Stay, or Stay Away

These three response factors—physiological, cognitive, and emotional—operating together lead the guests to make one of two choices: to become patrons (i.e., come and stay) or to give their business elsewhere (i.e., stay away) (see far right of Figure 3-1). Leaving the service and its delivery out of the equation, the guest can decide that the experience of the service environment was, on the whole, positive or negative. Servicescape perceptions can encourage the guest to stay longer and come again, or go away and stay away. Hospitality organizations must work hard to create environments that encourage the longer stays and repeat visits that result in increased revenues.

The model in Figure 3-1 should help hospitality managers to choose and arrange environmental factors so as to provide servicescapes that enhance the service and its delivery and that guests, in their infinite variety, will generally respond to in a positive way.

LESSONS LEARNED

1. Envision and create the service setting from the guest's point of view, not your own.

2. Use signs and symbols to make it easy for guests to go where they want to go and to know where they are, whether in your physical space or on your Web site.

3. Make sure that the functional parts of the setting work and work the way the guest expects.

4. Design the space to fit the guest's needs, wants, and expectations.

5. Theming can add quality and value to the setting by making it memorable.

6. Realize that for each guest both other guests and employees are part of the setting.

7. Supply information-rich environments when and where guests have time to appreciate and enjoy them; use information-lean environments when and where guests are trying to figure out what they should do or where they should go.

8. Do not overload the environment with information; recognize that most people can process only small amounts of unfamiliar information at one time.

9. Know and manage the cognitive, physiological, and emotional impact of your environment on guests.

10. Manage the environment to maintain the guest's feeling of safety and security.

11. Recognize that guests can differ in mood, expectations, and experience from one experience to the next; what was a wow for a guest today may only be an as-expected tomorrow.

1. Consider how theming a guest experience adds value or improves the quality of the guest experience. Compare two similar experiences you have had, such as one restaurant that offered a themed experience and another that did not. What differences did you note between the quality and value of the two experiences?

2. Why should managers pay attention to the environmental setting in which the guest experience occurs?

3. Reflect on the service environments of two different hospitality organizations, one that felt good to you and one that felt uncomfortable. Use the factors in the model in Figure 3-1 to determine why they felt different.

4. Imagine yourself as a first-time visitor to your town or your campus.

   A. How hard or how easy would it be to direct yourself to the location where you are right now?

   B. How could you make finding this location easier for an unfamiliar visitor, using the ideas suggested in this chapter?

5. Think about the environmental and "people" factors that make you feel safe and secure in the location where you live.

   A. To what extent are these same factors applicable to hospitality environments?

   B. Have you ever been in a hospitality setting in which you did not feel safe and secure? What more could or should the organization have done to enhance your feelings of safety and security?

6. Consider the places you go as a guest or customer.

   A. Are these environments too rich or too lean with information, and why do you make that judgment?

   B. How would you change those environments to make the amount of information in those environments just right for achieving whatever it is you need to do when you are in that particular situation?

1. The hospitality service product is largely intangible. Observe and report how one or more hospitality organizations with which you are familiar use environmental design cues to give a degree of tangibility to this intangible service product.

2. Using Figure 3-1 as your reference, go to a hospitality organization and take note of as many environmental factors as you can. Which ones seem to have been "managed" by someone? Which factors can and cannot be managed by the local manager? Which ones seem managed well and which ones do not?

A number of themed establishments try to represent different eras in history. While accurately representing history can be both educational and entertaining, different periods in history have had very different norms, mores, and construction and safety standards. In particular, many of the attitudes and policies toward women, minorities, and non-Christians in the eighteenth and nineteenth centuries would be considered highly offensive today. To some extent, a themed establishment wants to remain "true" to its historical basis. For example, think of a historic area like Colonial Williamsburg that tries to represent and recreate life in the eighteenth century. To what extent should an establishment try to be historically accurate, versus artificially injecting modern construction and interpersonal standards into the experience especially in regard to the way the actors behave when providing their services?

CASE STUDIES

Safety at the Downtown Hotel

It is 2012. Faramarz has recently purchased the Downtown Hotel, a 125-unit facility in downtown Central City, a large city in the northeast. The Downtown Hotel was originally a Holiday Inn, built in 1990 and owned by the parent company, InterContinental Hotels Group, rather than a franchisee. The hotel was later rebranded as a Holiday Inn Express Since its launch in 1991, Holiday Inn Express had grown from 0 to 500 properties by 1996, and had locations throughout the United States, Europe, the Middle East, Africa, and the Asia Pacific. When the Central City Holiday Inn was built, it was located near the bustling central business district but in a neighborhood that was typical of the older northeast working-class ethnic neighborhoods. Although most Holiday Inn hotels built in or near central business districts at that time were many stories tall, a zoning peculiarity on this site restricted the building to two levels.

Around 2000, as part of restructuring at InterContinental Hotels Group, the property in Central City was sold. By this time, the neighborhood in which the hotel was located had become more dangerous, the inner-city central district was less desirable to businesses, and the hotel building had begun to look dated. Faramarz knew these facts but bought the property anyway; the price was right, and he anticipated that he could revitalize it. The building was still structurally sound and located next to an interstate highway. It still had a 50 percent occupancy rate, although the rate had been gradually falling over the past few years. Faramarz attributed the falling occupancy rate to poor management and facility deterioration; he thought he could do better.

Faramarz spent considerable money refurbishing the property. When he was finished, the rooms were nicely decorated, the amenities appropriate for the intended market segment, and the exterior pleasant to look at.

The design of the hotel was typical of early 1990s construction: two levels of rooms facing the street with exterior entrances to rooms on both levels, the guests on the second level entering their rooms from an open balcony facing the street. Guests parked their cars in front of the rooms in an unfenced lot. The original bushes and trees that were planted years ago were now fully mature and, in combination with the two-level building structure, gave the property a shaded country feel.

Now that he had enhanced the attractiveness of his building and its rooms, Faramarz wanted to develop a strategy to improve the Downtown Hotel's occupancy rate. His basic information source was guest comment cards and mystery shoppers. The common theme of their feedback was that while they appreciated the modernization and the country feel of the place, they felt rather unsafe here. Many guests said that they did not intend to return to the hotel on future visits to Central City. Faramarz could see that he had a problem but didn't know quite how to solve it.

★ ★ ★

Based on the ideas in this chapter and what your own common sense tells you (and any interviews you might obtain with hotel personnel), develop a strategy for making Faramarz's guests feel safer at the Downtown Hotel.

Fine Dining at the Silver Slipper

After profitable careers in the stock brokerage industry, Fred and Song Yi attended Chef Elmo's School of Culinary Arts. When they graduated, they fulfilled their dream of many years: They opened their own fine-dining restaurant, The Silver Slipper.

They found a building in what they concluded was an excellent location. It had originally been a Denny's Restaurant. The next owner, Bella Starr, had converted the family restaurant into a steakhouse, the Tombstone Restaurant and Saloon. She left most of the Denny's decor intact but superimposed on the interior the rough timbers and boards that Americans have come to expect in their western steakhouses.

Buying the Tombstone Restaurant and Saloon used up a large chunk of Fred and Song Yi's available capital. They decided that since their focus was to be excellent food, they would invest the rest of their funds in an upgrade of the kitchen. They patterned their kitchen after the model fine-dining kitchens at Chef Elmo's School. The couple realized that the dining area needed refurbishing and upgrading, but they couldn't do everything at once. They decided to struggle along with the vinyl upholstery, plastic furnishings, and rough-hewn timbers and boards until their superb meals had generated some profits. After all, guests came to a fine-dining restaurant for fine dining, not for the decor. They knew that some of Europe's finest restaurants, with the highest prices, were simple and basic almost to the point of bareness. They had graduated at the top of their culinary class, had served apprenticeships at excellent restaurants, and knew they could provide tastier culinary creations than any other chefs in town.

The big night came; Fred and Song Yi were open for business! Their reputations as trained chefs had preceded them, and many guests arrived in response to the excitement created by the new fine-dining opportunity. Fred and Song Yi received many compliments on the excellence of the food. But more than a few guest comment cards also referred to how expensive the meals were.

Although comments on the food continued to be highly favorable, the crowds of diners began to dwindle as the initial excitement wore off. Within a few weeks, though the small numbers of diners still willing to pay premium prices continued to rave about the food, Fred and Song Yi saw that they had to do something or they weren't going to make it. Song Yi even had to begin selling mutual funds on the side.

Fred wrote a letter to Chef Elmo, asking him for advice. Chef Elmo offered to "help out in the kitchen" for a weekend, after which he would give his frank opinion as to how Fred and Song Yi should proceed.

★ ★ ★

What do you think Chef Elmo will tell Fred and Song Yi is wrong with their new business endeavor? What advice do you think he will give them?

ADDITIONAL READINGS

Augustin, S. 2009. *Place Advantage: Applied Psychology for Interior Architecture*. Hoboken, NJ: John Wiley & Sons.

Baker, S. M., Holland, J., & Kaufman-Scarborough, C. 2007. How consumers with disabilities perceive "welcome" in retail servicescapes: A critical incident study. *The Journal of Services Marketing*, 21, 160–173.

Bigne, J. E., & Andreu, L. 2004. Emotions in segmentation: An empirical study. *Annals of Tourism Research*, 31 (3), 682–696.

Bitner, M. J. 1990. Evaluating service encounters: The effect of physical surroundings and employee responses. *Journal of Marketing*, 54 (2), 69–82.

Caru, A., & Cova, B. 2007. *Consuming Experience*. London: Routledge.

Countryman, C. C., & Jang, S. 2006. The effects of atmospheric elements on customer impression: The case of hotel lobbies. *International Journal of Contemporary Hospitality Management*, 18, 534–545.

Ek, R., Larsen, J., Bulh Hornskov, S., & Kjaer Mansfeldt, O. 2008. A dynamic framework of tourist experiences: Space time and performances in the experience economy. *Scandinavian Journal of Hospitality and Tourism*, 8 (2), 122–140.

Ezeh, C., & Harris, L. C. 2007. Servicescape research: A review and a research agenda. *Marketing Review*, 7 (1), 59–78.

George, B. P. 2006. Wine tourist motivation and the perceived importance of servicescape: A study conducted in Goa, India. *Tourism Review*, 61 (3), 15–19.

Grove, S. J., & Fisk, R. P. 1997. The impact of other customers on service experiences: A critical incident examination of "getting along." *Journal of Retailing*, 73 (1), 63–85.

Hall, C. M. 2008. Servicescapes, designscapes, branding, and the creation of place-identity: South of Litchfield, Christchurch. *Journal of Travel & Tourism Marketing*, 25 (3), 233–250.

Heide, M. 2006. Atmosphere: Conceptual issues and implications for hospitality management. *Scandinavian Journal of Hospitality and Tourism*, 6 (4), 271–286.

Heide, M., Laerdal, K., & Grønhaug, K. 2007. The design and management of ambience— Implications for hotel architecture and service. *Tourism Management*, 28, 1315–1325.

Hilliard, T. W., & Baloglu, S. 2008. Safety and security as part of the hotel servicescape for meeting planners. *Journal of Convention & Event Tourism*, 9 (1), 15–34.

Hoffman, K. D., Kelley, S. W., & Chung, B. C. 2003. A CIT investigation of servicescape failures and associated recovery strategies. *Journal of Services Marketing*, 17, 322–340.

Hwang, L. J. J. 2007. The hotel servicescape for Chinese female travelers. *Advances in Hospitality and Leisure*, 3, 231–241.

Jang, R. S. C. 2008. DINESCAPE: A scale for customers' perception of dining environments. *Journal of Foodservice Business Research*, 11, 2–22.

Kotler, P. 1973. Atmospherics as a marketing tool. *Journal of Retailing*, 49 (4), 48–64.

Kwortnik, R. J. 2008. Shipscape influence on the leisure cruise experience. *International Journal of Culture, Tourism and Hospitality Research*, 2 (4), 289–311.

Lin, I. Y. 2004. Evaluating a servicescape: The effect of cognition and emotion. *International Journal of Hospitality Management*, 23, 163–178.

Lugosi, P. 2008. Hospitality spaces, hospitable moments: Consumer encounters and affective experiences in commercial. *Journal of Foodservice*, 19, 139–149.

Mehrabian, A., & Russell, J. A. 1974. *An Approach to Environmental Psychology*. Cambridge, MA: MIT Press.

Morgan, M., Watson, P., & Hemmington, N. 2008. Drama in the dining room: Theatrical perspectives on the foodservice encounter. *Journal of Foodservice*, 19, 111–118.

Mossberg, L. 2008. Extraordinary experiences through storytelling. *Scandinavian Journal of Hospitality and Tourism*, 8 (3), 195–210.

Namasivayam, K., & Mattila, A. S. 2007. Accounting for the joint effects of the servicescape and service exchange on consumers' satisfaction evaluations. *Journal of Hospitality & Tourism Research*, 31 (1), 3–18.

Newman, A. J. 2007. Uncovering. *The Service Industries Journal*, 27 (1-2), 15–28.

Nguyen, N. 2006. The collective impact of service workers and servicescape on the corporate image formation. *International Journal of Hospitality Management*, 25, 227–244.

Oh, H., Fiore, A. M., & Jeoung, M. 2007. Measuring experience economy concepts: Tourism applications. *Journal of Travel Research*, 46, 119–132.

Pareigis, J., Edvardsson, B., & Enquist, B. 2008. The role and design of the service environment in creating favourable customer experiences. Paper presented at the 11th International QMOD conference, Helsingborg, Sweden.

Patricio, L., Fisk, R. P., & Falcao e Cunha, J. 2008. Designing multi-interface service experiences: The service experience blueprint. *Journal of Service Research*, 10, 318–334.

Pullman, M. E., & Gross, M. A. 2004. Ability of experience design elements to elicit emotions and loyalty behaviors. *Decision Sciences*, 35, 551–578.

Rafaeli, A., & Vilnai-Yavetz, I. 2004. Emotion as a connection of physical artifacts and organizations. *Organization Science*, 15, 671–686.

Rosenbaum, M. S. 2005. The symbolic servicescape: Your kind is welcomed here. *Journal of Consumer Behavior*, 4, 257–267.

Rosenbaum, M. S. 2009. Restorative servicescapes: Restoring directed attention in third places. *Journal of Service Management*, 20, 173–191.

Sherry, J. F. (ed.). 1997. *Servicescapes: The Concept of Place in Contemporary Markets*. Lincolnwood, IL: NTC Business Books.

Sulek, J. M., & Hensley, R. L. 2004. The relative importance of food, atmosphere, and fairness of wait: The case of a full-service restaurant. *Cornell Hotel and Restaurant Quarterly*, 45, 235–247.

Tombs, A., & McColl-Kennedy, J. R. 2003. Social-servicescape conceptual model. *Marketing Theory*, 3, 447–458.

Vilnai-Yavetz, I., & Rafaeli, A. 2006. Aesthetics and professionalism of virtual servicescapes. *Journal of Service Research*, 8, 245–259.

Voss, C., Roth, A. V., & Chase, R. B. 2008. Experience, service operations strategy, and services as destinations: Foundations and exploratory investigation. *Production and Operations Management*, 17, 247–266.

Wall, E. A., & Berry, L. L. 2007. The combined effects of the physical environment and employee behavior on customer perception of restaurant service quality. *Cornell Hotel and Restaurant Administration Quarterly*, 48, 59–69.

Walter, U. 2008. The meeting aspect and the physical setting: Are they important for the guest experience? *Journal of Foodservice*, 19, 87–95.

Zemke, D. M. V., & Shoemaker, S. 2007. Scent across a crowded room: Exploring the effect of ambient scent on social interactions. *International Journal of Hospitality Management*, 26, 927–940.

Zemke, D. M. V., & Shoemaker, S. 2008. A sociable atmosphere: Ambient scent's effect on social interaction. *Cornell Hospitality Quarterly*, 49, 317–329.

NOTES

[1]Pine, B. J., & Gilmore, J. H. 1999. *The Experience Economy: Work Is Theatre and Every Business a Stage.* Boston, MA: Harvard Business School Press.

[2]http://www.unusualhotelsoftheworld.com/, accessed September 28, 2010.

[3]Huelat, B. 2003. *Healing Environments: Design for the Body, Mind & Spirit.* Arlington, VA: Peecapress.

[4]Volzer, R. 2006. West Indies panache: The Windsor of Lakewood Ranch, Bradenton, Florida. *Nursing Homes*, 55 (3), 49–55.

[5]Weiss, R., Feinstein, A. H., & Dalbor, M. 2004. Customer satisfaction of theme restaurant attributes and their influence on return intent. *Journal of Foodservice Business Research*, 7 (1), 23–41.

[6]Fjellman, S. M. 1992. *Vinyl Leaves: Walt Disney World and America.* Boulder, CO: Westview Press, p. 257.

[7]Mossberg, L. 2008. Extraordinary experiences through storytelling. *Scandinavian Journal of Hospitality and Tourism*, 8 (3), 195–210, 204.

[8]See for example, Hui, M. K., Dube, L., & Chebat, J. 1997. The impact of music on consumers' reactions to waiting for services. *Journal of Retailing*, 73, 87–104; Magnini, V. P., & Thelen, S. T. 2008. The influence of music on perceptions of brand personality, décor, and service quality: The case of classical music in a fine-dining restaurant. *Journal of Hospitality Marketing & Management*, 16, 286–300; Morin, S., Dubé, L., & Chebat, J. 2007. The role of pleasant music in servicescapes: A test of the dual model of environmental perception. *Journal of Retailing*, 83, 115–130.

[9]Caldwell, C., & Hibbert, S. A. 2002. The influence of music tempo and musical preference on restaurant patron's behavior. *Psychology & Marketing*, 19, 895–917.

[10]North, A. C., Hargreaves, D. J., & McKendrick, J. 1997. In store music affects product choice. *Nature*, 390, November 13.

[11]Waldrep, Shelton. S. 1995. Monuments to Walt, in *Inside the Mouse: Work and Play at Disney World.* Durham, NC: Duke University Press, pp. 212–213.

[12]Koenig, David. D. 1994. *Mouse Tales: A Behind-the-Ears Look at Disneyland.* Irvine, CA: Bonaventure Press, pp. 42–43.

[13]Pugh, S. D., Dietz, J., Wiley, J. W., & Brooks, S. M. 2002. Driving service effectiveness through employee-customer linkages. *Academy of Management Executive*, 16 (4), 73–84.

[14]Episode OF0209. http://www.foodnetwork.com/food-detectives/liquid-nitrogen-cocktails/index.html, accessed September 16, 2010. Air date, July 16, 2009.

[15]The structure of the following discussion is adapted from Bitner, M. J. 1992. Servicescapes: The impact of physical surroundings on customers and employees. *Journal of Marketing*, 56 (2), 57–71. See also Kim, W. G., & Moon, Y. J. 2008. Customers' cognitive, emotional, and actionable response to the servicescape: A test of the moderating effect of the restaurant type. *International Journal of Hospitality Management*, 28, 144–156.

[16]Parish, J. T., Berry, L. L., & Lam, S. Y. 2008. The effect of servicescape on service workers. *Journal of Service Research*, 10, 220–238.

[17]Walt Disney. *Famous Quotes.* 1994. Printed for Walt Disney Theme Parks and Resorts, p. 29.

[18]Bitner, M. J., Ostrom, A. L., & Meuter, M. L. 2002. Implementing successful self service strategies. *Academy of Management Executive*, 16 (4), 96–108.

[19]Business Wire. 2009. Ten years later Westin hotels is still the best in bed. May 19.

[20]Sewell, C., & Brown, P. B. 2002. *Customers for Life*. New York: Doubleday.

[21]Trottman, M. 2007. To clarify sloppy signage airports hire 'wayfinders.' *The Wall Street Journal*, October 9, pp. B1, B2.

[22]Berry, L. L., Wall, E. A., & Carbone, L. P. 2006. Service clues and customer assessment of the service experience. *Academy of Management Perspectives*, 20, 43–57.

CHAPTER 4

Developing the Hospitality Culture: Everyone Serves!

HOSPITALITY PRINCIPLE: DEFINE AND SUSTAIN A TOTAL SERVICE CULTURE

I see it as my job to set the example, but it is an example I enjoy setting.

—J. W. Marriott Jr., Chairman and CEO, Marriott International

My role? Well you know I was stumped one day when a little boy asked, "Do you draw Mickey Mouse?" I had to admit I do not draw anymore. "Then you think up all the jokes and ideas?" "No," I said, "I don't do that." Finally, he looked up at me and said, "Mr. Disney, just what do you do?" "Well," I said, "sometimes I think of myself as a little bee. I go from one area of the studio to another and gather pollen and sort of stimulate everyone. I guess that's the job I do."

—Walt Disney

LEARNING OBJECTIVES

After reading this chapter, you should understand:

- Why a hospitality organization's culture is so important to service success.

- Why the organization's leaders are so important to defining, developing, teaching, and maintaining its culture.

- What essential roles the organization's beliefs, values, and norms play.

- How the organization communicates its culture to its employees—through laws, language, stories, legends, heroes, symbols, and rituals.

- How the organization can accomplish the difficult task of changing its culture, if that becomes necessary.

- What research reveals about organizational cultures.

When you go to the Walt Disney World Resort, fly on Southwest Airlines, shop at Nordstrom, or stay at a Ritz-Carlton hotel, you can sense something special about the organization and the people who work there. If customers of these organizations are asked about the experience, they invariably describe it as better than they expected. What's even more amazing is that their employees will also tell you that the organizations are different. The Disney cast members talk about their commitment to the quality of "the show" they produce for park visitors. The Ritz-Carlton and Nordstrom employees talk about their commitment to guest service, and Southwest Airlines employees talk about their commitment to providing a unique and pleasurable flying experience. Not only do employees talk about these corporate values—they believe in them. And they demonstrate their commitment to the customer in a thousand different ways every day. The hospitality manager seeking excellence can learn a great deal by examining how these organizations create and sustain their culture of service excellence.

THE IMPORTANCE OF LEADERS

Getting everyone in the organization committed to high levels of guest service is a daunting challenge. Not only did Walt Disney, Herb Kelleher of Southwest Airlines, and Horst Schultz of Ritz-Carlton spend their personal time and energy necessary to create and sustain the **organizational culture** that still defines the corporate values for which their organizations are famous; they also got their employees and managers to believe in the culture. They knew that, as leaders, they were responsible for defining the culture. They all had a strong commitment to excellent service, and they communicated it—through their words and deeds—clearly and consistently to those inside and outside the organization.

Can managers who are not the presidents or founders of organizations have the same kind of influence on the culture that these famous leaders have had? They certainly can, and they must, although managers and supervisors are more likely to serve more as translators and teachers of a top manager's cultural values and beliefs than as definers of their own unit's culture. The most important influence on any organizational culture is the behavior of the organization's leader. Viewing this influence from the bottom of the organizational chart, employees try to behave as their supervisors do, supervisors are influenced by the behavior of their managers, the role models for managers are their own managers, and so on until top-level managers, and especially the organization's leaders, become the role models for the whole organization and the ultimate definers of each organization's cultural values.

Supervisory personnel at all levels, then, must realize how important they are as cultural keepers, teachers, and translators. If they do not perform this function well in everything they say, do, and write, service delivery will suffer. Managers must not only consistently walk the walk and talk the talk of excellent service; they must constantly remind all employees that they supervise to do the same. Isadore Sharp, founder of Four Seasons, says, "Employees are natural boss watchers. Everything their bosses say and do tells employees their real concerns, their real goals, priorities, and values."[1] If any manager moving through the service environment sees any employee doing something inconsistent with the culture and ignores it, that manager sends a message to all employees that such behavior is a legitimate option and that not everybody has to focus on guest service all the time. It doesn't matter if that employee is officially supervised by that manager or not. When any manager ignores any employee action that impacts the show or the guest experience negatively, the message is sent loud and clear to everyone that it does not matter that much. After a few instances of managers saying one thing but rewarding or not punishing another, everyone learns the real level of service commitment that is expected.

Sustaining the quality of the customer experience is everyone's job. Not only must all the public and private statements and actions support the idea that everyone serves; the organizational reward system, training programs, and measures of achievement must also support and reinforce this message. When managers publicly and loudly celebrate the service achievements of their employees, they send a very strong message to everyone else about what the organization believes in and what its culture values.

Culture and Reputation

A company's culture, like a person's character, drives its reputation. Companies whose culture honor customers, employees, and shareholders usually have excellent reputations with all three groups. These organizations recognize the importance of a strong culture in the competitive marketplace, a strong culture that everyone believes in, understands, and supports. All organizations have a culture, whether or not anyone spends any time worrying about it, shaping it, or teaching it. Managers who do not effectively manage their organizations' cultures encourage weak organizational cultures or, worse yet, cultures that are structured and defined by someone or a group that may not be concerned with or may even seek to subvert the organization's mission. Unmanaged cultures give weak and inconsistent guidance to their members on what the organization needs them to do, why, how, and when.

Managers of effective hospitality organizations, on the other hand, understand the value of a strong culture and do whatever they can to reaffirm and support what the organization values and believes. If the culture values excellent service, the members learn that providing excellent service is what they are supposed to do. The stronger this cultural norm is and the more the members accept and believe in it, the more likely it is that they will try to do whatever they can to create and sustain service excellence.

Unfortunately, many managers don't understand their responsibilities in managing the culture to get this level of employee commitment, and both their employees and customers can tell. Successful hospitality managers spend enormous amounts of time and energy on training new employees in the organization's culture, reminding their existing employees of the cultural values, and rewarding and reinforcing these values at every opportunity. Although there are always other things to do, these managers make the time to reinforce culture.

Gaylord Palms in Orlando is a great example of a company that intentionally built on its Grand Tradition heritage to create a culture that would ensure that everyone in it was committed to and would deliver excellent customer service. Its goal was to get the top scores, "5s", on its customer satisfaction measures and it set out to build a culture that would inspire its employees to get them. Upon opening, its general manager strategically defined a path by which this organization would create and sustain a strong customer-centric culture. He started by emphasizing Gaylord Entertainment

Company's customer-focused vision and a set of values based on the unique history and entertainment traditions of the Grand Ole Opry. He then selected a leadership team that would appreciate and teach these cultural values and beliefs to all employees (or STARS, as they are termed at Gaylord) as they were hired, oriented, and trained. Gaylord used a variety of communication tools to build trust in and affirm management's commitment to the culture. The term *STARS First* was created to send a strong message of its commitment to the staff, and management backed it up by creating a unique *employee guarantee*. This guarantee permitted direct access to top management for any employee anywhere who felt that the promised employment relationship was not being delivered. The guarantee was created to build trust that management really believed in its STARS First cultural value.

So, does building a customer-centered culture really work? The metrics collected by the Gaylord Palms showed that it really does. Not only did it achieve a strong showing in the 5s, but it also gathered every meeting planning award and best-place-to-work award in its market.[2] When this culture was later implemented in other Gaylord properties, it led to the same results in employee and customer satisfaction and market performance.

Few hospitality organizations have the opportunity to create a culture in a brand new operation, as Gaylord Palms did. Its employees understood and participated enthusiastically in the organization's beliefs and values from the very beginning. The Gaylord experience, however, offers a model of how to create new cultural values and beliefs even in existing organizations by systematically managing the culture. Its own success in transferring its guest-focused culture to other Gaylord Hotels shows how management can use a culture-based strategy to refocus strong employee commitment to a service excellence vision even where this commitment has been weak.

The Gaylord Palms Hotel in Orlando, Florida.

Image courtesy of Gaylord Entertainment Company

SERVICE BASICS

1
Look Everyone In The
Eyes And Smile

2
Speak First And Last

3
Look Sharp

4
Know Your Stuff

5
Discover And Delight

6
Make It Right

VISION

STAR employees
delivering
flawless service
to customers
seeking meeting,
convention
and leisure
experiences.

Gaylord Hotels uses its vision, presented on this card, to emphasize for its employees the key aspects of its hospitality focus.

Image courtesy of Gaylord Entertainment Company

The Manager's Most Important Responsibility

This chapter presents the concept of corporate culture, why and how excellent managers communicate culture to employees, the value of creating a strong culture versus a weak culture, how to change an existing culture, and how managers can work with their culture to ensure that it supports the organizational mission of service excellence. Everyone has been in an organization that feels warm, friendly, and helpful, perhaps for reasons they can't quite explain. Similarly, everyone has been in an organization that feels cold, aloof, uncaring, and impersonal. While most people can readily give examples of organizations that fit the two types, few can really explain what makes the two types different.

Making culture different in the right ways is the hospitality manager's responsibility. Fred Cerrone is the founder and CEO of Hotel Equities, a hotel management company. Adopting a practice used by many of the exemplar hospitality organizations, Cerrone asks all his associates to carry a card that defines the company's missions and values. Each day, the general manager of each hotel reviews one of the values listed on the card with the staff. Says Cerrone, "That's a way to instill the culture into our hotels and throughout the organization. Now, our more than 700 employees 'get it.'"[3] Indeed, some leading writers go so far as to maintain that defining and sustaining the culture is every manager's most important responsibility.

THE IMPORTANCE OF CULTURE

In Chapter 2, we talked about defining a service strategy. Strategy is no more than a piece of paper without a supporting culture. The organization's strategy must be connected to its culture. No matter how brilliant and well thought out a strategy is, it will fail if it doesn't fit with the organization's cultural values and beliefs.

Strategy and Employee Commitment

The firm's competitive strategy provides the basis for such critical decisions as how the organization will be structured, what type of service it wants to deliver, what market niche it seeks to fill, what production and service delivery system it will use, who it will hire, and how it will train, reward, promote, and evaluate those people. But only employee commitment to implementing all those critical decisions can turn plans into actions. All the plans in the world are useless without employee understanding, commitment, and support.

Hospitality organizations that seek to provide an exceptional service experience require an especially high level of commitment and understanding from their employees. The Boulders, a luxury property in Arizona, has the vision statement, "Seek opportunities to create memories." This vision, supported by ten principles, is emphasized through the use of coaches, orientation, training, and employee recognition programs.[4] The vision does not spell out specific actions to take, but emphasizes how the employees should look for opportunities to deliver excellent service.

Because the guest experience is intangible to some extent, and because each moment during the experience is so critical to determining guest satisfaction, employees must not only understand the vision, mission, and strategy of the organization but also have the skills needed to provide the service, knowledge of the guests they serve, and an ability to respond quickly to the many variations in guest expectations. However, knowledge, skills, and abilities are not enough. Employees must also have high levels of motivation to deliver the hospitality experience consistently, in the way it should be done. Culture is the organization's software that tells well-trained, motivated employees how and why to do what when a customer is standing in front of them. Consequently, a strong and focused organizational culture becomes an especially important managerial emphasis in hospitality organizations.

Culture as a Competitive Advantage

An organization's culture can be a significant competitive advantage if it has value to its members, is unique, and cannot be easily copied by others. If an organization has a strong culture that others cannot readily duplicate, it can use that culture to attract both customers and employees. A good strategy is to identify other organizations with successful cultures and try to emulate the processes used to create those cultures in your own company. For example, Southwest Airlines has a thriving culture that others can use as a benchmark for their own. A big part of that culture is "Living the Southwest Way," which means "displaying a Warrior Spirit" (work hard, desire to be the best, be courageous, display a sense of urgency, persevere, and innovate), with a "Servant's Heart" (follow the Golden Rule, adhere to the basic principles, treat others with respect, put others first, be egalitarian, demonstrate proactive customer service, and embrace the SWA family), and embracing a "Fun-LUVing Attitude" (have fun, don't take yourself too seriously, maintain perspective [balance], celebrate successes, enjoy your work, and be a passionate team player).[5]

Working in a culture where the employees truly have the *spirit* is very different from working in a culture where the norm is for employees to work only the typical nine-to-five job. More importantly, being a customer who encounters this type of culture is unique and fun. The Southwest culture represents a competitive advantage for them over other airlines.

Management by Culture!

The stronger the culture, the less necessary it is to rely on the typical bureaucratic management controls—policies, procedures, and managerial directives—found in traditional industrial organizations. If the culture can effectively substitute for such expensive control mechanisms, that in itself is a pretty good reason for the hospitality organization to spend the time and money needed to build a strong culture. JetBlue teaches its employees its five core values and tells them to use them instead of a rule book in making their decisions. The five values are safety, integrity, caring, fun, and passion. JetBlue believes that if employees keep these in mind as they do their jobs, they will always make the best possible decision for the customer and the company. Since hospitality organizations must find ways to delegate more decision-making responsibility and empower their employees, especially their guest-contact employees, they must rely on strong cultural values to ensure that their people do the right things the right way for their guests.

A strong culture can also help employees guide guests properly even when the manager is not nearby. Guests are not passive; they almost always participate in coproducing their own hospitality experience under the guidance of employees. Unlike a manufacturing organization, where the production process is fairly predictable, the process of providing a hospitality experience is subject to incredible variation. As many different things can happen as there are different types of people. Since defining and training for all the possibilities is impossible, the hospitality organization must rely on its employees to understand what each guest expects and fulfill that expectation for every guest every time. The more uncertain the task, the more employees must depend on corporate values instead of managerial instructions, formal policies, and established procedures to guide their behavior.[6]

An Example: The Chef

In some cases, professional values can substitute for or complement values of the organization. The cultural values of the professional chef are particularly strong. While much of any culinary program is devoted to teaching the principles of cooking, implicit in all the culinary training is the cultural value of preparing a consistent fine-dining experience. Regardless of program or type of culinary training, one central value stands out: The chef must strive for flawless production of the food delivered in a fine-dining experience for every guest every time. Indeed, some casual dining chains have sent their cooks to culinary courses not so much to learn how to cook, since the chain's recipes are standardized, but to learn how to respect the culinary cultural values of product quality and consistency so that the diner at a Chili's or Olive Garden, like the diner at a five-star Parisian restaurant, will have a consistently prepared meal.

Culture as a Competency

If an organization's culture is strong, it becomes another core competency. As would be true for other core competencies, the organization that seeks to do something incompatible with its culture is likely to fail. If, for example, members of an organization's culture believe they should provide a high-value service experience, any manager trying to implement a cost-saving move that somehow jeopardizes their ability to provide that experience will meet resistance.

The basic principle is simple. If the organization is committed to a strategy of service excellence, its cultural norms, beliefs, and values must support service excellence. Otherwise, excellence will not happen.

The uniform of the chef helps reinforce the professional norms of providing consistent quality to every guest.

© Cengage Learning, 2012

Culture Defined

An organization's culture is a way of behaving, thinking, and acting that is learned and shared by the organization's members. A more formal definition is one that follows: the shared philosophies, ideologies, values, assumptions, beliefs, attitudes, and norms that knit a community of different people together. All these interrelated qualities reveal a group's agreement, implicit or explicit, on how its members should approach decisions and problems. In other words, culture is the way people in the organization act and think as they go about doing their jobs. "It's the way we do things around here." Any culture is also dynamic and constantly changing as anyone who has followed the changes in teen music and dress for the past decade can readily confirm. A culture both influences its members and in turn is influenced by its members. The interaction between members over time as they deal with changing circumstances and changing membership means that cultures will change.

Culture and the Outside World

Culture helps an organization's members deal with two core issues that all organizations must resolve: how to relate to the world outside of the organization, and how the organization's members should relate to one another. Noted cultural scholar Ed Schein calls culture a "pattern of basic assumptions—invented, discovered, or developed by a given group as it learns to cope with its problems of external adaptation and internal interaction—that has worked well enough to be considered valid and, therefore, to be taught to new members as the correct way to perceive, think, and feel in relation to those problems."[7]

Some managers define how their organizations should deal with the outside world by taking a closed or negative view of the outside environment and encouraging an "us-versus-them" cultural mindset. Members of such a culture are unreceptive to new ideas from the outside; they tend to discard or downplay common industry practices or innovations, and are generally secretive about what their organization is doing and protective of its "proprietary knowledge." On the other hand, managers trying to create an open-culture organization constantly encourage their people to learn, grow, and develop by interacting with others in the industry, to benchmark against best-practice organizations wherever they can be found, and to consider ideas and innovations developed outside the organizational boundaries. Not surprisingly, people in these open, learning organizations adapt more quickly to changes in customer expectations and respond better to customer needs than those in organizations with closed or negative cultures.

Culture and the Internal Organization: X and Y

Relating to the outside world refers to how the members of the organization see the world, what assumptions they make about the organization's relationship to that world, and how members are supposed to respond to external events. Relating to one another inside the culture refers to how the members see their collective mission, the ways they interact or interrelate with each other to accomplish that mission, and the assumptions they should use in making decisions about those things they control—their functional areas, interpersonal relationships, and attitudes toward change and adaptation. With regard to internal interaction, a culture can be democratic, supportive, friendly, informal, and participatory in its decision making, or it can be formal, rigid, bureaucratic, and autocratic, allowing only those at the top of the organization to make decisions. These two extremes reflect the distinction made famous by management scholar Douglas McGregor in his classic discussion of Theory X and Theory Y management styles. These two theories represent two very different sets of assumptions managers can make about how people behave. Theory Y managers assume that people like to work, derive real satisfaction from their work, and want to do a good job. Theory X managers assume that people will work only as hard as they are made to work. In life, of course, most managers fall somewhere between these extremes. People entering one culture type from another quickly learn that the behaviors and actions managers rewarded and respected in their former organization may not be respected or rewarded by managers in the new one. Part of the employee hiring process should include an introduction to the new culture to help new hires learn the cultural norms, values, and beliefs.

Teaching the New Values

Since everyone brings to a new job the cultural assumptions of past experiences, managers of excellent hospitality organizations know they must start teaching new cultural values to employees from day one. Orientation is considered essential in hospitality organizations, and companies known for their strong cultures—like Disney, The Ritz-Carlton, Gaylord, and Four Seasons—earned that reputation by spending considerable time and money on teaching their cultures to new employees. Gaylord Hotels is a good example. Management believes that it is important to socialize its new employees to the Gaylord culture as soon as they join the organization. Its orientation begins with two days of training that everybody attends, with 60 percent of the time dedicated to teaching culture. Gaylord believes that this cultural training is critical to defining what the company is and what its values are to all who join it. Everyone learns the cultural value of Gaylord's STARS First commitment through the employee guarantee and the many avenues available for employee communications. Orientation is followed by one to four weeks in the individual departments, where new employees get training in both job skills and further training in the Gaylord culture and its values. STARS learn that there is not supposed to be any difference between serving a guest and serving each other. This initial orientation is followed ninety days later by an "orientation class reunion" to ensure the STARS know their benefits, are comfortable in their job roles, and can see how to apply the flawless service philosophy in their specific departments or areas.

Culture Fills the Gaps

The cultural teachings become employee beliefs about how things should be, values of what has worth, and norms of behavior. They provide guidance to the culture's members as they interact with each other and their customers. In Schein's terms, they guide the members in how they should perceive the world around them, feel about the events they face, and think about what they do and don't do within their jobs. Many bureaucratic organizations believe that the best way to make sure employees do the right thing in their jobs is to establish extensive rules and regulations to cover every possible contingency. Ideally, in that view, there would be a rule for every possibility. Excellent hospitality organizations, knowing that rules and procedures cannot cover everything, spend their time defining and teaching the culture so that their employees will know how they should act in treating their guests and one another. These organizations teach their employees as much as they can, and then rely on culture to fill in the inevitable gaps between what can be predicted and what actually happens when guests enter the service setting.

BELIEFS, VALUES, AND NORMS

Culture-driven organizations seek to define the beliefs, values, and norms of the organization through what their managers do, say, and write as well as by who they reward, recognize, and promote. Let's take a closer look at what we mean by beliefs, values, and norms.[8]

Beliefs

Beliefs form the ideological core of the culture. Beliefs define the relationships between causes and effects for the organizational members. A belief is how people in organizations make sense of their relationships with the external world and its influence on the internal organization. If culture is a set of assumptions about how things operate, beliefs are formed to help the people inside the organization make sense of how those assumptions influence what they do inside the organization.

Let's consider a simple illustration. If the people in an organization assume that the marketplace rewards those organizations that provide good service and punishes those that don't, the importance of providing good customer service becomes a cultural belief. It's something that everyone believes in. Obviously, most beliefs are more complex than this; a multitude of assumptions about how the environment operates may translate into a whole system of sense-making beliefs. The point here is that every organization's members make a number of assumptions about the world and develop beliefs that reflect how they will respond as part of an organization to those assumptions. The management of an organization that understands the importance of these beliefs will take an active role in defining both the assumptions and the beliefs that those assumptions create.

Values

Values are preferences for certain behaviors or certain outcomes over others. Values define for the members what is right and wrong, preferred and not preferred, desirable behavior and undesirable behavior. Obviously, values can be a strong influence on employee behavior within an organizational culture. If management sends a clear signal to all employees that providing good customer service is an important value to the organization, then the employees know they should adopt this value. Consequently, they are more likely to behave in ways that ensure that the customer has a good service experience.

Norms

Norms are standards of behavior that define how people are expected to act while part of the organization. The typical organization has an intricate set of norms. Some are immediately obvious, and some require the advice and counsel of veteran employees who have learned the norms over time by watching what works and what doesn't work, what gets rewarded, and what gets punished.

Most outstanding hospitality organizations have norms of greeting a guest warmly, smiling, and making eye contact to show interest in the guest. Some use the ten/five foot rule. Once guests are within ten feet of employees—window washers, engineers, and ground crews, as well as guest-contact persons—they are within the "hospitality zone" and the behavior norm is for employees to make eye contact and smile. Once guests are within five feet of employees, the behavior norm is to briefly speak to or engage the guest. Some organizations print the service norms on cards (like the Gaylord Palms does with their "Service Basics" on their employee card as shown on page 121), supplied to every employee to serve as the guidelines for service.

Cultural norms are defined and shaped for the hospitality employee not only by fellow employees and supervisors but also by guests who make their expectations plain. Such guests are an advantage that hospitality organizations have over manufacturing organizations because these guests become potent assistants to the managers in monitoring, reinforcing, and shaping employee behavior. At Disney, the guest service guidelines are so well established that even the guests often know them. If a ride operator in the Magic Kingdom fails to make eye contact or doesn't smile, a park patron may comment about the deviation from the service norm ("What's the matter? Did Goofy step on your toe?") or offer a reminder. Ride operators learn quickly what is expected of them by the constant hints, looks, glares, and comments guests make. Guest expectations of normal behavior help shape employee behavior. As with many organizations that make sure their guests know their commitment to service excellence, Disney's guests help reinforce the norms of behavior; they demand that Disney cast members live up to their reputation for providing a high-quality Disney experience.

Norms in Advertising

Many hospitality organizations use advertising as a means to sell their services, to show the guest visually what the guest experience should look like. Since the employees see the same ads, they also learn the norms of behavior that guests will expect, and this advertising serves to train them just as it informs prospective guests. The guest arrives with predefined expectations, and the hospitality employees know what they are and also know that they had better meet or exceed those expectations or the guest will be unhappy and dissatisfied.

Norms of Appearance

In addition to the norms of behavior, most hospitality organizations have norms of appearance and standards of personal grooming. For example, employees may not be allowed to have hair that extends below a certain length; only women may have pierced ears and earrings must be smaller than a certain size; fingernails may not be excessively long or colored in unusual ways; and necklaces, bracelets, beards, moustaches, visible tattoos are not allowed, and so forth. Although such norms can lead to criticism about restrictions on personal freedom of expression regarding appearance, hospitality organizations must meet guest expectations in this regard, as in all areas of service. If Ritz-Carlton guests expect to see clean-cut employees greeting them upon check-in, then the Ritz-Carlton had better hire clean-cut employees. Disney wants its employees to have a conventional appearance; anything other than the "*Disney Look*" would detract from the guest's experience of the Disney show. On the other hand, the Disney's norms would not be consistent with the culture at a Hard Rock Cafe, Harley Davidson Cafe, or Jekyll and Hyde Club. While organizations where employees do not have direct contact with external customers can ignore such personal-appearance concerns, most hospitality organizations cannot. The latter must carefully define and enforce their norms of appearance to ensure that employees have the look guests expect.

We have seen that advertising can help predefine guest expectations. Here is an example of how an appearance norm at a southern resort hotel affected the appearance and expectations of the hotel's convention clientele. Traditionally, this hotel had required that the men on its management team dress in blazers and ties, and the women in blazers and skirts. Whenever meeting planners visited the hotel to discuss potential convention business, they could see by the outfits of the hotel managers that the culture was clearly somewhat formal. When these meeting planners went back to their organizations, they reported to their members that the attire for the convention, even though it was to be held in the sunny south, would be jackets and ties, and jackets/skirts or dresses. Now that the hotel's management has stopped requiring its team to wear jackets and instead requires short-sleeve shirts with collars, or skirts and blouses, the entire atmosphere of the meetings held in the hotel has changed. Meeting planners, adopting the new appearance norm, now report to their convention attendees that the meeting attire will be informal and relaxed.

Folkways and Mores

Folkways are the customary, habitual ways in which organizational members act or think, without reflecting upon them. Shaking hands (or not shaking hands), addressing everyone by first or last name, and wearing or not wearing a tie would all be examples of folkways. In a restaurant, a folkway might be to roll silverware when there is nothing else to do in the quiet times between crowds. An organization's mores are folkways that go beyond being polite. These are customary behaviors that must be followed to preserve the organization's efficient operation and survival. Mores require certain acts and forbid others. By indicating what is right and wrong, they form the basis of the organization's code of ethics and accepted behaviors.

CULTURE AND THE ENVIRONMENT

The organization's culture, then, represents a shared learning process that continues over time as the people inside the organization change, grow, and develop while responding to a world that does the same. The world external to the organization (consisting of the physical, technological, and cultural environment) defines the activities and patterns of interactions for the organization's members who have to deal with that external world. Ed Schein says,

One must never forget that the environment initially determines the possibilities, options, and constraints for a group, and thus forces the group to specify its primary task or function if it is to survive at all. The environment thus initially influences the formation of a culture, but once the culture is present in the form of shared assumptions, those assumptions, in turn, influence what will be perceived and defined as the environment.[9]

Learning the Culture, Learning from the Culture

As new people join the organization, they learn the culture from both formal company practices such as training and reward systems and informal social interaction with fellow employees, supervisors, and subordinates. They learn the right way and the wrong way to do things in that particular culture. The point is that culture is an important influence on how people inside organizations behave while performing their jobs, how they make decisions, how they relate to others, and how they handle new situations.

The guidance that culture can give in handling unusual situations becomes especially meaningful in hospitality organizations. Unlike manufacturing organizations, where the jobs in the production process can be clearly defined in advance through engineering methods and bureaucratic control mechanisms, the hospitality industry is full of unusual events. People ask unbelievably odd questions, make the most outrageous requests, and behave in unpredictable ways. Without a cultural value system to guide them, employees in hospitality organizations would frequently fail the guest because they would not know how their organization wants them to respond to these unusual events. While most product manufacturers need to focus on teaching employees only the hows of producing the product, the hospitality organization must also teach its employees the whys. Developing, reinforcing, and communicating clear cultural norms about what is and is not the right way to deal with customers is a very effective way to teach those whys. A sign frequently seen in customer-focused organizations says:

Rule 1: The customer is always right.
Rule 2: If you think the customer is wrong, re-read Rule 1.

While no organization believes that all customers are always right in all situations, the two principles are a good guide to behavior in those organizations that want to remind their employees of the organization's fundamental value structure. This sign is a strong symbolic reminder of this important cultural value.

Like everybody else, employees need to make sense out of their environment and how to behave within it. Culture helps them do so. When people collectively make assumptions about how the world operates, they form beliefs that help them make sense of those assumptions, collectively decide upon what is valued, and then define norms that enforce and carry forward those values in the day-to-day behavior of the members.

It sounds more complicated than it is. Essentially, managers who recognize these concepts and their worth to the organization spend considerable time and effort clarifying and articulating the assumptions, shaping the belief system, and making clear the organizational values to all the members. Members of every culture want to make sense of what they are supposed to do when dealing with those inside and outside the organization and will find a way to do so with or without management help. Hospitality managers wanting to ensure that their primary cultural value is service excellence will continually and consistently emphasize and define that critical value for the entire organization through everything they say, do, and write.

Subcultures

Cultures can often split into subcultures. Usually, the more people involved in the culture and the harder it is for them to stay in communication with one another, the more likely it is that the organization will see some subcultures form. Subcultures can be good or bad, supportive or destructive, and consistent with or contrary to the larger corporate culture. Since culture relies on interactions to sustain itself, people who work together may well create a subculture of their own, especially if they don't interact much with other organizational units. Organizations that depend greatly on part-time employees are especially susceptible to subculture formation; the part-timers may not spend enough hours in the greater organization to absorb its culture or care enough about the organization and its members to substitute its values for their own. The organization will want to do what it can to ensure that the subcultures are consistent with the core cultural values even if some specific behaviors, beliefs, and norms do vary somewhat from the desired culture. Communication is the key to sustaining the overall culture.

The authors of *Inside the Mouse* show how the large size of the entire Walt Disney World Resort operation has led to the development of subcultures.[10] The categorizing and subdividing of employees by place (Tomorrowland versus Frontierland), type (food and beverage versus attractions operator), shift (weekend versus weekday), and amount of work (full-time versus part-time) have the effect of forming many and clearly distinguishable subcultures. Cast members tend to associate with others like themselves, who are doing things like what they do in areas where they are likely to meet one another frequently. After all, a culture is a shared experience, and the more it is shared, the more definable it becomes for those sharing it. Pirates of the Caribbean people tend to hang out with other Pirates of the Caribbean people, Haunted Mansion people hang out with other Haunted Mansion people, and so forth.

The subcultures forming within the overall culture can be a managerial challenge if they operate in ways that do not support the overall corporate culture. The Jungle Cruise operators have a tendency to see themselves as excellent stand-up comedians and compete against one another for the best comedy routine during a Jungle Cruise ride. Although some humor can enhance the show for guests, this subcultural competition promotes values that, if carried to an extreme, could directly conflict with the overall Disney culture. Deviations from the accepted scripts might become so outlandish as to violate the overall cultural value of providing a wholesome and non-offensive family entertainment experience. Although the worst violators eventually get caught, the damage to the overall Disney experience for some guests may by then be irreparable. The overall culture must be strong enough to override the subcultures on issues important to the organization's survival. While some cultural variation may be tolerated, the overall culture has to be defined and reinforced by management in ways sufficiently strong that the central values of the organization come through in the customer experience.

Subcultures of Nations

Just like subcultures in organizations, organizations themselves can be thought of as subcultures of ethnic populations, nations, or even entire geographic regions. When an organization seeks to open a branch or start a business in a cultural setting it is not accustomed to, it can often have unexpected challenges. Disney was unprepared for the challenges that opening EuroDisney (now Disneyland Paris) would have. The French saw this as an attempt to teach American values as superior to French and resisted it. Four Seasons Hotels learned from this and decided to take a very different approach when it opened its Four Seasons Hotel King George V Paris. After doing a service quality audit to identify some of the differences between French and North American business culture, David Richey, the auditor, stated, "There were three things we talked to Four Seasons' executives about, mostly related to employee attitude. First the staff had an inability to apologize or empathize. ... Second, the team had a very tough time doing anything that could be described as selling. This is also typically European. For example, say your glass is empty at the bar. In Paris they may not ask you if you want another drink. Third, the staff were rules and policy oriented. If something went wrong they would refer to the manual instead of focusing on satisfying the guest."[11]

The point is simple. Just as hospitality managers must pay attention to and manage how they relate to the subcultures that may form in their organizations, they must recognize that they must also pay attention to and manage how they relate to the larger culture in which their organization is embedded. People will bring to work their cultural values, and if there is conflict between those cultural values and those of the organization, the managers will need to find ways to bring them together. The Paris Four Seasons, for example, recognized that its employee of the month and year recognition programs might be seen as controversial unless presented as congruent with the French, Anglo-Saxon culture and not as an American scheme.

COMMUNICATING THE CULTURE

While the substance of culture is a set of assumptions that lead to beliefs, values, and norms, culture is communicated to those inside and outside the organization in a variety of ways, including laws, language, stories, legends, heroes, symbols, and rituals. In these ways, people can express, affirm, and communicate their shared beliefs, values, and norms to each other and to those outside the organization. Each way is important in helping the members learn, implement, teach, and reinforce the shared culture. They should be used together and become part of an overall message to members of what the culture stands for. The more these communications support each other in sending a single clear message to the organizational membership, the stronger the impact of that message will be.

The Gaylord Palms' opening manager knew that communicating culture was critical. Much of the effort to communicate the culture took place in the hiring process, so that new entrants immediately learned the emphasis placed on being customer centered. The process started with hiring people who fit with the Palms' culture. But management knew that this culture had to be reinforced on an ongoing basis. As described earlier in this chapter, this included emphasizing the culture in employee orientation, follow-up training, and through the wallet cards that detail the Gaylord values for easy reference.

Leading hospitality organizations know the importance of these elements in defining the organizational culture. They manage their cultural mechanisms in a holistic way to reinforce, clearly and consistently, those organizational values that they expect all employees to have in mind when they meet, greet, and serve customers. Learning the culture becomes part of the training for all new employees. Managers and other experienced employees, internal communications media, and organizational reward structures all continue to teach, reinforce, and celebrate the corporate culture thereafter.

Laws

The laws of an organization are its rules, policies, and regulations—the norms that are so important that they need to be written down so everyone knows exactly what they are. They tell the members what behaviors are expected within that culture and also detail the consequences of violating the norm.

Two norms are so important to Disney that they are corporate policies—in effect, laws. First, a cast member in costume must not walk in an area where the costume is inappropriate. An employee in the futuristic Tomorrowland cannot go to Frontierland. Nor may an Epcot World Showcase member of the China Pavilion be found in costume in the Moroccan Pavilion. Second, cast members portraying Disney characters must stay completely in character; they must maintain and fulfill the character expectations of Disney guests. They cannot speak, be seen out of costume, take off any part of the costume in public, or do anything else that might destroy the sense of fantasy for the children (of all ages). Indeed, a policy forbids transporting any character costume in a public area unless it is in a black bag that completely covers all its parts so no child (of any age) will see a favorite fantasy character "in pieces." A cast member violating either norm can be fired.

Language

In addition to the common language of the larger social culture, each organization develops a language of its own, which is frequently incomprehensible to outsiders. The special language is an important vehicle both for communicating the common cultural elements to which the language refers and in reaffirming the identity with the culture that those who speak this language share. Terms an insider uses to talk with another insider communicate an important concept quickly and also distinguish that person from an outsider.

For example, everyone at Disney uses certain important terms that carry strong cultural messages. All employees recruited by Casting are called *cast members*. This term sends two important messages. First, everyone is equally part of the overall cast of the organization, a concept reinforced by the use of first names alone on all name tags. Second, the term reminds cast members that they are playing "roles" that help make up the Disney show. This show concept is reinforced by the use of other terms such as *on stage*, to define all situations and areas where cast members are in front of their customers, and *back stage*, to define areas the customers cannot see. Law enforcement staff are called *security hosts*, and everyone's uniforms are costumes that are checked out daily from wardrobe. In other words, the language of the culture is carefully constructed to ensure that cast members constantly think of themselves as participants in an ongoing stage production designed to create a magical fantasy experience. So effective is this training in language that Smith and Eisenberg report that no Disneyland Park employee they talked to during their thirty-five half-hour interviews used any of the traditional terms for *uniforms*, *customers*, or *amusement park*, instead using only *costumes*, *guests*, and *property*.[12]

Stories, Legends, and Heroes

Stories, legends, and heroes are another way of transmitting cultural beliefs, values, and norms. They communicate proper behaviors and the right and wrong way to do things. The best at building culture use stories extensively. Disney, Four Seasons, Gaylord, and the Ritz-Carlton all have their collection of stories that are used by managers to teach the culture. The Ritz-Carlton is especially noted for using teaching stories and its managers tell many. For example, to teach going the extra mile to serve a customer, the *New Gold Standard* reports how managers use the following letter from a guest as a story to teach its values:

"My wife [accidentally] broke a bottle of makeup that she had brought along and left it in pieces on the counter in the bathroom because she wanted to use as much of it as possible. We came back to the room one day to find a note sitting beside the broken makeup bottle from housekeeping offering to replace the broken bottle they didn't even break."[13]

The best service-oriented companies want to obtain only top scores in customer evaluations, and stories provide a means to define and teach employees what customer-guests will find inspiring enough to give such high evaluations. Some companies, like Disney, have a rich history of stories to draw on. Disney managers have used examples from the *Lion King* to teach the value and importance of the guest service commitment, or used the song "Be Our Guest" from *Beauty and the Beast* to build similarly inspirational stories about providing excellent guest service. New companies, like the Gaylord Palms, don't have this past to draw upon but can invent them. To take advantage of the power of stories as a training tool, the Palms' management created a letter from a fictitious customer when it opened to illustrate what the intangible mission of flawless service meant through the customer's eyes until it could collect real customers' letters. In short, the best service-oriented companies collect and use stories to teach employees about what the service they want to provide looks like. To accomplish this, they use real examples with real employees whom everyone knows; those that don't have real examples create heroes with stories to teach the culture.

American Express calls those employees who have provided exceptional service to customers "Great Performers." To help illustrate this point to new employees, American Express tells them stories about their Great Performers. New employees hear, for example, about two customer service people in Florida who got money to a woman in a foreign war zone and helped her get passage on a ship out of the country; travel agents in Columbus, Georgia, who paid a French tourist's bail so he could get out of jail after being arrested for speeding; an employee who drove through a blizzard to take food and blankets to stranded travelers at Kennedy Airport; and an employee who got up in the middle of the night to take an Amex card to a customer stranded at Boston's Logan Airport. Any hospitality organization has its heroes—employees who have gone above and beyond the call of duty—and their stories should be preserved and shared. American Express distributes its Great Performers booklets to all employees worldwide.

Four Seasons also has a rich reservoir of stories to draw upon. Stories about the Power of Personal Service are used to illustrate what this term means in real examples that anyone in their organization can understand and use. One story, for example, tells of an employee who accidentally overheard a guest telling his wife how embarrassed he felt as he was the only one without a black tie at a black tie function. The employee pulled him aside and said he thought he might have a solution. After asking the man to take a seat in his office, he went into a back room, took off his own tuxedo, put on his civilian clothes, rushed to the laundry to clean his tuxedo, and then called in the seamstress to fit the cleaned tux to the guest. What makes this story so rich is that it teaches the values management wants shared by all Four Seasons all of Four Seasons' employees. It also shows clearly the connection between customer service and two important business outcomes. First, the guest turned out to be the chairman and CEO of a leading consulting organization, who after this experience directed all his company's business, worth millions in food and lodging, to Four Seasons. Second, the man took every opportunity to tell people in his speeches and conversations what Four Seasons did for him. These testimonials from a leading businessman proved to be priceless word of mouth advertising. Teaching the culture through stories can leave a lasting impression on employees as they come to see how the abstract idea of customer service translates into specific employee actions that lead to outcomes that benefit both their company and them.

All organizations can and should use stories, heroes, myths, and legends to help teach their culture, to communicate the values and behaviors that the organization seeks from its employees while performing their jobs and to serve as role models for new situations. Most people love stories. It's so much easier to emotionally connect to a story of what a hero did than to listen to someone lecturing about customer responsiveness in a formal training class. Not only are stories more memorable because of this emotional connection than a few arbitrary points listed on a classroom PowerPoint, but the tales can be embellished in the retelling and the culture thereby made more inspiring. Tales of "old Joe" and what wondrous things he did while serving customers teach employees the desired responses to customer concerns and reaffirm the organization's cultural values. When Gaylord Palms opened, it had no stories to tell, so its opening general manager invented some to show the kind of service he wanted his STARS to deliver and asked his managers to ask employees at weekly meetings for examples that would replace the fictitious ones with real ones as time went on. Stories are felt to be so powerful in teaching culture at the Gaylord Palms that they are collected in a database so managers needing a particular type of story to tell can find one even if their own employees have had no examples to share.

Every hospitality organization should capture and preserve the stories and tales of its people, who do amazing things, create magical moments, to wow guests. The effort will yield a wonderful array of inspiring stories for all employees and send a strong message about what the organization values and desires in its employees.

Symbols

A **symbol** is a physical object that has significance beyond itself, a sign that communicates an unspoken message. Cultural symbols are everywhere in organizations. A window office, an office on the top floor, or a desk and office in a particular location communicate information about the status and organizational power of the person within that transcends the mere physical objects involved. At Walt Disney World Resort, Mickey's famous mouse ears are everywhere. The plants are grown in mouse-ear shapes, the anniversary service pins are mouse ears, awards are mouse ears, the souvenir balloons are ear shaped, the entrance to Team Disney is framed by ears, and Disney's Hollywood Studios landmark water tower (The Earful Tower) has mouse ears on it. Mouse ears are subtly hidden everywhere around the property and serve as a constant symbolic reminder of where Disney began. Not even the employees know where all the mouse ears are. There is even a Web site devoted to Hidden Mickeys. While this may seem overdone, it ties into the cultural values as they serve as a constant reminder of the reason behind why everyone is there—it all started with a mouse.

Rituals

Rituals are symbolic acts that people perform to gain and maintain membership or identity within an organization. At most hospitality organizations, all employees go through a similar training program. Rituals are mainly informational; new employees learn the organizational basics and cultural heritage. But, like military boot camp or initiation into a sorority, it also has ritualistic significance because everyone goes through the experience upon entry into the company to learn and share the common culture. Most hospitality organizations develop elaborate ritual celebrations of service excellence. These can range from a simple event like a departmental pizza party to honor those receiving positive comments on customer comment cards to elaborate employee of the year award ceremonies that resemble a major gala. The point is that what the organization celebrates ritualistically

The Team Disney Administration Building uses its architecture as a symbolic reminder of Disney's culture.

and how much effort it makes to celebrate tells the members a lot about what the culture believes in and holds valuable.

Gaylord Palms' management gave extra effort to the development of rituals and celebrations that would reinforce its culture and affirm its commitment to its employees.[14] They created rituals and celebrations specifically designed to reinforce the organization's vision and values. One ritual was designed for celebrating promotions. When a STAR got promoted, the person was put on a three-wheeled bicycle and pedaled around the hotel by his or her new supervisor. The bike would be followed by a camera-toting paparazzo waving a sign and making noise. If the idea was to make the newly promoted person feel special and recognized, this simple celebration certainly did that. As the person was peddled around the hotel's ten acres both front of the house and back, everyone could see, hear, and celebrate the event. Indeed, even guests would sometimes join in the parade.

A second celebration that was specifically designed to reinforce the culture and its values is the All STARS rally that is held quarterly. These rallies provide a mechanism to publicly celebrate management's commitment to open communications, to reinforce the importance of the company's values, and to highlight the fun STARS have doing their jobs. They celebrate successes of individual contributors, by selecting STARS in the hotel that best represent each of the six values seen on the pocket card shown earlier. The STARS are selected by a committee comprised of former winners. A three-minute video is prepared on each person and shown at the rally along with the awarding of a plaque. These are emotionally charged entertaining events that make the STARS feel valued, recognized, and appreciated while teaching all in attendance what the company values, recognizes, and appreciates. Value award winners are honored by being included in the Value Wall of Fame, which details the history of value award recipients over the years.

At the end of the year, a corporate-wide process selects the best representative of each value, who is flown to Gaylord Entertainment's headquarters at Nashville with his or her family for a corporate-level celebration. The winners have dinner on the stage of Gaylord's famous Grand Ole Opry and get $1500 to give to a charity of their choice. It is seen by the employees as an important event in their lives and seen by management as an important tool for teaching the organization's culture and values.

Leaders Teach the Culture

Managers of effective hospitality organizations constantly teach the culture to their employees, reinforcing the values, mores, and laws. Strong cultures are reinforced by a strong commitment by top management to the cultural values. Ed Schein suggests that the *only thing* of real importance that leaders do is to create and maintain the organization's culture.[15] Effective leaders don't just talk about the culture; they act on it every day. They personally model their commitment to the service mission, and they do it visibly. They back up slogans with dramatic, sometimes costly, actions. To instill values, they stress two-way communications, opening their doors to all employees and using weekly work-group meetings to not only inform and inspire but also to discuss and solve service problems. They put values into action by treating employees exactly as they want employees to treat their customers.[16] They use rituals to recognize and reward the behaviors that the culture values, and they praise the heroes whose actions have reflected worthy cultural values in the stories they tell. Other employees can use these hero stories as models for their own actions.

Ed Schein offers further insights about how leaders can embed the culture, especially at the time the organization is being formed.[17] Initially, the leader defines and articulates a set of beliefs and assumptions about how the organization will operate. According to Schein, "At this stage the leader needs both vision and the ability to articulate it and enforce it."[18] Since new members join the organization with mixed assumptions and beliefs, the leader must carefully and comprehensively define the organization's culture. Schein says, "It is intrinsic to the leadership role to create order out of chaos, and leaders are expected to provide their own assumptions as an initial road map into an uncertain future."[19] This process creates the definition of the corporate culture, embeds it in the organization's consciousness, and shows what behaviors are reinforced. Whatever the leader responds to emotionally or with great passion becomes a powerful signal to which subordinates also respond. Thus, during the period of an organization's creation, the leader must spend some thoughtful time defining what is important, how the organization's members should interpret the world they face, and what principles should guide their actions. Once the organization's culture is in place, the leader constantly adjusts and fine-tunes it as markets, operating environments, and personnel change.

Schein suggests that leaders can use five primary mechanisms to define and strengthen the organization's culture: "(1) what leaders pay attention to, measure, and control; (2) leader reactions to critical incidents and organizational crises; (3) deliberate role modeling, teaching, and coaching by leaders; (4) criteria for allocation of rewards and status; (5) criteria for recruitment, selection, promotion, retirement, and excommunication."[20]

Setting the Example

Bill Marriott Jr. provides a good example of how a leader can help to sustain the culture. He is famous for dropping in at a hotel and chatting with everyone he sees. He has been known to get up early in the morning and wander into the Marriott kitchens to make sure the pancakes are being cooked properly. This intense commitment to personal contact with each and every Marriott employee and visible interest in the details of his operations have become so well known among the Marriott organization that his mere presence on any Marriott property serves as a reminder of the Marriott commitment to service quality.[21]

Kimpton Hotels & Restaurants maintains a culture based on Bill Kimpton's vision. Although Bill Kimpton died in 2001, the culture he created lives on through the organization's new leadership. According to Niki Leondakis, chief operating officer, "one of the things we do at employee orientation is talk to every one of our employees. Once a year, I and one of our senior executives travel around the country on the Kimpton National Tour and bring together all the employees at each hotel. We talk about the culture of care. It means caring for your co-workers, caring for our guests, caring for the environment, our community, our investors."[22]

The clear commitment to the customer-service culture, demonstrated through the actions of those on the top of the organizational chart, sends a strong message to all employees that everyone is responsible for maintaining a high-quality customer experience. This same modeling behavior can be seen in the many hotel managers who visibly and consistently stop to pick up small scraps of paper and debris on the floors as they walk through their properties. Employees see and emulate this care and attention to detail.

A leading hotelier in Orlando has earned a reputation among his employees and fellow hoteliers alike as a can-do manager. A story is told about how he took a chance and bought a bankrupt hotel with very little money and a whole lot of courage. When he was seen mowing his own property's lawn, a legend was born that here was a guy who would do what it took to get the work accomplished. He reinforced the message by his attire. His typical working outfit was blue jeans and a polo shirt. He intentionally wore shoes with soles that he could use to rub out black marks on his tiled floors and was frequently seen doing exactly that. His employees learned, by reputation and by deed, that this owner was ready to work at any job that needed doing. Since he also had a big sign on the interstate that advertised different room rates for each night, he earned a reputation as a relentless competitor. His strategy was to fill his rooms at rates that would allow him to capture his variable costs plus whatever else the market could bear. His flexibility in room rates and his nightly phone calls to his front desk manager, asking about the percentage of rooms sold rather than revenues, sent a powerful message to his organization that its goal was to fill the rooms every night. By his own actions, dress, and style, he has been extraordinarily effective in teaching his employees at all organizational levels the cultural values and norms that he wants for his organization.

Hospitality managers must stay close to both their employees and their guests. Only by walking around can they see for themselves that the quality of guest experiences is high, that concerns of guests and employees are being met, and that everyone remains focused on the guest. Unlike the manufacturing industry, which can rely on statistical reports to tell managers how things are going on the production line, hospitality managers inform themselves about how things are going by staying as close as possible to the point where the service experience is produced. They must use the classic managerial technique of "management by walking around." As Norman Brinker put it, "There's no substitute for spending time with people in their own environment. You not only meet everybody personally, you are able to see and hear for yourself what's going on."[23] Many restaurant managers are told to meet every guest and to make at least one table visit to talk to them; hotel managers spend time in their lobbies to observe the reactions of guests; and bed and breakfast operators monitor the looks on guests' faces to make sure the experience

Being out among employees and guests, and ensuring service standards are met are effective ways to reinforce a company's culture, as exhibited here by an award-winning supervisor at Marriott hotels.

Photo courtesy Marriott International

is going well. All these guestology techniques are based on the simple idea that the reason for the organization's existence and basis for its success is the customer. For successful organizations, being out with the customer is an important organizational value and not just a company slogan, and managers from the top down must set the example. As most of them know, the pressures of day-to-day administrative responsibilities can easily push aside this fundamental ingredient in service success, so they build customer-contact time into their schedules. Orlando's Grand Cypress Hyatt has each manager assigned to a door-duty time, to send the message to customers and employees alike that it is important to Hyatt that everyone be aware of the guest experience: Even managers must spend some time at the door talking to guests and watching their body language as they enter and leave.

Guests Teach the Culture

Hospitality organizations often have the help of guests in teaching and reinforcing the values, beliefs, and norms expected of the employees. As management scholar Van Maanen reports from his observations of Disneyland Park,

> *Ride operators learn how different categories of customers respond to them and the parts they are playing on stage. For example, infants and small children are generally timid, if not frightened, in their presence. School age children are somewhat curious, aware that the operator is at work playing a role but sometimes in awe of the role itself. Nonetheless, the children can be quite critical of any flaw in the operator's performance. Teenagers, especially males in groups, present problems because they sometimes go to great lengths to embarrass, challenge, ridicule, or outwit an operator.... The point here is that ride operators learn what the public (or at least their idealized version of the public) expects of their role and find it easier to conform to such expectations than not. Moreover, they discover that when they are bright and lively, others respond to them in like ways.*[24]

Culture and the Organization Chart

Schein suggests that a leader can use other, secondary mechanisms to reinforce or define the organization's culture.[25] A leader can define the value of a functional area by placing that area at the bottom or near the top of the organizational chart. For example, placing the quality assurance function near the top of the chart and requiring its manager to report to a high-level executive tells the organization's employees that the leader values quality. The way in which the leader designs the organizational systems and procedures will also tell everyone in the organization a great deal about what is valued. McDonald's

The use of physical space can also communicate aspects of culture, such as how much employees are really valued. Contrast these two physical spaces for employees.

Image copyright Matt Niebuhr, 2010. Used under license from Shutterstock.com

Image copyright Pell Studio, 2010. Used under license from Shutterstock.com

sends a strong value message through its quality checklist and by the procedures it uses to maintain its standards of cleanliness to guarantee its customers the freshness of each hamburger it sells. McDonald's spends a great deal of money sending quality control people out to individual restaurants to check on these key items, to let restaurant managers know what is important, and to make sure that customers get what they expect. All McDonald's employees know what's on the quality checklist and how seriously the organization takes these inspections, so the checklist helps to define the cultural values of cleanliness and quality. Employees know that what is expected is inspected.

Culture and Physical Space

The layout of physical space is another secondary mechanism that can send a cultural message. For example, office size and location are traditional symbols of status and prestige. By putting the executive chef in the big office out front, the leader tells the rest of the organization that the chef plays an important role in the organizational culture and that producing food of high quality is an important organizational function. If the employee break room is put in leftover space, not very nice, and generally non-hospitable, this sends a very different message of the value of employees than a well-lit, well-furnished, and appealing employee cafeteria. Finally, the formal, published statements of the company's mission and vision hanging on the walls not only teach employees the philosophy, creeds, and beliefs by which the organization lives but show them that the organization believes in them enough to display them where all employees can be reminded of them. Although some organizations may not say what they really mean in these public statements, the excellent hospitality organization will do so clearly, concisely, consistently, and publicly.

Culture and Leadership Skills

The success with which leaders use the mechanisms discussed above to convey cultural values is a good measure of their leadership skills. When they concentrate on using them together in a holistic way, they can ensure that all mechanisms convey to employees a consistent set of cultural beliefs, values, and norms. Consistency is important as a powerful reinforcer of the culture. The more consistently these mechanisms are used, the more powerfully reinforced the culture will be. Leaders must take care about what they do, say, and write to ensure that the messages they send are what is intended and explicit. What the leader gets angry or excited about tells everyone what is important. A leader who expresses outrage over a service failure caused by a careless employee sends a strong message to all the employees that good service matters. A story is told of how Bill Marriott Sr. fired an employee on the spot for insulting a guest. When this story got around the organization, there was no question in anyone's mind of the guest orientation that Marriott valued.

At Southwest: Maintaining a Strong Culture

Truly outstanding hospitality organizations engage all their members in teaching each other the organization's culture. Good managers create the opportunities for this teaching and learning to happen. For example, Southwest Airlines created a Culture Committee, whose responsibility was perpetuating the Southwest Spirit.

The Culture Committee was created in 1990 "to take the lead in preserving the airline's unique culture."

The Culture Committee was created to pull together people who exemplify Southwest's culture. Most of the original committee had ten or so years at Southwest and embraced Southwest's maverick, caring, irreverent way of doing things. They were all great in their individual jobs and were hand-picked for their creativity, expertise, energy, enthusiasm, and most importantly, Southwest Spirit. For the two years they serve on the committee, they engage in leadership activities that protect the company's unique and highly valued culture. Committee members have been known to visit stations with equipment and paint in hand to remodel a break room. Others have gone to one of Southwest's maintenance facilities to serve pizza and ice cream to maintenance employees. Still others simply show up periodically at various field locations to lend a helping hand.

Their labor is really a labor of love; their payoffs are the relationships they build with other workers, the knowledge that they have sparked worthwhile and fun endeavors, and most importantly, the satisfaction of having been a vital part of keeping the Southwest Spirit alive.[26]

Originally, the committee was made up of 38 people. It has since expanded to well over 100 individuals, with representatives from each station and part of the airline.[27] Even after members end their terms on the committee, these alumni members tend to stay active in support of Culture Committee initiatives.

The Culture Committee has helped maintain Southwest's culture throughout its growth. Because of its culture, Southwest's employees maintain a strong customer-service-oriented company, repeatedly making the company one of the highest-rated airlines in terms of customer satisfaction and one that is currently recognized by the Great Place to Work Institute list as one of the top five best companies to work for in America.

CHANGING THE CULTURE

The world changes and the people inside the organization change. The culture must also evolve to help members cope with the new realities that the organization faces. Even a culture that starts out with a strong customer orientation may change over time as the managers, customers, and employees change. No matter how good a job the founder did in defining the culture and getting everyone to buy into it, the next generation of managers must work, perhaps even harder, to sustain those cultural values that should endure while changing those that need changing. They have available, of course, all the tools discussed in this chapter to do this. The communication tools of symbols, legends, language, stories, heroes, and rituals need constant attention to sustain the cultural values in the face of changing circumstances.

Denny's Restaurants

The most difficult task of all is changing an entire culture that is not service oriented. When a negative culture is pervasive throughout an organization, it can be very challenging to make a change to a positive culture, even when the culture is causing major problems.

In 1997, Denny's restaurants operated 1652 restaurants, and was generally seen as a successful company. But over the next few years, repeated claims of racial discrimination were made that seemed to indicate that racism was ingrained in Denny's culture. In one instance, several black teenagers were refused service unless they paid for their meal in advance; in another, six black Secret Service agents were forced to wait an hour for service while their white counterparts were seated and served promptly; multiple cases emerged of other black customers being forced to pay a cover charge and prepay their meals while white customers seated and served at the same time did not have to; and of Denny's thousand-plus restaurants, there was only one black franchisee and none of the suppliers for the company were from companies owned by minorities. Denny's CEO at the time, Jerome Richardson, publicly stated that Denny's did not discriminate and that negative events were isolated incidents. It did not seem that he really thought racism was an issue. Richardson was quoted as saying, "We hire from the population. We get the good with the bad. But yeah, it makes you wonder if this wasn't blown out of proportion" and "If our African-American guests were mistreated, was it because of racism? I can't tell you. It's impossible to know what's in a person's heart."[28] In subsequent lawsuits, it seemed that racism was simply ingrained in Denny's culture. For example, one lawyer said that a former manager talked of training he had received on how to deal with what was considered too many blacks in a restaurant at one time, a policy the manager said the company referred to as "a blackout."[29] Although the company seemed to make some efforts to change, the lawsuits kept coming. While they never admitted guilt, Denny's agreed to settle a class-action lawsuit for $54 million to 295,000 customers, the largest public accommodation settlement ever at that time.[30] Yet, despite the bad publicity and high costs, the culture did not change.

Change did not begin until new leadership came to the company. In 1995, Jim Adamson was brought in as CEO, and the culture began to change from the top down. In his first meeting as CEO, he told employees, "Anyone who doesn't like the direction this train is moving had better jump off now … and I will fire you if you discriminate."[31] Management began to deal with its racial problems instead of trying to explain them away.[32]

Through the change in culture, which began at the top, Denny's radically changed the way it treated minorities. Within a few years, half of Denny's employees were minorities, 32 percent of supervisory positions were held by minorities, there were dozens of black-owned franchises, and millions of dollars of supplies were purchased from minority-owned suppliers. Perhaps even more impressive, *Fortune* magazine later named Denny's parent (Advantica Restaurant Group, Inc.) the number one of "America's 50 Best Corporations for Minorities" for two years in a row.

Changing a company's culture is a difficult task. It often requires new leadership with a true commitment to the new ideas. Simply providing training or mentioning supposed cultural values in orientation will not work if upper management does not truly embrace the behaviors it hopes its line employees will engage in by what it says, does, and writes every day.

WHAT WE KNOW ABOUT CULTURE

Here are some principles about organizational culture that seem to hold generally true.

- Leaders define the culture (or redefine it if necessary), teach it, and sustain it. Doing so may be their biggest responsibility in the organization.
- An organizational culture that emphasizes interpersonal relationships is uniformly more attractive to professionals than a culture that focuses on work tasks.[33]
- Strong cultures are worth building; they can provide employee guidance in uncertain situations, when company policies or procedures are unavailable or unwritten.
- Subcultures will form in larger organizations. A strong culture will increase the likelihood of keeping the subcultures consistent with the overall culture values in important areas.
- Sustaining the culture requires constant attention to the means of communicating culture so that they all consistently reinforce and teach the organization's beliefs, values, and norms of behavior to all employees.
- Excellent hospitality organizations hire and retain employees who fit their culture and get rid of those who do not. The fit between the individual and the culture is strongly related to turnover, commitment, and satisfaction.[34]

LESSONS LEARNED

1. Leaders define and teach organizational culture to everyone by what they say and do every day, and by what they reward.

2. Culture fills in the gaps for employees between what they've been taught and what they must do to satisfy the guest.

3. To create a culture of success, celebrate success—publicly.

4. Leaders think carefully about how everything they say, do, or write ties into supporting the cultural values of guest service.

5. Leaders find heroes, tell stories, and repeat legends to reinforce the important cultural values.

6. Leaders know that one of their most important jobs is to teach culture.

7. Leaders celebrate employee actions that help fulfill the customer service mission.

REVIEW QUESTIONS

1. Recall any organization in which you were heavily involved as an employee or as a student.

   A. How would you describe the culture of that organization?

   B. What did the managers or leaders do or not do to cause the culture to be as you described it?

   C. What ideas in this chapter could the managers or leaders have used to improve the organizational culture?

   D. How does culture relate to managing the guest experience in hospitality organizations?

2. Why is culture such an important concept to guest service organizations? How does culture influence the guest experience?

3. What is the difference between a strong and a weak culture? What can a manager do to create a strong culture?

4. Does a culture exist whether a manager does anything about it or not?

5. How are stories important to building and sustaining a strong culture?

   A. Give examples of stories you have heard that helped teach cultural values.

   B. How does all that relate to managing the guest experience in hospitality organizations?

6. "Walking the walk" is an expression that one hears in hospitality organizations in connection with the leaders. What are some possible meanings of the concept in the hospitality context?

ACTIVITIES

1. Divide into groups. Come up with a list of what factors or aspects make up an organizational culture. Which characteristics are the most important?

2. Find a hospitality organization that has a strong, clearly defined service culture. You may work for one yourself or have friends who do. How does the organization create

and sustain that culture? What training methods, incentives for managers and employees, and communications techniques are used to create and define the culture? If you know of an organization that has a weak, muddled, unfocused culture, talk about that organization, too.

ETHICS IN BUSINESS

In this chapter, we talked about how companies set standards for appearance and personal grooming. This is done to ensure a certain image of the service providers and help reflect the culture of the organization. These standards are also based on customer expectations. That said, when do these standards go too far? Suppose that a hotel wants employees without moustaches or beards. Is this reasonable? What if it violates a potential employee's religious beliefs? How much of a role should the government play in regulating what employers can specify as reasonable? At one extreme, you could argue that employers should be able to do whatever they want (which could therefore include selecting people based on gender, race, etc.). At the other extreme, the government could prohibit any sort of regulation that is not clearly and directly job related (and so, make any sort of appearance policy illegal). What do you think is ethically appropriate?

CASE STUDY

Doug's Fried Chicken

Within four years of assuming the presidency, Judy Hart brought the market share of Doug's Fried Chicken from 2 percent to 20 percent. She was a risk-taking, innovative entrepreneur. She increased the chain from 400 outlets to 1743 and rapidly expanded into 27 countries. "I've got to be involved in a continual go-go growth cycle. Because of my successful track record, the franchisees and the board go along with any programs I propose," Hart believed. Hart was flamboyant and sensational. She shifted the annual franchisee convention from Des Moines, Iowa, to New York. She moved headquarters from a converted post office into a new $5.8 million building.

Then, one Friday afternoon, Doug's board of directors dismissed Hart from the presidency. "Judy," said Chairman Doug Jones, "for a while we liked your 'full-steam-ahead' attitude. But you can't seem to slow down. You're trying to change too many things too fast."

The board elevated John Davis, vice president for finance, to the position of president. Davis was a conservative, accommodating executive who watched budgets closely and believed in rigorously controlled expansion. He emphasized fiscal responsibility. Davis set up a centralized purchasing system (which Judy Hart had always opposed). Board Chairman Doug Jones was pleased; he considered Davis to be "in tune with the mood of the board and the franchisees at this point in time."

Judy Hart was unemployed over the weekend. Then she was enthusiastically hired by Berger's Burgers, a company that had achieved financial stability only in the last couple of years. Now they were in a strong cash position. "Judy," said Horace Berger, chairman of the board, "we think we're ready to take off. We want to triple the number of Berger's Burgers outlets within three years. Can you do it?"

"Can do, Mr. Berger," said Judy happily. "But first we've got to refurbish this tacky headquarters building and change the site of the annual convention. I envision a truly spectacular party for the franchisees in Las Vegas...."

★ ★ ★

1. How do you explain Judy Hart's unceremonious dumping from Doug's and her warm welcome at Berger's?

2. Did Doug's make the right decision? Did Berger?

Ashkanasy, N. M., Wilderom, C. P. M., & Peterson, M. F. (eds.). 2010. *The Handbook of Organizational Culture and Climate,* 2nd edition. Thousand Oaks, CA: Sage.

Bellou, V. 2007. Achieving long-term customer satisfaction through organizational culture: Evidence from the health care sector. *Managing Service Quality,* 17, 510–522.

Collison, J., Cohen, D., Ford, R. C., Newstrom, J., & McLaughlin, F. S. 2002. *SHRM Fun Work Environment Survey.* Alexandria, VA: SHRM Research.

Crotts, J., Dickson, D. D., & Ford, R. C. 2005. Aligning organizational processes with mission: The case of service excellence. *Academy of Management Executive,* 19 (3), 54–68.

Davidson, C. G. M. 2003. Does organizational climate add to service quality in hotels? *International Journal of Contemporary Hospitality Management,* 15 (4), 206–213.

Davidson, M., Manning, M., Timo, N., & Ryder, P. 2001. The dimensions of climate in four- and five-star Australian hotels. *Journal of Hospitality and Tourism Research,* 25, 444–460.

Deal, T. E., & Key, M. K. 1998. *Corporate Celebration.* San Francisco, CA: Berrett-Koehler.

Derry, M. A., & Shaw, R. N. 1999. An investigation of the relationship between employee turnover and organizational culture. *Journal of Hospitality and Tourism Research,* 23 (4), 387–400.

Dwyer, L., Teal, G., & Kemp, S. 1998. Organizational culture & strategic management in a resort hotel. *Asia Pacific Journal of Tourism Research,* 3 (1), 27–36.

Fiol, M. C. 2002. Capitalizing on paradox: The role of language in transforming organizational identities. *Organizational Science,* 13, 653–666.

Ford, R. C., Heisler, W., & McCreary, W. C. 2008. Leading change with the 5P model: A case study of "complexing" the WDW Swan-Dolphin hotels. *Cornell Hotel and Restaurant Quarterly,* 49 (2), 191–205.

Ford, R. C., McLaughlin, F. M., & Newstrom, J. W. 2004. Questions and answers about fun at work. *Human Resource Planning,* 26 (4), 18–33.

Ford, R. C., Wilderom, C. P. M., & Caparella, J. 2008. Strategically crafting a customer-focused culture: An inductive case study. *Journal of Strategy and Management,* 1, 143–167.

Freiberg, K., & Freiberg, J. 1996. *Nuts!* Austin, TX: Bard Press.

Gioia, D. A. 1986. Symbols, scripts, and sensemaking, in H. P. Sims (ed.), *The Thinking Organization.* San Francisco, CA: Jossey-Bass, pp. 49–74.

Gordon, G. G., & DiTomaso, N. 1992. Predicting corporate performance from organizational culture. *Journal of Management Studies,* 29, 783–799.

Klidas, A., van den Berg, P. T., & Wilderom, C. P. M. 2007. Managing employee empowerment in luxury hotels in Europe. *International Journal of Service Industry Management,* 18 (1), 70–88.

Kotter, J. P., & Heskett, J. L. 1992. *Corporate Culture and Performance.* New York: Free Press.

Kusluvan, Z., & Karamustafa, K. 2003. Organizational culture and its impacts on employee attitudes and behaviors in tourism and hospitality organizations, in Z. Kusluvan (ed.), *Managing Employee Attitudes and Behaviors in the Tourism and Hospitality Industry.* Hauppauge, NY: Nova Science Publishers, pp. 453–487.

Ogbonna, E., & Harris, L. C. 2002. Managing organizational culture: Insights from the hospitality industry. *Human Resource Management Journal,* 12 (1), 33–53.

Ostroff, C., Kiniki, A., & Tamkins, M. 2004. Organizational culture and climate, in W. C. Borman, D. R. Ilgen, R. J. Klimoski, and I. B. Weiner (eds.), *Handbook of Psychology: Industrial and Organizational Psychology*, vol. 12. New York: John Wiley & Sons, pp. 565–594.

Peters, T. 1994. *The Pursuit of Wow!* New York: Vintage.

Schein, E. 2004. *Organization Culture and Leadership*. San Francisco, CA: Jossey-Bass.

Schneider, B. 1980. The service organization: Climate is crucial. *Organizational Dynamics*, 9 (2), 52–65.

Schneider, B., & Bowen, D. E. 1985. Employee and customer perception of service in banks: Replication and extension. *Journal of Applied Psychology*, 70, 423–433.

Schneider, B., White, S. S., & Paul, M. C. 1998. Linking service climate and customer perceptions of service quality: Test of a causal model. *Journal of Applied Psychology*, 83, 150–163.

Simons, T. 2008. *The Integrity Dividend*. San Francisco, CA: Jossey-Bass.

Simpson, S., & Cacioppe, R. 2001. Unwritten ground rules: Transforming organization culture to achieve key business objectives and outstanding customer service. *Leadership & Organization Development Journal*, 22 (8), 394–401.

Testa, M. R. 2004. Cultural similarity and service leadership: A look at the cruise industry. *Managing Service Quality*, 14, 402–413.

Torvald, O., Larsen, S., & Marnburg, E. 2005. Organizational culture and performance-evidence from the fast food restaurant industry. *Food Service Technology*, 5, 23–34.

Trice, H. M., & Beyer, J. M. 1993. *The Cultures of Work Organizations*. Englewood Cliffs, NJ: Prentice Hall.

Van Maanen, J. 1992. Displacing Disney: Some notes on the flow of culture. *Qualitative Sociology*, 15 (1), 5–35.

NOTES

[1]Sharp, I. 2009. *Four Seasons: The Story of a Business Philosophy*. New York: Penguin Group, p. 101.

[2]Ford, R. C., Wilderom, C. P. M., & Caparella, J. 2008. Strategically crafting a customer-focused culture: An inductive case study. *Journal of Strategy and Management*, 1, 143–167.

[3]Ricca, S. 2009. Commitment to culture. *Hotel and Motel Management*, 244 (5), 28–29.

[4]Enz, C. A., & Siguaw, J. A. 2000. Best practices in service quality. *Cornell Hotel and Restaurant Administration Quarterly*, 41 (5), 20–29.

[5]http://www.southwest.com/careers/culture.html, accessed September 4, 2009.

[6]For more information on this point, see Davidow, W. H., & Uttal, B. 1989. *Total Customer Service*. New York: Harper, pp. 96–97.

[7]Schein, E. 2004. *Organization Culture and Leadership*. San Francisco: Jossey-Bass.

[8]For the definitions in this section, we are indebted to Trice, H. M., & Beyer, J. M. 1993. *The Cultures of Work Organizations*. Englewood Cliffs, NJ: Prentice Hall, pp. 33–34.

[9]Schein, 51.

[10]Kuenz, J., Willis, S., & Waldrep, S. (eds.). 1995. *Inside the Mouse: Work and Play at Disney World, The Project on Disney*. Durham, NC: Duke University Press.

[11]Hallowell, R., Bowen, D., & Knoop, C.-I. 2002. Four Seasons goes to Paris. *Academy of Management Executive*, 16 (4), 19.

[12]Van Maanen, J. 1991. The smile factory: Work at Disneyland, in P. J. Frost et al. (eds.), *Reframing Organizational Culture*. Newbury Park, CA: Sage Publications, p. 66.

[13]Michelli, J. A. 2008. *The New Gold Standard: 5 Leadership Principles for Creating a Legendary Customer Experience Courtesy of the Ritz-Carlton Hotel Company*. New York: McGraw-Hill, p. 181.

[14]Deal, T. E., & Key, M. K. 1998. *Corporate Celebration*. San Francisco: Berrett-Koehler.

[15]Schein, 2.

[16]Davidow & Uttal, 107.

[17]Schein, 317–320.

[18]Ibid., 317.

[19]Ibid., 318.

[20]Ibid., 224–225.

[21]Gregersen, H. B., & Black, J. S. 2002. J. W. Marriott, Jr., on growing the legacy. *Academy of Management Executive*, 16 (2), 33–39.

[22]Wolff, C. 2008. What makes Kimpton cool. *Lodging Hospitality*, 11 (8), 42–43.

[23]Brinker, N., & Phillips, D. T. 1996. *On the Brink: The Life and Leadership of Norman Brinker*. Arlington, TX: Summit Publishing Group, p. 191.

[24]Van Maanen, 70–71.

[25]For the discussion of secondary mechanisms here, we are indebted to Schein, 237–242.

[26]http://www.southwest.com/about_swa/airborne.html, accessed September 7, 2009.

[27]McGee-Cooper, A., Trammell, D., & Looper, G. 2008. The power of LUV: An inside peek at the innovative culture committee of Southwest Airlines. *Reflections: The SoL Journal*, 9 (1), 49–55.

[28]Howard, J. 1994. Service with a sneer. *New York Times*, November 6, sec. 6, p. 43.

[29]LaBaton, S. 1994. Denny's restaurants to pay $54 million in race bias suits. *New York Times*, May 25.

[30]Rice, F. 1996. Denny's changes its spots. *Fortune*, 133 (May 13), pp. 133–134.

[31]Rice, 133.

[32]After lawsuit, Denny's restaurant chain buries its racist image. *Lubbock Avalanche-Journal*, April 6, 2002. http://www.lubbockonline.com/stories/040602/nat_0406020065.shtml.

[33]Sheridan, J. E. 1992. Organizational culture and employee retention. *Academy of Management Journal*, 35 (5), 1036–1056.

[34]O'Reilley, C. A., III, Chatman, F., & Caldwell, D. F. 1991. People and organizational culture: A profile comparison approach to assessing person-organization fit. *Academy of Management Journal*, 34 (3), 487–516.

SECTION 2

The Hospitality Service Staff

We're not in the coffee business, serving people; we are in the people business, serving coffee.

—Howard Schultz, CEO, Starbucks Coffee

CHAPTER 5

Staffing for Service

HOSPITALITY PRINCIPLE: FIND AND HIRE PEOPLE WHO LOVE TO SERVE

If someone isn't smiling during the interview, what in the world would make you think they will be smiling when faced with a line of customers all in a hurry for service, service, service?

—T. Scott Gross, *Positively Outrageous Service*

It is delusional to expect your employees to be extraordinary and differentiate your organization if your employee systems are basically the same as those in other organizations.

—Daniel M. Cable, *Change to Strange*

LEARNING OBJECTIVES

After reading this chapter, you should understand:

- The process of recruiting employees who will give excellent guest service.

- Internal and external recruitment strategies that organizations use.

- Standard approaches and techniques for screening and interviewing job candidates.

- Employee skills, traits, and general abilities that have been found to lead to guest service excellence.

- The importance of a strong service orientation for all organizational employees, not just those on the frontline serving guests.

- The importance of a diversified workforce to hospitality organizations.

KEY TERMS AND CONCEPTS

recruitment	emotional labor	unstructured interview
service naturals	emotional relationship	structured interviews
selection	surface acting	behavioral interviews
human resource planning	deep acting	situational interviews
KSAs	hiring from within	assessment center
job analysis	succession plans	on-boarding

When you check into a hotel, most of the time things go ... as expected. You drive up to the hotel, get your luggage out, go to the front desk, give the agent your name. She interacts with you pleasantly while she finds your reservation, handles the check-in, gives you your key, and has the luggage sent up to the room. You let yourself into your room without incident. You maybe watch TV to relax after your trip, and then you go to sleep. If someone were to ask you, "How were the employees of that hotel?" you might think back to your front desk experience and say "fine." But this answer overlooks the large number of people that were hired, trained, and coordinated to make your check-in meet your expectations.

So, who are all the people involved? There was the reservationist who took your reservation, the manager who hired and scheduled the reservationist, the valet who parked your car, the bellperson who took your luggage, the doorman who let you in to the hotel, the front desk agent (whom you did remember), the front desk manager who scheduled enough people to be on staff to ensure that your check-in occurred in a reasonable amount of time, the housekeeper who cleaned the room, the maintenance person who made sure the light bulbs and TV remotes were working, and of course, the executive staff who were responsible for the higher level management activities that ensured the profitability and efficiency of the hotel. It took literally dozens of people to get you checked into your room ... as expected. All those people had to be hired, trained, paid, and managed.

This chapter begins a discussion of the human resource issues involved in managing the guest experience, by reviewing the first issue: hiring the right people, who can deliver the experience your guests expect. Chapter 6 will look at what is involved in training and developing the employees you have hired, and Chapter 7 will examine the financial and nonfinancial factors involved in motivating quality employee service. The final chapter of this section will consider these human resource management issues as they apply to your guests who can be considered as quasi-employees coproducing their own hospitality experiences.

THE MANY EMPLOYEES OF THE HOSPITALITY INDUSTRY

Providing either a tangible or an intangible service product requires many different employees doing many different jobs. Most obvious are the front-of-house employees who interact with the guest. They are directly responsible for providing the value and quality of an exceptional experience because they are the interface between the guests and the company. Back-of-house employees or what is sometimes called the *heart of the house* help create the service experience. They fix the rides, cook the meals, clean the sheets, and so forth so that the guest's experience meets or exceeds expectations.

Management also plays a critical role. They hire the employees, train, evaluate, reward, discipline, celebrate, promote, and oversee all the other tasks that must be done to ensure that there is someone at the right time and place ready to serve the guest. Beyond these tasks, there are laws and regulations that must be followed; accounts that must be balanced; financial statements that must be created; strategies that must be developed and implemented; marketing and sales that must be done. All these tasks—and the people who perform them—are critical for a successful business.

Serving the Guests

Scott Gross, in his *Positively Outrageous Service*,[1] provides numerous examples of how exceptional customer service can make the service experience extraordinary. One such service experience occurred at a Hampton Inn at the St. Louis Airport. A guest arrived very late at night, with an important 9 a.m. meeting the next morning. Unfortunately, his luggage didn't make it, but he needed to look fresh and clean for this important meeting. Upon hearing the dilemma, the night auditor suggested that the guest get clothes and other essentials at a Wal-Mart store, which stayed open late. Because the guest had flown in and had no way to get there, the night auditor gave the guest directions *and* the keys to his car!

While many people are involved in the delivery of any service experience, it is the frontline or customer-contact employee, with whom the guest interacts, that has the most direct influence. This employee—the front desk agent, the restaurant server, the character at a theme park, the driver of the bus, the flight attendant—is frequently the one that can turn a guest experience into a wow that is memorable. This can be done in a variety of ways, but one way is to add something extra and unexpected to the experience. The story is often told of a Southwest flight attendant who hid in the overhead compartment to surprise boarding guests with an unexpected greeting. Those who were greeted this way still talk about the pleasant and memorable experience this provided them on an otherwise as expected flight. Such an employee can make the

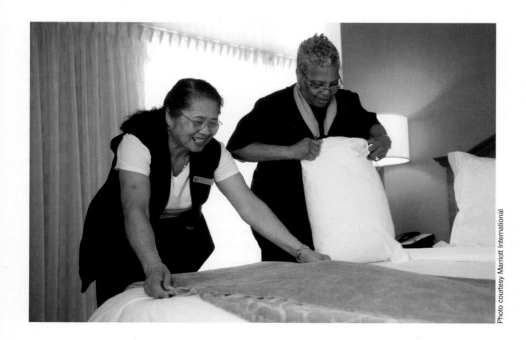

Many employees contribute to the service experience, beyond those often seen by the guest

Photo courtesy Marriott International

service experience something special, worthy of being told to friends or recorded in books about great service experiences, by adding an extra service to an already outstanding service product.

The hotel employees in the preceding examples illustrate the role of the hospitality employee in adding this extra. In the first example, in which a guest checks routinely into a hotel, the service was as expected, simple, polite, and efficient but not especially memorable. The flight attendant, in the second example, however, made the experience memorable by going above-and-beyond what was expected. And by doing more, he created a memorable guest experience that helped the guest in an unexpected way. For this guest, it was a wow!

Supporting the Service

If employees are to deliver excellent service, there must be something excellent to deliver in the first place. And just as guest-contact employees must have the right abilities and motivation to interact appropriately and engagingly with guests, so employees in non-contact positions must have the right abilities and motivation to do their jobs if an excellent service experience is going to result. For example, Spain's El Bulli is considered by some to be the best restaurant in the world. It is open only seven months a year, the dining room had fewer than 50 seats, and there is only one seating per night. The restaurant claimed to receive over a million reservations a year but accommodated only about 8000 diners in a single season. And yet the dining experience was supported by over 40 chefs![2] The guest might interact directly with only a few employees (e.g., maitre'd, server, wine steward), and while those employees provide exceptional service, they were not what made the restaurant so special. People go to such restaurants (if they can get in) for the magic occurring out of sight in the kitchen. Of course, getting into El Bulli will become even harder, as it is scheduled to close for two years in 2012 to become an academy for advanced culinary study. Chef Ferran Adrià plans to reopen El Bulli in 2014, but in a re-imagined way. As with any restaurant, whatever new form El Bulli will take will require careful consideration of the sort of talent that will operate behind the scenes.

Almost any service encounter requires some back-of-the-house people providing support to those interacting with guests. Rooms must be cleaned, laundry must be done, beds must be made, buildings and rides must be maintained, and dishes must be washed. The work of some support services is obvious—a skilled chef is clearly involved in the preparation of a meal served at a fine restaurant. Other functions are less obvious—the Walt Disney World Resort in Orlando, Florida, is supported by a full-time fire department, employing roughly 150 firefighters, emergency medical technicians, and paramedics, who are seen only when needed.

The Role of the Manager

Hospitality is such a labor-intensive industry that there must also be managers to supervise, coach, and coordinate the many employees doing the different jobs. Supervisors and managers have a number of important roles, from checking employees' work to creating work schedules, supplying necessary equipment and supplies, providing training, and conducting performance evaluations. Yet managers in service firms are faced with very different issues than managers in product-producing firms.[3] For example, managers in service firms have to rely on subjective assessments, such as customer satisfaction and loyalty, to determine the effectiveness of their decisions and their employees' behaviors. Furthermore, the simultaneous production and consumption of services makes the hospitality

Both front-of-house and back-of-house employees must work together to provide an exceptional service experience

Photo courtesy Marriott International

managerial role complex and difficult to spell out. In addition to their administrative responsibilities, hospitality managers are held accountable for success on qualitative measures, and often perform a customer-service role as well. Finding and hiring managers with these capabilities is at least as important, critical, and challenging as hiring customer-service employees.

LOVING TO SERVE

While employees in different positions will obviously play different roles and have different levels of customer contact, ultimately, the hospitality industry comes down to providing service. Each employee helps deliver that service, either directly or indirectly. When one comes across employees who deliver exceptional customer service experiences, they really stand out.

Scott Gross calls these people "**service naturals**" because they instinctively give great service when provided the opportunity. These are the employees who can change a regular interaction into something special that the guest will both appreciate and remember. Through this experience, the server connects with the guest in a way that builds a relationship. Though often very brief, this relationship somehow makes an emotional connection that leaves the guest feeling good about the experience and believing that something was special and memorable about it. The challenge for hospitality organizations seeking excellence is to find and hire these people who can make these connections with guests.

Gross estimates that Service Naturals represent only one in ten of the available workforce. As he states, "Ten percent can't get enough of their customers. Five percent want to be left alone. The vast majority, when it comes to customers, can take 'em or leave 'em."[4] If Gross's percentages are accurate, he raises two major challenges for hospitality managers. First, they need to work hard at developing a process that will systematically

It is critical for exceptional service organizations to find the employees who love to serve

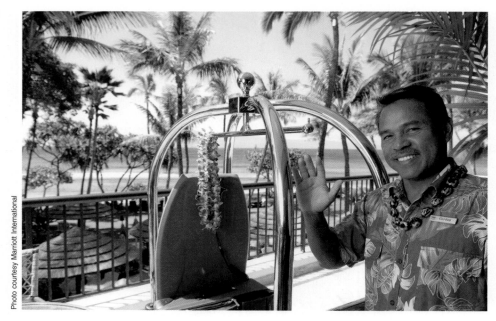

Photo courtesy Marriott International

find, recruit, and select those 10 percent who are truly committed to providing excellent service. Second, they must work even harder to develop an effective process for showing the rest how to provide the same quality of service that the naturals do naturally. Because naturally talented people are so rare in the labor pool, the organization must identify what skills are lacking in the people they do hire and train them in those skills.

Given the challenges of recruiting and hiring good employees in the hospitality industry, some organizations are tempted to place the service naturals in the guest-contact jobs and hire the rest for support jobs, which don't have direct contact with the guest. Since not all jobs in hospitality organizations require extensive guest contact, putting people not naturally good at service in these behind-the-scenes jobs might seem like a way out. The truly excellent organizations, however, recognize the fallacy of this reasoning. They know that *all* employees are somehow involved in serving either external, paying guests or internal fellow workers. Knowing that service effectiveness depends on everyone throughout the organization taking service responsibility seriously, these outstanding organizations try not to hire anyone unwilling or unable to provide outstanding service. There are simply very few places to hide employees who may be outstanding technically but have no service skills.

Many hospitality companies say they hire the "best and the brightest." Others claim to follow the mantra "select the best and train the rest." But in reality, the process of getting employees into service roles can prove to be a challenge for all companies. Entry-level jobs in the hospitality industry are often known for long hours, difficult conditions, and low pay. By its very nature, the business of hospitality often means being open twenty-four hours a day, including on holidays and weekends. It is an industry known for its high turnover, and finding qualified applicants can prove to be quite a challenge. For all the rhetoric about hiring the best and the brightest, it is not uncommon to hear managers say, "If the candidate has a pulse, he's hired!"[5] The exemplar or benchmark organizations know that this is a recipe for service disaster. They know that the **recruitment** and **selection** process must be carefully planned and executed.

Although all companies clearly want to have high-ability, motivated employees, the best-performing companies are those that have gained a competitive edge by developing recruitment, training, placement, and reward and recognition programs that motivate all employees to provide outstanding service for customers. It all begins with recruitment and selection. If the organization can somehow attract and select the best potential employees, it will gain a significant advantage over those organizations that do not systematically seek out and find these guest-focused people.

The selection process, in theory, is straightforward. First, figure out exactly what you are looking for; second, recruit a pool of good candidates; third, select the best in the pool; fourth, bring the best candidates on board; fifth, make the new hires feel welcome; and sixth, manage any potential future turnover of employees strategically. Each step requires a number of critical decisions. How do you know who your best candidates are and what does a great candidate look like? Do you look for applicants from inside or outside your company? What tools do you use to collect information (e.g., interviews, psychological testing, references)? How do you combine the information you collect to decide who you should hire? How do you make the new hire feel genuinely welcomed and show your appreciation to that person for agreeing to join your organization?

THE FIRST STEP: STUDY THE JOB

Human Resource Planning

Selecting the best person for the job should begin by first looking not at the applicants but at the job. First, you should engage in **human resource planning**. Human resource planning is the process of analyzing an organization's current human resource capabilities and the organization's human resource needs that are required to meet organizational objectives. Based on your organizational strategy, you must determine what knowledge, skills, and abilities (**KSAs**) employees must possess to accomplish your goals, what levels of KSAs currently exist in your organization, and how you expect both your organization and people to develop over time.

HR planning not only is directed at today's employee needs but also should be done with a longer-run perspective. While most recruitment activity is focused on filling jobs that are currently vacant, some effort should be given to anticipating the long-term employment needs of the organization. If, for example, you are planning to build a new hotel or expand an existing one, you must consider whether or not job candidates with the necessary KSAs will be available for hire when the project is done. If not, plans need to be developed to recruit from distant labor markets, retrain people in the current labor market, or hire away qualified employees from their current employers. Each of these strategies has costs and benefits that should be carefully weighed, but each also offers a planned path to find the employees needed when it is time to hire.

HR planning may reveal that you have too many employees (and so layoffs may be necessary), current KSAs are inappropriate, or your organization needs to acquire more people with more skills. You may also determine that you can acquire the new skills by training current employees (a topic covered in Chapter 6) or by motivating and empowering your employees (Chapter 7), but commonly you will find that the best way to acquire the needed KSAs is by hiring new employees.

Job Analysis

After HR planning, but before you start looking for a new employees, you must take the time to carefully analyze exactly what sort of job you are going to fill. A careful, thorough **job analysis** allows the organization to identify the exact job specifications and required competencies for each job classification and type (Figure 5-1). A job analysis will tell you if you need physically strong people to assist park visitors into a ride, skilled lifeguards to keep people safe in the water parks, or multilingual people to speak to foreign guests.

Many organizations spend a considerable sum of money identifying the KSAs associated with each major job or job category and then develop measures to test applicants on the degree to which they have these KSAs. A carefully developed measurement process ensures that the tests are both valid and reliable to provide an effective and legally defensible means for putting the right candidates in the right jobs. Further, a careful job analysis to develop accurate selection measures has the added benefit of identifying training needs and building reward structures that are directly connected to the critical knowledge, skills, and abilities closely linked with job performance.

While the KSA approach is the most widely used strategy for selection in industrial organizations, using it in the hospitality organization is more difficult because of service intangibility and variability in guest expectations. Measuring the strength, height, and manual dexterity competencies necessary for a manufacturing job is far easier than measuring friendliness, ability to stay calm under guest criticism, integrity, and willingness to help—all necessary to provide excellent guest service. For this reason, hospitality organizations must go beyond KSAs and consider other factors such as *employee attitudes*. Indeed, many hospitality organizations find attitude so important that they use this staffing principle: Hire for attitude; train for skill. From the guest's perspective, another way of expressing this idea is found in a commonly heard hospitality saying, "Guests don't care how much you

FIGURE 5-1 The Knowledge, Skills, and Abilities Required for an Assistant Front Desk Manager in a Major European Hotel
© Cengage Learning 2012

- Ability to work in a fast-paced environment.
- Outstanding flexibility; must be able to work under stress and pressure and reflect at all times, even under difficult conditions, a positive can-do attitude and the best image of the hotel.
- Ability to analyze complex statistical data and make judgments accordingly.
- Ability to deal effectively with internal and external customers, some of whom will require high levels of patience, tact and diplomacy to difuse anger, collect accurate information, and resolve conflicts.
- High school diploma required. Degree with hospitality focus preferred.
- Minimum 2 years previous front desk experience required.
- Experience with reservation information systems required.
- Experience in a luxury property of comparable size preferred.
- Operational and/or sales experience required.
- Must be able to deal correctly with confidential information and must be discreet.
- Must be fluent in French and English and must be able to address any kind of information in an adequate manner.
- Must be well groomed and maintain impeccable hygiene standards.
- Extensive walking required and ability to stand on feet for a long time.
- Hours may vary based upon organizational needs and operational demands.
- Strong leadership skills.
- Excellent oral and written communication skills in English and French. Dutch is an asset. German and/or Spanish is a plus.

know until they know how much you care." Of course, you cannot forget that you need to hire people with the right skills to perform the job, or at least the right abilities to be successfully trained on the job, but employee attitudes can also be an important factor in whether a company provides service excellence or a service failure.

Study Your Best Performers

The intangibility of the guest experience and the uniqueness of what each guest expects from it have led some hospitality organizations to use a secondary strategy for identifying good candidates: study the organization's best performers and identify their personal traits, tendencies, talents, and personality characteristics. Then, find candidates who match this profile.

Instead of identifying the KSAs that particular jobs seem to require or will require in the future, this approach starts by defining the KSAs of currently successful employees. In essence, this is benchmarking against your own very best practitioners of the job. The idea is that if you hire only employees who have traits, skills, abilities, tendencies, talents, and personality characteristics that are similar to those found in the current strong job performers, they should be more successful than new employees who don't have those same characteristics. If you want to find a successful new job performer, find an existing successful job performer and hire someone as nearly like that person (in terms of KSAs and attitudes) as possible. The trick, of course, is to discern the distinguishing characteristics that enable your strong performers to succeed.

Develop Talent Profiles

Many organizations have followed the strategy of identifying talent profiles that is based on work by the Gallup Corporation, S.R.I., J.D. Power, and other similar organizations. The idea here is to look at an organization's strong performers and, based on their talents, develop talent profiles for each major job category. Then, they use these benchmark profiles to screen new applicants. For example, theme park ticket sellers have traditionally been hired and rewarded on their ability to handle large sums of money transactions quickly and accurately. Careful analysis has shown that the best ticket sellers have additional talents. In effect, the ticket seller is the first point of contact between a theme park and its guests. Newly arriving guests are not typically knowledgeable about the many ticket package options. They often need to talk to a person who can quickly and easily identify what guests really want to do and then sell them the most appropriate ticket package. The talents required of the employee who can do this well include having very good empathetic listening, interpersonal, and coaching skills in addition to the ability to handle large sums of money rapidly and carefully. The successful ticket seller is really something of a vacation planner. Once the talent profile of successful ticket sellers is identified, a reassessment of both the selection process and the reward structure for this job can be done.

The use of this approach can even be extended to look at the mix of talents in entire departments. If an analysis of a particular department shows that the current composition of people does not include some vital talent for departmental success, the selection process can ensure that the next person hired will have an ample supply of the missing ingredient.

Companies like Choice Hotels and Marriott International have made identifying leadership competencies a priority. By identifying appropriate competencies, senior managers can be more effective in selecting and developing future leaders. Competencies are usually identified by examining the characteristics of current high performers. Once identified, these competencies are then formalized, defined, and described so that one knows when they are being demonstrated. Choice Hotels uses a database of employees' competencies for help in internal selection, promotion, and succession planning. Marriott uses its competency system, called the Benchstrength Management System, to help ensure that high-potential managers are given assignments that help their development and prepare them for future assignments.[6] Table 5.1 shows some of the key competencies needed for leadership in the hospitality industry.

Competency-Based Approaches: Disadvantages

Competency-based approaches to selection have a few drawbacks. Designing them for a single job or single job category can be quite expensive unless the organization has a lot of people doing that job. While Marriott employs so many hotel assistant managers that developing a competency profile becomes worthwhile, an independent hotel may not believe that the considerable expense of having a professional organization come in to do this work can be recaptured in any selection efficiencies gained. Further, as the necessary competencies change, so too must the selection measures. Finally, it is not clear how

TABLE 5.1 Leadership Competency Model for the Lodging Industry.

FACTOR	DIMENSION
Self management	Ethics and integrity
	Time management
	Flexibility and adaptability
	Self-development
Strategic positioning	Awareness of customer needs
	Commitment to quality
	Managing stakeholders
	Concern for community
Implementation	Planning
	Directing others
	Reengineering
Critical thinking	Strategic orientation
	Decision making
	Analysis
	Risk taking and innovation
Communication	Speaking with impact
	Facilitating open communication
	Active listening
Interpersonal	Building networks
	Managing conflict
	Embracing diversity
Leadership	Teamwork orientation
	Fostering motivation
	Fortitude
	Developing others
	Embracing change
	Leadership versatility
Industry knowledge	Business and industry expertise

Source: From Exhibit 2, pg. 23, Leadership Competency Model for the Lodging Industry. In Chung-Herrera, B. G. Enz, Cathy A., and Lankau M. J. (2003). "Grooming Future Hospitality Leaders: A Competencies Model", *Cornell Hotel and Restaurant Administration Quarterly*, 44 (3) 17-25. Reproduced with permission.

helpful developing a competency profile is for a specific job in the long run if the company plans to promote employees into other jobs in the future. Because of this, companies like Marriott and Choice have developed more generic competency measures, which help avoid some limitations of the single-job measures.

Nonetheless, all competency measures are essentially anchored on the successful practitioners in the current organization. If the organization wants diversity in opinion, training, talents, and personalities to promote change and organizational growth, the use of the mix of existing executives to establish the norms for who should be hired in the future may impede gaining the benefits of a diverse workforce. To avoid these potential problems, competency measures should be considered as only one tool in the selection process.

Other Key Characteristics for Service Personnel

While certain KSAs or competencies can be identified for a specific job, there are some known characteristics that are needed by employees who are actually serving customers, clients, or guests. One is enthusiasm. To provide exceptional service, guest-contact employees must have *an enthusiastic approach to life*. Enthusiasm is contagious, and guests come to most hospitality organizations expecting to be served by employees who are enthusiastic about the service itself, the organization, and the opportunity to provide service. There are very few guests who do not want and expect a feel-good guest experience that only enthusiastic employees can deliver.

Enthusiastic employees show their enthusiasm in many ways, but one important way is to put on a "show" for their guests. Scott Gross devotes a significant part of *Positively Outrageous Service* to the importance of hiring and training people who can create the show. He believes a touch of spontaneous, unrehearsed showmanship can sometimes provide the margin of difference between a hospitality experience that merely meets the guest's expectations and one that is truly memorable. Enthusiastic hospitality "showpeople" engage guests in their performances and enable guests to remember the experience. Whether it is the server who bursts unexpectedly into a song during a restaurant meal, the bus driver who delivers a comedic monologue during the ride to an off-airport rental car location, or the amusement park employee who spontaneously turns an unexpected delay for an attraction into a "good show," the point is the same.

Employees who are recruited, hired, and trained to not only perform their jobs in exceptional ways but also create a good show for the guests add value to the guest experience in important ways. First, they make the experience memorable and help keep the hospitality organization in the top of the guest's mind, increasing the likelihood of return or repurchase. Who can forget the Southwest attendant who surprises newly boarded passengers by singing the preflight safety instructions to rap music? This entails more than just "doing the job." Sometimes, guests will get extra value from being entertained while dealing with boring, routine activities like boarding a plane.

Employing servers who interact with guests in this way creates a competitive advantage since no competitor can design into its service experience the same feeling of a unique and personalized show for the guest that the well-selected, well-trained, enthusiastic employee can. The opportunity to provide a show for the guest is a terrific opportunity for properly selected employees to show their enthusiasm in a fun way. An organization that encourages its employees to take every opportunity to be creative and individualistic with guests, connect with guests, and use their showmanship tells employees that the company

Service personnel need to demonstrate an authentic sense of concern for their guests

Photo courtesy Darden Restaurants

appreciates their skills and trusts them to do the right thing with customers. For servers who sought the job partly for the opportunity to demonstrate their creativity and originality, this is a fun part of the job.

Employees with guest-contact responsibilities should *demonstrate an authentic sense of concern* for their guests. They must be upbeat, cheerful, enthusiastic, and genuinely interested in serving the guest, even when the guest is not reciprocally positive and even when they themselves don't feel upbeat or positive. This requires them to engage in **emotional labor**, which can be just as tiring as physical labor.[7] When hiring individuals into customer-contact roles, companies must select individuals with the ability to not only do their jobs but also make a connection with guests in an **emotional relationship**. Putting on a happy face when you yourself are having a bad day is difficult. When employees' true emotions are not consistent with the types of emotions the company and the customer want them to display, they can act in one of two ways: **surface acting**, where they modify their facial expressions, or **deep acting**, where they modify their inner feelings.[8]

Not everyone, no matter how service oriented, can make or act as if they can make this heavy emotional commitment consistently. All hospitality employees have had guests who push them to their limits and thus challenge their genuine commitment to provide great service. Some positions require listening to complaining guests all day, and for most employees, a point comes when they can endure it no longer. It may take a day, a week, or years, but this type of negative experience eventually exacts its toll on the employee and results in burnout. Sometimes, it doesn't even take negative experience. Some employees burn out because they tire of acting the same positive, upbeat way in the same job every day. Watch a fast-food server greet everyone with the same smile and the same affected cheery greeting and wonder how long that person has performed this same ritual. Employees who engage in surface acting experience more negative effects than those who are able to engage in deep acting.[9] At some point, most people switch into an "automatic-pilot mode" because they can't perform the emotional labor of their jobs any longer.

They have lost the emotional commitment to treat guests with sincerity. Bowen and Schneider term this emotional commitment *a passion for service*, and they have developed a questionnaire for measuring it. More importantly, their research reports that a passion for service is highly correlated with positive service outcomes.

Finally, because service employees will be interacting with the guests, they should also be polite, considerate, and willing to make a genuine effort to help other people. For example, during the hiring process, observe how candidates treat the receptionist before the interview. To put these general abilities together would lead to selecting someone who has the ability to handle emotional labor, can put on a consistent show in front of guests, cares about the quality of the performance and the guest's reaction to it, and does it all with gusto.

THE SECOND STEP: RECRUIT A POOL OF QUALIFIED CANDIDATES

Once you know what you are looking for in new employees, you need a diverse pool of qualified applicants from which you can select them. Where do you find them? The most basic choice here is, do you consider people from inside the company or outside?

Whether the company looks inside or outside may depend partially on the level of positions to be filled. If they are entry level, recruiting will occur mainly from outside. If above entry level, the company will have to decide whether to promote from within or look outside.

Hiring Internal Candidates

Many companies prefer internal recruitment for several reasons. In fact, the practice of **hiring from within** is often seen as a best practice of human resource management.[10] Hiring internal candidates has a number of advantages, as described below. But it is no panacea, and the decision to hire from within needs to be considered in light of both its advantages and disadvantages.

The Known Quantity

The most important advantage of promoting from within is that you have much more information—and more accurate information—about your current employees than you do about external candidates.[11] The internal candidate is a known quantity. That person's performance has been available for observation and evaluation every day, and the person's strengths and weaknesses are generally known. Because some external candidates will interview well and some poorly, managers doing the hiring can make mistakes. On the other hand, the good and bad qualities of a person observed every day are evident. Perhaps even more importantly, the present employee has shown loyalty to the organization by staying on and seeking higher levels of responsibility and challenge. For these reasons, many organizations prefer a known inside candidate over an outsider. Because customer relationships are so important in hospitality organizations, it makes considerable sense to promote current employees who have proven successful in their job, have shown a commitment to customer service, know and like the company culture, may be connected to the company's customers, and are familiar with the organization's mission and commitment to guest service.

Internal Equity

The second reason for internal hiring is internal equity. Many hospitality organizations employ people from varied backgrounds and with different levels of training and education. Many employees, except those in some technical areas and those with unique qualifications and experience, start at the same entry-level point. Each has an equal opportunity to prove a commitment to service excellence if they wish to get promoted. At a hotel front desk, you might find a recent college graduate, an older person who has changed careers, and a person with a high school or technical school degree—all working side by side and trying to impress the front desk manager with their merits for promotion. If an outsider gets the vacancy at a higher level, these hard-working employees will not feel fairly treated. They helped the organization achieve its success; now they should be recognized for their contributions and allowed to share the rewards.

The Shangri-La Group subscribes to this internal promotion approach. Says Kenneth Wai Shiu-kee, Island Shangri-La, Hong Kong area's director of human resources, "We believe that to build a career in the hotel service, it is useful to accumulate knowledge and experience from the start. The first-hand experience of what delivering the service product is like will prove useful when an employee moves on to more senior decision-making positions. Our policy of internal promotion helps us promote this attitude among staff. The steadying effect it has on our workforce also helps us make good succession planning. We invest heavily in training for our staff, not just to improve their performance but also to prepare them for career advancement when opportunities arise from our rapid business growth. The group also benefits from having experienced employees well-versed in our corporate culture."[12]

Experience

Most people, as just mentioned, start in the hospitality industry by taking entry-level jobs. Companies want their employees to know the business from the ground up. This hiring strategy is usually uncompetitive and unattractive for college graduates who have not acquired such experience through co-op or intern programs. While most graduates appreciate the need to take the entry-level jobs as an opportunity to prove themselves, many are unwilling to accept the relatively low starting salaries that hospitality organizations offer. This is becoming an even greater issue for the industry as students graduating from college increasingly start their careers with tens of thousands of dollars of debt. These students cannot afford low starting salaries even when they have hope of future promotions and pay raises.

The hospitality industry has, consequently, often relied on growing its own from non-college talent or finding college students who are so committed to the industry that they will give up current rewards to enter it. In a tight labor market, the belief in the need to start everyone at the entry level has caused the industry some difficulty. Bright college graduates interested in the hospitality industry often have better options even in other service industries. The entry-level approach makes attracting MBAs and other advanced-degree holders especially difficult. While this is less of an issue in a loose labor market (i.e., when a lot of people are looking for jobs), there is always a shortage of truly excellent workers, even when there is high unemployment.

Hiring from within makes it possible to gain the employee commitment needed while maintaining the entry-level salary structure. The well-managed hospitality organizations have systems in place to recognize potential and have training programs available to develop that potential. Although they miss out on some college-trained applicants, they are able to build a strong workforce based on their own internal processes. Whether the costs of these internal development programs are worth the trade-off—for not paying higher entry-level salaries—is still debated, but college graduates are often not willing to make the heavy financial sacrifice that the industry asks of them.

Another experience-related point in favor of hiring from within the organization—if the job to be filled is at the managerial or supervisory level—is the belief that you cannot manage someone doing something you've never done. Although hospitality experience and real-life examples can be acquired in one company and brought to another, the most relevant experience and examples are obviously those that are acquired internally. The core competence of hospitality organizations is providing service, and unless you have had experience in providing service, felt the pressure of guests in your face, and found ways to resolve guest problems on the spot, you don't really know what it's like. Given the uniqueness of organizations, and the particulars of companies' cultures, promoting employees from within helps preserve the investment you have made in employees, and keeps that company-specific knowledge working for you. You are in the business of providing an outstanding guest experience and, as a manager, of establishing and sustaining a guest-focused culture within the organization. You need to have real examples from your own experience that help you tell your employees how to provide excellent guest service.

Knowing the Culture

Organizations like to promote internal candidates because much of the training in the organizational culture has already been done. Internal candidates already know the company's beliefs and values and have proven themselves to be comfortable in that culture. The cultural learning curve for promoted internal candidates is substantially reduced as they already know the office political structure, the corporate goals, the real way things get done inside the organization, and what the organization really believes in and rewards.

Lower Cost

Internal recruitment also has the general advantage of reducing costs. There is no need to pay for advertisements and travel expenses of candidates to be interviewed, and the decision often requires less time, which saves money. Also, candidates can be considered before a position is even open, and the company can begin developing them to take on the new responsibility when it becomes available. This way, when an opening does occur, it takes less time to fill the position. Additionally, cost savings occur because there are fewer eligible employees and ultimately fewer applicants for a given position than would be the case had external candidates also been considered. A well-prepared company can use internal selection successfully to move good people up through the organization. But if not well prepared, it may find itself forced to select from a pool of less qualified employees.

Another advantage of internal selection is that it can reduce turnover. Employee turnover is greatest among new hires, so promoting internally helps decrease the chance that the position will need to be filled again in the near future. Recruiting is an expensive process and reducing turnover reduces costs. Promoting good performers from within will reduce turnover by giving the high performers assurance that the company will let them grow and reward them for their loyalty and dedication. As Len Berry puts it, excellent companies "hire entry-level people who share the company's values and, based on performance and leadership potential, promote them into positions of greater responsibility."[13]

Internal Search Strategies

A pool of internal candidates can be created in one of two ways: job postings or a review of personnel records. Many organizations announce open positions to employees via a company Intranet, bulletin boards, newsletters, or other means of communication. Sometimes, employees are informed of openings before they are publicly announced, thus giving internal candidates the first chance to apply for positions.

Some companies use their employee records to identify potentially qualified candidates. For example, Hilton Hotels uses a computer application that tracks such factors as employee profiles, past performance ratings, employment history, skill sets, employee interests and career aspirations, willingness to relocate, and languages spoken. Hilton can instantly access the records of qualified candidates from across its entire set of properties and determine who might be a good fit for, say, a new general manager position in San Diego. This technology provides decision makers with instant access to a potentially large pool of applicants for whom they already have good performance and competency data.[14] It also helps employees manage their careers by matching their preferences and qualifications with the requirements of open positions. Employees can then see what they need to do to prepare for positions with greater responsibility.

Some companies, like Darden Restaurants, manage internal promotions and transfers even more proactively. They develop **succession plans**, in which employee careers are planned over a long period, including the progression through a number of key positions or key locations. When a position becomes available, the company already has a list of finalists for that job, or even a person already identified to take on a new role. Succession plans allow a company to identify talented personnel and put them through appropriate training and increasingly challenging job positions to prepare them for taking on greater responsibility.

Hiring External Candidates

Not every job can be filled by an internal candidate. For example, the only source of candidates for entry-level jobs is the external labor market. Nor do organizations always want to promote only from within. Internal recruitment is by definition limiting. A company's internal labor pool is almost always smaller than the total labor pool. In some circumstances, looking outside the company for new employees has a number of advantages.

New Ideas and Fresh Perspectives

One problem with hiring internally—which usually involves promotions and transfers—is that it limits the diversity of experience of the candidate population. When companies hire only from within for everything except entry-level positions, everyone's experience comes from the same organization. Employees may learn very well how business is done in their company, but they may have no idea of how other companies are doing the same things, and in particular how others might be handling certain problems in a better way. Some companies have come to rely on hiring from the benchmark organizations as a way to reduce their own training costs while obtaining the talent they need to be competitive. This strategy can be expensive as hiring someone away from an existing external job will generally cost more than developing such a person internally, but for some specialized or senior positions, the benefits gained may be worth the cost (and may actually reduce training costs).

Difficulties with Internal Candidates

The company that promotes from within often promotes its best line-level employees into supervisory or managerial roles but good line-level employees do not always make good managers, nor do all of them want to become managers. For example, by promoting the best front desk agent to front desk supervisor, the company may be losing a great agent with great customer service skills and acquiring a bad manager with poor leadership abilities. Convincing a bellman or waitress to become a manager may be difficult as employees in tipped positions frequently make more money than their supervisors. Unless organizations are willing to develop employees systematically to take on the greater responsibilities of higher-level positions, promotion from within might do more harm than good. Similarly, if a culture change is desired, or if a particular talent is unavailable in the internal labor pool, adhering to the practice of promoting from within can fail to produce the characteristics required in new leaders.

Specific Skills and Knowledge

While hiring from within can be a means to motivate and retain lower-level staff interested in a promotion, external candidates may be desirable when a needed ability or combination of abilities in a specific job is unavailable among existing employees. Although most hospitality leaders can tell many stories of general managers who worked their way up from entry-level positions, many aspects of running a hospitality business may require particular knowledge and training that a firm may not always be able to provide internally.

For example, the knowledge of accounting, IT, finance, human resources, law, marketing, revenue management, statistics, and strategy that a general manager needs in order to run a profitable hotel cannot necessarily be "picked up" along the way without some sort of external education or experience at the same level at a different company. Many hospitality organizations must look outside for information systems skills that are not generally acquired through the experience-based internal-development career paths. While organizations would like to promote internal candidates, the technological revolution is happening so fast that the traditional in-house training processes are often not able to keep up. The hospitality industry increasingly looks to the more technologically advanced industries for filling positions that require application of up-to-date technologies to emerging hospitality focus areas. The same phenomenon has occurred in the finance area, where the increasing need to have employees skilled in asset-management and capital-budgeting techniques has meant that the traditional approach of growing the necessary skills internally doesn't work well enough or fast enough to keep up with the rapid pace of change.

In short, the hospitality industry is becoming more sophisticated. Companies are recognizing that to acquire specific sorts of skills and experiences, they have to look outside the company for people with particular education, experience, or a good combination of the two. Because the pace at which technologies are changing is so rapid, and because the sophistication of the business of hospitality is increasing, the traditional strategy of "start at the bottom and grow your way to the top by watching others doing it as we've always done it" can no longer be viewed as necessarily the best way to fill all positions.

Diversity

Another concern with promotion from within is that it can limit diversity at higher organizational levels. If a company hires only from within, its diversity in higher-level positions is limited by the employee demographics already present. For example, if women are slightly more likely to leave a company than men, it becomes increasingly unlikely that women will achieve the highest levels when the company hires only from within. Hiring from outside the firm allows a company to enhance its diversity by seeking candidates from different applicant pools.

Of course, simply hiring externally does not guarantee diversity. Enhancing diversity takes a concerted effort to seek diverse applicant pools and to have managers willing to hire people who do not necessarily look or sound like themselves. One company that has clearly made such an effort is Marriott International. In 2003, Marriott's board of directors established the Committee for Excellence, chaired by a member of its board, to monitor the progress of the company's diversity initiatives. The committee's programs are designed to increase the diversity of Marriott's workforce, hotel ownership, and suppliers. And the initiative has paid off. While maintaining its presence on *Fortune*'s list of 100 Best Companies to Work For, Marriott has also been listed repeatedly as one of the "40 Best Companies for Diversity" by *Black Enterprise* Magazine, "Top 50 Companies for Diversity" by DiversityInc, "50 Best Companies for Latinas to Work For in the U.S." by *LATINA Style* magazine, a "Diversity Elite 60" company by *Hispanic Business* magazine, and "Top 50 Companies for Executive Women" by the National Association for Female Executives.[15] Making a clear commitment to diversity begins at the top of the organization and has helped to keep Marriott one of the most highly regarded lodging companies in the world.

Embracing diversity is not about being politically correct. It is good business. Clearly you have to act within the law. U.S. Federal laws prohibit discrimination on the basis of race, color, national origin, sex, religion, age (if 40 and over), disability status, veteran status, and genetic information. Some (but not all) jurisdictions prohibit discrimination on the basis of sexual orientation and gender identity. Beyond the legal and moral need to comply with antidiscrimination laws, contemporary hospitality organizations have three other very good reasons to foster diversity in their staff. First, thanks to advances in transportation and communication, global travel patterns, and the breaking down of many cultural and racial barriers, increasingly guests are from diverse cultural and demographic populations. In some service settings, these diverse guests expect that service providers will be similar to themselves or will at least understand the expectations of people like themselves. They want servers who speak their language, figuratively and perhaps literally. Many large airlines try to hire multilingual flight attendants and reimburse attendants for taking language lessons or classes. United Airlines offers classes for flight attendants in Air Spanish, Air Portuguese, and Air Japanese. Attendants learn the forty or so words necessary to greet, board, and serve native speakers of these languages and use a smile and hand gestures for everything else.[16] When the Gaylord Opryland Hotel was preparing to host a large international meeting, it gave its 7000 employees special training in international guest service. The grand training finale was an all-day international marketplace; employees won prizes by participating in games while dining on international foods.[17] Although no workforce will be as diverse as the broad cultural range of guests, staffing strategies should be designed to hire guest-contact employees sufficiently insightful to read cues indicating the expectations of guests from different cultures and backgrounds and flexible enough to meet those varied expectations.

A second reason for interest in diversity is that employing a diversified workforce, by tapping all available segments of the general labor pool, will result in *a better workforce* than if the organization limits its hiring to select parts of the labor pool. In a competitive environment, all organizations must look at the entire labor pool for the best employees, regardless of background, cultural heritage, or other differences. The best organizations gain a competitive advantage by seeking out and recruiting talent wherever it may be found. Recognizing and appreciating diversity can be a stimulus to develop innovative ways to recruit. Knowing that Orlando, Florida, has a large Moroccan population, one hotelier sought them out. Since few other hospitality organizations recognize this group's size or bother to understand its proud cultural heritage, this hotel has gained a unique and valuable advantage by recruiting from this relatively untapped resource.

A third reason a company should embrace diversity is that its labor pool and its customers are becoming more diverse. Companies should therefore be proactive so that they are prepared for the inevitable demographic shifts that they will be seeing. According to the Census Bureau, roughly 35 percent of the U.S. population is a racial or ethnic minority. The Census Bureau projects that by 2050 only 52.8 percent of the U.S. population will be comprised of white, non-Hispanics.[18] In short, businesses need to accept and be prepared for diversity, whether they like it or not. There is no longer a typical hospitality employee for whom the organization can design one-size-fits-all selection, training, and reward systems. Dual-career couples, same-sex partners, single mothers with child care responsibilities, grown children with elder care responsibilities—all these and many other demographics are apt to be represented in the hospitality organization's workforce. The manager of the modern hospitality organization must be sensitive to the needs of employees from these varied backgrounds and lifestyles.

No matter how diverse the hospitality organization's workforce, the fact remains that guest-contact personnel will be different in most ways from the guests they serve. For example, most restaurant servers are younger than the patrons. The organization must hire people who are adept at interacting with the great variety of guests, who can take a reading of guest expectations during the first few moments of the service encounter, and who enjoy the challenge of providing personalized service to today's multicultural hospitality clientele.

External Search Strategies

When looking to hire externally, companies can develop an appropriate pool of applicants in many ways. Figure 5-2 lists important external-search strategies. For large hospitality organizations in cities and towns, where the tourism and hospitality industries dominate, these strategies are especially important to provide the tremendous number of people that the hospitality industry needs. The smart hospitality companies go where the growth is; thus, growth plus replacement needs add up to a big recruitment job. Seasonal fluctuations in demand for hospitality services only compound the problem by requiring intensive recruitment and selection drives to prepare for an expected seasonal rush. Even in tighter

The modern workforce is increasingly diverse, and the best hospitality companies prepare for, manage, and embrace their diversity to get the best applicants and ideas

FIGURE **5-2** Some Sources Used for External Recruitment

Advertising

A message containing general information about the job and the organization is placed in various media, such as newspapers, radio, and television. These media can have a local, regional, or national audience and can serve the general public or a specific segment of population.

Associations and Unions

Many occupations have state, regional, or national associations that hold meetings, publish newsletters, and represent the interests of the occupation. Such associations frequently have job-placement units (e.g., the International Council on Hotel, Restaurant and Institutional Education, CHRIE).

Colleges and Secondary Schools

Organization members are sent to colleges and schools to meet with individuals or groups of students to provide specific information about the organization or their jobs and to answer any questions. They may also perform the first review of applicants. The organization's members may visit, for example, Cornell University's School of Hotel Administration or University of Central Florida's Rosen College of Hospitality Management.

Employee Referral Programs

When using this word of mouth technique, employees are provided with information about job openings and asked to refer individuals to the company. Often, the employee is given a bonus if the referred individual is selected. Should the applicant be rejected, the employee is customarily given a brief explanation.

Employment Agencies

The firm contacts an organization whose main purpose is to locate job seekers. The company provides the agency with information about the job, which the agency then passes along to its clients. Clients can be either employed or unemployed. Agencies can be either public or private. Fees may be charged to either or both the client seeking a job and the company seeking applicants. Global Hospitality, Marshall-Alan Associates, and Presley Consultants are executive search firms that specialize in the hospitality industry.

Employment Events, Job Fairs, Career Fairs

These events are specially organized to attract a large number of potential candidates to a specific location on a certain day, who are then interviewed for jobs. These events can be held in conjunction with other organizations and may be in one's own labor market or in a distant location where unemployment is high. Job fairs are also increasingly being held in central business-district locations where any potential employee can talk to recruiters from sponsoring organizations. For example, the Roosevelt Hotel in New Orleans, which was closed because of Hurricane Katrina, received 5000 applications for 400 jobs when they held a four-day job fair (*Times Picayune*, May 13, 2009).

The Internet

The firm can either post information about open positions on its own Web site or contract with an Internet recruiting service. These services are online job centers that offer many organizations a site for listing jobs across many job categories and locations. Job seekers can access the job center and view job postings according to job title, company name, geographic location, and so on. Some centers will perform an initial match between applicant characteristics and company job requirements. Résumés of applicants who are well matched to the job requirements are forwarded to the company for future contact. The CareerBuilder and Monster web sites are two examples.

Temporary Employment Firms

Companies sometimes need to fill short-term positions that do not warrant commitment of resources to recruit, select, and train people. Temporary employment firms, like Kelly Services and Manpower, help to fill such vacancies. Job contracts are generally limited to less than a year, and companies pay a given hourly rate. Although some temporary workers hope they may be considered for permanent employment, others like the flexibility and variation that working for temporary employment firms offers.

Walk-Ins

Unsolicited individuals sometimes initiate contact with the organization. The number depends on such factors as the nature of the business, the level of the positions open, the image of the company, the frequency of job openings, and how close the labor market is to the hiring company. For example, many people want to work at the Phantom Ranch in Arizona but it gets few walk-in applicants as it is located at the foot of the Grand Canyon.

Source: From GATEWOOD/FEILD/BARRICK. *Human Resource Selection, 6E.* © 2008 by South-Western, a part of Cengage Learning, Inc. Reproduced by permission. www.cengage.com/permissions.

economic times or in situations with limited seasonal variation, the high turnover in the hospitality industry makes recruitment a constant challenge, and controlling costs becomes even more important. In the end, regardless of the specific economic or business situation, a major challenge for all hospitality organizations is how to both create and maintain a qualified external labor pool in a cost-effective way. The key point, however, is that every job will be seen as a great opportunity by some group of people, and the external search strategy should begin by considering who those people are and where to find them.

Public Advertising

Although there is much discussion of how the Internet is replacing print media, help-wanted advertisements are still a very common method for advertising job openings. Almost all newspapers still print help-wanted ads in the traditional way in which they have been printed for decades.

In addition to the advertising in newspapers, magazines, and weeklies targeting potential employees, aggressive recruiters use more creative means to reach people who may not read the help-wanted ads, may not be thinking about changing jobs, or may not even be thinking about working. Just as marketers segment their markets to find likely candidates for their products and services, recruitment managers increasingly segment their markets to reach and attract job candidates. For example, when the Wynn Hotel in Las Vegas was opening a sister property, Encore, it needed to hire for every position: roughly 6000 new employees, including room concierge, dealers, room attendants, management staff, security, and valet. To fill these positions, their managers believed they needed approximately 60,000 applicants. As part of their recruitment effort, Wynn used skywriting to advertise its openings. Planes flew up and down the California coast leaving messages over every major beach and even over a Los Angeles Angels versus Boston Red Sox baseball game. They received over 25,000 applications on the first day, and they would have received more had not the sheer volume of response crashed their server.

This type of public advertising can also attract interest from employees who are currently working for someone else. These people might not have thought about working for the organization doing the advertising until they happened to see or hear the ad, which might suggest to them an intriguing opportunity. If these people are at all dissatisfied with their current jobs, the possibility of interesting them in your organization becomes even greater. Even though they aren't looking for a job, their interest may be captured by a billboard; an advertisement at the bus terminal, television, or radio ad; or a skywriting campaign.

Some public advertising can, however, create problems. For example, having a sign on the marquee of a fast-food restaurant may be an efficient way to advertise for new employees, but it potentially sends a negative message to customers: We don't have enough employees, so our fast-food experience may be a lot slower today. Care must be taken so that any recruitment effort sends the right message to employees, potential employees, guests, and potential guests.

The Internet

The widespread use and accessibility of the Internet has turned Internet recruiting into a multibillion dollar industry. Companies can use Internet job sites, like Monster, to advertise their positions. Job seekers examine what is available and look for additional information on jobs that interest them. This method can help attract a large number of possible applicants, and applicants can consider a large number of possible jobs. The problem with this approach, however, is that hiring companies cannot always tell which applicants are really interested in a given job and which ones are not really serious, so a large amount of useless information may be generated.

The Internet also helps to fit employees to jobs and companies they want. Unlike some web sites that only post job openings—like a modern help-wanted section—some others ask job seekers questions to assess their fitness for positions or about what they are looking for in a new position. For example, you might be asked if you had managerial responsibility in a previous job, or whether you prefer to work for a large or small company. A job site can then use the information it collects to try to create a fit between the qualifications and preferences of applicants and the characteristics of jobs and companies.

Some companies are trying to stay on top of technological trends to reach out to potential applicants. Some companies have developed Facebook, LinkedIn, and MySpace pages as part of their recruiting efforts. These efforts help employers find and attract young, tech-savvy candidates and may make such employers stand out from their competitors—at least, until all companies start recruiting this way. Of course, this approach is also not without its risks. Companies with blogs and Web pages must update their content continuously or they won't look credible. Also, these pages create opportunities for any company detractors to have more of a voice. While companies should take advantage of current technology to enhance their recruiting efforts, they need to understand how their use of technology can be used against them. Further, they must be prepared to commit the necessary resources to monitor and use the technology well or the entire effort may actually hinder recruitment efforts.

Some, companies also use their own Web sites to advertise openings. By using a structured online application form, an employer can use screening technology to eliminate those candidates who are not a good fit for either the company or the advertised job. The technology also makes it easier to follow up with those candidates who may indeed be qualified. All major hotels' Web sites have links for careers from their main page that allow users to search for available jobs with the company, often by location, job characteristics, job title, and so forth.

Furthermore, as already mentioned, companies use the Internet to facilitate recruitment by allowing applicants to post their résumés on job search web sites like CareerBuilder and Monster. Here, applicants can advertise their skills and have the Web site help match their skills to positions that fit their skill set. This approach can give job seekers far more exposure to opportunities than previous paper-and-pencil job searches; however, if not properly managed, they can also create too much information to be useful to either party.

The Internet is also affecting the type and quantity of information on both candidates and companies. Job seekers are increasingly using their social networks to find job opportunities. People looking for jobs can make large amounts of personal information publicly available by posting it on sites like LinkedIn and Facebook. Prospective employers have begun to examine these sites to learn more about job candidates. People seeking jobs should therefore think carefully about what information and pictures they post or allow on their sites. Job seekers can also use networking opportunities, such as LinkedIn, Plaxo, and others, to look for jobs by networking with their online contacts, finding out about job opportunities, and so forth.

In short, the Internet has dramatically changed the way in which people look for, apply for, and find out about jobs. While the Internet has not replaced older ways in which companies and job seekers find each other, it certainly has added a host of new communication methods. Although many jobs will still be filled in traditional ways, the information made available through the Internet has changed the job search and recruitment process dramatically.

Niches

Targeting specific segments of the labor market to identify potential employees is another recruiting strategy. Some organizations target high schools, minorities, associations of disabled people, homeless people, or senior citizens. They structure the job opportunities and marketing to appeal to the needs and limitations of that particular segment of the employment pool. For example, many hospitality organizations find that some of their best employees are older, retired people, so they target that group. Retired seniors are often lonely, bored, looking for something to do that will bring them into positive contact with other people, or, realizing that they retired too early, need a job to supplement their Social Security. Many guest-contact jobs can provide this opportunity for them. Organizations that originally recruited older people because of labor shortages have often found to their pleasant surprise that their older employees not only have better attendance records than younger employees but they bring an enthusiasm for and experience in helping and interacting with guests that makes them great customer-focused employees.

For example, McDonald's offers McMasters, a nationwide program that identifies, recruits, and trains workers aged fifty-five years and older. It features job coaches as well as a referral program that alerts older workers to other opportunities at McDonald's. Workers hired through McDonald's referral program are immediately teamed up with a partner—an experienced worker who helps the employee through the initial training.

McDonald's employs about three workers per restaurant who are sixty or older, and they are looking to increase that number.

Professional Networks and Placement Services

Successful hospitality managers join professional organizations to find both good employees and good ideas about how to find good employees. The amount of movement back and forth across hospitality organizations causes these professional networks to be strong and informative. Some organizations seek to represent an entire industry (like the American Hotel & Lodging Association), a segment within the industry (like the Asian American Hotel Owners Association), specific professions (like the Society for Human Resource Management), or even particular networks of individuals (like the Cornell Hotel Society). While jobs can be found in many ways, networking is still one of the most effective to find out about potential jobs and potential employees, network, and enable the personal face-to-face connection that can make a potential employee stand out in a large pool of applicants and ultimately set up and serve as an initial interview.

Student Recruiting

An important strategy for finding the many people that the hospitality industry needs is student recruiting. A number of programs develop pools of potential employees among young people who are either still in school or have recently graduated. Being young, full of energy, recently educated on state-of-the-art methods, and enthusiastic, students are often ideal hospitality employees. In addition, they come to the job with the anticipation of learning and growing and are, therefore, quite comfortable with structured work requirements and extensive training. The most common recruiting strategy is the traditional campus visit by a company recruiter. The institution's placement office schedules eligible students to meet with the recruiter and provides an interview space on campus. The recruiter may interview graduating senior applicants for full-time jobs and undergraduates for summer internships. A variation on this idea is the job fair, where many employers come to the campus on the same day and set up booths where they can meet with potential employees.

Organizations can sometimes get students to work for them as part of a school experience, such as co-op, internship, or work-experience programs. Nearly all hospitality programs, most schools of business, some other academic majors, and many high schools and junior colleges encourage their students to get some real-world work experience while they are taking academic course work. For example, Cornell University's School of Hotel Administration requires students to work 800 hours in the hospitality field before graduation. The student not only makes some money to help cover education costs but benefits from seeing the practical application of classroom theory in the real world. This sort of relevant work experience can add value to a college student's résumé or high school student's college application.

The company also benefits from these programs as it gains access to an eager, young, energetic labor pool that does not expect a permanent employment commitment. The smart organizations, however, keep a close eye on these student employees and make sure that impressive student workers know of the company's interest. They offer these students scholarships or put them in special work experiences that prepare them to be fully trained employees upon graduation. Unfortunately, not all organizations use these programs well, and they can work to the student's and the industry's disadvantage. Some short-sighted organizations place young, part-time students only in simple, quickly learned, highly repetitive, and monotonous jobs that provide little learning experience and even less personal growth. The fast-food industry has burned out many students in this way. Putting students in these jobs not only keeps turnover high but, more importantly,

FIGURE **5-3** Sample Internship Programs from Major Hotel Companies
© Cengage Learning 2012

Four Seasons Internships

Four Seasons offers global internship opportunities to undergraduates and graduates who want to get a head start in their career. An internship allows you to experience the Four Seasons culture, learn our standards, and gain exposure to various areas of a hotel or resort.

Marriott Internships

Marriott offers paid internships that provide true hands-on work experience to prepare you for leadership in the professional world. You will focus on one professional area, with possibilities to explore other business operations.

Starwood Summer Intern Program

Starwood offers summer opportunities in our hotels which foster students' professional development, understanding of hotel operations and career planning for placement after graduation. Starwood provides each summer intern with experiences comparable to entry-level, full-time professionals in the field of hospitality.

---

has discouraged many bright young people from seeking careers in the food-service industry. These companies have unfortunately taught many young people that the industry is full of jobs suitable only for burger flippers.

Enlightened organizations, taking a longer-term view of the need to get and keep young people interested in the hospitality industry, have designed their work-experience programs to provide some real learning opportunities and growth challenges. The point is that student-recruitment programs can be designed and used to get not only employees who learn, earn, and contribute to the business today but also employees who will be eager to stay in the industry tomorrow upon graduation. The best organizations know how to use these work-experience programs to identify the better students and keep them after they graduate. Since many of these same organizations also place a high premium on dues paying, these programs give the students the opportunity to pay their dues in these entry-level jobs while they are still in school and put themselves in a better position for promotion to higher-level and better-paying jobs by the time they graduate. Figure 5-3 presents descriptions of internship programs at several major hotels.

Helped by the current federal funding emphasis on school-to-work programs and stronger ties between hospitality companies and academic institutions, the hospitality industry has found a variety of ways to effectively create opportunities to attract students. This is a constant issue because of the large number of new employees required by this industry's growth rate and the high turnover common in the industry. Even while there are a lot of students looking for work, and particularly when economic times return to lower unemployment, it is always critical to find highly skilled and motivated new talent.

Employee Referrals

Another large and successful source of employees for many hospitality organizations is referrals by current employees. A great way to get the kind of new employees you want is to ask your star employees to find them. Your good employees know what your organization is like, perform well in it, obviously like working for you, and can therefore be your best recruiters and spokespersons in the labor market. A bonus of this strategy is that existing employees who bring in their friends feel responsible for them and their performance. They exert positive peer pressure and encourage the new employees they sponsored to do well, which acts to the organization's benefit. Some organizations pay a bonus to their existing employees if they bring in a job candidate who is hired and stays through a probationary period. The reward might be monetary, or it could be something else that has value to employees, such as a free weekend trip to a nice resort area, dinner at a special place, or some other inducement. A common characteristic of *Fortune*'s Best Companies to Work For is the presence of an employee referral program.[19]

Employers of Choice

A company's reputation can also aid in recruitment. Publications like *Fortune* magazine, *Fortune Small Business*, and *HR Magazine* list companies that they evaluate to be Employers of Choice. These employers are characterized as being good places to work, where the organization makes efforts to create and maintain a humane and respectful workplace. As described by the Society for Human Resource Management, "They're the kinds of places at which we all want to work. Where talent and teamwork are highly esteemed; where everyone is encouraged to reach their potential and given opportunities for advancement; where employers respect and care about their workers, and workers, in turn, care about the company and its customers."[20] In other words, these companies hold out for the best employees, invest in those people so they grow and develop, provide challenges and keep them motivated in their current jobs, and offer them future opportunities with the organization. These companies see higher average returns on investment than those not on the list.

Interestingly, although so much time and energy are devoted to high-quality customer service in the hotel industry, only four hotel and restaurant companies made *Fortune*'s 100 Best Companies to Work For list in 2009 (Starbucks, at 24; Marriott International, at 78; Four Seasons Hotel and Resorts, at 92; and Kimpton Hotel and Restaurants, at 95).[21] Of course, there are other such lists—such as *Best Company to Work for Women, Best Companies for Minorities, Best Small and Medium Companies to Work for,* and even many local surveys within specific cities—and many different companies fill these lists. Nonetheless, the high-quality treatment of customers on which the industry prides itself does not seem always to be matched by similar treatment of its internal customers, at least in the view of these list makers.

Some companies try to enhance their reputation by building a positive image in the community. Southwest Airlines provides an excellent example of how a company can establish an exceptional community reputation. In addition to providing multiple educational programs and opportunities that have earned it the reputation for growing and developing its people, Southwest has spent much time and money making itself into a good neighbor. Each year, Southwest details its contributions in its Southwest Cares Report.[22] Each year's report details the previous year's activities related to environmental conservation, donations of money and tickets to charitable causes, number of employee hours devoted to charitable causes, and so forth.

Similarly, Marriott (among various activities) sponsors Spirit to Serve Days, where employees participate in various activities to benefit local nonprofits, schools, parks, hospitals, and charitable organizations. Such activities support Marriott's culture, demonstrate the company's support of its people, community, and environment, and make for good public relations too.

Marriott's employees show their Spirit to Serve by contributing to local charitable causes

Photo courtesy Marriott International

Even when the labor market is tight, Southwest and Marriott have a talented and deep labor pool. Being a good neighbor is good public relations, enhancing the company's positive reputation among potential employees and motivating satisfied employees to tell their friends that this is a great place to work.

Walk-Ins

Some hospitality organizations rely extensively on walk-ins. Here, they have a significant advantage over the manufacturing and industrial sector. A prospective employee curious about what goes on cannot casually walk into a General Motors assembly plant in Arlington, Texas, to see and feel what it is like. Almost anyone can casually walk into a hotel or restaurant and get a pretty good idea of what it might be like to work there. Indeed, many Disney employees are people who fell in love with the place after visiting with family or friends. One employee said that, after visiting the Magic Kingdom with her family, she planned for twenty years to work there. After her children grew up, she sold her home and moved to Orlando to work in the parks because she wanted to be one of the people who made other people happy. Students in hospitality management programs tell similar tales of a great experience in a hotel, restaurant, or other hospitality organization that excited them about the industry. As a result of that experience, they found out what they wanted to do when they grew up.

The Competition

Scott Gross adds another strategy: Seek out excellent employees in similar service jobs elsewhere. Again, unlike the manufacturing sector, where a potential employer is not going to be able to walk in and watch the best workers on a competitor's factory assembly line, watching customer-contact employees do their jobs in the hospitality industry is easy.

Every time you receive service or watch someone receiving service, you can evaluate the server as a potential employee in your own organization. Gross hands his business card to those who really impress him and tells them to come see him if they are interested in another job. Hiring people because you saw them working well elsewhere has the advantage of starting off the new relationship on the right footing: New employees found in this way will be flattered that you sought them out and asked. Everyone likes to be recognized, and if, by asking people to consider a job opportunity, you do a better job of recognizing them than their boss has done, you may very well land some excellent candidates. A variation on this strategy is to ask good people, whether they work for you or not, if they know about other good people. A surprisingly large part of the existing workforce is networked with people who are like themselves or have similar jobs. Using the network to build a candidate pool can be a rewarding strategy.

Call-Back File

Usually, there are more applicants than positions. Companies can call unsuccessful applicants back several months later to see if they are still interested. Even applicants who dropped out because they found other jobs might now be interested if the positions they took didn't turn out to be what they hoped for. They were once interested and might be again.

The Final Applicant Pool

No matter how the set of applicants is acquired—through internal selection, via a job posting system, using the Internet, or through public advertising—the selection decision will come down to two factors. First, how choosy can the company be in the selection process; and second, how well can the employee's performance be predicted.

Being choosy means having enough applicants apply for a position so that you can select the better ones and not hire others. Obviously, to make a decision, you need at least two applicants for a given position. But companies want much more than that. When opening its new hotels, the Gaylord Palms hired 1400 full-time employees from a pool of 14,000 applicants.[23] Similarly, as noted earlier, the Wynn Hotel sought to attract a pool of 60,000 applicants to fill 6000 openings. The point is if you have not built a sufficiently large labor pool to select from, you cannot be picky; you cannot choose to hire better people.

But being picky is not enough. You also need to be able to predict who will be better employees. Companies must be able to collect information on each applicant that can be used to identify good performers—and ideally the best performers. This process of gathering information on applicants constitutes the third step in the selection process.

THE THIRD STEP: SELECT THE BEST CANDIDATE

With a pool of applicants assembled, the next step is to determine who will be hired into the company. The selection process sounds disarmingly simple: figure out what an ideal candidate looks like, collect information on potential candidates, and then select the person who best matches the ideal. The people hired should be able to offer the quality of service that guests expect and that makes hospitality experiences memorable. They should be able to handle the stress of providing service, especially when a service failure occurs.

They must handle failure smoothly and successfully enough to satisfy the guest. Finally, they must act in such a way that each and every guest feels specially treated, safe, and secure. Anyone who has had both good and bad service experiences knows that companies perform the selection function with varying degrees of success.

Screening and Evaluating Applicants

Once you know what you want in a candidate, you must collect information on your applicants to make the best hiring decision. Many tools are available to help collect this information efficiently so as to make accurate hiring decisions. There is, of course, a trade-off. The more information that is collected, the better the potential decision can be; however, collecting more information takes both time and money. Companies must therefore carefully consider how they evaluate applicants in order to make efficient and effective hiring decisions.

The Application Form

Application forms are the first screen an employer should use in deciding whom to hire. A typical application form will include the applicant's employment history, education level, and conviction record if any. The form should be designed such that responses provide enough information to permit reasonable decisions about whom to keep in the pool and whom to drop. Obviously, a major trade-off is involved here. The recruitment strategy should be designed to bring in as many legitimate candidates as possible but also screen out unsuitable candidates. The advertising should state what qualifications, work experience, or training are minimum requirements for employment. The application form serves as a preliminary check on whether or not the candidates do in fact have the appropriate occupational qualifications. Job requirements should be clearly stated, so that they do not inadvertently amount to discriminatory hiring practices or eliminate candidates who could perform superbly in the role.

Technology is changing the form that applications can take. Sometimes, the application form can be built into a telephone application system. Applicants are encouraged to call a job hotline to find out about job openings and apply for those that interest them. A telephone application-and-screening process collects basic information about the candidate. If the information matches the organization's predetermined criteria, the automated interview ends with a request for a faxed, mailed, or e-mailed résumé. Optical character recognition (OCR) systems can scan résumés, evaluate each candidate's suitability for the job, and provide summarized information. These systems allow applications to be processed in larger numbers and with greater speed. They also allow organizations to be more flexible with their résumé screening, searching their database of résumés for applicants to see if any fit with the jobs openings on hand. Many companies allow—and some require—applicants to apply for jobs via the Web or kiosks in the organization's facilities. Online systems allow people to search and apply for jobs at their own convenience. These automated systems allow organizations to use computerized screening programs that save a great deal of time and money when compared to manually screening the many candidates who apply.

Traditionally, applicants have often needed to complete paper-and-pencil applications during business hours in a company's human resource department. But some people can't fill out applications in person, because they are already working elsewhere during these hours or are living in a different geographic area. The use of technology in the application process allows people to apply for jobs at any time of any day or night.

These 24/7 automated recruiting systems—just a phone call or click away for most potential applicants—are particularly useful for people who may not be able to call or come in during the usual work day and are a comparative advantage for firms.

The Interview

If the applicant passes the initial screen, the organization will most likely schedule an interview to determine if the information on the application checks out. That is, they will seek to determine if the applicant seems to fit the organization, see if the candidate is really committed to service excellence, and tell the candidate what the job is actually like. The interview is the most common method used by employers to help select employees. Research, however, has also shown it is often the least accurate.

Not surprisingly, the accuracy of an interview is largely determined by how well it is planned and how consistently it is used. When interviewers make up questions as they go along, have no predetermined way to score applicants, or rely purely on their memory, they are conducting what is called an **unstructured interview**. Probing questions (e.g., "Tell me about yourself and why you're interested in or qualified for this job") can sometimes add valuable information, but they can also yield information that differs in quality and amount from candidate to candidate because of interviewer differences in ability to ask and interpret appropriate questions. Without training, interviewers can be overly influenced by their own mood, the attractiveness of the candidate, personal biases, and the quality of the candidate interviewed just before.

Most writers believe that interviewing should follow a structured pattern. **Structured interviews** increase the likelihood that interviewers will assess all candidates according to the same criteria. When large numbers of interviewers interview large numbers of candidates, consistency becomes both organizationally and legally important. A structured array of questions ensures that the interviewer collects the necessary personal and job-related data. A properly designed and administered structured interview ensures that the questions are job related, consistently scored, and asked of all candidates. Research shows that such interviews can be valid predictors of job performance.[24] Typically, a structured interview will include questions that address past experiences, work competencies, willingness to do the job as designed, and commitment to service.

Structured Interviews   Because past performance is often the best predictor of future performance, one would ideally assess an applicant's prior performance in order to make a hiring decision. Unfortunately, that information is generally not available, or perhaps the person has actually never performed the job before. A valuable way to assess a candidate, though, is to see how he or she has or would have responded to particular situations.

In the hospitality industry, **behavioral interviews** are often the most effective way to assess applicant's qualifications on critical criteria. Behavioral interviewing is based on trying to specifically evaluate some instances of past performance to help predict future performance. So, unlike most interviews, in which applicants get questions like "Tell me about yourself" and "What are your strengths and weaknesses?" behavioral interviews try to capture past behaviors and performance. They might include questions like "Give me an example of how you helped to resolve a customer's problem," or "Tell me about a time when you had to make an unpopular decision and the consequences of your choice."

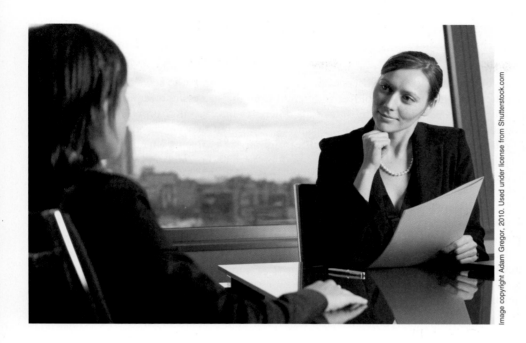

The employment interview, whether structured or unstructured, is one of the most commonly used methods for selection

Sometimes, and particularly for entry-level positions, applicants simply do not have the experience to answer the questions typically asked in a behavioral interview. Depending on the pool of applicants, companies may want to employ **situational interviews**. Like behavioral interviews, situational interviews aim to assess performance, but they involve hypothetical situations rather than actual past experiences. So, questions might include "How would you handle a guest whose reservation cannot be found and the hotel is full?"

For a structured interview system to be successful, the interview questions should be based on a careful job analysis, and the questions should be clearly related to specific KSAs that you want in an employee. Furthermore, interviewers should be trained in how to conduct interviews and evaluate candidates. A structured interview—be it behavioral or situational—involves more than just giving interviewers the same set of questions and the same scoring sheet.

Work Competencies   The second group of questions that should be included in a structured interview are those related to work competencies. A good structured interview should be closely connected to job analysis, so that the questions clearly help evaluate the characteristics of an applicant that are relevant to the job in question. For example, the interviewer assesses the competence of an applicant for a hotel front desk position by asking specific questions about check-in and check-out procedures and processes. Although hotels use customized systems and vary the routine, the steps of checking guests in and out are basically the same across all hotels. This part of the interview can be objectively scored, based on the candidate's correct and incorrect responses to job-related questions.

Doing the Job as Designed   The third part of a structured interview should assess the candidate's willingness to do the job as it is designed. The interviewer might ask questions about such aspects of the job as the applicant's willingness to work overtime, long shifts, or weekends. Many hospitality workers have to work when others do not. If candidates can't or won't be available when needed, they are probably not a good fit.

Commitment to Service   For positions with customer contact, interviewers will want to include questions that help to assess each applicant's commitment to service. The reality is that the successful hospitality employee is different from the successful traditional manufacturing employee, and the interview must take the difference into account. Frontline hospitality employees must be able to do the task assigned to them, but they also need interpersonal skills to relate to the guests and creativity skills to fix service problems when they occur. Service employees perform a wide array of tasks, both physical and mental, and yet throughout all of it, they must demonstrate a sincere and genuine sense of concern for their guests. Since applicants may try to hide their true feelings during an interview to get the job offer, interviewers must try to determine which of the candidates are the true service naturals,[25] who genuinely want do deliver exceptional customer service. Interviewers can try to assess this service orientation by asking situational-stress-type questions that focus on the service experience, and in particular, guest service problems.[26] Employees must respond quickly, appropriately, and creatively when the organization fails the guest in some way. The nature and critical importance of each aspect of service delivery make it essential to assess the applicant's attitude and personality before that person is hired and put out in front of guests.

The best hospitality companies also know that commitment to service is not limited to frontline employees. Indeed, ensuring that managerial candidates possess a high commitment to service may be more important because the commitment of managers to service quality positively affects those around them. Even when managers do not interact much with guests, their commitment to service influences their team members' behaviors, and helps the company deliver excellent customer service.[27]

Psychological Tests

Psychologists have developed a variety of tests to distinguish one person from another along different dimensions. Tests of mental ability measure logical reasoning, intelligence, conceptual foresight, ability to spot semantic relationships, spatial organization, memory span, and a number of other cognitive factors. Some measures of personality traits and behavioral predispositions have also been developed and validated for use in the selection process. For example, service orientation is associated with gregarious and outgoing personalities who make a conscientious effort to help others. Psychological tests have also been used to assess applicant integrity, such as how likely they are to engage in theft or risky behaviors at work.

Personality Traits   Managers often talk about hiring the right type of person for a job, or someone with the right disposition. So it should be no surprise that some employers try to assess the personalities of applicants in order to make better hiring decisions.

Research indicates that personality can be reliably measured and summarized along five dimensions:

1. *Extroversion.* The degree to which someone is talkative, sociable, active, aggressive, and excitable.
2. *Agreeableness.* The degree to which someone is trusting, amiable, generous, tolerant, honest, cooperative, and flexible.
3. *Conscientiousness.* The degree to which someone is dependable and organized, conforms to the needs of the job, and perseveres on tasks.

4. *Emotional stability.* The degree to which someone is secure, calm, independent, and autonomous.
5. *Openness to experience.* The degree to which someone is intellectual, philosophical, insightful, creative, artistic, and curious.

Of these five, conscientiousness is generally considered to be the most valid predictor of job performance.[28] Common sense suggests that people who are more organized, thorough, and dependable are likely to be better-performing employees.

Emotional stability has also been shown to be associated with job performance. Since the quality and value of hospitality experiences exist only in the minds and memories of guests, hospitality employees are often uncertain about whether they are delivering the experience as guests expect them to. Emotionally stable servers are much more likely to deal with this uncertainty in a positive, confident way. If the service turns out to be less than the guest expects and the guest complains, emotionally stable employees are more able to deal with the stress of complaints and work to resolve the complaints quickly, fairly, and with a smile.

While conscientiousness and emotional stability are correlated with job performance across jobs, extroversion has been shown to be an effective predictor of job performance in occupations where interactions with others are a major job component. Extroverts tend to be sociable, gregarious, assertive, and energetic. They are therefore more likely to get along well with others and seek out relationships and interpersonal interactions. Research suggests that extroverts are better at socializing or initiating contacts with others (e.g., customers, coworkers, and supervisors). They enjoy interacting with the customer and are more likely to perform better in service jobs, where interaction is a critical component of successful performance.

Cognitive Ability   While many managers think personality is the best predictor of job performance, in fact, decades of research has shown that cognitive ability may be the best.[29] This finding has been replicated across a wide variety of settings and occupational groups. Research has shown that general mental ability (GMA) can account for up to one third of the variance in performance ratings for complex, managerial jobs, and up to 16 percent of the variance in performance for less complex, semiskilled positions.[30] These results have led some to argue that GMA should be used as the primary basis on which to make selection decisions. As Norman Brinker says, "Look for people ... who are smart. Remember, sinners can repent, but stupidity is forever."[31]

GMA is the ability to learn and process information. In part, GMA influences performance because it affects how quickly one can acquire the knowledge and skills needed to perform the requirements of the position. Given that modern jobs change frequently—in duties, responsibilities, technology—smarter employees, on average, perform better. GMA also helps employees process more information simultaneously. For a server waiting on multiple tables; for a front desk agent juggling check-ins, questions, and phone calls; or an amusement ride attendant paying attention to the line, safety apparatus, and customer questions, higher GMA gives the capability to perform better. Although GMA is not the only predictor of success, it is a good predictor of performance and an important criterion to use in selection decisions.

Integrity Tests   Integrity tests predict the predisposition of job applicants to engage in theft, drug taking, and dishonest or otherwise disruptive work behaviors. It includes questions like "Excluding pills you got from a doctor (prescriptions), which of the following drugs do you use?" [A. Cocaine, Coke, Snow, Crack; B. LSD, Acid, Mescaline, Peyote; C. Heroin, Opium; D. None.] It might seem that some applicants would not answer questions on an integrity test honestly, if they do indeed steal, take drugs, or drink at work.

Selection tests—of personality, cognitive ability, and integrity—are not very commonly used, although there is mounting research evidence of their validity for predicting job performance

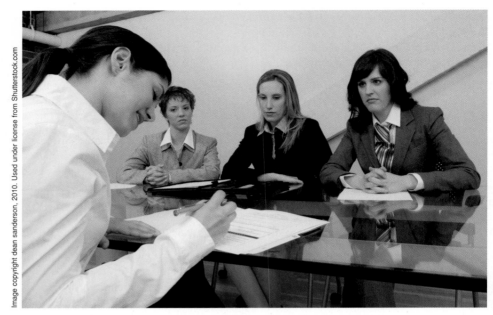

Image copyright dean sanderson, 2010. Used under license from Shutterstock.com

But the evidence is strong that many people will indicate their misbehavior. In two separate uses of integrity testing in actual hiring in two hotel companies, roughly 30 percent of applicants indicated that they engaged in such risky behaviors.[32] Research shows that integrity tests can predict theft, illegal activities, drug use, absenteeism, tardiness, performance ratings, violence, and workers compensation claims.[33] They have also predicted these behaviors for various types of jobs and for both current employees and job applicants.

Despite the research evidence, integrity tests are not commonly used in the hospitality industry or elsewhere. But since they are relatively inexpensive and show evidence of ability to screen out undesirable candidates, they seem to be a promising tool in selecting the best candidate.

Assessment Centers

An **assessment center** is a battery of tests that are used to measure the KSAs of a group of individuals. This can be used either for the purpose of selecting individuals for higher-level positions or as a tool to help develop the participants' careers. Assessment centers often include interviews, psychological testing, and a variety of exercises involving administrative tasks, group exercises, cases analyses, and managerial exercises. While assessment centers can come in many forms, they typically measure seven key sets of KSAs: organizing and planning, problem solving, drive, influencing others, consideration and awareness of others, stress tolerance, and communication.[34]

Assessment centers require a significant time and resource commitment from organizations. Because of the large number of people involved and the types of devices used as part of the assessment center, the participants must be able to devote a significant amount of time to the process, and the company must provide the necessary space over this time. Furthermore, assessment centers require trained assessors to help score performance on all the measuring tools and provide feedback to participants. This investment, though, can have a substantial payoff. Assessment centers typically have high validity, and help predict performance beyond even cognitive ability and personality tests.[35]

References, Background Checks, and Drug Tests

It is also a fairly common practice to check a candidate's references. This may involve soliciting letters of recommendation, calling former employers, or requesting from candidates names of individuals who can attest to their character. Since most people are sensible enough to provide references from individuals who will write nice things about them, reference checks don't usually provide much useful information. Nonetheless, it is generally worthwhile to follow up on these references. If a given reference doesn't have good things to say, or worse, if the name given in the reference is fake, it clearly indicates a potential problem. Although many candidates can provide glowing references that may not really predict much, the skilled manager will still look for specific examples in the references that can attest to the KSAs and competencies needed for the job.

Once a candidate gets to the point of hiring, a criminal or background check and/or a drug test will often be conducted. Most hospitality organizations do these checks routinely to protect themselves and their guests. Obviously, a hotel's baby-sitting service must avoid hiring convicted child molesters. Indeed, no organization that sends its employees out unsupervised to provide a service can afford to employ someone who has not been thoroughly checked out before the hire is made. Similarly, hotel employees may have easy access to guests' belongings because some jobs require that they have keys to their rooms. Many services also involve handling cash. For all these reasons, a background check is critical when employees are dealing directly with customers or valuables. Learning that you hired a person who could damage your organization's reputation is not only embarrassing; much worse are the legal cases that can arise if a customer sues you for not exercising due diligence in your hiring practices.

Companies also want to screen out those who use illegal drugs, as drug use leads to greater absenteeism and greater likelihood of being fired or being in accidents, which results in higher medical expenses. Furthermore, because many drugs are by definition illegal, courts have generally accepted the use of drug tests in hiring, even if employers cannot provide a clear link between drug use and job characteristics.

THE FOURTH STEP: HIRE THE BEST APPLICANT

After all the information has been collected on potential applicants, selecting the right people from the applicants becomes the next critical step, in ensuring that the company gets the employees who will provide the level of service that the organization expects. While finding and hiring the right people is challenging for all organizations, it is especially difficult for the hospitality industry. Although many jobs require definable skills that can be identified, measured, and tested, the hospitality industry has the extra challenge of ensuring that the guest-contact employees they hire not only have the competency to perform the task skills but also have the interpersonal skills necessary to interact successfully with the guests and the creative skills to fix the inevitable service failures. The difference between a good and a great guest experience is so often the indefinable *extra* that the employee adds to the experience. Finding, hiring, training, and rewarding the employee who happily and naturally gives that extra effort is one of the biggest challenges for hospitality organizations.

The hiring decision must thus be made while balancing a number of factors. Does the person have the right personality to be successful in a service-based role? Is the person smart enough to handle a dynamic environment, master the training, and learn the job efficiently? Does the person's experience suggest that he or she will perform

Walt Disney World's
Casting Center

effectively in creating memorable guest experiences? Does this person have the potential to grow into greater roles in the future? In short, is there a good fit between the person and the work environment? There is no simple way to collect information to help answer all these questions; all these issues should nonetheless be kept in mind when making the hiring decision. The purpose of all the different selection devices—the application blank, the interview, and the various psychological tests—is to collect information to answer these questions and help companies hire the kind of employee who can make the company's service experience truly stand out.

Of course, most applicants for a given position will not be hired. Even so, those making hiring decisions should try to maintain good relationships with all applicants. Someone not hired today may be offered a job tomorrow. The hospitality industry has very high turnover, so although there may not be an opportunity for a given candidate on Friday, the job could be vacant on Monday. Additionally, prospective applicants can also be prospective customers. If you treat applicants badly, they may not only refuse to work for you; they and their friends may not want to stay in your hotel or eat at your restaurant. Word of mouth is a powerful force in the service industry, and negative comments can hurt a business even more than positive ones can help. All applicants should be treated courteously and with respect. Even if they are not selected as employees today, they might become good employees or valued customers tomorrow.

Disney offers an example of how guestologists think about hiring. It knows that meeting its very large labor needs will require it to process a very large number of applicants. The Casting Center is not only designed to handle this volume of people but is an impressive reminder of the culture and values of Disney itself. Even if applicants do not get a job offer (and most will not), everyone leaves the Casting Center with a positive impression of how they were treated by the process and a strong reminder of Disney's commitment to guest service. The experience not only pays off in how those that are hired feel about working for an organization with this strong culture of customer service, but it also impresses the many who are not hired but may be future customers.

THE FIFTH STEP: MAKE THE NEW HIRE FEEL WELCOME

Once the job offer is made and the selected applicant hired, the staffing process may seem to be complete. Indeed, many companies think and act this way too. However, the staffing process is not done until the organization has "on-boarded" the new employee. **On-boarding** should be designed to ensure that the new hire feels genuinely welcomed. After all, the organization spent a lot of time and money finding the right person to hire and convincing that applicant to accept the job offer. Now the organization should find ways to tell its new employees how welcome they are. The way the employees feel welcomed on their first day of employment may well set the tone for the rest of their career with that company.

On-boarding is the process of getting the new employee started in both a new company and a new job. Some of it is just common sense: people, especially the new supervisor, should be ready to greet the new person, the necessary paperwork should be complete, the office—if there is one for the position—should be ready with a computer, telephone, and other equipment and supplies. Many companies have formal orientation programs, and everything should be set up for the new employee to participate in one. While this process may all seem logical, surprisingly, many companies do not thoughtfully prepare for the arrival of new employees, and the result can be unpleasant. You only get one chance to make a first impression, and the best companies don't miss that chance.

As we discussed in Chapter 4, culture is critically important to most companies, and so communicating this culture to new employees is an absolute necessity for properly on-boarding a new employee. Since a lot of time and money have gone into the selection process, it is important to ensure that this investment is solidified by giving the new employee a sincere welcome to show that the company is as excited about the employee joining it as the employee is in accepting the job.

Because Gaylord's Opryland needs to employ a large number of people, it has developed a Convention of the STARS as an innovative way to on-board its new hires in groups. Since Opryland's primary business is as a convention hotel, it sets up its on-boarding process to resemble a convention. It gives new hires name badges with lanyards and tote bags, has keynote speakers, breakout sessions by functional area, a trade show floor with booth displays, entertainment, and even a banquet. This event not only makes the new employees feel very welcome but also effectively introduces them to how Opryland delivers the convention experience.

THE SIXTH STEP: TURNOVER—SELECTING PEOPLE OUT OF AN ORGANIZATION

Although you must expend significant time, money, and effort to hire people into your company, turnover is an inevitable part of business, and particularly in the hospitality industry. While selection is usually considered as the process of choosing employees from a pool of applicants, turnover can also be seen as selection of a sort. While those acquired are selected into the company, those leaving the company are essentially "selected out" of the company's workforce. While many companies give a lot of attention to the process of selecting people into the company, the process of turnover is often less strategically managed. If you know it isn't a good idea to hire randomly, why would you leave the process of turnover up to chance?

The hospitality industry is known for having high turnover. This can be voluntary, where employees choose to leave, or involuntary, where the choice is made for them by the organization. Hospitality jobs often involve working in unpleasant conditions (such as hot kitchens) or during undesirable hours (holidays, nights, weekends). The hospitality industry also often pays less than other industries and attracts turnover-prone applicants who see it as a short-term job commitment or an industry where their career aspirations cannot be met.[36] High turnover is the result.

Turnover can be costly for organizations. Direct costs are associated with the selection of a replacement for a departing employee, namely the cost of advertising for an opening, processing applications, and conducting background checks. Additionally, because new people must be trained in skills that departing people already had, turnover also increases training costs. These turnover, selection, and training-cost numbers show why organizations are frequently torn between designing a job task in a way that makes it challenging, complicated, and interesting (to reduce turnover) and designing the task to be quickly learned and easy to do (to reduce training costs). In the former situation, if the strategy does not reduce the turnover typically found in the hospitality industry, the organization will be constantly investing heavily in new employees who won't stay long enough to justify the cost of training. On the other hand, the simple, boring, and repetitive jobs are the ones that tend to have high levels of turnover. Obviously, this is something of a chicken-and-egg problem: more interesting jobs might lead to lower turnover, but most organizations are unwilling to pay the costs to find out.

Turnover also has an important indirect cost: the cost of disappointed customers. Guests frequently build relationships with servers, and being served again and again by the same person is part of the value they receive from an organization's guest experience. If turnover is high, these relationships are destroyed or don't get built at all, and a powerful means for retaining repeat guests is lost. New employees are also less productive than experienced employees, and it takes time for them to learn their new tasks as efficiently. Turnover can also create morale problems. As Jerry Newman describes his experiences in the fast-food industry, where turnover is very high, the other employees don't even bother to learn your name when you begin your job. Because turnover is so high, it isn't worth the effort. Instead, they will learn your name only after you have come back to work a few times.[37]

Because of the direct and indirect costs, turnover can be quite harmful. For entry-level positions in the hotel industry, some estimate that replacing a single departing employee costs 30 percent of that individual's annual pay.[38] For positions of greater complexity, some estimate the cost of turnover to be upwards of two times an individual's salary.[39] Clearly, if turnover is high, a company risks being at a significant competitive disadvantage.

On the other hand, turnover is not always a bad thing. While turnover always involves costs, it can actually benefit an organization. For example, the selection process is never going to be perfect, no matter how carefully planned and implemented it is. So, if the poor performers leave and are replaced by better employees, the organization will benefit in the long run. Customer service can be improved by shedding the employees who do not embrace the company's mission. Turnover also creates the opportunity to take advantage of the benefits of external selection. If the size of the company's workforce is not growing, turnover provides a means to hire employees from the outside with new ideas, new education, and different skills and perspectives, possibly from backgrounds that will enhance the company's diversity. Finally, if turnover occurs at upper levels, the door is opened for junior talent to move up. Talented junior people who see openings filled from within may stay, rather than moving to other firms that give them such opportunities.

Every company has turnover, but before assuming that all turnover is bad, the causes and consequences of this turnover should be investigated. Why are people leaving? Is it because of higher pay at competitors' firms, an unpleasant work environment, a poor manager, or something out of the company's control? Who is leaving? Is it high performers, low performers, new employees, long-tenured employees, a specific demographic group, or does it seem random?

Once a company understands who is leaving and why, it can begin to manage the turnover process effectively. Seeing who leaves and who stays, who succeeds and who fails helps provide a better understanding of what you are looking for in a candidate. Thus, this sixth step leads back into the first step—study the job—and the selection process becomes an ongoing cycle with the potential for continuous improvement.

EMPLOYING THE BEST TO SERVE YOUR GUESTS

To provide excellent service, the organization needs employees with the right knowledge, skills, abilities, and attitudes. To get the right people, the company needs to know what to look for, where to look to recruit talented workers, and the right ways to collect the information on job applicants. Successful staffing depends on a clear understanding of what the jobs require and of the personal characteristics that lead to success in these positions.

The best hospitality companies use a consistent and rigorous method to find, select, and hire the best talent. They also know that staffing does not just stop once an applicant is hired. Selection can continue as positions open up within the company, and internal candidates may make the best hires for these positions. Also, sometimes employees need to be "selected out" of the company, and this turnover process should be monitored and maintained with as much care and thought as the processes that bring people into the company.

Staffing is the first step in having the right human resources within your company to provide the level of service that you want to give your customers. But it is only the beginning. Hiring the best does not necessarily mean that employees will perform the best (although it certainly does help). Employees need to be trained in how to do their jobs, and they need to be motivated to perform their jobs well. These two steps are the focus of our next two chapters.

LESSONS LEARNED

1. Find the best people; train the rest.

2. Recruit creatively: Use the major search strategies, but try to think of new ones.

3. Carefully consider whether you should look inside or outside your company for new talent.

4. Build a large candidate pool; it will improve the odds of finding good people.

5. Carefully check applicants; are they the people you want serving your guests?

6. Know and hire the knowledge, skills, and abilities necessary to provide outstanding service.

7. Look for technical competence, strong interpersonal skills, and creative problem-solving ability.

8. Looking at internal candidates first sends a positive message to all employees about the kind of company they are working for.

9. Seek diverse candidates to enhance awareness of new ideas and trends.

10. Manage turnover with as much rigor as you manage the selection process.

11. You only get one chance to make a first impression with your new employees; make it a good one.

REVIEW QUESTIONS

1. Why are hiring and promoting from within so popular in the hospitality industry? What are the disadvantages of this strategy?

2. Assume that you are in a tight labor market for entry-level employees.

   A. Do any of the recruitment strategies described in the chapter seem more or less appropriate under those circumstances?

   B. What innovative ideas do you have that might improve your ability to recruit outstanding entry-level employees?

3. Recruiting applicants is only half the task.

   A. Indicate several techniques you would use to select those you want to hire.

   B. Assume that you are hiring a server for a casual-dining restaurant. What KSAs would you look for?

   C. Assume that you are hiring a hotel front desk agent. What KSAs would you look for?

   D. Are the front desk agent KSAs different from those for the restaurant server?

   E. What problem-solving skills would you look for in either type of candidate?

4. Assume that you are interviewing candidates for a position that involves selling your hotel as a convention site.

   A. What questions would you ask of candidates?

   B. What questions are you not legally permitted to ask? Why?

5. Do certain personality traits seem to be typical of the best hospitality employees who have served you as a guest? How do these traits compare with those mentioned in the chapter?

6. When Scott Gross meets good employees in other hospitality organizations, he gives them his business card as a means of suggesting that they might want to give him a call for a job interview.

   A. Do you have any problems with the ethics of this method, which is not uncommon in the business world?

   B. Suppose that a competitor sent someone into your employee parking lot to put job-interview invitations under the windshields. Would you view this situation differently? Why or why not?

7. When Lone Star Steakhouse & Saloon needs staff, they print a large announcement on guest checks: Now Hiring Energetic Outgoing Servers! What do you think of this technique?

ACTIVITY

Find a hospitality organization that will tell you about its employee selection processes and procedures. How does the organization determine which recruits are likely to succeed as hospitality employees? What selection methods do they use? How well are the organization's predictors of employee success working?

ETHICS IN BUSINESS

As part of its screening process, after candidates fill out an application, the Family-Happy Hotel and Restaurant scours the Internet looking for blogs and Facebook entries for these prospective employees. Often, it discovers a job candidate looking drunk in a Facebook photo or acting in a way that would be embarrassing if a customer saw that person once employed. Typically, these photos aren't on the candidate's social networking site but are posted on various sites of his or her friends and acquaintances. Family-Happy's management has decided that these behaviors are not consistent with the image they want to project of the organization, and so they remove from consideration any individuals for whom they discover such images. Besides, there are enough people looking for jobs that they can be picky when hiring, and in any case they need some way to narrow down the pool of applicants.

Do you feel the company's policy is ethically defensible?

CASE STUDIES

Choosing a Manager

The director of management development for the Long Stay Suites was required to recommend someone for a high-level management position in the company. Careful screening of all present employees narrowed the selection to two men: John Jarvis and Satya Patel. After lengthy interviews, the following information was accumulated.

John Jarvis had a tenure of three years with the company. He was very seldom absent from work and had obtained a college degree in hospitality administration by taking evening courses. His superiors rated his management potential as promising. The one complaint voiced against him was that he appeared impatient and overly ambitious. During his interview with the director of management development, Jarvis indicated that promotions had not come along fast enough for him and that unless he received this promotion he would seek employment with another major hospitality organization. He hinted that he had received offers.

Satya Patel was several years older than Jarvis. He had been with the company since graduation from a nearby university six years previously. He was rated by his superiors as a steady, dependable employee, apparently very intelligent, but he had been given little opportunity to display his talent. Three years ago, he had turned down a more responsible position at one of the organization's branches in another city. He said he didn't want to relocate, and the job required some traveling. Since that time he had not been given another opportunity to move upward in the organization.

In considering the recommendation he would make, the director of managerial development recalled a comment Patel had made during his interview: "I'm confident that you will recognize the importance of seniority when you make your final recommendation."

★ ★ ★

1. Weigh the pros and cons of promoting Jarvis or Patel.

2. Which one would you recommend for the position, and why?

3. Ideally, what additional information would you like to have before making a recommendation?

Regal Five-Star Hotel

During her first year as personnel manager of the Regal Five-Star Hotel, Margarita Gonzalez became increasingly aware of a possible morale problem among the housekeeping staff. Employee absenteeism and tardiness were rising. Coffee breaks were being extended beyond the allowed fifteen minutes. According to the grapevine, employees were not happy with working conditions or with the workload.

Although Gonzalez was aware that turnover had been rising, she was surprised to receive data indicating that it had exceeded 50 percent among the housekeeping staff over the past year. She reviewed the year's resignations. They accounted for 95 percent of the turnover. The other 5 percent were workers who had been terminated as unsatisfactory. Approximately 25 percent of the resignations were women, whose stated reasons for resigning were "husband being transferred to another city" and "leaving to devote more time to home and family." Gonzalez viewed these resignations as beyond the hotel's control and ignored them. The remaining resignations occurred for four reasons, in the following frequency of occurrence: (1) left to get salary increase, (2) left to get greater opportunity for advancement, (3) left to get different type of work, (4) personal reasons.

Margarita Gonzalez reviewed the criteria for hiring housekeepers, from desirable to undesirable in the hotel's view: under 25; single or newly married without children; husband in armed forces or for other reasons temporarily in the area; divorced with children; early twenties to early thirties; family fully established; husband permanently employed in the area; children fully grown. The hiring policy was obviously designed to appeal to women who seriously needed an income but who did not need a high income.

★ ★ ★

1. How should Gonzalez change the Regal Five-Star Hotel hiring policies, if at all?

Cruising Travel Agency

Ho-Chien Lee is a manager at a travel agency that specializes in cruises. Among his other administrative duties at Cruising Travel Agency, he hires and trains entry-level employees.

The typical agency job applicant is fresh out of college, excited about the future of travel, and confident that some of the world's problems can be relieved if hard-working people have a chance to relax on a cruise. Most applicants understand that travel-agency jobs are at the entry level. In return for these ideals and this ambition, the agency offers minimal training, little chance for advancement, considerable job security, low pay, and long working hours at night and on weekends.

For several years, job applicants have been plentiful. In recent months, the number of applications has dwindled.

Lee recently expressed his concern to Mary Ammerman, sitting at the next desk. "Where are we going to get fresh new employees? How can we keep the good people

we have at the lower levels? I can't for the life of me see why so many stay on at Cruising Travel. Of course, the best ones go somewhere else for more money and faster promotions. But I'm surprised that any of them at all stay. I wonder what they get out of it. And how can we help them to get more out of their jobs?"

Mary Ammerman said she didn't know. As a matter of fact, she thought to herself, she wasn't getting all that much out of her own job.

★ ★ ★

1. How would you describe the staffing situation at Cruising Travel Agency?

2. Do you think hospitality-related organizations like this agency make a mistake in hiring college graduates at the entry level?

ADDITIONAL READINGS

Carlson, K. D., & Connerley, M. L. 2003. The staffing cycles framework: Viewing staffing as a system of decision events. *Journal of Management*, 29, 51–78.

Carlson, K. D., Connerley, M. L., Mecham, R. L., III. 2002. Recruitment evaluation: The case for assessing the quality of applicants attracted. *Personnel Psychology*, 55, 461–490.

Cascio, W. F., & Boudreau, J. W. 2008. *Investing in People*. Upper Saddle River, NJ: Pearson Education.

Crotts, J. C., Ford, R. C., Heung, V. C., & Ngai, E. W. T. 2009. Organizational alignment and hospitality firm performance. *International Journal of Culture, Tourism and Hospitality Research*, 3, 3–12.

Davidson, M. C. G., Timo, N., & Wang, Y. 2010. How much does labour turnover cost? A case study of Australian four- and five-star hotels. *International Journal of Contemporary Hospitality Management*, 22, 451–466.

Deery, M. 2008. Talent management, work-life balance and retention strategies. *International Journal of Contemporary Hospitality Management*, 20, 792–806.

Gatewood, R. D., Field, H. S., & Barrick, M. 2008. *Human Resource Selection*, 6th edition. Mason, OH: Thompson.

Gross, T. S. 2004. *Positively Outrageous Service*, 2nd edition. New York: Warner Books.

Guion, R. M., & Highhouse, S. 2006. *Essentials of Personnel Assessment and Selection*. Mahwah, NJ: Lawrence Erlbaum Associates.

Hinkin, T. R., & Tracey, J. B. 2000. The cost of turnover: Putting a price on the learning curve. *Cornell Hotel and Restaurant Administration Quarterly*, 41, 14–21.

Hinkin, T. R., & Tracey, J. B. 2010. What makes it so great? An analysis of human resource practices among fortune's best companies to work for. *Cornell Hospitality Quarterly*, 51 (2), 158–170.

Huffcutt, A. I., Weekley, J. A., Wiesner, W. H., & Degroot, T. G. 2001. Comparison of situational and behavioral description interview questions for higher-level positions. *Personnel Psychology*, 54, 619–644.

Lockyer, C., & Scholarios, D. 2004. Selecting hotel staff: Why best practice does not always work. *International Journal of Contemporary Hospitality Management*, 16, 125–135.

Milman, A., & Ricci, P. 2004. Predicting job retention of hourly employees in the lodging industry. *Journal of Hospitality and Tourism Management*, 11, 23–41.

Moncarz, E., Zhao, J., & Kay, C. 2009. An exploratory study of US lodging properties' organizational practices on employee turnover and retention. *International Journal of Hospitality Management*, 21, 437–458.

Morgeson, F. P., Reider, M. H., & Campion, M. A. 2005. Selecting individuals in team settings: The importance of social skills, personality characteristics, and teamwork knowledge. *Personnel Psychology*, 58, 583–611.

Newman, J. 2007. *My Secret Life on the McJob*. New York: McGraw-Hill.

Pettersen, N., & Durivage, A. 2008. *The Structured Interview: Enhancing Staff Selection*. Quebec, Canada: Presses de l'Universite du Quebec.

Ployhart, R. E. 2004. Organizational staffing: A multilevel review, synthesis, and model. *Research in Personnel and Human Resources Management*, 23, 121–176.

Ployhart, R. E. 2006. Staffing in the 21st century: New challenges and strategic opportunities. *Journal of Management*, 32, 868–897.

Ployhart, R. E., Schneider, B., & Schmitt, N. 2006. *Staffing Organizations: Contemporary Practice and Theory*, 3rd edition. Mahwah, NJ: Lawrence Erlbaum Associates.

Ryan, A. M., McFarland, L., Baron, H., & Page, R. 1999. An international look at selection practices: Nation and culture as explanations for variability in practice. *Personnel Psychology*, 52, 359–391.

Schmitt, N., Cortina, J. M., Ingerick, M. J., & Wiechmann, D. 2003. Personnel selection and employee performance, in I. B. Weiner (ed.-in-chief) and W. C. Borman, D. R. Ilgen, and R. J. Klimoski (eds.), *Handbook of Psychology*, vol. 12. Hoboken, NJ: John Wiley & Sons.

Simons, T., & Hinkin, T. 2001. The effect of employee turnover on hotel profits. *Cornell Hotel and Restaurant Administration Quarterly*, 42, 65–69.

Sturman, M. C., & Sherwyn, D. 2009. The utility of integrity testing for controlling workers' compensation costs. *Cornell Hospitality Quarterly*, 50, 432–445.

Tracey, J. B., Sturman, M. C., & Tews, M. J. 2007. Ability versus personality: Factors that predict employee job performance. *Cornell Hotel and Restaurant Administration Quarterly*, 48, 313–322.

Wildes, V. 2007. Attracting and retaining good servers: How internal service quality moderates occupational stigma. *International Journal of Hospitality Management*, 26, 4–19.

[1]Gross, T. S. 2004. *Positively Outrageous Service*, 2nd edition. New York: Warner Books, p. 8.

[2]World's 50 best restaurants. *Restaurant Magazine*, http://www.theworlds50best.com/restaurants/restaurant_01.html, accessed April 21, 2008.

[3]Bowen, J., & Ford, R. C. 1992. Managing service organizations: Does having a "thing" make a difference? *Journal of Management*, 28, 447–469.

[4]Gross, 2004, 149.

[5]Tracey, J. B., Sturman, M. C., & Tews, M. J. 2007. Hiring for attitude and skill: The role of general mental ability and conscientious in predicting performance for new and experienced employees. *Cornell Hotel and Restaurant Administration Quarterly*, 32, 313–322.

[6]Chung-Herrera, B. G., Enz, C. A., & Lankau, M. J. 2003. Grooming future hospitality leaders: A competencies model. *Cornell Hotel and Restaurant Administration Quarterly*, 44 (3), 17–25.

[7]Johanson, M. M., & Woods, R. H. 2008. Recognizing the emotional element in service excellence. *Cornell Hospitality Quarterly*, 49, 310–316.

[8]Rupp, D. E., & Spencer, S. 2006. When customers lash out: The effects of customer interactional injustice on emotional labor and the mediating role of discrete emotions. *Journal of Applied Psychology*, 91, 971–978.

[9]Ibid.

[10]Hinkin, T., & Tracey, J. 2000. The cost of turnover: Putting a price on the learning curve. *Cornell Hotel and Restaurant Administration Quarterly*, 41, 14–21; Pfeffer, J. 2005. Producing sustainable competitive advantage through the effective management of people. *Academy of Management Executive*, 9, 95–106.

[11]Sturman, M. C., Cheramie, R. A., & Cashen, L. H. 2002. How to compare apples and oranges: Balancing the past job performance of internal candidates with selection tests of external applicants. *Cornell Hotel and Restaurant Administration Quarterly*, 43 (4), 27–40.

[12]Wong, C. 2007. Internal recruitment benefits hotel group. *South China Morning Post*, Hong Kong, July 28, 24.

[13]Berry, L. L. 1999. *Discovering the Soul of Service: The Nine Drivers of Sustainable Business Success*. New York: The Free Press, p. 45.

[14]Needleman, S. E. 2008. Demand rises for talent-management software. *Wall Street Journal On-Line*, January 15, http://online.wsj.com/article/SB120035522634389823.html, accessed July 22, 2009.

[15]http://www.marriott.com/corporateinfo/culture/Diversity.mi, accessed September 30, 2010.

[16]Susan Carey. 1998. Flight attendants master airplane Spanish (40 Words). *Wall Street Journal*, November 23, B-1.

[17]Guest relations—Individual property (150 rooms and more). 1998. *Lodging*, 23 (8), 127.

[18]U.S. Census Bureau. 2002. *Census 2000 Modified Race Data, MR(31)-CO.txt.* Washington, DC: U.S. Government Printing Office.

[19]Hinkin, T. R., & Tracey, J. B. 2010. What makes it so great? An analysis of human resource practices among Fortune's Best Companies to Work For. *Cornell Hospitality Quarterly*, 51 (2) 158–170.

[20]http://moss07.shrm.org/Publications/hrmagazine/EditorialContent/Pages/0709bptw.aspx, accessed July 14, 2009.

[21]http://www.greatplacetowork.com/best/list-bestusa-2009.htm, accessed July 14, 2009.

[22]See http://www.southwest.com/about_swa/southwest_cares/southwest_cares.html, accessed September 30, 2010.

[23]Ford, R. C., Wilderom, C. P. M., & Caparella, J. 2008. Strategically crafting a customer-focused culture: An inductive case study. *Journal of Strategy and Management*, 1, 143–167.

[24]For an extensive review of research on employment interviews, see Macan, T. 2009. The employment interview: A review of current studies and directions for future research. *Human Resource Management Review*, 19, 203–218.

[25]Gross, 2004.

[26]Johanson, M. M., & Woods, R. H. 2008. Recognizing the emotional element in service excellence. *Cornell Hospitality Quarterly*, 49, 310–316.

[27]Ones, Deniz S. 2005. Personality at work: Raising awareness and correcting misconceptions. *Human Performance*, 18 (4), 389–404.

[28]Tracey, Sturman, & Tews, 2007.

[29]See, for example, Gottfredson, L. S. 1997. Why *g* matters: The complexity of everyday life. *Intelligence*, 24, 79–132; Schmidt, F. L. 2002. The role of general cognitive ability and job performance: Why there cannot be a debate. *Human Performance*, 15, 187–210.

[30]See Hunter, J. E. 1986. Cognitive ability, cognitive aptitudes, job knowledge, and job performance. *Journal of Vocational Behavior*, 29, 340–362; Hunter, J. E., & Hunter, R. F. 1984. Validity and utility of alternate predictors of job performance. *Psychological Bulletin*, 96, 72–98; Ree, M. J., & Earles, J. A. 1992. Intelligence is the best predictor of job performance. *Current Directions in Psychological Science*, 1, 86–89; Schmitt, N., Gooding, R. Z., Noe, R. A., & Kirsch, M. 1984. Meta-analyses of validity studies published between 1964 and 1982 and the investigation of study characteristics. *Personnel Psychology*, 37, 407–422.

[31]Brinker, N., & Phillips, D. T. 1996. *On the Brink: The Life and Leadership of Norman Brinker*. Arlington, TX: The Summit Publishing Group, p. 191.

[32]Sturman, M. C., & Sherwyn D. 2009. The utility of integrity testing for controlling workers' compensation costs. *Cornell Hospitality Quarterly*, 50, 432–445.

[33]Berry, C. M., P. R. Sackett, and S. Wiemann. 2007. A review of recent developments in integrity test research. *Personnel Psychology* 60, 271–301.

[34]Arthur, W., Jr., Day, E. A., McNelly, T. L., & Edens, P. S. 2003. A meta-analysis of the criterion-related validity of assessment center dimensions. *Personnel Psychology*, 56, 125–154.

[35]Meriac, J. P., Hoffman, B. J., Woehr, D. J., & Fleisher, M. S. 2008. Further evidence for the validity of assessment center dimensions: A meta-analysis of the incremental criterion-related validity of dimension ratings. *Journal of Applied Psychology*, 93, 1042–1052.

[36]Sturman, M. C. 2001. The compensation conundrum. Does the hospitality industry short-change its employees—and itself? *Cornell Hotel and Restaurant Administration Quarterly*, 42 (4), 70–76.

[37]Newman, J. 2007. *My Secret Life on the McJob*. New York: McGraw Hill.

[38]Hinkin, T. R., & Tracey, J. B. 2000. The cost of turnover. *Cornell Hotel and Restaurant Administration Quarterly*, 41 (3), 14–21.

[39]Casio, W. F., & Boudreau, J. W. 2008. *Investing in People: Financial Impact of Human Resource Initiatives*. Upper Saddle River, NJ: Pearson Education, Inc.

CHAPTER 6

Training and Developing Employees to Serve

HOSPITALITY PRINCIPLE: TRAIN YOUR EMPLOYEES, THEN TRAIN THEM SOME MORE

The how and why of every operation may be clear as day to you, but it's clear as mud to a brand new employee. You wouldn't believe the number of employees who say "I never could figure out exactly what they wanted me to do." They usually say that on their way out the door.

—T. Scott Gross, *Positively Outrageous Service*

LEARNING OBJECTIVES

After reading this chapter, you should understand:

- The importance of training and development to hospitality organizations.

- The principles and methods used by hospitality organizations to train and develop their employees.

- Methods used by hospitality organizations to measure the effectiveness of training.

KEY TERMS AND CONCEPTS

external training

internal training

mentoring

coaching

apprenticeship

on-the-job training

cross-functional training

classroom training

simulation

audiovisual training

computer-assisted instruction

training at home

employee development

Heskett, Sasser, and Hart tell the story about a bellman at a Sheraton Hotel who when confronted with an unusual problem implemented an ingenious solution.[1] A departing guest had locked his car keys in his trunk while checking out. The car was parked in the middle of the driveway that handled all the arriving and departing traffic and, if not immediately moved, would bring the entire check-in/check-out process to a halt. The bellman called for a floor jack, which he had had the foresight to store away nearby, jacked the car up, and rolled it away from the middle of the driveway. He told the guest he had called for a locksmith, estimated how long it would take for the locksmith to arrive, and promised to keep the guest informed as events unfolded. The traffic problem was solved, the guest's car problem was promptly addressed, and the guest was spared the embarrassment of being the cause of everyone else's delay.

Teaching such resourcefulness to new employees is difficult, but every new employee in the area learned from the bellman's example what a Sheraton employee is expected to do to solve a guest's problem. The bellman had the big picture: He knew that a creative solution was expected of him, and he delivered one.

Len Berry and colleagues identified in their extensive research five key factors that customers use to judge the overall quality of service.[2] Of these five, four are directly related to the ability of the service employee to deliver service in the way the customer expects, and the fifth, on tangibles, addresses the appearance of the service employee. The first four factors are reliability (the ability of the organization and its employees to deliver service consistently, reliably, and accurately), responsiveness (the willingness of the organization's employees to provide prompt service and help customers), assurance (the employee's knowledge, courtesy, and ability to convey trust), and empathy (the employee's willingness to provide caring and individualized attention to each customer).

While the hospitality organization's service product, environment, and nonhuman components of the delivery system are clearly important in forming the guest's impression of the guest experience, guestologists know that the individual hospitality employee delivering the service can make or break the organization's relationship with the guest in each and every encounter, or moment of truth. Service marketing scholar Mary Jo Bitner sums up the research on this subject: "First and foremost, customer satisfaction depends directly and most immediately on the management and monitoring of individual service encounters."[3] Everyone remembers a truly bad service experience that was caused by an indifferent, uncaring, discourteous, or ignorant employee. One awful experience can overshadow the rest of the outstanding experiences that the customer may have had with the organization. The customer may never return. In addition, that customer may tell everyone within hearing about the one bad experience, so no one who hears will come either and, even worse, this customer may create a blog or Web site and describe the bad experience. Disney estimates that each guest has seventy-four service encounters in a single visit to its theme parks.[4] Disney managers know how important it is to manage every one of these encounters, by selecting and training the right people to provide the consistent quality of guest service that customers expect.

The impact of a negative experience on the organization's reputation can be devastating. The disappointed guest won't come back and will spread the bad word. Excellent hospitality organizations recognize the value of investing time and money on employee training and development to prevent service disasters. Engineers can design an efficient service delivery system for a great service product, and the human resources department can select the right people, but those efforts are not enough. Companies that consistently deliver high-quality guest experiences also extensively and continuously train their employees.

EMPLOYEE TRAINING

In the United States alone, roughly $100 billion is spent annually on organizational training. Although this figure translates to about $800 per employee on average, the best organizations spend a lot more. The Ritz-Carlton hotel company, for example, provides a minimum of 310 hours of training for new employees within their first year. They also pair new employees with mentors to ensure that the former understand how to do their jobs successfully.[5] Overall, they spend 10 percent of their payroll cost on training.[6] The Ritz-Carlton knows the value of ensuring that employees have the ability, skills, and knowledge to deliver the high-quality service that their customers expect.

Hospitality organizations face the special challenge of training not only in the required job or task skills; they must also teach the server how to solve inevitable problems creatively and how to interact positively with guests. A car going down the assembly line doesn't care if the auto worker has a bad attitude. The customer facing the bartender at a private club, the front desk agent at a hotel, or the ticket seller at an amusement park certainly does. Guest service employees must be trained to do the required job task consistently for each guest in real time with a sense of sincere caring, with many people looking over their shoulder. This is a major training task. It goes far beyond the simple requirements of training someone to mix a martini, check in a guest to the proper hotel room, or receive money and make change.

We shall describe three exemplary training programs, to show how outstanding organizations train their employees.

Training at Starwood Hotels

Starwood Hotels and Resorts Worldwide has an extensive portfolio of hotel brands—Sheraton, Le Méridien, Four Points by Sheraton, The Luxury Collection, Westin, Element, W Hotels, Aloft Hotels, and St. Regis—and uses a correspondingly extensive training program to ensure that they deliver the proper service product for each distinctive brand. For Starwood Hotels, the service product is all about being "on brand," and so employees must fully understand what that means.

As in most companies, new Starwood employees receive an orientation. They learn about the brand of the hotel for which they now work, the history of that specific brand and Starwood Hotels in general, and something about the entire line of Starwood brands. This general orientation sets up the next three phases of training, which over roughly the next two years are designed to build and shape employee attitudes, skills, and behaviors. These next three phases deliver what Starwood calls *service culture training*.

The phases are all about teaching employees what it means to be on brand. While the general training strategy may be universal for all Starwood Hotels, the programs are customized to each individual brand. The first phase, delivered within the first few months of employment, lays the foundation. It emphasizes the idea of branding and its link to customer loyalty. Through classroom content, shared experiences, and storytelling, new employees learn each brand's core values. They also learn the brand's success profile, which describes what success looks like for an employee of that brand.

The second phase of training, delivered a few months later, emphasizes how the employee can bring the brand's core values to life. Again, all the training is aimed at making every aspect of employee and customer experiences on brand, including specific words (e.g., employees at Westin are called "associates"; employees at W Hotels are called "talent"), conversational tone, background music, customer interactions, and so on.

The third phase of the training emphasizes how employees should be "living the brand." While the first two phases are delivered mainly through classroom instruction, the third phase takes place in a variety of non-classroom settings. It includes activities in pre-shift meetings, e-learning modules, video content, and self-learning exercises.

Overall, Starwood sees training as essential to its success. In their effort to build world-class brands, Starwood's management recognizes that all employees need to understand the unique culture, approach, and attitude associated with the brands for which they work. They believe that delivering an exceptional service experience unique to each brand will build customer loyalty to that brand, and ultimately financial success.

Training at Disney

Disney uses an extensive training program to teach new employees how to do their assigned jobs and how to deal with guests in a manner consistent with guest expectations about what the Disney experience should be and how employees who deliver it should act. Visitors to Walt Disney World Resort not only assume that employees will be competent at the technical aspects of their jobs but also have high expectations about the level of employee caring, consistency, and enthusiasm. While a street cleaner inside the Magic Kingdom can quickly learn the mechanics of operating a pickup broom and dustpan, learning how to do it the Disney way takes more time. The street sweeper is to many guests the always-handy expert on where everything is, the available extra person to snap a group photo, or the symbol of continuing reassurance that the park is clean, safe, and friendly for all. To prepare that person properly for those multiple roles is an essential training task.

Disney's innovative Traditions training program is made mandatory for all new employees from street sweepers to senior management. The program teaches everyone the company's history, achievements, quality standards, and philosophy; details the responsibilities of new cast members in creating the Disney show; and provides a tour of the property. It becomes the first exposure for new employees to the culture that unites all Disney cast members in a common bond. Here, they are taught the four parts of the Disney mission in their order of importance: safety, courtesy, show, and efficiency. They also receive an introduction to company policies and procedures, a summary of recreational and social benefits available, and an introduction and orientation to each cast member's new work area. Above all, and regardless of their job assignments, cast members learn that their foremost job requirement is creating happiness in guests. A supervisor or mentor then teaches the new employee the necessary job skills. The Traditions training is a combination of classroom experiences, with both instructors and interactive videos at Disney University, which is later followed by on-the-job training. After a set period of time, the new cast members are evaluated to ensure that the training provided was sufficient to teach them the Disney way and their individual job responsibilities.

Wall-to-Wall Training at Scandinavian Airline Services

Other organizations also appreciate the value of including every employee in a training program. When Jan Carlzon took over the ailing Scandinavian Airline Services (SAS) in 1980, he immediately recognized the deficiencies in the airline's strategy and in its employees' understanding of the airline's mission. He launched a service quality training program for all 20,000 employees that eventually cost several million dollars at a time when SAS was losing $17 million a year. Because it involved training every employee throughout the airline, this concept became known as wall-to-wall training. Karl Albrecht, the author of *At America's Service*, says, "He [Jan Carlzon] wanted the message [of service quality importance] presented in its original, compelling, unfiltered, undiminished form to every SAS employee."[7] Albrecht suggests that this was the first time a major corporation used a 100 percent training process to help create an organization-wide cultural change. Every employee, from shop workers to top managers, went through a two-day workshop entitled The New SAS.

This program was so successful in creating a total organizational enthusiasm for service excellence that Carlzon initiated a second program in 1983. This follow-up was designed to teach everyone in the organization how to read the company's financial statements. Carlzon believed that if employees could understand these statements, they would better understand where the revenues came from, where the money went, how much it cost to run the company, and how much each employee could influence profit. Carlzon said, "I didn't think I could get a 1,000 percent improvement, but I knew I could get one percent from 1,000 smaller things." The success of these wall-to-wall training efforts at SAS encouraged other organizations to train their entire workforce, including British Airways, which trained all its 37,000 employees.[8]

Hospitality service providers should be trained not only in the skills necessary to deliver the service and interaction expected; they should also be taught the company's cultural values, practices, strategies, products, and policies. This knowledge helps them figure out how to fix a problem when a customer is unhappy. Unless they understand the corporate values and beliefs, they cannot know what the company expects them to do. Because the guest defines the quality and value of the guest experience, hospitality service providers should also learn about their customers' expectations, competitors' services and strategies, industry trends and developments, and the general business environment. Even a cab driver needs to know more than how to drive a car to meet the service expectations of the rider in the back seat.

Berry's Five Training Principles

Len Berry recommends that service companies, including hospitality organizations, should follow five key principles in developing an effective training strategy[9]:

1. Focus on critical skills and knowledge.
2. Start strong and teach the big picture.
3. Formalize learning as a process.
4. Use multiple learning approaches.
5. Seek continuous improvement.

We shall discuss each of these in turn.

Critical Skills

Berry's first principle involves identifying the skills that service employees simply must have. A hospitality organization can identify these critical skills through a systematic analysis of the service, delivery systems, and staff. They can also determine them by asking their guests and employees. The guests can tell you what employee skills are related to their own satisfaction, and employees can be trained to ask the guests what it takes. The organization can survey regular customers who know the business well. Employees should become involved in the design of training as they have a pretty good idea of what critical skills they need for their positions. Ask the best service providers in the organization. Study the servers who do things well to understand what everyone else needs to learn. Study what the best do and what they know.

The Big Picture

In an earlier chapter, we stressed the importance of teaching the organization's culture to give employees a way to make sense out of their jobs and how they do them. The best organizations do this consistently and well to show employees the big picture. Teaching the big picture means teaching employees the organization's overall values, purposes, and culture, and how what they do helps the organization succeed. This is what Jan Carlzon did with SAS, and it paid handsome dividends for this organization. Once he told the employees what things they did that helped and what they did that hurt the organization, they could understand for themselves how their performance and skills added to the airline's success.

New employees in any organization are usually eager to learn the organization's core values and what the company is all about, so they can see how their jobs fit into the big picture. When an employee is later confronted with a problem situation that doesn't exist in a handbook or training manual, the core values learned and accepted during training should lead that employee to do the right thing for the customer. Since so many situations in services are unplanned and unplannable, teaching the big picture and the culture's core values is especially critical. People who are taught the values and beliefs from the first day are far more likely to make the right choice for the customer and the organization when the situation calls for both personal judgment and decisive action.

Formalized Learning

Formalizing learning refers to the process of building learning into the job, making learning mandatory for everyone, and institutionalizing that expectation. Give employees learning opportunities, and do it on company time. By putting their money where their values are, the best hospitality organizations send a strong message to employees that learning is vital to the organization and that everyone must participate.

Gaylord Palms has made a strong commitment to employee learning and linked formal training programs to the company's mission and strategic objectives. For example, it set an objective of promoting from within and designed a curriculum to teach its employees how to achieve that objective.

Varied Approaches

Because different employees will learn differently, using a variety of learning approaches is also important. Berry recommends leaving no opportunity unexplored. In addition to traditional methods, he suggests that organizations sponsor book clubs, send employees out to observe exceptional organizations in the service industry to benchmark against the best, and constantly practice the necessary skills through a variety of means.

Continuous Improvement

A commitment to continuous improvement is essential. The initial training found at most organizations provides the KSAs that enable employees to begin doing their jobs. But training shouldn't stop there. The best service organizations and their employees want continuing employee improvement through on-the-job training and supervision, special training sessions, video demonstrations, online courses, and the full range of training methods available to modern organizations.

DEVELOPING A TRAINING PROGRAM

What Do We Need to Improve?

Training should always be preceded by a needs assessment to determine if perceived organizational problems or weaknesses should be addressed by training or by some other strategy. What do we need to improve? Will training give it to us? For example, a service problem might be initially identified as a training issue, to be solved by offering servers a short training session. Upon closer examination, however, the issue might turn out to be a fault in the nonhuman part of the service delivery system. For example, constant guest complaints about slow beverage service at a local restaurant might seem at first to require training for the servers. But maybe the coolers in the beverage service area are too small. Or perhaps there are simply not enough servers on staff to manage the volume of orders. All the server training in the world cannot correct a flaw in some other part of the service delivery system.

Needs assessment takes place at three levels: organizational, task, and individual. The organizational analysis seeks to identify which skills and competencies the organization needs and whether or not it has them already. If, for example, the organizational analysis reveals a need for several new restaurant managers in the Boston market and people to fill that need are not available, the organization would initiate a training program to prepare either existing employees or new entrants to be restaurant managers in that market.

The second level of analysis is the task. What tasks need to be performed? Are they being done well, or is training needed? Most training in the hospitality industry is at the task level, either to prepare new or newly promoted employees to perform the necessary job tasks or to retrain existing employees when existing task requirements change. At the third level, that of the individual, the organization reviews the performance of people doing tasks to determine if they are performing up to job standards. For example, low customer satisfaction scores may reveal that employees need to be better trained in customer interaction skills. Once the organization has assessed its needs at these three levels, it can set up training programs to meet them. Table 6.1 shows examples of training programs commonly found in the hospitality industry.

Solving the Guest's Problem

The needs assessment also leads to identifying the objectives of training and learning goals. If the needs analysis reveals a lack of some important employee skill, the training objective would be to ensure that each employee needing that specific skill to perform effectively has it. If, for example, guest comment cards show general dissatisfaction with the effectiveness of a hotel's front desk agents in checking guests in and out, the training objective would be to improve their mastery of the check-in and check-out procedures.

With the objectives known, specific learning goals should be specified. It should be clear to both the trainer and trainee what is supposed to be learned during the training process. Continuing the above example, what do front desk agents need to learn in order to improve their mastery of the check-in and check-out procedures? Depending on the situation, it could require better customer service skills, or perhaps better knowledge of the company's information systems. Once you are clear on your learning goals, it is much more straightforward to design a training program to accomplish those specific needs. This is what is ultimately needed for a training program in order to improve employee job performance.

Guest feedback about service problems or failures should serve as an important trigger for evaluating relevant parts of the service delivery system and for considering training as one way to solve the problems. It should concern you if your guests are dissatisfied with your employees' performance, whether your needs assessment has revealed a problem or not. Training may or may not be the answer. Service failure could be a result of strategic issues (misidentifying the needs of the market), inadequate staffing (providing an insufficient quantity of staff to deliver services in expected time frames), poor selection (hiring people without the right skills or capability to learn the job), or delivery service issues (not having the right equipment to do the job correctly). The environment may cause a service failure (such as an approaching hurricane or a major earthquake that forces a resort to evacuate), and a poorly designed service delivery system can lead to poor service (e.g., the layout of the hotel kitchen and the hotel's rooms makes it impossible for room service to deliver food while still hot). Of course, training cannot fix the inadequacies that led to these failures. However, if you have enough employees to handle the demand, if your systems are properly designed, if the environment or setting doesn't interfere, if employees are ready and willing to perform, and if they have the capability to learn, training can give them the specific skills they need to provide the desired service quality and value to the customer.

Effective hospitality organizations constantly measure and monitor the performance of their staff, systems, and service products to identify problems. Many problems in delivering the guest experience are caused by the people comprising the delivery system. If managers learn about these problems quickly, either from surveying guests or from their own observations, and identify their connection to training issues, they can quickly institute corrective training to address the issue before other guests have the same problems.

External Training

Some large organizations can afford internal training departments. Others rely on individual managers, high-performing employees, and supervisors to provide the training for both new and existing employees. If companies choose to go outside, they generally turn to training consultants or independent training organizations. These **external training** companies range from small organizations with an expertise and reputation in training within some specialized area of a particular industry to large multinationals that offer training programs on just about any skill, area, or topic imaginable.

Universities and colleges are also important sources of training as their faculty members frequently have job or industry expertise and the teaching experience and ability to convey it. Many universities offer night, week-end, or online classes to accommodate degree-seeking employees who cannot attend classes during the typical workweek. Also offered are various forms of executive education, including short courses during the summer, periodic courses over the year, or custom training programs developed for specific companies. Universities offer a lot of potential options for delivering training to workforce members wanting to supplement their education and skills. The people teaching knowledge and skills to college students can also teach your employees.

TABLE 6.1   Examples of the Types of Training Programs Offered in the Hospitality Industry

Mandatory training
  EEO/diversity training
  Orientation
  Safety training

Skills-oriented training
  Basic skills training
  Computer training
  Crisis training
  Cross-functional training
  Language training
  Retraining
  Specialized skills training

Competency-oriented training
  Communications training
  Customer service training
  Ethics/values training
  Remedial/basic education
  Team training
  Wellness/health training

Managerial training
  Change-management training
  Cross-cultural training
  Leadership training
  Performance feedback and management training

© Cengage Learning 2012.

While many companies contract with training organizations that develop and deliver customized on-site training, others send their employees to more generic, often less expensive, external programs. If the required training is in a highly specialized area or if only a few people need it, a company-specific program would probably not be worth the expenditure, so employees needing training are sent outside to get it. Advanced techniques of financial management, information systems design and use, Web design, and new marketing strategies are examples of specialized programs frequently offered through universities and other organizations that provide generic training for the general public. These programs may lack specific application to the hospitality industry or firm, but on the plus side they are relatively inexpensive.

Training in even more general topics such as supervision, human relations, and service orientation is frequently available through these same organizations. Universities offer similar programs through their executive development and continuing education programs. These programs can be fairly inexpensive and one or two key employees may be sent to get important training if producing a specially tailored in-house program would cost too much. Frequently, trade associations offer programs that focus on topics of interest to their members, such as working with unions, new purchasing techniques, sanitation in food-service organizations, and the rules and regulations defined by the Americans with Disabilities Act. The common benefit of membership in trade associations is that the organizations can collectively hire an expert consultant, or use someone from a member organization who has mastered a topic to educate and train others in the industry. Trade associations also frequently offer certification programs in topic areas of interest to their members. The Educational Institute of the American Hotel and Lodging Association, Educational Foundation of the National Restaurant Association, the Professional Convention Management Association, and the Destination Marketing Association International have all developed training products for their members.

Internal Training

In-house training departments are found in larger hospitality organizations. Every major company has an **internal training** unit that provides programs to its employees. Hilton, Hyatt, Marriott, McDonald's, Holiday Inn Worldwide, Sheraton Hotels, Darden and Disney are all multiunit organizations that have internal training departments. Some companies have even set up their own "universities," such as The Ritz-Carlton's *Leadership Center*, instituted in 2000.[10] With courses like *Onboarding New Talent … Everything Matters*, *The 21st Century Luxury Experience*, and *It's All About Leadership*, the center supports the growth and expansion of the company's products and services and helps provide training to the company's employees. The Leadership Center also provides training to other companies interested in learning about The Ritz-Carlton's approach to customer service and employee development. In fact, roughly one third of the participants in the center's programs come from outside the company.[11]

Training Costs

Although some organizations keep all training in-house to preserve organizational security and culture, the usual determinant of whether to use in-house or outside training is cost. The number and location of employees who need training and the level of expertise they need to acquire determine the cost. If only a few employees need highly technical training, it will be expensive for the organization to deliver it. If the employees are scattered at multiple locations, the training will cost even more. But if those employees need only basic skills training, the organization will probably offer it internally. If many employees at a single location need training, the organization will probably find a way to do its own training. The high employee turnover that is a basic problem for many hospitality organizations can influence the decision. An organization of 2,500 employees with an annual employee turnover rate of 80 percent has the same basic training requirements for new employees as an organization of 20,000 employees with a 10 percent turnover.

Likewise, the level of expertise that the training must develop has an important impact on the training cost. If considerable employee expertise will be required, training costs will be high. Offering 100 training hours to 10 employees who will be responsible for operating a sophisticated point-of-sale electronic system, like ticket sellers in a theme park, might cost about as much as offering 5 training hours to 200 employees hired to work at a fast-food drive-through window.

TRAINING METHODS

The most common training method is on-the-job training. Other common methods are classroom presentations, simulations, audiovisual programs, home study, and computer-assisted instruction (see Table 6.2). Training programs deliver their content in varied ways. Many rely on extensive interpersonal contact, such as coaching and mentoring. Other training programs use a combination of presentation techniques with increasing emphasis on Web-based methods, as computers have become more widely available and people more comfortable with this way of learning. Table 6.2 shows a variety of training methods, ranging from those with high personal contact to those with high reliance on technology and no or little personal contact. We now discuss the characteristics of each of these programs.

TABLE 6.2   Different Methods of Employee Training

Mentoring	A formal relationship between junior and senior colleagues. The mentor gives advice regarding functioning in the organization and career development.
Coaching	One person who has necessary knowledge instructs other individuals on a one-to-one or small group basis.
Apprenticeship	Trainees spend a set period of time learning a craft or trade under the guidance of an experienced master.
On-the-job training	The employee learns the job by doing. The individual is placed in the work situation and a supervisor or coworker instructs the employee on how the job is done directly at the work station.
Cross-functional training	The trainee moves through a series of job assignments over specific time frames.
Classroom training	Content is delivered to trainees using a lecture-based format.
Simulation	The employee practices the job in a simulated work environment.
Audiovisual training	Training using video, such as through DVDs or online content.
Computer-assisted instruction	A computer program guides the trainee through a preprogrammed training course. The training is conducted on a computer, often at the schedule of the trainee, and at the trainee's desired pace.
Training at home	Self-paced and self-directed learning where individuals learn the material in his or her own time, and away from the job site.

Mentoring

Mentoring is a relationship in which an experienced manager is paired up with an individual early in the latter's career or when new to the company. The purpose of the relationship is for the experienced employee to convey interpersonal, organizational, and developmental skills. Mentoring can help employees acclimate to a new organization quicker, reduce stress by providing an efficient way for employees to get help, and allow employees to better develop their own careers within the company by using the advice of their more experienced mentors.

Research has shown mentoring to be associated with a number of beneficial outcomes, including higher job performance, motivation, satisfaction, helping of others, and lower turnover and stress.[12] It is important to point out that while the research shows a number of statistically significant relationships associated with mentoring, the size of these effects is modest. Thus, while beneficial, the overall value of mentoring should not be overestimated.

Coaching

Coaching involves a relationship between an individual (a teacher, supervisor, or trainer) and either an individual or a team of employees. Coaching requires a strong relationship between the coach and the individual(s) being trained, but it is not the same as mentoring. Whereas mentoring focuses on providing career advice, coaching focuses on building skills or competencies.

Coaching requires opportunities for both observation and feedback. Coaches need to be able to explain appropriate behaviors, articulate why certain actions need to be taken, provide suggestions to improve performance, and reinforce desired behaviors. Coaching may be conducted by outside consultants, specialists within the organization, supervisors, or by particularly skilled peers.

Apprenticeships

An **apprenticeship** is a training program that combines on-the-job training with related instruction so that a worker learns how to perform a highly skilled craft or trade. In exchange for the instruction, the apprentice works for the trainer or training organization for an agreed period of time. Apprenticeship programs can be run by individual employees, trade groups, unions, or employer associations.

Apprenticeships are historically and most typically found in construction or related jobs (e.g., carpenter, electrician, plumbing). In the hospitality industry, though, apprenticeships are still common in food-related occupations (e.g., baker, butcher, chef, pastry chef).

In the United States, apprenticeships need to be certified by the Department of Labor. Practices vary widely around the world. While apprenticeships are not very common in the United States, they are a major component of the educational system in Germany and cover many more occupations than in the United States. Apprenticeships are still common around the world, and while they share some common elements (i.e., time spent under the supervision of a master of the given craft), the nature of the programs varies by country.

On-the-Job Training

One of the best ways to learn something is to actually do it. **On-the-job training** comprises having an experienced employee help a new employee actually do the job. One-on-one supervised experiences are a typical on-the-job training method. The trainee may attend a short classroom introduction and then go to a work station, where a supervisor or trainer can demonstrate, observe, correct, and review the employee performing the required tasks. Because the skills required to do some jobs are often unique, the only cost-effective training method to perform them is to put new employees into the actual job and let them learn the job by doing them in real time, under close supervision.

Hospitality organizations use the on-the-job training technique extensively because many tasks are best learned by doing, while supervisors or coworkers with more experience are standing by to assist. Veteran servers help new ones; a new front desk clerk will often quickly find himself checking guests into the hotel, but with an experienced employee standing close by to ensure that all procedures are properly followed. Many a small organization, like Ralph's Restaurant on the corner, does the same thing. If Ralph can't hire someone with the experience he needs for one of the restaurant's many jobs, or can't afford to send a new employee to an external training course, then the most efficient and cost-effective training method is for Ralph to teach the new employee "Ralph's Way" of washing dishes, making spaghetti, or serving meals.

If managers are conducting the training, they themselves may benefit from on-the-job training as the training specialists can coach them while training their employees. Jenny Lucas, director of education and development for Loews Hotels, says, "Our training managers are out there, watching training being delivered, watching managers in action, doing spot checks, and giving feedback afterward."[13]

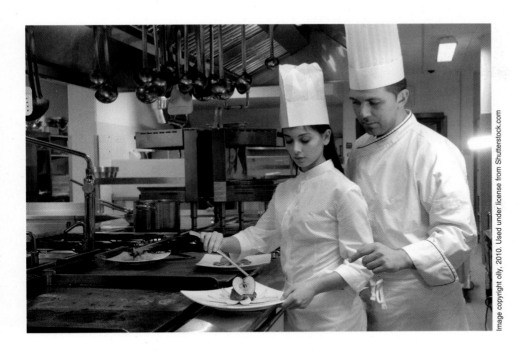

New chefs often train under the watchful eye and careful guidance of a master chef.

Besides sometimes being the only way to train an employee in a job with varied and changing duties, on-the-job training has added advantages. First, employees find out directly what the job requires because they are actually doing it. There is no question about how well the training carries over to the actual task, because the trainee is *doing* the actual task. Another advantage is that the company is actually getting some productivity out of new employees, whereas if they were in classrooms, they would not be contributing to achieving organizational goals.

Of course, on-the-job training has its drawbacks. Because the trainee is actually doing the job, errors due to lack of experience may directly affect the customer and the organization's reputation for service. The impact of poor service delivered by untrained new employees can be compounded if management does not take its commitment to on-the-job training seriously. Jerry Newman describes his first day on the job at a cash register in a fast-food restaurant.[14] At first, a manager stood with him and gave him some guidance, but once the lunch rush started, the manager disappeared to do other tasks. Although he had told Jerry "I'll be here if you need me," Jerry was left totally on his own. Customers noticed his poor performance and were not favorably impressed.

On-the-job training can be a very effective way to help employees learn a new job, but it needs to be carefully planned and implemented. Is the job one that can actually be learned by doing? Are experienced employees ready, willing, and able to provide the necessary assistance? What are the business- and service-related consequences of having a new employee learn by doing on the job? In short, learning by doing can be a great way to learn, but companies that want to preserve their reputation for providing excellent customer service do not use it to force new employees to "sink or swim."

Cross-Functional Training

Cross-functional training enlarges the workforce's capabilities to do different jobs. Gaylord's Opryland Hotel cross-trains its front desk personnel and telephone-reservation agents so that each can help out the other. The front desk often needs help when many people wish to check in or check out within a short period of time. The hotel has set up a separate registration desk in the lobby, and when the lines at the front desk begin to reach unacceptable levels, these cross-trained agents are called to the separate desk to help serve guests. Some hotels cross-train employees from many departments on how to provide banquet service. On banquet days, current employees can be temporarily redistributed rather than hiring more employees. Since all hospitality organizations have similar variability in their demand patterns, cross-functional training is often necessary to handle the sudden surge in guests at different points in the service delivery system. At the same time, it provides task variety and higher interest levels for employees, which has significant benefits in employee motivation and morale. Cross-functional training is often a win-win-win for guests, hospitality organizations, and employees.

Classroom Training

Another common training method is training in a classroom environment. **Classroom training** can follow a variety of formats. The most usual is the lecture presentation. A knowledgeable expert speaks to employees so that they will learn the necessary skill or knowledge in the available lecture time. This listen-and-learn approach is based on the assumption that an expert can train the uninformed by speaking to them. That this assumption has been questioned by research on how people actually learn doesn't seem to deter its continued use. University teachers and students alike know that not everyone listens and not everyone can learn by listening.

Nonetheless, the method has advantages: It is inexpensive, time efficient, and to the point. If a top performer in the company stands up and tells you what she knows, she may not feel the need to develop elaborate visual aids, instructional screens, or anything else that takes time and money to produce. She and the company may assume that since she has been there, done that, and done it well, she is obviously worth listening to and will have great credibility with employees. Most of the time, these assumptions prove accurate. This strategy should be combined with on-the-job training and mentoring to help reinforce the important points made in the classroom presentation.

Another basic classroom technique is the interactive case study. Here, the organization provides learners with case material for discussion. The material may be related to the skill they need to learn, or it may be material to teach the more general skills of decision making or problem solving. This technique requires a skilled facilitator, to keep the discussion focused and the learners engaged.

More recently, with the increasing organizational emphasis on teams and leadership, team-based training has become popular. Leaderless groups may be given a problem to solve or an issue to address and asked to form collaborative problem-solving teams to tackle it. People learn to work together, but they also learn about discovering and sharing the tremendous amount of knowledge that often exists within a team. Smart managers believe in training their people to take advantage of the wisdom of teams; other managers never discover their value.

The modern approach to classroom learning emphasizes learner involvement and frequently uses a mixture of educational formats to reach as many types of learners as possible. While some can learn from listening or watching, others can learn only by doing. Those facilitating classroom experiences mix short lectures or videos with case or problem discussions with role playing to engage and retain active learner interest.

Classroom learning provides an efficient means to instruct a large number of employees.

Image copyright VladKol, 2010. Used under license from Shutterstock.com

Simulation

While learning by doing is often the most effective way to train new employees in certain areas, the consequences of failure may be too great or expensive to allow the employee to fail in real time with real guests and equipment. Sometimes, employees should learn by practicing a task in a controlled and safe environment, a **simulation**.

Airlines provide the clearest example. They use sophisticated flight simulators to teach their pilots how to fly different airplanes into different airports and how to prepare for emergency situations. They create a virtual airplane with all the controls, physical layout of a cockpit, and simulated motions so that pilots flying the simulator feel like they really are flying an aircraft. You do not want to use on-the-job, real-time training to teach a pilot what to do if two of the airplane's four engines fail or if the airplane flies into a flock of seagulls and has to ditch in New York's Hudson River!

Simulation can be used in a variety of settings. Some hotel companies use employees to act as guests with a complaint in a mock check-in scenario. Often based on real experiences at the hotel, the simulation lets the new employee learn by doing without the risk of mishandling a real situation and losing a real guest's business. One luxury hotel chain uses a simulation for its new bartenders. A preset number of orders come in, and the new bartender has to make the drinks in precise proportions within a certain length of time. To help prepare everyone for the real opening night, new restaurants will often have a mock opening, with chefs making meals and servers taking orders from each other or from local dignitaries who are served a free meal.

Success in a simulation does not automatically mean success in a real situation. And simulations can be a very expensive way to train employees, even if they are not as sophisticated as flight simulators. But in situations where employees need hands-on experience to truly learn how to do their jobs and service failures are costly to risk in real time, simulations can be an effective way to teach employees the skills they need.

Learning in small groups can help develop both skills and the ability to work in teams.

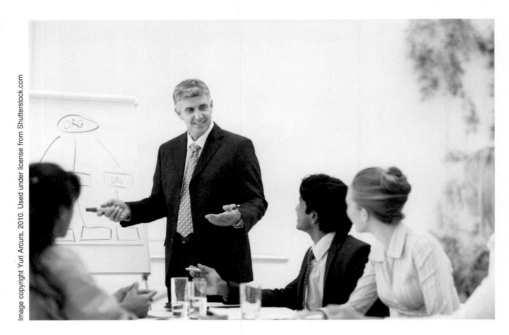

Image copyright Yuri Arcurs, 2010. Used under license from Shutterstock.com

Simulations provide a safe way for airline pilots to practice their skills without the risk of harming guests.

Image copyright Jordan Tan, 2010. Used under license from Shutterstock.com

Audiovisual Training

Another major training technique involves using videos, either through DVDs or delivered on-line, collectively referred to as **audiovisual training**. Audiovisual training is frequently used in conjunction with a live presentation as a way to bring in new material beyond the expertise of the classroom presenter or to add variety to the presentation. For many hospitality organizations, videos are a cost-effective strategy. A centralized training department can make or buy video presentations and then ship them to individual units, all over the world if need be, or host them on a Web site. Smaller, independent hospitality organizations can obtain a wealth of video instruction through either commercial retailers or their trade associations. Larger organizations often create their own.

Starwood Hotels uses DVD videos to supplement many aspects of its various training modules. Obviously, having business leaders from the entire company share their experiences with every new employee would be prohibitively costly and time consuming, so Starwood uses a DVD video presentation to provide what it calls *Lessons from Leadership*. The DVD video includes testimonials and examples from leaders throughout the company—from the corporate level (the CEO), to the different business units, to the different divisions, to property leaders—about what the service culture means to them. The use of these realistic on-the-job examples from company leaders helps teach and inspire new employees to deliver the appropriate customer service experience.

In view of the traditionally high turnover in the hotel industry and the constant need to train new employees, an instantly available video is useful and practical. New employees can watch it by themselves anytime and learn the basics of how, for example, housekeeping is to be performed in a W Hotel. Darden's restaurants uses a series of videos to educate new employees about its various restaurant brands, including Red Lobster, Olive Garden, Seasons 52, and Bahama Breeze. New servers learn how the different menu items are to be prepared and served, how guests are to be greeted, and how the waitstaff are supposed to do their job. Darden's goal for its standardized training is to teach its people to provide the same high-quality restaurant experience in every facility throughout the entire chain.

Indeed, one of video training's many advantages is to standardize the presentation of the material so that everyone learns from the same source of information and learns how to do the required tasks in the same way. Being able to offer the same high-quality experience every time in every location is quite important for a multi-unit operation like a chain, franchised restaurant, or branded hotel where guests have standardized expectations about what the organization is supposed to do, how it provides its service, and what it looks like.

DVD and online videos are also relatively cost effective when organizational locations are numerous and widely dispersed. The cost and logistics to send a corporate trainer to every location of a brand every time a new employee is hired would be prohibitive, but sending training DVD videos to every part of the world or providing access to streaming video through the Web is easy. A well-designed and well-produced video can do an excellent job of holding the new employee's attention, portraying outstanding role models of expected service behavior and stressing important points. With professional actors or star employees in a video showing the correct means of providing guest service, a new employee can see far more easily what the expected behavior is than if an instructor spoke for several hours.

Videos can also overcome language barriers. Homewood Suites created a training video to meet the needs of its multilingual housekeeping staff. The videos demonstrate procedures, but no words are used.[15] Truly, a picture is worth a thousand words when it comes to training in the highly diverse hospitality industry.

The making of videos can itself be used as a training technique. The organization can call upon its best employees in the training video's subject area and ask them to create and produce the video. Such a home-made video lets the participants see that the organization appreciates the quality of their job performance, gives them ownership in the training role, and provides live role models for the new employees to follow. Making a video is an enjoyable and status-enhancing recognition reward for service jobs well done, though it takes time away from other activities.

Streaming video, video conferencing, and Webinars (seminars conducted via the World Wide Web) are often used to conduct training simultaneously in multiple locations. Live transmissions allow participants from around the world to ask questions and interact with the instructor. Also, the content can be saved and downloaded as desired by others who need the training but could not participate in the live session.

The cost of broadcasting live training sessions to remote employees is declining rapidly. Once the company has acquired the technology to deliver this sort of training, the incremental cost of additional training sessions can be minimal. After the technology is in place, companies can have their own experts share their knowledge with the entire company, and both present and future employees can learn from the content. The increasing availability of video conference and teleconference facilities, advances in Internet technology, and the escalating costs of sending people to central training locations are making streamed and live video presentations increasingly desirable training options, especially when employees and service units are geographically dispersed. DVDs and videos come quite close to providing the just-in-time education and training that is needed in industries like hospitality where organizational requirements, guest expectations, available technologies, and employees are diverse and change rapidly.

Of course, DVDs and on demand, streaming video have limitations. The key issue is the extent to which managers and new employees take them seriously. Jerry Newman describes one example of being "trained" in the fast-food industry. He was sent into a back closet with a video player and told to come out after he had watched a training video. No one emphasized that the video was important; no one checked to see if Jerry had learned anything; no one even checked to be sure he watched the video. It was simply something that "had to get done" to satisfy a corporate policy. As is true of all forms of training, videos will work only if management is committed to their use and if trainees take them seriously.

Computer-Assisted Instruction

As with all other areas of business, technology has changed the way training can be delivered. **Computer-assisted Instruction**, such as with Webinars and streaming video, can allow interactions between instructor and learners across the world. Expertise can be delivered anytime, anyplace, to anyone who is online. These advances are expanding the reach of much classroom training and are even blurring the distinctions between classroom and at-home training. Computers can help with on-the-job training, as technology can monitor an employee's speed on check-ins, accuracy in placing orders, and so forth. For example, Choice Hotels has a training initiative called ResCoach. Distributed by CD, the program is a self-paced course that teaches the basics of telephone etiquette and reservations selling. This training is then followed up with on-site workshops, and its effectiveness is tested through three random phone calls each month to every hotel property.[16]

Hyatt has created its own Hyatt Leadership Network, which makes hundreds of training programs available to any Hyatt employee anywhere and anytime. If a manager needs refresher training on how to conduct a performance appraisal, there is a program for that. If a new property management system requires employee training on its use, there is a program for that too. The network contains so many training programs that some managers now assign specific topics as part of an employee's improvement plan to overcome weaknesses identified in a performance review.

The newer technologies mean that colleges and universities no longer have a monopoly on education in their geographical areas. These developments are a boon to the hospitality industry, as many organizations are multi-unit and geographically dispersed. Getting their people to an educational center or a centralized training program is costly, difficult, and sometimes impossible. Getting these same people to log onto the Internet is comparatively easy, and the amount of information, knowledge, and training they can obtain through this medium is enormous. Internet capabilities make just-in-time education a reality as the people needing training can log on to the appropriate site at exactly the time they need it.

Training at Home

Self-study is another major training method, and **training at home** can prove efficient and effective for both employees and organizations. Here, a trade association or private training organization produces materials that people can receive in their homes by mail or online and study at their own learning pace. When they have gone through the materials, they take an exam online, at home, or at a central location often with a proctor. The American Hotel and Lodging Association uses self-study material extensively for programs leading to industry-recognized certification and diplomas. The self-study is ideally backed up with classroom experience, but the geographic dispersion of hotels makes offering classes difficult except in cities where a lot of hotels are clustered. Universities offer online courses, allowing people to take courses on their own time and often at their own pace. Self-study courses work well in the hospitality industry; they provide skill and knowledge training in topics unique to the hotel business at times and locations convenient for employees—after hours and at home.

Further Approaches to Training

Training can be very specific or somewhat general. The specific is typically used for new entrants who must quickly start performing a job skill well to justify their salary. Consequently, the major training costs tend to be for skills training. It can cover a wide variety of topics, ranging from literacy to complex electronic systems. According to the American Management Association, companies report that over one-third of applicants tested by major U.S. companies lacked sufficient reading and math skills to do the job they sought. Some restaurateurs even find it necessary to teach employees basic hygiene, including teaching food handlers how to wash their hands.

Large hotels may need to provide training just to teach new employees to know their way around. The Wynn hotel and resort complex in Las Vegas has a novel training program for new employees. The resort is so large—with dozens of places to eat, an extensive casino environment, many shops, a nightclub, a theatre, and so on—that new employees need the basic skill of knowing to their way around the property. To help acquaint them with the entire facility, they are asked to participate in a scavenger hunt, searching the property for artwork, items, landmarks, and so forth, and in the process they learn about the entire resort.

There are other types of training that companies offer for specific outcomes. For example, *retraining* is often made available to employees who have burned out, have become unable to perform their current jobs because of technological developments, or whose jobs have been eliminated. Disney has operated a retraining program for many years that tries to sprinkle "Pixie Dust" on employees who have become disenchanted with their present jobs or have otherwise lost their enthusiasm. In the program, it retrains such employees for new jobs that might help them recapture their enthusiasm or rethink why they are unhappy with their existing jobs, to regain the spirit of doing it the way the guests expect.

To encourage employees to be more effective and responsive to guests, outstanding hospitality organizations offer *training in special competencies*, such as working as a team, creative problem solving, communications, relationships, leadership, and guest service orientation. These organizations realize that having the job skills is only part of the service requirement for their employees.

Companies have learned that *diversity training*, attitudinal training, and other efforts to change how people look at other people can have significant payoffs in improving the way their service employees interact with each other and with the many types of guests. There are more than fifty languages spoken by employees at the Waldorf Astoria in New York City, and employees come from an even greater number of different cultural backgrounds. In today's diverse environment, companies need to train employees in how to get along with and understand each other and their guests.

The Message: Guest Service

One benefit of training is to remind the employees of what management thinks is important. Sending people to a training program that focuses attention on service sends a powerful message to all employees that management cares enough about both its commitment to service and its employees to invest time and money in its people to improve service quality. Any training tends to make employees feel more positively about the topic covered because they recognize the training as a visible show of organizational commitment to improve the area.

CHALLENGES AND PITFALLS OF TRAINING

While training can help a company prepare its employees to provide excellent service, problems often arise. Common causes are a failure to establish training objectives, measure results, and analyze training costs and benefits.

Know Your Training Objectives

Training programs can run into trouble if the precise nature and objective of the training are unknown or imperfectly defined, or if the expected outcome of the training is hard to define or measure. Such programs are hard to justify or defend when senior management reviews the training budgets. Typical examples of areas in which the effectiveness of training is difficult to measure are *human relations* and *supervisory skills*. Since these terms are vague and situationally defined, knowing what and how much training to offer to improve trainees in these areas and how to measure results is difficult. Hospitality organizations quite naturally want their employees to have a service orientation, but the concept is as hard to define as it is to know whether the training has resulted in such an outcome. Such training is important, without question. What exactly that training should be and how to measure its effectiveness are much more difficult to determine.

Measuring Training Effectiveness

If you don't know what your training is or is not accomplishing, you cannot know whether it is making your organization more effective. Four basic measurement methods are available to assess training's effectiveness.[17] These approaches range in complexity, expense, and accuracy.

Participant Feedback

The easiest, cheapest, and most commonly used measure of assessing training effectiveness is to simply ask the participants what they think about it. They fill out a questionnaire based on general evaluation criteria and respond to questions such as "How valuable was this training?". Although asking such questions has merit, responses to these questionnaires tend to reflect the entertainment value of the training rather than its effectiveness. Such evaluations, therefore, have relatively little usefulness for accurate program evaluation. They tell you if the participants enjoyed the training, but not much more.

Content Mastery

Another way to assess a training program is to test participants for content mastery. After all, if the point of the training was to learn a specific skill, competency, or content area, it should be possible to design a test to determine whether participants learned what they were supposed to learn. These measures can be as simple as paper-and-pencil tests similar to academic exams or as elaborate as on-the-job demonstrations of how well participants mastered the skill.

Of course, doing well on a test does not mean that the employee will retain that knowledge or use it on the job. Such evaluations also run the risk of having instructors "teach to the test," essentially training people how to do well on the final exam and not necessarily how to be better performing employees.

Behavioral Change

A more advanced level of training evaluation is to assess the behavioral change in the participant. Many people quickly forget what they learn in classroom settings, especially if they don't apply it. "Use it or lose it," as the saying goes. College students often say they learn a subject well enough to get through the final exam and then flush all the information out of their brains. To be effective in any meaningful way, training must be followed by real and lasting behavioral changes when the employee returns to the job. If the training is well designed, and connected to mastering specific service-related behaviors that are reinforced by positive results on the job, then positive, measurable behavioral change should result.

One function of supervisors is to evaluate the behaviors of their subordinates. If the training affects subordinate behaviors, then the training results should be included in supervisory evaluations. Supervisors can observe employee behaviors and assess the extent to which the desired behaviors are exhibited. Companies can also use mystery shoppers to find out what behaviors their employees exhibit when interacting with guests. Feedback from actual customers concerning employee behavior is also a valuable way to learn if the training was effective.

Organizational Performance

The ultimate and most sophisticated level of evaluating training effectiveness is to watch what happens to the measures of overall organizational performance. The training may be well received, the employees may remember most of it upon completion, and they may continue to use it on the job, but the training is useless unless it eventually contributes to overall organizational effectiveness. To maintain the organization's competitive position, the training objectives, and the training program require constant monitoring to make sure they continue to prepare employees to provide the level of service expected by an ever-changing customer.

The problem with this sort of training evaluation is that it is difficult to know precisely how organizational results change due to a specific training program. If booking agents receive training and then room occupancy increases, is this increase a result of the training or changes in the economy? If front desk agents receive customer service training and then scores on measures of customer satisfaction improve, how confidently can the company attribute the gain to the training program? Knowing the exact effects of training on organization-level outcomes is very difficult.

Even so, organizations must try. One way to approach this is to measure changes in key outcomes, like the number of guest complaints before and after training or customer satisfaction ratings. Or an organization could use paid mystery shoppers to sample the level of service before and after the training. The point of any such technique is to measure the value added by training. With no "before" measurement, the organization has little way to know if the measurement after the training represents any improvement. Here, larger organizations have an advantage as they can use people from different parts of their organization to test different types of training and statistically determine whether or not one training type is more effective than another in terms of reducing guest complaints or increasing positive comments. Another strategy might be for the organization to survey the attitudes of its own employees toward guests both before and after the training. Since there is a positive relationship between guest and employee attitudes, measuring employee attitudes can indicate how your guests will perceive the service experience before and after training.

While measuring the impact of training on the organization as a whole is quite challenging, all training programs should nonetheless be implemented with the goal of increasing organizational effectiveness. Training should help make your employees more effective, which should ultimately result in greater customer satisfaction, greater market share, higher profits, and other key results.

Getting Good Value from Training

Training programs have obvious direct costs, but they involve indirect or opportunity costs as well; all the time that trainees and instructors spend away from their regular jobs costs money. Training is too expensive for the organization to train everybody in everything, so it must try to get the best value for its money by using those training programs that give the greatest positive results for the training dollar expended. Too many organizations fall victim to consultants selling programs of unproven usefulness and value. Organizations should make the effort to ascertain the value of each training program, and they should assess if each training program provides the desired results and greater guest satisfaction.

When a Great Training Program Can Hurt You

Sometimes, even a great training program can have negative results. Some companies find hiring trained employees away from competitors is easier and less expensive than developing their own training programs. For example, employees from The Ritz-Carlton are very marketable, as competing luxury hotels know that these employees have been given excellent preparation and training in their jobs. Similarly, one chain of Japanese steak houses spends almost no money on training its chefs; instead, the owners travel to competing restaurants and try to find chefs who are already excellent at what they do. This restaurant chain finds that providing higher pay to attract another organization's experienced chefs is more cost effective than training new chefs and paying them until they become as proficient as desired. The same sort of "hunting" or "poaching" of employees occurs in many sectors of the service industry, including casino dealers, restaurant servers, and tour guides.

The Ritz-Carlton knows that it risks losing its investment in well-trained employees. Its strategy is to not only provide exceptional training on how to deliver the top-level service in which it takes pride but also to select employees who find their fit into The Ritz-Carlton culture to be so strong that they will stay. The Ritz-Carlton also knows that showing employees opportunities for growth in the company is another way to help retain their highly trained employees. No matter what retention strategies a company uses, the fact remains that it is not only the guests who can recognize exceptional training. Competitors can see it too, and so the risks associated with providing such training should be kept in mind.

EMPLOYEE DEVELOPMENT

Norman Brinker of Chili's said, "People either shrivel or grow. Commit to helping people help themselves."[18] Walt Disney said, "Get in. Be part of it and then move up."[19] CEOs of the best hospitality organizations agree. They provide many opportunities for employees to grow and develop, and they give employees the opportunity to work their way up through their individual efforts. Employee growth can be facilitated by means of the many techniques covered in this chapter. Organizations should make it possible for employees with ambition, ability, and a willingness to expend the effort to rise as high as they want to. Career paths should be made available and visible. The current leaders of many hospitality organizations took advantage of the educational opportunities and the promotional paths available and worked their way to the top. When each entry-level employee can see the same possibility, it provides a general feeling of opportunity for all. The desire to learn, the encouragement of learning, and the assumption that learning can lead to advancement should be an important part of the organization's culture.

Employee development involves a combination of work experience, education, and training. Training typically focuses on teaching people how to do the new jobs for which they have been hired or to overcome deficiencies they may have in performing their current jobs. Employee development, on the other hand, is typically focused on getting people ready for their future. Training tends to look at the present to identify and correct employee deficiencies in performing the job today. Development looks forward to identify the skills, competencies, and areas of knowledge that the employee will need in order to be successful tomorrow. One problem with employee development is that knowing exactly what the future will bring is impossible. Therefore, employee development programs tend to emphasize more general managerial, problem-solving, and leadership skills. Measuring these general development programs and evaluating their effectiveness is difficult.

Career Paths and the Right Experience

Preparing for Organizational Needs

In spite of the challenges in predicting what the future will bring, organizations need to prepare for how they will meet it. Many companies plan to grow and they need to have people who are ready to rise to higher-level positions as that expansion occurs. Current expansion in China and India, for example, will see the opening of thousands of new hotels over the next twenty years. These hotels will need general managers, executive teams, trainers, managers, supervisors, and staff. You cannot prepare for this sort of expansion without giving careful consideration to where the people will come from and what KSAs they will need in order to perform well in those positions.

Companies often want employees to follow certain preferred career paths that will effectively prepare them to move up into future assignments. For example, some hotel chains require their employees to have a full range of experiences, in the front-of-house, back-of-house, marketing, sales, food and beverage, and rooms divisions, before they can be considered for general manager positions. Ensuring that these experiences are provided for potential managers in a chain with dozens of hotels takes careful planning and career tracking of employees.

The most effective organizations know that they cannot simply promote someone from a functional task into a management position and hope for the best. Training must be designed to help newly promoted managers make the transition, but the employee must already possess at least some of the necessary knowledge and skills that turning a "super doer" into a supervisor will require.

Giving Employees the Chance to Advance

Employees tend to believe that the longer a person is with a company, the more that person is worth to the company. Many organizations support that belief by celebrating anniversary dates with parties and pins to show that the organization recognizes and appreciates the employee's commitment to the organization.

However, pins and parties are not enough. The outstanding service organizations recognize that most, but not always all, individuals' need for personal growth and development must also be satisfied in well-designed career development paths. The hotel housekeeper should be able to see a path upward through the organization that can be successfully traveled with hard work, dedication, and effort. Too many organizations typecast their employees, and these people know that no one expects them to go very far. Indeed, some employees lack the ability, training, or desire to move up and are satisfied with their present positions. Trying to convince a successful bellman at a resort hotel to abandon his tip money and move up as front desk manager is a tough sell because many bellmen are not willing to give up their higher income (much of it in tips) for the lower salary of an entry-level manager with only the hope of long-term career growth prospects.

On the other hand, very few people picture themselves doing in the far future the same thing they are doing today. Humans have a need to grow and develop. People who are helping the organization succeed today should also be getting prepared to help it succeed in the future, and most of them want to. The outstanding organizations provide career paths with development support that give talented people the opportunity to realize their dreams.

The opportunity is symbolically important, even if employees don't choose to take it. For example, the Gaylord Palms Resort sets as a goal to get 60 percent of its leadership from internal promotions. To do so, it offers three levels of leadership training. The first and most basic level is offered to all its employees (STARS). The second is for individuals who have been promoted into leadership positions and is designed to give them the tools and skills to help them be effective in their new roles. The third level, for those in positions above entry leadership, provides advanced training in the core processes and procedures needed to operate the hotel, with a special emphasis on the finance and people sides of the business.[20] Even those Gaylord employees who do not enter the leadership program appreciate the fact that their organization makes the opportunity available to any who aspire to lead.

Education

While experience and in-house training are clearly valuable in the preparation for some tasks, certain jobs require formal education. For example, knowledge of accounting, finance, human resources, information systems, marketing, and organizational behavior is necessary for taking on many managerial roles in modern businesses. Chefs are often required to have formalized instruction. Academics, such as the authors of this book, strongly believe that formalized education can help train people to perform well in new areas, think critically, and communicate more effectively. These skills, available primarily through formal education, may be the best way to prepare today's employee for the unknown challenges of tomorrow's competitive environment. Some companies make sure to provide opportunities for employees to get the education that they need to grow and develop within the organization.

Tuition Refunds

A good example of how to provide formal education is the traditional employee tuition-refund policy that many organizations use to encourage employee development. Companies may pay tuition in advance for certain programs, or they may reimburse employees upon the successful completion of a course. Of course, the providing of such programs needs to be thought out in advance. Will employees have to reimburse the company for education payments if they leave the company within a certain length of time? What is *successful* completion of a course? A? A or B? Not failing? And what courses should employees be allowed to take?

Companies may want to reimburse only for courses directly related to the employee's existing job. This limitation controls the potential tuition expense and makes it more likely that the organization will receive some direct business value for the expense. On the other hand, it might be better for both the company and the employees if the company pays for any course regardless of field. Doing so expands the total pool of knowledge available to the organization. Consider what could happen if a group of people who are studying different topics in different majors are brought together in a quality circle or problem-solving group session to work on an organizational matter. A variety of learning experiences expands the creative potential of both the employees and the organization and, therefore, increases the possibility of finding new and innovative ways to perform existing jobs and prepare for the future.

Supporting General Education

Supporting any legitimate employee effort to improve, grow, and learn is in the employer's interest. Such support lets employees know that the organization values their potential as much as it values their current contributions. Even more important is employee awareness that the company supports a learning environment. An organization that actively promotes learning of all kinds sends a powerful message to its employees that it believes the only way it will stay competitive is to learn continuously. These learning organizations promote the active seeking of new knowledge that not only benefits the individual but the entire organization by building its total pool of knowledge. No matter how irrelevant the material may seem, the creative employee will use it to connect to organizational needs.

The organization will eventually benefit from whatever creativity the educational experience spurred and from the increased loyalty and feeling of support that any employee gets from working for an organization that supports employee learning. Forward-looking organizations understand that most of their profits in ten years will come from products or services they don't even know about today. Restricting educational reimbursement programs to those courses the organization thinks are important today may be as erroneous as trying to predict which products will be around ten years from now.

On the other hand, companies are in business to make money, and the present needs of the business must often be put ahead of the employee's needs for long-term growth and development, important though they may be. Obviously, not all employers can afford to let all employees take time off for tuition-paid courses, nor can many employers even pay partial subsidies for classes taken on an employee's own time. In difficult economic periods, companies may have to worry more about which employees to lay off than about funding coursework that may have some return in the future. Employee development, like any business cost, must be considered in the context of the broader business picture. While supporting employee growth needs is desirable and beneficial, business needs must come first if the organization hopes to survive in the long run.

The Competition Is Watching

While paying attention to immediate business needs is critically important, many organizations are too short-sighted and don't offer any development programs. Their employees may feel permanently stuck where they are and, as a result, may feel that the only path to career advancement lies in opportunities outside their present company. Some organizations seem to think that keeping their best service employees at the guest-contact level is smart. Their employees are likely targets for competitors, who seek out stuck people and invite them to join an opportunity to grow and develop.

At Outback

A good example of an organization that provides advancement opportunities at the managerial level is Outback Steakhouses. The company starts by recruiting the best restaurant operators it can find. Then, it offers them something most corporate restaurants do not: a chance to participate financially in their own restaurant. Many restaurant operators share a common dream of running their own restaurant. They will tell you that they will work for someone else only until they can save up enough money to buy their own. Outback has recognized this dream and has invited the best operators to run Outback restaurants with an ownership interest. This part-ownership gives them a direct payoff for their ability to run their restaurants well through sharing in the profits that they help to generate. It is a true win-win for both Outback and the operator. Outback gains excellent restaurant operators, and for a relatively small financial commitment, the operators gain an equity interest in an excellent restaurant.

They Want Your Best

At least some of your competitors will always seek to hire your best people. Scott Gross is out in your restaurant or resort right now, handing his business card to your best employees. Ignoring the needs of the employee to grow and develop may be a money-saving short-run strategy, but it will be a long-run expense. Not giving employees opportunities to grow means that the hospitality organization itself may not grow and develop either. The best employees you need for your future can always find opportunities elsewhere to use their talents if you don't give them the chance. The key idea behind organization development is that everyone must continue to grow and develop. Skill and knowledge development is a continuous process. It must be ongoing to meet the ongoing changes in the guest's expectations. It is a never-ending journey.

LESSONS LEARNED

1. Teach employees not only job-related skills but also interpersonal skills and creative problem-solving techniques.

2. Do not train just to do training; know what outcomes you expect from your training dollars, and measure your training results to be sure you get them.

3. Before training people, check the delivery system technology; the problem may lie there.

4. Develop your people for your organization's future.

5. Do more than just believe in your people; champion their training and development.

6. Reward behaviors learned through training to keep them alive.

REVIEW QUESTIONS

1. Virtually all organizations give their employees some training.

   A. "Training frontline employees is more important to hospitality organizations than to manufacturing organizations, because hospitality employees are dealing with people, not widgets." Do you agree or disagree? Discuss.

   B. How can organizations try to find out if the training they provided was effective? Can they ever be sure?

2. This chapter presents Berry's five principles of training. How would you set up a training program to apply these principles to restaurant servers?

3. How should a training program for fine dining and casual dining waitstaff be different?

4. The chapter presents several types of training. Match several of those training types to employee types and job types. For example, which techniques described in the chapter might be most effective with restaurant servers? Ride operators at a theme park? Agents at an information booth on a cruise ship?

   A. How do you like to be trained or instructed? Which method or methods work best for you, and why?

   B. If the class shares responses to that last question, how do you account for the differences among students?

C. How does all that relate to managing the guest experience in hospitality organizations?

5. What does it mean to *develop* employees anyway? Why is it particularly important to develop employees in hospitality organizations?

6. Some types of hospitality organizations typically experience (and accept) a high rate of entry-level employee turnover. Do you think these organizations should develop their entry-level employees to reduce turnover? Or would they simply be spending money to develop employees who will be moving on anyway, possibly to competitors?

ACTIVITIES

1. Interview three friends who have held jobs. Find out which of the chapter's training methods were used to train them. To what extent were any of your friends "developed" as well?

2. Divide into groups. For the group members who have held jobs, make a list of the different training methods that their organizations used. How are they similar to or different from the methods described in the text?

3. The next few times you visit a service provider, take particular notice of your servers. Although you did not see the training they received, do they seem to be conforming to some training and doing the job as it was designed to be done? If not, where are they going wrong, and why?

4. Interview four employees at a restaurant or hotel to discuss their training. Report your findings to the class.

ETHICS IN BUSINESS

In service jobs, training often involves in some ways "manipulating" the customer. This could be training a service worker how to calm down an angry customer, or might go as far as how to manipulate a customer to purchase a product even if the customer may not really need it. Ethically, when does this sort of training go too far? Servers can be trained to perform certain actions in order to increase tips. This may not improve the level of service, but creates subtle changes that research has shown have led to larger tip sizes. Is this appropriate? Salespeople can be trained to identify psychological characteristics of a potential customer and make a sales pitch in a way that evidence suggests is more likely to get that customer to agree to a purchase. Some employees are trained in high pressure sales techniques, based on the evidence that some customers are effectively manipulated in this way, resulting in sales of products that the customer may not really need. What level of customer "manipulation" is ethically appropriate? Can anything be justified in terms of increasing organizational profits as long as it is not illegal, or should companies have additional standards?

CASE STUDIES

The Beef and Reef Mystery Guest

Sally Salkind has worked for two years as a server at the Beef and Reef Restaurant while getting her degree in hospitality management. As a national restaurant chain, the Beef and Reef has specific written standards about how guest service should be provided and posts those standards in the kitchen, where all employees can see them. The chain also allows local managers considerable latitude in training employees and providing service, so long as unit financial results are satisfactory. Most of the servers go "by the book" in serving guests, figuring that the company knows best and that they can't go wrong by following company standards. But Sally has developed her own very successful way of opening the service encounter and delivering service thereafter. Since manager Bill Gordy has had nothing but good things to say about her performance, she has continued to serve guests in her own style. Apparently the guests like it; her tips are among the highest and her average check is the highest in the restaurant.

Early one evening, the manager, Bill Gordy, informed the servers of a rumor he had heard at a national meeting: corporate headquarters intended to use more mystery shoppers in the following month. He said, "I know you all do the best job possible, and I appreciate it, but next month, let's all lift our service to a new level." About two weeks later, as Sally Salkind started to walk to greet a couple who had just been seated, Bill Gordy whispered to her, "Mystery shoppers. I can tell them a mile away. Do it by the book, Sally, and you'll be fine."

Sally tried to do it by the book: "Good evening. I'm Sally and I'm going to be your server tonight." But then she got tongue-tied. She couldn't remember if procedure called for her to solicit a beverage order, recite the specials, or encourage the party to choose an appetizer. The rest of the meal went the same way. The party of two had to ask for information that Sally usually related in her comfortable, natural way. But when called upon to do it by the numbers, she couldn't remember what the numbers were. She had never been so happy to see two people leave.

Several days later, Bill Gordy called Sally into his office and reprimanded her for not following standard serving procedures at the very time when following procedures was most important.

"Sally, I had been considering promoting you to head server, but I can't promote somebody who can't follow simple instructions."

Sally went quickly from surprise, to shock, to anger. She asked Bill Gordy why, if the procedures posted on the kitchen wall were so important, he had never said anything about them in her two years with the restaurant.

"I'm not dumb, Bill. I can learn as well as anyone. But you never told me that I had to learn that stuff, much less taught me how to do it. You threw me in the water, and, fortunately, I could swim. I did darn well on my own, using my own talents plus some things I learned in my hospitality courses. How can you expect me to change my whole way of doing things with 20 seconds notice?"

Bill Gordy didn't have an answer for Sally's question. He simply reiterated his criticism, told her that she had embarrassed him and the restaurant in front of "a big shot from headquarters," and sent her back to her station.

Sally had been thinking of trying to get a permanent position with the Beef and Reef organization after she finished her studies, but she decided that she didn't want to work for an outfit that gave her little training in how to do the job, complimented her for the way she did it, then criticized her because she didn't follow formal procedures and memorize the silly little phrases. She would stick around for now because the tip income was good, but she would be looking.

* * *

1. What went wrong? Who was at fault?

2. Discuss the pros and cons of a strict set of serving standards for everybody.

Flint Hill Beef and Lamb

Just before graduating with a degree in hospitality management, Sally Salkind interviewed with several hospitality organizations. She was most impressed with Beef and Lamb, a medium-sized restaurant chain founded by Bob Beef and Larry Lamb. She was particularly impressed that Bob and Larry had come to campus to do the interviewing themselves.

Sally got along well with Bob and Larry. They invited her to corporate headquarters for further interviews, and the impression she made on other Beef and Lamb executives was exceeded only by the impression that they made on her. On the second day of her interview series, she was surprised to be offered a selection of several assistant manager positions in different cities. She had relatives and friends in central North Carolina, so she picked Flint Hill, NC, a growing community near Charlotte. The week after her college graduation, she headed for Flint Hill exuberant with optimism.

Smith Hamilton, manager of the Flint Hill Beef and Lamb, had only the day before been told that he was being sent an assistant manager. When Sally entered the restaurant, eager to begin the career that she had trained for, make a good impression, and justify the faith that Larry and Bob had shown in her, Smith Hamilton barely gave her the time of day. He told her he was busy but said that she should "make herself useful." Sally was quite surprised to receive such a reception at the local level, since she had been treated so beautifully by the company founders, but she resolved not to be down about it.

Sally spent her first day walking around in the restaurant, meeting people, taking notes, asking questions of employees and guests, and generally getting the lay of the land. Since Smith Hamilton was too busy to talk to her on the second day, she spent it in much the same way. By the end of the week, with no help from Hamilton, Sally had gathered valuable information, given it much thought, and saw numerous ways in which the already successful operation of the restaurant could be improved.

The next day, she made her presentation to manager Smith Hamilton. She was too excited to notice that he kept looking at his watch. When she finished, he said: "Young lady, I have made money with this Beef and Lamb restaurant every year since I have been here. I have 18 years of experience in the business, and I've got this restaurant set up just like I want it. Sure, I never went to college, but I know the food business. All you have is book learning. These ideas of yours might look good on a homework assignment, but they will not work in Flint Hill, North Carolina. I don't want all these 'point of sale' machines you talk about; they aren't worth the money. Neither are any of your other ideas. Maybe you ought to interview with Beef and Reef; your highfalutin college notions might be just what that outfit needs. Or you can stick with me and learn something about the restaurant business."

★ ★ ★

1. How did things go so wrong?

2. Should Sally bear any part of the blame? Should the institution where she received her training in hospitality bear some blame?

3. If you were Sally, what would you say to Smith Hamilton, and what would you do? Would you "stick with him and learn something about the restaurant business"?

ADDITIONAL READINGS

Anderson, D. N., Groves, D. L., Lengfelder, J., & Timothy, D. 2001. A research approach to training: A case study of mystery guest methodology. *International Journal of Contemporary Hospitality Management*, 13, 93–102.

Baum, T. 2002. Skills and training for the hospitality sector: A review of issues. *Journal of Vocational Education and Training*, 54, 343–364.

Baum, T., & Devine, F. 2007. Skills and training in the hotel sector: The case of front office employment in Northern Ireland. *Tourism and Hospitality Research*, 7, 269–280.

Blanchard, P. N., & Thacker, J. W. 2010. *Effective Training: Systems, Strategies, and Practices*, 4th edition. Upper Saddle River, NJ: Prentice Hall.

Colquitt, J. A., LePine, J. A., & Noe, R. A. 2000. Toward an integrative theory of training motivation: A meta-analytic path analysis of 20 years of research. *Journal of Applied Psychology*, 85, 678–707.

Ellis, A. P. J., Bell, B. S., Ployhart, R. E., Hollenbeck, J. R., & Ilgen, D. R. 2005. An evaluation of generic teamwork skills training with action teams: Effects on cognitive and skill-based outcomes. *Personnel Psychology*, 58, 641–672.

Grau-Gumbau, R., Agut-Nieto, S., Llorens-Gumbau, S., & Martinez-Martinez, I. M. 2002. Managerial training needs: A study of Spanish tourism organizations. *Tourism and Hospitality Research*, 3, 234–244.

Hicks, G. J., & Walker, M. D. 2008. Training in the timeshare industry. *Tourism and Hospitality Research*, 6, 296–300.

Kline, S., & Harris, K. 2008. ROI is MIA: Why are hoteliers failing to demand the ROI of training? *International Journal of Contemporary Hospitality Management*, 20, 45–59.

Magnini, V. P., & Honeycutt, E. D., Jr. 2005. Face recognition and name recall: Training implications for the hospitality industry. *Cornell Hotel and Restaurant Administration Quarterly*, 46, 69–78.

Maxwell, G., Watson, S., & Quail, S. 2004. Quality service in the international hotel sector: A catalyst for strategic human resource development? *Journal of European Industrial Training*, 28, 159–182.

Noe, R. A. 2005. *Employee Training and Development*, 3rd edition. New York: McGraw-Hill.

Poulston, J. 2008. Hospitality workplace problems and poor training: A close relationship. *International Journal of Contemporary Hospitality Management*, 20, 412–427.

Rivera, M., DiPietro, R. B., Murphy, K. S., & Muller, C. C. 2008. Multi-unit managers: Training needs and competencies for casual dining restaurants. *International Journal of Contemporary Hospitality Management*, 20, 616–630.

Smith, E., & Kemmis, R. B. 2010. What industry wants: Employers' preferences for training. *Education and Training*, 52, 214–225.

Tews, M. J., & Tracey, J. B. 2009. Helping managers help themselves: The use and utility of on-the-job interventions to improve the impact of interpersonal skills training. *Cornell Hospitality Quarterly*, 50, 245–258.

Tracey, J. B., & Tews, M. J. 1995. Training effectiveness: Accounting for individual characteristics and the work environment. *Cornell Hotel and Restaurant Administration Quarterly*, 36 (6), 36–42.

Winfred, A., Jr., Bennett, W., Jr., Edens, P. S., & Bell, S. T. 2003. Effectiveness of training in organizations: A meta-analysis of design and evaluation features. *Journal of Applied Psychology*, 88, 234–245.

NOTES

[1]Heskett, J. L., Sasser, W. E., Jr., & Hart, C. W. L. 1990. *Service Breakthroughs: Changing the Rules of the Game*. New York: The Free Press, p. 109.

[2]Parasuraman, A., Zeithaml, V. A., & Berry, L. L. 1988. SERVQUAL: A multiple-item scale for measuring consumer perceptions of service quality. *Journal of Retailing*, 64, 12–40.

[3]Bitner, M. J. 1990. Evaluating service encounters: The effects of physical surroundings and employee responses. *Journal of Marketing*, 54, 69–82.

[4]Bitner, M. J. 1995. Building service relationships: It's all about promises. *Academy of Marketing Science*, 23, 248.

[5]http://corporate.ritzcarlton.com/en/Careers/FAQs.htm, accessed August 31, 2009.

[6]Gavin, T., Johnson, G., & Barbian, J. 2003. The 2003 training top 100. *Training*, 40 (3), 18–38.

[7]Albrecht, K. 1988. *At America's Service: How Your Company Can Join the Customer Service Revolution*. New York: Warner Books, p. 185.

[8]Ibid.

[9]Berry, 191.

[10]http://corporate.ritzcarlton.com/en/LeadershipCenter/Default.htm, accessed October 1, 2010.

[11]Johnson, G. 2003. Nine tactics to take your corporate university from good to great. *Training*, 40 (7), 38–42.

[12]Eby, L. T., Allen, T. D., Evans, S. C., Ng, T., & DuBois, D. 2008. Does mentoring matter? A multidisciplinary meta-analysis comparing mentored and non-mentored individuals. *Journal of Vocational Behavior*, 72, 254–267.

[13]Dolezalek, H. 2008. We train to please. *Training*, 45 (3), 34–35.

[14]Newman, J. 2007. *My Secret Life on the McJob*. New York: McGraw Hill.

[15]Acculturate, educate and Motivate. 2004. *Training*, 41 (12), 10–11.

[16]Outstanding training initiatives. 2006. *Training*, 43 (3), 64–66.

[17]Kirkpatrick, D. L. 1994. *Evaluating Training Programs: The Four Levels*. San Francisco, CA: Berrett-Koehler.

[18]Brinker, Norman, & Phillips, Donald T. 1996. *On the Brink: The Life and Leadership of Norman Brinker*. Arlington, TX: The Summit Publishing Group, p. 194.

[19]Walt Disney. 1994. *Famous Quotes*, p. 55. Printed for Walt Disney Theme Parks and Resorts.

[20]Ford, R. C., Wildermon, C. P. M., & Caparella, J. C. 2008. Strategically crafting a customer-focused culture: An inductive study. *Journal of Strategy and Management*, 1, 143–167.

CHAPTER 7

Serving with a Smile: Motivating Exceptional Service

HOSPITALITY PRINCIPLE: MOTIVATE AND EMPOWER YOUR EMPLOYEES

Profit is the applause you get for taking care of your customers and creating a motivating environment for your people.

—Ken Blanchard, in *Leading at a Higher Level*

People often say that motivation doesn't last. Well, neither does bathing—that's why we recommend it daily.

—Zig Ziglar, author, salesperson, and motivational speaker

LEARNING OBJECTIVES

After reading this chapter, you should understand:

- How hospitality organizations motivate their employees to provide outstanding guest service.

- How organizations reinforce and reward guest-centered employees.

- How outstanding hospitality organizations fulfill employee needs.

- How playing roles can improve guest service.

- How modern hospitality organizations enhance guest service by empowering employees.

- How leadership and authority work in organizations and why employees accept authority.

KEY TERMS AND CONCEPTS

motivation

formal group

informal group

recognition program

empowerment

positive reinforcement

expectancy theory

self-efficacy

role theory

emotional labor

goal setting

SMART criteria

Management by Objectives (MBO)

authority-acceptance theory

equity theory

behavioral integrity

The service setting is superb, the best employees have been hired and trained, and all the mechanical and back-of-the-house aspects of the delivery system are flawless—so far, so good. Now it's up to that frontline employee you've worked so hard to hire and train to deliver. In almost all guest experiences, the guest-contact employee can make the difference between a satisfied guest and a dissatisfied guest. This employee is also the one who can turn a satisfied guest into a wowed guest. In the manufacturing sector, the tire or automobile on the assembly line doesn't really care about the scowl on the employee's face, the sarcastic comments, or the bad attitude. But people who seek guest experiences are very aware of how employees treat them. If the hotel gift-shop clerk makes a comment that offends a guest, the guest will obviously be angry at the employee. Yet, in all likelihood, the guest will also be angry at the hotel that hired and trained the employee. Because the guest service employee is so important in the guest's determination of value and quality, hospitality organizations that strive for *positively outrageous service*[1] take great care, as we have seen in previous chapters, in the hiring, training, and development of their employees. But this is not enough to ensure exceptional service.

This chapter focuses on motivating and empowering the hospitality employee to provide a high-quality guest experience. Since quality and value are defined by the guest, the employee who provides the guest experience must be not only well trained, but highly motivated to meet the guest's quality and value expectations and do so consistently. If the role of the hospitality service provider is this important to the organization, the role of the hospitality manager—whose leadership and managerial skills are the most important influence on employee work attitudes and job behaviors—is vital.

MOTIVATING EMPLOYEES

A family was checking in at the Hyatt Grand Cypress on a busy night. The hotel was full, the family's reservation had not been properly handled, and the husband, wife, and three tired children were upset. The front desk employee assessed the situation and acted promptly. She took some quarters out of the petty cash drawer and gave them to the kids to go and play the video games and gave the parents vouchers for free drinks in the lobby bar while she went to find a manager to straighten out the problem. The parents were happy, the kids were happy, and the front desk person had defused a tense situation.

In contrast, consider the experiences of Tom Farmer and Shane Atchison. They had a confirmed reservation at a hotel, which was held for late arrival with a major credit card. Yet, when they arrived at 2 a.m., they were refused rooms. Tom and Shane publicized their service experience with an open complaint to the hotel called "Yours is a Very Bad Hotel" that became an Internet sensation.[2] They reported that "Mike the Night Clerk" was "deeply unapologetic," "had done nothing about finding [them] accommodation elsewhere," and when they suggested that he should have lined up other rooms in advance, Mike the Night Clerk "bristled!" Maintaining that the customers were wrong to be upset that their "guaranteed" room was not saved for them, Mike told them, "I have nothing to apologize to you for." After the Internet posting, representatives of the hotel did apologize and reportedly improved their training and overbooking policies, but the damage was done: A Google search in 2010 of "Yours is a Very Bad Hotel" yielded thousands of results! This bad hotel story is only one of many. Customers and even employees have set up thousands of protest sites to complain about how companies have treated them. These days, through the power of the Internet, one unhappy guest or employee can create a public relations disaster for a company.

Both of the above cases began in a similar way: A reservation was not properly handled. But because of the employees' actions, the results were markedly different. The Hyatt employee took a creative path to solving a guest problem, not because she had to, but because she wanted to. Something or someone motivated this employee to act to satisfy a customer despite a problem that was not of her making. On the other hand, Mike the Night Clerk could not have cared less. The challenge for hospitality managers is to discover what makes employees do not only what is in their job descriptions efficiently and competently but also the extra things that can make the difference for guests and organizations.

The best hospitality organizations have learned the importance of using their employees from the neck up as well as from the neck down. Every guest experience is unique, and any manager who believes it is possible to predefine policies and procedures for handling any and all guest experiences is mistaken. Employees should know that they are encouraged, empowered, and trusted to handle all of the many and varied situations that come up in the guest service areas for which they are responsible. Even if employees were properly selected and trained, management must continue to encourage them do their jobs with responsibility, skill, enthusiasm, and fun. But how?

What Motivates People?

Motivation is a simple idea that is difficult to put into practice. To motivate means to instill a desire within a person that encourages the person to act. In the organizational setting, motivation rests on the idea that people are driven to achieve their own ends and satisfy their own needs. They will give up some control over their own behavior to organizations they join because they believe they will have greater opportunities to achieve their goals and meet their needs by joining an organization than by not joining.

Organizations of all kinds offer us inducements to join them and incentives and rewards to stay with them. In return, they expect us to make organizational contributions as the price of membership. For example, we may join a social group, either on or off the job, to satisfy our needs for friendship and belonging. We may join hotels, restaurants, and cruise line organizations to satisfy our social needs (a great group to work with), achievement needs (a job that lets me show my talents), recognition needs (management appreciates my skills here), and, perhaps most important to most members of business organizations, economic needs (I need the money to pay my bills, feed my family, and survive). In other words, people join hospitality organizations seeking a wide variety of incentives and rewards, for which they will, in return, contribute their knowledge, skills, abilities, loyalty, and effort. The challenge for the hospitality manager is to discover what incentives and rewards each employee requires as reasons to give up at least some personal control to the organization and exert effort on its behalf. Finding the right combination of incentives and rewards is the hard part of motivation, as employees—like guests—are highly individual persons with their own sets of needs, wants, expectations, capabilities, and behaviors. Managers of hospitality employees need to use the same guestology principles with their internal guests—employees—that they use with their external guest-customers.

In motivating employees, the role of the manager is critical. Managers must (1) understand what employees need and want so that rewards can be aligned with these interests, (2) know what tools are at their disposal to help motivate employees, (3) understand how employees react to both financial and nonfinancial rewards and how these rewards motivate employees to perform, and (4) understand how their roles as managers and leaders are critical for doing all this effectively and in a way that is seen as fair and trustworthy. This is no easy task, as employees' needs and environmental conditions are always changing. Precisely because of these difficulties, though, a manager's effectiveness as a leader can be judged in large part by how well that person performs in each of these four roles.

THE NEEDS PEOPLE HAVE

Before managers can know how to create systems to motivate and reward employees, they need to figure out what their employees need and want. Theories that try to explain people's needs are numerous.[3] In general, they suggest that people seek to fulfill four levels of needs when joining organizations. The four needs are survival needs, social needs, recognition needs, and achievement needs. Of course, the degree to which these needs drive behavior will differ from person to person, for any given person at different times, and from organization to organization. The task of hospitality managers is to identify which needs are driving the behavior of their employees and then to offer them the combination of incentives and rewards that will satisfy or help satisfy those needs. Offering the most effective combination best motivates employees to exert effort.

Survival Needs

In general, the most basic employee need is survival. To meet employee survival needs, the most obvious inducement is money provided though a paycheck. While people join organizations for a wide variety of reasons, most people who seek to work for a business do so in large part because they need to earn a living. For many people across the world, the primary need satisfied by employment is earning enough to pay rent, buy food, and acquire the other basics of living. People do not worry much about their social, recognition, or achievement needs if they are concerned about how they are going to get their next meal, feed their family, find a safe place to stay, or buy warm clothes in the winter. Before offering employees incentives or rewards that can help satisfy their other needs, managers must ensure that their employees are paid enough to meet their survival needs.

This issue is especially important for most entry-level employees, who are at the bottom of the pay scale. If they are to be the first—and sometimes the only—point of contact with the company's guests, they must not be worried that they may be unable to meet their basic needs. To help them do so means offering incentives like scheduling enough hours, working around child or elder care responsibilities, and helping them find affordable health care for their families. If Fred Yang is the first person the guest sees when entering your hotel, restaurant, or casino, a first impression of a worried Fred, as he thinks about how long it will be until he has to start his second job or where he is going to sleep tonight, may not be the positive encounter that the organization wants the guest to have.

Social Needs

Most people enjoy being a part of a group or team. This sense of belonging can be helpful in managing employee direction and behavior in the workplace. Indeed, as studies at the Hawthorne Plant of the Western Electric Company showed many years ago, whether employees feel that they do or don't belong greatly influences what they will or won't do in the workplace. Although the main purpose of a work group, obviously, is to work, the group often fulfills the need of members to *belong*.

When employees join any organization, they join a **formal group**. This includes the company as a whole, but may also be the team they join, or the shift they work. In addition, employees may belong to an **informal group** at the workplace. An informal group refers to a social group that forms without guidance from the organization. The managerial focus here, therefore, should be to establish an environment wherein employees can work in harmony with informal and formal work groups to support each employee's effort to achieve group goals, which will—directly or indirectly—help achieve the organizational goal.

The first managerial challenge in meeting employee belonging needs, then, is to identify those informal groups, in addition to the work groups, to which employees belong. This is not always obvious or easy to do. The second challenge is to discover those informal groups' goals. The last is to develop a path to fit the informal groups' goals and the organizations' work group goals together to ensure the satisfaction of both groups' goals, and, ultimately, the satisfaction of the employees in their informal groups and in their organizational groups.

Social groups form alongside or as part of work groups for a variety of reasons. People who work together tend to have things in common: what they do, when they do it, and who they do it with. They not only work together on the job every day but also may associate off the job. They have things in common to talk about, shared experiences, and constant reminders of their common basis for acquaintance, which serve as reasons to continue their on-the-job relationships. Since the best hospitality organizations use careful

People who work together often associate off the job. Groups at work can also create social groups outside of the work environment.

Photo courtesy of Marriott International

hiring criteria, these people tend to share even more commonalities, which bind them as a group. They frequently are young, share similar values and beliefs, and have many personality traits in common. When you take similar people and put them together in a work setting, you have the basis for forming a work group that is also a friendship group.

Another benefit of formal and informal groups in the workplace is that they provide the opportunity to share. Sharing thoughts and ideas about the job has obvious organizational benefits. But being able to share the dreams, ambitions, challenges, joys, and problems of life with someone has great benefits to most people. Groups give the individual a sympathetic ear, reassurance of self-worth, and help and assistance in times of challenges to the individual. The more that group members identify with their group, the more they will look to their groups to affirm their worth, acknowledge their successes, and recognize their achievements. Research shows that the more employees identify with their groups, the more they are willing to engage in helping behaviors, both to coworkers and to the company as a whole.[4] Organizations benefit by finding ways to incorporate informal group goals into the organizational goals.

Recognition Needs

Although the need for recognition is stronger in some people than others, everybody likes to be appreciated. The need for recognition refers to employees' desire for praise and attention from colleagues and superiors.

Recognition needs can be satisfied in a number of ways. Most obviously, a formal recognition program is one way to acknowledge and appreciate stellar performance. But recognition need not always be formalized. It can be conducted on a specified schedule or ad hoc, formal or informal, individual or collective, private or public, and monetary or nonmonetary.[5] Letting employees know they did a good job has a number of advantages. It lets employees know that what they did is indeed desired behavior, and it demonstrates to employees that management is aware of their behaviors and likes what they see. Employee recognition, be it formal or informal, is key to preserving and building the desired organizational culture.

Certainly, the level of employee needs for recognition varies. Some employees desire public recognition, while others are embarrassed by it. Individual recognition may also be more effective in individualistic cultures like the United States and the Netherlands, than in more collectivist cultures like China and Indonesia. Recognition needs also vary by generation, with younger employees desiring more formal and informal recognition than their baby-boomer-generation counterparts.[6] Once again, it is important for a manager to identify the level and form of recognition that different employees want so that this need can be filled appropriately.

Achievement Needs

Employees like to believe that what they do is important and the companies they work for do important things. If employees think that their level of service really makes a difference to their customers, the profession, or the community, they will feel a legitimate sense of importance. They will have pride in the jobs they do and in the company for which they do those jobs. If the employees believe what they are doing is important, they will be highly energized to give incredible effort to make that important task happen. Tales of Disney's early days report employees who worked incredibly long hours with energy and enthusiasm because they were so committed to what the organization was trying to accomplish. Everyone wanted so badly for Walt's wonderland to work that they gave it their all. "I ran my ass off," says one veteran. "I lost fifteen pounds in the first sixty days.

You never walked; you got behind the scenes and ran. There was always a fire to put out. I went fourteen months straight without a day off."[7]

Seeing Disneyland or some other facility open and succeed creates an incredibly good feeling of success and achievement in those who made it happen. Additionally, if the community thinks that the hotel, theme park, or convention center plays a major role in its economic health, all the employees who work there will feel good about their contributions to their community. They will have pride in the job they do and in the organization for which they do that job. Finding ways to show employees that they are contributing to making a real difference in something they feel is important and valued is a key talent of managers in successful hospitality firms. They know how to get the spark of enthusiasm, extra effort, and the strong commitment that a dedicated missionary feels and a clock watcher never does.

Achievement needs can also be fulfilled while satisfying social needs. Since groups offer members the opportunity to achieve something greater by being a part of the group than would have been possible individually, the value of the group becomes greater than merely helping to satisfy social needs. Employment in organizations with strong corporate cultures, whose objectives are respected by the society as a whole, is valuable to both the group and individual. Asking the group to help accomplish the valued, respected organizational purpose becomes a powerful motivational tool for the organization and a potent means for keeping the individual and the group positively involved in the organization's mission. When employees strongly identify with the property and share in the goal of providing exceptional service, they are highly motivated to achieve exemplary customer satisfaction ratings.

THE REWARDS PEOPLE WANT

Once managers know what employees need, they can begin to develop ways to meet those needs. To do so, managers have a variety of financial and nonfinancial tools at their disposal. They include financial rewards like wages, bonuses, and group incentives. The most effective

Although employees work for different reasons, working for money is a primary motivation for seeking employment around the world.

Image copyright Vinicius Tupinamba, 2010. Used under license from Shutterstock.com hospitality companies also use nonfinancial rewards, like formal recognition programs, to motivate exceptional performance. The best managers also change jobs for employees to make the work more rewarding, including making the job itself more fun and empowering employees to more effectively use their knowledge and skills to achieve superb performance.

Financial Rewards

Money serves different purposes for different people. Some employees need money mainly for food, shelter, and clothing. Others use money to acquire various luxuries. For all employees, money plays some role in motivating them to perform, but because different people have different needs, desires, and preferences, the best managers realize that money and paychecks are a tricky incentive or reward to manage effectively.

As seen in Figure 7-1, money can be offered as an incentive or a reward for employee performance in a variety of ways, and can be used to satisfy a variety of needs. For example, annual performance bonuses reward individual performance. Group financial incentives reward team success and focus employees on working in a group to achieve common goals. Individual tips can encourage high-quality customer service, while pooled tips can encourage servers to work together. Ownership in the company (through stock) helps employees realize that their own success depends on the company's overall success. Depending on how almost any financial reward is presented, it can help satisfy employees' needs, reinforce what is expected from employees, and encourage certain future behaviors. In these ways, pay methods can be designed to help focus employees on achieving high performance. However, because financial incentives change behaviors, managers need to stay alert to ensure that what they are rewarding is what they want employees to do.

Although most people need a job for the income it provides, money alone can go only so far in helping to create the type of personal and emotional attachment to a company that motivates its employees to provide customers with a wow experience. Many reasons why people behave as they do are unrelated to money (e.g., being with people they like, joining civic and religious organizations, raising children, helping a stranger, volunteering in the community, caring for parents). Smart managers know that in addition to monetary incentives, nonfinancial incentives—like friendship, fun working environment, recognition, praise, personal growth, and achievement—can often produce individual effort that money could never buy.

The point is this: Managers must discover what needs each employee is seeking to fulfill in the employment relationship and then offer different incentives for different employees that make it possible for each to meet those needs. Managers also need to think beyond incentives, on the way jobs are designed and the authority granted to employees, as a means to motivate exceptional performance.

Recognizing a Job Well Done

The purpose of a **recognition program** is to say, publicly and officially, thank you for a job well done. A survey of U.S. firms revealed that nearly 90 percent of companies have recognition programs, and about 70 percent of firms have both formal and informal recognition programs. They recognize not only exceptional performance, but a variety of other accomplishments, like sales performance, innovative suggestions, safety performance, and attendance.[8] The recognition rewards reinforce behaviors that represent the company's cultural values and achievement of the service mission. In the service industry, these awards show employees that their efforts to deliver a wow experience to customers are desired, valued, and appreciated.

FIGURE 7-1 Financial Incentive and Reward Options

© Cengage Learning 2012

PAY FORM	DEFINITION	HOW PERFORMANCE IS ASSESSED	EXAMPLE
Merit raise	An increase in base pay (i.e., a raise) that is tied to individual performance.	Managers review individual performance.	A manager gives an employee a 4% annual raise to reward exceptional performance on the job.
Annual performance bonus	A one-time lump sum payment made to an employee based on a performance evaluation.	Managers review individual performance.	A manager gives an employee a lump sum bonus of $10,000 that year to reward exceptional service.
Spot bonus	A one-time payment made to an employee who exhibited great performance through some specific act.	Managers observe or customers report a specific incident of exceptional performance.	A manager gives an employee a $100 bonus for handling a difficult guest complaint to the guest's satisfaction.
Individual tips	Voluntary payments given to service providers by customers after providers deliver service.	Customers assess the service received during the service encounter.	A customer gives a server a tip at the end of a meal.
Pooled tips	When all customer tips are put into a common "collection" and are then divided proportionally between the servers on duty.	Customers assess the service received during the service encounter.	At the end of a shift, all servers on duty during the shift divide the total customer tips.
Recognition program	A program designed to provide a reward (financial and/or symbolic) to employees who achieve a notable goal.	Managers assess performance over a period (monthly, annual, etc.) or employees nominate their peers.	The CEO publicly recognizes the rooms agent who takes the most reservations in a year with a ceremony, a plaque, and a check for $5000.
Group incentive plan	A bonus paid to all employees of a group for successfully meeting a specific goal.	Managers assess individual, team, or company-wide performance.	Employees each receive a $100 bonus for each month that customer satisfaction ratings exceed a certain level.
Compensation through ownership	Enabling employees to own a portion of the company, e.g., common stock or stock options.	Because of stock ownership, employee wealth is tied to how well the market values the company.	Company gives employees the option to purchase 500 shares of stock at $20 per share. If the stock price goes above $20, the employees will benefit.

Fairmont Hotels & Resorts launched a recognition program designed to reinforce the company's service culture. The program featured different award levels, such as Memory Maker for outstanding demonstrations of thoughtfulness and creativity, and Star of the Month for employees nominated by their peers for consistently demonstrating superior performance.[9] The awards helped support the organizational culture of appreciation and recognition for everyone, from housekeepers to senior management, and for all Fairmont employees around the world. Winners received gift certificates in small denominations (typically $10–50 in value) that could be redeemed with thousands of merchants around the world. Surveys of Fairmont's employees after the program was implemented revealed that employees felt more recognition for a job well done, felt that the best performers were more likely to receive recognition, and felt that they were being recognized in a way that was personally meaningful. Surveys also showed that employee levels of engagement increased significantly following the program's inception.[10]

While many programs offer cash awards alone, many others offer symbolic, non-cash rewards, or gifts, like plaques or certificates, merchandise with the company logo, gift certificates, jewelry, office accessories, household items, recreational items, and electronic goods.[11] A key advantage of these non-cash awards is that they often create a lasting memory of the experience for the employee, which proves more effective in achieving employee satisfaction than cash awards. While cash is usually spent immediately on things that people may or may not remember, non-cash rewards tend to serve as long-lasting reminders of company appreciation. Moreover, the cost of non-cash awards, from the plaque on the wall to the trophy on the desk to photos from the special vacation, is often insignificant when compared to the high level of recognition. For example, a special pin that announces an employee's outstanding service may cost only $20, but its emotional impact on the employee, wearing it for all to see and perhaps keeping it for a lifetime, is far greater than the impact of simply receiving a twenty-dollar bill. The way the reward is presented can also be a powerful symbol. Having the CEO of the company personally recognize excellent performance sends a clear signal that indeed stellar performance is valued.

Marriott Hotels uses a recognition program, called the Award of Excellence, to recognize its best performing employees. Showing the company's commitment to this award, Bill Marriott (at the far right) participates in the awards ceremony.

Photo courtesy of Marriott International

Making the Job Fun

Not all rewards for working well have to come in the form of cash, an incentive, a plaque, or a prize item. Sometimes, the work itself can be its own reward. Walt Disney said, "You don't work for a dollar—you work to create and have fun."[12] Chili's Norman Brinker said, "If you have fun at what you do, you'll never work a day in your life. Make work like play—and play like hell."[13]

Some jobs may never be fun, but to whatever extent managers can establish an enjoyable atmosphere, the organization will benefit. Fun is contagious. People having fun at work tend to infect peers as well as guest-customers. Customers of hospitality organizations expect to deal with happy people; they expect to be greeted with a smile. A happy work setting can not only enhance sales but, as research has shown, can improve employee retention, morale, and recruitment.[14] It is simply more enjoyable to go to work in an organization that is fun than in one that is not. Of course, the fun has to help achieve the organization's goals. As one manager stated, "We don't take ourselves seriously, but we take what we do very seriously." You want the job to be fun but not in ways that employees are just playing around and ignoring their job duties and customer service responsibilities.

Minimizing the Negatives

Another way to make a job enjoyable is to eliminate or minimize the things that make it uninteresting or unpleasant. In all jobs, there exist some parts that are never fun or interesting or challenging, but they must be done. Managers can motivate employees by providing fun ways to minimize these less attractive aspects. Good managers add fun elements to jobs to break the monotony, boredom, or annoyances. Anyone operating the It's a Small World attraction at the Magic Kingdom must receive some relief from the constant repetition of the attraction's distinctive theme song. Likewise, anyone walking backward loading a constant stream of guests on Epcot's Spaceship Earth while ensuring that guests are properly seated needs a break from this repetitive task. If employees have jobs like these, managers should consider rotating them to other jobs in other locations from time to time, or find other fun ways to break the routine or escape the monotony.

Motivating employees whose jobs contain monotony and boredom is hard enough. Motivating employees whose jobs have downright unpleasant aspects is even more difficult. Imagine being an airline lost-baggage representative, a customer service representative dealing with passengers of late or cancelled flights, or a front desk agent who has to listen politely while an angry customer lodges a complaint. While jobs requiring extensive physical labor can be fatiguing, jobs like these, requiring polite and reasonable interactions in the face of angry or difficult customers can be equally fatiguing. Although these tasks are emotionally taxing, they must be done by someone.

Managers of the best organizations appreciate the emotional price that these employees pay and seek to minimize or compensate for the negative aspects of all jobs. Some organizations offer stress-reduction programs, such as physical exercise and time off from the stressful aspects of jobs. Others offer counseling. The most common approach is to encourage employees to apply their professional standards (e.g., a nurse dealing with a dying infant), use scripted behaviors (e.g., "Welcome to McDonalds, how may I serve you?"), or use other strategies listed above that allow the employee to cope with the stress-creating situation.

Angry and unhappy guests present a challenge. Managers must find ways to help employees who have to deal with such guests so that they don't lose their ability to do their jobs or angrily retaliate against an angry customer. But, as we shall discuss later in this book, dissatisfied guests are also an opportunity for the company, and the people who interact with these guests must be skilled, emotionally ready to deal with them, and effective at maintaining their professional poise while solving the problems that caused the dissatisfaction.

Empowering the Employee

In addition to motivating employees through incentives, by means of recognition programs, and by making the work environment more enjoyable, organizations can find ways for employees grow and develop while at the same time helping to fulfill the company's mission. One important way is **empowerment**.

What Is Empowerment?

Empowerment[15] is the assignment of decision-making responsibility to an individual. It requires sharing information and organizational knowledge that enable empowered employees to understand and contribute to organizational performance, giving them the authority to make decisions that influence organizational outcomes and rewarding them based on the organization's performance.[16] The concept of empowerment is broader than the traditional concepts of delegation, decentralization, and participatory management. Empowerment can stretch responsibility for decision making beyond a specific decision area within a job to include decision responsibility for the entire job and for knowing how performing on that job fits within the organization's overall purpose and mission. It sends a powerful message to the employee that he or she is trusted. Empowered employees know that their managers trust them to make the right decision at the right time to enable the guest to get the service expected. Since no one can predict everything that can happen when a guest has a moment of truth with an employee, it is impossible to prescribe in advance how to deal with all guest encounters. Empowered employees know what to do, know what their company expects of them, have the ability to do it, and can make the difference between an *ow* situation and a *wow* situation.

One of the most widely known examples of empowerment in hospitality is the approach used by The Ritz-Carlton. Empowerment there extends beyond simply planning how work is done: It is a core component of The Ritz-Carlton culture. Indeed, empowerment is number three in the company's twelve service values: "I am empowered to create unique, memorable, and personal experiences for our guests." If guests are unhappy, The Ritz-Carlton employees have up to $2,000 to make them happy again without approval from upper management.[17] That amount was chosen, says John Timmerman, vice president of quality and program management at The Ritz-Carlton, at a level where "an employee would never second guess themselves."[18] That is, the authorized amount is high enough to cover just about any steps that an employee might need to take to satisfy a customer. As Joseph A. Michelli describes it, "This financial authority is the living embodiment of trust and power conferred to each staff member at The Ritz-Carlton."[19]

Although empowerment may make the job more fun for employees, it presents them with an opportunity for growth and development, which makes the job more interesting. The organization also benefits from employees who are not only well trained but also authorized to use their skills and capabilities to provide an outstanding guest experience. As the legendary restaurateur Norman Brinker said, "You can achieve so much more by empowering people to achieve on their own. Don't be too hands-on."[20] The empowered server can personalize the service experience to meet or exceed each guest's expectations and can take whatever steps are necessary to prevent or recover from service failure.

Some organizations talk the talk of employee empowerment without giving employees any real power or authority to implement decisions. The purpose of employee empowerment is not only to ensure that effective decisions are made by the right employees but also to provide a mechanism by which responsibility for job-related decisions is vested either in individuals or in work teams.[21] Empowerment also means that management is willing to share relevant information about and control over factors related to effective job performance.

Empowerment helps achieve the company's mission. For example, Hyatt felt that it was not doing enough to provide authentic hospitality to its most loyal customers. Hyatt began a program that empowered employees to perform what it called *random acts of generosity*. Member customers in their Gold Passport loyalty program might suddenly find that their bar tab was paid, or they might receive a complimentary massage, or their family's breakfast might be paid for by the hotel—all because an empowered employee saw a way to enhance the guest's hotel stay. The company could have dictated a set of policies that told employees how to surprise and delight guests (such as, if guests do X, then give them Y). Instead, Hyatt trusted employees to see a situation and then decide on how to provide a wow element to a customer's experience.

When successfully implemented, empowerment has several benefits for both employees and managers. It tells employees that the organization trusts them to know what to do, how to do it, and trusts them to do it. Nothing frustrates people more than being hired and trained to do a job, and then having the manager constantly look over their shoulders to be sure they are doing it right. Empowerment treats employees as respected adults. Managerial unwillingness to allow employees to make the decisions they are both capable of making and willing to make can lead to a loss of employee self-respect, a loss of self-confidence that they can do their jobs, and a loss of interest in doing them. Empowerment builds self-respect, self-confidence, and interest.

Empowerment also benefits the hospitality manager. No one can be everywhere all the time. How employees behave when an overly controlling manager is away or unavailable can be a problem. Employees can be either helpless or empowered. Those who cannot make decisions on their own become helpless, and ultimately useless (or worse) when their boss is away, but the empowered do their jobs as their managers hoped they would even without managerial oversight. Another benefit is that organizations simply cannot train people to solve every problem that may occur in their jobs. But if employees know the organization's mission and goals and understand and believe in the organization's culture, they can be empowered to make the right decisions. Former Southwest Airlines CEO Herb Kelleher said, "I can't anticipate all of the situations that will arise at the stations across our system. So what we tell our people is, 'Hey, we can't anticipate all these things; you handle them the best way possible. You make a judgment and use your discretion; we trust you'll do the right thing. If we think you've done something erroneous, we'll let you know—without criticism, without backbiting.'"[22] No one can anticipate, train, and prepare for every possible problem, outcome, or customer request. Empowerment can fill the gaps when the circumstances are new, unique, or unexpected.

Empowerment Implementation

Successful implementation of employee empowerment requires companies to take some key steps. Empowerment cannot simply be decreed; it requires an investment in training employees so that they know how to use their new decision-making freedom effectively. Companies must also recognize that empowerment cannot solve all problems, so it should be implemented only where the keys are present.

The five keys to implementing an effective empowerment program are as follows:

1. *Training.* Empowerment requires an investment in employee training. Employees must learn to understand their areas of responsibility thoroughly. Then they must learn how to make sound decisions within their areas.
2. *Willingness.* Empowerment requires employees to not only be ready and able to make decisions about their jobs but also be willing to do so. If the employees are uninterested in the company and its future, empowering them to make decisions will be risky.
3. *Measurement.* Employees must have goals or standards against which the results of their decisions can be measured. Otherwise, they will not know either what they should do or if their decisions were good or bad.
4. *Incentives.* Rewards need to be attached to successful performance. To be most effective, an incentive system rewards employees for making good decisions. Rewards help reinforce the goals of the program and make it clear to employees that using their empowerment appropriately is worthwhile.
5. *Managerial buy-in.* Management must be willing to accept empowered employees, let them make their own decisions, and not interfere. An empowerment program will not work if managers cannot learn to trust the capabilities of empowered employees. If managers who let their people make decisions end up changing, overriding, or otherwise not using these decisions, employees were not really empowered in the first place.

Limitations and Potential of Empowerment

Of course, not all organizations can benefit equally from employee empowerment. Empowerment may be less appropriate if (1) the basic business strategy emphasizes low-cost, high-volume operations, (2) the tie to most customers is short term, (3) technology used is simple and routine, (4) the business environment is highly predictable, and (5) employees have low growth needs, low social needs, and weak interpersonal skills. Alternatively, employee empowerment can be highly successful and rewarding if (1) service is customized or personalized, (2) customer relationships are long term, (3) technology used is complex, (4) the environment is unpredictable, and (5) employees have high growth needs, social needs, and strong interpersonal skills. Under these circumstances, the potential gains from employee empowerment are significant.[23] Although the hospitality industry generally does not use complex technology, nearly every guest-contact situation is customized and unique. If you have chosen the right employees (with respect to point 5), employee empowerment will lead to most guest-contact decisions benefiting the organization.

Degrees of Empowerment

Of course, empowerment is not an absolute; it has degrees. Managers may find that more is not necessarily better. Employees need to be capable of making appropriate decisions. Robert Teerlink, former head of Harley-Davidson, said, "If you empower idiots, you get dumb decisions faster."[23] A manager may choose to provide higher degrees of empowerment for some individuals and teams doing certain tasks than for others. Indeed, even within a given employee's job or a given group's task responsibilities, different decision areas can be empowered to different degrees. A restaurant chain, for example, may empower its restaurant managers with complete authority to resolve customer complaints but may not let the same managers make even minor modifications to the menu.

Since the workforce is so diverse, some employees will be better suited for empowerment than others. Part-time employees or contract (temporary) employees may not be interested enough in the goals of the organization or in a long-term relationship with it to be good candidates for empowerment programs. One art of good management is to determine what degree of empowerment to extend to different employees based on an assessment of the five keys discussed earlier.

Unintended Consequences of Empowerment

Empowerment can lead to problems if empowered employees make decisions that are disadvantageous to other employees or to the organization as a whole. For example, if a desk agent allows guests to check out two hours late, the housekeeping staff may have difficulty in preparing the room for the next guests, especially if another empowered desk agent allows them to check in early. The actions or decisions of an empowered employee must not be allowed to affect other employees negatively in the performance of their jobs as that will in turn affect the organization's ability to deliver a service experience that meets their guests' expectations.

REWARDING EMPLOYEES FOR PERFORMANCE

Once you have hired functionally qualified people, trained them, and have identified their various needs, you have the challenge of keeping them interested in the specifics of their jobs. Knowing what employees need and want is only half the battle; you need to figure out how you are going to connect rewards and behaviors so that, in the process of fulfilling their needs, you elicit from employees the exceptional performance that you desire. You may satisfy these needs through financial incentives, job restructuring, recognition programs, and empowerment. The key issue is to understand how these motivational tools work to produce the desired behaviors.

The Power of Positive Reinforcement

A well-accepted psychological principle is that if you reward desired behaviors and don't reward undesired behaviors, you will get more of the desired behaviors and fewer of the undesired ones. Rewarding desired behaviors is called **positive reinforcement**. While the idea seems simple enough, providing appropriate positive reinforcement is no simple task. Rewarding the wrong behavior can create as many problems as not rewarding the right behavior. Managers need to review their words and actions constantly and carefully to ensure that the behaviors being rewarded are the behaviors that the organization really wanted.

All rewards need to be scrutinized carefully to determine exactly what is being incentivized. GuestFirst Hotels, for example, may tell its employees that they should make every effort to satisfy the guest, but GuestFirst managers actually evaluate and reward only according to whether employees meet the budget numbers. This type of managerial misdirection is called *the folly of rewarding A while hoping for B* and it is folly for any organization whose managers engage in it. Depending on how the reward systems are constructed, individual bonuses may discourage teamwork; a group incentive system may cause employees to provide too many free upgrades; a profit-sharing plan may focus employees on short-term cost-cutting rather than long-term exceptional customer service. Over time, everyone figures out exactly what behaviors are being rewarded. As a result, most employees will focus on management's actions and not their words about the importance of customer service.

At the Buffet

A popular buffet restaurant decided to add a greeter position to welcome guests as they entered the restaurant. Manager Gail Bowman told newly hired Charles Jones explicitly that his primary responsibility was to greet and welcome the guests. However, as time went on, to keep Jones busy when guests were not entering the restaurant, Bowman added responsibilities to the position—such as checking periodically to make sure there were enough trays or that the butter dish was always full. Jones quickly realized that Bowman never complimented him for properly greeting the guests, nor did she ever say anything to him when he missed a guest because he was too busy with his other duties. But if he ever let the buffet line run out of trays or butter, Bowman strongly reprimanded him. By her actions or lack of action, Bowman redefined the job description. She made her real priorities clear (in the mind of Charles Jones, at least), and he adjusted his actions accordingly.

The point is that *what we reward tends to be what gets done.* Managers must remember to reinforce preferred behaviors by providing the right incentives in the right amounts at the right times. If we want our employees to exert appropriate effort, we must be clear and consistent about what we reward.

LINKING PERFORMANCE AND REWARDS

A critical part of the manager's job, in addition to identifying the mix of incentives or rewards that each employee needs, wants, and expects, is to define how each employee can get those rewards. **Expectancy theory** maintains that organizations need to relate rewards directly to performance. If employees believe or expect (1) that they can achieve a certain performance level by putting in a certain level of effort, (2) that achieving this performance level will lead to promised rewards, and (3) if employees value these rewards sufficiently, they will be motivated to put in the effort necessary to get the rewards. While employees must of course have the right abilities and be trained appropriately so that they have the capabilities to perform, offering desired rewards and establishing expectations that effort will lead to receiving those rewards is a critical managerial responsibility.

Based on expectancy theory, managers must take several essential steps in order to motivate employees to perform effectively. First, they must give their employees confidence that their skills, training, and capabilities are adequate for doing what is necessary to receive rewards if they put in the effort. That is, employees must possess sufficient **self-efficacy**. Second, managers must ensure that employees believe that if they exert effort and perform their jobs well, management will deliver the rewards as promised. If employees do not have sufficient trust in management, reward systems will simply not have the desired effect. Third, they must provide the array of rewards that employees believe are important and worthwhile to satisfying their needs. Whether it is the value or recognition that the award provides, employees must want the reward for the system to motivate high performance.

This theory puts a major burden on managers to *manage.* Managers need to ensure that their employees are properly trained; that they have the right people in the right jobs to do the work; that they identify, offer, and then deliver the rewards that have value to their employees; and that they behave fairly toward them. If Mary is told that she will get a trip to Hawaii she has always wanted if she books the big convention she has been working on and she succeeds, then management had better give her the trip to Hawaii. Otherwise, she and everyone she talks to will not be very motivated to give the job much effort in the future as they will not believe that management will deliver on its promises.

A manager who fails to meet an internal customer's expectations will need to find and fix that failure with the same commitment and effort that the manager would use to find and fix a failure in meeting the expectations of an external guest.

CLARIFYING EMPLOYEES' ROLES

Managers are responsible for clarifying job roles for their employees by explaining how they fit within the overall organizational effort, by providing clear job descriptions, by setting clear and specific goals, by reinforcing cultural norms and values, and by continuously communicating the expected role behaviors of employees in their jobs through everything managers say, do, and write. Employees who know their roles will be better able to focus their efforts on productive activities and avoid wasting energy on unproductive activities.

Role Theory

Role theory is a way to explain how the organization, group, or work team influences the behavior of its members. People behave in their roles in fairly predictable patterns, which are usually influenced by others. A person may be a church member, a student, a parent, a civic-group member as well as an employee. Each role has different expectations of the person and, while playing the role, the person is continuously influenced by others watching the person behave. A student behaves, for the most part, as a student is expected to behave, and a Hard Rock Café employee usually behaves as one would expect from a Hard Rock Café employee. Guests or other employees may give a funny look or make a critical comment to a frowning hotel desk agent or receptionist, because a frown is not part of their expectations for those roles. Anyone observing a mother ignoring her child in danger will scowl or even speak up. People continually tell us by word, facial expression, body language, or deed how they think we should be behaving in a particular situation.

As seen in Figure 7-2, based on classic research in the field,[24] role-playing situations have two major elements: role senders and the role receiver or focal person. Role senders are all those who let us know what role they expect us to play and then try to tell us how to behave in performing the role by sending us verbal and nonverbal cues. The

FIGURE **7-2 The Way Roles Affect Behaviors**
© Cengage Learning 2012

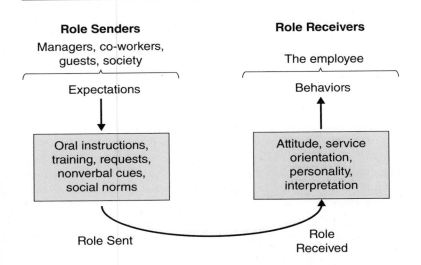

instruction and training that the boss sends, the cues that coworkers and guests send, and the social norms that our society sends help define the expectations they all have of us in the guest service role. The role receiver or focal person is the employee. Employees observe and receive all the expectations that people are sending them and interpret this information to form the behaviors they think people want from them. Each employee then decides to comply or not to comply with those expectations and acts or does not act accordingly.

The Cast Member Role

Disney uses the concept of role in a unique way to enhance the nature and performance of the job. By using the term *cast member* for all employees, Disney emphasizes the idea that everyone in the organizational cast is playing a role in a public performance. The terms *on stage* and *off stage* are also used to reinforce this notion in the minds of all employees. The idea that employees comprise a cast putting on a show has many organizational benefits, but perhaps the biggest is to get people to think of their jobs as roles. They understand that what they are asked to do in those roles is part of a performance for their guests or audience. This mind-set gives new and greater importance to every job throughout the organization. Now, instead of thinking "I am merely a street sweeper," which may demean the employee's many years of education and experience, the street-sweeping cast member can look at the task as the playing of a role. In a theatrical production, nothing is demeaning or lowly about playing the role of a street sweeper. After all, you're not really a street sweeper but rather a cast member or actor doing an excellent job of playing a street sweeper. This attitude helps eliminate role conflicts. The distinction between the real you and what you're capable of doing or being in real life on the one hand and your skillful performance of the street sweeper's role on the other is clear.

Role Conflicts

This continual process of playing different roles is full of potential and real conflicts for guest-service employees. A person who is sent different role expectations by different people may feel conflict and confusion. If the guest expects one thing and the company policy requires another, the employee faces the difficult choice of determining which way to go, which role to play. Conflict can also occur when the supervisor sends out conflicting role expectations, when the role expectations conflict with the employee's fundamental values or beliefs, or when the roles themselves come into conflict. If Sally's husband asks her to come home early for the children's birthday party and Sally's boss asks her to work an extra shift tonight, Sally's roles as wife/mother and employee will conflict.

Clarifying the Role

Managers need to spend time and energy in minimizing employee role conflict and maximizing role clarity. People like to know what is expected of them. When the organization and its leadership don't spend the necessary time clarifying employee role expectations, the potential for conflict is great. Effective hospitality training programs clearly define roles for their employees and thereby minimize the conflicts they will have to face. When they have finished training and begin to serve guests, service providers should know their roles thoroughly. For example, when Disney cast members go "on stage" to perform, they know that the priority of the elements in the roles they play is safety, courtesy, show, and efficiency. Safety is never to be compromised. If a cast member has a choice of two actions, one safer and the other showier, the cast member feels no role conflict in taking the safe action.

Emotional Labor and Role Playing

Frontline hospitality employees who interact with guests have to be good at performing what is termed **emotional labor**. These employees not only need the skills, ability, and knowledge to perform the service, which may require some physical labor, but also need whatever it takes to perform the service in a certain way. Hardly anyone naturally smiles all the time, nor can anyone's natural response to a guest's needs always be empathetic. But smiles and sympathy are part of the hospitality employee's job, even when it's hard. It is especially difficult for most people to act positive and empathetic when things go wrong and an angry, upset, or unreasonable guest is yelling at them.

The effort required to deal with guests in these situations is emotional labor. It can be at least as draining on the employee as physical labor. Just as a positive attitude can be contagious, so too can a negative one. How can employees avoid getting caught up in the emotional reactions of guests? One way is by thinking of the job as playing a role in a theatrical performance to decrease the personal wear and tear of this emotional labor. Instead of actually paying the emotional price of getting personally involved in every guest's needs, the employee can display the emotional response that would be required of someone acting as if he or she were personally involved in every guest's needs. The emotional labor expended in genuinely feeling the emotions responding to the many needs and problems of guests could wear anybody out long before a work shift was over. Performing the job as an acting role makes it possible for hospitality employees to perform well without becoming emotionally exhausted.

The research on this topic suggests that role playing is actually better for the employee and the organization than genuine emotional involvement.[25] According to Ashforth and Humphrey, "Given the repetitive and scripted nature of many service roles, one may develop habitual routines for...acting such that emotional labor becomes relatively effortless."[26] Individuals who strongly identify with their organizational roles are apt to feel more authentic when they are conforming to role expectations, even if they are only acting to display rather than actually feeling the emotional involvement required of the role.[27] Further, acting like a certain type of person tends to commit one to becoming that type of person, especially if one volunteers to play the role to a public audience.[28]

SETTING GOALS

Another way managers can clarify their expectations for employees, and at the same time motivate better performance, is by setting goals. Most managers are familiar with the value for the overall organization of **goal setting** for individual employees and units. Research has repeatedly shown that setting specific and challenging (but attainable) goals leads to higher performance levels than expressing vague goals or telling people to "do their best."[29] Goals should satisfy the **SMART criteria**, that is, goals should be Specific, Measureable, Attainable, Result oriented, and Time bound. Specific and measurable goals allow people to know where they are supposed to be heading and what it will look like when they get there.[30] They are a powerful means to achieve attainable, result-oriented, and time-bound outcomes. Goal setting that follows these SMART rules is an excellent motivational tool. They allow people to self-manage since they can show clearly and objectively whether behaviors at work are leading toward or away from the set goals. They provide a means to keep everyone's efforts aligned with the organizational purpose since the goals are directly connected to the organization's mission. Finally, specific and measurable goals are a way to keep people from wasting time doing things that do not need doing. When goal setting is used in conjunction with a clear mission statement, a strong organizational culture, the right incentives, and appropriate training, people will be more productive, more satisfied, and happier.

The goal-setting process has two desirable organizational outcomes. First, it produces a logical and complete plan of how each part of the organization will contribute to the overall success of the hotel, convention bureau, or local attraction. Second, it demonstrates to all members of the organization how what they do adds value to that organization's ability to achieve its mission. Employees perform more effectively when they know how they are contributing to organizational success, and the goal-setting process communicates in specific terms what they need to do in order to make their contribution.

An Example: Management by Objectives

Organizations often make their goal-setting process systematic by incorporating Peter Drucker's **Management by Objectives (MBO)**.[31] MBO is a process of having each employee set specific and measurable goals and then using the achievement of those goals as a key driver for that employee's performance assessment. Its great value to both organization and employee is that it forces specification of job responsibilities in a contract-like written document that allows everyone to know exactly what they are supposed to do and how they will be evaluated on it.

The heart of traditional MBO is the *manager's letter*, written by employees to managers and not vice versa. In the letter, employees express their understanding of their own job objectives and the manager's job objectives, their own goals for the coming period (e.g., the following quarter or year), the obstacles to meeting them, the standards by which they expect to be evaluated, and the specifics of what they plan to do to meet the goals. The employee and manager discuss the letter until they reach an agreement about its contents.

Preparation of the letter involves a rich discussion by employee and supervisor about the employee's goals and job objectives, with a breakdown of job responsibilities into detailed sub-objectives and specific activities. The letter opens up communication between supervisor and employee about how each contributes to the overall organizational mission. Employees should leave the final discussion of a properly done *manager's letter* with a full understanding of what their jobs are for the coming period, how their performance is going to be evaluated, and how their performance fits into the fulfillment of their supervisor's job responsibilities, the supervisor's goals, and the overall organizational mission. The letter represents a formal agreement between employee and supervisor that tells the employee what to do during the forthcoming period and how the supervisor will evaluate the employee at the end of the period.

As a communication tool, the letter is exceptional. As a performance-measurement and employee-direction tool, it is as good as management theory can offer, because the standards against which performance will be measured are mutually determined and clearly understood by managers and employees. Combining the benefits of solid communication about employee expectations with the benefits of specific goal setting makes these letters a powerful device for aligning everyone in the organization with the mission and motivates them to perform.[32] As a means for telling the right people the right things to do, MBO can play a large part in organizational success—placing the right people in the right jobs doing the right things in the right ways with sufficient commitment and effort to get the mission accomplished.

Of course, MBO and goal setting are not perfect and doing them well can be a challenge for the hospitality manager. Managers have to estimate correctly what goals to emphasize, for themselves and their employees, or run the risk of being wrong at the end of the period. Also, if the manager does not know what employees are doing, should be doing, and what they are capable of doing, having a thoughtful discussion about the contents of the manager's letter will be difficult or pointless. Furthermore, because they can be spaced out as far as a year, the periodic nature of performance reviews can lead to inflexibility in responding to rapid changes in the organization's environment.

Setting clear and measurable goals is an important but difficult thing to do. Doing it well takes time and effort, especially for tasks whose performance outcomes are difficult to measure. But the benefits achieved by working with employees to set goals make the effort worthwhile. Even if organizations do not want to use a formal MBO approach, they should have some sort of goal-setting process in place.

PROVIDING THE RIGHT DIRECTION

We have emphasized in this chapter the critical role that managers play in motivating employees. Managers need to know what theories of motivation they can apply to motivate employees, what needs their employees have, and how to offer rewards that meet those needs in order to elicit exceptional performance. Managers also need to have sufficient administrative or transactional skills to take care of the basic job-related requirements of their employees. They must be able to handle the paperwork, administrative procedures, and policies that directly influence each employee's ability to perform the job. A manager who forgets to submit the proper payroll, doesn't get the computer fixed, or schedules too few people to work on a shift creates situations in which the most enthused, energetic employee can't succeed. Good managers are those who thoroughly and competently attend to these basic and routine job requirements of employees.

Managers also have another critical tool to manage their employees. By the nature of their role, managers are given formal authority to help run the company. How they use this authority, and how employees respond to it, is another important mechanism to understand for directing employee behaviors.

Managers and Authority

To many managers, authority is the power to yell at someone because you are the boss. These managers are still comfortable with the outmoded idea that the boss tells subordinates to jump and lets them ask how high on the way up. "I don't have to motivate my people. I tell them what to do, and they do it"—Such managers are less comfortable with the fact that, in the contemporary working environment, they may get little or no cooperation, high turnover, low morale, and a hostile work force. Employees working for these managers are not usually motivated to provide the exceptional service for which hospitality organizations strive.

People generally don't want to work for authoritarian managers. Such managers lower employee morale, increase turnover, and hurt the company culture. And yet, hospitality managers and supervisors need to get people to accept direction and work hard on behalf of the organization. How do they *exercise their authority* without being *authoritarian*?

Authority-Acceptance Theory

While not all managers have the characteristics of great leaders, they all possess the power and responsibility to direct subordinate behaviors because of the very nature of the managerial job. Managers who wish others to work well for them have to understand why people follow (or don't follow) directions and do (or don't do) what managers ask them to do. According to classic management writer Chester Barnard's **authority-acceptance theory**, authority is the quality of a directive that causes someone else to accept the directive and to do as directed.[33] If someone instructs you to bring a keg of beer from the cooler and you do it, that directive has authority for you. If you do not do it, that directive does not have authority for you. So, whether a directive has authority or not is determined by the directive receiver, not the sender or person in authority. The organization gives the manager formal powers; the individual gives the manager authority. In much the same way that value is defined by the guest and rewards defined by the employee, authority has to be accepted by the employee or there is no authority.

The factors influencing the acceptance of managerial authority lie in the nature of the sender and receiver, their relationships to the organization and to each other, and in the nature of the communication itself. The manager must understand and pay attention to these factors that influence employee acceptance of direction. Just as governments must ultimately rely on the consent of the governed, so too must hospitality organizations.

Preconditions for Employee Acceptance of Authority

Four preconditions must be met before an employee will accept managerial authority. However, even if the preconditions are met, the employee may still not accept the directive. But if they are not met, the employee either will not or cannot accept the directive.

1. *The employee must understand the directive.* If the employee does not understand the directive, compliance is impossible. Many employees have listened carefully and then later wondered what the manager was talking about or what the manager wanted done. Many employees have thought they understood a directive and then found that they did not, because the communication was too confusing or too general. For example, Area Regional Supervisor Jones tells Store Manager Smith, "Get rid of the trouble with the refrigerator at the Garden Grill Restaurant." Smith removes the troublesome refrigerator, scraps it, and replaces it with a new one, when Jones really wanted the old one repaired. The two employees had different meanings for "get rid of the trouble." Even though they both "understood" the communication, their understandings were different. A manager who has not checked to see if the communication was understood has not exercised authority. Employees who are supposed to comply with a directive cannot do what they do not understand.

2. *The employee must believe that the directive is consistent with the organization's goals.* An airline flight attendant notices that the exit to a plane has oil on the floor, which might endanger the safety of deplaning passengers. The pilot tells the attendant to allow the passengers off the plane anyway. Because so many training sessions have stressed the primary importance of passenger safety, the attendant may well ignore the pilot and keep the passengers on the plane until the oil is cleaned up. Without a reasonable explanation for departing from safety standards, the attendant would not see the directive as consistent with the organization's goals. All experienced managers know that employees hesitate to follow such directives. If a directive appears to conflict with an organizational goal, accepted policy, tradition, or past practice, the manager must spend the time to explain why this time it is different.

   A special violation of this precondition is the role conflict caused by conflicting directives from two or more managers. Both directives are sent down, but they cannot both support the organization's effort. The employee will either accept one and reject the other or do nothing.

3. *The employee must believe that the directive is consistent with the employee's own goals.* This precondition is related to whatever motivated the employee to affiliate with the organization in the first place. If carrying out the directive will result in the employee having to do something that will make the organization less attractive to the employee, the directive may be disobeyed or (more usually) evaded. Such directives are inconsistent with the employee's personal motives, which are the basis for accepting any directives at all. If the directive is totally inconsistent with goals or principles that are important to the employee, and the directive cannot be ignored or avoided, the employee may resign. Accepting or rejecting managerial or supervisory authority is a result of the employee carefully weighing the balance between the inducements offered and the contributions expected in return. If inducements offered are equal to or more than the contributions expected, directives will be accepted. If required contributions outweigh inducements, directives will not be carried out.

4. *The employee must be physically and mentally able to carry out the directive.* This precondition may seem too obvious to mention. Yet, we are sometimes asked to do the impossible. A woman with a bad back is told to carry heavy cases of liquor. An employee allergic to detergent is told to take a temporary assignment in the hotel laundry. The manager who gives directives without knowing each employee's capabilities soon finds out that if it can't be done, it won't.

Securing Employee Compliance with Directives

Once the preconditions to the acceptance of authority are understood, how do managers actually secure compliance with their directives? When you are a manager, what will you need to do to ensure that your subordinates do what you ask of them? The compliance necessary for a smoothly functioning organization comes about for four reasons.

1. *Effective managers issue directives that comply with the four preconditions.* The effective executive communicates directives that are accepted. Directives that do not comply with the preconditions are not obeyed. Poor managers ignore the preconditions primarily for one reason: They don't know any better. They think their formal organizational positions give them the right to issue commands of all types. Many managers believe they have absolute authority over their subordinates. This belief is confirmed by many organizational experiences in which managers' subordinates do indeed comply with their commands, but it can also lead to those managers having subordinates leave for more fulfilling positions. Effective managers know that "absolute" authority is absolute only as long as the four preconditions are not violated. If managers meet the preconditions, employees allow them to use their authority. Once the manager begins to ignore the preconditions, employees begin to ignore the directives.

2. *Effective managers ensure not just clear communication from the manager to the subordinate, but also from the subordinate to the manager and between subordinates.* Managers may forget that the organizational view and knowledge they have is different from those of their subordinates. It is easy to forget that information you have frequent and easy access to is not available to your employees. Managers who know what their subordinates don't know often forget to share what they know, and the resulting communication gap can lead to employee misunderstandings and failure to do what needs to be done. A manager needs to make sure that all employees have the information they need to do their jobs correctly and that the information can flow freely among the employees who need it to effectively deliver the service product.

Good communication is essential for a good manager. Managers must ensure that they are understood; they must also make sure they understand their subordinates' needs.

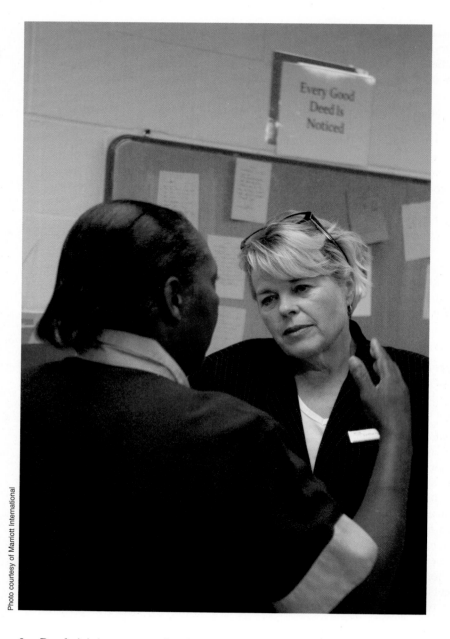

Photo courtesy of Marriott International

3. *People joining an organization expect to do job-related tasks.* Another reason for compliance is that people expect to be given directions, instructions, and sometimes commands regarding certain aspects of their behavior in organizations. They obey directives within these "zones of acceptance" without question. Directives fall into one of three classes: clearly acceptable, clearly unacceptable, and questionable.

If Lois Evans tells her assistant, Bill Elliot, to come into her office to install a new spreadsheet program on her computer, the order would fall within Elliot's zone of acceptance. Elliot knew when he took the job that Evans might tell him to do software installations. On the other hand, if Evans asks Elliot to come over to her apartment for drinks and software installation, Elliot would probably refuse. He would not consider such overtime work outside the office to be an acceptable part of the job.

Many directives fall into a third area: the questionable zone. If Evans asks Elliot to make the coffee, or get a birthday card for Mr. Evans, or do some other task that is not part of the job but is not really outrageous, Elliot may be unsure about whether to follow the directive and might have to think about it.

The width of the acceptance zone depends on the extent to which the organization fulfills the member's needs. The fanatical member of a cult might literally be willing to do anything to advance the cult's cause. Most organizational members, however loyal and hard working they may be, are not nearly so fanatical.

4. *Members enforce each other's compliance.* Most members want "their" organization to run smoothly. If it does, they can gain the benefits that they anticipated when they joined. Therefore, group members will bring social pressure to bear on any member unwilling to accept authority. Employees realize that they cannot achieve their own personal goals if the organization fails. An organization cannot succeed if its members will not accept authority and take direction. Therefore, any member who denies a directive or will not cooperate represents a threat to those members who identify with and work toward organizational goals for their own reasons. Accordingly, the group takes an active interest in maintaining every member's compliance with organizational directives.

The informal group plays this important enforcement role in support of the formal organization's authority structure. If the informal group wants a decision implemented, it is usually implemented. If a decision is not agreeable to the informal group, its members can find many effective ways of holding up implementation.

Organizations promote their best and most expert employees, give them titles to remind everyone of their rank, and give them control over information and resources—among which are rewards. The more important the rewards that a manager controls are to an employee, the more able that manager will be to get that employee to accept authority. Determining which resources are important to employees is a key responsibility of managers seeking to retain the enthusiastic commitment of their employees. Managers able to provide these rewards can elicit effort, productivity, enthusiasm, and other contributions that the hospitality organization seeks from employees—all without unduly exercising their authority. The essential point here is that the greater the benefits or inducements (intrinsic or extrinsic) that the organization provides to its members, the more willing they are to accept orders from the organizational leadership. Effective managers find ways to keep the inducements/contributions balance tilted heavily in favor of the employee. They know what inducements are available, try to identify those that are important to the employee, and provide that array of inducements.

Managing Fairly

Employees want to be treated fairly by their managers and the organization, and successful managers seek ways to ensure that they are. According to **equity theory**, we compare what we get out of an endeavor (the outputs) to what we put into it (our inputs) and draw a conclusion as to the fairness of the ratio of the two. We may have an internal standard of comparison, or we may compare ourselves to other people both inside and outside our organizations. If we think that we are getting a fair deal, we are satisfied. If we think that we are getting less than we deserve, we feel unfairly treated. According to the theory, and common sense, employees who feel fairly treated are more motivated to perform on behalf of their organization than employees who feel unfairly treated.

The difficulties lie in figuring out how or with whom your employees are comparing their inputs and outputs and, if the comparison is external, in trying to understand how employees value the inputs and outputs of both parties. Managers who seek the superior performance that distinguishes excellent organizations from the merely average must be alert to the equity comparisons that their employees make. Employees are, ultimately, volunteers. They can choose to leave their jobs whenever they want to. And nothing undermines voluntary performance faster than a feeling of being treated inequitably. Research shows that employee feelings of inequity lead to lower performance, less positive customer engagement, greater dissatisfaction, and increased turnover.

Justice in the Workplace

In the last few decades, research on equity theory has expanded into consideration of organizational justice to examine how fair and unfair treatment by managers, supervisors, and coworkers affects employee behaviors. Regarding employee reactions to how fairly or justly they are treated, four forms of justice have been examined: distributive justice (i.e., fairness of decision-making outcomes), procedural justice (i.e., fairness of decision-making processes), interpersonal justice (i.e., fairness of treatment), and informational justice (i.e., fairness of communication). A multitude of studies confirm what common sense suggests: When employees feel treated fairly by their organization and other organizational members, they tend to be more committed to their organization, have higher levels of job satisfaction and performance, and engage in more helping behaviors and fewer harmful behaviors.[34] Employees who feel unjustly treated tend to call in sick more often, have poor morale, and may even steal from the company. They also do not sound or act happy with their customers.

At the other extreme, employees who initially feel that they got more than others in similar situations eventually conclude that they deserve what they got. For a short time they may feel guilty that they were overly rewarded and may work harder to justify what they got, especially in the eyes of their fellow workers. For example, an employee who has received an apparently unjustified pay increase may come to work earlier and stay late—but only for a few weeks, if that long.

Whether to keep salary figures private or make them public is an organizational concern. When people do not know what others are getting paid, they tend to assume wider salary disparities than what actually exist. These assumptions can lead to feelings of inequity. Some academics advocate publishing everyone's salary, in the hope that accurate information will reduce feelings of inequity, if in fact salaries are equitable. When everyone's pay is published, no one has to guess what someone else is being paid. And everyone can see what behavior gets the highest rewards. However, since organizations realize that equity is in the eyes of the beholder, many of them are reluctant to publish actual payroll data because of privacy concerns and because they fear raising equity concerns in the minds of employees who might have thought their salaries were fair until they saw the full salary figures. Some organizations publish pay ranges for jobs that all can see, in hopes of demonstrating that the ranges are equitable.

Managers and Leaders

Managers must take care of the administrative duties, but managers can do more than exercise their authority, to direct the way work is done. Managers who are also leaders do other things that transform the organization and the people working in it. Leadership skills include the ability to identify and provide those rewards that the individual employee wants from membership in the organization. Although fear and the threat of punishment may be powerful short-term motivators, it is the ability of the manager to fulfill employee needs that invokes energetic employee commitment to organizational goals in the long run. Employee needs must be identified and satisfied if managers want employees to give their enthusiasm, effort, commitment, and effective job performance.

Leadership has been defined and described in many ways. A description applicable to the hospitality industry is one provided by Kouzes and Posner, who state that "leadership is ultimately about creating a way for people to contribute to making something extraordinary happen."[35] So while a manager may simply tell subordinates what to do, a leader inspires employees not only to complete their job tasks, but to make the extra effort needed to provide exceptional service.

The power of effective leadership is undeniable. Kerry Miller, former Vice President of People Development for Bertucci's Restaurants, explains, "I think that when you get behind a true leader, you're more jazzed up to get into work every day because you know that person is supportive of what you're doing."[36] Effective leadership motivates employees to focus their efforts on achieving the organization's goals. Great leaders *get the job done* because others want to help them achieve the goals and objectives they have mutually set. Great leadership obviously includes short-term achievement, but it also involves employee development and engagement so that employees are motivated and capable of achieving their own long-term goals, as well as helping to achieve organizational goals.[37]

Leading with Integrity

A leader's responsibilities are many: to inspire, challenge, and create a shared purpose among employees; to promote employee engagement, set goals, offer feedback, provide inspiration, and set the example that motivates employees to go the extra mile. But it all begins, says Tony Simons, author of *The Integrity Dividend*, with establishing trust. Simons explains, "Any leader's word is his or her most potent tool, and an effective leader devotes much attention to developing and preserving the power of that word. It is not about being nice. It is not about being ethical. It is about being more effective by developing and preserving your credibility.... Behavioral integrity is not everything it takes to lead, but it is a necessary ingredient of huge consequence and huge challenge."[38]

Behavioral integrity describes the fit between what the leader says and what the leader does.[39] When subordinates trust their leaders, they are more satisfied with their own work, more committed to the company, better performers, and more willing to perform beyond what is required by the job description.[40] If leaders fail to keep their promises, they lose their effectiveness. If promised rewards are not given, employees become skeptical and less likely to engage in behaviors that were supposed to be rewarded. If leaders do not behave with integrity, they are going to create dissatisfaction and turnover.

Motivating employees is a complex balancing act. The best organizations place many tools at the manager's disposal to help encourage employee performance, but if the manager does not lead with integrity, these tools are ineffective.

Leaders and the Changing Environment

As hospitality leaders try to strike the inducements-contributions balance that will motivate employees to perform at their best, they must remain responsive to the ever-changing environment: increased diversity, more work teams, greater global competition, cultural shifts, new technologies—the list goes on. As a result, future leaders will need to be more culturally aware and be able to incorporate multiple perspectives, appreciate cross-cultural and cross-generational differences, understand both individual and team needs, and function effectively in complex environments.[41] All these factors will make determining rewards that fulfill employee needs more difficult.

MOTIVATION, EMPLOYEE SATISFACTION, AND GUEST SATISFACTION

Because people are complex, there is no simple way to motivate everybody. While realizing the critical role of financial rewards in the world of work, managers must also realize that money will not solve all motivational problems. Recognition and feedback can also be motivational, if managers have the leadership and management skills to provide these nonfinancial rewards effectively. The work itself can be highly motivating if designed appropriately. A complicating factor is that jobs cannot be designed only to motivate employees. Job designers must also consider the company's culture, the types of employees selected, the training they receive, and the way the service product is delivered.

Ideally, the manager gets it all right. Employees are offered the incentives that best fit their needs, managers structure jobs to make them motivating, employees understand their roles and how their behaviors can lead to rewards, and managers provide clear leadership, exercise managerial authority effectively and appropriately, and lead with integrity. All parties to the "contract" do their jobs—employer contributions match the incentives that employees seek. The result (ideally) is a satisfied and productive workforce.

Do Satisfied Employees Perform Well?

But is it safe to assume that a satisfied workforce is going to be a productive workforce? Certainly, employee satisfaction leads to several beneficial outcomes, including lower turnover. Some even argue that employee satisfaction is essential if the employee is to be motivated to maintain maximum effort and performance. These satisfied employees will yield satisfied customers, or so the argument goes. Unfortunately, research does not support this idea. Having happy employees does not necessarily mean that you will have either good performers or happy customers.

Research combining the results from more than 300 studies shows that employee job satisfaction explains less than 10 percent of the variance in employee performance.[42] Employees often love their jobs even when they don't do them very well. Conversely, some dissatisfied employees may take enough pride in their work to provide excellent customer service despite their dissatisfaction. Other factors, such as employee ability and role perception, have a much greater impact on performance than does job satisfaction. Similarly, a review of nearly two dozen studies shows that employee satisfaction explains only about 5 percent of the variance in customer satisfaction ratings. Customer satisfaction does not seem to depend on employee satisfaction. Managers need to avoid the trap of concluding that because their employees are happy, they must also be performing well and satisfying customers. Don't think that you can simply look at employee satisfaction as a measure of how well the employee is performing or how well you've done as a manager.

Are High Performers Satisfied?

The relationship between employee performance and employee satisfaction may actually be the other way around: high performance *may lead to* high satisfaction. Here is the reasoning.[43] Good management practices—primarily offering the right inducements to employees and showing employees that the inducements will become rewards if employees exert appropriate effort—motivate employees to put forth that effort. But effort is not

An employee's happiness does not necessarily mean they will perform better. Often, high performance actually leads to high employee satisfaction. However, increasing satisfaction does improve retention.

Image copyright Monkey Business Images, 2010. Used under license from Shutterstock.com

enough to achieve the performance that will lead to rewards. Employees must have accurate perceptions of their organizational roles; otherwise they may be putting forth effort in the wrong direction. Employees must also have the traits and abilities that will enable them to achieve desired performance levels. When motivated employees with the right traits and abilities properly understand their organizational roles, high levels of performance result.

Up to this point, we don't know whether employees are satisfied or not! Only after employees receive their rewards (both external and internal) and compare them to the promised, anticipated rewards will they make the equity determination of whether the rewards are fair or not. If fair, they are satisfied; if not fair, they are not satisfied.

Are the Customers of Satisfied High Performers Also Satisfied?

But what about the guests? Are they satisfied? Many companies with satisfied employees have gone bankrupt. The big question is whether employee satisfaction is generally accompanied by guest satisfaction. Fortunately, research suggests that if employees know what to do, feel that the company values and rewards good customer service, and are well-managed, the result will be both high employee satisfaction *and* high guest satisfaction.[44] As we have previously shown, employee satisfaction is not enough in and of itself to motivate or enable employees to give customers a wow experience. But because satisfied employees tend to stay, learn the culture, and be engaged, it is an important piece of the customer service puzzle.

To deliver great customer service, you need to have the right culture, hire the right people, and motivate them to perform. But even all of this may not be sufficient to ensure exceptional service experiences. An additional managerial challenge is to make sure the customers do their part in coproducing the service experience, know the roles they are supposed to play, and have the capabilities to perform them successfully. And that is the subject of the next chapter.

LESSONS LEARNED

1. Set clear, measurable standards that define expectations for job performance. Constantly reinforce these standards by setting examples; let employees know that the standards are important; reward employees when they meet these standards.

2. Walk the talk; set the example. Employees respond more to what you do than to what you say.

3. Make all tasks and goals measurable; people like to know how well they're doing.

4. Pay attention to communication; people can't do what they don't know about or don't understand.

5. Be fair, ethical, and equitable. People need to feel they are being treated equitably. If you don't show people why reward differentials are made between employees, they will assume the worst.

6. Reward behaviors you want, and don't reward behaviors you don't want.

7. Praise, praise, praise. Look for reasons to reinforce people doing the right things. Privately re-educate and coach those doing the wrong things.

8. Show employees the relationships between their personal goals, group goals, and organizational goals. Find win-win-wins.

9. People give you the right to direct them. Know how to earn that right.

10. Don't just support your frontline employees; trust them as well.

11. Give people a chance to grow and get better, and then reward them for it.

12. Your frontline employees are heroes; make their jobs fair, fun, interesting, and important.

REVIEW QUESTIONS

1. If you have ever been employed, what if anything did you want from your job other than a paycheck?

   A. If you are employed now, have your job expectations changed from those of the past?

   B. What are your job expectations from the position you hope to hold in ten years?

2. If you have been employed, can you recall times when you were upset due to the boss ignoring your good work because the boss was giving complete attention to another employee who was complaining or doing a bad job? If so, what managerial lesson did this teach you? How would you use that lesson to determine or change your own managerial style?

3. What does it mean to be empowered? Give some situations in which you were empowered.

   A. How did you handle empowerment? How did you feel?

   B. Compare those situations to a few in which you were not empowered. How did you handle the latter, and how did you feel?

C. If you were a hotel or restaurant manager, can you think of some job functions that you would hesitate to empower your employees to perform? Why?

D. Why is it particularly important to empower the frontline people who interact with hospitality guests? Or is it?

4. Consider a restaurant meal in which much of the service is provided one on one, server to guest. How important is teamwork to the success of this guest experience?

5. The authority-acceptance theory suggests that people must accept authority or it does not really exist. Do you agree or disagree?

A. Give examples of situations you have been in where people did not follow direct orders. Did they refuse because the conditions for authority acceptance detailed in the chapter were not met, or for other reasons?

B. What do managers need to know to ensure that their authority is accepted?

C. How does all that relate to managing the guest experience in hospitality organizations?

D. Does authority-acceptance theory seem to you to have more or less relevance to the hospitality industry as compared to most industries?

ACTIVITIES

1. Find a hospitality organization that seems to have succeeded in motivating its frontline employees to give outstanding service. How do they do it? If you work for an organization that does not sufficiently motivate you, what is the organization doing or not doing that causes you to be unmotivated?

2. Find an organization that seems to try to make its hospitality jobs fun and interesting. What do they do, and how well does it work? If you or your friends have jobs that do not provide fun and are not interesting, why is that so? Does the organization seem to care whether you are interested and having fun? Why or why not?

3. Interview three line employees from two hospitality organizations and find out what motivates them to perform well.

ETHICS IN BUSINESS

Rewards can change behavior, but you need to design your pay system carefully to be sure you want the behaviors your pay plan is actually encouraging. Below is a list of pay plans and their desired goals. What might be the unintended consequences of each system? How might each form of pay inadvertently motivate employees to behave inappropriately?

GOAL	PAY SYSTEM
To encourage teamwork among servers	Change from individual tips to pooled tips
To encourage front desk agents to "up-sell" customers to more expensive rooms	Provide a bonus for each luxury suite sold
To achieve higher customer satisfaction	Provide bonuses if customer satisfaction ratings average above 4 on a 5-point feedback card given to all guests
To improve the hotel's financial performance	Give company stock to all employees
To encourage employees to get higher performance evaluations	Provide merit raises and bonuses for higher evaluations
To encourage employee retention	Implement a recognition program to reward employees on their five-, ten-, fifteen-, and twenty-year anniversaries

CASE STUDIES

Hartsell Hotels

While he was still in college, Bill Hartsell decided that he wanted to own hotels. When he graduated, he borrowed some money, bought a bankrupt property, and created the first Hartsell Hotel. The hotel presented constant problems, but Bill was highly motivated and worked twelve to sixteen hours a day, six or seven days a week. He did as much of the work as he could himself, from making beds to preparing light meals in the hotel coffee shop.

The hard work paid off. Bill succeeded with his original hotel, bought two more, and increased his staff accordingly. He made a determined effort to hire young people, old people, women, minorities, and the handicapped, and he paid them as well as he could. Bill felt a genuine sense of responsibility to his employees and to the community. After five years, Bill had 300 employees.

Bill hired three recent hospitality graduates, intending to move them into responsible management positions after a training period. At his first meeting with them, Bill made his position plain: "No one at Hartsell Hotels works harder than I do. I'm the first to arrive and the last to leave. I work most weekends. I'm paying you

well. I'm offering you a chance for rapid advancement. But don't think in terms of a 40-hour work week. I want you to work as hard as I do and act as if this business were your own. Is that clear?" In unison the three responded, "Yes, sir, Mr. Hartsell."

Three months later, they had all left to take jobs with Marriott, Hilton, and Sheraton.

★ ★ ★

1. What, if anything, was wrong with Mr. Hartsell's approach? Why did the new employees leave, and what might have motivated them to stay?

2. Were Mr. Hartsell's expectations for his new employees unrealistic? If so, why?

3. What inconsistencies, if any, do you see between the goals of the three new employees and Mr. Hartsell's goals?

4. Could those inconsistencies have been resolved? How?

Farney Spa and Fish Camp

Farney Spa and Fish Camp has found its niche; it caters to women who want to combine the facilities of a luxury spa with fishing opportunities. Sally Blade, supervisor in charge of fishing guides at Farney Spa and Fish Camp, has a problem with one of the fishing guides. All guides

are supposed to be at work by 5:30 a.m. They must have their skiffs ready for operation by 6:30 a.m. But Mary Lou Day is almost always late for work. She arrives any time between 5:40 and 6:15 a.m. Once she gets to work, she is excellent. She is easily the best guide in the camp and always gets her boat prepared early, even after arriving late. She is qualified for a promotion except that she has not been in her present position long enough. She understands and accepts that situation, but she hopes to move up into management some day.

Day's frequent tardiness is causing problems. Other guides, without Day's willingness or ability, are using Day's lateness to justify their own. Sally Blade feels that she cannot crack down on the other guides without cracking down on Day as well. Sally has had several talks with Mary Lou. She always promises to do better, but she never does. Sally has even suggested a different reporting and leaving time for Mary Lou, to accommodate fishing parties that don't like to head out onto the lake so early, but Mary Lou does not like the idea of being treated differently. "After all," she says, "I always get my skiff ready on time, my guests like the service I provide, and I always get my boat back and cleaned up by quitting time, don't I?" Mary Lou has even suggested that she may quit if the organization cannot be "flexible enough to let one good employee be a few minutes late every so often, without bugging me about it. There are other fish camps on this lake, you know."

★ ★ ★

1. Mary Lou Day is Sally Blade's best fishing guide. Is Mary Lou justified in asking that Sally "cut her some slack"? Should Sally comply?

2. If you think Mary Lou should meet the same work requirements that are imposed on the other guides, how would you motivate her to do so?

Jubilee Hotels Corp.

Jubilee Hotels Corp. was having problems with negative worker attitudes and low productivity at its Hartwell, Alabama, hotel. To turn things around, JHC decided in 2007 to change the operation of the Hartwell hotel completely. The hotel would be run with a minimum of supervision. The employees themselves would take over such traditional management prerogatives as making job assignments, scheduling coffee breaks, interviewing prospective employees, and even deciding on pay raises.

The new system eliminated several layers of management and supervisory personnel and assigned three primary areas of responsibility—front desk, housekeeping, and office duties—to self-managing teams of seven to fourteen workers per shift. The former middle managers, divided among the primary areas, retained some supervisory authority but had not nearly as much as before. The workers rotated between the dull and the interesting jobs. The teams made all necessary management decisions.

For several years, the new system was a success in many ways. Unit costs decreased by 10 percent compared to costs under the old system, translating into a savings of $2 million per year. Turnover dropped to only 5 percent. Quality of work life and economic results were good.

Notwithstanding the plan's success, in 2010 the hotel began the transition back to a traditional organizational and management system, as an accompaniment to a major expansion. JHC introduced more specialized job classifications and more supervisors, and they reduced opportunities for employee participation. The company added seven management positions to the hotel, including controller, engineering manager, and services manager. Management took back the right to make decisions about pay raises.

Professor Andrew Stubbs analyzed what had happened at Hartwell for his hospitality class: "The basic problem was that in this functional organization, many managers became nervous about what functions they could perform after the hotel workers themselves were given so many responsibilities. In addition, they resented being left out of things; upper-level management's enthusiasm for enriching the jobs of the workers didn't take into account the feelings of the middle managers. Where was their enrichment?"

★ ★ ★

1. Do you agree with the professor's assessment of what went wrong?

2. What does the Jubilee Hotels experience tell you about applying work team, enrichment, and incentives principles in real life?

3. What do you think will happen to the hotel once it fully returns to a "traditional" management system?

ADDITIONAL READINGS

Berger, L. A., & Berger, D. R. 2008. *The Compensation Handbook*, 5th edition. New York: McGraw-Hill.

Bettencourt, L. A., & Brown, S. W. 1997. Contact employees: Relationships among workplace fairness, job satisfaction and prosocial behaviors. *Journal of Retailing*, 73(1), 39–61.

Chiang, C. F., Jang, S. C., Canter, B., & Prince, B. 2008. An expectancy theory model for hotel employee motivation: Examining the moderating role of communication satisfaction. *Journal of Hospitality and Tourism Administration*, 9, 327–351.

Cropanzano, R., Bowen, D., & Gilliland, S. W. 2007. The management of organizational justice. *Academy of Management Perspectives*, 21(4), 34–48.

Dong, L. C., Droege, S. B., & Johnson, N. B. 2002. Incentives and self-interest: Balancing revenue and rewards in China's tourism industry. *Tourism and Hospitality Research*, 4, 69–77.

Gill, A., Fitzgerald, S., Bhutani, S., Mand, H., & Sharma, S. 2010. The relationship between transformational leadership and employee desire for empowerment. *International Journal of Contemporary Hospitality Management*, 22, 263–273.

Gill, A., & Mathur, N. 2007. Improving employee dedication and pro-social behavior. *International Journal of Contemporary Hospitality Management*, 19, 328–334.

Herzberg, F., Mausner, B., & Snyderman, B. B. 1959. *The Motivation to Work*. New York: Wiley.

Latham, G. P., & Pinder, C. C. 2005. Work motivation theory and research at the dawn of the twenty-first century. *Annual Review of Psychology*, 56, 485–516.

Lundberg, C., Gudmundson, A., & Andersson, T. D. 2009. Herzberg's Two-Factor Theory of work motivation tested empirically on seasonal workers in hospitality and tourism. *Tourism Management*, 30, 890–899.

Lynn, M., & McCall, M. 2009. Techniques for increasing server' tips: How generalizable are they? *Cornell Hospitality Quarterly*, 50, 198–208.

Milkovich, G. T., & Newman, J. M. 2005. *Compensation*, 8th edition. New York: McGraw-Hill.

Mitchell, T. R., & Daniels, D. 2003. Motivation, in I. B. Weiner (ed. in chief) and W. C. Borman, D. R. Ilgen, and R. J. Klimoski (eds.), *Handbook of Psychology*, volume 12. Hoboken, NJ: John Wiley & Sons.

Simons, T. 2008. *The Integrity Dividend*. San Francisco, CA: Jossey-Bass.

Sturman, M. C. 2001. The compensation conundrum: Does the hospitality industry shortchange its employees—and itself? *Cornell Hotel and Restaurant Administration Quarterly*, 42, 70–76.

Umashankar, V., & Kulkami, A. 2002. Employee motivation and empowerment in hospitality, rhetoric or reality - Some observations from India. *Journal of Services Research*, 2, 31–53.

NOTES

[1]Gross, T. S. 2004. *Positively Outrageous Service*. Kaplan Publishing: New York, p. 147.

[2]There are many Web pages that present the entire slideshow. More information is available at http://www.snopes.com/business/consumer/badhotel.asp; the presentation can be seen at http://www2.oakland.edu/users/oakley/Teaching_files/Yours%20Is%20a%20Very%20Bad%20Hotel.pdf.

[3]Latham, G. P. 2007. *Work Motivation: History, Theory, Research, and Practice.* Thousand Oaks, CA: Sage Publications.

[4]Blader, S. L., & Tyler T. R. 2009. Testing and extending the group engagement model: Linkages between social identity, procedural justice, economic outcomes, and extrarole behavior. *Journal of Applied Psychology*, 94, 445–464.

[5]Brun, J. P., & Dugas, N. 2008. An analysis of employee recognition: Perspectives on human resources practices. *The International Journal of Human Resource Management*, 19, 716–730.

[6]Busch, P., Venkitachalam, K., & Richards, D. 2008. Generational differences in soft knowledge situations: Status, needs for recognition, workplace commitment and idealism. *Knowledge and Process Management*, 15, 45–58.

[7]Koenig, D. 1994. *Mouse Tales: A Behind-the-Ears Look at Disneyland.* Irvine, CA: Bonaventure Press, p. 27.

[8]WorldatWork. 2008. *Trends in Employee Recognition: A Survey of World-at-Work Members.* Washington, DC: WorldatWork.

[9]Smith, M., & Irvine, D. 2009. The power of Fairmont Hotels and Resorts' strategic employee recognition program. *Workspan*, 52 (8), 28–32.

[10]Ibid.

[11]WorldatWork, 2008.

[12]*Walt Disney: Famous Quotes.* 1994. Printed for Walt Disney Theme Parks and Resorts, p. 36.

[13]Brinker, N., & Phillips, D. T. 1996. *On the Brink: The Life and Leadership of Norman Brinker.* Arlington, TX: The Summit Publishing Group, p. 195.

[14]Ford, R. C., McLaughlin, F. S., & Newstrom, J. W. 2004. Questions and answers about fun at work. *Human Resource Planning*, 26 (4), 18–33.

[15]This discussion of empowerment is based Ford, R. C., & Fottler, M. D. 1995. Empowerment: A matter of degree. *Academy of Management Executive*, 9 (3), 21–28.

[16]Bowen, D. E., & Lawler, E. E., III. 1992. The empowerment of service workers: What, why, how, and when. *Sloan Management Review*, 33 (1), 31–39.

[17]Barker, J. 2008. Power to the people. *Incentive*, 182 (2), 34–37.

[18]Ibid, 36.

[19]Michelli, J. 2008. *The New Gold Standard: 5 Leadership Principles for Creating a Legendary Customer Experience Courtesy of the Ritz-Carlton Hotel Company.* New York: McGraw-Hill, p. 110.

[20]Brinker & Phillips, 192.

[21]Plunkett, L. C., & Fournier, R. 1991. *Participative Management: Implementing Empowerment.* New York: John Wiley, p. 5.

[22]Freiberg, K., & Freiberg, J. 1996. *Nuts! Southwest Airlines' Crazy Recipe for Business and Personal Success.* Austin, TX: Bard Press, p. 289.

[23]See Bowen and Lawler, 31–39.

[24]Katz, D. M., & Kahn, R. L. 1966. *The Social Psychology of Organizations.* Wiley: New York.

[25]Varca, P. E. 2009. Emotional empathy and front line employees: Does it make sense to care about the customer? *Journal of Services Marketing*, 23, 51–56.

[26]Ashforth, B. E., & Humphrey, R. H. 1993. Emotional labor in service roles. *Academy of Management Review*, 18, 94.

[27]Ibid., 98.

[28]Ibid., 102.

[29]Locke, E. A., & Latham, G. P. 2006. New directions in goal-setting theory. *Current Directions in Psychological Science*, 15 (5), 265–268.

[30]Zeithaml, V. A., & Bitner, M. J. 1996. *Services Marketing*. New York: McGraw-Hill, p. 76.

[31]Drucker, P. F. 1954. *The Practice of Management*. NY: Harper.

[32]Crotts, J., Dickson, D., & Ford, R. C. 2005. Aligning organizational processes with mission: The case of service excellence. *Academy of Management Executive*, 19 (3), 54–68.

[33]See Barnard, C. I. 1968. *The Functions of the Executive*. Cambridge, MA: Harvard University Press, Chapter 12.

[34]For example, Colquitt, J. A., Conlon, D. E., Wesson, M. J., Porter, C. O. L. H., & Ng, K. Y. 2001. Justice at the millennium: A meta-analytic review of 25 years of organizational justice research. *Journal of Applied Psychology*, 86, 425–445; Cohen-Charash, Y., & Spector, P. E. 2001. The role of justice in organizations: A meta-analysis. *Organizational Behavior and Human Decision Processes*, 86, 278–321.

[35]Kouzes, J., & Posner, B. 2007. *The Leadership Challenge*. San Francisco, CA: Jossey Bass.

[36]Simons, T. 2008. *The Integrity Dividend*. San Francisco, CA: Jossey-Bass, p. 25.

[37]Blanchard, K. 2007. *Leading at a Higher Level*. Upper Saddle River, NJ: Prentice Hall.

[38]Simons, 223

[39]Ibid., 5.

[40]Dirks, K. T., & Ferrin, D. L. 2002. Trust in leadership: Meta-analytic findings and implications for research and practice. *Journal of Applied Psychology*, 87, 611–628.

[41]Avolio, B. J., Sosik, J. J., Jung, D. I., & Berson, Y. 2003. Leadership models, methods, and applications, in W. C. Borman, D. R. Ilgen, and R. J. Klimoski (eds.), *Handbook of Psychology*, vol. 12. New York: Wiley, pp. 277–307.

[42]Judge, T. A., Thorensen, C. J., Bono, J. E., & Patton, G. K. 2001. The job satisfaction-job performance relationship: A qualitative and quantitative review. *Psychological Bulletin*, 127, 376–407.

[43]For this reasoning, we are indebted to Porter, L. W., & Lawler, E. E., III. 1968. *Managerial Attitudes and Performance*. Homewood, IL: Richard D. Irwin, Inc., p. 17.

[44]Akdere, M. 2009. A multilevel examination of quality-focused human resource practices and firm performance: Evidence from the US healthcare industry. *The International Journal of Human Resource Management*, 20, 1945–1964; Way, S. A., Sturman, M. C., & Raab, C. 2010. What matters more? Contrasting the effects of job satisfaction and service climate on hotel F&B managers' job performance. *Cornell Hospitality Quarterly*, 51, 379–397.

CHAPTER 8

Involving the Guest:
The Co-Creation of Value

HOSPITALITY PRINCIPLE:
EMPOWER GUESTS
TO CO-CREATE THEIR EXPERIENCES

If you can't get it for yourself, who's going to get it for you?

—Fritz Perls, father of gestalt psychology

LEARNING OBJECTIVES

After reading this chapter, you should understand:

- How, when, and why hospitality organizations encourage or empower guests to help provide their own guest experiences.

- Which strategies most effectively involve the guest in co-creating the experience.

- What the advantages and disadvantages of guest involvement are for the organization and guest.

- Why hospitality organizations must sometimes "fire the guest" and how to do it.

GUESTS CO-CREATE VALUE

In the traditional firm-centric view of organizations, management decides what the guests want and designs a delivery system to provide it. The guest-centric view is that the guest-ologist seeks to identify what the customers want and involves them in the co-creation of the experience, before, during, or after the actual experience itself. Guest involvement leads to their **co-creating** the value and quality of that experience. If guests are involved in the design of the experience, through focus groups or by providing feedback on their prior experiences, they have the opportunity to co-create the experience before it happens. For example, a prepare-a-meal franchise will offer busy people the opportunity to come to a location where ingredients, recipes, utensils, and expertise are available for customers to co-create a week's worth of meals to take home and freeze. They cook their own meals. On a more complex level, guestologists at Disney use guest feedback to determine what aspects of the Disney experience are working well and which need to be redesigned. In today's instant-access-to-information environment, the hospitality organization can access guest comments via a designated complaint Web page, blogs (e.g., Marriot's blogs.marriott Web site), or social networking sites to find out what its guests are saying about things that make them satisfied and dissatisfied even by tweeting their opinions while they are still co-creating the service. Table 8.1 lists some popular social networking and blog Web sites. Guests can also co-create knowledge by posting reviews about their travel experiences, on sites like those listed in Table 8.2.

During the hospitality experience, management can use a variety of strategies to engage the guests in the **co-production** of that experience so that they co-create quality and value. This chapter focuses on these strategies. A later chapter will present strategies that management can use to engage its guests in co-creating value *after* the experience, for example, customer satisfaction surveys to pinpoint service failures and follow up on errors.

Noted management strategists Prahalad and Ramaswamy suggested that a customer co-creation of value is predicated on the rapid change in technology that allows today's customers to know more, share more, and compare more about their experiences than ever before. As a result, customers can learn what organizations are really doing in dealing with their guests by talking to others, on social networks or information-sharing Web sites (e.g., TripAdvisor); what they should pay, by visiting auction Web sites; and what the quality and value of the service product is.[1] The Web gives the guest the opportunity to interact directly with the hospitality organization and tell it what that guest really wants. It is up to the organization to find ways to listen, and guestologists always find ways. The point is that today's guest expects to co-produce the experience and co-create its value and quality in some way, and hospitality organizations need to find the means to fulfill that expectation.

There are several processes that can be used to engage the guest with the organization before, during, and after the hospitality experience. Some writers categorize the types of guest engagement into marketers, information providers, and co-producers. The discussion below will use a more elaborate categorization.

TABLE 8.1   Popular Social Networking and Blog Sites

WEB SITE	WHAT IT IS OR DOES
BlackCareerZone	A career and job search site for black professionals
Doostang	By invitation only, chiefly for financial services
85Broads	For female professionals and executives
Facebook	A social networking giant
GoogleGroups	A wide array of easily created shared interest groups
Jigsaw	A social network for business contacts with profiles
LatPro	For bilingual or Hispanic professionals
LinkedIn	A social network targeting professionals
Meetup	Helps groups of people with shared interests plan meetings and form off-line clubs in local communities around the world
CareerBuilder.com	One of the largest online job sites in the United States
My.Monster.com	Networks of Monster help-wanted opportunities
MySpace.com	A social network pioneer; social network and content sharing site for the jobs market
MyWorkster.com	Connects students, alumni, employers, companies, and the university community to foster professional growth and interconnectivity for college communities
Plaxo.com	A business and professional network; tailored to family, friends, or business
QuintCareers.com	Job search site with expert advice
Ryze.com	Business networking; member-created, themed networks
Saludos.com	Hispanic employment service for jobs promotes work force diversity and offers free résumé postings to qualified bilingual and college-trained professionals
Vault.com	A career information Web site, providing employee surveys of top employers, career advice, job listings, and career guides to individual industries; networks allowing anonymity
Windows Live Groups	A service that allows users to form their own community groups; an on-line service provided by Microsoft as part of its Windows Live services
Youtube.com	Site to watch, share, upload, and discover videos
Ziggs.com	White pages and free people search for professionals; for job data and profile sharing

© Cengage Learning 2012.

TABLE 8.2   Web Sites for Finding and Posting Reviews Related to Travel and Hospitality Services

WEB SITE	WHAT IT IS OR DOES
Consumersearch	Reviews mostly consumer goods, but also includes reviews related to travel.
Epinions	Reviews mostly consumer goods, but also includes reviews related to travel.
Fodors	Allows members to read and write reviews about travel experiences, share tips, and ask travel-related questions.
IgoUgo	A web site that allows users to plan trips, read and write reviews, create travel journals, and share photos.
TripAdvisor	Offers advice from travelers and a variety of travel planning tools.
Virtualtourist	Provides user-generated travel content from around the world. Includes tips, reviews, and photos from travelers sharing their experiences.
Yelp	A social networking site that provides reviews of businesses and services. Includes travel-related reviews, such as for hotels and restaurants, but also of other businesses and non-business locations.

© Cengage Learning 2012.

THE GUEST CAN HELP!

In the traditional manufacturing organization, the people involved in the core production tasks are insulated from external interruptions by layers of strategic planners and middle managers. The people providing many hospitality services, in contrast, are right out in the open where the guests can see and even interact with them. In many circumstances, the guests will take the primary role in co-producing the service themselves. Obvious examples are salad bars in restaurants and self-service check-ins at airports. Other obvious examples are the growing number of self-service technologies like Web-based restaurant, airline, and hotel reservations sites.

A crucial implication for hospitality organizations when they involve guests in co-producing the guest experience, either indirectly as observers or directly as participants, is that they must remain constantly aware that a server or a Web screen is likely to be the point of contact between the organization and the guest. Instead of relying on highly paid, experienced, and loyal executives or well-trained sales representatives serving as the point of contact with customers and the outside world, the hospitality organization must rely on its frontline servers or a Web page to represent the company. Both the server and the Web site represent the initial moments of truth for creating the guest's first impression of the organization. Each year, for millions of Disney park visitors, Southwest Airlines passengers, Olive Garden restaurant diners, and Marriott hotel guests, the visible, front-line employees answer questions, solve problems, provide services, and keep their organizations operating smoothly and efficiently. These employees not only produce the magic that guests expect, but they do it while the guests are watching, participating, and asking a million questions about everything. Unlike the automobile assembly-line production employee who can work undistracted in a controlled and structured environment, these employees must produce the guest experience consistently and flawlessly while coping with the many uncertainties that interacting constantly with guests can create.

Guests as Quasi-Employees

Hospitality organizations know they must help manage the confusion, stress, and uncertainty guests can create for their employees while on their jobs. One way is by training the employees in both job skills and the management of guest co-production. Another effective strategy for managing this confusion is to think of guests as quasi-employees and "manage" them accordingly.[2]

These unpaid "employees" must have the knowledge, skills, and abilities (KSAs) to successfully co-produce the service experience. This means organizations need to design a service product, an environment, and a delivery system that match the KSAs the customers bring to the experience. It may also mean that companies need to "train" the customers on how to take advantage of the service product. If it is to the advantage of both guests and organization to involve guests in the experience, the organization must take on the responsibility of figuring out how best to enable these quasi-employees to succeed in doing their tasks within the experience. Unlike customers of the typical manufacturing organization, guests are actually paying the hospitality organization to be successfully managed—putting an extra burden on management to manage them effectively.

Benjamin Schneider and David Bowen recommend a three-step strategy for managing these quasi-employees[3]:

1. Carefully and completely define the roles you want guests to play. In effect, do a job analysis, similar to that developed in Chapter 5 for employees. Define the knowledge, skills, and abilities required to perform the jobs identified as desirable and appropriate for guests.

2. Make sure that guests know exactly what you expect them to do and that they are physically able, mentally prepared, and sufficiently skilled to do those tasks. Show guests that performing the tasks is to their benefit. Give them a reason to do the tasks well.
3. Once task performance is underway, evaluate the guest's ability and willingness to perform well. In effect, conduct a performance appraisal on the guest to ensure that the experience being co-produced is meeting the guest's expectations. If it is not, identify what needs to be fixed. Does the guest need further training? Is something about the setting or delivery system impeding the guest's success?

Of course, the customers should not co-produce those parts of the experience where their performance may be too dangerous for them, time consuming, or when it would be too difficult for the customer to master the necessary skills. Airline passengers don't help fly the plane, although they may be asked to make sure they pick up their trash so that the plane can be prepared for its next flight more quickly. By assessing each component of the entire guest experience carefully, the hospitality provider can identify those parts of it that might be designed to discourage, encourage, or even require guest co-production. A restaurant could offer a low-price self-service buffet to *discourage* patrons requesting expensive waitstaff, a hotel might provide self-service check-in kiosks to *encourage* its guests to avoid waiting for an available front desk agent, or an airline might *require* self-check-ins with a kiosk assistant available only to help when guests have computer problems. In each of these instances, customers can choose to have an employee serve them (and wait for service) or they can produce their own service product: go get their salads, access their hotel rooms, or print their own boarding passes.

The Organization Decides

Some hospitality organizations do not offer the guest any choice; they either design parts of the experience in ways that make **guest participation** impossible or structure it so that the guest must participate to some extent. A quick-serve restaurant is quick-serve and inexpensive because it requires customers to serve as their own order-takers, servers, and table clearers. Without the cost of servers bustling about taking a variety of customized orders, filling glasses, and picking up dirty dishes, McDonald's and Burger King can save money and offer a quick, less expensive food product than a fine-dining restaurant can. In the fast-food service setting, the customer must participate somewhat but cannot be allowed to take over completely. The efficiency of the quick-serve process is based on a carefully engineered food-production system that ensures a consistent quality and safe food product. Allowing customers to cook their own burgers and fries would significantly interfere with production efficiency while creating substantial food safety and sanitation problems. The quick-serve restaurant gains efficiency by letting the customers serve themselves in the part of the service delivery system that takes place in front of the counter. They do not allow customers behind the counter, where they can slow down the production process or jeopardize food safety.

Organizations need to think through when and where to let guests co-produce their own experience and how much co-production there should be. Sometimes guest participation makes sense for the organization and the guest, and sometimes it does not. The challenge is to identify which situation is best regarding the amount of co-production that leads to the greatest value for the guest.[4]

STRATEGIES FOR INVOLVING THE GUEST

A guest can be involved with a hospitality organization in several ways: as a consultant or source of expertise and quality information, as a marketer, as part of the environment for other guests, as co-producer of the experience, or as a manager of the service providers and systems. Some of these involvements may sound unlikely, but they are all common.

Guests as Unpaid Consultants

When the hospitality organization asks its guests what they like or dislike about the guest experience, they become unpaid consultants and act as quality control inspectors. Since their input regarding their experiences will become part of the information that management uses to review and adjust the service product, environment, and delivery system, the guests are acting as expert consultants in giving this important feedback to the organization. Using outsiders in this way is not unique to hospitality firms; many other types of organizations systematically invite their suppliers, customers, and even communities to provide feedback about how they are doing. Southwest Airlines extended the consulting role to include the hiring process. It invited its frequent flyers to participate in interviewing prospective flight attendants.[5] Companies are also employing new technologies to gain feedback. Intercontinental Hotel Group launched an initiative to create an online community that allows members in its loyalty program to share feedback on their hotel experiences. After all, who is better to judge whether a person has the qualifications to be an effective flight attendant or if a hotel stay was up to expectations than the most valuable customers of the company?

Organizations also frequently invite customers to participate as members of focus groups. As discussed in a later chapter on assessing service quality, these groups are designed to give expert feedback about the service experience to the service provider, and no one can be more expert on that experience or its quality and value than the customers themselves.

Guests as Marketers

Everyone has asked a friend or colleague about a hospitality experience. The person who just came back from a terrific meal, a resort stay that was beyond expectations, or an amazing cruise is eager to talk about it. Likewise, the person who just returned from a ruined dining experience, terrible hotel stay, or the cruise with bad food and service is equally eager to talk about it—perhaps more so. Guests are excellent marketers for good or bad service. They are asked by their friends and acquaintances for their opinion in both face-to-face communications and through Web-based social networking media, and this "word of mouth" can make or break a hospitality organization. Recognizing the power of this marketing medium—the customer—especially when the service experience is bad, is an important part of the manager's responsibility and will be covered in greater detail in the chapter on fixing service failures (Chapter 13).

A more recent development in using guests to co-produce marketing is the group coupon sites. The basic idea is to get people to organize into large enough groups so that they can qualify for a discount or special rate on a service. Web sites like Groupon and Living-Social negotiate with retailers for a special price on items like spa services, paintball, or specialty restaurants. The Groupon site lists one retailer a day but the deal becomes official only when a fixed number of people sign up for it. These sites reward people for marketing. With LivingSocial, a person can get a specific deal free if he or she gets three others to sign up for it. Both sites give dollar rewards to users who recruit friends. In other words, these sites use guests to market to other guests using their social networks in a powerful way. The communications technology used today in combination with the existing social networking sites offer amazing opportunities to use guests as active marketers for a wide variety of hospitality organizations.

Guests as Part of Each Other's Experience

If you enjoy simply watching other guests, you may think of them as part of the service environment. If other guests are especially important to your enjoyment of your experience, you might even consider them a part of the service product itself. The line is not always clear. For example, most people don't like to go to an empty restaurant or movie theatre; enjoying the experience along with other people, even strangers, is part of the package. Going to a water park when it is comfortably full and when it is almost empty are very different experiences. Water parks, like many other service situations where the emphasis is on "having fun," rely to some extent on other customers being part of the fun. Thus, many people get great enjoyment out of watching other people, ordinary folks just like themselves, act as bit players in a Universal or Disney Hollywood Studios film-making demonstration. For those doing the acting, the guest experience obviously includes the opportunity to participate in the movie simulation. For observers, however, those customers doing something unusual are perhaps best considered as part of the service environment. Though interesting, unusual, or amusing, watching them is not really the reason why you came to the amusement park, water park, or gaming casino.

This principle of encouraging customers to be either directly or indirectly part of other guests' experiences is evident in new Web-sharing technologies—for example, video clips on YouTube—but it has been a practice in hospitality for quite a while. For example, at one of Coney Island's earliest amusement parks, Steeplechase, there was a stadium set up next to a rotating Barrel of Love so that the customers could watch others fall down in a tangle with complete strangers and look foolish. For them, the opportunity to watch other people falling down awkwardly was an important part of the amusement experience. Indeed, the founder of Steeplechase Park early in the twentieth century, George Tilyou, was one of the first to recognize that a successful amusement park provided its customers the opportunity to observe the most entertaining experience of all: other people. In his park, the visitors were the main show. According to amusement parks authority Gary Kyriazi, "Tilyou felt that people will pay any price in order to provide their own entertainment."[6]

After couples had finished the Steeplechase ride, they would walk down a corridor and then find themselves on a brightly lit stage called the Insanitarium. Unknown to them, crowds of people would be sitting in bleachers watching them. As Kyriazi describes the scene, "Suddenly, strong air jets would lift the women's dresses (exposed ankles were rare at the time) and blow the men's hats off. A clown would prod the men with an electric stinger. When they tried to escape, piles of barrels on either side of the exit gangway would begin to sway and appear to tumble down on them as they made their escape." They could then join the crowd beyond the glare of the stage lights and laugh at others going through what Kyriazi calls "the same light, humorous torment."[7]

Although standards have changed, and modern hospitality organizations do not see torment, even if "light and humorous," as a service they want to provide outside of Halloween "fright nights," the principle that guests enjoy watching guests is as true today as it was then. Successful operators make sure to offer plenty of opportunities for guests to observe other guests.

Although a case can be made for considering other guests as part of the service product itself or as supervisors under certain circumstances, they are most often a part of the service environment. Like any other environmental element, they can be a neutral influence, they can damage the experience for others, or they can enhance it. Movies, concerts, and Broadway plays all rely on the audience to help create the mood. All these entertainments are more enjoyable with a full house than they are when empty. The laughter and other reactions of people surrounding the customer become an important part of the customer's

Guests observing guests at George Tilyou's Steeplechase Park, Coney Island. The Human Roulette Wheel (top). The Hoop-La (bottom).

Courtesy of Seth Kaufman, Whirl-i-gig. Used with permission.

environment. Indeed, some attractions rely on paid professionals or electronically created cues to generate applause, laughter, or other emotional responses that create the right setting for the service experience. At the other extreme, everyone has had an experience ruined by a crying baby, a public family squabble, or a thoughtless bunch of loud talkers on cell phones. For better or worse, other guests are part of the hospitality servicescape and, therefore, need to be managed like any other environmental element.

Guests as Co-producers

Perhaps the most important way in which guests can participate, other than simply being there, is as active co-producers of the guest experience. During all or parts of the service experience, they can actually become participants in the production and delivery system. This participation can be as simple as having guests serve themselves at a fast-food restaurant, preparing their own salads at the salad bar, or carrying their own bags at the golf course to

Guests are often part of each other's experience in casino gaming.

Image copyright Yuri Arcurs, 2010. Used under license from Shutterstock.com

substitute for the job of a paid employee. The value of guest co-production can be substantial for the organization. While this may be a more costly strategy under some circumstances, in general, every time guests co-produce at least some of their own experiences, they are replacing some or all of the labor that the organization would otherwise have to pay to do the same thing, while often improving the quality and value of their own experience.

Starwood has created the Make a Green Choice program as a way to encourage its guests to co-produce some of their hotel experience by opting out of its daily room service. If guests make no effort to co-produce the hotel's environmental experience, linens and towels are cleaned as usual; however, if the guests indicates that they do not need the room cleaned, Starwood gives them a $5 gift card and loyalty points to reward their participation. Starwood reports that they have had an 8 to 12 percent participation rate and that it is growing. At one hotel, the co-production initiative amounted to 188 rooms that did not need to be cleaned per night.[8] Assuming a housekeeper cleans fifteen rooms a day, that equates to 12.5 fewer housekeepers being needed. But there is more. Hotels that encourage customer participation reduce not only labor costs but also water, sewer, energy, chemical, and linen expenses—a win for the environment as well. Starwood's Sheraton Seattle, for example, used 900,000 fewer gallons of water and 9000 fewer gallons of chemicals in one year.

Advantages of Co-production for the Organization

The organization gains several advantages by having the guests co-produce their experience. First, co-production may reduce employee costs.[9] Generally, the more guests do for themselves, the fewer employees the organization needs to employ. In addition to being an obvious labor-saving strategy, co-production allows the organization to use the talents of its employees better. If guests are allowed, encouraged, or required to take care of some of their own basic requirements or perform routine tasks, employees are freed up to do more elaborate or complicated tasks that the guests would not enjoy or do successfully, and tasks that would simply not be suitable for guests. For example, at some restaurants, patrons are allowed to make their own reservations on the Web. Maitre d's take fewer reservation phone calls, which permits them to spend more time responding to guests who need information or advice. In effect, by letting the guests schedule themselves through the Web, the quality of the restaurant service goes up with no increase in costs.

A buffet is a common method of co-production, allowing guests to select what and how much they want, but also allowing the company to hire fewer service personnel, thereby saving money.

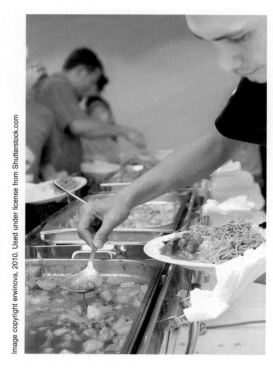

Image copyright erwinova, 2010. Used under license from Shutterstock.com

In a similar fashion, the strategy of offering buffets at lunch is an effective way for restaurants to stay open at lunch time without overextending their waitstaff. Many servers are unhappy working at lunch time, because the check sizes (and tips) are lower. People tired out from working at lunch cannot work as efficiently at the dinner hour. A buffet provides meals with a minimal use of waitstaff, the diner gets a good price on the meal, the restaurant gets more utilization of its physical plant, increases total revenue by being open more hours and serving more diners, and the restaurant provides a better work situation for its servers.

Advantages of Co-production for the Guest

For the guest, co-production has a number of advantages. First, it can decrease the opportunity for service failure while increasing the perception, and perhaps the actuality, of service quality. Since the guests themselves define value and quality, handling production themselves means they can produce exactly what they want. If guests fix their own salads at the salad bar in exactly the way they want them, how can they complain if the salads aren't perfect? Guests can pile on their favorite salad items in their favorite quantities and avoid the items they dislike. They end up feeling they got the very salad they wanted. This opportunity creates the perception of real value.

Second, the opportunity for self-service typically reduces the time required for service. A simple example is the customer at the airport who chooses to use the self-check-in kiosk instead of standing in line to wait for a counter clerk. Fast-food restaurants make their reputation and define their market niche on the basis of saving time for their customers who are too busy to eat in a full-service restaurant.

Third, self-service reduces the risk of unpleasant surprises for guests. If diners walk through a cafeteria's buffet line, they can see exactly what the food products are, instead of ordering off a menu and hoping for the best. While not everything tastes as good as it looks, choosing one's own meal from a cafeteria line or buffet can reduce the perception of risk in comparison with ordering meals unseen, from a menu.

Self-serve kiosks at airports allow guests who want to use them to save time.

Image copyright Jacqueline Abromeit, 2010. Used under license from Shutterstock.com

Disadvantages of Co-production for the Organization

Permitting or requiring guest participation may also have disadvantages for the organization. First, in this litigious society, participation exposes the organization to legal risk. Having a guest handle a hot pot in a cook-your-own fondue restaurant could lead to a major burn and lawsuit. Second, the organization may have to spend extra money to train the customer contact employees so that they can add to their usual serving jobs the task of both recognizing when guests are ready to co-produce and when they are not and, then, communicating effectively and easily about what guests are supposed to do. These employees are responsible for instructing the guests in how to provide the service for themselves and for monitoring the experience to prevent the guests from creating any disasters. Every guest is different and comes to the guest experience with different skills, knowledge, abilities, and expectations for the service itself. Servers who train and oversee guests must be alert, observant, and well trained in recognizing guests' capabilities to co-produce and in how to coach all types of guests through the experience. This training cost increases as guest use of self-service technologies increases. Hiring and training people to perform the necessary job skills at, say, a modern copy center is one thing, but to allow or encourage self-service, the organization must go beyond basic job skills to hire and train people who can successfully teach customers to use computers, scanners, and copy machines. One of the most interesting challenges of self-service technologies is to ensure that customers do not fail while using the technologies or get confused and discouraged to the point they abandon the use of the technology and the company offering it.[10]

This means that successful hospitality organizations must not only train their guest-contact employees to recognize when guests are ready, willing, and able to participate in the co-production of their experiences but also carefully design their service systems and service setting to accommodate the variations in guest capabilities. Teaching employees to recognize the difference between customers who are able to co-produce and those who are not is important.[11]

If guests co-produce their experience, the service delivery system and the service environment must be user friendly. If the organization wants the guest to follow a predetermined sequence of operations to create the desired experience, it must have people to guide them, excellent directional signs, or, for on-line services, a Web layout that is intuitively obvious to people from varied cultures. Only then can the organization be reasonably sure that all types of guests will do what they are supposed to do when and where they are supposed to do it. Signs in a self-serve cafeteria must indicate clearly where the entry point is, where the trays, silverware, and napkins are, and how the diner is supposed to proceed through the food selection and payment procedure. Someone unfamiliar with a cafeteria restaurant might have no idea how to navigate this service delivery process. The cafeteria workers must be alert to confused-looking people wandering around looking for signs, directions, and instructions on how to participate successfully in this food delivery process.

Involving guests in the service delivery system also has an impact on the cost and layout of the environment. Most hospitality organizations already spend time and energy ensuring that the traditional front-of-the-house areas meet guests' expectations in terms of appearance and quality, but those organizations that involve guests in the service delivery system spend the money to ensure that back-of-the-house areas meet their expectations as well. Making the back of the house a part of the "show" has an obvious impact on how the equipment is laid out, what it looks like, how shiny and clean it is kept, how the personnel are dressed, and what skills they must have to work alongside the guests in service co-production. Instead of having not particularly articulate cooks in greasy aprons

At 'Let's Dish!', guests create their own meals, which they then take home to eat later. Although the service product is all about the guest participating and enjoying the cooking of the product, employees must be ready to step in and assist those guests who need help.

Photo courtesy of Let's Dish!/Slate LD, LLC.

producing meals in an out-of-sight kitchen, involvement of the guest in a food-production system means that the organization must hire employees who can communicate easily with diners, maintain a neat appearance, and ensure that the kitchen and other visible food preparation areas are always clean and healthy looking to meet the guest's expectations. All this is expensive because the costs of the uniforms, the extra interpersonal skills required of the employees, and the rearrangement of the food-production area to allow the guest to be involved in the food-production process will add to the costs of the production system.

Guest involvement expands the role of the guest-contact employee. Now the employee must have the skills and abilities to be a coach, trainer, teacher, standard setter, fixer of problems, and manager of the guest flow through the delivery system. Hospitality employees must know how to get guests engaged in co-production and also how to get them to disengage. If guests enjoy co-production and are reluctant to disengage, the organization that does not want to hurry its guests may have to add extra capacity.

Clearly, when guests become co-producers, the traditional role of server in the guest experience requires redefinition, and servers need additional training in the new roles they must play if co-production is to work to the organization's advantage.

Disadvantages of Co-production for the Guest

From the guest's perspective, co-production can have disadvantages.[12] The most obvious one is that paying guests may resent having to produce any part of that for which they are paying. Some task-oriented guests don't particularly want much guest-server interaction; they just want, for example, a quick meal. A production-line approach suits them just fine. Other guests insist and thrive on close personal attention and are willing to pay for it, or they may be uncomfortable with the technology used in place of the personal service. If shifting part of the guest-experience production to guests themselves results in a perception of less TLC, some guests will be dissatisfied.

Another possible disadvantage is that guests may fail to co-produce the service properly. If you find that the items you assembled from the salad bar don't taste as good as you thought they would, or if your experiment with some new food selections from the buffet was not a success, you will not have co-produced a wow for yourself. Similarly, a customer may mistakenly select the wrong option when using an automated kiosk, be frustrated by the experience, and perhaps may not be able to figure out how to fix the error. While hospitality organizations that seek to provide excellent service may want to utilize the advantages of guest co-production, when problems occur, they can't blame the guest for the unsatisfactory experience. Hospitality organizations know that people tend to take credit for their successes and attribute failures to someone else—usually the company.[13] Excellent providers of customer service try to protect guests against self-service failures and create opportunities for their success. They want you to have the satisfying experience you expected when you chose them rather than a competitor. They may let you try again or offer to help. The risk is nonetheless present that the guest may co-produce an unsatisfactory experience.

The High Cost of Failure

While unsatisfactory or unsuccessful co-production can be a minor annoyance to a restaurant patron, it can be disastrous if the cost of failure is great. If you run a dude ranch and let inexperienced riders go off alone on horseback, the result may be humiliation, broken bones, or worse—plus a law suit. Or imagine a situation in which you co-produce a fondue meal with a peer, boss, or significant other—and fail. The best hospitality organizations make every effort to ensure that guests succeed as co-producers, but the risk of failure is always there. If the costs of failure are too high, the organization must tactfully intervene to keep the guest from failing. The server must be sensitive and aware enough to recognize when a guest is about to fail, must take over before the failure occurs, or fix the failure, and be able to do all these things with sufficient grace that the guest is not embarrassed by failing when others all around are succeeding. These requirements add up to high expectations for a low paid, entry-level employee.

Motivating Guests to Co-produce

Guests can safely participate when they have the necessary knowledge, skills, and abilities to create the service product, but guests must be motivated to participate in the process. Like employees, guests will be motivated to "perform" when they can see some economic, psychological, or social benefits in participation.[14] Some experiences can be completed only if co-produced. Psychiatric treatment will fail if the patient refuses to be involved. In any large geographically spread service setting—like a zoo, museum, food court, cruise ship, or national park—customers who want a particular array of experiences must schedule them for themselves. If customers don't plan out their time and physically move themselves around, they are unlikely to enjoy the experience.

Many guests are motivated to participate because of the economic incentives available to those who take a role in their own guest experience. Others are motivated by their personalities or their familiarity with the experience being offered, or they are simply looking for something to do while waiting for the other parts of the guest experience to take place. Some guests just want to be a part of whatever it is they're involved in at the moment, no matter what, and constantly look for such opportunities. Some people always park their own cars, carry their own luggage, or walk up the stairs for the benefit of the exercise, or because they like to demonstrate for themselves (and anyone else who may watch) that they are physically fit enough to do these things. Others like to show how mentally fit or technically adept they are by doing things for themselves—whether it be by making their own online travel reservations or baiting their own hooks on a deep-sea fishing trip. Of course, some people also think they do a better job than an employee could do.

Finally, some people just like to be the center of attention and seek opportunities to be "on stage." In a simple situation, Joe wants to show his friends how well known he is at Ralph's Restaurant, so he goes and gets his own coffee or refills his partner's ice water instead of waiting for the server. Even more on stage is the person who volunteers to sing in a karaoke bar or be drenched by Shamu in the SeaWorld demonstration. Many people enjoy showing off, and hospitality organizations should try to provide appropriate opportunities for them somewhere in the service delivery system.

The Guest as a Substitute for Management

Guests can serve in a quasi-managerial role as unofficial supervisors and motivators of employees; they can even supervise and train other guests.

Guests as Supervisors

Guests have more contact with the service personnel, speak with them more often, and see more of their job performance than the organization's supervisors do. Guests have the opportunity and the motivation to act as supervisors and provide immediate feedback as to whether an employee is making them happy or unhappy. After all, the guest is paying for the service and is, therefore, motivated to tell the server (who to the guest receiving the service is the organization) what the guest thinks about the service, the server, and the organization.

Hospitality employees are trying to produce memorable guest experiences; the guests themselves will let the employees know how well they have succeeded. The more familiar guests are with the organization, the more they know about what level of service should be provided and the more qualified they are to provide technical feedback. All these guest activities and functions are in a sense supervisory because the guests are observing, guiding, and motivating employees and, in many cases, "paying" them for good or poor service with a large or small tip.

Everyone has watched an unhappy guest tell an employee that the employee is not providing the service properly. That guest is in effect performing a supervisory function: providing feedback to the employee. Anyone watching characters in the Magic Kingdom interact with the children will soon see that the children are supervising the actions and behavior of the characters better than any supervisor ever could. The children will immediately respond to any deviation from character or any flaw in the character performance. They give constant feedback to cast members to let them know if they are not doing something right. Although supervisors also monitor the behavior of cast members as they perform their character roles, their job is, in a sense, much simpler than that of supervisors in the manufacturing sector. The typical auto assembly-line worker never has a car talk to him, smile at him when he installs the brakes correctly, participate in the production, or complain when he doesn't. The hospitality supervisor must worry about guests doing all these things. In the hospitality organization, guests talk, smile, co-produce, give directions, and complain. They assess the performance of servers and, through tips, compensate certain employees for the services they provide. Having guests constantly monitoring and responding to the employee's job performance is a substantial aid to the supervisory responsibility.

Guests as Motivators

Having guests participate in supervision can be highly motivating to employees when guests tell them in both verbal and nonverbal ways what a good job they are doing. Most hospitality employees find great enjoyment in meeting and exceeding the expectations of guests. Chefs love to be challenged by guests who are knowledgeable about the culinary arts. Hospitality employees usually enjoy the opportunity to be challenged by a guest who shares an interest or expertise in the subject of the experience. College professors often find the students who ask the most difficult questions to be the most fun to have in class. Most hospitality employees are constantly tested by the variety in guest expectations and ability to perform their responsibilities in the service delivery process. In the Magic Kingdom, the challenge of making all children happy by responding to their unique needs and personalities makes the job of playing a Disney character a high-status and highly sought-after job. It's fun to show off what you can really do when you have an appreciative audience.

Guests as Supervisors and Trainers for Other Guests

Guests can also supervise and train each other. Learning how to stand in line seems like an obvious skill until one encounters people from other cultures who do not believe in standing in line. Someone has to train the untrained to stand in line in an orderly way, and the people already in line will do that. Watch the customers already standing in line the next time you see someone break into a line and you'll witness a training session in line standing. Most guests of hospitality organizations, like most employees, are anxious to fulfill their responsibilities and do their jobs well. They can be seen watching other people to learn what their own behavior should be in the various tasks of the co-production process.

Waiting lines are often located to allow guests not being served to observe guests who are being served; by the time the guests in the airport security line get to the screener, they know pretty much what they are supposed to do.

We all learn from watching others, and with so many people in most hospitality situations on a typical day or occasion, we can learn what we're supposed to do to enjoy the experience by observing others. The first-time guest at a basketball game learns from others when to chant "airball" and enjoys the game all the more for chanting.

The organization can also use videos of experienced guests to show waiting guests what they are supposed to do. At most amusement parks, television monitors are set up so waiting guests can see what role will be expected of them when their turn comes to participate in the attraction or get on the ride. If the organization can use its guests to train at least some of the other guests, it can save itself the cost of those employees who would be required to train those guests and minimize the time spent explaining to the next guest what the last guest just did. The cost and time savings can be substantial.

Likewise, guests can supervise other guests in the performance of the roles they need to successfully perform to be satisfied with the experience. Many guests are more than willing to tell other guests where to go or not go, when they are behaving inappropriately or doing something that might be dangerous or detrimental to both their own and others' experiences. Managing guests as they manage other guests is a tricky task as there are costs and benefits of letting guests train and supervise one another that must be carefully balanced to avoid guest dissatisfaction.

DETERMINING WHEN GUEST PARTICIPATION MAKES SENSE

Sometimes, both the organization and the guest benefit from guest participation and sometimes not. Distinguishing when, where, and how much the guest should or should not be involved in any part of the guest experience depends on a variety of factors. Generally speaking, co-producing the service is in the interest of guests when they can gain value, reduce risk, or improve the quality of the experience. Co-production is in the organization's interest when it can save money, increase production efficiency, or differentiate its service from that of competitors in a key way. Each opportunity for guest participation should be assessed on these criteria and designed into the hospitality organization when the factors are favorable and designed out when they are not.

Enriching the Wait

Sometimes, situations encouraging guest participation evolve when guests are required to wait for service. Organizations should try to decrease the feeling that the wait is too long by giving guests something to do, ideally something that will enrich the overall experience. A good example is getting a group of people sitting on a delayed flight to participate in a singalong, a technique frequently attributed to Southwest Airlines. Passengers get the opportunity to keep active while they are waiting for their flight to take off, and the singing may even enhance the experience by providing a pleasant way to pass the time.

Co-producing Value

While some hospitality situations require participation and some guests look for opportunities to participate no matter what, almost everyone is happy to co-produce if it adds value to their experience. By definition, value can be added by reducing costs (for the same quality), increasing quality (for the same costs), or both. Costs include not only the price but also the other costs incurred by being involved in the guest experience. For example, if a potential guest sees a long line outside her favorite restaurant, the time cost of waiting for the next available table may be so great that she willingly goes to a nearby cafeteria or fast-food restaurant—to reduce the time cost of getting a meal. The guest may experience a decrease in quality but expects the greater decrease in overall cost to compensate for it. Similarly, guests who want to be sure of service quality may want to participate in providing service. Those guests derive additional value from knowing that they are getting the service "their way." Even non-hospitality organizations like Home Depot have learned that they can make a lot of money serving customers who want to co-create the quality and value of their home repair by doing it themselves. Customers look to Home Depot not only to provide a fair price on the building products but also to give the necessary instruction or help to do the job correctly.

Another cost of co-production for the guest is risk, the risk that the service may not meet expectations. Guests who co-produce their experiences minimize the risk that a hospitality employee will not provide exactly what is wanted. Many people now surf the Internet looking for hotel accommodations and flight reservations. They believe that the travel agent or airline they contact may be more interested in selling them the most profitable travel package than in finding the price, times, or routes they want.

Key Factors: Time and Control

Several dimensions of providing service can help us distinguish between situations when guests can beneficially be involved in co-production and when they should not. The research suggests, surprisingly, that only two factors are important: time and control. Each of these is of two kinds: real and perceived.[15]

With respect to time, the *feeling* of how long something takes is as important to the guest as how long it *actually* takes. In Chapter 11, on waiting lines, these real and perceived factors are discussed in detail. The same is true for control. The amount of control over the quality of, value of, risk involved in, or efficiency of the experience that guests think they acquire by participating is as important in determining the value of participation as the actual control guests have. As an example, many resort facilities offer a climbing wall for their guests to enjoy the feeling of rock climbing. The walls are designed to allow climbers to choose their own path up the wall and experience the exhilaration of a successful rock climb. On the other hand, every climber is required to wear a safety harness to ensure that the occasional slips and falls do not turn into a disastrous experience. Climbers enjoy the illusion that they are in control of the situation, when in reality the harnesses cover up any mistakes.

Cutting Costs, Increasing Capacity

From the organization's point of view, the most obvious reason to incorporate the guest into the guest experience is to save money. As noted earlier, whenever the guest produces or co-produces the service, the guest is providing labor the organization would otherwise have to hire. The second reason is to increase production efficiency or increase capacity utilization. If a restaurant offers a buffet at lunch, it provides a meal product at a time of day when waitstaff are sometimes unavailable or unwilling to work. The restaurant still has the opportunity to derive income from its physical plant and food-production capacity without overusing its human resources. In a similar sense, many other organizations can add self-service capacity to handle surges or unevenness in guest demand. A hotel can offer its check-in and check-out guests an automated option if they don't want to wait in

Sometimes, after the organization creates the servicescape, it is entirely up to the guest to produce the service experience, such as in this nature walk.

Photograph by Joel N. Sturman.

line, or a rental-car agency can offer automated check-in, check-out service for its regular customers. In this way, the organization can maintain a constant staffing level while still being able to accommodate the variability in customer demand for this service. Letting customers co-produce this part of the service experience increases the number of customers who can be handled without increasing labor costs.

Guest Participation as a Differentiation Strategy

Organizations can also use guest participation as part of a product differentiation strategy. The obvious example is the cook-your-own restaurant that sells the experience of doing it yourself to distinguish itself from other restaurants. While the physical part of the service product is food, the entire service product also includes the experience. These restaurants often try to make the cooking a social experience, making reservations for groups of friends, and providing the environment that produces not only food people want and the opportunity to enjoy cooking their own meals but also the fun of the social experience. Other examples abound, such as self-service gas stations, car-rental agencies, cafeterias, and banking services. Boston Market offers a take-home product but no delivery service. This combination distinguishes it from both the quick-serve drive-through and home-delivery restaurants. Having the customer come inside gives Boston Market the opportunity to sell more products than it could if the customer was ordering over the phone or reading off the menu at the drive-through window. This guest participation strategy helps Boston Market position itself as a quick and convenient stop for busy people.

Building Commitment

A final reason for letting guests participate is to build guest commitment and repeat business. If a guest feels the organization trusts her enough to let her provide her own service, the guest feels a bond and a commitment to this place where everybody knows her name. Getting the guest involved in the guest experience is a positive way for the guest to feel ownership in that experience and a loyalty to the organization that provides this opportunity.[16] Pouring one's own coffee at the coffee shop may be a way of getting a coffee cup filled fast, but it also may be a way for that guest and the organization to express their tie to each other. Many organizations try hard to build such relationships because they recognize the lifetime value of a loyal repeat customer. Loyalty programs such as frequent-flyer and frequent-guest programs are designed to build this attachment so that customers come back time after time to the organization that "knows" them.

The Bottom Line: Costs Versus Benefits

The key to deciding when to offer the guest the opportunity to participate is to do a simple cost-benefit analysis (e.g., see Table 8.3). The organization needs to be sure, for both itself and the guest, that the benefits of participation outweigh the costs. The organization will want to look closely at the costs it will incur: the costs of extra training or more elaborate skill requirements for employees, extra or simpler equipment necessary for guest use, and extra effort to lay out the service delivery system in a way that is user friendly. In essence, these are the costs of training a guest to be a quasi-employee.

Help Wanted: Co-producer

As it would in assessing any job position it wants to fill, the organization must ask itself the following questions: What are the KSAs necessary for a guest to perform successfully as a quasi-employee? Are we likely to find these KSAs in our job candidates/guests? What is the motivation of guests to participate, and how do we appeal to that motivation? What are the training requirements for successful performance in the guest-employee role, and do we have the time and personnel necessary to train guests in the proper performance of that role? Will guests come back and use that skill if we spend the time and money to train them? If so, the expenditure of time and money may be worthwhile. Is it cheaper, faster, or more efficient for the organization to provide the service or to allow the guest to do it? Are role models (especially other guests) available to help with the training, and

TABLE 8.3 Advantages and Disadvantages of Guests Co-producing Service

FOR GUEST		FOR ORGANIZATION	
ADVANTAGES	DISADVANTAGES	ADVANTAGES	DISADVANTAGES
Reduces service costs	May frustrate guest	Reduces labor costs	Increases liability risk
Increases interest	May diminish service level	Improves quality	Guest training costs
Saves service time	May not have needed KSAs	Reduces service failures	Increases needs for employee training
Improves quality	Requires a learning-curve period	New market niche	Increases design costs
Reduces risk		Enriches employee jobs	May interfere with other units
Chance to show off			Variability in guests

how can we physically structure the service environment to use these models? Are there interactions with other guests or other parts of the organization that letting guests provide their own experience will interfere with or harm?

To employ guests effectively in the guest experience, they must have the ability to participate, the knowledge of how to participate, and the motivation to help produce their own service experience at a level that meets or exceeds their expectations. Since the guests have come to your place to receive some service, they must see a reason to do something for themselves. Thus, the role they perform in the guest experience must be clearly defined.[17] In addition, some guests just want to do things for themselves and will do so if given the opportunity. These people get satisfaction out of serving themselves and being in control of the situation. Some people, on the other hand, do not want to do anything to help provide their own experience. If they are paying for it, why should they provide it? Organizations that see mutual benefits to co-production and try to encourage it must always have a backup plan to accommodate the fact that some guests will and some guests won't want to participate in the experience. Those organizations that find ways of using guests as much as possible will, however, decrease their costs and increase the value and quality of the service for those guests who co-produce.

Inviting Guests to Participate: Guidelines

The basic point is that some, but not all, situations lend themselves to using self-service or guest participation for all guests. Two strategies are available to the hospitality organization contemplating how to gain the advantages of using guest participation while not incurring the disadvantages. First, they can let customers in their targeted market segment know that everyone entering the service setting must provide some of the service themselves. No one goes into a McDonald's expecting table service. The second strategy is to segment the service process so that guests entering the service setting can choose to participate or not. Some restaurants have learned that some guests wish to gain the advantages of serving themselves while others come to the restaurant expecting service and are willing to pay for it. To accommodate this, guests can decide whether to order off the menu or choose from the buffet.

Other ideas about when to include the guest in the experience are suggested in Table 8.4. It describes several situations in which both the guest and the organization may benefit. Obviously, the ideal is when both benefit in some meaningful way so that the experience is at least what the guest expected, and perhaps more.

ONE LAST POINT: FIRING THE GUEST

In a sense, all guests co-produce—or have the potential to co-produce—the hospitality experience for others simply by being in each other's company. If a well-mannered, well-dressed guest sits quietly and passively within the service setting, that guest may be no more than a minor enhancement, an adornment, to the experience of other guests. Unfortunately, despite the old saying that the customer is always right, all organizations know that the customer is sometimes wrong by any reasonable standard; certain extreme behaviors are unacceptable in any hospitality setting. Guests get drunk, become verbally and physically abusive, refuse to comply with reasonable organizational rules and policies, and make outrageous demands.

Not all employees work out; not all guests work out either. Sometimes, the guest's "job performance" as a co-producing quasi-employee is so unsatisfactory that the organization must—as a last resort and employing clearly defined procedures—**fire the guest**.

TABLE 8.4   Guidelines for Deciding Whether Guests Should Participate

1. Would guests derive value or satisfaction from participating in the co-production of the service experience? Are they ready, willing, and able to co-produce their service experience?
2. Can you clearly communicate to guests when and how they are expected to participate in the service experience, and can you make it clear to guests when and why they may not participate?
3. Can you make it advantageous for guests to co-produce, thereby replacing employees and reducing labor costs?
4. Are your employees doing routine, repetitive, easy-to-learn tasks that could be performed by guests or guest-friendly equipment? Can guests participate in co-creating the service experience with little or no training?
5. Can guest participation speed the delivery of the service experience and eliminate waits?
6. Are your guests trying to avoid your service personnel (to avoid giving tips, perhaps) in a way that shows that some guests prefer to co-produce their service experience?
7. Can guests participate in the service experience without being a risk to themselves, other guests, or employees?
8. Are your customer-contact employees ready, willing, and able to help guests co-produce?
9. Can you design your service experience to permit those guests who can and want to co-produce to do so, and so that guests who do not want to co-produce do not have to?

© Cengage Learning 2012.

Firing Airline Passengers

Customer aggression is an unfortunate part of a service employee's workday, causing emotional exhaustion and absenteeism.[18] The best hospitality companies recognize this reality, and will intervene to support their employees when necessary. Southwest Airlines, while always committed to customer service, has also worked diligently to protect its employees from such customers. Herb Kelleher, cofounder of Southwest Airlines, has said, "When we encounter a customer like that, we say to him, 'We don't want to see you again because of the way you treat our people.' " Kelleher made the point that the customer is not always right. If a passenger is abusive to a Southwest employee, Kelleher was known to have called the passenger on the phone. Customer complaints to management are common; management complaints to customers are unusual. Employees appreciate this kind of support.[19]

The airlines in particular have trouble with guests. In one month in 2006, over 1300 incidents occurred on British aircraft flights, including passengers becoming angry at flight crews, punching attendants, trying to open an emergency door, head-butting a copilot, and trying to break into the cockpit. This is nearly double what it had been in the previous year.[20]

Airlines are taking actions to reduce and address air rage. After a drunken passenger struck one of his flight attendants on the head with a bottle, the chairman of Virgin Atlantic Airways was able to achieve a British lifetime air-travel ban on the perpetrator. In the fall of 2002, British Airways extended giving yellow soccer-style "warning cards" to passengers who seemed to be losing control on the ground after a successful use of them to control irate in-air passengers. Some airlines now equip each plane with a set of plastic handcuffs and provide flight attendants with conflict resolution training. The causes of these incidents seem to be the record numbers of people wanting to fly, more passengers per plane with less room to stretch and move around, the increased frequency of airline delays, free liquor in first and business classes, and the smoking ban. Some passengers think the airlines have, to some extent, brought the unpleasant incidents upon themselves.

Other organizations fire customers too. In June 2007, Spring Nextel fired 1000 of its customers. In a letter terminating service to those customers, it was quoted as saying, "The number of inquiries you have made to us ... has led us to determine that we are unable to meet your current wireless needs.... We understand that having to switch to another wireless carrier may be an inconvenience.... So, a credit has been applied to your account to bring your current balance to zero."[21]

Abrupt Firings

The termination of the hospitality relationship must occasionally be dramatic and abrupt, perhaps even implemented by a security guard, a large person wearing an "Events Staff" t-shirt, or a "bouncer." Dramatic "firings" should occur when customers threaten the well-being or safety of other customers, employees, or themselves. No organization should tolerate customers who are threatening, excessively rude or loud, or dangerous to others or themselves. If any customer threatens or endangers the physical and mental health of an employee, that employee should be empowered to tell the offender to go elsewhere for the service, as this organization is unable to continue rendering it. Employees should also be trained on how to recognize such situations and the procedures involved to get the assistance necessary to conduct the abrupt firing.

Subtle Firings

Customers can also be fired subtly. Everyone realizes that organizations place their advertising so that their target markets will see it, as in beer commercials accompanying televised athletic events. But organizational advertising can also be carefully placed so that some customers never see the ads for a service, never get promotional mailings, or are never offered premiums for using the service. Sometimes, this strategy is more overt, such as a cruise line's refusal to allow unaccompanied children under eighteen to book passage, or a resort hotel's unwillingness to book a convention of ex-convicts, or a sign in a gift shop "No Shoes, No Shirt, No Service."

Maintaining Guest Dignity

Not even hospitality organizations are required to extend unlimited hospitality. They should of course give guests the benefit of the doubt. However, in the case of those few guests who are demonstrably unable to participate appropriately in the experience that all have come to the hospitality provider to enjoy, the organization should not hesitate to hand them their hats and show them the exit. If at all possible, however, the dismissal should be accomplished with minimal harm to the guest's physical or mental well-being and dignity. The guest, like any employee, who feels unfairly treated, who is really angry about being dismissed or fired, can become a source of long-term negative publicity and bad-mouthing.

Although the firing of a guest is a response to a guest failure of some kind, the organization must realize that it has also failed in some way. The rude, troublesome guest had expectations—whether reasonable and realistic or not—and the organization failed to meet them.

1. Train your service personnel to coach, monitor, and supervise the co-production of guests, and hire people who enjoy this kind of activity.

2. Train your guests to participate before you let them do so; be sure they have the KSAs.

3. Motivate guests who derive value and quality from participation to co-produce.

4. Encourage guests to help monitor the service behavior of your employees.

5. Structure guest experiences in ways that encourage other guests to train your guests; provide preshow videos or otherwise prepare your guests to engage in the experience.

6. The more guests do for themselves, the less you have to do for them.

7. Guest involvement can improve efficiency and capacity utilization, especially at peak demand times.

8. If you have to fire a guest, try to preserve the guest's dignity.

1. Name some ways or situations in which guest involvement in the co-production of a restaurant experience can be useful to the organization.

   A. Name some ways in which it can be useful to the restaurant guest.

   B. What KSAs should restaurant guests have to be successful co-producers?

   C. "Train them if they need it; motivate them if they need it; and keep it simple, undemanding." Would that formula promote successful guest co-production?

2. Name some ways or situations in which guest involvement in the co-production of a restaurant experience would not be useful or might be harmful to the organization.

   A. When might co-production in a restaurant not be useful to guests? When might it be harmful?

   B. What can the organization do to discourage co-production in those situations?

3. Suggest some ways in which a restaurant, a hotel, a theme park, a tour bus, and a travel agent might achieve a higher level of guest co-production that would benefit both the organization and the guest. Was it more difficult to apply the co-production idea to some of those hospitality or hospitality-related organizations than to others? If so, why?

4. Under what circumstances do you think the organization is justified in firing a guest? Think of a hospitality situation in which you would almost but not quite fire a guest. See whether your classmates agree with you or whether they would fire the guest.

5. Some hospitality authors suggest that guests should be managed as if they were quasi-employees.

   A. Who do you suppose these authors think should do this managing?

   B. Whoever these managers are, should they be selected differently for their jobs because of the type of "management responsibilities" their jobs will entail?

   C. Should they be trained differently?

ACTIVITY

1. Find a hospitality situation in which the guest is required to co-produce the service experience. Try to find something more challenging than a salad bar or receptacle labeled "Trash." Describe and evaluate how the organization prepares its employees and its guests for successful guest participation. How effective is the co-production strategy? What incentives are offered to guests to encourage their participation? In what ways is this guest participation beneficial for the guest, the organization, or both?

2. Interview a manager or supervisor within a hospitality organization to find out what the organization will and will not let guests do regarding co-producing the guest experience. Try to get some examples of guests co-producing excessively—trying to do more for themselves than the organization wants them to—and find out how the manager, supervisor, or server handled those situations. Report your findings to the class.

3. Interview a teacher who seems to believe in classroom "co-production," even if not under that term, and find out why the teacher does so and how the teacher got that way. Bring back your findings for discussion in groups. Discuss the extent to which you are required or invited to co-produce your own education, and how you feel about it.

ETHICS IN BUSINESS

By definition, the co-production process requires certain actions on the part of the customer. But how much is the customer obligated to do? A fast-food restaurant uses co-production to facilitate efficiency. In order to provide cheaper prices, individuals clear their own tables. What if a customer does not clear his or her own table? At a buffet, co-production occurs when customers go up to the buffet and serve themselves. For health reasons, each time you visit a buffet you are to take a new plate. What if a customer does not want to do this? At the buffet, customers can take what they want. Typically, buffets do not allow customers to take leftovers home. So if any remaining food cannot be brought home, what responsibility does a customer have to not waste food? At a fine-dining establishment, part of the co-production is that others in the restaurant dress and act the part appropriate for that establishment. What responsibility does a customer have to dress appropriately? What if a customer chooses to be loud, talk on a cell phone, or otherwise act in a way that others typically deem inappropriate for that environment? In short, what are the ethical responsibilities of consumers in the co-production process to engage in the expected behaviors that enable the service experience?

CASE STUDY

Over the Bounding Main

Luke Dwyer and Sue Mayes met when they were both crewing on a yacht in a round-the-world sailing race. They married, started a software business on a shoe-string, came up with several innovative ideas that enabled them to attain financial security, and then started looking for a way of life that would be more fun if perhaps not as profitable. Running a bed and breakfast was one possibility, but it seemed rather tame.

Then Sue saw an article in a shipping magazine about the *Shingo Maru*, a small 1920s-vintage freighter for sale. Luke and Sue sent off for a set of the freighter's plans, looked them over with a maritime architect, and decided to convert the ship into a kind of floating wilderness experience. They figured that a certain part of the cruise clientele must be tired of the typical big-boat cruise, where all you did was sit around on deck or by the pool all day, eat huge fattening meals, and drink all night while watching mediocre entertainment and waiting for the midnight buffet. Luke and Sue would give guests an opportunity not to be pampered but to take part in an experience they would remember for the rest of their lives: helping to sail a ship around the world or, for the less committed, some part of it.

About a million dollars and four years later, the conversion was complete, and Sue was breaking a bottle of champagne against the prow of the now-christened *Windenwaves*, a classic square-rigged, three-masted sailing ship with a top mast five stories high. The ports of call on its maiden voyage were going to be romantic-sounding, faraway places that most people experienced only through the novels of Joseph Conrad and Robert Louis Stevenson: Bali, Zanzibar, Bora Bora, Fiji, the Galapagos Islands, Tahiti, Samoa, Barbados, and Antigua. About half the time would be spent sightseeing in these ports and about half the time at sea. The hired crew of twelve, all of them veteran sailors, would help the three dozen paying guests learn to climb the masts, stand proper watch, navigate by the stars, steer, repair

sails, and all the other standard shipboard activities. For the privilege of co-producing their own sailing experience, the guests were to pay anywhere from $4,500 for a one-month onboard stay to $60,000 for the full eighteen-month round-the-world trip.

After about six months, approximately half of the passenger-guests had experienced the thrill of a lifetime. The other half wanted their money back. They didn't enjoy sleeping in bunks in one big dorm-type room, getting seasick, using a hose for a shower, being without TV, eating canned and dried foods (the ship had no refrigeration), and having little privacy. Some guests just couldn't "learn the ropes," and the experienced sailors among the crew didn't seem to be able to teach them how. One guest, who later claimed that he had been forced to climb the five-story mainmast, curled up into a paralyzed ball and had to be airlifted by helicopter to shore. He later sued the Dwyers and Windenwaves Partners Ltd. for $750,000 and won; the Dwyers had not thought to get insurance protection against such an action.

The delighted guests thought their trip on the *Windenwaves* was a high point in their lives, and not just because of the climb up that five-story mast. Said one, "Everybody who's been on a sailboat dreams of a trip like this. We saw places and things we would never get to see in any other way." The disappointed guests were really disappointed. They saw no reason why they should pay so much money and have to do so much of the work themselves. Said one, "I wanted a relaxing cruise. They treated me like a common sailor; made me scrub the decks and empty the slop. At those prices, who needs it? Next time, I'm going on the Disney Magic."

1. Which dangers of co-production became realities for Luke and Sue?

2. How might they have headed off those dangers by planning more thoroughly?

ADDITIONAL READINGS

Anitsal, I., & Schumann, D. W. 2007. Toward a conceptualization of customer productivity: The customer's perspective on transforming customer labor into customer outcomes using technology-based self-service options. *The Journal of Marketing Theory and Practice*, 15 (4), 349–353.

Berry, L. L., Carbone, P. L., & Haeckey, S. 2002. Managing the total customer experience. *Sloan Management Review*, 43 (Spring), 85–89.

Bettencourt, L. A. 1997. Customer voluntary performance: Customers as partners in service delivery. *Journal of Retailing*, 73, 383–406.

Bitner, M. J., Faranda, W. T., Hubbert, A. R., & Zeithaml, V. A. 1997. Customer contributions and roles in service delivery. *International Journal of Service Industry Management*, 8, 193–205.

Bowers, M. R., & Martin, C. L. 2007. Trading places redux: Employees as customers, customers as employees. *Journal of Services Marketing*, 21, 88–98.

Chang, H. L., & Yang, C. H. 2008. Do airline self-service check-in kiosks meet the needs of passengers? *Tourism Management*, 29, 980–993.

Chase, R. 1978. Where does the customer fit in a service operation? *Harvard Business Review*, 56 (6), 137–142.

Dabholkar, P. A., & Bagozzi, R. P. 2002. An attitudinal model of technology-based self-service: Moderating effects of consumer traits and situational factors. *Journal of the Academy of Marketing Science*, 30, 184–201.

Gentile, C., Spillera, N., & Nocia, G. 2007. How to sustain the customer experience: An overview of experience components that co-create value with the customer. *European Management Journal*, 25, 395–410.

Goodwin, C. F. 1990. "I Can Do It Myself": Training the service consumer to contribute to service productivity. *Journal of Services Marketing*, 2 (4), 71–78.

Halbesleben, J. R. B., & Buckley, M. R. 2004. Managing customers as employees of the firm: New challenges for human resource management. *Personnel Review*, 33 (3), 351–372.

Harris, L. C., & Reynolds, K. L. 2004. Jaycustomer behavior: An exploration of types and motives in the hospitality industry. *Journal of Services Marketing*, 18, 339–357.

Honebein, P. C., Cammarano, R. F. 2006. Customers at work. *Marketing Management*, 15, 797–818.

Hsieh, A. T., & Yen, C. H. 2005. The effect of customer participation on service providers' job stress. *Services Industry Journal*, 25, 891–905.

Kristensson, P., Matthing, J., & Johansson, N. 2008. Key strategies for the successful involvement of customers in the co-creation of new technology-based services. *International Journal of Service Industry Management*, 19, 474–491.

Lovelock, C., & Young, R. 1979. Look to customers to increase productivity. *Harvard Business Review*, 57 (3), 168–178.

Matthing, J., Sandén, B., & Edvardsson, B. 2004. New service development: Learning from and with customers. *International Journal of Service Industry Management*, 15, 479–498.

Piccoli, G., Anglada, L. D., & Watson, R. T. 2005. Using information technology to improve customer service. *Journal of Quality Assurance in Hospitality & Tourism*, 5 (1), 3–26.

Pini, F. M., 2009. The role of customers in interactive co-creation practices: The Italian scenario. *Knowledge, Technology & Policy*, 22 (1), 61–69.

Prahalad, C. K., & Ramaswamy, V. 2004. Co-creating unique value with customers. *Strategy & Leadership*, 32 (3), 4–9.

Sierra, J. J., & McQuitty, S. 2005. Service providers and customers: Social exchange theory and service loyalty. *Journal of Services Marketing*, 19, 392–400.

Verhoef, P. C., Lemon, K. N., Parasuraman, A., Roggeveen, A., Tsiros, M., & Schlesinger, L. A. 2009. Customer experience creation: Determinants, dynamics and management strategies. *Journal of Retailing*, 85, 31–41.

Wu, C. H., 2007. The impact of customer-to-customer interaction and customer homogeneity on customer satisfaction in tourism service: The service encounter prospective. *Tourism Management*, 28, 1518–1528.

Zhao, X., Mattila, A. S., & Tao, L. E. 2008. The role of post-training self-efficacy in customers' use of self service technologies. *International Journal of Service Industry Management*, 19, 492–505.

NOTES

[1]Prahalad, C. K., & Ramaswamy, V. 2004. Co-creation experiences: The next practice in value creation. *Journal of Interactive Marketing*, 18 (13), 5–14. For a classic discussion of value co-creation see Vargo, S. L., & Lusch, R. F. 2004. Evolving to a new dominant logic for marketing. *Journal of Marketing*, 68, 1–17.

[2]Ford, R. C., & Bowen, J. T. 2004. Getting guests to work for you. *Journal of Foodservice Business Research*, 6 (3), 37–53. Also see Bowen, D. E. 1986. Managing customers as human resources in service organizations. *Human Resource Management*, 25, 371–383; and Bettencourt, L. A. 1997. Customer voluntary performance: Customers as partners in service delivery. *Journal of Retailing*, 73, 383–406.

[3]Schneider, B., & Bowen, D. E. 1995. *Winning the Service Game*. Boston: Harvard Business School Press, pp. 88–89.

[4]For an elaborate discussion of this trade-off, see Etgar, M. 2008. A descriptive model of the consumer co-production process. *Journal of the Academy of Marketing Science*, 36, 97–108.

[5]Heskett, J. L., Jones, T. O., Loveman, G. W., & Sasser, W. E. 1994. Putting the service-profit chain to work. *Harvard Business Review*, 72 (2), 172.

[6]Kyriazi, G. 1976. *The Great American Amusement Parks: A Pictorial History*. Secaucus, NJ: Citadel Press, p. 82.

[7]Ibid., 87.

[8]http://www.greenlodgingnews.com/Starwood-Makes-Wise-Business-Move-With-Make-Green-Choice, accessed October 13, 2010.

[9]For evidence that customer coproduction does not always save time or cost, see Hsieh, A. T., Yen, C. H., & Chin, K. C. 2004. Participative customers as partial employees and service provider workload. *International Journal of Service Industry Management*, 15, 187–189.

[10]Bitner, M. J., Ostrom, A. L., & Meuter, M. L. 2002. Implementing self-service technologies. *Academy of Management Executive*, 16 (4), 96–108.

[11]Bateson, J. 2002. Are your customers good enough for your service business? *Academy of Management Executive*, 16 (4), 110–120.

[12]Reinders, M. J., Dabholkar, A. P., & Frambach, R. T. 2008. Consequences of forcing consumers to use technology-based self-service. *Journal of Service Research*, 11 (3), 107–123.

[13]Bendapudi, N., & Leone, R. P. 2003. Psychological implications of customer participation in co-production. *Journal of Marketing*, 67, 14–28.

[14]Etgar, 2008.

[15]Bateson, J. E. G. 1985. Self-service consumer: An exploratory study. *Journal of Retailing*, 61 (3), 49–76.

[16]For further discussion and examples of this point, see Bendapudi, N., & Berry, L. L. 1997. Customers' motivations for maintaining relationships with service providers. *Journal of Retailing*, 73 (1), 15–37.

[17]Kelley, S. W., Skinner, S. J., & Donnelly, J. H., Jr. 1992. Organizational socialization of service customers. *Journal of Business Research*, 25 (3), 197–214.

[18]Grandey, A. A., Dickter, D. N., & Sin, H. P. 2004. The customer is not always right: Customer aggression and emotion regulation of service employees. *Journal of Organizational Behavior*, 25, 397–418.

[19]Heskett, J. L., Sasser, W. E., Jr., & Schlesinger, L. A. 1997. *The Service Profit Chain: How Leading Companies Link Profit and Growth to Loyalty, Satisfaction, and Value.* New York: John Wiley & Sons, p. 238.

[20]Starmer-Smith, C. 2006. Air rage incidents double in two years: Alcohol and illicit smoking contribute to a big increase in violence on planes. *Telegraph*, November 25, http://www.telegraph.co.uk/travel/737102/Air-rage-incidents-double-in-two-years.html, accessed July 21, 2009.

[21]http://gizmodo.com/gadgets/announcements/sprint-dumps-needy-customers-275374.php, accessed July 21, 2009.

The Hospitality Service Delivery System

Design systems that allow you to do the job right the first time. All the smiles in the world are not going to help you if your service is not what the participant wants.

—Joseph J. Bannon, Hospitality academic, educator, and author.

CHAPTER 9

Communicating for Service

HOSPITALITY PRINCIPLE: GLUE THE GUEST EXPERIENCE ELEMENTS TOGETHER WITH INFORMATION

Like a human being, a company has to have an internal communication mechanism, a "nervous system," to coordinate its actions.

—Bill Gates, chairman and co-founder, Microsoft Corporation.

If you make customers unhappy in the physical world, they might each tell 6 friends. If you make customers unhappy on the Internet, they can each tell 6,000 friends.

—Jeff Bezos, founder, Amazon.com

Communicate everything you can to your associates. The more they know, the more they care.

—Sam Walton, founder, Wal-Mart

LEARNING OBJECTIVES

After reading this chapter, you should understand:

- The importance and uses of information to hospitality organizations.
- Ways in which information enhances the service product, setting, and delivery system.
- The sophisticated information systems that hospitality organizations are now using and their advantages and disadvantages.
- The impact of the Internet on communication with customers and employees.
- The hospitality organization itself as a large information-processing system.

THE CHALLENGE OF MANAGING INFORMATION

A traveler was waiting for her breakfast to be served at a business hotel. Within a reasonable time, the server brought her eggs and bacon. She looked at the bacon and realized it was too undercooked to eat. She moved it to the side and proceeded to eat the rest of her meal. During a routine visit to the tables, the manager asked how the breakfast was. All right, she said, except the bacon was not cooked properly. The manager apologized and went on to another table. A short time later, the server appeared and asked the same question. The second time the traveler was annoyed. Not only did the restaurant do nothing about the poorly cooked bacon; the manager didn't even share the information with the server so that he would know of a problem with one of his customers.

At another restaurant, a guest wants to order a bottle of wine and is presented with a wine menu longer than some novels. Hundreds of options are provided, choices of different varietals from regions around the world. After pretending to study the list for a period of time, the guest simply gives up. Frustrated, he decides to just have water with his dinner. The frustration and embarrassment of not knowing what to do with the information available diminishes the quality of the dining experience and, at the same time, the restaurant loses a profitable sale.

Both situations illustrate the challenge of **managing information**. In the first case, the manager did not communicate important information to the server to alert him about a possible problem with one of his customers. The manager had the information but did not communicate it, so the server was unable to make the dining experience better. In the second illustration, the guest was provided with a near encyclopedia of wine, but he could not use any of it.

Creating a system that manages information effectively is one of the most important and challenging issues facing any hospitality organization. Information is data that informs, and an **information system** is a method to get data that informs to those who need to be informed. A well-designed information system gets the right information to the right person in the right format at the right time so that it adds value to that person's decisions. The right person in hospitality organizations could be an employee, the manager, the guest, a supplier, a combination of all these people, or many others. Information that does not add value to either the guest's or the organization's decisions is useless. Informing a guest standing in line waiting for a table at a Ralph's Restaurant that they had plenty of empty tables last night is not only useless, it is infuriating. Similarly, receiving a free-beverage coupon in the mail the day after the offer expires does not enhance the potential guest's fondness for the sending organization.

Informing the Guest

Since service is by definition intangible, the information that the hospitality organization provides to help the guest make the intangible tangible is a critical concern of the information system. What information should the organization provide, where, in what format, and in what quantity, in order to help create the experience that the customer expects? If the experience is a formal dinner, the restaurant should organize all the information it provides to the patron to cue the perception that this is a formal-dining environment, and an excellent one at that. The restaurant should be set up to look appropriate for a formal-dining experience. The chef should have the clean white coat and chef's hat that announce, "I am a chef, not a mere cook; I create a fine-dining experience, not merely cook food." The silverware and plates should be elegant, and the rest of the environment should communicate the message *fine-dining experience*. While the focus of a fine-dining experience is usually the food, the total experience includes everything from the food, to the environment, to the delivery system that provides the service. The restaurant must manage the many bits of information that the guest tastes, touches, hears, sees, and smells to be sure that each one contributes to helping that guest define the intangible elegance of a fine-dining experience in the way that the restaurant wants the guest to define it.

Cues Communicate

Regardless of the hospitality experience being offered, all informational cues in the service setting should be carefully thought out to communicate what the organization wants to communicate to the guest about the quality and value of the experience.[1] If the experience is themed, all cues should support the theme and none contradict or detract from it. The less tangible the service, the more important consistent communication will be. By recognizing that information is the glue that connects the service product, the service environment, and the delivery system together to make a *whole* experience for the guest, the organization should use information to make the guest experience seamless. The organization can manage its information and use the available information technology to tie together all the elements of the guest experience to ensure that the guest enjoys it and will want to come back. Similarly, an organization that looks at each manager and employee as a customer for its information can design the organization's information system to facilitate the optimal flow of useful information to those people. Information systems can even connect all parts of the industry supply chain so that vendors, suppliers, and distributors can know what they need to provide, in what quantities, and when, all to ensure that the organization can deliver a seamless guest experience.

Adding Quality and Value through Information

Organizations can use information in many ways to add quality and value to the service experience. Occasionally, information technology becomes so important that it can even transform the organization itself.

Information can help employees personalize the service to make each customer, client, or guest feel special. For example, having caller ID to allow the service representative to address the customer by name when answering the customer's phone call adds a special touch to the experience. Information and information technology can improve the service. While a barcode on a retail product or an RFID (radio frequency information device) on a gaming chip provides the basis for recording the transaction, it also provides a wealth of other information that enhances the service experience for both the organization and the customer. For casinos, having a real-time record of which customers are betting what provides for more accurate player tracking, better bet recognition, and labor-cost savings.

With an RFID reader at each table, casinos can track bets, ensure that customers get the comp meals and rooms they deserve, and check to see if any player is using a banned betting system.[2] Just as retail stores can track inventory and sales patterns with these information systems, casinos can track players. Even more interesting is the opportunity to keep track of what types of products or bets the customer is buying or making so that options can be suggested or offered as an enhanced service. If you buy a book online from Amazon.com, the online retailer may let you know about choices others buying the book you bought have made, track previous searches, or even offer new books on the same subject the next time you visit its Web site. Also, cross-selling between organizations is possible. If you purchase an airplane ticket using any of the many Internet retailers, you will be presented with opportunities to purchase an array of other services, including hotel rooms and rental cars.

Finally, information technology can transform an organization or even an industry. Online bookstores and travel Web sites, customized print-on-demand book publishers, e-book readers, social networking sites, and the amazing array of applications on smartphones are all transforming their respective industries in important ways. The easier, cheaper, and faster provision of information and services for customers made possible by advancing information technology, especially in innovative Web-based applications, has rapidly changed the dynamics of many industries. When Google became a verb, it meant the end of the encyclopedia business. When JetBlue offers those whom it twitters special discounts on airfares, the rest of the airlines will have to respond to this competitive initiative or risk losing contact with an entire segment of customers.

Radio frequency information devices (RFIDs) on gaming chips allow casinos to know where, when, and how much people are betting, giving management a wealth of information that can be used to create greater efficiencies in the casino and to enhance the guest experience.

Image copyright Peter Baxter, 2010. Used under license from Shutterstock.com

New Information from Virtual Worlds

Even more dramatic has been the technology that enhances information quality through the creation of virtual worlds, where customers can have an experience without leaving their homes. Rather than look at a two-dimensional picture, guests can take virtual tours on Web sites like synthtravels, a virtual-reality travel agency.[3] It, and others like it, can arrange virtual tours of art museums, VIP homes, and even red light districts. Second Life and other massive multiplayer online games offer a window into online virtual worlds, where people can gather, buy, sell, and generally do the same things that they do in the real world. Starwood used Second Life to test market the design of a new concept hotel, Aloft, and to observe how avatar visitors used the space and furniture.[4] Indeed, Second Life can be so real that one writer discussed the dilemma when a man's avatar married a woman's avatar in his Second Life virtual identity while still married to his real wife. The article asked the question "Is this man cheating on his wife?"[5] Virtual experiences have grown so popular that there are protests when companies eliminate or modify them in ways that are unpopular with their players. Disney, for example, closed down its free Virtual Magic Kingdom in 2009 and immediately was inundated by people representing the 1 million avatars who wanted to stay in the virtual theme park.[6]

Getting Information Where It Needs to Go

The challenge for hospitality managers, then, is to gather the data that can inform, organize the data into information, and distribute that information to the people—both customers and employees—who need it just when they need it. Hospitality organizations that are effective in getting information to where it needs to be recognize that providing information is in itself a service to guests, often as important as the primary service itself, and a necessity for employees.

Just as it is important to develop information systems that get the right information to the right person at the right time, it is equally important to develop systems and procedures to prevent the wrong information from getting to the wrong person at the wrong time. Every organization needs a plan that not only protects sensitive information from unauthorized access but also details other information rules, such as who can say what to whom when a major disaster strikes, who will talk to the press when a guest complains publicly, or who is the spokesperson for the organization on key decisions and policy. When information is not managed well, the information that is in the public domain will confuse and not inform. When statements that shouldn't have been made are made, they may even lead to law suits. Employees need to be taught what not to say as much as what to say. In this era of instant communication, they also need to be reminded of what information they have that should not be shared on their social networking site.

The whole challenge of information systems is to figure out exactly how to provide only the required information just when and where it is required. Designers of information systems must, therefore, identify the information needs of both guests and hospitality employees in regard to all three components of the guest experience: the service product itself, the service setting, and the delivery system. Let's talk about information as it relates to each of these elements.

INFORMATION AND THE SERVICE PRODUCT

Information about services offered is usually found within the environment rather than as part of the service product itself. Chapter 3 showed the many ways in which the hospitality organization can plant cues or information in the service setting. Such "tangibilizing" leads guests to favorable judgments about the quality and value of the guest experience. Just as doctors hang diploma certificates on the wall, restaurants display food reviews, and hotels display American Automobile Association ratings, all in the effort to say to guests, "This experience will definitely be good and may be a wow." Similarly, sensory information can communicate a message about the guest experience. The smell of bread baking, fresh flowers, or even antiseptic will communicate information to guests that can help make an intangible experience tangible. We shall presently speak in more detail about information in the service setting.

With the dramatic growth of the Web and its use by hospitality guests for making reservations, co-producing experiences, and giving feedback, there is increasing concern with ensuring that the self-service capabilities of Web-based services meet customers' expectations. After all, it can be just as frustrating for a guest to wait for a Web page to load as it is to wait for the phone to be answered or to be served in a restaurant. There are many aspects of guests' use of self-service technologies for hospitality organizations to plan for and manage. Besides the obvious things like "do they work?" "will they work fast enough?" or "will they work consistently?" managers must think through and plan for the different users' needs, wants, expectations, and capabilities just as they would with any aspect of the hospitality experience.[7]

Information as Product: FreshPoint

A good illustration of a sophisticated information and decision system properly used is that developed by Orlando's FreshPoint. FreshPoint sells more fresh fruits and vegetables to central Florida restaurants, hotels, theme parks, and other hospitality customers than all its competition combined, and its information system is one of the big reasons why. FreshPoint has developed its information system so that it can accurately predict what all its customers will need and when they will need it. In effect, FreshPoint has moved beyond the business of supplying fruits and vegetables into the business of managing its customer inventories. Its computerized models are so accurate that FreshPoint frequently knows better than its customers what they need, how much, and when. This is important to FreshPoint because its Orlando location is about a week away from its suppliers, and fruits and vegetables are extremely perishable. Since freshness is critical to most chefs, effective inventory management is a competitive advantage. Through the capabilities of its information system, FreshPoint is able to become responsible for the freshness and adequacy of fruits and vegetables for its foodservice customers. For one large customer, FreshPoint has taken over the management of more than 50 percent of its inventory, and its purchasers are no longer required to physically place those orders.

FreshPoint uses what is called an **economic ordering quantity (EOQ)** model to determine the optimum number of units to reorder. Based on the EOQ model, the customer's inventory is monitored, future demand estimated, and orders generated automatically via EDI (Electronic Data Interchange) for next-day delivery. Although most of its customers do not have the technical capability to connect to its inventory management system through its EDI, FreshPoint predicts demand patterns for them anyway and uses its decision models to monitor called-in or Web orders for accuracy and completeness. When customers call in or log onto its online ordering system, they are prompted to order items they typically request, alerted when their orders are not large enough to accommodate a big weekend or large convention, advised when they made a mistake on quantity, and made aware of special deals and products. With this information in its database, FreshPoint can call and help its customers avoid a problem before it happens. Work is also underway to allow users to simply select menu items, and the system

Photo courtesy of FreshPoint, and Kent Shoemaker.

Although FreshPoint delivers food items to its customers, its competitive advantage is the information services it supplies to help its customers order the right items at the right time in the right quantities.

will both determine what ingredients they need *and* determine the most efficient way for the customers to receive the product. FreshPoint's market share attests to the appreciation its restaurants have for the help FreshPoint's information system provides.

Giving Employees the Information They Need

Employees also need relevant, timely, and accurate information to do their jobs effectively. When you consider information to be a service product, the employee is an **internal customer** for that product. For this internal customer, the service provided is the delivery of the information that the employee needs for making decisions about how to satisfy external customers. This information-as-product is provided to the internal customer by an employee or information-gathering unit acting as an internal "service organization."

For example, if your hotel is hosting a conference with more than 10,000 attendees, and they are all ready for dinner, your employees need up-to-date information to deliver exceptional service. The Gaylord Opryland Resort and Convention Center uses an **integrated information system** to help employees serve guests at their four full-service restaurants more effectively. Using a small hand-held wireless device, employees find out what tables are available, can clear and close any table, or can update seating arrangements from anywhere in the four restaurants. Employees can get immediate information on wait times, can find out if a table's food has been ordered, if a quoted wait time is about to expire, or even if it is a repeat customer's birthday. All this information allows employees to be more efficient, as well as deliver better service. The information provided to employees allows them to fulfill the company's mission. As Rickie Hall, the senior vice president and chief information officer says, "It's all about the guest service."[8]

Providing information is the service product for many internal employees/customers, and all hospitality organizations seek to provide it as effectively and efficiently as possible. Indeed, the entire movement toward frontline employee empowerment that characterizes benchmark hospitality organizations depends upon employees having easy access to needed information. Without some systematic way to provide it, empowerment would be impossible. Managers and empowered employees alike must have information to make good decisions and to measure the results of their decision-making activity.

INFORMATION AND THE SERVICE SETTING

The service setting and its features and aspects can provide several kinds of useful information for guests.

The Environment and the Service

First, the service setting can be a source of information related to the service itself, and that information must be efficiently and effectively provided. If the tangible product in the guest experience is a quick-service meal, the patron needs to know how to get quick service, which quick-service meals are available, and when the meal is ready. Signs are therefore placed in the service environment to facilitate quick customer access to the order taker, menus are posted in easy-to-find places to aid the diner in selecting the meal, a picture of what the meal looks like may be located next to each menu item so that the diner knows what the menu item is, and the customer order number may be displayed on an overhead video screen to let the customer know as soon as the order is ready.

Many hotels have attractive graphics on their Web sites showing room interiors or offering panoramic 360 degree views of a sleeping room or other places in and around the hotel. Some even allow the site visitor to take a virtual tour of the hotel and the surrounding destination. These visuals of the setting help to make the service tangible for potential guests.

Many hotels provide images of their rooms on-line so guests can see what they are booking.

Image courtesy of Marriott International.

The Environment as Information System

In a larger sense, the service environment itself can be thought of as an information system of sorts by the way it is themed and laid out. Not only does the environment provide information on the location of various points of interest, but the environment itself becomes part of the service and therefore influences the customer's perception of the service.[9]

The information embedded in the environment can enhance or detract from the service experience. This information can be in the form of carefully located walls and shrubbery that tell guests where they should not go and paths that tell them where they should. Simple orientation maps tell customers where they are, and arrows and signs allow customers to obtain the information they need to fully enjoy the service experience.

Casinos have long known this, and their environments are carefully designed to send the desired messages to the customers. Interiors of casinos are full of information. Signs are carefully located to quickly show where different restaurants, bars, the theatre, and the night club are located. In addition to signage, casinos use environmental stimuli—such as architectural design, colors, furnishings, textures, lighting, ceiling height, and aromas—for both functional and marketing purposes.[10] Casinos know that the longer they can keep customers inside their establishment, the laws of probability will ultimately lead to financial success. Casinos are designed not only to enhance the customers' experience, but also to present information that keeps them there longer.

Customer-Provided Information

Guests do not need to wait for companies to provide information to them. There are now many sources of information available to customers to help evaluate a hospitality experience before they decide to have it. In the previous chapter, we listed a number of Web sites where customers post information about their experiences to share with anyone who wants it. There are numerous other online sources for customers to post reviews and find information on nearly any hospitality organization that exists in any part of the world: their prices, service quality, quality of destination attractions, and anything else the inquiring visitor might wish to know. New sites are being created all the time in response to customers' demands for this sort of information. Figure 9-1 provides a list of some—but certainly not all—Web sites.

FIGURE **9-1** Some Web Sites Hospitality Customers Can Use

© Cengage Learning 2012

Guests Sharing Information with Other Guests

Foders: User-generated reviews of hotels and restaurants

Consumeraffairs: Consumers can give their opinions and try to get needs met

Consumerist: Spotlights poor customer service

Cruisecritic: Reviews boat by boat and port by port

IgoUgo: Travel advice, deals, reviews from other travelers

Ripoffreport: Gives consumers a chance to fight back against erring service providers

TripAdvisor: Reviews lodging places, travel packages, and other travel services

Virtualtourist: Source for user-generated travel content and reviews

World66: Open content travel guide, with user-posted information on destinations from around the world

(continued)

FIGURE **9-1** Some Web Sites Hospitality Customers Can Use
© Cengage Learning 2012
(continued)

Finding Deals or Comparing Prices

AirlineConsolidator: Sells unsold seats from airlines at steep discounts

Bingtravel: Searches for prices and offers predictions on whether to buy now or wait

Ctrip: For information on hotels, flights, and cars in China

Cheaptickets: For plane tickets, hotel rooms, car rentals, events, and cruises

ebookers: For flights, hotels, car rentals, cruises, and travel insurance

eLong: For flights and hotels in China

Expedia: Travel agency for airlines, rental cars, and lodging

FareCompare: Search for discounted first-class seats, historical data

Flyingfees: Compare airline fares with all included fees and extras

hotels: Search for airfares, hotel deals, and vacation packages

Hotwire: Offers discounts; supplier not disclosed until after purchase

Kayak: For both online agencies and suppliers

lastminute: Search for last minute deals

Opodo: Travel agent search site

Orbitz: Travel agency for airlines, rental cars, and lodging

Priceline: Allows travelers to bid on fares

Shoretrips: Links and reviews of shore trips

SideStep: Searches online agencies and suppliers

travelocity: Travel agency for airlines, rental cars, and lodging

travelzoo: Search to find best air fares from other search engines

Usaca: Sells unsold seats from airline at steep discounts

Yapta: Notifies of price drops and refund possibilities

zuji: Travel guide and engine for flights, hotels, rail travel, cruises, and packages in a number of Asia Pacific countries

Information Tools for Guests

away: Provides ideas and recommendations based on user-specified travel interests

cdc.gov: Center for Disease Control posts cruise-ship inspection scores

DisneyFamilyTravel: Go-to source of family-oriented travel

Flightstats: Notice of flight changes, cancellations, or delays

frommers: Travel guide intended to give a local's perspective on worldwide destinations.

goby: To help find area attractions

Gusto: Hotels, mostly North America-centric

HotelShark: Composite summary of hotel reviews

IgoUgo: Provides background information on person writing review

lonelyplanet: Provides reviews and information for responsible tourism

maps.google: Provides information and driving directions

maps: Provides information and driving directions

Mytravelguide: Source of travel information around the world by city

OpenTable: Finds restaurants and makes bookings

realtravel: Source of travel information for the United States and Canada

Roadfood: Lists memorable eateries along highways and back roads of America

roadsideamerica: Source of information for odd, strange, or otherwise peculiar destinations around the United States

trails: Information and travel guides for hiking and biking

travbuddy: An online community for meeting other travelers and sharing travel reviews, photos, and blogs

Travelmuse: Online travel planning Web site

Trazzler: A Web site specializing in local travel opportunities

TripIt: Puts all confirmation numbers in one document

TripWiser: A site for users to share travel interests, experiences, plans, and advice

Tripwolf: A worldwide travel guide

uptake: A travel site that allows users to ask travel questions and find answers and recommendations based on their preferences

Walkscore: Walkability of more than 2500 neighborhoods

Wayn: Lifestyle and travel social network

Whereivebeen: A Facebook application that marks where users have traveled on a color-coded map

Zoomandgo: Reviews and video clips of hotels and vacations

Companies definitely need to pay attention to guest-provided content. Because potential customers are making purchase decisions in part (and sometimes entirely) based on this information, technology has allowed "word of mouth" to travel far beyond what it ever could even just one decade ago. Some people habitually evaluate anything they do. Others only post comments when something particularly good or, more often, particularly bad happens. A bad customer experience can hurt a company more than losing a customer or those friends whom the customer tells about the experience: It will likely lose many potential guests with Internet access who are trying to find information about the quality of its service. In this information-rich environment, many hospitality organizations have created new monitoring units whose only responsibility is to track and correct, if necessary, what is being said about the company on the Web.

INFORMATION AND THE DELIVERY SYSTEM

Finally, and perhaps most obviously, information is required to make the service delivery system work. That system includes both people and the processes by which the service and any accompanying tangible product are delivered to the customer. Here again, the nature of the service product and the delivery system unique to that product and guest will determine what the information system ideally should be. If the end result of the service is a properly prepared hotel room, the information system needs to be set up in a way that communicates to the front desk agent that the room is properly serviced and ready for a guest. Such an information system could be as simple as having the housekeeper bring the room key back to the front desk only after the room has been cleaned. In this way, no guest could be checked into a dirty, unprepared room because the key wouldn't be at the desk.

Really Knowing Your Customers

Many hotels seek to provide more than just a simple clean room, and their information systems are designed to provide this extra level of guest service. The Wyndham Hotels and Resorts uses data warehousing applications to allow customers enrolled in its frequent-guest programs to use its Web site to configure rooms to their liking. Members of Wyndham ByRequest can log on and create a detailed guest profile of their preferences (what floor they like, nearness to elevator, pillows, drinks, etc.). This information is combined with members' guest history data to customize and thereby enhance their experience at any Wyndham hotel. This technology allows frontline employees to access comprehensive guest information stored in Wyndham's database. Housekeepers are empowered and enabled, for example, to customize rooms and amenities for individual guests without the need of supervisory intervention or direction.[11]

The Ritz-Carlton Hotels also has a similar database, called Mystique, for its guests. It goes further, however, as it asks its employees to listen for and record any information that can be used to help The Ritz-Carlton Hotels improve or add value to a guest's experience. For example, if a floor sweeper overhears guests talking about celebrating their anniversary, the sweeper is supposed to pass the information along so that the hotel can take some notice of this special event. The employees help deliver the wow Ritz-Carlton experience by inputting useful information into the organization's information system.[12]

Delivering Freshness

In restaurants, the information system can improve service delivery by including in the database information about the freshness of the food products used to prepare the meals. Chefs could know how fresh an ingredient is on the basis of its freshness date. Labels with date of production or purchase on food products, "day dots" on fresh-food items, and online inventory systems are all examples of how an information system can be designed to ensure that the chefs have the information they need to make the right decisions about using or not using the available ingredients to produce the fresh meals they are responsible for preparing. Though the information is related to the product—the ingredients—and to the service delivery system, its primary purpose is to ensure that product delivery is "just-in-time"—available fresh when the chef needs it.[13]

Ensuring freshness has another dimension that information systems can help manage: food safety. With the increased emphasis on food safety caused by disease outbreaks linked to fresh food, traceability to identify where fresh fruits and vegetables were grown and processed has become an important part of the information kept on the food supply chain. Some growers place RFIDs on their shipments so the buyer can trace the source back to the specific location using a GPS. Buyers can even view the location, using geographic information programs like Google Earth. In one instance where a contaminated supply of vegetables was found, a Google Earth picture of where the produce was grown showed a barn next to the growing field that housed contaminants that had spilled onto the field.

Information on Service Quality

Perhaps one of the more important uses of service delivery information systems is in the systematic gathering of information on service quality. Acquiring this information, organizing it into a usable form, and disseminating it to managers and service providers is critical to ensuring that service delivery and other problems are identified and resolved. Inputting the fact into the information system that a guest is annoyed because she is allergic to the feather pillows typically used in the rooms is important, but the information is worthless unless the manager and other employees responsible for guest satisfaction are able to access that same information promptly. Finally, the information system must be designed so that the person concerned follows up on this information to ensure high service quality in the future.

Information to the People

The information system can be used to ensure that all the people involved in delivering the service have the information they need to do their jobs in the best possible way. Here is where the most powerful applications of modern information technology have been developed. Providing the hospitality employee with the information necessary to satisfy and even wow the guest is an effective way to add value to the guest experience.

At Hyatt

Every employee phone at the Hyatt hotels has a caller ID system that allows any employee to greet the caller by name when answering the phone. To a hotel manager, this information "allows the guest to experience a higher level of guest satisfaction and find greater value in the hotel's service." To the guest, it's "a nice personal touch." The technology provides information that was previously unavailable; it gives the service delivery employee the opportunity to add quality and value to the guest experience. The system should be designed to accommodate multiple users who want the same information at the same time. If simultaneously (1) a telephone operator is attempting to find a particular guest for a telephone caller, (2) the front desk agent is trying to find the name of the same guest on the database, and (3) the restaurant is trying to bill the same guest for tonight's meal, the need for multiple access to databases becomes obvious. As the Wyndham example showed, even the frontline housekeepers need access to the database to do their part in providing a guest experience that exceeds expectations.

High Tech Becomes High Touch

In many other situations, information systems make it possible for the organization and its employees to provide service to customers quickly and efficiently. As technology has advanced and customers have become accustomed to self-service kiosks in various venues (e.g., airports, rental cars, retail stores), self-serve devices have become increasingly accepted in hotel environments, and even in some of the luxury establishments.[14]

The use of technology is a challenging issue for hospitality organizations, as they want to capture the benefits and economies that technology offers without losing the human contact that is so vital to the guest experience. The key, not surprisingly, is giving guests what they want, need, and expect.

Says Pierre-Louis Giacotto, General Manager of the Sofitel Chicago O'Hare, "I believe that self-service in luxury and higher end establishments can dilute customer service if that is the only method offered. However, if technology is in addition to the traditional way of checking in, I don't see a problem at all."[15] Walter Brindell, Vice President of Rooms for Hyatt Hotels and Resorts, echoes the point: "You have to have both, depending on your market. Some customers need personal interaction and others prefer the availability of technology that they can control, select, and orchestrate themselves."[16]

Hospitality organizations therefore try to use as much technology behind the scenes as they can, primarily to save on back-of-the-house labor costs and give the customer a choice of service options in the front of the house.

Technology for Expertise

In many ways, information technology now allows the hospitality organization to provide expert skills without paying experts to provide them. A concierge who knows every good restaurant in town or how to get last-minute tickets to a sold-out play is a valuable hotel asset and is generally paid accordingly. Acquiring this level of expertise takes time and experience, and the organization and the guest pay for that expertise. On the other hand, if this knowledge is online, through a guest-room Internet connection, accessible through a touch-screen device in the lobby, or even available through an employee who can easily find it in a computerized database, the cost to the guest and the organization of accessing that information is reduced while the quality of the information and the ease of access are increased.

The Web is also making it possible for customers to provide expertise to each other, and guests increasingly want to get this information for themselves. Rather than asking a concierge for the information, they prefer to do a Google search for nearby restaurants and walking tours themselves, ask for suggestions from other guests on Web sites like TripAdvisor and food411, search blogs, or text their friends for suggestions. With billions of text messages sent every day, there is a lot of communication going on besides what the organization itself offers. Guests may use Second Life avatars or access virtual customer environments, which can range from discussion blogs about the organization's ability to deliver the guest experience to product prototyping.[17] This trend has resulted in hotels reducing costs as they do not need to staff as many people at the concierge desk while still providing the service their guests want and expect. Further, it provides an opportunity for hotels that traditionally do not offer this level of service to provide their guests with this information via the Web. There are increasing opportunities for hospitality organizations to use information and information technology to enhance the hospitality experience, or they can enhance the guest experience by providing the guest with easy access to information. The best organizations are constantly seeking them out to enhance their guests' experiences.

Centralized Reservations at Hyatt

Like most hotel chains, Hyatt has a centralized reservation system that all callers reach when calling in for rooms or access via the Web. Hyatt's reservationists have access to the entire inventory of rooms available in all Hyatt properties and can help the caller find a room that best matches the desired price point and time when the caller wants to come. Instead of calling each Hyatt hotel, the person needing a room calls the centralized reservation system and speaks to a reservationist, who offers complete information about how best to meet that person's lodging needs.

Cross-Selling

Even better, from an organizational perspective, is that having the information system set up in this manner allows the organization to **cross-sell** its other products and services. A potential guest calling the Hyatt reservation number for a hotel room can also be offered a room upgrade or other available products or services. The net result of this integrated reservation information system is to ensure that the guest becomes aware of the many options that Hyatt provides. The reservationist can not only sell a room in one location for one hotel, but is empowered with the expertise to offer hotel rooms for every night at every location the traveler will visit. Travel agents and Web sites do the same type of cross-selling when they book hotel rooms, arrange for rental cars, and offer other services when people call in or log in to make airplane reservations.

The Front and the Back of the House

The hospitality service delivery information system ties together the front of the house with the back of the house. Coordination between those people and operations serving the guest and those people and operations serving those who serve the guest is critical in providing a seamless experience for the guest. The guest does not care that the communications system between the cook and the server is faulty. The guest cares only about the quality of the overall restaurant experience, and the organization is responsible for serving the ordered food in a timely and appropriate manner.

Point-of-Sale Systems

Point-of-sale (POS) systems have been developed to help managers, servers, and cooks do their jobs better. The server enters the order on a touchscreen or handheld wireless touch screen device, and it is transmitted back to the cook station for preparation. POS systems ensure that the orders are entered in the proper sequence so that the hot foods are served hot and the cold foods are served cold and not the other way around.

Some systems help the cooks do their jobs more effectively, such as by accompanying each order with a display of the recipe and a picture of the final plated meal so the cook can verify if the meal being produced matches the standard.[18] This extra

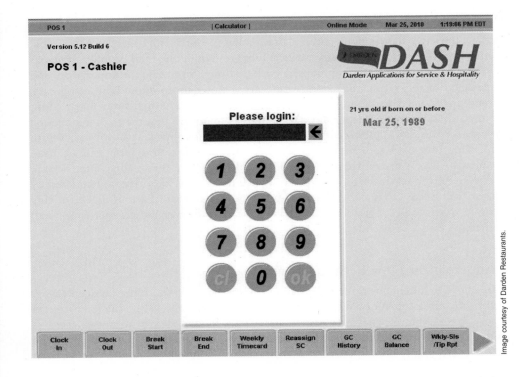

POS systems, like those used by Darden, track a myriad of data on employees, food sales, and financial information.

Image courtesy of Darden Restaurants.

informational feature lets cooks self-monitor their work; they can review the proper preparation procedures for the meals they are producing to assure a consistent, high-quality meal.

Modern POS systems are so powerful they can provide information that influences almost any dimension of the business. For example, some POS systems can produce financial reports, track individual server performance, determine which menu items are big sellers, track inventory, and even post the nutritional information of different menu items.[19] They can also support strategic decision making. For example, by tracking coupon use and sales, a system can determine whether a promotional campaign is profitable. POS systems also collect and analyze data to make sales forecasts, provide inventory recommendations, and create employee schedules that meet employee preferences and reduce labor costs. Some systems help with guest retention, by identifying lapsed customers and sending them a coupon.[20] In short, advances in POS systems are allowing managers to gather and use vast amounts of information quickly and easily. The information they provide can then help managers improve nearly every operational and strategic decision they make.

The Daily Count

Another illustration of how an information system can improve experiences for customers and performance results for the company is a **daily count** system, like the one used at Disney. Every guest entering the park is counted and added to the total in the park at that time. Based upon its extensive attendance database and knowledge of arrival-rate distributions, Disney can accurately predict after the first hour of operation how many guests will come into the park during the whole day. This information can then be used to inform the food and beverage people how much food needs to be taken from central storage facilities and brought into the park's various restaurant and food-service locations, and how many salads, soups, and other prepared food items need to be on hand.

Further, the same data is made available to human resources managers to ensure that an appropriate number of employees are scheduled to handle the total number of guests Disney now knows will be coming into the park that day. Similarly, the supervisors and area managers of the various attractions can access this data to know how many cars, boats, and trains need to be available for their attractions. The first-hour guest count can be used in a number of important decision areas to ensure that the park is prepared to serve all of the day's guests with the level of service quality that Disney strives to provide. This one data source flowing through the information system can be used simultaneously across the entire service experience to improve the quality of the service delivery system, the service setting, and the service itself. The information generated by the system will make the many different experiences a guest will have of higher quality than would otherwise be possible and enables Disney to deliver these experiences with high efficiency and consistency.

The Information Flow between Levels

The last major requirement of the information system, as it relates to the service delivery system, is providing for information flows across organizational levels. This level-to-level flow can be as simple as an employee newsletter or a routing slip, or as complicated as an online, real-time, data-retrieval and decision system. Information can also be provided through a centralized database or intranet made available through computer connections to all employees, so they can access the specific information they need to interpret corporate policy, identify the dates and places of training opportunities, or the availability of alternative jobs.

All these methods, whether on paper or in electronic form, are ways in which hospitality managers can reinforce the organizational culture, motivate employees, and educate them to enhance the guest experience. Of course, many other communication channels flow up and down between management and employees. For example, employee-of-the-month programs allow the organization to communicate to all employees by example what types of behavior are desired and rewarded. Employee suggestion programs are another way for management to pick up new ideas and other types of information from their employees that let it quickly identify problem areas in the service delivery system. Building an information system into the design, structure, and operation of the hospitality organization is vital to gather and distribute the necessary information in a timely way to manage and monitor the contribution of all parts of the organization to the quality and value of each guest's experience.

DECISION SUPPORT SYSTEMS

With computers collecting so much information across so many aspects of the hospitality business, many companies are finding that they now have vast databases with information on customers and their behaviors. Data come from centralized reservation, POS, and Mystique-type property management systems. As discussed earlier in the Wyndham and The Ritz-Carlton Hotels examples, data also come from customers who voluntarily provide information that can be entered into a database for future reference. It is possible for companies to purchase consumer data containing demographic information and information on past purchasing behavior. Organizations like National Demographics make a business of collecting and providing such data, and some state driver-license bureaus make money by selling information about their licensed drivers. In order to sell targeted advertising, some companies have added "history sniffing" capabilities to their web sites so that they can surreptitiously track what other sites their users are visiting. All these data clearly have the potential to provide more information about one's guests, and what they want and expect from the hospitality organization. But having a lot of data does not mean you have good information. You have to use the data to change how you make decisions, and there are a number of ways technology can help accomplish this task.

Systems that go beyond getting information to the right person at the right time, and actually help improve business decisions, are called **decision support systems (DSS)**. Built into these systems are analytical methods and decision rules that either help a decision maker make a decision or, in some cases, replace the decision maker altogether. An example of a decision system that aids a decision maker would be an automatic warning that signals a manager when an inventory level of a critical product gets low, a computer icon that flashes on a computer screen to warn a cruise-ship engineer that a piece of equipment is heating up or malfunctioning, or a report that alerts a manager if a worker has not received mandatory training within a specified amount of time since she was hired.

A DSS can help support decision making in a number of ways. Most obviously, it can help collect, synthesize, and present data in meaningful ways. DSSs frequently generate reports that help in both tactical and strategic decision making. DSSs can also provide recommendations. One way to generate recommendations is to model how experts make decisions. That is, a DSS can be programmed to mimic the process used by a recognized expert; once captured in a computer program, this expertise can be shared with anyone who uses the system. DSSs can use sophisticated algorithms and statistical methods to analyze data and present recommendations based on these models' results.

Using Data to Drive Decisions

In general, DSSs collect and present information. It is up to the user to ask the right questions. Capturing the power of information systems and DSSs to improve an organization's decision making capabilities requires gathering the right data, finding the right experts, and using the right models. DSSs can support organizational decision making using a variety of approaches.

Modeling Decisions

Some decisions can be modeled because the environment in which they occur is generally predictable. Since situations that call for such decisions recur frequently, it is worth the organization's time and trouble to develop a mathematical model describing the situation and to discover the appropriate decision rule. For example, if a pressure sensor in a Tunnel of Love ride registers a change in the weight of the car carrying guests, the DSS which monitors the ride makes the "decision" to shut the ride down because past experience has shown that someone has probably left the car and started walking on the track. Since this behavior is dangerous, the DSS is programmed to check the weight sensor continuously to ensure that no person is walking where people shouldn't be. If someone is out of place, the system shuts the ride down until the operator can check. Other illustrations of automatic decision making can be seen in recommended staffing and preparation levels of certain food items based on statistical projections, prepositioning taxis in locations and at times that match demand patterns, and rerouting buses based on analysis of real-time load factors.

As is true of any procedure designed to improve service to customers, the organization needs to assess the relationship between the value and the cost of the information before it establishes such a system. Because professional chefs are artists and not accountants, they may not get around to gathering and organizing data about ingredient supplies often enough to justify the expense and sophistication of an online system. Just because a company has a lot of data does not mean its systems necessarily support the types of decisions it needs to make. If the input of data is haphazard, or the available data irrelevant, the value of the frequently out-of-date or inaccurate information would be low and the expense of installing a sophisticated system unjustified.

Statistical Analysis

Another way to use available data is to statistically analyze it to detect relationships. Statistical data analysis can either be used to test certain expectations (e.g., test to see if prepositioning taxis led to quicker response times to customer calls) or be exploratory in nature (e.g., looking to see what variables are related to greater spending at the hotel spa). Statistical analysis is relatively easy to use. Microsoft Excel has a Data Analysis tool, and there are many statistical packages available in the market. The challenge is that the person conducting the analysis must understand the basics of how to use and interpret statistics. Someone must also be willing and able to devote the time to organize the data and perform the desired analyses. While this may be a task the authors of this book, professors that they are, enjoy, it is not a task many others may relish. Furthermore, as companies gain more data, it is possible that the sheer size of the database will make it unmanageable for statistical analysis on a single computer. So, while statistical analysis is actually within the reach of many hotels, restaurants, casinos, and other service providers, many are unable to drill down into their data to take full advantage of the large amount they collect.

Data Mining

When companies have massive datasets, completely analyzing the data is simply not feasible. Often, companies do not have the time or expertise to conduct sophisticated statistical analyses to take advantage of the true potential their huge data stores may provide. The process of **data mining** has emerged to help resolve these issues.

Data mining is a largely automated process that uses statistical analyses to search massive datasets for useful and meaningful patterns. The process is user friendly as it does not require complete understanding of the underlying analytical methods. The system identifies relationships in the data that can then be used in a variety of ways to improve the ability of the organization to satisfy its customers. In hotel marketing, for example, data mining allows the organization to create more focused direct-mail campaigns, offer more effective seasonal promotions, time and place its ad campaigns better, define which market segments are growing most rapidly, and determine the number of rooms to reserve for wholesale customers and business travelers.[21]

Data mining, however, can be expensive, requiring sophisticated software and hardware to analyze large amounts of data. Nonetheless, it is a technology being employed by many large hospitality companies, including Hilton, Starwood, Marriott, and Harrah's. Because these large companies can combine information from many properties, they have the potential to track their best customers and create highly targeted promotional campaigns. For instance, Harrah's Hotels and Casinos combine information from every customer transaction, including which casino games the customer prefers and psychographic and demographic information on the customer. Analyzing these data, the system can determine which customers are potentially the most profitable, and then provide appropriately customized incentives to attract their repeat business. For example, customers who live outside the Las Vegas area received complimentary hotel rooms or transportation, while drive-in customers received food, entertainment, or cash incentives.[22] Harrah's also estimates that it has saved over $20 million by not offering incentives to customers who were unlikely to return.[23]

Data mining, of course, does not guarantee finding information that will help improve either business success or the guest experience. Although it generally requires a substantial investment, it is a technology that many companies with large amounts of data can turn into information that will enable them to get a better idea of what guests want, how they behave, and perhaps how they can be influenced to become more loyal, profitable, and satisfied.

Using Information

Market Segmentation

By finding out more about individual customers, companies have found that they can customize their products to serve customers more personally. Rather than treating all customers the same, there is an increased emphasis on relationship marketing, or the *market-segment-of-one* concept, which has been made possible through the increasing power of computers to store, analyze, and interpret large quantities of information. The idea is to find out so much about customers that the organization can treat each person as a separate "market." When customers return warranty cards on products, fill out the online customer feedback surveys, send in for discount coupons, or request free company-logo coffee mugs, they provide information that companies can use to gain a better understanding of their customers and their unique needs. As discussed earlier in the Wyndham and The Ritz-Carlton Hotels examples, customers themselves may voluntarily provide information when they know it will enhance their experience or employees may be asked to listen, learn more about their customers, and enter what they hear and learn into the database for future reference. Knowing the individual customers better allows the company to customize and target its marketing campaigns, offer the services that they know specific individuals want, and, ultimately, best meet the guests' needs with the goal of providing a wow experience.

Identifying and Targeting Your Best and Worst Customers

Just as market segmentation helps identify the different preferences and purchasing behaviors of customers, gathering customer information can be used to identify how profitable each customer is. The fact is that not all customers are equally profitable. In truth, some are simply unprofitable. Instead of taking a "come one, come all" approach to customers and guests, more and more organizations are using information to determine customer value. Organizations use this information to establish closer relationships with their best guests. These customers are targeted to encourage their repeat business and continued loyalty. At the other extreme, companies can use information technology to identify unprofitable customers, allowing the company to change how it markets to this segment, and sometimes even severing relationships with them.

Using information on purchasing behavior, Dorothy Lane Market, a small supermarket chain that offers gourmet food and attentive customer service, identifies its best and worst customers with sophisticated technology. It knows that 30 percent of its customers generate 80 percent of its profits, and 1 percent of its customers are responsible for 11 percent of its profits.[24] Instead of advertising in newspapers and providing coupons to everyone, the market uses the Internet and direct mailing to provide specific incentives to its best customers. For example, during a milk price war, select customers received coupons to purchase milk at $1.49 per gallon; those who simply stopped in off the street paid $ 3.89.[25] Similarly, Harrah's Casino has different room rates, depending on their estimate of customer value.[26] Harrah's is willing to take a loss on a single room to attract a customer who will spend a significant amount of time gambling in the casino; those who are not expected to spend time at the casino pay a much higher rate.

While a few customers are often responsible for much of a company's profits, it is also true that some customers actually cost a company more than it gains. These customers demand more attention than they may be warranted given their spending and profitability.[27] Companies may want to get rid of these customers to become more profitable. The danger, of course, is that the organization may be cutting loose presently unprofitable customers who might generate large future profits or who might, if treated well, recommend the organization to potentially profitable friends.[28]

Collaborative Filters

Internet-based programs allow customers to make information about themselves available to companies and each other through collaborative filtering and social networking sites.[29] Collaborative filters can be found on many Web sites, like Amazon, eBay, and iTunes, where customer patterns are gathered and organized. This allows the customers to see what others searching in ways like them have purchased (Amazon) or listened to (iTunes) while adding their information to the database. An innovative software agent program called Firefly, designed in the middle 1990s, organized and categorized individual's judgments about music and then compared them with those of others like that person in a single database. The program was able to know what you liked, what you liked to do, and what you were likely to do in the future. It could then act as your personal intelligence agent. Firefly built vivid profiles of the people that used its Web site and sorted them to recommend new products and services based on what people like themselves are doing. In effect, it allowed the powerful influence of informal word-of-mouth marketing to be used even from strangers whose recommendations you'd never heard before.[30] Although the development of collaborative filters has been slowed somewhat by the need to ensure privacy, these filters offer powerful tools for providing experiences and products to targeted customers whose own database history indicates their specific preferences.

Social networking sites, on the other hand, reduce the concerns with privacy as they are created by the people themselves. People willingly share their data and personal information to any who find their Web site and view their public profile. While some restrict access to more personal information, it is surprising how many do not. With the growing popularity of the iPhone and similar wireless communication devices with their ever-increasing information-sharing applications like Facebook and Latitude, more people (and companies) can learn more about other people than ever before. One interesting application is offered by one company, Sense Network, which has found a way to track wireless communicators whether the person wants to be tracked or not. This company avoids privacy concerns by not identifying specific people holding the phones and tracks electronic dots representing individual cell phone users as they move in a geographical area. Observing customer behaviors by tracking the movement of cell-based communicators by day and time across their maps allows the company to see what people are really doing and where they are.[31]

Problems with Information Systems

Although no hospitality organization is going to give up its information system, these systems have potential and actual problems associated with them. One is **information overload**, the tendency of the system to produce and transmit too much data. A second is the creation of a false sense of information preciseness. Since these systems produce such apparently accurate numbers, managers tend to focus on the numbers instead of on less definite but often more important qualitative and human factors. Another problem is that an information system can produce bad information that looks good. Still another major concern is that organizations have crucial and sometimes proprietary information within their system, so maintaining security is an issue. Finally, the costs of installing and learning the systems must be matched against the benefits those systems can confer. These points will be discussed in turn.

Information Overload

Information systems are helpful and have revolutionized business, but they are far from perfect. The most obvious problem in the hospitality industry is the possibility of creating information overload for both guests and employees. As anyone who has ever done a Google search knows, too much information is as bad as not enough. While sophisticated systems are designed to provide only the right information to the right person when that person needs it, many information systems (and search engines) provide a lot of raw data, and leave it to the recipients to discover whatever information they need in the pile. Indeed, many systems are designed by having systems planners ask users what information they need. Human nature being what it is, most users will ask for as much information as they can get, instead of only as much as they really need. Most people believe having too much is better than not having enough; their proof is that they have seen people disciplined for having too little information but never for having too much. Another aspect of this same issue is that when asked, most people indicate that they use many informational data sources, instead of mentioning the one or two they actually use. Not wanting to admit ignorance or own up to how little information they use, they ask for a lot and then get lost in the pile.

Travelocity offers an example of how a company dealt with a very large information overload problem. Every month, Travelocity received 30,000 customer survey results, 50,000 emails, and notes sent by a half-million calls that it did not have enough employee time to read and respond to. Its managers knew that in this large pile of information, however, was important information about customer problems, sources of dissatisfaction, and issues that needed their response and resolution. Their solution was to turn to software based on *text analysis*. These programs can scrutinize text documents, quickly identify crucial terms and concepts, and put this information into an easily searchable format. Other companies have used this same technology to keep track of blogs and other online communications that may mention the company's name. This customer-created information on the Internet can be a gold mine of useful data about how its customers view the company and the service it provides. Data mining offers one promising way for organizations to dig out from under this information overload.[32] As Domino's Pizza found out much to their surprise, a practical joke by two employees in North Carolina, who put a fictitious video on YouTube showing them putting cheese sticks up their nose and then sneezing the sticks into a sandwich they were making, can become a national marketing problem requiring quick reaction. If an organization has no way of sorting through the large volume of information that is on the Web to know that something like the Domino's video is out there, then it has no opportunity to get the right information to the right person at the right time in the right format so that the person can fix it.

Focusing on the Numbers

A second problem with information systems is the tendency to get tied up in numbers. Since computers excel in transmitting, organizing, and analyzing numbers, much information is provided in numeric form. While this aids accurate conversion of data into information, it does tend to focus attention on only those things that can be quantified or somehow expressed in numerical terms. Unfortunately, much of a manager's job focuses on subjective, qualitative information and not quantitative data. The availability of numerical information creates an overemphasis in decision making on such information and an underemphasis on qualitative information.

Bad Information

Related to the problem of falling in love with numbers is the third problem with information systems: that of assuming that the numbers are accurate when they may not be. The saying "garbage in, garbage out" is quite true. A sophisticated information system can quickly get a lot of bad data to a lot of people. If bad data get into the organization's decision-making structure, that bad data will be used in many decision situations. The results can be worse than garbage: they can be catastrophic. Bad information leads to bad decisions. A ship captain who gets a false reading of crossing traffic in a narrow ship channel can make a steering error that collides with rather than avoids another ship. Likewise, bad information widely circulated by means of a sophisticated information and decision system can lead to disaster.

Maintaining Security

A fourth potential problem with information systems is security, or maintaining the integrity of the database. An organization's information system must be protected so that another organization cannot access its confidential or proprietary data, or worse yet, crash the system or destroy the data. In this era of telecommuting and managers working at home or on the road with wireless connections to the information system, protecting the integrity of the database from unauthorized or inappropriate access is an important concern. As the newspaper headlines often report, when employees are able to download sensitive information on laptop hard drives or flash drives, they can also misplace them, sell the information, or leak it to the press. Moreover, if hackers can get into Defense Department and CIA computers—as they have—competitors may find ways to get into your database as well. Protecting against such unauthorized entry is a big problem and big expense for organizations. The problem exists even internally, as database managers need to ensure that unauthorized persons cannot obtain confidential employee data. Outsiders and company insiders need to be prevented from snooping around in the organization's database.

Value Versus Cost

Another problem is determining the true value and true cost of the information. Even though it often seems like it in this era of instant access to endless amounts of information on the Web, information is not really free. Buying computers, routers, and servers, hiring programmers, Web designers, operating a network, and maintaining an accurate and user-friendly information system are hugely expensive. On the other side of the expense are the largely intangible benefits of employees having access to the right information at the right time in the right format to do their jobs. How does one measure the value of an employee being able to instantaneously access a guest database so that the guest is identified by name, a piece of information the guest wants is immediately available, and the guest's unique expectations are known so that they can be met?

Obviously, the difference in price between a hotel room at the Four Seasons and the Econolodge is one way to estimate the presumed value of these information-driven

Image copyright Amy Walters, 2010. Used under license from Shutterstock.com

Adding new technology adds costs, in both equipment and personnel. State-of-the-art computer systems add potential for huge customer databases, data mining initiatives, and powerful decision support systems, but you also have to be able to purchase, support, and maintain the new technology.

services to a guest. If guests didn't think these amenities were worth the price, they wouldn't select the Four Seasons. Since many guests do, they must place a value on these services, but their exact value in relation to their cost is usually impossible to establish. Deciding how much better a decision was because the manager had the right information available is all but impossible. Yet, most organizations believe their systems are worth the cost and give them a competitive advantage over others that do not have the same capabilities. The problem is that when budget time comes and paybacks on investments are calculated, defending information system upgrades and improvements is difficult because evaluating the exact contribution of the system is so challenging.

Though determining costs and benefits of information systems is complex, companies can make estimates. Consider how Google has forged its entire business model and financial success on understanding the value of information. In part, Google computes what it calls Page-Rank to estimate the relevance of information on Web pages to over 2 billion search terms. Google also factors in the full content of a page to consider its relevance to a search query in addition to the quantity and quality of the sites that are linked to a given Web page.[33] At the same time, Google uses data collected from every search and advertising click (millions a day) to estimate a host of metrics, all aimed at helping estimate the value of information to users and advertisers.[34] The result is a completely different way of doing business than nearly all other companies: Google gives away its best services, doesn't set prices for the advertisements it sells to support its business, makes businesses bid for advertising, and even turns away advertisers if its algorithms determining value and relevance suggest the ad has a poor fit.

Learning the System

The final problem with information systems involves the costs of learning how to use the new system and evolving tools that become available. People with decision-making responsibilities are the very group who need to learn how to use the organization's information system. At the same time, because these individuals are often those who have been out of school the longest, they frequently are the very people who are most uncomfortable and unfamiliar with it. Worse yet, given the problems in quantifying the value of the technology, these are the same people who make the decisions about buying the equipment and investing in the system. Obviously, a lot of learning has to take place before those who are uncomfortable with new technology–such as those who are uneasy talking about tweets and mayorships; don't know the difference between MMSs, SMSs, and RSSs; and don't really understand how many Gs their phones have– are at ease when using the new systems. Nonetheless, it is critical to get employees familiar with the technology necessary for them to make high-quality decisions. Even though increasingly user-friendly software has made it easier for these managers to learn and use the powerful technology available to them, the challenge for them will be that as soon as they master one technology, a newer and more powerful one will come along and they will need to learn that one. The rapid changes in what technology can do in managing information will require managers to rapidly adapt to new situations. With so many other things to worry about in performing their jobs, many managers' use of technology can be predicted by what was available when they were growing up rather than what is available to them now. This can cause a challenge when trying to communicate needed information to people from different technological generations.

THE HOSPITALITY ORGANIZATION AS AN INFORMATION SYSTEM

Perhaps the easiest way to understand how information ties the hospitality organization together is by considering the organization itself as a big information system. The main purpose of the information network is to provide each person with whatever information that person needs to serve the customer when that person needs it. Looking at the organization in that way, everyone becomes a transmission point on the organizational network—gathering, sending, and processing information into a user-friendly format. Those responsible for designing the **organization as an information system** must consider how all these network participants are linked together along with what information each participant needs to provide to others and what information each participant needs to have provided by others. If a Delta Airlines customer service representative is responsible for telling an inquiring customer exactly how to get from Arrival Gate #72 to the limousine service phones by Baggage Carousel #1, the information system had better be designed to obtain and provide that information to the representative when the phone rings. Likewise, if the Delta customer service desk needs to know that Flight 1582 is arriving late and will have to rebook passengers with missed connections, the late arriving pilot needs to communicate that information to the person scheduling staff at the customer service desk. The Delta system design will therefore require communication linkages, across all parts of the organization, providing access to all information needed by the customer service representatives so that the person responsible can solve customer problems. Reengineering the organization and its information system around the customer's needs is a necessity in our present-day competitive marketplace.

Integrated Systems

Retail stores illustrate how organizations can design their entire physical and record-keeping setup around an integrated information system. The system has structure and, to gain the full benefit of the information system and its database, the organization designs its other functions to accommodate the requirements of that structure. Here's how it might work at a Cracker Barrel gift shop. The shop's POS system uses barcodes on the items similar to the way in which restaurants use their POS systems. When a customer brings an item to the counter to pay for it, the employee responsible for registering the sale runs a scanner wand over its barcode to gather the price and quantity information from a central database and then register that information on the customer's receipt. At the same time, the inventory of that product is adjusted to reflect the sale of one unit, and the customer payment is added to the daily sales cash or credit ledger, the gift shop's daily profit-and-loss figures, the particular salesperson's record of sales for the day, and other corporate databases that collect information about how the shop's operations are doing. This simple act of running scanners over product barcodes ultimately leads to information that tells Cracker Barrel management how the product is selling, how the store is doing, and how the salespersons are producing.

When all the parts of an organization are connected via technology, the company collects a wealth of data over time. The best hospitality companies use this integrated information system philosophy to determine how well all parts of their service operations are working, and what can be done to better meet customer needs, improve efficiency, and continuously improve their service product.

The Primacy of Information

The logic of organizing around the availability and flow of information changes the way in which jobs are organized and tasks are performed. It may even drive changes in the sequence of operations and the organization of departmental units. The organization should be designed in a way that responds to information requirements. Jobs and departments dealing with uncertain, ever-changing, ambiguous situations require a lot of information to ensure that the managers, employees, and co-producing guests making decisions in those units can get all the information they need to create a successful service product. Jobs or units that are relatively insulated from uncertainty, ambiguity, and changing circumstance may not require the same volume or quality of information; they can anticipate that whatever happened or was true yesterday will pretty much be the same today and tomorrow. In either case, though, the final goal—to create a great service product—remains the same.

Organizational units facing uncertainty need to add the information capacity that will allow the necessary information to be gathered, or they must find ways to reduce the need for that information. Both strategies involve integrating the organizational design into the information system and vice versa. We shall now take a more detailed look at these two strategies.

Increasing Capacity

When the organization must increase its information-handling capacity, its system designers must consider the ways in which information is transmitted across the organization. The system will need to be designed in a way to filter and analyze data so that unnecessary or distracting information is not offered while the essential information is presented in a clear and readily usable format. Furthermore, the system will have to create redundant sources of critical information. Information that a decision maker absolutely must not miss should be provided in more than one channel of communication to ensure that the manager has it when it is needed. That way, if one channel breaks down or fails to get the information to the person needing it, it can be provided through another means. A simple example would be sending someone an e-mail, followed by a text message, followed by a fax, followed by a mailed hard copy, with the same information in all four communications. Building in this redundancy obviously creates additional demand upon the information system, and organizations should carefully consider what information is so important that it needs to be sent in more than one way.

Reducing Need

An alternative to building additional information-processing capacity into the organization is reducing the need to handle information. One major way to do this is to create self-contained decision-making units with employees who are empowered and enabled to make decisions about their areas of responsibility. By increasing the number of decisions made at the point where the information is generated, usage of the information channels is reduced. This is the classic strategy of decentralized decision making or, in the more current literature, the growing use of individual or group empowerment. The idea here is that with proper training in asking for job-related data and turning it into information used for decision making, the individual employee or department can make many decisions that would otherwise have been routed up the administrative chain of command. If a furious guest is standing in front of the employee, that guest does not want to wait until some unseen manager gives approval for resolving a problem. This is why The Ritz-Carlton Hotels gives its employees the authority to use up to $2000 to resolve a customer's problem without seeking permission from a supervisor. As Vivian Deuschl, Vice President of Public Relations, says, "I've come to learn that the least costly solution is the one that happens immediately. The longer and higher a customer complaint lives in an organization, the more it grows."[35] The time and effort it takes to check with a supervisor or higher-level organizational unit can use up information channel capacity, but even worse for a hospitality organization, it also slows down the response to the problem.

Everybody Online

The most effective strategy for increasing the information flow is to give all employees access to a company intranet with immediate and easy access to the corporate database. Increasingly, rather than sending masses of hard copy information through the traditional communication channels, organizations are putting information online so that any employee with a computer connection can ask for it. Many organizations have an expanded intranet that allows any employee to ask any manager any relevant question over the internal e-mail system or even tweet them. The flow of information back and forth across all levels of the organization is incredibly enhanced by this technique. The recent move by many organizations to connect to external Web sites with the amazing databases and informational resources available on the Internet means that even more information is available to anyone who needs it whenever they need it. Frontline employees now have access to much the same information that their bosses do and, with proper education about corporate goals and training in decision making, can make decisions in specified job-related areas of the same quality that their bosses could in previous eras. Of course, this clearly underscores the importance of hiring the right people, training them, and motivating them in a way that leads to the effective use of this information and improved decision making and service.

Implications for Service

The impact that these communication systems have on empowering frontline employees to do their jobs better, faster, and cheaper is astonishing and will grow even more so in the future. These changes have important implications for middle managers and supervisors in the hospitality organization, who historically were responsible for transmitting information from senior managers to frontline employees. The impact that these technological trends have on organizational design, frontline-employee responsibilities, and need for middle managers is profound. When a frontline employee can obtain any information needed, training required, or questions answered via the Web, the information-processing responsibilities and requirements of the traditional middle manager and supervisor are greatly changed. Information technology has changed and will continue to change the way organizations are managed, responsibilities are organized, and the reporting relationships are structured; it has also changed in a fundamental way the nature and role of hospitality employees who are concerned with delivering high-quality guest experiences.

Designers of the information systems for hospitality organizations must be aware of the three components of the guest experience—service product, service setting, and service delivery system—and the best information system would integrate all three. Such a total information system would simultaneously be providing information to guests, management, guest-contact servers, and back-of-the-house staff, just when they need it 24/7. Achieving this end requires system designers to pay close attention to the needs of users, their capabilities, and the time available to them to find and use the information provided. It would not do any good to provide thirty pages of statistical output to a person who doesn't understand statistics or who doesn't have the time to sort through the pile of data to find the necessary information. If you're out of food in your restaurant, you don't want to review statistical predictions of how much food you were supposed to use this week, the sales forecast for next week, or the summary data for last week. You simply want to connect with somebody who can get some more food to you. You need all that other information, but not right now. When you're in the weeds, you don't care what the chemical composition of the weed killer is, as long as you have some. The list of chemicals may be data, but it is not information.

LESSONS LEARNED

1. Know the unique informational needs of each internal and external customer, and satisfy them.

2. Know the value of information to each customer, internal and external.

3. Know the cost of providing that information.

4. Make information available in a format that each customer expects, can use, and will use.

5. Ensure access to information to all in the organization who need it, and exclude access to those who do not.

6. Make organizational information available on-line, but make sure it is secure.

7. Make information flow in as many directions as possible.

8. Make it easy to get feedback from customer-contact employees to management.

REVIEW QUESTIONS

1. What is the difference between providing a guest with information and actually communicating with that guest? Give an example of each. How can hospitality organizations know if information has been communicated effectively to both guests and employees?

2. How is this chapter on communications related to meeting or exceeding the expectations of guests? Is an effective organizational information system important for providing quality to guests, providing value, or both equally, and why?

3. Think about a restaurant you go to frequently. The server probably listened to you place your order and then wrote the information down on a pad or entered it into a POS terminal. What decisions and activities might this order then trigger or affect throughout the entire restaurant organization? (Hint: Think about immediate, on-the-spot matters, but also about inventory, staffing, menu selection, profit and loss calculations, etc.)

4. Think of several different hospitality organizations with which you are familiar.

   A. What are some significant decisions that those organizations must make?
   B. Which of those decisions should perhaps be made by computer systems and which by a well-informed manager?
   C. What differences do you note between the two types of decisions?

5. Some think of organizations as big information systems. According to that idea, the only function and responsibility of a hospitality organization is getting the right information to the right person at the right time so people can make the right decisions that will enable the providing of outstanding guest service.

   A. To what extent does that kind of thinking make sense to you?
   B. Does this idea of the organization as information system correspond to what you yourself have actually experienced in organizations?

1. Interview a local hospitality manager. Find out what information technologies at that hospitality location are the most advanced and most basic. Does the manager want any technology that is not available? Find out which technology the manager thinks the organization could least afford to do without. Report back to the class.

2. Interview service employees at four levels within an organization. Ask them how they learn what's going on in the organization. What communication devices, channels, and sources do they use or have access to? Then compare the differences between information sources of the different levels. If any of the employees don't seem to be getting the adequate, timely information that they need or want, what strategies or devices could be used to improve the information flow?

Many restaurants now use the Internet to communicate with customers. This includes providing background information on the restaurant, menu items, contact information, and so forth. Some restaurants also allow customers to provide comments about the restaurant. Imagine you are a restaurant owner and have such a site. Most of the time, the site provides complimentary information and that helps business. But once in a while, someone complains. Because it is your own Web site, you have the power to delete the comment. Would you? Would any of the following factors affect your decision?

1. What if the post is anonymous versus signed?

2. What if the post complains about a specific server and gives the name?

3. What if the post uses profanity?

4. What if you think, but don't know for sure, that the post is possibly fictitious?

5. What if you simply disagree with the posting? Would you delete it? Would you respond?

CASE STUDIES

At the Country Club

While waiting to tee off at the country club, Lillian Hollowell and Sarah Dinsmore were arguing about handheld computers.

Hollowell, president of Conglomerate Restaurants, spoke this way: "Sarah, I don't know how I got along before our restaurants purchased point-of-sale handheld units. I got them to improve communication between the servers and the kitchen, but they have really made my job easier, too. They instantly give me sales data I can combine with other databases. I can convert reams of numbers into colorful charts and graphs that my managers can easily understand. These units have enabled me to get more useful information, make decisions, and have more time for golf. I don't have to depend any longer on summary reports from the branch restaurants. I have instant access to my company's database, so I can call up info on current and past performance of any of my units, along with comparative industry and economic information from outside databases. If I see something out of the ordinary, I can get right to the restaurant manager responsible and check it out, or hold a teleconference with several managers."

Sarah Dinsmore was president of International Restaurants. Although the chain had 1400 units, it specialized in friendly, personal attention. Sarah thought of her organization as high touch, as opposed to her high-tech rival: "I want no part of those POS units. You don't see the fine restaurants in Europe cluttered up with those machines. The blasted things churn out a ton of data, but I still can't get much information. I've tried three different POS systems and I despised them all. If you want to do anything beyond the simplest operation, then you need to be very familiar with the system. I don't have the time to gain that familiarity, so I've turned my link in our current system over to my executive assistant. She knows how to run it and I don't think I'll ever need to learn. Besides, when I go to a restaurant with handheld POS terminals, the servers as often as not are so busy punching in my order that they forget to make eye contact and they fail to give me the personal attention I expect. I think they spend too much time with the technology and not enough with me."

1. Will Sarah Dinsmore be able to function effectively for very long with this attitude, or will she eventually have to learn how to use the data that the POS units make available?

2. How can she gain the advantages of high tech without losing the high touch she believes is a differentiating hallmark of her restaurants? Or is this a trade-off situation in which you can't do both?

Fine Family Motels

The reservation agents at the 105 units of the Fine Family Motels chain worked hard, but the chain's occupancy rate seemed to keep drifting lower. When that rate hit 58 percent, management realized that something had to be done.

While most locations had an acceptable occupancy rate, a few low-occupancy locations pulled down the overall rate. Unfortunately, the low-occupancy properties seemed to shift around from month to month. The local reservation agents, travel agents, and airline reservation networks weren't notified of the low-occupancy areas until the problem became acute. The company was willing to offer discounts of up to 50 percent in the low-occupancy properties to fill rooms, if it could identify them promptly and get the information out to tour organizations, online distributors, travel wholesalers, and other client sources.

1. What technological changes would benefit Fine Family Motels?

2. What structural changes might they make necessary?

3. How might Fine Family Motels use the World Wide Web to improve its occupancy rates?

Albayrak, S., & Milosevic, D. 2006. Multi-domain strategy coordination approach for optimal resource usage in agent-based filtering framework. *Web Intelligence and Agent Systems*, 4 (2), 239–253.

Albayrak, S., Wollny, S., Varone, N., & Milosevic, A. D. 2005. Agent technology for personalized information filtering: The PIA-System. *Proceedings of the 2005 ACM Symposium on Applied Computing*, Santa Fe, NM.

Alford, P., & Clarke, S. 2009. Information technology and tourism a theoretical critique. *Technovation*, 29 (9), 580–587.

Blecher, L., & Yeh, R. J. 2008. Forecasting meal participation in university residential dining facilities. *Journal of Foodservice Business Research*, 11, 352–362.

Buhalis, D., & Law, R. 2008. Progress in information technology and tourism management: 20 years on and 10 years after the Internet: The state of eTourism research. *Tourism Management*, 29, 609–623.

Buhalis, D., & Zoge, M. 2007. The strategic impact of the Internet on the tourism industry. *Information and Communication Technologies in Tourism*, 19, 481–492.

Chan, F. T. S., Chan, H. K., Ip, R. W. L., & Lau, H. C. W. 2007. A decision support system for supplier selection in the airline industry. *Proceedings of the Institution of Mechanical Engineers*, 221 (Part B), 721–758.

Chang, S. E., & Chou, Y. C. 2007. A virtual enterprise-based information system architecture for the tourism industry. *International Journal of Technology Management*, 38, 374–391.

Chathoth, P. K. 2007. The impact of information technology on hotel operations, service management and transaction costs: A conceptual framework for full-service hotel firms. *International Journal of Hospitality Management*, 26, 395–408.

Delen, D., & Sirakaya, E. 2006. Determining the efficacy of data-mining methods in predicting gaming ballot outcomes. *Journal of Hospitality & Tourism Research*, 30, 313–332.

Green, Y. N. J., & Weaver, P. A. 2008. Approaches, techniques, and information technology systems in the restaurants and food service industries: A qualitative study in sales forecasting. *International Journal of Hospitality & Tourism*, 9, 164–191.

Jain, J. 2008. Back to the future: Meet the hotel guest of 2020. *Hotel Marketing*, September 18, accessed August 8, 2009.

Kim, D. Y. 2009. The moderating effect of individual and organizational factors on information technology acceptance: The case of U.S. CVBs' internet marketing. *Journal of Travel and Tourism Marketing*, 26, 329–343.

Kim, D. Y., & Park, O. 2009. A study on American meeting planners' attitudes toward and adoption of technology in the workplace. *Tourism & Hospitality Research*, 9, 209–223.

Kim, W., Jeong, S., & Ham, S. 2005. The effect of information technology on performance in upscale hotels. *Information Technology in Hospitality*, 4 (1), 15–22.

Lankton, N. K., & Wilson, E. V. 2007. Antecedents and dimensions of online service expectations. *IEEE Transactions on Engineering Management*, 54, 776–788.

Law, R., & Jogaratnam, G. 2005. A study of hotel information technology applications. *International Journal of Contemporary Hospitality Management*, 17, 170–180.

Law, R., Mok, H., & Goh, C. 2007. Data mining in tourism demand analysis: A retrospective analysis. *Lecture Notes in Computer Science*, 4632, 508–515.

Leung, R., & Law, R. 2007. Information technology publications in leading tourism journals: A study of 1985 to 2004. *Information Technology & Tourism*, 9, 133–144.

Magnini, V. P., Honeycutt, E. D., Jr., & Hodge, S. K. 2003. Data mining for hotel firms: Use and limitations. *Cornell Hotel and Restaurant Administration Quarterly*, 44, 94–105.

Ngai, E. W. T., Xiu, L., & Chau, D. C. K. 2009. Application of data mining techniques in customer relationship management: A literature review and classification. *Expert Systems with Applications*, 36, 2592–2602.

O'Connor, P., & Murphy, J. 2004. Research on information technology in the hospitality industry. *International Journal of Hospitality Management*, 23, 473–484.

Oronsky, C. R., & Chathoth, P. K. 2007. An exploratory study examining information technology adoption and implementation in full-service restaurant firms. *International Journal of Hospitality Management*, 26, 941–956.

Peters, M., Withalm, J., & Wölfel, W. 2008. Capability maturity models for SMEs and collaborative networked organisations in tourism. *Information and Communication Technologies in Tourism*, 17, 568–579.

Piccoli, G. 2008. A framework for evaluating the business value of customer data in hospitality. *Journal of Hospitality Marketing & Management*, 17 (1-2), 4–29.

Piccoli, G. 2008. Information technology in hotel management. *Cornell Hotel and Restaurant Administration Quarterly*, 49 (3), 282–296.

Piccoli, G., Brohman, M., Watson, R., Parasuraman, A. 2004. Net-based customer service systems: Evolution and revolution in web site functionalities. *Journal of Decision Sciences*, 35, 423–455.

Power, D. J., & Sharda, R. 2007. Model-driven decision support systems: Concepts and research directions. *Decision Support Systems*, 43, 1044–1061.

Racherla, P., & Hu, C. 2008. eCRM system adoption by hospitality organizations: A technology-organization-environment (TOE) framework. *Journal of Hospitality Marketing & Management*, 17 (1), 30–58.

Song, H., & Li, G. 2008. Tourism demand modeling and forecasting: A review of recent research. *Tourism management*, 29, 203–220.

Tseng, L. 2009. Using the extension of DEMATEL to integrate hotel service quality perceptions into a cause–effect model in uncertainty. *Expert Systems with Applications*, 36, 9015–9023.

Wang, Y., & Qualls, W. 2007. Towards a theoretical model of technology adoption in hospitality organizations. *International Journal of Hospitality Management*, 26, 560–573.

Ye, Q., Law, R., & Gu, B. 2009. The impact of online user reviews on hotel room sales. *International Journal of Hospitality Management*, 28, 180–182.

Yu, G., Schwartz, Z. 2006. Forecasting short time-series tourism demand with artificial intelligence models. *Journal of Travel Research*, 45, 194–203.

Yuan, Y. L., Gretzel, U., & Fesenmaier, D. R. 2006. The role of information technology use in American convention and visitors bureaus. *Tourism Management*, 27, 326–341.

[1]Berry, L., & Bendapudi, N. 2005. Clueing in customers. *Harvard Business Review*, 81 (2), 100–106.

[2]Recognizing an opportunity, 2005. *Casino Journal*, June, pp. 26, 52.

[3]Vencat, E. F. 2007. Window seats: Virtual tours provide exploration without jet lag, hassles, or crowds. *Newsweek*, May 28, p. E22.

[4]Lyons, K. 2008. Towards a theoretically-grounded framework for evaluating immersive business models and applications: Analysis of venues in second life. *Journal of Virtual Worlds Research*, 1 (1), 1–19.

[5]Alter, A. 2007. Is this man cheating on his wife? *Wall Street Journal*, August 10, pp. W1, W8.

[6]Sanders, P. 2008. Fans resist end of virtual Disneyland. *Wall Street Journal*, May 20, pp. B1, B2.

[7]Bitner, M. J., Ostrom, A. L., & Meuter, M. L. 2002. Implementing successful self-service technologies. *Academy of Management Executive*, 16 (4), 96–109.

[8]Rubinstein, E. 2005. Gaylord Hotels extends reservations, table seating systems to increase customer service quotients with solutions from NTN. *Nation's Restaurant News*, 39 (26), 29–30.

[9]Johnson, L., Mayer, K. J., & Champaner, E. 2004. Customer atmospherics from a customer's perspective: A re-examination. *UNLV Gaming Research & Review Journal*, 8 (2), 1–10.

[10]Mayer, K. J., & Johnson, L. 2003. A customer-based assessment of casino atmospherics. *UNLV Gaming Research & Review Journal*, 7 (1), 21–31.

[11]Piccoli, G., Anglada, L., & Watson, R. 2004. Using information technology to improve customer service: Evaluating the impact of strategic opportunity. *Journal of Quality Assurance in Hospitality and Tourism*, 5 (1), 3–26.

[12]Michelli, J. A. 2008. *The New Gold Standard: 5 Leadership Principles for Creating a Legendary Customer Experience Courtesy of The Ritz-Carlton Hotel Company*. New York: McGraw-Hill.

[13]For an interesting application, see Ngai, E. W. T., Suk, F. F. C., & Lo, S. Y. Y. 2008. Development of an RFID-based Sushi management system: The case of a conveyer belt Sushi restaurant. *International Journal of Production Economics*, 112, 630–645.

[14]Ibid.

[15]Carlin, M. L. 2008. High touch vs. touch screen: Exploring the pros and cons of self-service in hotels. *Hospitality Technology*, January/February.

[16]Ibid.

[17]Nambisan, F., & Nambisan, P. 2008. How to profit from a better "virtual customer environment." *MIT Sloan Management Review*, 49 (3), 53–61.

[18]Manion, C., & Demicco, F. J. 2004. Handheld wireless point of sale systems in the restaurant industry. *Journal of Foodservice Business Research*, 7 (2), 103–111.

[19]Lorden, A. L., & Volpe, C. 2008; POS system trends. 2009. *Hospitality Technology*, December.

[20]Lorden & Volpe, 2008.

[21]Magnini, V. P., Honeycutt, E. D., Jr., & Hodge, S. K. 2003. Data mining for hotel firms: Use and limitations. *Cornell Hotel and Restaurant Administration Quarterly*, 44, 94–105.

[22]Nickell, J. A. 2002. Welcome to Harrah's. *Business 2.0*, April. See also Loveman, G. 2003. Diamonds in the data mine. *Harvard Business Review*, May, pp. 109–113.

[23]Levinson, M. 2001. Harrah's knows what you did last night. *Darwin Magazine*, May.

[24]Young, M. L. 2003. For the worst customers. *CIO Insight*, 1 (34), 51.

[25]Ibid.

[26]Numbers game: Taking retailers' cues, Harrah's taps into science of gambling. 2004. *Wall Street Journal*, November 22.

[27]Zeithaml, V. A., Rust, R. T., & Lemon, K. N. 2001. The customer pyramid: Creating and serving profitable customers. *California Management Review*, 43 (4), 119–142.

[28]Reinartz, W. J., & Kumar, V. 2002. The mismanagement of customer loyalty. *Harvard Business Review*, July, 86–94.

[29]Adomavicius, G., & Tuzhilin, A. 2005. Toward the next generation of recommender systems: A survey of the state of the art and possible extensions. *IEEE Transactions on Knowledge and Data Engineering*, 17, 734–749.

[30]Wikipedia entry on Firefly, accessed August 1, 2009.

[31]Levinson, B., & Gibson, E. 2009. An unwelcome delivery. *Business Week*, May 4, p. 15.

[32]Morrison, S. 2008. So many, many words. *Wall Street Journal*, January 28, R6.

[33]http://www.google.com/corporate/tech.html, retrieved October 19, 2009.

[34]Levy, S. 2009. The secrets of Googlenomics. *Wired*, 17 (6), 108.

[35]Michelli, 2008. 111.

CHAPTER 10

Planning the Service Delivery System

HOSPITALITY PRINCIPLE: PROVIDE SEAMLESS SERVICE DELIVERY

Being nice to people is just 20% of providing good customer service. The important part is designing systems that allow you to do the job right the first time.

—Carl Sewell, *Customers for Life*

LEARNING OBJECTIVES

After reading this chapter, you should understand:

- How to plan, design, analyze, and check the hospitality organization's service delivery system.

- How to design a delivery system using several methods, such as flow-charting, blueprinting, the universal service map, and PERT/CPM.

- How to use fishbone analysis, poka-yokes, and other methods to locate the source of problems and prevent their occurrence or reoccurrence.

- How to use a cross-functional organizational design to deliver a service product.

PLANNING AND DESIGNING THE SERVICE DELIVERY SYSTEM

Check the System First

Horst Schulze, former chief operating officer of The Ritz-Carlton Hotels, liked to tell the story of how one hotel manager solved the problem of delays in serving room-service breakfasts. After several guests complained to the manager about their breakfasts being brought to the rooms both slow and cold, the manager knew he had to investigate. The traditional managerial solution to the problem would have been to call in and loudly criticize the offending room-service manager for technical incompetence and poor supervisory skills. The then properly disciplined manager would return to the kitchen, gather the room-service staff around, and yell at them. After all, in most organizations, blame rolls downhill to the lowest-level employee.

Schulze used the example to illustrate a different problem-solving approach. The manager organized a team of room-service people and asked them to study the problem, find out why the meals were not getting to guests within a reasonable time, and suggest ways to solve whatever problem they found. The team did exactly that. They studied the problem at great length and found that the cause was the unavailability of service elevators needed by the room-service people to get the meals quickly to their guests. They studied why the elevators were unavailable and even had a room-service employee spend an entire morning in the elevators with a stopwatch to see where the elevators were, what they were being used for, and why they were unavailable when the room-service people needed them.

Short-Sheeted

What the team found astonished Schulze and the manager. The whole problem could be traced to a faulty management decision about how many bed sheets each floor was allowed to stock (called the "par") for the housekeepers. The decision had left some floors with too few sheets, and the housekeepers were using the elevators to hunt for extra sheets to finish cleaning the rooms on their floors. The elevators were therefore unavailable to the room-service delivery people when they needed them, cold meals intended to be hot were delivered late, and the guests got angry. Because a manager trying to save on the cost of sheets had stocked too few, the rest of the system was disrupted. This cost-saving move drove up the costs of room service (because the hotel did not charge for meals when guests complained) and housekeeping labor (because housekeepers were spending their time in elevators instead of making beds). Trying to solve a problem in one part of the service delivery system created problems for another part. The total impact was to drive up costs and cause guest dissatisfaction.

Lessons Learned

What manager would ever have thought that the late-breakfast problem would be solved by adding more bed sheets to the available supply on each floor? Schulze drew three lessons from this story. First, managers aren't smart enough, or don't have enough time or information, to prevent or solve all the problems by themselves. Therefore, they tend to find the simplest, quickest solution, which is usually based on their assumption that a subordinate isn't sufficiently motivated, trained, or supervised. These managers rely on the traditional theory that "if you correct the person, you correct the problem." Second, employees may have a better chance of finding the root causes of a problem than the manager. After all, those in the middle of the situation often know more about what is really going on than the manager. According to Schulze, not using the talents, intelligence, and job-related knowledge of these people is worse than dumb. Finally, the most important lesson is that every problem should be addressed first from the perspective of the entire service delivery system. Although a person may end up being the cause of a service failure, Schulze believed that the fault is frequently in the system and not the person. Simply putting out one small fire ("we are spending too much money on sheets") without thinking about the system can cause big problems elsewhere.

Designing and Checking the Service Delivery System

We have said all along that the service delivery system includes all aspects of the service experience—service product, service setting, and service delivery—and hospitality managers need to think about the entire process that delivers the service to the guest and about the systems that are needed to make the process work flawlessly. Developing a service product that meets guests' needs and having well-trained, motivated, enthusiastic employees using the right information, equipment, and tools to deliver the product to guests within a well-designed service environment are all necessary, but these are not sufficient. The key component of a flawless service experience is making sure that the entire service delivery system, the process by which the service is delivered to the guest, is designed so that it effectively integrates the many elements of the experience to make it happen in the way that the customer expects.

Richard Metters and Ann Marucheck maintain that "the urgency for rigorous study to guide service managers in improving the design, competitiveness, efficiency, and effectiveness of service delivery, both at the firm and industry levels, has never been greater."[1] Achieving guest delight and avoiding service failure can both be greatly affected by delivery system design. Every hospitality organization should spend whatever studying and planning time and energy it takes to get the system right. It is a crucially important topic.

The total quality management movement, which emphasized that everyone is responsible for quality—not just the quality control department—has taught organizational leaders several important lessons. First, achieving total quality requires consideration of the entire system—from initial design, to using whatever raw materials and inputs that are needed, to the finished product. Second, everyone is responsible for delivering and monitoring quality; in hospitality, everyone is responsible for the quality of the guest experience. Third, the system needs to be checked for problems before people are blamed. Hospitality managers must find the *root causes* of problems and implement solutions to avoid future problems, and these root causes often lie in the system.

Too many times, hospitality managers assume that the employee has made an error when in reality the fault lies in a bad system, which makes it difficult, if not impossible, for the employee to deliver the service experience with the excellence that the organization,

Behind the scenes at a busy restaurant; a service delivery system must be carefully planned to ensure that every guest is delighted by both the service and the service product.

Image copyright rehoboth foto, 2010. Used under license from Shutterstock.com

the employee, and the guest would like. Talk with frontline servers at hotels, restaurants, or any hospitality organization, and they will tell you how frustrated they become when the service systems are inadequate for them to do the jobs they are hired and paid to do, and which they really want to do well. When the service delivery system fails, everyone loses. The guest is unhappy, the employee is frustrated, and the organization may lose a guest and all the profits that the guest's future business represents.

The Goal: Fail No Guest; Delight Every Guest

The hospitality manager must spend the extra time and effort to plan and organize the service delivery system so that it works right every time. To achieve the companion goals of failing no guest and delighting every guest, successfully planning the entire guest experience (the cycle of service) and focusing on an effective delivery system are critical. While we don't want to downplay the contributions of production management techniques and the solutions that industrial engineers have found for problems in manufacturing organizations, these tools cannot guarantee the success of any hospitality organization's service delivery system because *the guest* is always the ultimate judge of the quality and value of the guest experience. Service delivery system designers must, therefore, ensure that they design the experience from the guest's point of view and not their own. Too many organizations design their service production processes for employee convenience or efficiency. Although the system should be user-friendly for employees, the outstanding hospitality providers organize the service around the guest's needs, expectations, capabilities, and actual behaviors. The delivery of any service should always be smooth, seamless, and transparent from the guest's point of view.

Some Guiding Principles

Given the goal of providing exceptional customer service, and learning from the lessons of The Ritz-Carlton example (and indeed, all the examples in this book), here are some principles to keep in mind. Study your customers in minute detail, build a service delivery system that will provide the experience they expect from your organization, monitor that system closely, create accurate early-warning measures for each possible failure point, engage everyone in the organization in watching those measures, and follow up on everything that doesn't meet your guests' expectations for whatever reason. If failures occur repeatedly at certain points, change the system design. If service standards are unmet, find out why. If the organization has a service guarantee, be sure that the delivery system can meet and exceed that guarantee.

Although excellent hospitality organizations do their best to keep service failures from happening by keeping a careful eye on all the places where the system might fail, they know that failures are inevitable. Therefore, they plan for how to recover from the inevitable failures. They design systems that ensure success, avoid failure, and recover from failure on the key drivers of guest satisfaction.

DEVELOPING THE SERVICE DELIVERY SYSTEM

After almost fifty years of research, Joseph Juran published the **Juran Trilogy** in 1986. It defined the three management processes that Juran thought were required by all organizations to improve: quality planning, quality control, and quality improvement. Quality planning involves identifying customers, determining their needs, creating a product or service to meet those needs, and then developing a system to deliver the product or service. Quality control with respect to the hospitality industry means making sure that the system is delivering the service in the most effective way. Errors as the product or service is being delivered, whether due to inadequate planning or faulty execution, are prevented or minimized through quality control. Quality improvement involves after-the-fact analysis of the errors and failures that have contributed to poor quality and improving the delivery process to reduce or eliminate future errors based on that analysis.

The influence of Juran's Trilogy can be seen in Table 10-1. It shows the when, what, who, and how of a comprehensive service delivery system and the service experience that it provides. It reminds us that an exceptional customer service experience begins even before the guest walks through the door. It also reminds us that the needs, wants, expectations, capabilities, and behaviors of the targeted guests are the starting point of any delivery system. The table shows that the overall process consists of three phases: planning, monitoring, and assessing/improving the service delivery system. These three phases are the focus of this final section of the book. If the process was well planned and designed, then the organization is ready to deliver the desired service, in a way that should elicit a wow reaction.

This chapter focuses on carefully planning the service experience. The next chapter focuses on a special case of planning—managing waits—because waits and queues are so pervasive in hospitality experiences. Chapter 12 describes how companies can better manage the delivery of each guest's experience by monitoring, measuring, and evaluating the quality of their service delivery as it is being delivered. Chapter 13 describes the process of service recovery, and how fixing service problems and learning from service errors after the service has been delivered can both help recover unsatisfied guests and lead to improvements in the entire service delivery system. No service system is foolproof, but the best managers take the time to plan out the guest experience with all available planning tools, monitor it while it is happening, and fix it when they find that it did not meet guest expectations. Since no one can manage what isn't measured, we will focus on tools that measure the service delivery system so that a flawless experience can be delivered to every guest every time.

TABLE 10-1 Planning the Delivery System, Monitoring the Service Experience, and Assessing the Experience to Improve the System

	Phase I: Planning the Service Delivery System	Phase II: Monitoring the Service Experience	Phase III: Assessing the Experience to Improve the System
When	**Before** the guest arrives, and while the guest is waiting for the service experience	**During** the guest's experience	**After** the guest's experience
What	Experience expected	Experience realized	Experience remembered
Who	Target customers	Actual customers	Past, current, and potential future customers
How	Setting service standards; blueprinting; Universal Service Map; fishbone analysis; PERT/CPM; simulations; forecasting demand; designing waits (queues); training; quality teams; poka-yokes; cross-functional organizational design	Applying service standards and job performance standards; managerial observation (MBWA); employee observation meeting terms of service guarantees; personal interviews and encounters with guests	**Guest assessment**: Comment cards; toll-free 800 numbers; surveys (mail and Web, phone, critical incidents); SERVQUAL; guest focus groups; mystery shoppers **Other data review**: Service failure reports; service guarantee utilization; interviews; customer complaints by category and type; employee feedback; sales and revenue reports; market share/capacity utilization **Further review**: Organizational design; service standards; training methods **Refer findings back to system planners**

© Cengage Learning 2012.

Planning the System

Any good delivery system begins with careful planning. Careful analysis and detailing of every step in the entire service delivery process will make the difference between having it mostly right and reaching the level of excellence that the very best service organizations deliver.

Service standards should be established early in the planning process. They are the company's expectations for how the different aspects of the service experience should be delivered every time to every guest. And, as is true when setting individual goals (discussed in Chapter 7), the criteria for service standards should be SMART: specific, measureable, attainable, results oriented, and time bound.

Some standards are widely used in the hospitality industry: twenty minutes to get a room-service breakfast, six minutes to check-in including waiting time, and less than that to get the first cup of morning coffee in the hotel restaurant. A special type of service standards (see Table 10-2) are those set by industry associations or other agencies that establish

TABLE 10-2 **Externally Developed Standards**

Some organizations test the accuracy of their internally developed standards by seeking external affirmation of their service quality. They do so in three basic ways: certifications, accreditations, and recognition by ranking organizations.

Certifications
The National Institute of Standards and Technology's Malcolm Baldrige Award and ISO 9000:2008 series certification are the external evaluations generally seen by hospitality and other service organizations as the best affirmation of their service quality. Many are now also seeking environmental certifications such as Leadership in Energy and Environmental Design (LEED), Green Lodging, BigGreenG, and various state-level certifications. Those organizations seeking to be ISO 9000-certified develop the supporting materials for showing their compliance with each standard and apply for a review. If the review finds that the firm meets the standards, the firm can advertise itself as being ISO 9000 certified. The International Organization for Standardization details its requirements on its Web site. These certifications may have little meaning to most guests, but to both employees and external business partners, the certifications are marks of quality that can be displayed proudly. Individuals can earn a Six Sigma Black Belt Quality certification from the American Society for Quality (ASQ) to affirm their mastery of the quality-improvement principles defined by the Design, Measure, Analyze, Improve, Control (DMAIC) methodology. A variety of other certifications are designed either for a specific employee category, such as those for cruise line counselors, meeting professionals, and sommeliers, or for specific industry groups, which in some cases are required by law to affirm compliance with quality standards such as the National Restaurant Association's ServSafe Food Safety Manager and the Hazardous Analysis and Critical Control Point (HACCP) certification.

Accreditations
Accreditation provides public notice that an organization has met standards of quality established by the accrediting group. Several professional organizations related to hospitality offer accreditation as a way for their members to affirm to their key stakeholders that they are of high quality. Examples are the Destination Management Accreditation Program (DMAP) initiated by Destination Marketing Association International (DMAI), the International Air Transport Association (IATA) accreditation for travel agents, and the International Cruise Council of Australia's (ICCA) Cruise Accreditation Program.

Recognitions
The various hospitality recognition programs are generally the most visible and important affirmations of quality to guests. They include evaluations and ratings by magazines like *Consumer Reports* and *Wine Spectator*, quality-rating organizations like J.D. Power and American Automobile Association, and print or online travel guides such as Michelin, Fodor, Rick Steeds, Lonely Planet, and TripAdvisor. These external organizations create and then apply service standards to evaluate hospitality organizations. Knowing that these standards and ratings exist and may be used by guests, hospitality organizations can use them as blueprints for developing a set of more detailed internal service standards that focus organization members on key drivers of guest satisfaction. Knowing that the guests using these external reviews are seeking a specific level of service when they arrive at a hotel, restaurant, cruise line, or an attraction not only gives the organization's management a set of standards to meet but also provides an opportunity and motivation to exceed those expectations and provide a wow experience, instead of merely meeting the standards.

Achieving these certifications, accreditations, and recognitions provides visible evidence to key customers and stakeholders of the organization's commitment to service excellence. A concierge who is a member of the Les Clefs d'Or proudly wears her crossed gold keys to show her mastery of the profession and commitment to high levels of guest service quality.

The external evaluations also provide an excellent means for organizations that have not yet developed internal service standards to begin the process of identifying what service factors are most important to their guests.

certification, accreditation, and recognition standards. Organizations or individuals are assessed on the degree to which they meet these standards and those assessments are then made public. Most standards, however, are specific to the organizations setting them and are designed to meet or beat the expectations of their targeted guests and often the competition as well. McDonald's sets standards for every task and includes them to create the "Full Field (now "Operating") Report" that their more than 950 field inspectors use to evaluate each McDonald's.[2] Airlines define how many minutes it should take for bags to get from the parked aircraft to the baggage-claim area. If they're not on the conveyor belts in that time, the service-quality standard has not been met. Many organizations use the number of rings for answering the phone in a guest service response area. If a reservationist, for example, hasn't picked up the phone within three rings, the service-quality standard has not been met. These are service-quality standards, established during the planning phase, that guide employees in what quality and kind of experience they are expected to deliver to guests.

Service standards are one of the most important tools that hospitality managers have to ensure that the service expectations of guests are at least being met. Service standards need to be established in the planning stage, before the guest is present. As we will discuss in subsequent chapters, they also need to be checked when the guest is present to be sure they are being met, and after the guest leaves to determine the degree to which every part of the service experience was delivered in the way it was planned.

Monitoring the Service Experience

Phase II in Table 10-1 involves monitoring the experience through measurement as the experience is happening, to be discussed in Chapter 12. We have said before that you can't manage what you don't measure, and this is especially true of service situations. Industrial engineers in manufacturing have taken methods measurement to the level of a precise science. The service industry in general, and the hospitality industry in particular, have lagged behind in understanding how to apply measurements to the largely intangible services that they offer. The need for measuring what is happening to the guest in every step of service delivery is critical in assuring continuing guest satisfaction and, if problems arise, in recognizing them, applying solutions, and in determining if the solutions have succeeded.

Organizations should measure the quality of service delivery against service standards whenever possible. Such standards help to make the intangible experience tangible for purposes of measurement and control. These standards, carefully created during the planning stage, are an excellent way to focus everyone on what is important to the guest. Saying to a server "I think you ought to work faster" is easy and might (or might not) improve the service experience of tonight's guests. However, in the long run, comparing a server's performance from last month against target levels for standards like "time until initial greeting," "time for delivery of food or drink," and "time to bring the bill" can be much more helpful. Indeed, in the best circumstances, when the measures are clear, fair, connected to providing excellence, and completely understood by the employees whose performance is being measured, employees will be able to measure and manage themselves on certain performance measurements. If done well, *self-management through self-measurement* is to everyone's benefit. If you teach employees what is important to their individual job success and then train them to measure how they are performing on those critical factors, you have the beginnings of a self-managing workforce and, when things go wrong, a self-healing system. Ideally, performance measures make it possible for employees to monitor their own delivery effectiveness while actually providing the service. If Kris Smith knows that the organizational maximum for answering her phone is three rings, and a computerized device displays a running record of how many average rings it takes Kris to answer a call, Kris knows at all times where she stands in relation to the company standard.

Assessing the Experience and Improving the System

After planning the system and monitoring the experience through measurement comes the last step: assessment and improvement. Collecting and analyzing information about what has actually occurred drives system improvement. Once the plan is clearly laid out and the results of implementing that plan adequately measured to yield insights into how well the system is operating, both management and employees have the information needed to redesign the system and fix the problems to yield continuing improvement in the guest experience.

In Table 10-1, in the "How" block of Phase III: Assessing the Experience to Improve the System, sales and revenue reports and market share/capacity utilization are included. The overall health of the business is a good indicator of whether or not guest service quality is where it should be. If the business is losing money, market share, capacity use, and so forth, these measures may indicate problems with the service product, setting, or delivery system. In other words, gathering and reviewing data generated by the tools described in the chapters to follow are important, but the overall success of the business itself is an indicator of whether or not you are providing the guest experience on which you built your business model.

The Blurred Lines

Figure 10-1 shows that the lines between the different phases of service are not sharply drawn. This figure helps us to organize across the following chapters what we know about managing a service delivery system so as to provide an exceptional experience. In reality,

FIGURE **10-1** The Phases of Service Delivery

© Cengage Learning 2012

the distinctions between the phases of producing services like hospitality experiences are not clear. A refrigerator is built in a distant factory, delivered to a store, and then purchased in that store. Each stage of the production and delivery system is clearly distinct. The borders between the phases of service delivery represent overlapping areas and are not distinct.

As noted above, planning for the service experience begins even before the guest walks through the door, and part of this planning involves preparing for the inevitable customer waits, represented by the upper gray area in Figure 10-1. The customer perceives the wait as part of the service experience, and if it is mishandled or too long, then the guest may feel that, overall, the entire service experience was disappointing. Another blurred line, represented by the lower gray area in Figure 10-1, represents service recovery or the correction of errors. They can be corrected either during the service or after the service. Obviously, the best time to catch, fix, apologize, and possibly compensate for failures is before the guest actually leaves.

Although organizations are not happy about guest complaints, all should welcome them as valuable feedback on how well they are meeting their guests' needs and expectations. Complaining guests give a clear indication that their service experience was in some way not a success. Because research shows that most dissatisfied guests do not complain, organizations need methods for measuring the success of all service experiences, not just experiences that guests complain about. Only in that way can organizations ensure that they are delivering the expected service, to every guest, every time.

Because organizations need systematic ways to learn how well they are doing in order to get better, they survey not only the guests that came in but also the ones in their target market who didn't, or those who didn't come back.

The Self-Healing System

As noted by Horst Schulze, even if you have all the characteristics and features of a high-quality hotel, its service delivery system can still fail from time to time. Schulze's goal was to use the people and the system designers to create what he termed a *self-healing system*, in which the employees can override the system and fix guest problems when it fails. The employees in a self-healing system are also responsible for telling management where the system has failed so that together they can fix it. Just as everyone is responsible for providing and maintaining quality, everyone is responsible for avoiding and fixing service failures.

The Cycle Goes On

The cycle of planning, monitoring, and assessing/improving should never stop. The service plan lays out what you think your service delivery system should do for the guest, the control measures tell you if what you planned is in fact happening, and the commitment to improvement focuses everyone's attention on analyzing the data collected to fix any identified problems and move toward a flawless guest experience. The measures used should also trigger recognition of "exceptions," variations from the plan.

In addition to including ways to measure how well the service is being rendered at every step of the delivery process, a good plan must also include ways to measure how the overall plan is succeeding. When guests are asked about their experience, most of them evaluate it holistically. They are often unable to identify how any one part of the experience influenced their determination of the total experience's value and their degree of satisfaction. They can, however, give an overall impression of service quality that can trigger managerial investigations. The guest may be unhappy with the dining experience at the restaurant, but until management sits down and carefully analyzes the data measuring each step in the entire guest experience, it may not recognize whether the dissatisfaction was caused by a long wait, a dirty bathroom, a cold appetizer, a rude server, or a messy entrance littered with cigarette butts. Knowing what the delivery system is supposed to do and analyzing data collected from the measures should trigger the necessary corrective actions.

PLANNING TECHNIQUES

The first step in service delivery system design is planning out the steps and processes in the entire system. Planning techniques focus on constructing or *diagramming* a thoroughly detailed step-by-step description of what the service delivery process involves and the service standards that must be met. Planning always starts with the guest and frequently begins with the moment when the guest becomes aware of the organization's ability to satisfy some need. The guest's expectations begin to build from that moment, long before the guest ever arrives at your front door. Since we know that what the guest expects forms the basis or criterion for determining how well the experience satisfies the guest, understanding those expectations becomes the first step in planning for and then providing any guest experience. This understanding forms the basis for the beginning of delivery system planning.

Detailing the delivery system by diagramming it has several immediate benefits to managers seeking to fail-safe the delivery of their service.[3] First, by writing it down, they can see on paper or on a computer screen, in a flowchart form that is easy to understand and study, how all parts of the system work. Second, the process of creating a diagram allows managers a visual means to show the service delivery process to others and how the various parts of the organization must work together. Third, having a visual representation of the service delivery system allows for thoughtful consideration of what processes guests should see and what should occur out of their line of vision. Fourth, it provides a means for comparing ideal service, as embodied in the diagram, with actual service, to identify aspects of the process that need improvement. Fifth, and perhaps most importantly, by focusing attention on component elements of the service delivery process, diagramming illustrates areas where problems are occurring and which areas need improvement.

Of the many planning techniques available, four basic ones are commonly used to develop a detailed plan for delivering the guest experience. The tools are blueprinting, the universal service map, fishbone analysis, PERT/CPM, and simulation. Each has its own advantages, but all are premised on the idea that a detailed written plan leads to a better system for managing the people, organization, and production processes that deliver the total guest experience. These tools are especially useful because they can readily incorporate the measurements necessary for control and analysis of problems that may appear in the system. After the plan is devised, managers can also use these techniques to focus on any part that guest feedback indicates might be a problem area. If effort and care are devoted to the plan, failures should be minimized. This is important because if situations are regularly permitted to get to the point where problem-solving and failure-recovery techniques become necessary, some guests will inevitably be lost to competitors.

Blueprinting

The most commonly discussed type of service diagramming is blueprinting. The entire service delivery process and its subprocesses are described in blueprint format as if one were building a house and needed a plan of what went where. In effect, a good **blueprint** defines every component part and activity, not just of the delivery system, but of the entire guest experience from the moment when the guest sees the front door or greeting sign to the time that the guest departs and moves out of sight.

A typical blueprint has five parts[4]:

1. *Physical evidence.* The tangible physical parts of the service experience that can impact customer assessment of quality and value.
2. *Customer actions.* The actions and behaviors of customers, which drive the creation of a blueprint.
3. *Onstage/visible contact-employee actions.* Things that customer-contact employees do as part of the face-to-face encounter and which customers see.
4. *Backstage/nonvisible contact-employee actions.* Things that customer-contact employees do out of sight of customers but which must happen for the experience to take place; this part of the blueprint also includes nonvisible interaction with customers (e.g., a customer's telephone call to make a reservation).
5. *Support processes.* Activities essential to providing the service but carried out by individuals and units that do not have direct contact with the customer (e.g., maintaining the company's information systems, food delivery, managing payroll).

Every event that is scheduled to happen from the start to the finish of the experience is laid out on a blueprint, as is every contingency that can reasonably be projected. Those points at which service failures are most likely to occur should be identified and early-warning mechanisms included.

The blueprint should attach times to the activities and processes involved in providing the service and the time for the entire guest experience. If an excellent service product in a compatible environment is provided in twenty minutes, a guest may feel rushed; if the service is provided within an hour, satisfied; if the service takes two hours to deliver, the guest may never return.

Finally, the purpose of blueprinting is not only to satisfy the guest but also to enable the organization to achieve its profit goal. Providing the service according to a well-designed blueprint will permit the organization to show a profit while maximizing the quality and value of guest experiences.

The Hot Dog Stand

Figure 10-2 details the complete service cycle for a street vendor's hot dog stand.[5] As diagrammed in the figure, the service begins with the vendor greeting the potential customer. The vendor takes the order, assembles a heated dog-and-bun combination, applies condiments and dressings, delivers the hot dog to the guest, and finally collects payment. The blueprint of the service also shows an arrow dropping from the application-of-condiments step to represent a potential area of failure where the vendor might incorrectly select and use the wrong condiment—kraut instead of relish, for example. If this happens, the next step shown in the figure is for the server to fix the problem by cleaning off the wrong condiment and returning to the application-of-condiments step. The blueprint also contains some other useful information. It provides time estimates for each step so that the total time of the service experience can be calculated. A "line of visibility" separates the events that the customer can see from those that can't be seen. Finally, the blueprint shows the customer tolerance time of the entire cycle.

FIGURE **10-2** Blueprint for a Hot Dog Stand

© Cengage Learning 2012

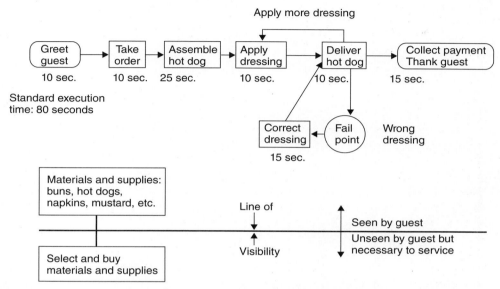

Source: Adapted from G. Lynn Shostack and Jane Kingman-Brundage. 1991. Reprinted with permission from *The AMA Handbook of Marketing for the Service Industry*, published by the American Marketing Association. How to Design a Service, Carole A. Congram and Margaret L. Friedman (eds.), p. 244.

The work-cycle times are calculated from carefully studying the process. The customer time tolerance is calculated by carefully studying the customers. The entire finished schematic clearly shows the planned sequence of activities and the measures for each step in the cycle of service. The blueprint becomes an easily communicated picture for analysis of the entire service cycle.

Obviously, this example is both simple and incomplete. The excellent regional manager or staff guestologist for a string of hot dog stands would want to extend this schematic to include the events that happen before the hungry customer arrives. The regional manager might start at the point where the overall strategy for the hot dog stand was established in the first place. Doing so would allow the manager to see all the other influences that have an impact on the total hot dog purchase experience, from establishing the nature and appearance of the sign that initially attracts the customer to the hot dog stand, to the many other intangible and tangible aspects of the actual hot dog experience. Smart managers start off their planning of the service delivery system by surveying their customers to determine the key elements of the experience from the customer's perspective. Once those key drivers are determined, the delivery system can be designed to ensure that the customer's expectations regarding those key drivers are met or exceeded. Once again, the customer drives system design.

One final factor necessary to a complete delivery system plan is the points at which customers may fail to do their part in co-producing the experience. A complete delivery system plan needs to account for the possibility that some customers may decline to participate at those points of the service delivery process where guest participation had been designed into the blueprint.

Even for a business that provides a simple service product like a hot dog stand, a service blueprint can identify how long service should take, potential fail points, and the complexity that can exist in the service delivery system.

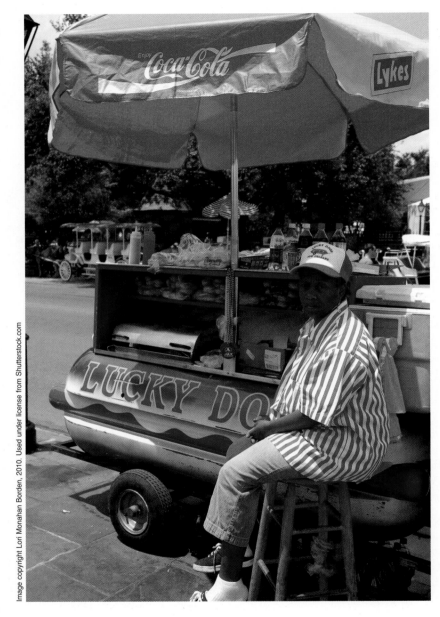

Image copyright Lori Monahan Borden, 2010. Used under license from Shutterstock.com

Adding Detail to Blueprints

Extending the simple example by incorporating all the fine points of hot dog vending would make for a more complicated but more complete process diagram. The blueprint could go into even greater detail by breaking down each step into even more specific subroutines (e.g., how long each hot dog should cook, ounces of condiments and their order of application). The blueprint for the hot dog stand would become even more complex if complementary products were added, such as sandwiches, sodas, or ice cream desserts.

Of course, more detail isn't always better. The level of detail should be sufficient to help improve decision making and service quality but should not go so far as to produce the customer becomes, in effect, a co-producer of the service experience. It is the point where passengers respond to the flight attendant's instruction to look around and pick up all their personal belongings before leaving the plane, or where the customer drives forward to pick up the food order at the McDonald's drive-through window. The activities above this line are also the point where customers decide about the value of the experience, which in turn decides whether or not they will return. By noting the activities above the line of guest interaction, the service manager can identify the critical events— the *moments of truth*—that influence this all-important decision process by the customer. By focusing on these actions (making the reservation, arriving at the hotel, checking in, checking out, etc.), the manager can do whatever is possible to influence the customers' experiences so that they decide to return.

Fishbone Analysis

While planning the delivery system, if a widespread and possibly system-wide service delivery problem is foreseen, as opposed to a more localized service failure, one technique that may be used is a cause-and-effect analysis, in the form of a **fishbone diagram**.[8] It provides a way to concentrate on the problem areas to avoid or recover from faulty service outcomes. The results of fishbone analysis are often used to make major changes in the delivery system.

Late Departures at Quickconnect Airlines

Figure 10-4 shows an application of **fishbone analysis** to a problem at a hypothetical regional connector airline, Quickconnect Airlines: too many planes departing late. That problem becomes the spine of the fish in the diagram. The general areas within which problems that could delay flights might arise are attached as bones to the spine. For example, "equipment" is required to get the planes off the ground on time and so becomes a potential source of delay. All the possible contributors to an equipment failure then become bones attached to the equipment bone, and so on with each resource and potential problems with it. The potential contributors to failure are typically identified through group discussion with the employees involved; they should know the reasons for late departures. Quickconnect's employees should be able to readily identify the possible trouble spots.

Resource Categories

The resources required for airplane takeoff can be categorized as equipment, personnel, procedures, supporting services and other. They are attached to the spine of the diagram. Within any one of them, a problem might arise that could cause the undesirable effect: late departures. Proceeding with the fishbone construction, the potential problems associated with each resource would then be identified, listed, and prioritized by the employee group working on this problem. This prioritizing technique, known as **Pareto analysis**, calls for arranging the potential causes of the problem based on the frequency in which they occur.

Table 10-3 presents an example based on actual transportation statistics from the Federal Aviation Administration (FAA), but for our hypothetical airline. The data representing the percentages of late flights associated with each cause are listed next to the cause in their order of frequency. The Pareto analysis reveals that about 90 percent of all late takeoffs are caused by only five of the approximately thirty possible causes listed by the FAA. The most frequent reason for delay at all airports combined was late arriving aircraft, at 36.2 percent, followed by late passengers (at 30.7 percent). The remaining causes, all contributing to fewer than 10 percent of the delays, include waiting for pushback, waiting for fueling, and mechanical problems with planes. These results revealed that the second leading cause of delays was due to giving preferential treatment to the passengers who least deserved it: those who arrived late for flights.

FIGURE **10-4** Fishbone Analysis: Reasons for Departure Delays for Quickconnect Airlines

© Cengage Learning 2012

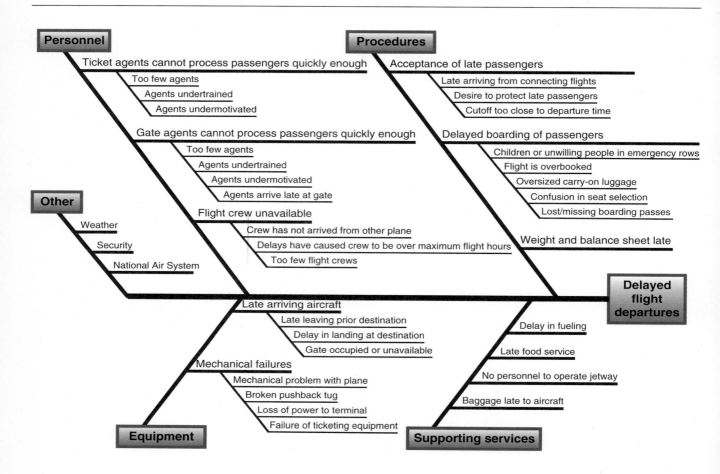

Airport Data

The data can also be analyzed by individual airports to see if the overall problems are the same as those found in each individual airport. As the data show, both the percentages and the reasons for delay at the Newark airport are different from those seen at the other airports. The fifth most frequent factor at Newark, "no personnel to operate jetway," does not appear as a problem for Washington Reagan, where "mechanical problem with plane" is a problem, one not found at Newark. By arranging the information in this way, managers looking for causes of service delivery failures have an easy-to-use analytical tool. For each potential failure point, they merely collect and arrange the data that the fishbone categories tell them to gather. Recognizing the problem—late flight departures—is the first step in improving the service delivery system, but then you must find out what caused the problem—late arriving aircraft and late passengers. You can't fix a problem if you don't know what caused it.

No More Waiting

Once the impact of late-arriving passengers was identified, the airline could decide that flights would no longer wait for them simply because they couldn't get to the airport on time. While this solution might contradict the airline's commitment to service, and gate

TABLE 10-3 Pareto Analysis of Flight Departure Delays

ALL STATIONS EXCEPT HUB			NEWARK			WASHINGTON (REAGAN NATIONAL)		
Cause of Delay	Percentage of Incidences	Cumulative Percentage	Cause of Delay	Percentage of Incidences	Cumulative Percentage	Cause of Delay	Percentage of Incidences	Cumulative Percentage
Late arriving aircraft	36.2%	36.2%	Late arriving aircraft	41.7%	47.1%	Late arriving aircraft	32.9%	32.9%
Late passengers	30.7%	66.9%	Late passengers	10.7%	52.4%	Late passengers	19.0%	51.9%
Waiting for pushback	8.8%	75.7%	Waiting for pushback	10.6%	73.7%	Waiting for pushback	19.0%	70.9%
Waiting for fueling	6.6%	82.3%	Waiting for fueling	10.7%	63.0%	Waiting for fueling	5.4%	87.2%
Mechanical problem with plane	5.1%	87.4%	No personnel to operate jetway	7.2%	80.9%	Mechanical problem with plane	10.9%	81.8%
Weather	5.0%	92.4%	Weather	5.2%	92.8%	Weather	9.8%	97.0%
Security delay	0.4%	92.8%	Security delay	6.7%	87.6%	Security delay	0.1%	97.1%

Source: Reprinted with permission of the Cornell H. R. A. Quarterly © Cornell University. All Rights Reserved.

agents naturally would want to help out late-arriving passengers, the airline was denying on-time service to the many passengers who made sure to get to the airport on time. By setting up this fishbone and comparing the survey data against the key factors, the airline could identify the problem and discover a solution that worked: don't wait on anybody. Of course, that solution might cause a customer-relations problem with late arrivals, but the airline might be willing to pay that price. Indeed, it is likely when the word gets out that the airline will not wait any more for late passengers, fewer passengers will arrive late. Furthermore, given that late passengers were a notable problem at non-hub airports, eliminating this cause of delays could actually lead to more on-time aircraft at hub airports, and thus a decline in the primary cause for late departures at these airports as well.

The individual parts of any delivery system can be broken down in the same way to discover the equipment, people, procedures, supporting services, and other factors that contribute to a service problem. Once managers measure each factor's contribution to the problem, finding a solution is relatively straightforward.

PERT/CPM

Building a Patio

Let's say you want to build a backyard patio for your new barbeque grill. You could design the patio with pencil and paper, go buy some bricks and landscaping timber, go out back to dig the foundation, realize that you don't have a shovel, go buy one at the hardware store, start digging the foundation, and, while you are doing that, have a chat with a neighbor who tells you that you need permission from the Neighborhood Homeowners Association before you can build a structure of that size on your property. Hospitality organizations obviously cannot operate that way. They cannot afford to start building a hotel and then find out that the county zoning ordinance will not allow it. When the planning and delivery of the service product involve different activities, and especially when those activities recur in a repeating cycle (like planning a convention or golf tournament), a helpful technique to use is PERT/CPM.

PERT/CPM Defined

The **PERT/CPM** planning technique, frequently used in the construction industry and the military, has many points of application in the hospitality industry as well. PERT stands for Program Evaluation Review Technique and CPM for Critical Path Method. Because these two techniques are similar, they have been merged into a single planning strategy and device referred to as *PERT/CPM*. PERT/CPM offers the benefits of any good planning tool. It provides to the manager a detailed, well-organized plan combined with a control measurement process for analyzing how well the plan is being executed. PERT/CPM is useful in planning major projects such as hosting a convention, building a convention center,[9] or opening a new hotel. PERT/CPM can also be used to plan a wide variety of smaller repetitive projects that have a beginning, an end, and a whole lot of things that must happen in between.

The steps in the PERT/CPM process are (1) identifying the activities that must be done to complete the project, (2) determining the sequence of activities, (3) estimating how long each activity will take, (4) creating and diagramming the network of activities, and (5) finding the **critical path**, which highlights the sequence of activities where no slack time is available and everything has to happen as planned or else the project will be delayed. The successful use of the process may depend on the accuracy of the estimates made in Step (3), and they are not always easy to make.

The Diagrams

Using a PERT/CPM diagram like that seen in Figure 10-5 allows the service manager to achieve several important objectives. First, the manager gains all the usual advantages of planning. Unforeseen events and activities can be identified. How long something will take to do is readily estimated. Everyone involved in the project has an easily understood picture, in the form of the PERT/CPM chart, that shows all the pieces of the project, the sequence in which they are laid out and must be accomplished, time estimates for finishing each project step, and the total time for completing the entire project. Finally, the PERT/CPM chart shows the items that must be done on time to get the project accomplished as scheduled, which activities can be done at the same time as other activities, and which must happen before others. PERT/CPM can be used to plan any activity that takes time, and it would be hard to find any service experience that doesn't take time.

Circles and Arrows

PERT/CPM diagrams are simple to create. They consist of circles or bubbles, representing completed events, and arrows representing the activities that must be done before an event can be considered completed. The arrows connect the circles, and the arrow points to the event for completion of which the activity is necessary. In Figure 10-5, Event 1 must be completed before work can be begun on activities leading to completed Event 2, and the same is true of Event 3. Only after completing Event 3 can work begin on Events 4, 5, and 6, which can be worked on independently of each other. Event 13 has three arrows pointing toward it, signifying that completion of Event 13 will first require completing Events 9, 10, and 12, and then completing the activities following them and leading up to Event 13. As the chart shows, Events 9, 10, and 12 themselves require that prior activities and events must be

FIGURE **10-5** A Simple PERT/CPM Chart

© Cengage Learning 2012

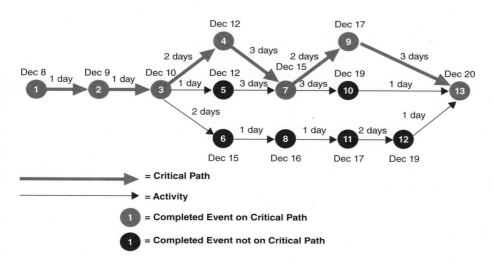

= Critical Path

= Activity

① = Completed Event on Critical Path

● = Completed Event not on Critical Path

completed before their own completion. The critical path indicated in the chart will be explained in more detail below, but, briefly, it is the sequence of events that must occur on time if the project is to be completed on time. It has no "slack" time (i.e., any time difference between when an event is scheduled for completion and when it must be completed for the entire project to end on time) in it as the other two paths do.

Tony's Deli

Let's leave abstract events and think about the new delicatessen Tony wants to open. The final event in the sequence, the final circle on his **PERT/CPM chart**, will be "Opening Day." One activity arrow leading up to that circle might be labeled "Hold three staff training sessions." But before those training sessions can be held, several other activities and events must take place. Tony must find a place to hold training, order training materials, hire and prepare a trainer, and hire the new deli personnel. Some of those activities can be done simultaneously. Their conclusion might be indicated in the diagram by a circle labeled "Preparations for training sessions finished." Also included in the diagram would be estimates of how long each activity will take. Summing the activity times will give Tony a pretty good estimate of how long it will take to have his delicatessen staff trained and available.

Complicated PERT/CPM networks are usually done on a computer. If organizations cannot afford to do their own programming, they can use off-the-shelf PERT/CPM computer programs. The owner of a small service organization might plug in the service delivery system's essential elements, and the computer will figure out the math and draw a schematic of the network.

Building the Network

Five steps are required to build a PERT/CPM network.

Step 1: Activity-event analysis.   The manager defines all events that must occur for the project to be completed, and all activities leading up to those events. The real fruits of the planning process occur at this step. By taking the time and making the effort, the manager can detail every activity in the project and uncover every step that must be taken.

Step 2: Activity-event sequencing.   Once the manager has defined the activities and events that must at some time occur, they can be placed in their proper sequence. Developing the sequence may reveal previously undiscovered or unknown events that must be scheduled. If you are describing how to tie a shoelace, you may forget event number one—that you must first have a shoelace—unless you sequence the process step by step.

Step 3: Activity time estimates.   The next step is for the manager to estimate how much time each activity will take so that an expected time for completing each event and the entire project can be calculated. The manager can use a simple and often-used formula to arrive at a weighted-average time estimate for each activity:

Expected time = (optimistic time + 4 times most likely time + pessimistic time) divided by 6

Step 4: Diagramming the project.   After all the events are sequenced, the activities detailed, and time estimates for each activity made, the pieces can be put together into the total-project diagram. As seen in Figure 10-5, each activity and event is set out in the diagrammed network along with the expected times.

Step 5: Identifying the critical path.   By summing up the activity times across the paths leading to the project completion, the manager can estimate the total time for completing the project and can identify the *critical path*, the CP of PERT/CPM, the sequence of activities that leaves no slack time. If these events don't happen on time, the project won't be finished as scheduled. Other paths in the network may have a time difference between when the events must happen and when they are scheduled to happen based on the calculation of activity times. In Figure 10-5, Event 6 must happen on December 15 or the entire project will get behind schedule, but Event 6 is scheduled for completion on December 12, so the project manager has some slack time. Even if Event 6 takes five days to complete instead of two, the delay won't affect the project completion date. Slack time also represents an opportunity to shift resources and attention away from events that finish earlier than they must and toward activities that need help.

The Big PERT/CPM Picture

In addition to showing the critical path, the projected completion time for the project, and the complete sequencing of activities needed to get the project done, the PERT/CPM network diagram provides a terrific visual of what is involved in the project. Using the diagram, the manager can show everyone what the whole project looks like, what each person's part in the project is, when each activity needs to be done, which activities are critical, and which events precede or follow each person's job. Even more helpful is that the manager now has a complete model that can be used to test what might happen under a different array of assumptions. What will happen, for example, if some of the pessimistic time estimates come true (whatever that could go wrong, did go wrong)? The PERT/CPM network diagram gives the manager an easy and quick way to substitute new numbers and revise the time schedule for total project completion if necessary. Obviously, every major project involves a whole lot of uncertainties. With this tool, however, the manager can plug in the uncertainties and refigure their impact on the project if they occur.

Holding a Convention

The PERT/CPM diagram in Figure 10-6 represents the steps necessary to prepare for and hold a convention. Convention manager Dorothy Barker went through all the steps noted above to determine the activities, their sequence, and the time estimates. Then she set up

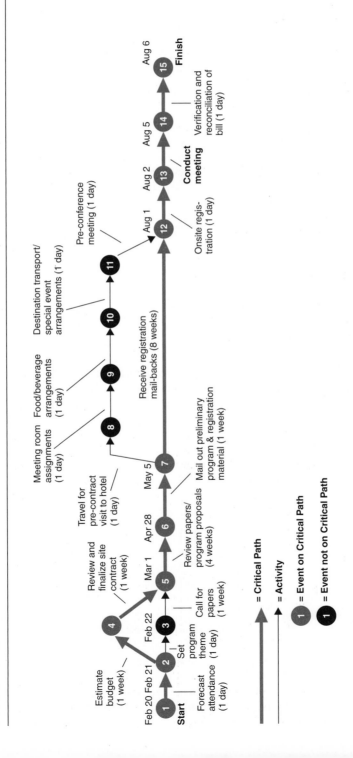

FIGURE **10-6** PERT/CPM Chart of the Steps Needed to Hold an Annual Convention

© Cengage Learning 2012

the PERT/CPM network to show the customer, the hotel staff members who will be critically involved in providing convention services, and herself all the things that must happen to complete a successful convention. This diagram can serve as a daily planning guide; it can be hung on the wall to show everyone what activities they need to accomplish each day. Since most convention managers have responsibility for more than one convention at a time, having these pictorial representations for each convention can help tremendously in keeping track of all the activities that each convention requires. A well-constructed and complete PERT/CPM chart can be used repeatedly because conventions generally have the same events and follow the same sequence of activities. The same would be true for servicing an airplane, for planning a restaurant or hotel opening, or a particular cruise in a cruise ship's annual schedule.

PERT/CPM can be used for any event, process, or experience that has a definable beginning and end to describe and detail the sequence of activities that must occur to complete all steps on schedule. Since the activities of hospitality organizations are often sequences or processes with a beginning and an end—from cooking and serving a meal, to cleaning and preparing a room for the next day's guests, to the entire guest experience itself—there are many possible applications of PERT/CPM to service situations.

Potential Disadvantages

The PERT/CPM process assumes that the activities leading to a project's completion are independent and can be clearly defined. That is not always the case. Also, the process depends on the accuracy of the time estimates. Since time estimates are made by fallible human beings, they may be incorrect, and it does not take many incorrect time estimates to throw off an entire project.

Simulations

A **simulation** is an imitation of the real thing. It may be doodled on a piece of paper with a pencil, or it may be done on a computer. Some simulations are big, like a computerized simulation of Epcot, and some are small, like a role-playing exercise at a company training session. Some simulations can consist of professional actors simulating the guest experience to show the observing employees and managers where problems in service delivery can occur. These simulations can reveal problems that the people who work there may not have thought about. They can also improvise customer mistakes to see if the system has safeguards built in to keep the customer from failing in the co-production experience or, if a failure does occur, to keep the customer from irreparably harming the value and quality of the experience. Organizations can use a wide variety of simulations when planning the service delivery system.

Computerized simulation techniques are the most sophisticated. They allow incredibly detailed simulation of a service delivery system and provide ways to measure and manipulate the system to see what might happen under different assumptions. Computers can also simulate behaviors of customers—with their infinite needs and ranges of behavior—on the receiving end of the system. The unique challenge in service delivery is that each customer is different. Because predicting exactly how any one customer will behave within the service experience is almost impossible, the opportunities for system failures are tremendous. Simulating customer behavior allows for a better comprehension of how that variability in customers affects the system's ability to deliver the service consistently at the expected level. Across the entire service experience, simulation can identify problems created by both the organization—in service design, environment, and delivery—and the customer.

At Epcot

Walt Disney World Resort used a computerized simulation model of Epcot during the planning and design of the park. Different patterns of guest behavior were modeled to make decisions about park capacity and where individual attractions, rest rooms, food-service facilities, and retail stores should be located. After the park opened, refinement and adjustment of the simulation model continued.

No one can know what any single guest might do inside the park during the course of a day, but knowledge of guest behaviors and statistical probabilities can yield relatively accurate predictions of how large groups of guests will behave. Probability distributions for all possible Epcot guest behaviors were developed and then built into the model. The resulting simulation accurately reflected the movements and behavior of a day's guests as they progressed through the park. The simulation model was then used to test and optimize such planning decisions as the location, size, and capacity of the attractions, restaurants, merchandise shops, and other facilities.

The Odyssey Restaurant

Here is a specific example of how the Epcot simulation led to a surprising discovery. In the early days of the park's construction, simulation runs were done to predict how guests would use Odyssey Restaurant, a large fast-food facility being built on an island in the lake between the Future World attractions section of the park and the World Showcase section. Studies had clearly shown that guests look for food near the exits of whatever attraction they happen to be leaving during peak mealtime periods. Since Odyssey Restaurant was somewhat remote from the exit of any attraction, the model predicted that rather than go to Odyssey, guests would head for the nearest fast-food locations placed at the exits of the Future World and World Showcase attractions. Unfortunately, there was not enough time to use the results of the simulation and relocate Odyssey. It opened and even though a bridge was constructed to make Odyssey more accessible, few guests used it—exactly as the simulation had predicted. Today, the facility is used for other purposes.

Computer Simulations for All

Not every organization will have the volume of customers to justify or pay for the creation of a full-scale computer model to study the service delivery system in detail. Nonetheless, with the increasing availability of computing power and smaller, more user-friendly software packages, even a Ralph's Restaurant on the corner may have economical access to a computerized simulation package. Simulations can be used for a variety of tasks, such as determining the optimal mix of tables in a restaurant,[10] scheduling tasks in a cafeteria,[11] or determining how many allergy-friendly rooms a hotel should have in its rooms inventory.[12] Already available to smaller service organizations is a computer program called a general-purpose system simulator (GPSS), which organizations can use to simulate their delivery systems. Even more widely available is Microsoft's Excel program, which can be used to create some types of simulations. Many simulations are focused on modeling and predicting waiting lines or queues, which is the subject of Chapter 11.

TARGETING SPECIFIC PROBLEM AREAS IN SERVICE DELIVERY SYSTEMS

Much of the planning process we have discussed in this chapter is designed to *make something good happen*: a wow service experience. Such planning deals with the entire service system and how the functional components work together to deliver the guest experience that customers want and expect. This planning is indeed critical to deliver an exceptional service experience by integrating all elements of the process. An equally important part of planning is to *keep something bad from happening:* problems and service failures. Such techniques as fishbone analysis and PERT/CPM charts can identify actual or potential problem areas in the system. In this section, we address some of the tools to plan for common delivery-systems problems before they occur since the best way to keep something bad from happening is to prevent it.

"A sandwich tossed is better than a customer lost." Arby's knows that their standard for tossing out sandwiches after they sit for a specific number of minutes not only prevents problems from occurring but also is less costly than recovering from an unhappy customer who got the poor-quality sandwich. Successful organizations use such strategies to identify and fix trouble spots before they become a problem for their guests.

Forecasting Demand to Prevent Problems

A major function of planning is to prevent problems. One strategy is forecasting and managing demand, which we will discuss in greater detail in Chapter 11. For example, if an analysis of the service delivery system indicates a potential service problem caused by excessive waits, a statistical analysis that forecasts demand might be an effective tool for discovering how much of a problem the waits might be and what can be done to address them before the doors open for the first customer. If a statistical prediction of the customer demand for a theme park on a particular day indicates that the park will be full, a preventive strategy will lead to the park's management calling in full staff, preparing extra food supplies, and having available the full capacity of each attraction. Restaurants may require reservations when the projected demand is high. Having a reservation system means that customer demand can be better matched with restaurant capacity and guests will not be disappointed with waiting when they come to the restaurant. In addition, the restaurant can know the number of diners to expect so that it can staff appropriately and have sufficient amounts of prepared items to ensure that the dining experience is enjoyable and trouble free. If the restaurant fails to plan, and customers are disappointed with a long wait, slow service, or out-of-stock menu items, their perception of the quality of the overall service experience will be poor, and a service failure will result. It is not uncommon to see Internet posts like "Good dinner, fair price, but I had to wait too long. I don't think it's worth the wait and don't see what all the hype's about. I'd suggest you go somewhere else." Keeping the wait down avoids that type of failure.

If the demand can be forecasted for a longer period of time, other proactive strategies can be implemented. If demand for the next quarter or next year, for example, is expected to increase by 20 percent, new capacity can be built, new employees hired and trained, and merchandise inventories increased to ensure that customers are not disappointed by long lines, unavailable souvenirs, or untrained and inadequate staff.

Training

Adequate training of employees before they ever get the chance to serve a customer can prevent failures. We discussed training in depth in Chapter 6, but the importance of training is worth repeating, not just for delivering the service product, but also for preventing service problems before they occur. For example, Olive Garden has all its employees available at least ten days before an opening to allow plenty of time to familiarize the new employees with the Olive Garden menu, standards of service, product offerings, and each other. By the time a new Olive Garden opens, the trained waitstaff knows the products they are serving, the systems for providing the Olive Garden experience to the guest, and the other members of the restaurant team.

The people who deliver any service need to know exactly what the total experience should consist of and need to be motivated to ensure that the guest experience happens in the way it is supposed to, every time, for every guest. Just as hospitals run disaster drills in conjunction with fire departments and rescue teams to prepare for unexpected, randomly occurring disasters, so can hospitality staff be trained, through practice, to handle both the expected and the unexpected.

Quality Teams

The use of quality teams is another preventive strategy. Recall how the Ritz-Carlton employees solved their service delivery system problem of late room-service breakfasts and how quality teams at the Quickconnect Airlines used a fishbone analysis to solve departure delays. Both show the value of letting the people directly involved in the service experience get together to identify service delivery system problems and recommend solutions to prevent their recurrence. Quite often, no one is in a better position to foresee and prevent problems than the people who have already experienced a wide range of problems and seen first-hand guest frustration with those problems.

Poka-Yokes

Trying to fix a problem once a customer has experienced it may be too late, so any devices or processes that can fail-safe the service delivery system or any part of it against human error are extremely desirable. Conceived by the late Shigeo Shingo, a Japanese quality improvement expert, **poka-yoke** (POH-kah YOH-kay)—the name Shingo gave these failure-preventing devices or procedures—means "mistake proofing" or "avoid mistakes" in Japanese. A poka-yoke basically involves inspection of the system for possible failure points and then finding or developing simple means to prevent, or immediately detect and correct, mistakes at those points. A poka-yoke is a proactive or preventive strategy for avoiding mistakes. Although it originated in the manufacturing sector, it can be used in planning and monitoring the service experience to keep it operating as flawlessly as possible.

Poka-yoke techniques can be of several forms, such as mechanical, electrical, or human. Since both the server and the customer can make mistakes during the service experience, both parties need to be mistake-proofed to the extent possible.

Here are some simple poka-yoke examples. Automobiles have many poka-yokes. To ensure that cars don't start moving when the ignition is turned on, the car is designed to not start unless the driver has a foot on the brake. Likewise, there are devices that prevent you from shifting a car into reverse when it is moving forward and devices that keep intoxicated drivers from starting their cars. Everywhere you look you can see examples. To ensure equity of service order and avoid disagreements, organizations ask customers to "take a number" or make a reservation. A surgeon's tray and a mechanic's wrench-set box may have a unique indentation for each item to ensure that no instrument is left inside a patient following surgery or wrench in an engine. Restaurants now buy different colored knives and cutting boards to prevent cross-contamination of food: Blue for fish, yellow for fowl, green for vegetables, and red for meat make it immediately apparent to all what should be on the cutting board and which knife should be used to cut it.

Types of Inspections

Shingo identified three types of inspections. In the services industry, they would be *source inspections*, in which potential mistakes are located at their source and fixed before they can get into the delivery system, *self-inspections*, in which people check their own work, and *successive inspections*, in which the person next in the service delivery system checks the quality and accuracy of the previous person's work. Mistakes can occur and poka-yokes can be used in all these inspection types.

An example of a source inspection is the chef monitoring the preprepared foods—such as salads, boned chicken, or whatever must be assembled in advance of the rush hour—to ensure that sufficient quantities of the items are available. An example of a self-inspection is the line cook personally comparing the order he has prepared against a picture of what the food display should look like before putting it on the service counter. An example of a successive inspection is the food server in a restaurant checking the food order on the counter before taking it out of the kitchen. Obviously, the closer to the source that errors or potential errors can be detected, the better.

Warnings and Controls

Poka-yokes are either "warnings that signal the existence of a problem or controls that stop production until the problem is resolved."[13] The *warning poka-yoke* occurs before an error is made. The *control poka-yoke* keeps a process from beginning or continuing after an error is made. A warning poka-yoke would be a light that flashes when the fries are ready to come out of the fryer. It signals the operator to remove the fries before they become overcooked. A control poka-yoke would be a device that turns a microwave oven off whenever the door is opened.

Warning and control poka-yokes can each be of three types. *Contact* poka-yokes monitor the item's physical characteristics to determine if they meet predefined specifications. Some restaurants cut their meats on scales to ensure that each cut is of the right weight before cooking. The second type of poka-yoke is based on the use of *fixed values* or constant numbers. It is used when a certain step is repeated—such as frying french fries—to ensure that the step is done the same way every time. McDonald's knows that a certain poundage of fries must be put in the fryer to make the fries taste the way McDonald's wants them to, so it designed a prepackaged bag containing a fixed value of potato pieces to ensure that the right quantity is placed in the fryer every time. The third type of poka-yoke is the *motion step*, or sequence method, used when more than one step is involved. This poka-yoke is useful in processes where an error-prone step must be completed correctly before the next step can take place. A simple example is the pop-up temperature gauge found in many turkeys. If the red button doesn't pop up, the turkey isn't done to the right temperature, and the turkey cannot move a step forward for further preparation until it does.

The tangible parts of the service experience can be mistake-proofed by poka-yokes just as readily as the tangibles in a manufacturing process. Preventing and quickly correcting service failures in the intangible aspects of service delivery is more challenging. Many service organizations try to avoid server errors during interactions with customers by standardizing or scripting what servers say and do during the service experience. These standards or scripts are poka-yokes designed to fail-safe the service delivery process. To whatever extent the servers can be prevented from making mistakes in routine aspects of the service by poke-yokes, it will reduce failure rates, and allow the servers to focus their efforts on the more creative, individualized aspects of guest service.

Poka-Yokes for Customers

Customers add a further complication to the service delivery process. They are frequently right in the middle of it and often responsible for co-producing it. Poka-yokes can be included to enable customers to prevent their own problems. For example, customers are irritated by a frequent fast-food service failure: leaving the drive-through only to find that they were served the wrong order. To avoid these failures, Burger King has installed poka-yoke video displays, called order confirmation units, at its drive-through windows so customers can verify the accuracy of the orders they are about to receive.

Customers can be prepared to do their part without error even before the service experience begins. The popular sign "No Shirt, No Shoes, No Service" prevents a customer error relating to attire and avoids the embarrassment for the customer and the organization of asking an improperly dressed customer to leave. During the service experience, the organization can develop poka-yokes to signal customers to do the right thing and avoid doing the wrong thing while co-producing their experience.

Speed Parking

Another example of a poka-yoke designed to help customers avoid failure is the speed-parking technique. Often seen at events where a lot of cars arrive at the same time, this system has the drivers line their cars up and park in successive spaces under the direction of a parking attendant. Each row is filled before cars go to the next row. This parking method is fast; it keeps all cars facing the same way and in line to park in the next available space. The method has led to the creation of a poka-yoke at some theme parks and other large attractions. When guests stream into the park every morning, the parking attendant writes down the time each row is filled. When evening comes and a family shows up lost and uncertain as to where their car might be, the attendant pulls out the yoke—a list of what sections were parked at what time. Th about what time they arrived at the parkin poka-yoke prevents a guest-caused failure

All poka-yokes should be simple, easy to at many points in most service delivery syst tifying something wrong and halting deliver do not use the term *poka-yoke*, they should for potential error sources as they plan the de preventing errors, if possible, and detecting e

A final point, emphasized by Shigeo Shing not simply to find and prevent errors, valuabl *tion to improve the system.* If the causes of servic improved, their number may not be substantial many poka-yokes are introduced.

Cross-Functional Project and Matrix

Sometimes, the problems in delivering a service sign or structure of the organization itself. A fui may not consistently provide the service experienc departments focus on their own individual goals ai faction across the entire experience. A guest doesi ager's goals and challenges or the food and bevera

Guests care about the quality and value of the entire experience they are paying for, and the individual organizational components need to be effectively connected in ways that unite them to focus everyone on ensuring guest satisfaction.

It may be helpful to consider the organization itself as an element of the service delivery process that effectively integrates and coordinates the activities of people working in different departments. Is the organization designed so that individual departments perform their functions smoothly, or is it designed so that the overall service delivery system functions smoothly? The two are often not the same.

One method of organizing people and groups to enable them to focus on the guest's needs, wants, and expectations across the boundaries of functional organizational units is by creating a temporary **cross-functional structure**. This term is also used to refer to a matrix structure where a group or project team is overlaid on the traditional functional organizational structure to work on a specific task or serve a particular customer for a limited time. Traditional organizational structures are characterized by a single line of authority running from top to bottom: You report to one person; that person reports to somebody else. This also tends to mean information flows in one direction: from the top down. A cross-functional organization is characterized by multiple lines of authority. You may report to more than one person; that person may do the same.

In hospitality organizations, many situations arise that call for focusing everyone's functional skills on solving a guest's problem or meeting a guest's expectation right now. Because so many functional areas must work in coordination with each other to deliver a whole service experience, information must flow between different functional groups. For example, a hotel's convention coordinator has to bring together all the functional areas of a hotel to meet the needs and expectations of the convention's meeting planner. In such a case, the convention coordinator acts as a project manager temporarily responsible for ensuring that everyone who needs to serve the customer is available and ready to do so. Cross-functional structures are especially useful in the hospitality industry, and, in fact, in any service-driven industry.

At The Ritz-Carlton

While discussing how The Ritz-Carlton Hotels won the Malcolm Baldrige Quality Award, Horst Schulze spoke about finding a cross-functional organizational solution to identify and correct system flaws. The Ritz-Carlton had used guest surveys to identify eighteen key guest-satisfaction measures. The Ritz-Carlton then hired a process manager for each hotel whose responsibility was to eliminate flaws and reduce work-cycle times by 50 percent in the systems that delivered the eighteen keys leading to guest satisfaction. The keys were deemed so important that this specific person was hired to enure that someone worried about them all the time, no matter which functional units responsible for the different keys. The Ritz-Carlton thereby avoided the potential ns of the functional orientation that come naturally to departments by authoriz-cess manager to cross all functional areas to ensure that someone was focused s guests and what satisfies them.

d Disadvantages of Cross-Functional Project ctures

he same focus on guest satisfaction as the Ritz-Carlton, other hospi-ject teams, matrix structures, and other cross-functional struc-s generally involve people working under more than one line nagers who believe that strict lines of authority are important have problems working with cross-functional structures. On the other hand, crossing functional areas and getting everyone focused on the guest can offer some important benefits. Table 10-4 compares the advantages and disadvantages of these organizational structures.

The Real Boss

Here is the bottom line on organizational design: Use whatever organizational design best enables every unit and every person to focus on the guest's needs, wants, and expectations. The Ritz-Carlton knows this, and Disney knows this. While the organization chart may show functional divisions with different people responsible for different areas like maintenance, front office, and housekeeping, everyone in these excellent hospitality organizations knows that *their real boss is the guest* and that their real organizational function is ensuring that their guest experience meets or exceeds their guest's expectations.

TABLE 10-4 Advantages and Disadvantages of Cross-Functional Project and Matrix Structures

ADVANTAGES	DISADVANTAGES
1. *Makes the guest, not the function, the focus.* If one person or team is responsible for satisfying guest needs, the focus of the organization is placed directly on the overall service needs of the guest, rather than the specific element of the experience delivered by any one functional department.	1. *Violates traditional "single line of authority."* Most companies are still organized to have a single and clear chain of command. Implementing a cross-functional structure changes this traditional form of management.
2. *Improved lateral exchange of information.* If multiple functional areas work together, different providers of services will communicate more with each other.	2. *Ambiguity about control.* Because different functional areas are involved, it can be unclear who is ultimately in charge or responsible for certain decisions, either for technical issues or human resource management issues.
3. *Improved vertical exchange of information.* The interactive process needed for cross-functional teams means that information will flow to, from, and through an organization's hierarchy more quickly. Cross-functional structures also lead to flatter (less hierarchical) organizations, with fewer levels through which information must pass.	3. *Creates organizational conflict between functional and project managers.* Even when units work together for certain projects, there are still functional activities that must be completed. Having cross-functional groups can create a conflict between managers of cross-functional teams and managers of functional areas, because they may have different, even conflicting, goals.
4. *Increased flexibility in use of human capital.* When different functional areas work together, it becomes easier to determine where there may be too many people, and where there are not enough employees. A cross-functional structure facilitates the ability of people to work in different areas.	4. *Creates interpersonal conflict.* Cross-functional structures require that individuals with different backgrounds, perspectives on work, time horizons, and goals work together. Such differences can lead to greater interpersonal conflict.
5. *Increased individual motivation and attitudes.* Through a cross-functional structure, individuals have a better sense of the entire service product being delivered. When employees see the entire product, as opposed to just a piece of it, they tend to be more motivated to perform better and have higher job satisfaction, organizational commitment, and morale.	5. *Creates insecurity and loss of status.* With a different organizational structure, some managers will lose some authority as more responsibility is given to cross-functional groups and project managers. This can reduce the perceived status of functional managerial roles and make some managers insecure with their reduced authority.
	6. *More costly for organization.* Cross-functional structures can lead to increased overhead and staff, more meetings, delayed decisions, and more information processing. All this can add to organizational costs.
	7. *More difficult for individuals.* Individuals working in cross-functional structures will face greater role ambiguity. Potentially conflicting instructions or orders may lead to personal stress.

LESSONS LEARNED

1. Check for system failure (e.g., not enough elevators; too many monorail trains) before blaming people.

2. Detailed planning can avoid most service failures.

3. Plan for guest failures and how to recover from them (more on this idea in Chapter 13).

4. Design the organization to ensure service excellence.

5. A bad system can defeat a good employee.

6. The goal: Fail no guest; delight every guest.

7. Problems will recur if you can't or don't find out what caused them.

8. Identifying problems is more than just fixing a single guest experience. It is an opportunity to improve the service delivery system.

9. Everyone is responsible for monitoring and maintaining the quality of the service delivery system; everyone is responsible for avoiding service failures.

10. There are many planning tools to help deliver excellent guest experiences. Use them as much as possible.

REVIEW QUESTIONS

1. Why is it important to check the delivery system first before checking to see whether employees are to blame for service failures?

2. Recall two types of hospitality organizations with which you are familiar.

   A. What people and nonpeople parts of each organization's service delivery system can you see? Not see?

   B. What steps does each organization take to ensure that you cannot see certain parts of the delivery system, and why does it take those steps?

   C. Are any parts of these two organizations' service delivery systems (e.g., the frontline server) more important than other parts? Or are all equally important because a service delivery system is only as strong as its weakest link?

3. If you opened a new restaurant, would you bother to blueprint your service delivery system? Why or why not?

   A. If you did a blueprint, would you show it to your employees and discuss it with them, which would take time and cost money, or simply teach them their jobs on a need-to-know basis? Or would you leave it up to them whether they studied the blueprint or not?

   B. The chapter referred to a service blueprint for a frontline bank employee that covered thirty-six 11-by-18 pages. How long would your restaurant blueprint be? Compare the relative usefulness of your blueprint with the bank-employee blueprint.

4. You have been asked to manage a local music festival.

   A. How would a PERT/CPM chart help you do this?

   B. What would its essential elements, the individual circles in the chart, be?

   C. What would your PERT/CPM chart look like? Sketch it out, indicating the critical path.

5. Describe several situations in which hospitality managers could use cross-functional project and matrix teams to improve the quality and/or value of the guest experience.

6. Providing a wow service and preventing service problems are two sides of the same coin. Discuss.

---

1. Apply a PERT/CPM chart to a guest service situation in a hospitality organization with which you are familiar.

2. Blueprint the service experience provided by a hospitality organization with which you are familiar, with emphasis on the delivery system.

3. Find a potential problem area in that blueprint and draw a simple fishbone diagram that you might use to prevent or resolve the problem.

The airlines, in essence, provide the service of getting guests from point A to point B safely. While there are clearly many parts to this service product, safety is a critical component that gets significant attention in the planning process. Fail-safes and various forms of security have been added to provide greater security for guests, but all these come at a cost. The U.S. government has recommended the use of cost-benefit analysis for assessing potentially new regulations. The regulatory safety goal is $1–10 million per life saved, meaning that a regulation costing this amount or less per life saved is worthwhile to implement. So, by these standards, hardened cockpit doors, which are estimated to cost $800,000 per life saved, seem like a good investment; however, the Federal Air Marshal Service, estimated to cost $180 million per life saved, seems a poor investment.

Safety is an issue for all parts of the hospitality industry. Measures could include maintaining heightened security at hotels and restaurants, having trained medical staff on hand, and putting more safety measures into all aspects of the service system. Hotels could hire a full-time doctor, have extensive security teams, hire dozens of more people to inspect and test all food products coming into the kitchen; and many, many more.

How should decisions about implementing greater safety measures be made? What ethical issues are involved? Can you put a value, or a budget, on a human life? Should a safety decision be made this way? If so, how do you estimate the value to put on a human life to help determine if an investment is worthwhile? Is $1–10 million the "right" range of values? If you should not make a formal calculation using a value for a human life, how should you make these sorts of decisions?

CASE STUDIES

Room for Improvement

Monique Kazer spends quite a bit of time on the road in her job as a salesperson for a company specializing in audiovisual equipment for convention hotels and centers. She works long hours, often dines late at night, and returns to her lodging place late, sometimes after midnight. Monique has asthma and is very sensitive to cigarette smoke, so she always requests a nonsmoking room at her hotel or motel.

Several weeks ago, tired after visiting three convention hotels, in Newark, Jersey City, and Hoboken, in one day, Monique arrived a few minutes after midnight at the Hospitality Inn, where she had a guaranteed reservation. The Hospitality Inn was a unit of the major chain with which her firm did business because of the deep discounts offered. She checked in and headed for Room 315, looking forward to a hot shower and good night's sleep; tomorrow was going to be even busier. As always, she checked the door for a no-smoking sign. When she entered, the smell of cigarettes, or possibly cigars, mixed with air-freshener spray, almost made her sick. She began to cough, and her throat started to close up.

She quickly backed out, shut the door, and returned to the front desk. At least she didn't have to wait in line at that time of night, thank goodness for that. Desk agent Hyun Cho had a magazine open on the area beneath the counter that she used as her desk, but she was not reading it because—as Monique saw it—she was obviously talking to a friend on the phone. She glanced at Monique a couple of times but continued to talk on the phone, making it clear that Monique would have to wait her turn. Ordinarily, Monique would have waited a few moments, but tonight she was not in the mood so she employed her last-ditch technique for gaining attention in such a situation: She reached over the counter, took the phone out of Cho's hand, and hung it up. The service encounter went downhill from there.

Monique didn't even give a red-faced Hyun Cho a chance to mention the phone hang-up: "I made a reservation for a nonsmoking room, and you people put me in a room full of smoking fumes. Just change my room and we'll let it go at that."

Cho was a fairly conscientious night desk agent, and she had actually been talking with her babysitter, but she was still steaming from having the phone taken from her in mid-sentence. Hyun said nothing, checked the hotel records with a glance, and then said to Monique: "That *is* a nonsmoking room!"

"Check again, Ms … (looking at her name tag)…. Cho. The room smells like a pre-war stag party."

"I don't care if it smells like hell warmed over. I don't need to check again, Ms…. (looking at the registration card)…. Ka-Zer. I can read and I know my rooms and I can tell you that Room 315 is for nonsmokers." She concluded triumphantly, "We changed it over last week!"

Monique whispered the first curse she had uttered in a year or two, and then said, "Just move me to a nonsmoking room that has been a nonsmoking room as long as you have been open."

"No, problem, Ms. Ka-Zer. (pause) Usually. But tonight, I'm sorry, we're filled up."

Monique tried to have the room fee canceled, but Hyun refused. "If you don't show up until after midnight, it's actually the next day. No cancellations or refunds under any circumstances after midnight." She played her hole card: "Company policy." Then she added, "You ought to do something about that cough."

Monique left—tired, defeated, and still coughing—and headed out into the night to find another room, if she could. If not, there was always the back seat of the rented Crown Vic.

1. How would you have handled this situation if you were Monique Kazer?

2. How would you have handled this situation if you were Hyun Cho?

3. What devices described in the chapter might system planners have used to prevent this service failure, and how might they have used them?

Room for More Improvement

As Monique Kazer rushed through the exit of the Hospitality Inn lobby, she almost knocked manager Roberta Morales down. Morales recognized Monique from previous visits and knew that Monique's firm gave Hospitality Inns across the region a lot of business. Morales realized that something was wrong and suspected that the something was a service failure.

"I'm the inn manager. Is there something I can do for you?" she said to Monique. She heard Monique's side of the story, took her to the cocktail lounge, bought her the beverage of her choice, and asked an assistant manager to chat with Monique while she went back to the front desk. After hearing Hyun Cho's side of the story ("she yanked the phone out of my hand and slammed it down"), Roberta Morales headed back to the lounge. She would speak further with Hyun Cho later on.

1. In a later chapter, you will be reading about some techniques for handling service failures. For now, what steps might you take to retain the patronage of Monique Kazer (and her entire organization)?

2. What steps would you take with regard to Hyun Cho and the failure at the front desk?

3. Using some hypothetical but realistic numbers, how much do you think it might end up costing Hospitality Inns if manager Roberta Morales is unable to recover from this failure and ends up losing the patronage of not only Monique Kazer but her entire firm?

ADDITIONAL READINGS

Biolos, J. 2002. Six sigma meets the service economy. *Harvard Management Update*, 7 (11), 3–5.

Bitner, M. J., Ostrom, A. L., & Morgan, F. N. 2008. Services blueprinting: A practical technique for service innovation. *California Management Review*, 50 (3), 66–94.

Bretthauer, K. 2004. Service management. *Decision Sciences*, 35, 325–332.

Carey, S. 2007. Calculating costs in the clouds. *The Wall Street Journal*, March 6, pp. B1, B12.

Chesbrough, H., & Spohrer, J. 2006. A research manifesto for services science. *Communications of the ACM*, 49 (7), 35–40.

Froehle, C. M., & Roth, A. V. 2004. New measurement scales for evaluating perceptions of the technology mediated customer service experience. *Journal of Operations Management*, 22, 1–21.

George, W. R., & Gibson, B. E. 1991. Blueprinting: A tool for managing quality in service, in Stephen W. Brown et al. (eds.), *Service Quality: Multidisciplinary and Multinational Perspectives*. Lexington, MA: Lexington Books, pp. 73–91.

Gross, D. 2009. Try the beef and broccoli: P.F. Chang's simple recipe for profits. *Newsweek*, May 25, pp. 29–30.

Hill, A. V., Collier, D. A., Froehle, C. M., Goodale, J. C., Metters, R. D., & Verma, R. 2002. Research opportunities in service process design. *Journal of Operations Management*, 20, 189–202.

Johnston, R. 2005. Service operations management: Return to roots. *International Journal of Service Industry Management*, 25, 1278–1297.

Jones, P. (ed.). 2008. *Handbook of Hospitality Operations and IT*. Burlington, MA: Butterworth-Heinemann.

Kimes, S. E. 2004. Restaurant revenue management: Implementation at Chevys Arrowhead. *Cornell Hotel and Restaurant Quarterly*, 45 (1), 52–67.

Kumar, S., Phillips, A., & Rupp, J. 2009. Using six sigma DMAIC to design a high-quality summer lodge operation. *Journal of Retail and Leisure Property*, 8, 173–191.

Kwortnik, R. J., & Thompson, G. M. 2009. Unifying service marketing and operations with service experience management. *Journal of Service Research*, 11, 389–406.

Kingman-Brundage, J. 1989. The ABCs of service system blueprinting, in M. J. Bitner and Lawrence A. Crosby (eds.), *Designing a Winning Service Strategy: 7th Annual Services Marketing Conference Proceedings*. Chicago: American Marketing Association, pp. 30–33.

Lewis, M., Young, B., Mathiassen, L., Rai, A., & Welke, R. 2007. Business process innovation based on stakeholder perceptions. *Information Knowledge Systems Management*, 6, 7–27.

Machuca, J. A. D., Gonzalez-Zamora, M., & Aguilar-Escobar, V. G. 2007. Services operations management research. *Journal of Operations Management*, 25 (3), 585–603.

Mahapatra, S. S., & Khan, M. S. 2006. A methodology for evaluation of service quality using neural networks. *Proceedings of the International Conference on Global Manufacturing and Innovation*, July 27–29, pp. 1–9.

March, L., & Fugazi, R. 2002. Applications of business process redesign in hotel daily operations: The impact of redesigning airport van pickup process on hotel customer satisfaction. *Journal of Quality Assurance in Hospitality & Tourism*, 3 (1/2), 19–33.

McCartney, S. 2008. Savvier airline schedules, fewer cheap fares. *Wall Street Journal*, October 21, p. D7.

Metters, R., & Marucheck, A. 2007. Service management: Academic issues and scholarly reflections from operations management researchers. *Decision Sciences*, 38 (2), 195–214.

Michaels, D. 2009. Airlines' expert on missing bags fights lost cause. *Wall Street Journal*, August 13, pp. A1, A4.

Morgan, I., & Rao, J. 2002. Aligning service strategy through super-measure management. *Academy of Management Executive*, 16 (4), 121–131.

Roth, A. V., & Menor, L. J. 2003. Insights into service operations management: A research agenda. *Productions and Operations Management*, 12 (2), 145–164.

Shostack, G. L. 1992. Understanding services through blueprinting, in Teresa A. Swartz, D. E. Bowen, and S. W. Brown (eds.), *Advances in Services Marketing, and Management: Research and Practice*, Vol. 1. Greenwich, CT: JAI Press, pp. 75–90.

Soltani, E., Lai, P.-C., Javadeen, S. R. S., & Gholipour, T. H. 2008. A review of the theory and practice of managing TQM: An integrative framework. *Total Quality Management & Business Excellence*, 19, 461–479.

Song, H., & Li, G. 2008. Tourism demand modeling and forecasting: A review of recent research. *Tourism Management*, 29, 203–220.

Stierand, M., & Sandt, J. 2007. Organizing haute-cuisine service processes: A case study. *Journal of Hospitality and Tourism Management*, 14, 24–36.

Swaminathan, J. M. 2001. Enabling customization using standardized operations. *California Management Review*, 43 (3), 125–135.

Testa, M. R., & Sipe, L. J. 2006. A systems approach to service quality: Tools for hospitality leaders. *Cornell Hotel and Restaurant Administration Quarterly*, 47 (1), 36–48.

Thompson, G. M., & Kwortnik, R. J. 2008. Pooling restaurant reservations to increase service efficiency. *Journal of Service Research*, 10 (4), 335–346.

Tsikriktsis, N., & Heineke, J. 2004. The impact of process innovation on customer dissatisfaction: Evidence from the U.S. domestic airline industry. *Decision Sciences*, 35, 129–142.

Wright, C. M., & Mechling, G. 2002. The importance of operations management problems in service organizations. *Omega*, 30, 77–87.

---

[1]Metters, R., & Marucheck, A. 2007. Service management: Academic issues and scholarly reflections from operations management researchers. *Decision Sciences*, 38, 196.

[2]Facella, P. 2009. *Everything I Know About Business I Learned at McDonald's: The 7 Leadership Principles that Drive Break Out Success*. New York: McGraw-Hill.

[3]Bitner, M. J., Ostrom, A. L., & Morgan, F. N. 2008. Service blueprinting: A practical technique for service innovation. *California Management Review*, 50 (3), 66–94.

[4]Ibid.

[5]For this discussion, we are indebted to Shostack, G. L., & Kingman-Brundage, J. 1991. How to design a service, in C. A. Congram and M. L. Friedman (eds.), *The AMA Handbook of Marketing for the Service Industry*. American Marketing Association, pp. 243–261.

[6]Albrecht, K. 1988. *At America's Service: How Your Company Can Join the Customer Service Revolution*. New York: Warner Books, p. 89.

[7]Shostack & Kingman-Brundage, 244. For more information on service blueprinting and service mapping, see Shostack, G. L. 1984. Designing services that deliver. *Harvard Business Review*, 62 (1), 133–139; and Kingman-Brundage, J. 1991. Technology, design, and service quality. *International Journal of Service Industry Management*, 2 (3), 47–59.

[8]Wyckoff, D. D. 1984. New tools for achieving service quality. *Cornell Hotel and Restaurant Administration Quarterly*, 25 (3), 78–91.

[9]See for example, McNeil, R. G., & Evans, R. A. 2004. So you want to build a convention center: The case of hope versus reality. *Journal of Convention and Event Tourism*, 6 (1&2), 23–43.

[10]Thompson, G. M., & Verma, R. 2003. Computer simulation in hospitality teaching, practice, and research. *Cornell Hotel and Restaurant Administration Quarterly*, 44, 85–93.

[11]Kuo, C., & Nelson, D. C. 2009. A simulation study of production task scheduling for a university cafeteria. *Cornell Hospitality Quarterly*, 50, 540–552.

[12]Dittman, D. A., & Hesford, J. W. 2007. Simulation-based optimization approach for investment decisions: A case study of Pure Allergy-Friendly Rooms. *Cornell Hotel and Restaurant Administration Quarterly*, 48, 88–100.

[13]Chase, R. B., & Stewart, D. M. 1994. Make your service fail-safe. *Sloan Management Review*, 35 (1), 36.

NOTES

CHAPTER 11

Waiting for Service

HOSPITALITY PRINCIPLE: MANAGE THE GUEST'S WAIT

Hurry up and wait.

—Old military saying

All things come to him who waits—provided he knows what he is waiting for.

—Woodrow T. Wilson

The other line always moves faster.

—Murphy's Law

LEARNING OBJECTIVES

After reading this chapter, you should understand:

- How to plan and manage the wait.

- How to make any wait for service as short and pleasant as possible.

- How to make any wait for service *seem* short and pleasant.

- How to plan for capacity shortages.

- How to manage the guest's perception of the wait.

- How to offset the wait's negative effects by managing the value of the experience provided to the guest.

- How to use queuing theory to plan the wait.

- How to simulate a wait.

How long we wait and how long we are willing to wait are fascinating subjects. While solid scientific evidence is hard to find, various estimates suggest that we wait in line about two to three years in a lifetime. To see a cardiologist in Minneapolis, you'll need to wait, on average, forty-seven days. To get a table for two at Citronelle, in Washington D.C., you may need to wait nearly three months for your reservation. Some parents put their children on the waiting lists for exclusive preparatory schools before their children are born. And, if you want season tickets for the Green Bay Packers or the Philadelphia Eagles, at the present rate the "line" is moving, you may need to wait several hundred years.

Nobody likes to wait in line. Yet, almost every hospitality organization relies on waiting lines or **queues** to match its serving capacity with the number of guests who want service. Planning and managing the wait of the customers are among any service provider's fundamental concerns. This chapter presents some strategies for planning and managing the reality and the perception of the guest's wait for service. These include both quantitative and perceptual strategies. The secret to managing the guest's wait effectively is to use all available techniques, in the right combination, to make a seemingly endless wait acceptable, perhaps even enjoyable, to the guest. Since nearly every service experience, whether in an actual queue or online, has a wait in it somewhere, planning for and **managing the wait** are sufficiently important to merit their own chapter.

In some respects, the wait is an inevitable part of the service experience since no organization can perfectly prepare itself to serve all guests, whenever and whatever they want. In another respect a wait is a service failure. When the wait between courses at a fine-dining restaurant is too short, because guests have anticipated a more leisurely experience, or a wait at a quick-serve drive-thru window is too long, the guest is disappointed. Even when the wait at a popular attraction is no surprise and, therefore, "meets the guest's expectations," the guest generally doesn't like it.

WHEN THE WAIT BEGINS

The guest experience often starts off not with a wow but a wait. The wait for service begins at the entrance to the restaurant, the automated message on the phone, the log-on to a Web site, or the line in front of Space Mountain at Walt Disney World Resort. The prospective guest or customer assesses the Space Mountain line, the number of cars in the restaurant's parking lot, the estimate in the automated message on the help-line, or the turning hourglass on the computer screen, and decides whether to walk to the next attraction, drive on to the next restaurant, hang up the phone, click to another Web site—or to wait. What makes that guest wait or leave can be anticipated and managed—if waiting lines are understood. If no other eating places are within eyesight, or the exceedingly hungry guest does not know what other restaurants are available nearby and doesn't have the wireless or GPS technology to find out, or the guest is absolutely convinced that he must eat in that restaurant because the quality or uniqueness of the dining experience is said to be unsurpassed, he will probably pull into the parking lot, walk inside, and wait in line.

High expectations of guests explain the large crowds usually standing outside an Outback Steakhouse or a Cheesecake Factory. The people waiting believe that the quality or the value of the dining experience will outweigh the costs to them of waiting, despite the full parking lot and the crowd standing in line outside the restaurant waiting to be served. In fact, sometimes guests view a line as a signal of quality. If there are two restaurants next to each other, one with a line and one without, a person might actually prefer the restaurant with the line, thinking that the one where people are waiting must be worth a wait. The same high expectations can explain the lines next to Space Mountain and the other popular attractions throughout the Walt Disney World Resort. In effect, each person makes an opportunity-cost judgment. If the expected benefits of the wait outweigh the costs (boredom and impatience, to name just two) of idly standing around, then the guest will wait. If they don't, the guest will leave and go elsewhere for the service.

For those customers who decide to wait rather than leave, how can planners be sure that the wait will be as short and as pleasant as possible? No matter how good the Space Mountain ride or the Cheesecake Factory meal is, if the customer begins the experience angry, distressed, or unhappy about having to wait for service, then that customer's expectations will be much harder to meet.

CAPACITY AND PSYCHOLOGY: KEYS TO MANAGING LINES

Managing the wait has two major components. First is to keep the wait as short as possible by planning for and building the appropriate capacity into the service facility to minimize the wait for the anticipated number of guests arriving at the anticipated rate. Second is to ensure that the guests who are waiting have their physiological and psychological needs and expectations met while they wait.

The capacity decision results from careful study of the expected demand pattern. Whether one is trying to plan for how many two-top versus four-top tables to place in a restaurant, how many registration booths to open at a convention, how many reservation agents to staff at each hour of the day, or how many blackjack tables to put in a casino, the need to make an accurate capacity estimate is the same. Planners must predict three factors that drive the capacity decision: how many people will arrive for the service, at what rate they will arrive, and how long the service will take.

If, on every day that the organization is open for business, the same number of people were to arrive for service every day, their arrivals were evenly spaced throughout the day, and serving each person took the same length of time, the capacity decision would be easy. For example, a psychiatrist can schedule eight patients per day, schedule them to arrive on the hour, then serve each patient for forty-five minutes and use the remaining fifteen minutes to write up notes on that patient and prepare for the next. That psychiatrist has an easy capacity decision (assuming that no emergencies occur and everyone is on time): one service facility (an office) containing one chair for the psychiatrist and one couch for the patient, plus other furnishings and equipment for one office. If the service is a guided tour through a museum, the service provider knows how long it will take, but the museum's planning staff must predict how many people will arrive for service. If the service experience has a less definite beginning and ending time, like a meal or a day at a ski resort, both the number of persons arriving for service and the average time taken to deliver each part of the network of events that make up a service experience will have to be estimated or predicted.[1] We will discuss several methods for making these predictions later in this chapter.

Capacity designs can affect perceptions of service quality. While a restaurant with too little capacity will fail to meet guest expectations for prompt service and short waits, a restaurant with too much capacity can also fail to meet guest expectations. A restaurant with too many seats will appear empty to diners and may lead them to conclude that the food or service is not up to par. This assumption predisposes guests to expect a poor experience. Further, they may feel foolish for choosing a restaurant that is so obviously unpopular. The chefs and the servers have two strikes against them, just because the restaurant designers put in too many seats.

Of course, from the restaurant owner's point of view, the excess capacity costs money! Fixed costs are tied up in unused tables, silverware, equipment, rent, and so forth. Too much capacity may mean higher variable costs as well. The manager may schedule too many servers who end up being paid simply to wait around.

Capacity

In an ideal world, planners would be able to determine the exact capacity required to serve each guest at the moment when the guest expects service. Each customer for Cheesecake Factory or Space Mountain would arrive just when a table or an empty car was available to receive the desired experience. Guests want that kind of service, and organizations want to provide it. Both are frequently disappointed.

What to Do?

Because people do not arrive at service operations in neat, ordered patterns, they sometimes have to wait for service. When hospitality managers see that waiting lines are becoming long, they have several choices.[2] Customer-focused research can identify the best options. The goal is to find the decision that ensures customer satisfaction with the lowest capital cost. Managers should choose the option that allows both customers and the organization to come out ahead.

1. *Close the Doors to Further Customers*. This choice is highly undesirable, but sometimes the movie theater manager or rock show entrepreneur must tell those waiting, "Sorry, we're sold out."
2. *Add Capacity*. Because this alternative is usually expensive, organizations do not usually choose it unless they believe the high demand causing the waiting lines will continue. The organization will be particularly hesitant to add capacity if its design-day capacity is already at a high percent level, meaning that the organization is already at or below capacity most of the time. Stopgap measures for adding capacity temporarily are sometimes available. For example, employees can be asked to work overtime or on flexible schedules, cross-trained employees can be reassigned from their normal areas to help unclog a service bottleneck, temporary help can be hired, or temporary changes in physical facilities can be made, like adding tents to provide additional exhibit space at a convention or busses for increasing capacity to move people at special events.
3. *Manage Demand*. Simply informing guests of when the busy and slack times occur may smooth out demand. Service providers can also schedule appointments or offer inducements to customers to use capacity at nonpeak demand times.

Requiring reservations at a restaurant is an example of the first method, and early-bird specials or discounts on airline travel or hotel rooms at off-peak times are examples of the second.

Some organizations, such as airlines and hotels, can ask that guests make reservations, even guaranteed reservations in some cases, to help manage demand. Customers are often willing to call for reservations with such organizations because they do not want to take a chance on not getting a flight or a room. No one wants to arrive at the cruise-ship dock only to find that all rooms are occupied. But many hospitality organizations do not have the market stature or have too many similar competitors for most customers to help them in their capacity decisions by requiring reservations. Guests will make reservations when the alternatives are few or they do not have the flexibility regarding time, desire, or distance to do something different if their primary choice is at capacity. Thus, guests are willing to pay for a guaranteed hotel-room reservation at the bottom of the Grand Canyon more than a year in advance to ensure that the room will be waiting for them after they walk to the end of the Bright Angel Trail. But, they may not see any value in making a reservation at the nearby Carrabba's since, if that restaurant is at capacity, many similar alternatives are probably available near Carrabba's.

Another way to manage demand is by shifting demand from peak-capacity use times to off-peak times by offering guests inducements to change their **arrival patterns**. When the wait times for popular attractions became excessive, Disney shifted demand by creating a special after-hours ticket called "Magic Kingdom's E-Ride Nights." The tickets were sold for under $15 and provided guests with unlimited access to the nine most popular attractions for an additional three hours after the normal park closing. To guarantee the guests minimal wait times on the nine attractions, the tickets sold each night were limited to a fixed number of guests and were sold in advance at the Disney resorts on a first-come, first-served basis. The actual number of tickets sold was limited to match the capacity of the nine attractions.

The guests who paid less than $15 for the right to spend an extra three hours after normal closing time to ride their favorite rides as many times as they wanted to were happy and thought they got a great deal. They did not have to stand in long lines with everybody else waiting for these rides during the day. Regular daytime guests were also happier; their lines were shorter because the E-Ride Nights guests were no longer in the lines during the day. In effect, Disney expanded park capacity by shifting demand, but unlike the power company that gives customers a lower rate at off-peak times or the restaurant that offers low-cost early-bird specials, Disney was able to charge more and guests were happy to pay; they felt they got good value for their money.

4. *Allow the Line to Form and Then Manage the Line by Diverting Customers.* When lines are unavoidable, one way to keep customers happy is by offering people waiting in line something else to do. Having a gift shop in a Hard Rock Cafe or Rainforest Cafe gives patrons an opportunity to go and do something while they wait for their table to be ready. These diversions not only benefit the guest by creating the perception that the experience has begun, but they can be highly profitable, sometimes more profitable than the service product itself. Rainforest Cafe even calls itself "A wild place to shop and eat." An organization may go so far as to close down some available capacity to ensure that people wait long enough to become "diverted" to the gift shop, with its high-margin items for sale. Or an organization may keep a phone caller on hold longer than absolutely necessary to present a recorded message promoting other services. Many restaurants suggest guests wait in the bar, where they can order drinks and appetizers, until their table is ready.

A related strategy is to upgrade a low-demand aspect of the organization's service to divert customers toward it and away from high-demand features. For example, a resort hotel could upgrade its pool bar to attract people away from the main lobby bar at peak times. A cruise ship could upgrade a currently underutilized restaurant to be family friendly so it takes pressure off the main dining facility. A golf course could upgrade its practice area with computerized swing-analysis equipment, to take pressure off the course during the most popular tee times.

From their own daily experience, most people can cite numerous examples of organizations that planned and managed the wait well or poorly. The best organizations know what steps they need to take when lines start to form.

5. *Do Nothing.* The organization can accept the fact that it will make customers unhappy with a wait and hope that they aren't so unhappy that they leave and vow never to return. Maybe lines form only rarely, and so the organization is not willing to spend money to address an occasional problem. Some establishments actually seem to benefit from doing nothing. For example, the long lines at some night clubs or restaurants signal an establishment that is trendy, in demand, and exclusive.

Design Day

Whether they realize it or not, or whether they do it consciously or not, all hospitality organizations use the design-day concept (also discussed in Chapter 2). The design day is the hypothetical day that the facility, attraction, or service was designed to handle comfortably, but not too comfortably. Planners set the design-day capacity to handle a predetermined amount of demand without compromising guest satisfaction. If demand is less than the design-day capacity, then guests are happy but the facility is underutilized. If demand exceeds the design-day capacity, then some guests will probably be unhappy. Planners know that waiting lines may form on design days, but they should not become so long that guests perceive a decline in the quality or value of their experience.

Benchmark organizations know just how long the lines can be and still remain within limits acceptable to guests. Some, like restaurants, even know how long a wait can be in each phase of the experience before guests become dissatisfied.[3] Others, such as a major theme park with a network of rides and events, may use a fifteen-minute average wait as a criterion across the entire park experience. On the design day, the park doesn't want anyone to wait longer than this average time in any queue because guest surveys have shown that the quality and value of the experience decline sharply beyond this time length. Because fifteen minutes is an average, it may take much longer for guests to get on a popular ride. However, based on the accumulated data, a fifteen-minute average may be the best balance between having too much capacity and not enough. A truly guest-focused theme park may set its design day at a very high level, say 80 to 90 percent—meaning that supply will be adequate for demand on 80 to 90 percent of the days of the year—because it appreciates the fact that most guests have traveled a long way, have limited vacation time, and have no choice but to wait once inside the park. To provide a guest experience with as little waiting as possible, the planners will set the design-day percentile high and build more capacity than might otherwise be practical. The cost of an unhappy guest to a major theme park that relies on return guest visits must be carefully balanced against the costs of building capacity.

The Capacity Day

Design days are the times when capacity is the best trade-off for both the guest and the facility—not ideal for either one, but satisfactory. Many organizational planners also calculate and use a **capacity day**, the maximum number of customers allowed in the facility in a day or at one time. This number is often set by the fire marshal based on the number of square feet each customer must have available. The capacity day may be set by the organization itself, to represent a point beyond which overall customer dissatisfaction with crowds, lines, or delays in service is unacceptable. Hospitality organizations know that guests disappointed because they did not have the guest experience at all are preferable to dissatisfied, angry ones who did.

QUEUING THEORY: MANAGING THE REALITY OF THE WAIT

Few organizations in any industry have the luxury of adjusting capacity quickly or managing demand by getting customers to show up when the organization wants them to, instead of when customers want to come. Most hospitality organizations must, therefore, rely on predicting and managing the inevitable waiting lines that are created when customers arrive looking for service.

The general problem for planners is that adding capacity costs money, such as by hiring more servers, but reduces the wait, which improves guest-experience quality, guest satisfaction, and guest loyalty. Reducing capacity saves money but increases the wait, which decreases guest-experience quality, guest satisfaction, and guest loyalty. How is the hospitality organization to find the proper cost-benefit balance?

The place to begin is in the use of **queuing theory**, sometimes called **waiting-line theory**, and the mathematical solutions that this technique offers. A typical queuing-theory problem facing an organizational planner might be: If an average of forty cars arrive per hour at a drive-thru window with a single server, and if the server takes an average of two minutes to fill an order, how long does the average car spend in line? During an average hour, how many minutes will the server be working and how many minutes idle? Most applications of waiting-line theory in the hospitality industry are based on the idea that people do not arrive in neat patterns. The typical approach is to sample the arrival and service patterns of guests and use this information to simulate the distribution that best matches the reality for the particular organization's guests. A restaurant might actually count all its guests over a period of time or sample them over a longer period using some appropriate sampling methodology and let the actual guest patterns represent the distribution of both arrival and service times.

Characteristics of Waiting Lines

All waiting lines have three characteristics that any model must include:

1. *Arrival Patterns: The Numbers of Guests Arriving and the Manner in Which They Enter the Waiting Line*. The arrivals could be random such as patrons to a restaurant, in bulk such as a busload of tourists, or in some other distribution that is difficult to describe, such as patients coming to a hospital emergency room in varying but not completely random intervals. Queue management is easiest when customer arrivals can be scheduled through reservations. Even if arrivals cannot be strictly scheduled, they may be controlled. Charging extra at peak times and offering discounts during the off-season would be examples of arrival-control strategies.

2. *Queue Discipline: How the Arriving Guests Are Served*. Options are first-come, first-served; last-come, first-served (not a formula for hospitality success), or some other set of service rules. For example, guests with reservations or wanting takeout food only may be served first, or restaurant parties of two may be served when a two-seat table is

available regardless of how many parties of three or more are in line ahead of them. Guests understand such a service rule.[4] They don't understand service rules that seem unfair to them or have no explanation. And, they really don't understand an implicit rule such as the following, which seems to be in effect at numerous service locations: "Answer a phone call from someone sitting at home before serving the customer or guest standing right in front of you who may have traveled miles to do business with you." The point is that a **queue discipline** must be obvious and familiar, or managers must find ways to carefully explain what the rules are and why they are fair.

The guests themselves can usually be counted on to maintain the discipline of the first-come, first-served queue. If someone breaks into the line in front of you, queue etiquette requires you to object and those in line behind you to support you. If the queue discipline in a certain grocery store line is first-come, first-served, no more than ten items, customers count each other's items and may forcefully object to a number over ten.

3. *Time for Service: How Long It Takes to Serve Guests.* The time boundaries of some service experiences can be carefully planned, like a flight from Boston to Atlanta, or a ride on a roller coaster car. But customers in most service settings vary, voluntarily or involuntarily, in the time it takes them to receive the service. Some diners want to eat and run; others wish to savor the meal. Likewise, some hospital emergency-room patients suffer from severe injuries while others have trivial problems. The amount of time it takes to serve the different customers can be as unpredictable as the people themselves. If the waiting-line model is to be an aid in managing the line, planners must take this variation into account. Although the previous examples involve people, waiting-line theory can be applied to anything that waits in line for something to happen to it. An automobile waiting in a fully automated painting line or a meal waiting to be served is as queued up and in need of managing as the newly arriving guest at the hotel front desk.

Line Types

Organizational planners must decide what line types will best meet customer needs and expectations. In the following discussion, "channel" refers to a *server*, and "phase" refers to a *step* in the service experience once it is underway.

Single-Channel, Single-Phase Queue

The basic line type is the **single-channel, single-phase queue**—one server, one step. This queue type is represented at the top in Figure 11-1. Mary Blaine has a one-chair hair salon. Customers come in, wait their turn, and have their hair cut in the single service phase. Indoor customers at some quick-serve restaurants stand in any one of several single-channel, single-phase queues. The customer looks the lines over, chooses one, stands in it waiting for service, and eventually reaches the counter to begin the single service phase. In that phase, the counter person takes the order, assembles and delivers it, and collects the money. Highway toll plazas and McDonald's counters are not the sites of multi-channel queues, even though they may have multiple servers. They consist of a group of single-channel, single-phase queues, with one server per queue.

Single-Channel, Multi-Phase Queue

The second queue type in the figure is the **single-channel, multi-phase queue**, such as a cafeteria line or the drive-thru at a limited-menu, quick-serve facility. Essentially, it is two or more single-channel, single-phase queues in sequence. The guest waits in one queue for

FIGURE 11-1 Some Basic Queue Types

© Cengage Learning 2012

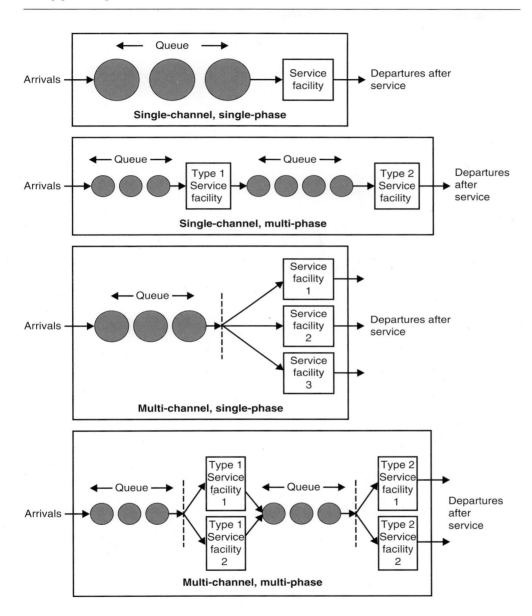

service from a single server, and then moves on to wait in another queue for another phase of service from another single server. At a typical drive-thru restaurant, customers queue up for the first phase. Each customer drives up to the order microphone, tries to understand what the person (the server, the single channel providing the first phase of service) inside the restaurant is saying, places an order (end of first phase) and then queues up again waiting to move forward to the window to receive and pay for the order (second phase, meaning another single channel for service with a single server). In this guest experience, the customer interacts with the organization twice, at two different places.

A drive-thru is a typical example of a single-channel, multi-phase queue.

Image copyright Ministr-84, 2010. Used under license from Shutterstock.com

Multi-Channel, Single-Phase Queue

A third type of queue is the **multi-channel, single-phase queue**. The customer begins in a single line that then feeds into multiple channels or stations for the service, each staffed by a server. The customer waits to get to the front of the single line, and then goes to the next available channel (server) for service. An example would be a bank or airport waiting line where everyone stands in a single queue, often snake-shaped to fit into available space, waiting for an open channel to any one of multiple servers. The queue discipline is to call the next person in the line to the next available teller, airline-counter attendant, telephone operator, or career counselor, who renders a single service in a single phase. The Federal Personnel Office uses this method for incoming telephone calls. The automated system tells each caller how many callers are ahead, so the caller can decide whether to wait or call back later. The single phase of service is to have a phone call answered. The multiple channels for obtaining this service are the many operators handling calls. The queue is managed by having the next available operator handle the next caller waiting in line. Many hospitality organizations find this method the most efficient way to manage their lines as it accounts well for the varying lengths of time that it takes to serve different customers. Everyone has had the experience of choosing to stand in one of several available single-channel lines—at the movie-theater refreshment stand, for example, or the hotel front desk—then watching all the other lines move much more quickly. The use of a multi-channel, single-phase system eliminates this feeling of unfairness or bad luck; everyone starts out in the same line. From the guest's perspective, the multi-channel, single-phase line feels faster as it moves people quickly to the multiple servers.[5]

Multi-Channel, Multi-Phase Queue

The last type of waiting line shown in Figure 11-1 is the most complicated to manage: the **multi-channel, multi-phase queue** system. Essentially, it is two or more multi-channel, single-phase queues in sequence. The guest waits to get to the front of one line, then goes to the next available server. After receiving the first phase of service, the guest then gets in another line, waits to arrive at the front, then goes to the next

Lines to check in at an airport are typically multi-channel, single-phase queues.

available server/channel to receive the next phase of service. Most airports use this queue type for security screening where the line for the first phase checks passenger documents and the second screens people and carry-ons. The Pepper Market, a cafeteria in Orlando's Coronado Springs Hotel, uses this pattern between its single-channel entry and exit points. At the entry point, the guest lines up to receive a "charge card" to be used at the different food stations. The guest then sees lines leading to each of several entrées and takes a place at the end of, say, the seafood line. The guest waits to become first in line, then goes to the next available seafood entrée server. The guest follows the same procedure for bread, dessert, vegetable, and so forth. The guest then gets in a checkout line and turns the charge card in to a cashier, who totals up all the purchases.

A hospitality organization will often have numerous queues linked in various combinations. For example, a restaurant will have a line for people waiting to be seated, a wait time while the server serves other customers in a queue ahead of you before taking your order, a line of orders queued up for processing by the cook, a queue of servers waiting while the food is being prepared, and a line of people at the checkout. To consider just the line of people waiting to be seated, it is a multi-channel, single-phase queue, if the restaurant tables are considered to be channels and being seated is considered to be a phase. Managing the wait times associated with single and multiple channels and phases is difficult, but it is critical for ensuring excellent guest service and minimizing service failures.

Virtual Queues

A final type of queue that is becoming increasingly popular is the **virtual queue** or the line that isn't visible. Most people don't like to stand in line, and the virtual queue enables them to avoid doing so. This type of queue, based on the idea underlying Disney's FASTPASS™,[6] was first introduced at Walt Disney World Resort in 1998 in response to a need to better manage waiting times to allow more efficient time use for guests and more efficient capacity use by the company. Disney found that guests using this virtual queue system spent significantly less time in lines, spent more per capita, saw significantly more attractions, and as a result had significantly higher overall levels of satisfaction. After a series of initial tests and refinements FASTPASS™ was expanded to all Disney Parks worldwide and is now used by millions of guests annually.

This virtual queue system is quite different from the waiting-line experience of most guests. When guests approach a FASTPASS™ attraction, they are instructed to insert their park admission ticket into a specially designated FASTPASS™ turnstile to enter a virtual queue in the computer. Based upon how many guests are in front of the ones who are just joining the virtual queue and the current flow of guests at the attraction, the computer estimates how long it will take for the newly arriving guest's space in the virtual queue to get to the front of the line. This estimated time is automatically printed out on each guest's FASTPASS™ ticket and is the designated time to return and gain immediate entry into the attraction with no wait. Customers can let the computer hold their space in the virtual line while they visit other attractions, eat, shop, or whatever they may want to do throughout the park before returning at any time within an assigned sixty-minute window. This sixty-minute flexibility was created to ensure that guests have the opportunity to engage in other activities during the wait time without worrying that they might be late for a specific entry time. They know that if they arrive back at the attraction within the sixty-minute window, they can walk right in.

A key point in making the FASTPASS™ system work is that guests always have a choice between a FASTPASS™ virtual line and the actual "stand by" line. It turns out that most of the guests in the standby line are people who are currently holding a FASTPASS™ ticket for another attraction and are using that time to experience a second attraction by standing in line for it. Since seeing attractions is a key driver for guest satisfaction, these guests are usually very satisfied, because they are able to see two attractions during the time they would have previously only been able to see one.

The FASTPASS™ system at Walt Disney World is a practical application of a virtual queue.

In addition to the primary benefits already described, the innovation of the FASTPASS™ virtual queue system provides many secondary benefits. During peak days, many guests previously waited in line as many as three to four hours in a day for the most popular attractions. The use of FASTPASS™ resulted in guests seeing more attractions during the day as well as greatly increased the utilization of the other secondary attractions in the park, which previously had little or no wait times. Another secondary benefit was that guests also used some of the time "freed up" from lines to engage in other revenue-producing activities, such as dining and shopping, without taking time away from visiting other attractions. Lower perceived wait times have led to higher customer satisfaction levels, and at the same time, Disney officials have seen increased revenues on food and merchandise per person in the parks.[7] Helping people to avoid standing in line benefits both Disney and its guests.

The virtual-queue concept has many potential applications in hospitality. Cruise ships and resorts are similar to theme parks in that guests have many activities from which to choose, so virtual queues could be used in the same way. Restaurants that hand out paging devices to indicate to guests when capacity is available can keep queued-up guests from having to stand in actual lines. These guests can spend time (and money) in nearby retail shopping or bar areas. Any free-standing attraction that experiences long lines for admission and entry is also a potential site for creating a virtual queue.

Which Queue to Use?

Guest preferences drive planners' decisions about queue types at the best organizations. McDonald's believes that using multiple single-channel, single-phase lines meets customer desires for quick service. Wendy's, Burger King, and most other quick-serve restaurants have a different opinion: They use the single-channel, multi-phase queue, with customers placing an order with a server at one location and moving to another server to pick it up. At some other quick-serve restaurants and many airline counters, all customers get into one line, often a "serpentine" line that snakes between posts and velvet ropes. Once customers reach the head of the line, they wait to enter whichever channel leads to the next available server or attendant. These different queue choices by company planners are based on their studies of what guests want in particular situations.

Common sense suggests that the best queue type for an organization to use is the one that guests perceive as enabling them to begin receiving service as quickly as possible. The guest-focused planner knows that the best line type is the one that customers prefer, and that may not be the type suggested by common sense. For example, guests may prefer to stand in a certain type of line because they think they will be served faster, even if they won't.

Anat Rafaeli and her colleagues suggest that planners need to consider at least four factors when choosing a queue type for a given situation.[8] Planners should select the queue that best provides customers with all the following:

1. A sense of progress toward their goal or service experience.
2. A sense of control over what is happening.
3. Activity.
4. A sense of fairness with how their wait was managed.

People generally seem to prefer the single serpentine queue—with several channels at the end of it, each leading to a server—even though the length of the single line can be intimidating. They don't have to think or worry about which line to choose, whether to

Virtual queues offer a means for guests to avoid long lines, like this one, and instead go on other rides while still "waiting their turn" at the original ride.

Image copyright jpskenn, 2010. Used under license from Shutterstock.com

change lines if the present line seems slow or another line seems to have gotten shorter, or whether someone joining the next line over will be unfairly served more quickly.

In short, while a single serpentine line may yield the same average wait as multiple lines, the variance in wait times is much smaller. With multiple lines, you have the chance to get through much quicker than customers in other lines, but you also run the risk of being much slower. The serpentine line guarantees first-come, first-served. It is also becoming more widely adopted—at hotels, banks, by Wendy's and Burger King, BestBuy, and many others. McDonald's, Wal-Mart, Target, and most grocery stores continue to employ multiple lines.

Line Simulation: A Gift Shop

While planners can use a statistical distribution to describe the arrival and service patterns of many standard queues, in some situations only a simulation will yield the quality of data necessary to explain and predict the reality of a particular queue. Here is how a simulation might work.

The Christmas Tree is an extremely successful Christmas-themed restaurant; their slogan, "Make every day like Christmas!" appeals to young and old. Because Christmas-related items are available in regular stores only during Christmas season, Rudolph's Gift Shop attached to the Christmas Tree does a huge business during the rest of the year. In fact, many customers shop at Rudolph's rather than dine at the Christmas Tree.

Rudolph's has twenty checkout counters, which if fully staffed would require two people at each, for a total of forty people. If on an average day only fifty customers are typically in the shop at any one time, then full staffing of the checkout counters would be an obvious waste of money because the probability of all fifty people moving to the checkout lines at the same time is extremely small. But, if Rudolph's opens only one checkout counter, a long line will soon form. Planners must decide what staffing level best balances the cost of staffing Rudolph's checkouts against the cost of lost customers who vow never to return because of the long lines or lost sales as customers abandon their carts full of Christmas items and walk out. How might planners help the shop manager to make this decision?

Observing the Flow

Over several weeks the shop manager can observe the flow of customers and time how long they are in the shop. If sufficient observations are made, the shop manager can create distributions that accurately describe customer arrival patterns, the quantity of items that they bring to the checkout stand, and their time spent in Rudolph's shopping for those items. With this information the manager can then simulate the shopping experiences of Rudolph's customers to determine how to staff the checkout counters appropriately at different times and on different days of the week. Here is how that might be done.

Allocation Wheels

In her office, the manager could set up the two roulette type wheels as shown in Figure 11-2. Spaces are allocated on the first wheel to represent, in percentage form, the time between customer arrivals at the checkout counters. From the observations already made, the shop knows that for 15 percent of their observations, the time between arrivals at checkout was zero minutes; people arrived simultaneously. For 20 percent the time between arrivals was one minute; for 25 percent, the time was two minutes; for 10 percent the time was three minutes. For another 10 percent, the time was four minutes; for 12 percent, five minutes; and for 8 percent, six minutes. The wheel has spaces reflecting the likelihood of each arrival time. To simulate the arrival patterns of the customers at checkout, the manager would merely spin the wheel and write on a chart the arrival interval noted in the section of the wheel when it stopped.

The second wheel in Figure 11-2 is, in similar fashion, portioned off to represent the observations about how long the customers took to go through the checkout process. This total would include the time to scan the purchased items, write the checks or pay cash, and wrap or bag the purchases. Since people vary in both quantity of purchases and speed of writing checks or making payment, the time for service and the proportions on the wheel representing those times would likewise vary. The observations might reveal

FIGURE **11-2** Wheels Representing Time Between Arrivals and Time for Service at Checkout

© Cengage Learning 2012

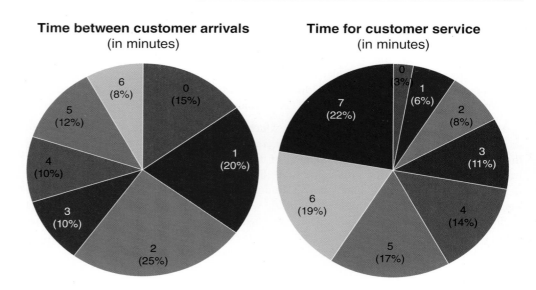

that customers were served with no wait three percent of the time, had a one-minute wait six percent of the time, a two-minute wait eight percent of the time, a three-minute wait 11% of the time, a four-minute wait 14% of the time, a five-minute wait 17% of the time, a six-minute wait 19% of the time, and a seven-minute wait 22% of the time.

Now the manager can execute the simulation by spinning the first wheel to randomly determine the time between customer arrivals and spinning the second wheel to determine how long each guest took to be served once in a checkout line. By recording the numbers on a simple chart that notes the time between arrivals, times for service and, finally, the time customers were waiting, the entire day's activities can be simulated to determine the maximum, minimum, and average length of time customers waited for service plus the total waiting time for all the customers. The chart would simulate a day's activities by beginning when the shop opens and recording the arrivals throughout the day until it closes. Running this simulation many times (typically more than 1000 on a computerized model) would allow Rudolph's manager and planning staff to draw some statistical conclusions about the length of waiting time, checkout capacity utilization, and the impact on waiting (and guest perception of the quality and value of the experience) that opening up more checkout stands and adding more capacity would have.

Although this is a fairly simple illustration and in all likelihood the entire simulation would be conducted on a computer, it does show the usefulness of mathematically determining the relationship between the service provider's capacity and the average waiting time for guests in a way that allows the hospitality organization to find the ideal balance between the two. This same technique can be used to determine the ideal number of monorails in a theme park, toll booths on a turnpike, front desk people in a hotel, servers and cooks in a restaurant, spaces in a parking lot, ski lifts on a ski slope, or any other application where an organization needs to balance the costs of providing capacity with the quality of the service experience.

Certain basic forces affect waiting lines, and they can be expressed mathematically. An explanation of the mathematics of waiting lines appears in the chapter appendix.

Balancing Capacity and Demand

Determining the proper balance between supply and demand requires more calculations than just the basics. The gift shop planners in the earlier example should gather more data about customer behaviors and expectations. If, for example, they find in interviewing or by simply observing customers that when the wait is longer than five minutes they will put down their selections and leave the shop without buying anything, then a wait longer than five minutes is unacceptable no matter what the remaining data might reveal. On the other hand, if the surveyed customers reveal that the uniqueness of the shop or the nature of the clientele makes waiting time an insignificant issue, then planners might recommend letting the lines grow without much adjustment. The essential feature of the calculation is to determine that point beyond which the length of the wait damages the quality of the guest experience beyond the level acceptable to the guest and the organization.

Once the capacity-and-demand balance decision has been made, planners must determine how to accommodate the inevitable lines created by uneven demand patterns. Here the challenge is to plan and manage the wait in such a way that the guest is satisfied with it. Two major dimensions are involved. The first is the way the time spent waiting *feels* to the guest, and the second dimension is how to minimize the negative effects of the wait by managing the *value* of the experience to the guest. The organization wants each guest to conclude that the experience was well worth the wait.

MANAGING THE PERCEPTION OF THE WAIT

Understanding what makes time fly while guests wait in line is a fundamental concern for planners seeking to improve the quality of the wait. Guestologists have found that time flies not only when they're having fun but also under other circumstances. Hospitality planners must remember that everyone is different, and these differences will influence how people feel about waiting in line. How customers feel about the wait is at least as important as how long the wait is.

1. *Occupied Time Feels Shorter Than Unoccupied Time*. If you are busy doing something while you are waiting, the time seems to go by faster. Most line waits can be made more enjoyable and made to feel less lengthy if guests can be distracted or diverted in some way.

   Disney planners are the masters of managing time waits by giving their guests something to divert them from thinking about the wait. If the line for a particular Walt Disney World Resort attraction has become extraordinarily long and a service failure is imminent, a strolling band or acrobats or some other distraction arrives to entertain and occupy the guests while they wait. For long lines, Universal Orlando Resort spaces television sets throughout the time which show a video or movie. People can watch an interesting program while moving toward the entrance to the attraction.

2. *Time Spent Waiting to Begin the Service Experience Will Feel Longer Than Time Actually Spent in the Experience Itself*. Hospitality planners, therefore, try to find ways to minimize how long the wait "feels." Theme parks and other entertainment

attractions may offer pre-attraction features, termed the *preshow*. Preshows make guests feel that they are already in the attraction, though they are mainly still standing in line. For example, people standing in line to get into the Walt Disney's Enchanted Tiki Room Under New Management hear a caged Audio-Animatronics bird telling bad jokes. Time seems to pass more quickly for guests when they are watching a preshow or a preview of the main attraction—almost as if the attraction itself has started.

Some airlines send roving people down long lines waiting to check in, to begin the contact with people and make them feel that someone is finally taking care of them. Avis Rental Car quickly gathers up people at the airport terminal contact point and shuttles them to an off-site facility where the line may be quite long and the wait substantial, but customers feel that Avis is at least doing something to take care of them. This strategy has the additional benefit of getting customers away from competing rental counters. Out at the off-site facility, they will wait longer in line because they cannot simply move to the competitor at the next counter.

Another way to make guests feel as if the experience has begun before it actually does is to use this "pre-experience" time to teach customers what they are supposed to do once they reach the actual event or attraction. The education provided during the wait can improve or enhance the service experience and actually becomes part of the experience. Many customers waiting in a fast-food line use their time to evaluate the menu items to select what they want. If they could walk right up to the counter, they would still need the time to review the menu options; they would then feel awkward about being at the front of a forming line unprepared to be served. For these customers having time to stand in a line is an advantage.

Many restaurants give patrons standing in line a menu to look over while awaiting their table. This gives customers something to do and not only speeds up the ordering process once customers are seated but also gives them the impression that the service experience has begun. Providing a complimentary beverage or snack if the wait is unusually long accomplishes the same purpose. Having a cocktail waitress serve waiting guests generally achieves the same goal and creates an additional revenue source.

3. *Anxious Waits Feel Longer Than More Relaxed Waits.* If people are afraid of what will happen to them once the service experience begins, the wait will seem longer. If people are sitting in an airplane that is obviously waiting for something to be fixed before it takes off, people may become quite anxious about what is wrong with the plane or what malfunction is holding it up, and the wait will feel long. If you are waiting in a hospital room, perhaps to receive the results of a diagnostic procedure, the wait will seem to drag. Sometimes, organizations want to create a little anxiety. The school principal may let the ill-behaved child waiting for punishment wait a little longer than necessary. Waiting to enter a scary ride at an amusement park can enhance the effect of the ride.

4. *Waits of Uncertain Length Feel Longer Than Certain Ones.* Anyone who has been at an airport waiting on a flight that is delayed for an unknown reason will know that such a wait feels endless. Waiting without knowing when the delay will be over causes any wait to feel much longer. Let your guests know what to expect. A time estimate can help the customer set a mental clock to let time pass more quickly until that preset time is reached. Telling phone callers how many callers are ahead of them in the phone queue serves the same purpose.

Norwegian Cruise Lines uses TV monitors throughout their ships to provide information on how full their various restaurants are. These "Restaurant Seating Guides" let guests know in real time how full each dining venue currently is, so they can decide which restaurant to go to with full knowledge of how long the wait, if any, will be.

Disney uses sign boards to tell guests how long before they will enter the attraction from that point in line. Generally, they overestimate the time because guests are always happy when they get to the ride faster than they thought they would but are never happy when they get there later. This is one reason patients want doctors to be on time for scheduled appointments. Once the appointment time is reached, in the patient's mind it is time to be served, and any time spent after that is uncertain and long.

5. *Unexplained Waits Feel Longer Than Explained Waits*. When you don't know what is holding up the line or causing the delay, the wait will feel longer than if you know the reason. If traffic stops and your view ahead is blocked so you can't see why, the wait will feel longer. If service is delayed, customers want to know why. Effective managers of waits will tell them or provide a visual cue that can explain the wait.

For example, a line at a restaurant can be structured so customers can see that all the tables are full, or at a bank so one can see that all the tellers are busy. On the other hand, effective managers of queues will ensure that front desk attendants or airline check-in staff doing something other than attending to waiting customers are kept out of sight of customers, so that they do not have to explain why their personnel are not serving customers. Restaurant managers try to keep empty tables out of sight; otherwise people queued up for a meal will think their wait does not have a legitimate explanation, and it will feel long. Restaurant guests do not buy the explanation, "That section is closed."

One author describes an airline experience that is familiar to many travelers.[9] He boarded a plane in San Francisco heading for Chicago. A broken toilet delayed the departure. The pilot and crew made an announcement about the problem and said that the flight would leave as soon as it was fixed. The pilot and crew gave frequent updates to the passengers and told them that the pilot was seeking permission to leave without one toilet operating. Every twenty minutes the author-passenger received a text message on his cell phone updating the departure time. After an hour of unsuccessful effort to repair the toilet, the pilot announced that he had decided the plane would not fly with only one toilet working. Instead, he told the passengers that they would have to disembark and leave later on another plane. Despite the uncertainty and annoyance over the broken fixture, the passengers were calm and understanding. The writer's seatmate said he found it reassuring that the captain himself had made the final announcement and explained his reasoning.

If this was the end of this story, it would be an excellent illustration of the value of explaining waits to customers, but the author went on to describe the chaos, anger, and frustration that occurred to these same passengers once they were back inside the terminal where no one would tell them anything and no one seemed to know what to do next. The contrast between the attitudes and reactions of guests who know why the wait is occurring and those who are uninformed is striking and serves as an important lesson to practitioners of guestology: Keep your guests informed as to why a wait is happening and what this means to them.

6. *Unfair Waits Feel Longer Than Fair Ones*. If customers feel that the queue discipline is consistently followed and fairly used, then the wait seems shorter than it does when people are allowed to get away with cutting in line, or people are served out of the apparent sequence of service order, violating the perceived queue discipline. Good organizations recognize this truth and manage their lines with this knowledge in mind. At times, VIP guests or some other special category of guest requires that the line discipline be broken. Airlines usually have a separate line for customers paying for first-class tickets. Passengers flying coach usually don't object to that special treatment since they know that the first-class passengers are paying for it. For VIPs, sometimes

the layout of waiting lines into twisting maze patterns enables VIPs to be integrated into the line flow so smoothly that those waiting do not usually notice that the discipline has been interrupted. But if they do notice, the airline personnel had better be prepared to hear about it.

When an organization needs to break the queue discipline, it must find some way to communicate a reason for the apparent unfairness that customers will accept after hearing it. Time-honored reasons are "Lady with a baby!" and "Women and children first!" Passengers needing assistance go onto planes first, and nobody minds. No one complains if a disabled person goes to the front of the line. Seating a party of four at a restaurant before seating waiting parties of six or more seldom creates guest complaints or problems for the restaurant; everyone knows that almost all tables are set up for smaller parties and that some juggling must be done to accommodate the larger group.

7. *Solo Waits Feel Longer Than Group Waits*. Waiting by yourself feels longer than waiting in a group of friends, or even in a group you don't know. Planners recognizing this perceptual issue try to organize their lines in such a way that people are grouped with other people. Under this logic, a double line would feel shorter than a single line, and a line structure that encourages people to interact so they feel like members of a group feels shorter than one in which the people are allowed to stay inside their own personal and highly individual spaces. Planners can arrange the seating in waiting room areas so as to promote interaction and a sense of being part of a group.

8. *Uncomfortable Waits Feel Longer Than Comfortable Ones*. All hospitality organizations dread seeing guests queued up in the hot sun, rain, or other uncomfortable conditions. Finding a way to keep people comfortable in outdoor queues while they wait to enter an air-conditioned environment is a real managerial challenge. Obviously, such devices as paddle fans, awnings, or artificially created shade can be useful for making the wait feel more comfortable and less lengthy.

9. *Interesting Waits Are Shorter Than Uninteresting Ones*. We have already said that occupied waits are shorter than unoccupied waits. This principle is true even if the activity in which one is occupied is only "busy work." But if you are occupied in doing something interesting while you wait, the time will seem even shorter. Bank of America found that when they provided television monitors in the bank lobby, customer perceptions of wait times decreased significantly.[10] Restaurants frequently have a bar with entertainment so that guests waiting for a table can have a drink and listen to some music. The time seems to pass more quickly that way.

10. *Happy Waits Are Shorter Than Sad Ones*. While this goes without saying in most situations, it is part of the perception of the waiting experience. Customers who are having fun, enjoying themselves, and feeling positive about the wait itself and the service experience to come will find the wait to be shorter than those who are unhappy, sullen, or feeling negative about waiting. Planners need to think of ways to keep happy customers happy and make unhappy customers feel better about waiting. Using clowns is one way to turn unhappy children into happy ones. Professional comics warm up their audiences; the comics get them laughing during the wait, to make sure that when the television cameras come on, the guests are ready to have fun and laugh.

The Emotional Wait State

In all these waiting situations and especially the last one, the customer's emotional state will significantly impact the wait for service. Different people react differently to anxiety, uncertainty, discomfort, and other perceptual influences on the waiting time. Planners should keep these different reactions in mind as they structure organizational queues.

Image copyright Karin Hildebrand Lau, 2010. Used under license from Shutterstock.com

Waiting in line can be frustrating and boring. Organizations need to manage the wait to avoid losing customer satisfaction.

Crowds and Clientele

If the waiting line to be managed is large and diverse, then the "typical customer" drives the design of the line and the associated wait. While planners should consider individual differences as much as possible in designing and managing waits, the line for large crowds must be designed to accommodate what the average guest expects when entering the wait process.

If the people in line are a more select clientele with identifiable features, such as a queue at an upscale restaurant or hotel, then variability in treatment of the waiting guests may be possible and even necessary to ensure that the quality of the entire experience, including the wait, meets the guest expectations for that upscale level of service. You want to make the wait enjoyable or at least less irritating, and that is harder to do with a mass-market audience than with a select, known clientele, for reasons other than the size of the crowd.

Waits in Contrast

In all these waiting situations, the contrast effect will also influence the perception of the wait. If a customer has just had a comfortable, totally explained, predictable wait, followed by a subsequent wait that is unpredictable, anxiety producing, and of uncertain length, the second wait will seem longer than if a well-managed wait had not just occurred. Similarly, if a customer has just had a long wait, a short one will feel even shorter in contrast. If the guest has just been waiting where employees were friendly and all servers were busy, that wait will seem shorter than a wait in which employees pay minimal attention to guests and some are engaged in activities other than serving people in line.

The key for planners is to remember that the customer, client, or guest perceives the wait. If the objective data say the average wait at your place should be acceptable to customers or the wait at your company is actually shorter than it is at a competitor's, that doesn't matter to customers who think they have waited too long for your service. Customers have mental clocks in their minds that tell them when the wait is too long or just right and extremely well managed. Managing the perception is as effective a technique as managing the actual waiting time, and if the organization is particularly good at managing perceptions, it can make even very long waits acceptable and tolerable to customers.

SERVICE VALUE AND THE WAIT

The more value the customer receives or expects to receive from the service, the more patiently the customer will wait. Since the customer defines the value of services rendered, the second major strategy for managing the perception of the wait is to manage the perceived value of the service for which the customer is waiting. This strategy can be implemented before, during, or even after the service is delivered.

Before Service

Before receiving the service, waiting customers can be provided with information (or even with some other service) that will enhance the value of the service that motivated them to enter the queue in the first place. A hotel, for example, can enhance the perceived value of the guest experience by offering guests waiting in line some sparkling water or champagne, or they may be entertained by a chamber-music group. Such thoughtful touches not only distract and occupy the guest, they also add value to the experiences that the hotel and restaurant are selling (and for which the guest must wait in line).

During Service

During the performance of the service itself, its value (to the customer and as defined by the customer) can be enhanced over the customer's expectations by many strategies. The organization will want to employ these strategies in any event, but the idea here is that if the service meets or exceeds expectations when the customer gets it, the wait was worth it.

In addition to providing customers with a service that is beyond their expectations in the first place, some more subtle actions can enhance the value of the service experience or increase the perceived cost of abandoning the wait. Some restaurants believe in hanging signed photographs of celebrities who have eaten in the restaurant; doctors display diplomas from their medical schools to indicate the high quality of their training. These touches tend to encourage the guest or patient to think that the meal or the medical treatment is worth the wait. As a more direct response to the wait, the server could apologize for it, which adds a personal touch that may increase the value of the experience for the guest. Hops Restaurant pursues a philosophy of "whatever-it-takes service," which also applies to those waiting for tables. As part of their strategy for "Lobby Comfort," guests are provided with samples from the menu while waiting for a table.[11] These are all examples of how the value of the service to the customer can be enhanced even as it is being delivered. These enhancements all make the wait seem shorter in retrospect; an excellent service experience diminishes the ill effects of the wait.

After Service

After the service, the value of the experience in the eyes of customers can sometimes be enhanced, so they feel better about having taken the time to wait on the service in the first place. Although advertising is generally used to attract the attention of potential customers, people who have already purchased services are even more attentive to ads than those who have not. The ads reinforce the wisdom of purchasing the service as well as waiting in line to do so. Of course, ads seen ahead of time can also reduce the effects of the wait while it is in progress; the ads have convinced customers that the experience will be good, so they wait more patiently. A phone call to a customer after the service experience, asking for feedback on it, can enhance the value of the experience and reduce the negative effects of the wait. Once Honda dealers started calling up customers after they left the dealership to ask about the quality of the service experiences, to remain competitive other dealers had to make the calls, too. This type of personal attention after the experience can help compensate for the wait before the experience.

Managing Waits in an Imperfect World

Planning and managing the waiting line are fundamental challenges for managers in the hospitality industry. The service cannot be stockpiled or inventoried, and planners must find the right balance between having enough capacity to fill demand and having so much capacity that some sits idle most of the time. In a perfect world, the flow of customers matches the supply exactly. When one guest leaves the restaurant, another walks in for lunch. When one guest finishes with the concierge, another arrives to ask a question, and so on across the entire range of services offered by organizations. In our less-than-perfect world, getting customers into the service setting and meeting their time expectations require effective queue planning and management. The critical point is to make it visibly clear to guests by everything that everyone in the organization does and says that they respect their customers' time, appreciate their tolerance of any waits, and that the company is doing everything it can to make waits fair, fast, comfortable, and as enjoyable as possible.

---

1. Plan for and manage the guest waits across their entire experience; don't just let them happen.

2. Know how long or whether your guests are willing to wait.

3. Know the arrival rates, queue discipline, and service rates for each wait and use the knowledge to calculate the length of each.

4. Make design-day decisions that best balance the costs of providing capacity with the costs of guest dissatisfaction from waits.

5. Design queues to best meet guest expectations.

6. Know the psychology of managing waiting lines.

7. Use waiting-line models to understand how your queues work.

8. Try to minimize the negative effects of the wait before, during, and after the guest experience.

9. Use virtual waits whenever possible.

10. Find out how much a dissatisfied guest costs you; that will motivate you to manage the wait for your guests more carefully.

LESSONS LEARNED

REVIEW QUESTIONS

1. "Just about every full-fledged guest experience has at least one wait somewhere within it." True or false?

   A. If false, name some guest experiences that do not involve a wait.

   B. Indicate some common front-of-the-house waits (as opposed to out-of-sight waits such as queued-up food orders) during a typical guest's experience at a casual restaurant such as Chili's, Olive Garden, or Red Lobster. Which ones should be managed, and which ones can be left alone to take care of themselves?

   C. Indicate some common back-of-the-house waits, unseen by the guest, during a typical guest's experience at such a casual restaurant. Which ones should be managed, and which ones can be left alone to take care of themselves?

2. Think of a pleasant or an enjoyable wait you have experienced within a hospitality setting. Think of an unpleasant or annoying wait.

   A. What strategies described in this chapter did the organization's managers use or fail to use that caused your wait to be one kind or the other?

   B. Did the managers employ any strategies not covered in the chapter?

3. What strategies are available to match the capacity of a hospitality organization with the demand for its services? Which strategies work best and under what circumstances?

4. This chapter explained how a theme park might use the design-day concept.

   A. How might the concept be used by a hotel, a restaurant, and an airline?

   B. Is the concept as applicable to those other organizations as to a theme park?

   C. If so, what are the common elements that facilitate applicability? If not, why is that?

5. Give some examples from your own experience of the different queue types shown in Figure 11-1. Did the queue type used seem to fit the situation? Was it readily apparent why the organization chose it? If you have to wait, which line type do you prefer and why?

6. You are the front desk manager of a popular hotel, and you are frustrated by the number of guests you see waiting impatiently in line to check in and check out. Compare the advantages and disadvantages (and the costs and benefits, if you can) of relieving this situation by considering the following alternatives.

   A. Set up and use simulation wheels like those in Figure 11-2.

   B. Use some of the techniques in the chapter for managing the feel of the wait.

   C. Cross-train some employees so they can help out at the front desk during busy times.

7. Some organizations, restaurants in particular, seem to take more interest in managing the wait in positive ways than others. How does an organization decide how much time and effort to place into managing the initial wait for service?

8. Although some academic people make a life's work out of queuing theory, many readers enjoy reading about the "psychological" methods for managing the wait more than they do studying "theory." Which is more important to manage the guest experience in hospitality organizations: the hard numbers of queuing theory or the softer psychological approach?

9. You may have heard someone say, or may have said yourself, "Whichever line I am in, the others always move faster." Can this be true?

1. Find a situation in which a hospitality organization has found a way to control or shift guest demand. Why does the organization employ this strategy? How effective is the strategy? What incentives are offered to guests to encourage them to seek the hospitality service at one time rather than another? How profitable do you think the strategy might be?

2. Study the waiting-line situations (movies, athletic events, fast-food outlets, etc.) in which you find yourself over a period of time. Evaluate how well the lines are being managed. Which line-management strategies described in this chapter might have been used to improve these situations?

Generally, people feel that "first come, first served" is fair and that people should not violate the order in a queue. But sometimes exceptions are made. When is it appropriate to make these exceptions? Imagine that you are managing a fine-dining restaurant, several patrons are waiting for tables, and you estimate roughly a forty-five-minute wait. When do you think is it appropriate to allow a newly arriving patron to bypass the line and be seated immediately?

- A Supreme Court justice shows up, and her security detail says that for security reasons, she cannot wait in the lobby, so she must either be seated immediately or will have to leave.
- A famous movie star arrives wanting a table.
- The owner of the company that supplies your alcohol arrives wanting a table.
- Your mother surprises you and comes by wanting a table.
- Your first-grade teacher is in line.
- You recognize one of the authors of this book in line waiting for a table.
- Someone shows up, at the right time, with a reservation.
- Someone shows up fifteen minutes late for a reservation.
- Someone shows up, thirty minutes late for a reservation.
- Someone shows up one hour late for a reservation.

What factors do you consider when making the decision to move someone to the head of the line? Why are some decisions "fair" and others "unfair"? Does a decision have to be fair for you to make the exception?

CASE STUDIES

The Front Desk

Jane Gianini, manager at the Thusly Manor, an upscale inn and golfing resort in the North Carolina mountains, was becoming increasingly concerned about the situation at the front desk. On several occasions during the past week, she walked by the desk and saw a line of waiting guests. Several other times she walked by and saw no guests at all.

The dramatic rise in personal income and tourism during the first part of the new millennium had caused a boom in the number of guests wanting to combine a stay in a fine hotel with some golfing on a beautiful hilly course. But success also brought problems for Thusly Manor, how to handle the increased numbers at the front desk among them. Gianini thought she had controlled the situation by implementing a new staffing procedure.

If her calculations were correct, the new procedure should have just about eliminated both the waiting lines and the front desk server down time. Nevertheless, she had seen guests lined up several times, and idle desk agents quite frequently.

When she first analyzed the data, she computed simple averages. To construct her present staffing schedule, she had found out how many guests arrived during each eight-hour shift on average and had divided that number by eight, to arrive at guest load per hour during a shift. She then staffed the front desk accordingly. She pulled the following data for the 8 A.M. to 4 P.M. shift from her files to check on whether she had analyzed it correctly when she had set up her present system.

Type of Service and Percent of Service Time Used

SERVICE TYPE	AVERAGE SERVICE TIME	PERCENT
I. Check-in/check-out	10 minutes	70%
II. Informational/misc. requests	5 minutes	30%

Frequency of Guest Arrivals at Front Desk

AVERAGE TIME BETWEEN ARRIVALS	PERCENT
0 minutes	30%
5 minutes	40%
10 minutes	20%
20 minutes	10%

1. What was wrong with Gianini's original analysis?

2. How should she have analyzed this problem?

Waiting for Gaudeaux

Grand Gaudeaux Cruise Lines specialized in taking passengers on luxury cruises to the Gaudeaux island chain in the Caribbean. Because of its financial success and good reputation in the industry, Grand Gaudeaux had recently been able to expand its passenger capacity by adding two brand-new, large ships to its fleet. The guest-satisfaction measurement team was meeting this morning with Steve Weitzman, CEO of Grand Gaudeaux, to discuss some surprising low guest-satisfaction ratings received from passengers on these two state-of-the-art ships. The company practice was to mail departing guests a survey about a week after their cruise, asking them a variety of questions. The recent data were troubling. Grand Gaudeaux had hoped to delight its guests by providing these new ships; instead, guests were reporting dissatisfaction.

The topic today was the dramatic downturn in the satisfaction scores. Knowing that this meeting was coming up and realizing the CEO's depth of concern, the measurement team had done some further investigation into guest opinions through a variety of means. The most interesting insight was gained from a series of focus groups in which guests from the newer, larger ships had indicated their frustration with the departure routine. It appeared that the larger the ship, the more difficult it was to get everyone ashore after the cruise ended. This long wait tended to give "cruisers" on the two newest ships an unsatisfactory last experience with Grand Gaudeaux Cruise Lines. Because of the "recency effect"—the psychological theory that the most recent events are best remembered and have greatest impact—the passenger problems in departing the ship were overshadowing the many excellent aspects of the cruise experience.

The team recognized some system solutions; for example, the port facility could be retrofitted with larger capacity to accommodate more departing passengers. Such a retrofit would involve significant expenditures. But even if the budget were available to make such improvements over the long run, the guest-satisfaction measurement team realized the acute need to improve the management of the passenger wait experience in the short run. The team knew of Weitzman's personal pride in and high hopes for the new ships. They knew he would want some answers as to what might be done to fix this source of guest dissatisfaction.

If you were on the guest-satisfaction measurement team, what steps would you recommend to Weitzman?

APPENDIX

THE MATHEMATICS OF WAITING LINES

The mathematics are quite simple for a single-channel, single-phase line. An understanding of a few calculations will reveal much about the dynamics of waiting lines.

In the following example, we will use a single-channel line for a hotel's front desk, with one server/agent at the desk. We will calculate the average amount of time that a guest stands in line and stands in the system (time in line plus time being served). In addition, we will determine the idle time of the front desk staff. These figures would be useful to a hotel manager wishing to control the waiting time for guests and to reduce the idle time for service personnel.[12]

These calculations for a single-channel, single-phase line, to illustrate the underlying principles of waiting-line management, can be done manually. However, more complicated line systems requiring more complex formulae should be (and can easily be) analyzed by computer. A standard spreadsheet products such as Excel can be used to perform such waiting-line analysis.

The Single-Channel, Single-Phase Case

The Chelten Hotel has a simple front desk with one service station. Ben Blake, the front-office manager, has been observing the line at the front desk for several weeks. Not wanting guests to wait in line too long, he wishes to calculate the average wait in line for his guests over a one-hour period. He also wants to know how much idle time his servers will have during that hour. Mr. Blake would like them to perform some routine tasks such as sort the mail and enter charges to guest accounts during their idle time.

Blake has compiled the following information for this one-hour period. For this example, we ignore variability and use averages to describe both arrival and service rates for the hotel guests:

The average time it takes to register a guest is four minutes; the hotel can register about fifteen guests per hour. This is the service rate, the units of server capacity per time period.

Ten guests are expected to arrive during the hour. This is the arrival rate.

The formulas use the following symbols:

$$A = \text{arrival rate per hour (10)}$$

$$r = \text{service rate per hour (15)}$$

1. *Average time a guest waits in line:*

$$W_q = A/r(A - r) \quad W_q = 10/15(15 - 10) \quad W_q = 0.133 \text{ hours or 8 minutes}$$

W_q means waiting time in the queue before being served. This calculation tells manager Blake that the average wait in the line for a guest is eight minutes. If that wait time is unacceptable to Blake, he may have to add another server.

2. *Average time spent in system:*

$$T_S = 1/(r - A) \quad T_S = 1/(15 - 10) \quad T_S = 0.2 \text{ hours or } 12 \text{ minutes}$$

T_S means the average time a guest waits in the system. This equation tells manager Blake that the average guest spends twelve minutes in the system, including both waiting time and service time.

3. *Average number of guests in line:*

$$L_q = A^2/r(r - A) \quad L_q = 10^2/15(15 - 10) \quad L_q = 1.33 \text{ guests}$$

L_q means the average length of the queue, in number of guests. Knowing that only 1.33 guests are in line at any one time, on average, reveals to Blake that the line's space requirements are minimal.

4. *Percent of time the server is busy:*

$$p = A/r \quad p = 10/15 \quad p = 67\%$$

p means the percentage of time the server is busy. The front desk registration procedure has one or more guests in it—either in line or being served—67 percent of the time, or about forty minutes out of every hour.

5. *Probability that there is no one in the system:*

$$P_0 = 1 - (A/r) \quad P_0 = 1 - (10/15) \quad P_0 = 33\%$$

P_0 means the probability that no one is in the system. This is obviously the inverse of the previous formula. If the wait-plus-registration system has someone in it about forty minutes out of each hour, it is empty for the other twenty minutes. Blake can use this information to assign other tasks to idle servers. Now that Blake has run his calculations, the registration agents can probably look forward to an expanded job description.

ADDITIONAL READINGS

Allon, G., & Federgruen, A. 2008. Service competition with general queuing facilities. *Operations Research*, 56, 827–849.

Bielen, F., & Demoulin, N. 2007. Waiting time influence on the satisfaction-loyalty relationship in services. *Managing Service Quality*, 17, 174–193.

Butcher, K., & Heffernan, T. 2006. Social regard: A link between waiting for service and service outcomes. *International Journal of Hospitality Management*, 25, 34–53.

Chambers, C., & Kouvelis, P. 2006. Modeling and managing the percentage of satisfied customers in hidden and revealed waiting line systems. *Production and Operations Management*, 15 (1), 103–116.

Dickson, D., Ford, R. C., & Laval, B. 2005. Managing real and virtual waits in hospitality and service organizations. *Cornell Hotel and Restaurant Administration Quarterly*, 46 (1), 52–68.

Dunnande-Moreau, A. 1999. Waiting for service: Ten years of empirical research. *International Journal of Service Industry management*, 10, 171–182.

Hwang, J. 2008. Restaurant table management to reduce customer waiting times. *Journal of Foodservice Research*, 11 (4), 334–351.

Hwang, J., & Lambert, C. U. 2005. Customers' identification of acceptable waiting times in a multi-stage restaurant system. *Journal of Foodservice Research*, 18 (1), 3–16.

Hwang, J., & Lambert, C. U. 2008. The interaction of major resources and their influence on waiting times in a multi-stage restaurant. *International Journal of Hospitality Management*, 29, 541–551.

Iravani, S. M. R., Kolfal, B., & Van Oyen, M. P. 2007. Call center labor cross-training: It's a small world after all. *Management Science*, 53, 1102–1112.

Katz, K., Larson, B. M., & Larson, R. 1991. Prescription for waiting-in-line blues: Entertain, enlighten, and engage. *Sloan Management Review*, 32 (4), 44–53.

Kumar, P., & Krishnamurthy, P. 2008. The impact of service-time uncertainty and anticipated congestion on customers' waiting-time decisions. *Journal of Service Research*, 10, 282–292.

Laval, B. 1975. Optimization of Walt Disney World monorail system through computer simulation. *Proceedings 8th Annual Simulation Symposium*, Tampa, FL. March 12–14, 1–10.

Maister, D. 1985. The psychology of waiting lines, in J. Czepiel, M. R. Solomon, and C. F. Suprenant (eds.), *The Service Encounter: Managing Employee/Customer Interaction in Service Businesses*. Lexington, MA: Lexington Books, pp. 113–124.

McDonnell, J. 2007. Music, scent and time preferences for waiting lines. *International Journal of Bank Marketing*, 25, 223–237.

McGuire, K. A., & Kimes, S. E. 2006. The perceived fairness of waitlist-management techniques for restaurants. *Cornell Hotel and Restaurant Quarterly*, 47 (2), 121–134.

Munichor, N., & Rafaeli, A. 2007. Numbers or apologies? Customer reactions to telephone waiting time fillers. *Journal of Applied Psychology*, 92, 511–518.

Norman, D. A. 2009. Designing waits that work. *MIT Sloan Management Review*, 50 (4), 23–28.

Pullman, M. E., & Rodgers, S. 2010. Capacity management for hospitality and tourism: A review of current approaches. *International Journal of Hospitality Management*, 29, 177–198.

Pullman, M. E., & Thompson, G. M. 2002. Evaluating capacity- and demand-management decisions at a ski resort. *Cornell Hotel and Restaurant Administration Quarterly*, 43 (6), 25–36.

Pullman, M. E., & Thompson, G. M. 2003. Strategies for integrating capacity with demand in service networks. *Journal of Service Research*, 5 (3), 169–183.

Rafaeli, A., Barron, G., & Haber, K. 2002. The effect of queue structure on perceptions. *Journal of Service Research*, 5 (3), 125–139.

Ryan, G., & Valverde, M. 2006. Waiting in line for online services: A qualitative study of the user's perspective. *Information Systems Journal*, 16, 181–211.

Seawright, K. K., & Sampson, S. E. 2006. A video method for empirically studying wait-perception bias. *Journal of Operations Management*, 25, 1055–1066.

Song, H., & Li, G. 2008. Tourism demand modeling and forecasting: A review of recent research. *Tourism Management*, 29 (2), 203–220.

Taylor, S. 1994. Waiting for service: The relationship between delays and evaluations of service. *Journal of Marketing*, 58, 56–69.

Wong, K. I., Wong, S. C., Yang, H., & Wu, J. H. 2008. Modeling urban taxi services with multiple user classes and vehicle models. *Transportation Research* Part B, 42, 985–1007.

NOTES

[1]For an interesting example of a ski resort network of waits, see Pullman, M. E., & Thompson, G. M. 2002. Evaluating capacity- and demand-management decisions at a ski resort. *Cornell Hotel and Restaurant Administration Quarterly*, 43 (6), 25–36.

[2]Adapted from Heskett, J. L., Sasser, W. E., Jr., & Hart, C. W. L. 1990. *Service Breakthroughs: Changing the Rules of the Game*. New York: The Free Press, pp. 138–141.

[3]See for example, Hwang, J., & Lambert, C. U. 2008. The interaction of major resources and their influence on waiting times in a multi-stage restaurant. *International Journal of Hospitality Management*, 29, 541–551.

[4]See McGuire, K. A., & Kimes, S. E. 2006. The perceived fairness of waitlist-management techniques for restaurants. *Cornell Hotel and Restaurant Quarterly*, 47 (2), 121–134.

[5]See, for example, Rafaeli, A., Barron, G., & Haber, K. 2002. The effect of queue structure on perceptions. *Journal of Service Research*, 5 (3), 125–139.

[6]Dickson, D., Ford, R. C., & Laval, B. 2005. Managing real and virtual waits in hospitality and service organizations. *Cornell Hotel and Restaurant Administration Quarterly*, 46 (1), 52–68.

[7]Wolfson, B. J. 2000. Disney chief financial officer sees changes raising customer satisfaction. *Orange County Register*, April 11, www.orcegister.com; and Reckard, E. S. 2000. More Disneyland rides to get shortcut system. *Los Angeles Times*, May 26, www.latimes.com

[8]Rafaeli, Barron, & Haber, 2002.

[9]Norman, D. A. 2009. Designing waits that work. *MIT Sloan Management Review*, 50 (4), 23–28.

[10]Thomke, S. 2003. R&D comes to services: Bank of America's pathbreaking experiments. *Harvard Business Review*, 81 (4), 70–79.

[11]Hops Restaurant, Bar & Brewery on tap for Toledo. 2000. *Toledo Business Journal*, 16 (8), 7. Policy is stated on the company's Web site, at http://www.hopsrestaurants.com/home/frame_who.asp, accessed 11/3/09.

[12]Although the following assumptions underlie these formulas, it is not necessary to understand them to follow the discussion: (1) Queue discipline is first-in, first-out; (2) No balking or reneging. Customers must accept service when it is offered, and no one quits or leaves the line; (3) Arrivals are accurately represented by a Poisson statistical distribution; (4) Service times must follow a negative exponential Poisson distribution; (5) Arrivals are independent; (6) Arrival rate does not change over time.

CHAPTER 12

Measuring and Managing Service Delivery

HOSPITALITY PRINCIPLE: PURSUE PERFECTION RELENTLESSLY

Unless you have 100% customer satisfaction—and I mean that they are excited about what you are doing—you have to improve.

—Horst Schulze, Former President, The Ritz-Carlton Hotel Company, L.L.C.

Good isn't good enough.

—Len Berry, Service Marketing Author and Scholar

Success is never final.

—J. Willard Marriott Jr., Chairman & CEO, Marriott International, Inc.

LEARNING OBJECTIVES

After reading this chapter, you should understand:

- How to measure the effectiveness of service delivery and of the overall guest experience.

- How to use methods of measuring service effectiveness, including service standards, process strategies, managerial observation, and employee assessment.

- How to acquire guest opinions of service effectiveness using comment cards, surveys (mail, Web, and phone), focus groups, and mystery shoppers.

- How to determine the costs and benefits of the different methods for acquiring guest opinions.

- How to use service guarantees.

- How to achieve continuous improvement in the experience provided to guests.

The service has been planned, and the guests have arrived. Now you must deliver the expected service experience. You hope to provide great service, but how will you know wheather you are succeeding? Accurately measuring what guests think about their hotel stay, restaurant meal, or some other service experience is a difficult challenge for hospitality organizations striving to achieve service excellence. Nevertheless, it must be done. All hospitality organizations face rising guest expectations and an increasing guest unwillingness to settle for less than they think they paid for. This new customer activism has made service quality more important than ever as managers strive to meet both heightened customer expectations and increasing competition.

This chapter focuses on finding out how the guest perceives the quality of the guest experience so that the hospitality manager can see, from the guest's perspective, where there are any problems. The critical challenge for hospitality managers seeking this information is to identify and implement the methods that best measure the quality of the experience from the guest's point of view *as the experience is occurring*. Measurements taken after the experience may be too late to enable recovery from failure, though they may be useful in improving the service experience for the future.

As we have stated throughout this text, the guest determines the quality and value of the service experience. Consequently, an acceptable experience for one guest might be a wow experience for another and totally unacceptable to a third. The subjective nature of the quality and value of a guest experience makes identifying and implementing the appropriate measurements particularly difficult.

One key to creating a flawless guest experience is that the organization must know what errors are being made, what failures are occurring. If you don't know it's broken, you can hardly fix it. Consequently, monitoring and measuring the quality of the guest experience with an eye out for flaws or failures is a crucial part of the hospitality organization's responsibility. Satisfied guests come back, and dissatisfied guests go elsewhere.

The best time to find out about possible service failures is before the guest ever arrives. The best mistake is one that never happens because the organization planned thoroughly to ensure that each part of the experience is flawless. But no matter how well the management planned the meal, scheduled the convention, or designed the hotel lobby, mistakes will happen. The organization wants to have measures in place to identify the mistakes as soon as possible—certainly before the guest leaves the service setting, while the information is still fresh in the guest's mind. Finding out about failure on the spot gives the organization the opportunity to recover. The worst time to learn of a service failure is after the guest has departed because the opportunity to fix it is substantially decreased once the guest has left the premises.

As we have discussed in prior chapters on planning the service experience with blueprinting, fishbone analysis, waiting-line simulations and other techniques, the most effective tool for ensuring quality is through planning to ensure that anything that might go wrong is anticipated and failsafed to the extent humanly possible. In this chapter we look at techniques for assessing and monitoring how successful this planning has been. Since achieving perfection in hospitality experiences is impossible no matter how thoroughly you plan, we will discuss the art and science of finding and fixing service failures in Chapter 13.

TECHNIQUES AND METHODS FOR ASSESSING SERVICE QUALITY

Process Strategies

Process strategies include various ways in which organizations can avoid failing their guests by monitoring the delivery while it is taking place, while it is in process. A process strategy is a means of comparing what is happening against what is supposed to happen, usually, but not always, expressed as a measurable service standard. Sometimes process strategies are the experience and training that managers and employees have in delivering the high-quality service experience that organizations want their customers to have. The idea behind process strategies is to design monitoring mechanisms into the delivery system to find and fix failures before they affect the quality of the guest experience. A supervisor can monitor telephone calls, a server can check the food order against what is served, or a machine can control the frying time of french fries to get them perfect every time. The advantage of process strategies is that they can catch errors before or as they occur, enabling prevention or immediate correction before the errors impact guest satisfaction beyond repair. Of course, organizations need to devote the resources to create and maintain the error-prevention system, and that has costs.

Hard Rock Cafe, for example, hires an additional person to stand at the end of the food preparation line to match the order against the food on the plate to be served, to catch discrepancies before the guest ever sees the order. Even though the traditional job description for wait staff includes this checking responsibility, the additional person reduces the possibility of error even further. The Opryland Hotel in Nashville cross-trains some of its employees in front-desk service so that they can be called upon in peak demand times when the front desk is extra busy. If line lengths threaten to exceed the service standard, this "swat team" staffs extra positions at the front desk to reduce the wait for the incoming or departing guests.

Service standards that can be applied while the service is in process provide employees with objective measures against which to monitor their own job performance while they are doing it. Specifying the maximum number of times the phone can ring before it is picked up is an example. Other process-related measurements that allow the organization to minimize errors or catch them while the guest experience is underway include the number of times a server should revisit a table during the meal, or the number of people who can stand in line before the manager adds extra personnel to the check-in.

Rusty Pelican Standards

Restaurants know that guests value prompt service. Figure 12-1 shows an example of some of the service standards from the Rusty Pelican Restaurant. Although the full document is nine pages long, Figure 12-1 shows the portion describing how the server should "approach the table and seat the guests." Because the servers themselves determined the standards, they were eager to monitor their own performance and try to meet or surpass the standards. Several benefits resulted. Service quality improved; increased server productivity meant that fewer servers were needed, which increased the tip income of servers;

The Rusty Pelican restaurant has created explicit service standards both to inform servers of the quality of service expected from them and to motivate better service as servers try to beat the standards. The figure on the following page shows just one of nine pages of standards for the restaurant.

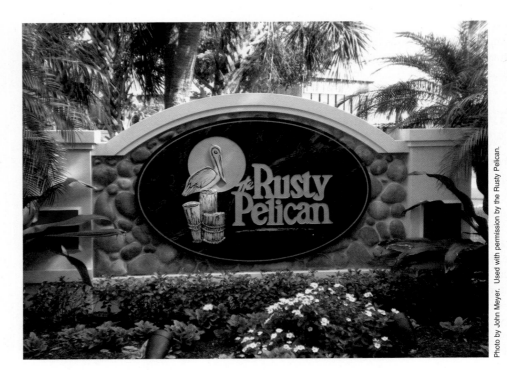

Photo by John Meyer. Used with permission by the Rusty Pelican.

customers (to management's surprise) were willing to pay more to receive better service, and servers identified a couple of bottlenecks—potential failure points—that interfered with prompt, reliable service. Smoothing out those points improved service quality even more.[1]

Continually checking the performance of organizational members against preestablished service standards while the service experience is in process is an excellent way to ensure a successful experience. Two other in-process methods of assessing the service quality of the experience while it is happening are managerial observation, sometimes called **management by walking around (MBWA)**, and employee observation and inquiry. If managers or employees ask a guest "how is it?" or see someone unhappy, they might be able to identify and fix a service failure immediately. Some standards of performance are embodied in organizational service guarantees, so organizations will want to keep the terms of these guarantees in mind while providing service. After providing the service experience to the guests but before they have left the premises, the organization may want to solicit their opinions about whether their expectations have been met.

The methods designed to assess quality while service is being provided are intended to ensure the success of individual service experiences. Also important for long-run organizational success is having methods in place for collecting data directly from guests after their experience, to identify the areas needing improvement to satisfy regular guests and attract new ones. Among these methods are comment cards; toll-free 800 numbers; e-mail, telephone, and Web surveys using various techniques; and **guest focus groups**. Mystery shopping is an additional widely used approach for gathering data about the quality of a service experience.

FIGURE **12-1** The Service Standards at the Rusty Pelican

Used with permission by the Rusty Pelican

Approach the table and seat the guests:

---

1. Server will approach the table and greet guests by name within one (1) minute.
    Immediately after the guest is seated:
    "Good evening Mr. or Mrs. Jones, welcome to the Rusty Pelican". Do not memorize greeting for all tables. Use creativity, vary wording to guests. Do not slouch, but stand up straight. Smile. Hold your tray at the side and not in front of you.
    If guests appear to be rushed, find out what time they must leave and make a notation on top of the check. For guests in a hurry or at lunch, you will discuss the menu and attempt to take order immediately during the greeting. Suggest faster service items.
    Suggest and sell a specific cocktail, appetizer. Use a head nod when making suggestions.
2. Suggest a cocktail to all guests at the table. "May I bring you a Fresh-Lime Margarita with Cuervo Gold and Grand Marnier, a glass or perhaps a bottle of Kendall Jackson Chardonnay?
    For non drinkers suggest "Mocktails" (virgin drinks such as virgin strawberry margaritas). Suggest bottled water. "May I bring you some water?" If response is yes..."we serve Pelligrino, Evian and Perrier. Which would you prefer?" If exotic drinks are not requested, then you may suggest juice, soft drinks, iced tea or coffee.
    Create a "Drink Special for a Day". Tell your guests about the ingredients. Remember to garnish all drinks as specified in the Mr. Boston liquor guide. If your guest would like a cocktail, UPSELL. If he/she orders a scotch on the rocks, ask them "Would you prefer Johnnie Walker Black or Chivas Regal?" Always give two choices.
    REMEMBER: Repeat back the order as the guest orders.
3. Suggest an Appetizer:
    "and how about a delicious _____ made with mouth watering _____ and a tangy _____ sauce, or my favorite _____ to begin your dinner? Encourage guests to share an appetizer!!!
    Use buzz words to entice and describe food and beverages. See attached list of buzz words.
    At lunch, for the benefit of the guest, the total order should be taken at this time, IF GUEST DESIRES.

The various methods differ in cost, accuracy, degree of guest inconvenience, and at what point in the guest experience they are used. Measuring service quality can have many organizational benefits, but as usual, the benefits must be balanced against the costs of obtaining them. The organization must balance the information needed and the research expertise required to gather and interpret the information against the available funds. As a rule, the more accurate and precise the data, the more expensive it is to acquire.

Measures of Service Quality

Managers of outstanding hospitality organizations try to develop measures for every part of the guest experience so that they can monitor where they are meeting or failing to meet their own definition of quality service. These measures are critical to ensure that the service is delivered to the customer as it should be. According to Phil Crosby in *Quality Is Free*, the price of not conforming to a quality standard can be calculated. That price is how much it costs to fix errors and failures that result from not meeting the quality standard in the first place. Although some may think that determining the cost of not answering phone calls within three rings is impossible, quality experts such as Crosby think it can and should be done.[2]

Some standards are built directly into the design of the service system. For example, a restaurant bar is designed to contain sufficient beer capacity and wine storage space to meet forecasted demand. Some standards are for employee use in anticipating guests coming in the door. To use the restaurant again as an example, if the restaurant has reliable predictions of how many customers come in on the different days of the week, those predictions can be used as a basis or standard for the number of salads that should be pre-prepared, the number of tables that should be pre-set, and the amount of silverware that should be rolled into napkins. If the prediction is correct and the standards for these aspects of the service are met, a service failure should not occur. A final group of standards is used after the guests have arrived and while the service is taking place, such as maximum number of minutes before greeting and number of visits to the table during the meal. Poka-yokes such as those described in Chapter 10 can be used to prevent failures in some of these activities.

Other examples of how performance standards can prevent failures might include annual hours of training required of service personnel, number of computer terminals to be purchased to serve anticipated demand, and number of banquet tables to be set up or other facilities to be available when the organization can reasonably predict requirements before the service experience ever begins.

Table 12-1 provides a summary of the methods and techniques available to hospitality organizations for monitoring and assessing the quality of the service experience while it is being delivered. They all depend on careful planning to set service standards, careful training to prepare the employees to meet those standards, and rewards for employees when the guest experience meets or exceeds the set standards.

Use Many Measures or Just One Super Measure?

Most hospitality organizations measure quality by developing and using standards in as many ways as they can. British Airways, for example, tracks some 350 indicators of quality, ranging from on-time performance, to aircraft cleanliness, to how much time to check in on a flight. It issues a monthly report on its key performance indicators to all of its managers, who can use these internally generated indicators in conjunction with the external customer surveys to assess the quality level of their airline.[3]

Others argue that a "super measure" capturing the most important factor in the experience is a better managerial strategy as it focuses everyone on that one important thing. At the other extreme from British Airways, Continental Airlines, now part of United Airlines, returned to profitability in the mid-1990s by using just one of the BA quality indicators—on-time performance—as a single super measure: Be On Time. For every month that the airline was in the top three of Department of Transportation monthly rankings of on-time flight arrivals, all Continental employees received a bonus. The airline extended the on-time concept throughout its system; everything—from baggage handling to aircraft cleanup—had to be on time. By 2000 Continental had become not only number one in on-time flight arrivals but was also rated number one in customer satisfaction by J.D. Power.[4]

TABLE 12-1 Techniques for Assessing Quality During the Service Experience

TECHNIQUE	ADVANTAGES	DISADVANTAGES
Job performance standards	• Translate service standards into behaviors that can be measured • Provide objective criteria for rewarding employees for doing what the standards require • Allow easy monitoring by supervisors and self-monitoring by employees of what they should be doing	• Can't cover all aspects of every service encounter • May discourage innovative solutions to customer requests falling outside service standards and prescribed behaviors
Managerial observation (MBWA)	• Management knows business, policies, procedures, and service standards • No technology or up-front costs required • No inconvenience to customers • Opportunity to recover from service failure • Opportunity to collect direct, specific guest feedback • Opportunity to identify service problems • Opportunity for immediate coaching or reinforcing of service-providing employees	• Management presence may influence service providers • Lacks statistical validity and reliability • Objective observation requires specialized training • Management may not know enough about situation to gather all the facts • Takes management time away from other duties
Employee observation	• Employees have first-hand knowledge of service delivery system obstacles • Customers volunteer service-quality feedback to service-providing employees • No inconvenience to customers • Opportunity to find and fix service failures immediately • Employee empowerment improves morale • Opportunity to collect detailed guest feedback • Minimal cost for data gathering and documentation	• Objective observation requires specialized training • Employees disinclined to report problems they created • Lacks statistical validity and reliability • Employee trust of management will influence what feedback is shared • Organizational system for collecting/analyzing customer feedback is required
Service guarantees	• Allow customers to see service standards and monitor them • Send employees strong message about organizational commitment to service quality • Document service failures • Enhance likelihood of guest complaining to allow fixing service failures	• Employees may try to avoid mentioning them or honoring them when invoked • Guarantee may not be written in a way that is consistent with the actual service product and may not be taken seriously • Managers may hide guarantee policy to avoid negative performance implications
Structured guest interviews	• Opportunity to collect detailed guest feedback • Ability to gather representative and valid sample of targeted customers • Opportunity to recover from service failure • Suggest that company is interested in customer opinions of service quality	• Require a significant investment in training and time • May not be a representative sample of guests • Difficult and expensive to collect a large sample of respondents • Recollection of specific service experience details may be lost • Memory of other service experiences may bias responses • Respondents tend to give socially desirable responses • Inconvenience makes incentives for participants necessary

Adapted from Robert C. Ford and Susan Bach, 1997. Measuring Service Quality: Tools for Gaining the Competitive Advantage. *FIU Hospitality Review* 15(1):86-87. Reprinted with permission.

Planning as described in Chapter 10 establishes a range of standards before and during the entire experience. If the standards are met, the experience should happen as it is supposed to happen. Now we need techniques and methods to assess how those plans work out in practice.

Service Standards

As discussed in Chapter 10, part of the process of planning a service delivery system is to develop service standards: the organization's expectations for how the different aspects of the service experience should be delivered every time to every guest. In a lot of ways, service standards in services organizations are the equivalent to quality-control standards in manufacturing organizations, except that no QC inspector can use calipers to measure the aspects of the service experience. Instead, service organizations try to invent surrogate measurement tools, such as service standards, to measure the essentially immeasurable service experience as it is being produced. The hope is that using such standards will enable catching and fixing bad experiences in a way similar to that in which the QC inspector catches and tosses bad ball bearings.

Job Performance Standards

The organization can help to ensure success by setting specific **job performance standards**. These standards for specific jobs, derived from the service standards, provide employees with clear and specific performance expectations for each major duty associated with their jobs. When guests are seated in a restaurant, they expect someone to attend to them within a reasonable time. Emeril Lagasse, famed chef, restaurateur, and television personality, tells how he implements his service standard that waiters must take a cocktail order within fifteen seconds of the guest being seated. Salt and pepper shakers are used to signal whether the standard has been met. The shakers are usually together. The person seating the guest subtly separates them, meaning that the drink order has not yet been taken. When servers take drink orders, they subtly put the shakers back together. This simple cue lets everyone see whether the standard has been met.[5] One additional benefit of setting and monitoring standards is that they can encourage employees who seek to meet or beat the standards to develop innovative solutions. Some servers create partnerships with other servers to cover for them when delays keep them from meeting a standard. If they are busy taking an order at a table, the partner will make the initial greeting for them to beat the standard.

On the other hand, the potential benefits of job performance standards may not be realized, and in fact may even become a disadvantage, if the performance standards are not carefully set. If standards are too limiting, employees may be reluctant to deviate from them if guests make unanticipated requests. Nonetheless, the potential benefits of well-designed standards can far outweigh the disadvantages. Performance standards make supervision easier (the manager can see if the employee is performing according to standards) and also facilitate self-management by employees (employees can see in clear terms what the organization's performance expectations are).

To help assess how well job performance standards are being met, employee performance can be monitored, by managers observing performance or by using technology such as a device that monitors how many rings it takes to answer each call, or by the employees self-monitoring their performance. One of the big challenges for managers here is to ensure that their employees do not feel they will be punished for reporting failures to meet standards because of something they did. While it's easy to report a failure someone else or the delivery system made, most people find it hard to report service failures they made.

Managers must make it clear to employees that doing what they can to fix service failures is their first responsibility and that not telling someone who can fix a problem they caused will get them in more trouble than reporting their mistakes.

The keys to the use of job performance standards are that (1) the standards must be clear and relevant to the service being delivered, (2) employees must know what they need to do, how they must perform, to meet those standards, and (3) the standards must be related to things the employee can control. To gain their benefits, though, managers must use job performance standards effectively. They must (1) ensure that they observe enough of each employee's performance so that the evaluation accurately represents how people actually perform, (2) differentiate between levels of service performance (don't just say everyone is great just to avoid confrontation), and (3) give honest feedback to employees of what they are doing effectively and ineffectively. By measuring the extent to which employees meet the standards, the organization will have a good indication of how well employees are doing their jobs in providing the service. By communicating these results to employees through performance feedback, good employees can maintain high performance levels and poorer performers know what they need to improve.

Managerial Observation of the Delivery Process

The simplest and least expensive technique for assessing the degree to which guest-service quality is meeting service standards while service is being delivered involves simply encouraging managers to keep their eyes open, especially to the interactions between employees and guests. Management by walking around, sometimes called in hospitality organizations "walking the front," means that managers are observing the operation first hand, looking for problems or inefficiencies, talking to both guests and employees to assess their reactions, and then recording and relaying any information that might improve service quality. Managers know their own business, its goals, capabilities, formal and informal service standards, and the job performance standards for their employees. They know when employees are delivering a high-quality experience. At their best, these observations do not interfere with service delivery or do not cause inconvenience to guests, and they often permit immediate correction of guest service problems. Further, managerial observation gives the boss the opportunity to reward the excellent employee immediately or counsel the employee who might not be delivering the service as the organization wants it delivered. It provides a modeling situation, a "teaching moment," in which a supervisor observing a service failure can show the employee how to fix the problem. When managers walk the front to serve as coaches and not as spies, their presence favorably influences employee attitudes and performance, and guest satisfaction.

There are, of course, drawbacks to this approach. Some managers may not have enough experience or training to fully understand what they are observing, or they may have biases which influence their objectivity. More importantly, when employees know that managers are observing the service delivery process, they invariably perform it differently. Additionally, although managerial observation may ensure the quality of the experience for a particular guest, managers can't watch every guest–employee interaction. The unobserved guest's reactions to unobserved experiences remain unknown to the manager.

Of course, hiring good managers can mitigate some of these drawbacks. Training them in methods of observing guest–server interactions and measuring servers' performance against quality standards can reduce both ignorance and personal bias. Unobtrusive observational techniques, random observations, and video cameras diminish employee awareness that the boss is watching. For example, many organizations tell their telephone operators and guests that all phone conversations may be "monitored for training purposes" to eliminate the observation bias by making it uncertain as to when management is actually listening in. The operators know that someone may always be listening, so they do the job by the book. Some larger companies use managers from one location to observe employees at another location as mystery shoppers for the same reason.

Employee Assessment of Guest Experiences

While valuable information can be obtained from managerial observation, employees themselves should be even more aware of how well they are delivering service. Just as managers can observe by walking around, service-providing employees can constantly monitor the guest experience and compare it against either formal standards set by management or informal standards set by their experience, training, and the organization's culture. The process of continuously comparing what they see against what they know they should be seeing enables them to find and fix guest problems, to improve the service as they are delivering it, and to report any findings or observations that might enable improvement of the delivery process.

Line employees are often the best people to find and fix service problems and innovatively adapt the service experience to meet each guest's expectations. They can also provide excellent feedback about the quality of guest experiences that supplements and adds detail to managerial observation. Line employees can provide input on issues such as cumbersome company policies and control procedures, managerial reporting structures, or other processes that inhibit effective service delivery. Because these employees are watching, talking, and listening to guests, they know firsthand about organizational impediments that prevent them from delivering a memorable service experience. The challenge as noted earlier is to make sure that all employees feel safe in reporting all the errors including those they have made. This is a delicate managerial task to build the level of trust that encourages employees to report their own failures. They have to believe from managers' words and deeds that it is better to tell about their failures than to cover them up.

Employee work teams and quality service circles are another source of feedback. The Ritz-Carlton Hotels uses work teams to gather feedback to develop "zero-defect" guest service strategies. Such techniques foster an understanding and appreciation of how each employee can directly influence service quality. Employee awareness of management's strong commitment to service quality is affirmed through work teams. They show not only management trust in employee judgment to correct service problems but also that management is willing to put its money where its mission is by paying for work time lost to team participation and employee training. The entire process of the employee empowerment movement discussed in Chapter 7 depends on such trust.

The Service Guarantee

To make their service standards clear to customers, companies can offer service guarantees, which may be expressed in simple statements such as "Satisfaction guaranteed or your money back; no questions asked" or in complex documents resembling contracts. A **service guarantee** is a publicly expressed, usually written promise either to satisfy guests or to compensate them for any failure in part or all of the service.[6] If both guests and employees know the service standards expressed in the guarantee, both parties can measure quality levels against them as service is being delivered.

Service guarantees are often considered only a marketing tool, to persuade potential guests unsure about an organization's quality to give it a try. They have the potential, however, to do much more for management. That is, they provide a means to encourage guests to tell the organization what they think of its service quality while sending a strong message to employees about the organization's commitment to provide an experience so good that it can be guaranteed. The guarantee gives guests a strong incentive to tell the organization when a service experience is not meeting their expectations, and it gives the organization a strong incentive to fix whatever problems there may be with its service, staff, or delivery systems, so future guests don't have the same problems. In 1989 Hampton Inn hotels were the first in the industry to offer an unconditional 100 percent satisfaction guarantee: "If you're not completely satisfied, we'll give you your night's stay for free." Every Hampton employee was empowered to approve this refund. According to Stephen Tax and Stephen Brown, the Hampton Inn organization "realized $11 million in additional revenue from the implementation of its service guarantee and scored the highest customer retention rate in the industry."[7]

Here are some examples of service guarantees:

100% Hampton Inn Guarantee: "Friendly service, clean rooms, comfortable surroundings, every time. If you're not satisfied, we don't expect you to pay. That's our commitment & your guarantee. That's 100% Hampton."

Whitbread Travel Inn: "Everything you want for a good night's sleep—100 percent satisfaction or your money back."

Embassy Suites Satisfaction Guarantee: "Embassy Suites Hotels offers an unconditional 100% Satisfaction Guarantee at all of its hotels. The unprecedented guarantee assures that guests will receive high-quality accommodations, clean, comfortable surroundings and friendly, efficient service. If guests are not completely satisfied, they are not expected to pay for that night."

Priceline's Sunshine Guarantee: "Travelers booking on Priceline will be refunded 100% of their air fare, hotel, and car rental if it rains more than 0.5 inches per day on half or more of the holiday. The policy is underwritten by WeatherBill which insures several destination guarantees of vacation perfect weather."

Organizational Advantages of Guarantees

A good service guarantee should meet several important criteria,[8] summarized in Table 12-2. The value of a good guarantee to both guests and the organization is significant. The service guarantee can have a powerful effect on customer intent to return by signaling an organization's commitment to quality to both employees and guests. As described by Chris Hart,[9] service guarantees provide several important benefits for measuring and improving the effectiveness of the service delivery system:

- The guarantee forces everyone to think about the service from the customer's point of view since the customer decides whether to invoke it.
- It pinpoints where the service failed since the customer must give the reason for invoking the guarantee, and that reason then becomes measurement data on the service delivery system. As Chapter 13 will show, a guest complaint helps a hospitality organization become better. Guarantees are an incentive to get customers to complain if their expectations (and the guarantee's terms) have not been met. These complaints help the organization fix whatever is wrong before many more customers have problems.
- It gets everyone to focus quickly on the problem at hand since the costs of making good on guarantees can be quite large. Once a customer invokes the guarantee, the cost in lost revenue directs management's attention to correcting the problem.

JetBlue's Customer Bill of Rights.

INFORMATION

JetBlue will notify customers of the following:
- Delays prior to scheduled departure
- Cancellations and their cause
- Diversions and their cause

CANCELLATIONS

All customers whose flight is cancelled by JetBlue will, at the customer's option, receive a full refund or reaccommodation on the next available JetBlue flight at no additional charge or fare. If JetBlue cancels a flight within 4 hours of scheduled departure and the cancellation is due to a *Controllable Irregularity*, JetBlue will also issue the customer a $100 Credit good for future travel on JetBlue.

DELAYS (Departure Delays or Onboard Ground Delays on Departure)

For customers whose flight is delayed 3 hours or more after scheduled departure, JetBlue will provide free movies on flights that are 2 hours or longer.

DEPARTURE DELAYS

1. Customers whose flight is delayed for 1-1:59 hours after scheduled departure time due to a *Controllable Irregularity* are entitled to a $25 Credit good for future travel on JetBlue.
2. Customers whose flight is delayed for 2-3:59 hours after scheduled departure time due to a *Controllable Irregularity* are entitled to a $50 Credit good for future travel on JetBlue.
3. Customers whose flight is delayed for 4-5:59 hours after scheduled departure time due to a *Controllable Irregularity* are entitled to a Credit good for future travel on JetBlue in the amount paid by the customer for the oneway trip less taxes and fees.
4. Customers whose flight is delayed for 6 or more hours after scheduled departure time due to a *Controllable Irregularity* are entitled to a Credit good for future travel on JetBlue in the amount paid by the customer for the roundtrip (or the oneway trip, doubled) trip less taxes and fees.

LAST UPDATED: 1/2010

JetBlue Airways' Customer Bill of Rights

Above all else, JetBlue Airways is dedicated to bringing humanity back to air travel. We strive to make every part of your experience as simple and as pleasant as possible. Unfortunately, there are times when things do not go as planned. If you're inconvenienced as a result, we think it is important that you know exactly what you can expect from us. That's why we created our Customer Bill of Rights. These Rights will always be subject to the highest level of safety and security for our customers and crewmembers.

ONBOARD GROUND DELAYS

JetBlue will provide customers experiencing an Onboard Ground Delay with 36 channels of DIRECTV®*, food and drink, access to clean restrooms and, as necessary, medical treatment. For customers who experience an Onboard Ground Delay for more than 5 hours, JetBlue will also take necessary action so that customers may deplane.

Arrivals:
1. Customers who experience an Onboard Ground Delay on Arrival for 1-1:59 hours after scheduled arrival time are entitled to a $50 Credit good for future travel on JetBlue.
2. Customers who experience an Onboard Ground Delay on Arrival for 2 hours or more after scheduled arrival time are entitled to a Credit good for future travel on JetBlue in the amount paid by the customer for the roundtrip (or the oneway trip, doubled) less taxes and fees.

Departures:
1. Customers who experience an Onboard Ground Delay on Departure after scheduled departure time for 3-3:59 hours are entitled to a $50 Credit good for future travel on JetBlue.
2. Customers who experience an Onboard Ground Delay on Departure after scheduled departure time for 4 or more hours are entitled to a Credit good for future travel on JetBlue in the amount paid by the customer for the roundtrip (or the oneway trip, doubled) less taxes and fees.

In-flight entertainment:
JetBlue offers 36 channels of DIRECTV® service on its flights in the Continental U.S. If our LiveTV™ system is inoperable on flights in the Continental U.S., customers are entitled to a $15 Credit good for future travel on JetBlue.

OVERBOOKINGS (As defined in JetBlue's Contract of Carriage)

Customers who are involuntarily denied boarding shall receive $1,000.

JetBlue Airways
118-29 Queens Blvd
Forest Hills, NY 11375

These Rights are subject to JetBlue's Contract of Carriage and, as applicable, the operational control of the flight crew, and apply to only JetBlue-operated flights.
*DIRECTV service is not available on flights outside the continental United States; however, where applicable, movies from JetBlue Features are offered complimentary on these routes.
This document is representative of what is reflected in JetBlue's Contract of Carriage, the legally binding document between JetBlue and its customers.

JetBlue Airways

- It enhances the likelihood of recovery from a service failure, because the guest is encouraged to demand instant recovery, instead of sending in a negative guest comment card and taking the business to a competitor.
- It sends a strong message to employees and customers alike that the organization takes its service quality seriously and will stand behind it.

If the company has a strong and well-understood service guarantee that its customers can and do readily invoke, everyone in the organization can learn much about the service delivery system from its use. Embassy Suites, for example, takes its guarantee so seriously that it has created multiple ways to inform guests about the guarantee, such as posting it on a lobby sign and having it mentioned by the person taking the reservation, the van driver, and the front desk agent. Using multiple means increases the likelihood that the guest will know about the guarantee and its message of quality, believe that the guarantee is real, and use it when things go wrong. The guarantee gives Embassy Suites the opportunity to fix any service failures before the guest leaves and to solicit feedback from its guests about any dissatisfaction with the hotel experience.[10]

TABLE 12-2 The Characteristics of a Good Service Guarantee[11]

1. *Unconditional.* The more asterisks attached to the bottom of the page and the more fine print, the less credible the guarantee will seem to both employees and customers. Few or no conditions should be required to use the guarantee.

2. *Transparent.* The guarantee must not appear to have any catches or special conditions. The guarantee should be clear and straightforward and all the "rules" should be known by the customer.

3. *Credible with a high perceived value.* If customers don't believe you will really make good, then they won't use the guarantee. They think "If it sounds too good to be true, it probably is." The classic illustration is Pizza Hut Delivery's 30-minutes-or-free guarantee, which was changed partly because people thought it was too good to be true.

4. *Focused on key features of the service.* The guarantee should focus on the services that the guests are most concerned about or the core features of the service product.

5. *Supported by significant compensation to the customer.* The remedy or compensation should cover the guest's dissatisfaction completely. If invoking the guarantee only partially solves the customer's problem or is of little consequence to the organization, neither the customer nor the service people will value the guarantee.

6. *Easy to understand and communicate.* Follow the old KISS rule: Keep It Simple Stupid. The more complicated the guarantee is, the less likely anyone will believe or use it.

7. *Easy for customers to invoke.* Invoking the guarantee and receiving its benefits should be painless for the guest. The harder a guarantee is to use, the less credible it will be and the less likely it will help identify serious service problems. Don't ask customers to fill out a bunch of forms and talk to several different departments to have their problem solved. It wasn't their fault you messed up so why should they have to do all the work to get it fixed?

8. *Easy to implement.* The policy must also be easy for the company to use. If employees do not have the authority to implement the guarantee or if internal bureaucratic hurdles unduly delay processing the guarantee, the customer will not perceive the company to be taking its guarantee seriously.

© Cengage Learning 2012.

Potential Disadvantages of Service Guarantees

Service guarantees do have some downsides. Perhaps the most obvious one is that employees will not always honor a guarantee when it is invoked. Supervisory commitment to the guarantee must be shown to reinforce for employees that the organization wants to make the guarantee known to guests and honor it without qualification or quibbling when guests invoke it. However, some supervisors may believe that reporting service guarantee use may negatively impact their annual reviews. They may avoid reporting the data generated by the service guarantee that could help to improve the service delivery system. Therefore, the organization must offer incentives to encourage managers, employees, as well as guests to invoke service guarantees. Companies must also be wary of guests who may inappropriately invoke the service guarantee. To avoid abuses of the guarantee, for example, Hampton keeps a database of customers who have invoked it and recommends another hotel to guests who repeatedly violate the company's trust. All parties must clearly understand what the guarantee covers in sufficiently specific terms so that they all take it seriously and use it only when it is appropriate.

Asking Guests the Right Questions

One of the best ways to find something out is simply to ask. Besides the manager and employees' informal observations and inquiries mentioned earlier, there are three additional in-process methods for acquiring the opinions of guests before they leave the service setting: informal queries by employees, formal inquiries by employees, and structured guest interviews.

Informal Queries by Employees

The most basic way to discover a service problem is simply to ask the guest. The desk agent who asks about your stay as you check out is a good example. Asking "Was everything OK?" may be the simplest and most effective way to find out if there was a problem. Some hotels ask employees to act informally as "lobby lizards" by randomly approaching guests on the property and asking about their experience. Of course, employees should be able to respond if the answer is "no." Don't ask this question unless you are prepared for a negative answer. Studies show that whether customers seek redress of a problem or simply let it go is determined by their perception of whether the organization really wants to hear about it and will act on it. Even customers who are reluctant to complain are more likely to do so if they perceive that the organization cares and will solve the problem.[12] Asking is a basic way to find out if your service has met the guest's standards.

Formal Inquiries by Employees

As noted earlier, employees are often in the best position to gather feedback from guests by just listening to them. But this role can be expanded in a more structured way. For example, rather than simply ask "How was your stay?" or "How was your meal?" a front desk agent or restaurant cashier can ask guests a series of carefully developed questions about their experience and then listen carefully to what they say and observe how they say it. Because guests may not always recall or report all the important details, employees recording guest reactions and responses in a systematic survey program can use questions that are professionally developed and validated, perhaps even scripted, to help ensure that the information gathered is useful and accurate for both immediate recovery from service failure (if discovered) and for further analysis.

Acquiring feedback in this way, before guests leave the premises, may allow recovery from service failures that might otherwise go unnoticed or unreported. Guests who have not yet left can be offered some compensating benefit or at least an apology to try to offset any failure. Employee training for many hospitality positions should, therefore, include appropriate service-recovery techniques, since research confirms that the organization benefits greatly from soliciting and quickly resolving guest complaints. As we shall discuss further in Chapter 13, effective hospitality managers know that recovering from service failures yields greater guest loyalty and repeat visits. In addition, because service quality information derived directly from the guest is highly believable to both employees and management, it motivates a quick recovery from service failures.

Structured Inquiries by Professional or Trained Interviewers

Face-to-face guest interviews provide rich information when trained interviewers, able to detect nuances in responses to open-ended questions, have the opportunity to probe guests for details about their experiences. These in-depth interviews can uncover previously unknown problems or new twists to known problems that might not be uncovered in a preprinted questionnaire or reflected well in numerical data. However, **structured guest interviews** are costly. The interviewers must be hired and trained, interview instruments must be custom designed, and they must be implemented on a clear and consistent schedule. Of course, it is impossible to conduct such in-depth interviews to all guests, so guests are typically selected at random. At theme parks and similar attractions, teams of interviewers roam the parks seeking guest responses. These conversations not only gather useful information about the guests' assessment of service quality but also enable the identification of any service failures that can be corrected while guests are still on the property.

As an alternative to hiring professional interviewers into your company, you may employ professionals skilled in customer intercepts to conduct the structured guest interviews. These consultants can design and implement the structured guest interview and provide a detailed report of the results to the organization. Because many businesses do not have the time, resources, or skills needed to design an appropriate structured interview, it is often more efficient to hire professionals to carry out this specialized task.

Regardless of who is conducting the interview, though, it is critical that accurate information is collected from guests. To get appropriate participation, inconvenienced guests must be compensated for participating. Without incentives, most guests see little personal benefit from participating in an interview unless, as with guest comment cards, they are motivated by being very satisfied or very dissatisfied with the service experience. Finally, for most experiences, the most desirable time to interview guests is at the conclusion when the experience is over but before the guest leaves in case there is a problem requiring resolution. Getting guests' attention and cooperation when they are most likely anxious to leave, however, can be a significant challenge.

MEASURING SERVICE QUALITY AFTER THE EXPERIENCE

Companies need good information from their guests in order to evaluate service performance and to make any needed changes. The service experience must be measured carefully and continuously, to make sure that it consistently meets guest expectations.

Service quality can be measured both during and after the service experience. Collecting information during the experience—by means of managers and employees comparing the actual service experience against service standards and other methods previously discussed—provides immediate information and may allow the company to repair the damage if service failures occur (service recovery is the topic of Chapter 13). Collecting information after the service generally allows more data to be accumulated and can yield a more representative sample of the organization's entire customer base. This sampling process allows more thorough analysis of the service systems. Results can be fed back to service planners who can then make changes and continuously improve the service.

Techniques to collect data directly from guests vary in cost, convenience, objectivity, and statistical validity. Informal methods are quick and easy, but generally lack validity. Formal methods generally can offer statistically valid, reliable, and useful measures of guest opinion that informal options cannot. Yet, even formal methods can range in sophistication, precision, validity, reliability, complexity, and difficulty of administration. The formal methods are generally more expensive than the informal ones.

The previously described methods of monitoring and assessing quality during service delivery and before guests have left the service setting are critically important in meeting the expectations of guests receiving service. But, to meet the goal of continuous improvement and to plan for future service success, hospitality organizations need methods for obtaining data from guests who have already experienced the service. The following pages describe several of these methods: comment cards, toll-free 800 numbers, mail and Web surveys, telephone surveys, critical-incidents surveys, the SERVQUAL instrument, and guest focus groups. A special service-assessment method called mystery shopping is also covered. Table 12-3 summarizes the techniques that may be used to assess service after the service experience.

TABLE 12-3 Techniques for Assessing Quality After the Service Experience

TECHNIQUE	ADVANTAGES	DISADVANTAGES
Comment cards	• Communicate company interest in customer opinions of service quality • Signed cards are an opportunity to recover from service failure • Low-to-moderate start-up cost • Minimal cost for data gathering and documentation • If printed in-house, can be modified easily to evaluate needs or new service products	• Self-selected sample of customers not statistically representative • Comments generally reflect extreme guest dissatisfaction or extreme satisfaction • Limited in information provided • Employees can influence results • Time lag between filling out and reading of card • Lack of specifics may make it difficult to use information to find real problem
Toll-free 800 numbers	• Permit potential and prior customers to ask questions, volunteer opinions on service • Opportunity to recover from service failure • No cost to callers	• Self-selected sample of customers not statistically representative • Comments generally reflect extreme guest dissatisfaction or extreme satisfaction • Time lag between experience and making phone call may cause important feedback to get lost in memory
Surveys: mail and Web, phone, critical incidents	• Gather info from potentially representative samples of targeted customers • Opportunity to recover from service failure • Allow follow-up discussion to probe into potential problems and opportunities in all parts of service experience • Send message that company cares enough about its service quality to spend money to ask customers what they think about it	• Recollection of details of a specific service experience can be inexact • Other service experiences may bias or confuse responses because of time lag • Inconvenience of participation makes offering incentives to participants necessary • Cost to construct questionnaire and then gather and analyze data from representative sample can be great • Responses may still represent only highly satisfied or dissatisfied guests
Guest focus groups	• Permit potential and prior customers to ask questions, volunteer opinions on service • Gather info from potentially representative samples of targeted customers • Send message that company cares enough about its service quality to spend money to ask customers what they think about it • Allow follow-up discussion of potential problems and opportunities identified by group	• Are very expensive • Rely on facilitator skill to enable group participation and focus discussion • Small sample can lead to misidentification of important or overemphasis on unimportant opportunities and challenges in total service experience

(continues)

TABLE 12-3 Techniques for Assessing Quality **After** the Service Experience
(*Continued*)

TECHNIQUE	ADVANTAGES	DISADVANTAGES
Mystery shoppers	• Unannounced observation by seemingly typical guests allows sampling of typical experience, not "dressed up" • Can be scheduled to observe/test specific training outcomes, times of day, or problem areas • Can be used to observe competing organizations • Provide more detailed data on all elements of service experience • Can be very accurate on objectively measured elements of experience • Are more accurate than guest feedback on subjective aspects of experience • Employees see shopper feedback as less subjective than manager's performance review	• Are expensive • May not be used often enough to gather statistically accurate data • Shopper biases, other experiences, and preferences can over- or underemphasize quality assessments

© Cengage Learning 2012.

Comment Cards

Other than asking guests the right questions before they leave, **comment cards** are the cheapest and easiest to use of all formal data collection methods. If properly designed, they are easy to tally and analyze. These advantages make them attractive for gathering guest-satisfaction data, especially for smaller organizations that cannot afford a quality assessment staff or consultants. Widely found throughout the hospitality industry, comment cards rely on voluntary guest participation. Guests rate the quality of the guest experience by responding to a few simple questions on a conveniently available form, typically a postcard. Guests deposit the form in a drop box, return it directly to the service provider, or mail it to the corporate office.

Increasingly, companies are using the Internet to implement the comment cards method. Companies provide Web addresses in visibly prominent areas on their printed material such as credit card receipts and bill copies; many post them in their ads, on their coupons, and any other place their customers might see them. Most organizations use a "contact us" link on their Web sites to provide a mailing address and contact names for those customers who prefer to write their comments to a specific person or functional area. Many paper comment cards include a Web address so that customers can complete the card online rather than on paper. Some companies such as Marriott and Olive Garden have completely replaced paper comment cards with electronic ones. The benefits of using the Internet to collect comment cards are that the data can be easily monitored, sorted, and analyzed, and the technology usually offers an easy way for the company to respond to customer comments.

What questions should appear on the comment cards? The organization studies its guests to determine their expectations and then embodies those expectations in the comment-card questions. If studies show a restaurant that its guests expect a friendly greeting, a properly setup table area, and overall cleanliness, its card will ask guests

Maxie's Supper Club, located in Ithaca New York, strives to provide great New Orleans-style food and warm professional service

Maxie's Supper Club and Oyster Bar

Maxie's Supper Club's Comment Card.

comments & suggestions

What do you like about Maxie's Supper Club?: _____

_____

_____

What would you change about Maxie's if you owned it?: _____

_____

_____

Name: _____

Address: _____

Email: _____ **Phone:** _____

☐ **Check here to receive our e-newsletter "SUPPER CLUB LIFE" every two months**

(••• **Your comment card will be entered into a monthly drawing for a free dinner for two** •••)

Maxie's Supper Club and Oyster Bar

about those elements of the guest experience. If an organization tries to differentiate itself from similar organizations, questions regarding the differentiating factors may appear on the comment card, so that the organization can gauge the success of its differentiation strategy.

Once the issues that the comment card should address are known, it should then be carefully designed. To do this, according to Bartkus and colleagues,[13] comments cards should adhere to the following guidelines:

1. Include a secure return mechanism (e.g., locked drop box or postage-paid mail)
2. Make introductory statements brief and neutral, not leading
3. Provide an opportunity to complete the comment card using the Internet
4. Limit the number of questions; don't make the survey too long
5. Provide enough writing space for open-ended questions
6. Make questions concise, and ask about only one issue in each question
7. For closed-ended questions, use at least five response points
8. Make questions neutral (e.g., "How was your stay") rather than containing positive cues (e.g., "What did we do especially well?") or negative ("Were there any problems with your stay?").

Of course, comment cards are available in many forms and styles. Consider the following examples:

- The West Inn and Suites[14] asks guests to evaluate the front desk, housekeeping, maintenance, and breakfast, in addition to providing general comments using a four-point scale (Excellent, Good, Fair, and Poor) with an opportunity to provide open-ended comments also.
- The Hilton Garden Inn at the Montreal Airport uses a ten-point scale to assess overall satisfaction and two questions related to the likelihood of return and overall value for price paid.
- The Rusty Pelican asks guests how often they visit, their favorite thing about the restaurant, what the restaurant should do to get them to visit more often, and whether they'd recommend the restaurant to a friend, and it provides a place for "other comments."

Completed comment cards indicate whether the organization is meeting the general expectations of the guests who take the time to fill them out. Written remarks about long waits for food, long lines at the front desk, or housekeeping problems reveal the weaknesses of the service delivery system, the personnel and their training, and the service product itself. Positive comments provide management with the opportunity to find and fix service delivery system problems, rework the service product, and, importantly, recognize employee performance. Positive comments can be used to reinforce the behaviors that lead to good guest service and create role models and stories about how to provide outstanding service that other employees can use in shaping their own behavior in their jobs. Negative comments can be used for individual coaching, departmental training (without mentioning specific employees) to illustrate behaviors that caused negative guest experiences, and as input for reviewing employee training programs. Using comment cards in these ways allows managers to coach and train employees about how to provide excellent guest service through the voices of the guests themselves.

Comments accumulated from cards may be categorized and plotted as numerical values on bar graphs and charts that visually display how guests perceived their experience. The plots will suggest whether service failures are occurring occasionally and randomly, or whether overall service quality might be deteriorating.

Disadvantages

The greatest disadvantage of comment cards is that many guests ignore them and don't fill them out, so the cards received are not likely to be a true general picture of guest perceptions. Typically, only 5 percent of customers are motivated to return comment cards, and they are usually either very satisfied or very dissatisfied with the service experience. Managers don't even know what percentage of the delighted total or the dissatisfied total these responses represent. The other 95 percent say nothing. Were they happy, unhappy, or indifferent? You might guess that they are indifferent, but there is a very good chance you would be wrong. A large percentage of dissatisfied guests fill out no cards, leave quietly, and never return. To help overcome the lack of response, some companies use incentives, like coupons or potential cash prizes, to encourage participation. These incentives do help increase participation, but of course they also cost additional money.

Another major disadvantage of comment cards, and in fact of many methods for acquiring feedback, is that the time lag between guest response and managerial review prevents on-the-spot correction of service gaps and failures. Once the moment of truth has passed and the angry or disappointed guest leaves after expressing negative responses on a comment card, the opportunity to recapture that guest's future business is diminished. Even worse, negative word-of-mouth advertising generated by dissatisfied guests cannot be corrected. Moreover, card usefulness can be impacted by employees themselves who may try to influence guests in filling them out. Some employees will watch guests while they fill out cards or even tell guests what to put down on the cards to influence the grades given, especially when scores may affect employees personally. If bonuses rest on comment-card scores, good comment cards will be kept and bad ones may disappear.

While guest comments and their visual representations are interesting and helpful to management, the information lacks statistical validity, one reason being that the random-sample requirement of most statistical techniques is not met because the guests who respond tend not to be representative of all customers that organization serves.

Because of the negatives associated with comment cards, some restaurants simply decide not to use them. For example, one of this book's authors asked the hostess at a Legal Sea Foods restaurant for a comment card. She said that the restaurant no longer uses them, and then asked if he would like to speak to a manager. Such a procedure conveys a simple yet powerful message: don't fill out a card; instead, tell us about your experience, and, if there is a problem, let us hear directly from you so we can try to fix it immediately.

Toll-Free 800 Numbers

Another way of measuring the quality of service is the customer-service 800 telephone number. This technique lets customers say what's on their minds twenty-four hours a day. This method also allows companies to get back in touch with customers to let them know how they addressed problems and comments. Like the guest comment cards, the usefulness of the 800 number depends upon the willingness of the guests to respond, and even the convenience of this method does not guarantee a representative response from all types of guests. Some companies also offer incentives such as coupons to encourage customers to call the 800 numbers. Others enter the caller into a lottery to win cash or other prizes.

New Technologies for Gathering Feedback

As technology changes and improves, companies are looking for new ways to get new and better information from their customers. The goal is to use new technology to solicit more representative feedback, get better response rates, and be able to use the information more effectively.

For example, Marriott's Fairfield Inns developed their Fairfield Inns Scorecard program as a means to get greater customer participation than comment cards, 800 numbers, or Web sites typically receive. At checkout, guests are asked to answer several brief questions on a computer touch screen while the receptionist is processing the bill. Responding by touching a computer screen is easy and the guests need to wait at least briefly as the bill is processed. Most guests are willing to share their opinions about the quality of their hotel stay while the experience is fresh in their minds. This provides much better information to Marriott than they would receive if they received comment cards from just the very happy or very unhappy customers.[15]

BD's Mongolian Barbeque uses an electronic customer comment card. This hand-held device is provided to each table at the end of a meal. Customers input data that are immediately processed. The technology encourages more customers to complete the evaluation and enables easier analysis of the data. For example, the company can look at evaluations by server and shift and can track the number of declined requests to complete the survey. Furthermore, by means of a wireless paging system, the device also alerts managers to serious guest problems (such as a guest indicating that she does not plan to patronize the operation again), allowing the manager to take immediate action.[16]

Hospitality organizations seeking feedback on their service experiences will find ways to take advantage of the Web generation's inclination to be in constant communication with everybody as much as possible. Some organizations are already providing addresses so that customers can tweet their reactions while they are still in the midst of their experiences.

Surveys

Mail/Web Surveys

Well-developed mail or Web-based surveys, sent to an appropriate and willing sample, can provide trustworthy information concerning guest satisfaction. Brinker International, the parent company of such restaurants as Chili's, On the Border Mexican Grill and Cantina, and Maggiano's Little Italy, has developed a variation that combines the mail survey and the frequent-diner card program. The feedback advantages of the survey join with the card's promotion of guest loyalty and return visits. Once Brinker obtains basic guest demographic information on an application form for the card, it not only can record the buying patterns for that customer whenever the card is used but it can use the guest's address information to follow up with mailed surveys that will collect valuable feedback on eating preferences and patterns.

Yet, while organizations can use mailed or Web surveys to their benefit, many uncontrollable factors can influence guest responses to them. Inaccurate and incomplete mailing lists or Web addresses, or a simple lack of interest in responding, can produce a participation rate too small to provide useful information. In addition, the time lag between the experience and filling out a survey can blur a guest's memory of details. Further, many people have so many experiences across their lives that it is difficult to recall specifics of any one of them, especially when it was brief or unmemorable. Trying to learn why the experience you provided is not memorable is impossible when customers can't remember anything about it.

While these surveys are usually used to generate reports full of numbers, the subtleties of the guest experience and guest perceptions cannot be fully expressed numerically. Also, averages may not be sufficiently informative. If some guests remember an experience as terrific and give it a high rating while an equal number of other guests rate it low as terrible, the numerical average would suggest that guest expectations were met on average.

Finally, formal mail or Web-based survey techniques require proper questionnaire development, validation, and data analysis, so they can be expensive.

Telephone Surveys and Interviews

Telephone surveys and interviews are another useful method for assessing customer perceptions of service. Car dealerships, for example, frequently use telephone surveys to measure customer satisfaction with a recent transaction. In the hospitality industry, some tour operators call their customers to obtain feedback about a recent vacation experience while paving the way for subsequent travel arrangements.

Telephone surveys and interviews are easy to conduct and can be inexpensive. If the company's own employees make the calls in their slack times, the only costs are for setting up a well-designed interview/questionnaire and a calling strategy/protocol that will yield the best possible statistical results. The data-collection process must ensure that the data are captured into a database that will permit solid analysis of the responses. Moreover, a telephone survey allows the immediate identification of service failures (or successes). The guest being called might well tell the interviewer about a failure that would not otherwise have been reported to anyone who might be able to fix it or offer restitution. Finally, the telephone survey allows the company caller to probe deeper into issues raised by the respondent in ways that no online or mailed questionnaire can. Only a face-to-face encounter is a better way of digging deeper to capture the whole story behind either a service success or failure in sufficient detail to ensure that the service experience was provided in the way it was supposed to be or to find out why it wasn't.

Unfortunately, although telephone interviews eliminate the inconvenience to guests of gathering information while guests are still in the service location, they do present other challenges. Telephone interviews can be expensive when organizations use a trained interviewer who uses a sophisticated questionnaire to solicit feedback from guests. When data analysis and expert interpretation are included, the total cost for a statistically valid survey can become quite high.

This technique, like surveys, also relies on retrospective information that can be blurred by the passage of time. If the service received was too brief or insignificant for guests to recall accurately, or if guests have no special motivation to participate, the information they provide is likely to be unreliable or incomplete. In addition, in this age of intense telephone solicitation, customers often regard telephone surveys as intrusions on their time and violations of their privacy. Annoyed respondents feeling resentment toward the organization for calling them at home are likely to bias the data. Red Lobster and Captain D's avoid some of these difficulties by building into their guest checks a code that asks every nth guest to call an 800 number to respond by pressing Touchtone buttons to questions about their experience at the restaurant. In return for participation, the restaurant offers coupons for free desserts or "two entrées for the price of one" when the guest visits the next time.

Critical-Incidents Surveys

Another important survey tool is the critical-incidents technique. Through interviews or paper-and-pencil surveys, customers are asked to identify and evaluate numerous moments—classified as dissatisfiers, neutral, or satisfiers—in their interactions with the organization. The survey lets the organization know which moments are critical to customer satisfaction, and the critical dissatisfiers can be traced back to their root causes and rectified.

In one study done by a cruise line, for example, passengers were asked to describe one positive and one negative aspect of their cruise either on board or at a port of call that might have impacted their decision to take another cruise with this company's ships. Analysis of the responses indicated that ten negative and eight positive categories or themes emerged as critical incidents and factors. Once the cruise line knew which incidents passengers viewed as most important in determining their post-cruise evaluations of satisfaction (e.g., service, staff, and food), it could concentrate on turning any incidents with negative ratings into positives.[17]

Servqual

Of the many service quality measures that have been developed,[18] one well-accepted technique is **SERVQUAL** (short for "service quality"), developed by A. Parasuraman and his associates. An adaptation of the SERVQUAL survey instrument, designed to evaluate service quality at Belle's Restaurant, is presented in Figure 12-2. SERVQUAL has been

FIGURE **12-2** Instrument for Measuring Guest Perceptions of Service Quality at Belle's Restaurant

---

DIRECTIONS:

Listed below are five features pertaining to Belle's Restaurant and the services they offer. We would like to know how important each of these features is to you when you evaluate a restaurant's quality. Please allocate a total of 100 points among the five features according to how important each feature is to you—the more important a feature is to you, the more points you should allocate to it. Please ensure that the points you allocate to the five features add up to 100.

1. The appearance of the restaurant's physical facilities, equipment, and personnel. _____ points
2. The ability of the restaurant to perform the promised service dependably and accurately. _____ points
3. The willingness of the restaurant to help customers and provide prompt service. _____ points
4. The knowledge and courtesy of the restaurant's employees and their ability to convey trust and confidence. _____ points
5. The caring, individualized attention the restaurant provides to its customers. _____ points

DIRECTIONS:

Based on your experience as a customer of restaurants, please think about the kind of restaurant that would deliver excellent service quality. Think about the kind of restaurant at which you would be pleased to eat. Please show the extent to which you think such a restaurant would possess the feature described by each statement. If you feel a feature is not at all essential for excellent restaurants such as the one you have in mind, circle the number "1" for Strongly Disagree. If you feel a feature is absolutely essential for excellent restaurants, circle "7" for Strongly Agree. If your feelings are less strong, circle one of the numbers in the middle. There are no right or wrong answers—all we are interested in is a number that truly reflects your feelings regarding restaurants that would deliver excellent service quality. [The 22 survey items for this section are the same as those in the next section, but without any reference to Belle's Restaurant.]

DIRECTIONS:

The following set of statements relate to your feelings about the service at Belle's Restaurant. For each statement, please show the extent to which you believe Belle's Restaurant has the feature described by the statement. Once again, circling a "1" means that you Strongly Disagree that Belle's Restaurant has that feature, and circling a "7" means that you Strongly Agree. You may circle any of the numbers in the middle that show how strong your feelings are. There are no right or wrong answers—all we are interested in is a number that best shows your perceptions about the service at Belle's Restaurant. **[On the instrument itself, the five category labels (Tangibles, etc.) would be omitted.]**

TANGIBLES

1. Belle's Restaurant has modern-looking equipment.
2. Belle's Restaurant's physical facilities are visually appealing.
3. Belle's Restaurant's employees are neat-appearing.
4. Materials associated with the service (such as menus) are visually appealing at Belle's Restaurant.

RELIABILITY

5. When Belle's Restaurant promises to do something by a certain time, it does so.
6. When you have a problem, Belle's Restaurant shows sincere interest in solving it.
7. Belle's Restaurant performs the service right the first time.
8. Belle's Restaurant provides its services in the way it promises to do so.
9. Belle's Restaurant insists on error-free service performance.

RESPONSIVENESS

10. Employees of Belle's Restaurant tell you exactly when services will be performed.
11. Employees of Belle's Restaurant give you prompt service.
12. Employees of Belle's Restaurant are always willing to help you.
13. Employees of Belle's Restaurant are never too busy to respond to your requests.

ASSURANCE

14. The behavior of Belle's Restaurant employees instills confidence in customers.
15. You feel safe in going to Belle's Restaurant and doing business with them.
16. Employees of Belle's Restaurant are consistently courteous to you.
17. Employees of Belle's Restaurant have the knowledge to answer your questions.

EMPATHY

18. Belle's Restaurant gives you individual attention.
19. Belle's Restaurant has operating hours convenient to all its customers.
20. Belle's Restaurant has employees who give you personal attention.
21. Belle's Restaurant has your best interests at heart.
22. Employees of Belle's Restaurant try to learn your specific needs.

Source: Adapted from A. Parasuraman, V. A. Zeithaml, and L. L. Berry. 1988. SERVQUAL: A Multiple-Item Scale for Measuring Consumer Perception of Service Quality. *Journal of Retailing.* 64(1): 38–40. Used with permission.

extensively researched to validate its psychometric properties. It measures the way customers perceive the quality of service experiences in five categories: tangibles (the physical facilities, equipment, and personnel), reliability (the organization's ability to perform the desired service dependably, accurately, and consistently), responsiveness (its willingness to provide prompt service and help customers), assurance (employee knowledge, courtesy, and ability to convey trust), and empathy (providing caring, individualized attention to customers).[19]

SERVQUAL also asks respondents to rate the relative importance of the five areas, so organizations can understand what matters most to customers. In each area SERVQUAL asks customers what they expected and what they actually have experienced, to identify service gaps at which organizations should direct attention. Figure 12-2 shows how the items on the SERVQUAL instrument might be adapted to a restaurant situation.

The SERVQUAL instrument reflects a point we have made throughout—the importance of the frontline server to service quality. While tangibles refer primarily to the setting and to the physical elements of the delivery system, and reliability reflects a combination of organizational ability and server ability, the remaining three elements— responsiveness, assurance, and empathy—are almost exclusively the responsibility of the frontline server.

If an organization's quality ratings on any of the SERVQUAL categories are unsatisfactory, it might consider setting up performance standards for the unsatisfactory items. For example, if the responsiveness ratings are unsatisfactory, standards could be established for promptness and helpfulness.

Focus Groups

Focus groups provide in-depth information on how guests view the service they receive. Typically, six to ten guests gather with a facilitator for several hours to discuss perceived problems and make suggestions. Researcher J. Santos used focus groups to discover the critical characteristics for e-service Web sites.[20] By asking participants to bring in examples of good and bad Web sites to the group discussions, researchers identified many important factors that were important to e-service. Many hospitality organizations routinely invite current or former guests to participate in focus groups to discover their feelings about and perceptions of existing or potential service experiences. Current guests are especially valuable because they can share their reactions and insights before they leave the premises, before they can forget the details of the service they just experienced. Focus-group guests are usually impressed that the company cares enough about their opinions to ask for them, and they use the free return admission, complimentary dinner, or other expression of appreciation that compensates them for their time.

Focus groups are useful but also expensive, time consuming, and labor intensive. They require a group facilitator, meeting space, travel and sometimes lodging expenses for the facilitator and participants, and, typically, some compensation to the participants. Since focus groups should represent the targeted customer market, correct selection of participants is crucial in obtaining accurate information. If the customer sample is not accurate or doesn't match the desired customer profile, the resulting information can lead to inappropriate conclusions about customer experiences. A large hospitality organization like a theme park can pick ideal and representative groups from its thousands of customers; an individual restaurant, a hotel, or a travel agency will have much greater difficulty in assembling a focus group that accurately represents the targeted customer profile.

Customers Evaluating Service on Their Own

We have reviewed a number of ways in which companies can solicit feedback from customers. However, with the Internet facilitating the spread of information, and with so much information available through social media sources, customers often don't wait for the company to ask them what they think. Individuals post blogs, post information to company Web sites, send in unsolicited letters and e-mails, provide reviews on Web sites like TripAdvisor, or express their opinions on discussion boards. When researching where to stay or eat, many people look for these unsolicited reviews in places like blogs, TripAdvisor, or Yelp with the hope of finding useful information about the quality of various service products.

While customers posting information on their own is generally out of the company's control, some organizations proactively monitor this information to look for problems. Many hoteliers monitor TripAdvisor to see if any complaints have been posted. Some organizations use search tools to scan through blogs for mentions of their establishments. Other companies are hiring consulting companies specifically devoted to monitoring and tracking social media comments and trends. Clearly, when considering unsolicited information, the company has no idea of who responded, if they actually stayed or ate at the establishment, are expressing a typical problem, have some ulterior motives, or are actually real customers trying to give useful reviews. Nonetheless, this information is widely available and it does affect customer decisions, and so the best companies pay attention and seek to address problems that may appear in these customer-generated sources.

Mystery Shoppers

Mystery shoppers or secret shoppers provide management with a relatively objective snapshot of the guest experience. While posing as guests, these sometimes trained and sometimes untrained observers methodically sample the service and its delivery, take note of the environment, and then send a systematic and detailed report of their experience back to management. They are often specifically instructed to determine if service standards were met (did the server introduce herself, did their drinks come in under three minutes, were they offered an appetizer, etc.). They can sample a restaurant meal, a trip on a cruise ship, or an overnight stay at a full-service resort hotel. Shopper reports generally include numerical ratings of their observations so that assessments of the guest experience can be compared over time and with other organizations. While employees usually know that their organization uses a mystery-shopper program, they don't know who the shoppers are or when they will shop. Owners of smaller organizations, such as independent restaurateurs or hoteliers, can hire an individual consultant or ask a personal friend or university class to conduct a mystery-shopper program. Larger organizations and national chains may employ a commercial service or use their own staff as shoppers.

Since visits by mystery shoppers are unannounced, employees cannot "dress up" their performance. Research shows that shoppers are especially accurate when reporting objective aspects of the service experience (e.g., Server uniforms clean? Paper towels/trash on rest room floors?) where service standards are clearly set. In addition, shoppers can be scheduled at specific times to assess the quality of service during various shifts, under diverse conditions, with different employees, and through the eyes of different types of shoppers.[21] For example, a hotel designed as a family resort employed a shopper and her children to assess the "family-friendly" factor at the property. The children said the front desk counters were too high and prevented them from seeing what was going on. As a result, a special registration desk was installed where young guests could check in and learn about the activities available for them at the hotel.

Mystery shoppers can also observe competing organizations in a particular market and systematically gather information on their service level, facilities, prices, and special packages. Some hotels employ mystery shoppers to test the ability of their properties to respond to anticipated service problems and service delivery failures. For example, shoppers can create a problem or intensify a situation by asking certain questions or requesting unique services to assess employee responses under pressure.

Mystery shoppers can also gauge the effectiveness of a particular training or incentive program by shopping at a hospitality organization before and after the training occurs or incentive is implemented. They are more accurate than customer surveys when the experience or service encounter being assessed is too brief for most guests to recall accurately. Finally, and most importantly, mystery shoppers give managers objective data to use in coaching employees identified by the mystery shopper as performing poorly or in praising those identified as performing well. Because the appraisal is provided not by a manager but by a real customer, employees are more likely to accept the assessment as objective and fair. A manager can collaborate on improvements with employees when the performance data come from customers themselves.

The main disadvantage of using a mystery shopper is the small size of the sample from which the shopper generates reports. Since anyone can have a bad day or a bad shift, a mystery shopper may base conclusions on unusual or atypical experiences. One or two observations are not a statistically valid sample of anything, but hiring enough mystery shoppers to yield a valid sample would be impractical and too expensive for many organizations. Further, the unique preferences, biases, or expectations of individual shoppers can unduly influence a report. Well-trained shoppers with specific information about the organization's service standards, instructions on what to observe, and guidelines for evaluating the experience avoid this pitfall.

One restaurant, for example, employed mystery shoppers for daily visits to units in the chain. The data confirmed that the benefits in improved customer service and headcount outweighed the costs of the daily shopper program. The mystery shoppers were reimbursed only up to a fixed amount, and they were required to bring at least one paying dinner partner. Not only did this approach generate positive revenues, but further analysis revealed that the shopper program had the effect of a marketing campaign using coupons to get customers to try the restaurant, as the mystery shoppers liked the restaurant so much they were returning again and again to eat.[22]

FINDING AND USING THE TECHNIQUE THAT FITS

Tables 12-1 and 12-3 provide an overview of quality assessment methods and show some advantages and disadvantages of each. Organizations should choose the techniques that fit their particular purposes. A luxury resort hotel, for example, may require more elaborate and expensive strategies to measure feedback since any reports of poor service can harm the reputation and bottom line of the hotel, the brand with which the hotel is affiliated, and the livelihood of countless employees up and down the line. The value to such a hotel of finding and correcting service failures so that it can deliver the service quality its guests expect is tremendous. Failing to meet guest expectations will quickly make the hotel and all services and business affiliated with it uncompetitive in a dynamic marketplace. On the other hand, a small independent restaurant whose owner loves to "interview" his patrons will probably not require sophisticated quality assessment methods.

Costs and level of expertise used to gather data also vary. An important question to ask is who should collect data: line employees, managers, consultants, or a professional survey research organization. Using line employees and managers is the least expensive alternative, but they also have the least expertise in research and may lack the communication skills to interview effectively. Consultants and survey organizations cost more, but they are better able to gather and interpret more detailed statistical data using more sophisticated techniques. Employee-surveyors cannot measure eye-pupil dilation; some professionals can.

Finally, the organization must consider when to request feedback. Is information to be collected during or after the service is delivered? The best companies do not limit themselves to one approach and hope for the best; they do both. Information collected during the service experience (such as by talking to guests, using management by walking around, monitoring adherence to service standards and guarantees, using employee assessments of the guest experience, or having the technology to receive immediate feedback on evaluations) allows companies to react immediately to any problems. This information, though, cannot be analyzed in depth (at least at that moment) because by its nature it requires quick decision making to respond to immediate customer concerns. Information collected after the service experience (such as through analyzing comment cards, toll-free numbers, surveys, and gathering reports from mystery shoppers) gives companies much more detailed information about service quality. Taking the time to conduct detailed analysis provides valuable information on trends in guest services and issues, indicates where problems might be emerging, and helps spot service problems that can perhaps be fixed before they escalate into large service failures.

Your Best Evaluators: The Guests

Regardless of the evaluation technique selected to measure service quality, one thing is certain. Guests evaluate service every time it is delivered, forming distinct opinions about its quality and value. All hospitality organizations that aspire to excellence must constantly assess the quality of their guest experience through their guests' eyes—while planning the experience, during the experience, and after it is over. Although guests will usually offer an unsolicited opinion only if they are very satisfied or dissatisfied with their experience, most guests are happy to offer an opinion if they are asked in the right way at the right time. Telephone surveyors calling on Friday night at dinner time will get the rejection they deserve. Hospitality managers striving for excellence need to find appropriate methods to elicit from guests the information necessary to ensure service that meets and exceeds guest expectations.

The Improvement Cycle Continues

Once the systems for identifying service failures and delivery system flaws have been put in place, the data that they have generated have been collected systematically, and the customers who were the source of complaints have been contacted and offered restitution, the organization can now use all of this information to revisit its planning process for the entire service experience. Knowing what has failed, and even what has not failed, provides the knowledge needed to reassess all aspects of the service experience to ensure that where it has not met guest expectations, it will do so in the future; where it has only met expectations, it might be improved to exceed them; and where it has exceeded expectations, it can learn why and how to extend the features that led to success to other parts of the experience. In other words, the benchmark organizations in hospitality or any service industry use information to learn how to improve. A key element in the continuous-improvement philosophy—which the best organizations use to drive continual reassessment of what they do—is to learn from their own history how to improve their future. The tools and techniques covered across the past several chapters are the means by which they gather the information needed to drive continuous improvement. Using these tools and techniques consistently and effectively is how the best stay the best.

LESSONS LEARNED

1. The quality of employee work and the quality of guest service can be different; manage so as to achieve high quality in both.

2. If you don't measure it, you can't manage it; if you don't manage it, you can't improve it.

3. Balance the value of service information obtained from guests with the cost of obtaining it.

4. Recognize the strengths and weaknesses of available assessment techniques.

5. The more sophisticated the information needed from guests, the more expensive it is to acquire.

6. If you want to become or stay the best, be proactive. Be driven to continuously learn and improve.

REVIEW QUESTIONS

1. Is it critically important for hospitality organizations to measure how satisfied guests are with service quality and value? Or is it sometimes sufficient for organizations simply to offer the best service they can and hope for the best?

2. Regarding the strengths and weaknesses of different methods for measuring service quality:

    A. What are the strengths and weaknesses of managerial observation?

    B. What are the strengths and weaknesses of guest comment cards?

    C. Why is the comment card technique used so frequently in spite of its weaknesses?

3. What provisions would you expect to find in a typical service guarantee for a restaurant?

    A. What are the advantages and disadvantages to restaurants of offering such a guarantee?

    B. How might the service guarantees of a quick-serve restaurant and a fine-dining restaurant differ?

    C. Why would a hotel be more apt to use a guarantee than a restaurant, or a restaurant than a hotel? Do the restaurants with which you are familiar have guarantees?

4. What are the advantages and disadvantages to hospitality organizations of mystery shoppers? In which types of hospitality organizations do you think mystery shoppers would be most and least effective?

5. To what extent should managers use a cost/benefit analysis when trying to determine which techniques to use to measure the guest's perception of the guest experience's quality and value?

ACTIVITIES

1. Collect guest comment cards or examine Web-based surveys from several hospitality organizations and compare the factors about which organizations solicit comments. What conclusions can you draw? If possible, interview the managers whose organizations make the cards or Web-surveys available to guests and ask how the managers use the results.

2. Imagine that you are a mystery shopper for a hotel. Write up a list of the activities in which you would engage, starting with deciding how long you will stay to do a thorough evaluation (twenty-four hours? forty-eight hours?). Develop service standards, such as for calling in to make a reservation. (What will your "number of rings" standard be? three rings? four rings?, and so forth.) What evaluation system will you use for the different hotel areas? Pass/fail? An excellent-through-poor scale?

3. Go mystery shopping. If appropriate, use some of the activities from your hotel evaluation list created for question 2. Or do a quick evaluation or service audit using "the three Ts"—Task, Treatment, Tangibles. Write up a brief description of what you found and observed on your shopping trip and send it to the manager of the service location.

4. Either in groups or individually, use Hart's criteria for a good service guarantee as presented in this chapter and create a guarantee for a real or imaginary hospitality organization.

ETHICS IN BUSINESS

A national restaurant chain in the United States has an interesting policy to help detect service problems. If any tip to a server is particularly low, the server must immediately report it to the manager. The manager then inquires as to what problem there might have been. If there was a problem, the manager can perhaps take some steps to correct the situation. This policy raises some interesting questions:

1. Is it appropriate to require servers to report low tips? The requirement may place the server in a very uncomfortable position. A server may have to report a low tip knowing it is justified because of his poor service, or the server may know that everything was fine and by reporting the low tip, she will be placing the customer in an uncomfortable and embarrassing situation. On the other hand, failure to report a low tip can result in the server being fired. Is it appropriate to put servers in this position?

2. What responsibility, if any, does a restaurant have to inform customers as to what is an appropriate tip? Many tourists from other countries do not know the "norm" in the United States to provide a tip of 15 percent–20 percent of check size. Even many Americans do not necessarily know this "norm." Should the company take steps to educate customers before causing them public embarrassment?

CASE STUDIES

Try Before You Buy: The Service Guarantee

Ed Jennings had never stayed at Super 10 Suites before, but he hadn't been very satisfied with the only other lodging establishment in Grover, Montana, a regular stop in his western sales territory, so he decided to try Super 10. The guarantee of service offered by Super 10 persuaded him to make the switch. It was basic, but it offered all that Ed wanted:

"Try before you buy. We guarantee that your rooms will be cleaned, inspected and ready, with all amenities in place, or you pay nothing! No questions asked. We want you to be happy in your choice of Super 10 Suites, Grover's finest."

Ed checked in late in the evening after a hard day on the road, went to his room, and looked around. The room wasn't exactly dirty, but it wasn't exactly clean either. There were small scraps of paper on the floor, some hair in the sink, and mold in the shower. He sat down in a chair, opened the complimentary bag of pretzels, and chewed on one while he thought about whether to stay or to leave.

"Oh, well, if it doesn't get any worse than this, I guess I can take it."

Without going into all the details, it did get worse. The hot water didn't work, the bed was lumpy, and the air conditioner failed during the night. A screaming baby in the next room kept Ed awake for several hours. When Ed checked out the next day, he informed the clerk that he was exercising his service guarantee; he wasn't going to pay. Of course the clerk asked why, and Ed explained the problems he had experienced.

"Your guarantee said the room would be clean and inspected, and it was not clean. There was hair in the sink, paper scraps on the floor, and mold in the shower."

"No," said the clerk. "The guarantee says that the room will be cleaned, and it was cleaned, last week. As for inspection, I inspected it myself."

Ed said, "When you inspected it, didn't you notice the scraps, the hair, and the mold?"

"This guarantee doesn't say anything about what I noticed or didn't notice. It just says the room was inspected. And before you even ask about the amenities, that's what the pretzels are—amenities."

"All that may be true," said Ed, "but this guarantee says 'No questions asked.' "

"Didn't you see the asterisk by that? Didn't you see the fine print?" asked the clerk. "The asterisk refers to our statement at the bottom that if you ask questions, this guarantee is null and void. This other asterisk, which apparently you didn't see either, says that 'This guarantee and the terms thereof shall be valid and its terms exercisable with respect to the cost of one night's room only, with all the covenants appertaining thereunto. Management shall retain its sole and exclusive right to interpret the terms of the guarantee.' In my opinion, and I'm the management this morning, we fulfilled our guarantee to you the guest, and then some."

Ed Jennings gave it up. He had sales calls to make. Mighty tired and upset, he headed out into the day.

What was wrong with this guarantee? Indicate as many faults as you can.

Standard Times at Happy's Restaurant

The top management at Happy's Restaurants, Inc., had assigned its new Work Methods and Standards Department the task of establishing "standard times" for the chain's units. Work Methods personnel went out into the restaurants as mystery shoppers and observed operations carefully. Work Methods then reported to management that the speed and efficiency of service in virtually all of the restaurants was in need of improvement.

Laura Martin, manager of a very successful and profitable Happy's Restaurant in South Carolina, got the e-mailed memo about the new "standard times for food and cocktail service" late one afternoon. A highly experienced server herself and a respected manager, Martin just laughed at the proposed standards and set the memo aside. She thought she had noticed some mystery shoppers making secret notes, so she had expected some kind of ivory-tower memo like this. It might look good on paper, but it just couldn't be done.

Next day at the afternoon meeting, Martin told her servers: "If you hear anything about new standard times and methods for serving food and drinks, don't pay any attention. As you know, we have all committed ourselves to getting the entrées to guests within eighteen minutes of taking their orders, but our average is sixteen minutes. We've been averaging sixteen for all the years I've been here, and our comment-card results on promptness are excellent. Because you are all terrific at your jobs, I'd say fifteen minutes is the absolute best we could do. But those bozos at headquarters say the new standard is all entrées to guests within fourteen minutes of taking the order." The servers looked at each other with disbelief, then they started to laugh.

"And they also think we can have the drinks on the tables within three minutes of first guest contact." The servers just rolled their eyes and smiled. "Don't worry," said Laura Martin. "I'll straighten this out in a hurry." Martin sent her boss an e-mail telling him that the new standards had to be a mistake because they were entirely unrealistic.

Her boss soon called her and straightened her out in a hurry: "Laura, the new standards will go into effect tomorrow. Work Methods has achieved improved results in several of our other chains already, and now all Happy's branches must conform. Sure, servers always resist at first, but they can meet the standards if you lay down the law, and if they use more efficient methods."

"Maybe that's true elsewhere," said Laura, "but I know my restaurant, my kitchen staff, my servers, and my guests, and I know we can't make fourteen minutes, even with these new methods they want us to use. Things can only be done so fast."

"Martin, call a meeting of your staff, explain that the new standard times will be met, teach your people the new methods, stick to managing your unit, and leave methods and times to the Work Methods and Standards Department. That's what we pay you for, and that's what we pay them for."

Martin tried her best, but her restaurant knew how she felt about the situation. The servers at this South Carolina Happy's Restaurant failed to meet the new work standards, and the head of the Work Methods and Standards Department blamed Laura Martin. He recommended that new talent should be located for her position.

1. What is the problem here?

2. Under what circumstances can such "by the minute" standards be made to work?

3. How would you determine service standards at your restaurant?

ADDITIONAL READINGS

Afify, M. F. 2008. Quality management. In P. Jones (ed.), *Handbook of Hospitality Operations and IT*. Oxford, UK: Butterworth-Heinemann, pp. 295–338.

Akbaba, A. 2006. Measuring service quality in the hotel industry: A study in a business hotel in Turkey. *International Journal of Hospitality Management*, 25, 170–192.

Baker, T., & Collier, D. A. 2005. The economic impact model for service guarantees. *Decision Sciences*, 36, 197–220.

Bell, C. R., Zemke, R., Bush, J., & Zielinski, D. 2007. *Managing Knock Your Socks Off Service*, 2nd edition. New York: AMACOM.

Bartkus, K. R., Howell, R. D., Hills, S. B., & Blackham, J. 2009. The quality of guest comment cards: An empirical study of U.S. lodging chains. *Journal of Travel Research*, 48, 162–176.

Beck, J., & Miao, L. 2003. Mystery shopping in lodging properties as a measurement of service quality. *Journal of Quality Assurance in Hospitality & Tourism*, 4 (1/2), 1–21.

Benítez, J. M., Martín, J. C., & Román, C. 2007. Using fuzzy number for measuring quality of service in the hotel industry. *Tourism Management*, 28, 544–555.

Berry, L. L., & Parasuraman, A. 2004. *Marketing Services: Competing Through Quality*. New York: Free Press.

Berry, L. L., Wall, E. A., & Carbone, L. P. 2006. Service clues and customer assessment of the service experience: Lessons from marketing. *Academy of Management Perspectives*, 20, 43–57.

Berry, L. L. 2009. Competing with quality service in good times and bad. *Business Horizons*, 52, 309–317.

Blind, K. 2006. A taxonomy of standards in the service sector: Theoretical discussion and empirical test. *The Service Industries Journal*, 26, 397–420.

Briggs, S., Sutherland, J., & Drummond, S. 2007. Are hotels serving quality: An exploratory study of service quality in the Scottish hotel sector. *Tourism Management*, 28, 1005–1019.

Buttle, F. 1996. SERVQUAL: Review, critique, research agenda. *European Journal of Marketing*, 30 (1), 8–32.

Caro, L. M., & Garcia, J. A. M. 2007. Developing a multidimensional and hierarchical service quality model for the travel agency industry. *Tourism Management*, 29, 706–720.

Chon, K. S., Kandampully, J., Mok, C., & Sparks, B. 2001. *Service Quality Management in Hospitality, Tourism, and Leisure*. New York: Routledge.

Chow, I. H.-S., Lau, V. P., Lo, T. W.-C., Sha, Z., & Yun, H. 2006. Service quality in restaurant operations in China: Decision-and experiential-oriented perspectives. *International Journal of Hospitality Management*, 26, 698–710.

Cronin, J. J., & Taylor, S. A. 1994. SERVPERF versus SERVQUAL: Reconciling performance-based and perceptions-minus-expectations measurement of service quality. *Journal of Marketing*, 58, 125–131.

Davis, C. 2003. The science of service: Analyzing the elements of quality assurance. *Business Travel News*, 20 (22), 6–10.

Fabien, L. 2005. Design and implementation of a service guarantee. *Journal of Services Marketing*, 19, 33–38.

Facella, P. 2009. *Everything I Know About Business I Learned at McDonald's*. New York: McGraw-Hill.

Haktanir, H., & Harris, P. 2005. Performance measurement practice in an independent hotel context. *International Journal of Contemporary Hospitality Management*, 17 (1), 39–50.

Hays, J. M., & Hill, A. V. 2006. Service guarantee strength: The key to service quality. *Journal of Operations Management*, 24, 753–764.

Hays, J. M., & Hill, A. V. 2006. An extended longitudinal study of the effects of a service guarantee. *Productions and Operations Management*, 15 (1), 117–131.

Hocutt, M. A., & Bowers, M. R. 2005. The impact of service guarantees on consumer responses in the hotel industry. *Journal of Hospitality & Leisure Marketing*, 31 (1), 5–23.

Hogreve, J., & Gremler, D. D. 2009. Twenty years of service guarantee research: A synthesis. *Journal of Service Research*, 11, 322–343.

Hudson, S., Hudson, P., & Miller, G. A. 2004. The measurement of service quality in the tour operating sector: A methodological comparison. *Journal of Travel Research*, 42, 305–312.

Ladhari, R. 2008. Alternative measures of service quality: A review. *Managing Service Quality*, 18 (1), 65–86.

Liden, S. B., & Edvardsson, B. 2003. Customer expectations on service guarantees. *Managing Service Quality*, 13, 338–348.

Liden, S. B., & Skalen, P. 2003. The effect of service guarantees on service recovery. *International Journal of Service Industry Management*, 14 (1), 36–58.

McCaskey, D., & Symes, S. 2004. Travel Inn: Everything you want for a good night's sleep – 100 percent satisfaction or your money back. *International Journal of Contemporary Hospitality Management*, 16, 166–174.

McCollough, M. A., & Gremler, D. D. 2004. A conceptual model and empirical examination of the effect of service guarantees on post-purchase consumption evaluations. *Managing Service Quality*, 14 (1), 58–74.

Maguire, S., Koh, S. C. L., & Huang, C. 2007. Identifying the range of customer listening tools: A logical pre-cursor to CRM? *Industrial Management and Data Systems*, 107, 567–586.

Min, H., & Min, H. 2006. The comparative evaluation of hotel service quality from a managerial perspective. *Journal of Hospitality Marketing & Management*, 13 (3/4), 53–77.

Morgan, I., & Rao, J. 2002. Aligning service strategy through super-measure management. *Academy of Management Executive*, 16 (4), 121–131.

Mukherjee, A., & Nath, P. 2005. An empirical assessment of comparative approaches to service quality measurement. *Journal of Services Marketing*, 19, 174–184.

Oh, H., & Parks, S. C. 1997. Customer satisfaction and service quality: A critical review of the literature and research implications for the hospitality industry. *Hospitality Research Journal*, 20 (3), 35–64.

Parasuraman, A., Zeithaml, V. A., & Berry, L. 1991. Refinement and reassessment of the SERVQUAL Scale. *Journal of Retailing*, 67, 420–450.

Petrick, J. F., Tonner, C., & Quinn, C. 2006. The utilization of critical incident technique to examine cruise passengers' repurchase intentions. *Journal of Travel Research*, 44, 273–280.

Prideaux, B., Moscardo, G., & Laws, E. 2006. *Managing Tourism and Hospitality Services: Theory and International Applications*. Oxfordshire, UK: ABI.

Pritchard, M. P., & Havitz, M. E. 2005. Destination appraisal: An analysis of critical incidents. *Annals of Tourism Research*, 33 (1), 25–46.

Ramdeen, C., Santos, J., & Chatfield, H. K. 2007. Measuring the cost of quality in a hotel restaurant operation. *International Journal of Contemporary Hospitality Management*, 19, 286–295.

Santos, J. 2003. E-service quality: A model of virtual service quality dimensions. *Managing Service Quality*, 13, 233–246.

Sowder, J. 2006. The 100% satisfaction guarantee: Ensuring quality at Hampton Inn. *National Productivity Review*, 15 (2), 53–66.

Susskind, A. M., Kacmar, K. M., & Borchgrevink, C. P. 2007. How organizational standards and coworker support improve restaurant service. *Cornell Hotel and Restaurant Administration Quarterly*, 48 (4), 370–379.

Testa, M. R., & Sipe, L. J. 2006. A systems approach to service quality: Tools for hospitality leaders. *Cornell Hotel and Restaurant Administration Quarterly*, 47 (1), 36–48.

Tsaur, S.-H., & Wang, C.-H. 2009. Tip collection strategies, service guarantees, and consumer evaluations of group package tours. *Journal of Travel Research* 47, 523–534.

van der Wiele, T., Hesselink, M., & van Iwaarden, J. 2005. Mystery shopping: A tool to develop insight into customer service provision. *Total Quality Management & Business Excellence*, 16, 529–541.

Wang, K. C., Hsieh, A. T., Chou, S. H., & Lin, Y. S. 2007. GPTCCC: An instrument for measuring group package tour service. *Tourism Management*, 28, 361–376.

Wilkins, H., Merrilees, B., & Herington, C. 2007. Towards an understanding of total service quality in hotels. *International Journal of Hospitality Management*, 26, 840–653.

Williams, C., & Buswell, J. 2003. *Service Quality in Leisure and Tourism*. Oxford, UK: CBI

Yang, C.-C. 2003. Establishment and applications of the integrated model of service quality measurement. *Managing Service Quality*, 13, 310–324.

---

[1]Wyckoff, D. D. 1984. New tools for achieving service quality. *Cornell Hotel and Restaurant Administration Quarterly*, 24 (6), 156.

[2]For a taxonomy of service standards, see Blind, K. 2006. A taxonomy of standards in the service sector: Theoretical discussion and empirical test. *The Service Industries Journal*, 26, 397–420.

[3]Prokesch, S. E. 1995. Competing on customer service: An interview with British Airways' Sir Colin Marshall. *Harvard Business Review*, 73 (6), 101–112.

[4]Morgan, I., & Rao, J. 2002. Aligning service strategy through super-measure management. *Academy of Management Executive*, 16 (4), 121–131.

[5]Tisch, J. M. 2004. *The Power of We*. Hoboken, NJ: John Wiley & Sons.

[6]For a thorough review of advantages and disadvantages of service guarantees, see Hogreve, J., & Gremler, D. D. 2009. Twenty years of service guarantee research: A synthesis. *Journal of Service Research*, 11, 322–343.

[7]Tax, S. S., & Brown, S. W. 1998. Recovering and learning from service failure. *Sloan Management Review*, 39 (3), 75.

[8]Fabien, L. 2005. Design and implementation of a service guarantee. *The Journal of Services Marketing*, 19, 33–38.

[9]Hart, C. W. L. 1988. The power of unconditional service guarantees. *Harvard Business Review*, 66 (4), 54–62.

[10]Hocutt, M. A., & Bowers, M. R. 2005. The impact of service guarantees on consumer responses in the hotel industry. *Journal of Hospitality & Leisure Marketing*, 31 (1), 5–23.

[11]Hart, 1988.

[12]Blodgett, J. G., Granbois, D. G., & Walters, R. G. 1993. The effects of perceived justice complainants' negative word-of-mouth behavior and repatronage intentions. *Journal of Retailing*, 69, 399–428.

[13]Bartkus, K. R., Howell, R. D., Hills, S. B., & Blackham, J. 2009. The quality of guest comment cards: An empirical study of U.S. lodging chains. *Journal of Travel Research*, 48, 162–176.

[14]http://www.westinnandsuites.com/guest-comments/index.cfm

NOTES

[15]Tax & Brown, 1998, p. 76.

[16]Ross, J. R. 2006. BD's chain solicits guest feedback with electronic comment cards. *Nation's Restaurant News*, May 8, p. 26.

[17]Petrick, J. F., Tonner, C., & Quinn, C. 2006. The utilization of critical incident technique to examine cruise passenger' repurchase intentions. *Journal of Travel Research*, 44 (3), 273–280.

[18]For a discussion of these alternative measures, see Ladhari, R. 2008. Alternative measures of service quality: A review. *Managing Service Quality*, 18 (1), 65–86; and Hudson, S., Hudson, P., & Miller, G. A. 2004. The measurement of service quality in the tour operating sector: A methodological comparison. *Journal of Travel Research*, 42, 305–312.

[19]Parasuraman, A., Zeithaml, V. A., & Berry, L. L. 1988. SERVQUAL: A multiple-item scale for measuring consumer perception of service quality. *Journal of Retailing*, 64, 12–40; Hospitality applications of SERVQUAL may be found in Knutson, B., Stevens, P., & Patton, M. 1995. DINESERV: Measuring service quality in quick service, casual/theme, and fine dining restaurants. *Journal of Hospitality and Leisure Marketing*, 3 (2), 35–44; Knutson, B., Stevens, P., Wullaert, C., Patton, M., & Yokoyama, F. 1991. LODGSERV: A service quality index for the lodging industry. *Hospitality Research Journal*, 14, 277–284; and Lee, Y. L., & Hing, N. 1995. Measuring quality in restaurant operations: An application of the SERVQUAL instrument. *International Journal of Hospitality Management*, 3, 293–310.

[20]Santos, J. 2003. E-service quality: A model of virtual service quality dimensions. *Managing Service Quality*, 13, 233–246.

[21]Miles, L. 1993. Rise of the mystery shopper. *Marketing* (March), 19. See also Morrall, K. 1994. Mystery shopping tests service and compliance. *Bank Marketing* (February), 13.

[22]Ford, R. C., Latham, G. P., & Lennox, G. In press. Mystery shoppers: A new tool for coaching employee performance improvement. *Organizational Dynamics*.

CHAPTER 13

Fixing Service Failures

HOSPITALITY PRINCIPLE: DON'T FAIL THE GUEST TWICE

You want your customers to tell you when you've screwed up, so that you can take care of the problem and take steps to ensure that it doesn't happen again—to them, or anybody. If they don't tell you they'll just walk away shaking their heads and they'll never come back. Worse, you're likely to alienate somebody in the future by doing exactly the same thing.

—Carl Sewell, *Customers for Life*

Do whatever is necessary to take care of guests.

—J. Willard Marriott, Jr., Chairman and CEO, Marriott International

LEARNING OBJECTIVES

After reading this chapter, you should understand:

- How guests respond when the guest experience fails to meet their expectations.

- How organizations should respond when the experience fails to meet guest expectations.

- Why fixing service failures quickly—on the spot, if possible—is so important.

- Why positive word of mouth is so valuable and bad word of mouth so harmful.

- Why the recovery method for handling a service failure is so important.

- How to learn from service failures.

- How guests evaluate the hospitality organization's recovery efforts.

- How to match the recovery strategy to the failure.

NO PERFECT SERVICE SYSTEMS

As we first stated in Chapter 1 and have reiterated throughout the book, providing a service is not like making a refrigerator on an assembly line where you can bring in an industrial engineer to study the production process that makes the refrigerator, see the product as it is being built, and check it for flaws after it is completed. While parts of most guest experiences are tangible and produced by a similar production process, like a kitchen in a restaurant that produces a dinner, the service that the guest experiences is only partially produced by a physical production process. The rest of the product is intangible. Add the fact that the product's value and quality are determined by the guest at the moment or over the period of consumption and you see why all the methods engineers in the world cannot build a 100 percent reliable, dependable service system. The guest sees, experiences, and evaluates the service. The guest decides what the experience was worth, whether it was worth returning for, whether to tell friends and neighbors that it was great or poor, and whether the overall experience was satisfactory. To succeed under these circumstances, any service delivery system has to be as nearly perfect as thoughtful planners can make it. The best systems must also have flexibility, allowing the appropriately trained and motivated employee to solve problems and ensure customer satisfaction.

When something goes wrong in the delivery of a service, it is called a **service failure**. As noted earlier, the best way to handle a service failure is to prevent it before it occurs. This involves building proactive or preventive strategies into the design of the service experience and its delivery system. These techniques, such as blueprinting, PERT/CPM, simulations, and fishbone analysis, were covered in Chapter 10. Yet, despite the greatest of efforts during the planning phase, and no matter how many poka-yokes, checks, or failsafes are put in place, not all failures can be prevented. Therefore, quality must be constantly monitored and measured during the delivery phase to minimize failure and ensure success. Measures can be used to collect information during the service delivery processes so that errors can be immediately identified and addressed, or after the service so that systems can be updated, corrected, or improved in such a way that future service is delivered more effectively. But when a failure does occur, steps should be taken to fix it, ideally on the spot, for the guest.

Chapter 12 discussed various methods used to collect information to measure service delivery quality. When these methods indicate that a guest has experienced a service failure, organizations must find ways to both fix the failure and improve their systems to prevent a recurrence of the failure. In this chapter, we shall focus on strategies for finding and fixing service failures. The methods we discuss are the result of both process and outcome service quality assessment strategies. Although service failures should be rare, and for the best hospitality organizations they are, this is such an important topic to managers committed to providing a great experience for each and every guest that it merits its own chapter.

Here is another reason for studying service failures intensely. In Chapter 10 we discussed the importance of assessing the service experience to improve the system. Tables 12-1 and 12-3 listed numerous ways for measuring service quality during and after the service experience, such as guest surveys, comment cards, employee feedback, focus groups, mystery shoppers, and others. All of these are important, and they may reveal many interesting findings regarding the delivery of service. But the information most likely to lead to service-delivery improvement is data about service failures. If the organization wanted to, it could review and study every aspect of the delivery system; however, if it did so, it would probably be analyzing many aspects that "ain't broke." Information about the service failure shows where something went wrong. The best way to improve the system and deliver better service in the future is to determine, by studying service failures, how to minimize them and refer those findings back to the system planners.

Stuck in the Snow

Service failures in the airline industry are a commonplace discussion topic among travelers, on the Internet, in newspapers, and on television. Compare the following two service failures by airlines and how they were handled.

Continental Flight 2816, operated by ExpressJet, was flying from Houston to Minneapolis. Weather conditions forced it to land in Rochester, Minnesota, at 12:28 A.M. on a Saturday where the passengers sat on the tarmac next to the terminal for the next 5½ hours with babies screaming, toilets overflowing, and the terminal tantalizingly near. The ExpressJet spokesperson said that no ground handlers were available to deplane the passengers at that hour of the morning. The airport said that was not true and that Delta's still available ground handlers repeatedly contacted them to ask permission to deplane the stranded passengers. The passengers' agony did not end when morning came and they could finally get off the plane. ExpressJet said that no buses were available to transport the stranded passengers to Minneapolis, their final destination. Moreover, the plane could not take off again as the crew was over its legal flying limit. When a relief crew finally got into Rochester to fly the plane to Minneapolis, the airline closed the toilets as no one had thought to get ground service to empty them. When the plane finally arrived in Minneapolis over nine hours after it landed in Rochester, the passengers stormed the ExpressJet counter to express their anger and dissatisfaction. As a last part of this story, the news media publicized this incident across the country as another example of an uncaring airline industry, causing

Stuck in the snow. The original cause of a service failure may be beyond a company's control, but what it does to manage the service failure can have dramatic effects on its reputation and future repatronage.

Congressional leaders to call for an expansion of passenger rights and reimbursement amounts.[1] Negative articles about the airline industry appear frequently in the newspapers, and just about everybody can tell stories of lost bags, indifferent and unhelpful desk agents, missed connections, or long unexplained waits. It is little wonder that the general frustration has led to formal efforts to regulate the industry more tightly and to informal airline passenger advice and advocacy. Web sites such as the one set up by Hendrick Noorderhaven in Europe help fliers win penalty payments for long delays, cancelled flights, and being bumped against their will.[2]

Contrast this service with that delivered by the motivated, empowered Scandinavian Air Service (SAS) purser in the following example. A planeload of SAS passengers was stuck at an airport because of snow. Because the purser knew that the SAS philosophy was to do whatever is necessary to satisfy the customers, or at least try to, she decided to offer them free coffee and biscuits. She went to the catering supervisor, a middle manager who outranked her, and asked for forty extra servings. Because each flight was allocated only so many cups of coffee and biscuits, the catering supervisor refused the request.

The purser could have let the system defeat her, but she noticed that the plane at the next gate belonged to Finnair, an airline that purchased food and drink from the SAS catering department. The SAS purser asked the Finnair purser to order the coffee and biscuits, because the catering supervisor was required by SAS regulations to fill the order for Finnair. The SAS purser then bought the coffee and biscuits from the Finnair purser with petty cash, and the stranded customers received a welcome snack.[3]

The purser solved a problem by finding a way around regulations and the catering supervisor. Through the empowered purser, the system "healed itself" without managerial intervention to achieve the airline's primary goal: customer satisfaction. Everybody was happy—except the angry, confused, bypassed catering supervisor. The system failed once when it could not accommodate the purser's desire to satisfy the customers, recovered briefly by giving the frontline purser the autonomy to solve the customer problems, then failed again in not telling a middle manager how to deal with the autonomy that had been granted to a subordinate.

Service failures can vary considerably across the dimensions of frequency, timing, and severity. A guest can experience a service failure anytime during a single experience or across multiple experiences. Failures can happen to first-time guests or long-time customers. Errors are more noticeable to long-time friends than they are to new customers. Since first impressions are so important, a failure occurring early may weigh more heavily than one occurring late. And obviously, big mistakes count more than little ones.

No matter how hard the organization works to prevent service failures in the first place by using the tools and methods covered earlier in this book, they can't avoid them all. If the organization fails once by not providing the expected guest experience, then not fixing this failure is failing the guest twice. This chapter shows the importance of finding and fixing service failures, the reasons why failures happen, and the strategies available to recover from and avoid future service failures.

SERVICE FAILURES: TYPES, WHERE, AND WHY
Types of Service Failures

A well-accepted categorization of service failures divides them into four types:

1. Service product failures—These include any failure in the core service products (e.g., cold or poorly prepared food, unavailable hotel room, or broken attraction),

service settings (e.g., dirty or smelly rooms, no directional signs, or overly worn carpets), and service systems (e.g., out-of-stock items, inoperative credit card machines, or disorganized servers).

2. Failure to meet explicit or implicit customer requests—These include any inability to provide what guests ask for, such as special requests on menu items, a nonsmoker being put in a smoking room, or not honoring a reservation.

3. Failures caused by employee actions or inactions—These include both intentional and unintentional acts such as showing rudeness or bad attitude or not presenting a meal or bill in a timely way.

4. Failures caused by other guests, random events, or circumstances beyond the control of the organization but which guests will still expect to be fixed.

Service failures can also occur for a combination of these four basic reasons. For example, a rude server may bring a salad that was poorly prepared by a supplier along with an entrée to a guest who asked that the salad come out first, thereby committing errors of the first three types. If the guest gets very angry, begins yelling and cursing at the server, and makes an unpleasant scene in the restaurant that ruins another party's evening, then the fourth type of service failure would occur. Regardless of the reason or combination of reasons, a service failure can dramatically reduce customer satisfaction and can have severe negative consequences for the business.

In a study that analyzed critical incidents during service encounters to identify the reasons for customers switching to other products or services, three common problems emerged.[4] The most common reasons people switched was due to failures in the service itself (such as mistakes committed by staff, technical failures, billing errors, or service catastrophes); they were mentioned by 44 percent of all respondents (noted by 11 percent as sole reason and 33 percent as one of two or more reasons). The second largest category of service failures involved employees' inappropriate actions, negative attitudes, or bad behaviors (noted by 34 percent). If employees were perceived as uncaring, impolite, rude, unresponsive, uncommunicative, or unknowledgeable (as in inexperienced, untrained, inept, out of date), they failed. The third largest category of reasons why people switched was unsatisfactory employee response to service failure (noted by 17 percent). When employees respond reluctantly, fail to respond with empathy or at all, or offer negative responses—for example, blaming the customer for service failure—customers understandably find those responses unsatisfactory and may switch even if the initial failure was not a sufficient motive to switch.[5] Summing those percentages reveals that when customers switch from one product or service to another, they do so more than half the time because of the way they were treated or spoken to by employees. Most of the time, service failures occur when the people part of the delivery system let customers down. The challenge this creates for managers is that the servers who create the failures are the same ones that must not only admit that they failed in order to fix it for the guests, but they must also trust their managers enough to tell them about their failures.

Customer Failure

Customer unhappiness is not always the hospitality organization's fault. Another source of failure is the customers themselves. The company may have done a perfect job of producing a meal to a customer's specifications, but the diner simply may not like the taste. For example, a diner might order halibut steak thinking it was a cut of beef; a guest may have ignored an "emergency exit only" sign and set off the alarm; or a guest may have lost a set of keys, a child, or money. Even though the organization does not create these problems—which are often beyond the organization's ability to manage no matter how much they train their people, perfect their systems and refine their services—the organization must still address them.

The organization should also be ready to handle those failures caused by other guests—the diner who sneezes on another diner's food, the sports bar Red Sox fan who tries to knock down the Yankee fan, the inconsiderate passenger who cuts in front of others at the airport security line, or loud talkers in a movie theater or concert hall. However, while doing everything in its power to rectify such situations, the hospitality organization should not admit liability for unfortunate, unavoidable occurrences that are not its fault. The Red Sox fan would probably have gone after the Yankee fan in any venue.

Attributing one's successes to oneself and one's failures to others is simple human nature. Guestologists know that. Hospitality organizations that want to keep guest-created service failures from destroying the guest experience and the guest's feelings about the organization build in strategies to help guests recover from their own failures so they can take a positive impression away from the service setting. Airlines have routines to help people who have lost their tickets complete their flights. Disney has routines to help parents who have lost their children in the parks find them again. The best organizations recognize the importance of helping guests solve the problems they create themselves—without making them look foolish or feel stupid while tired children or a spouse is looking on at the end of a long day in the park. Excellent organizations help these guests go home happy in spite of themselves.

Where Failures Happen

Though some moments of truth are especially susceptible to failure, an organizational failure to meet the customer's expectations can occur just about anywhere in the guest experience. This is why we spend so much time studying all aspects of the guest experience, identifying potential failure points, planning on how to prevent as many failures as possible, and being prepared to fix the inevitable failures. The best failure is one that is discovered before it happened, but no service experience can be totally flawless for every guest no matter how much managers plan. An organization needs to develop a way to find and fix failures and problems at the time guests are having their experience.

The service product may be inadequate, inappropriate, or fail in some other way to meet the customer's expectations. For example, the ordered hamburger may not look like the one advertised on TV that attracted the customer to the burger stand, or it may be undercooked, spoiled, or just not as good as the customer expected. A service failure is the result. The intangible part of the delivery system can also fail. If the burger took an hour to get to the customer at the burger stand or if the line wasn't managed properly, the delivery system itself may have failed. The people part of the delivery system can certainly fail. If the burger-stand counter person is unfriendly, inept, poorly trained, or rude, then the experience is unlikely to meet the customer's expectations. Finally, there can be a failure in the environment or setting if the customer feels that the ambient temperature is too cold, a sudden rainstorm ruins the meal, or one customer collides into another making them drop their meals. These points of possible failure must all be planned for and managed to ensure that the service experience meets and, hopefully, exceeds the customer's expectations.

Severity of Failure and Recovery

Service failure comes in degrees, ranging from catastrophic failures that make newspaper headlines, to those that are annoying, to insignificant slipups that are barely noticed. They also come in frequency from those that happen often to those that are rare. Customers tolerate most small and infrequent errors. They know that things don't work perfectly every time so they may brush off minor failures, especially if their prior experiences with that organization have been excellent and they expect to continue the relationship with it.[6] Failures can even include those of which the customer isn't aware. Some customer service experts believe the organization should apologize even for these failures as they provide an opportunity to "wow."

Along the severity continuum is an infinite range of service errors. Since the customer defines the quality of the service experience, the customer also defines the nature and severity of the service failure. Different customers can be very unhappy or just mildly unhappy about the same failure just as different customers can be very happy or mildly happy about the same service. Some service recoveries fix the customer's problems, and other recovery efforts make things worse. Sometimes the best a manager can do is to neutralize the angry customer.

THE IMPORTANCE OF FIXING SERVICE FAILURES

When a guest has a problem, one of three outcomes usually occurs. The problem is fixed and the formerly unhappy guest leaves happy; the problem isn't fixed and the unhappy guest leaves unhappy; or the organization tries to fix the problem and succeeds only in neutralizing the unhappy guest. In a study of a restaurant,[7] students were asked to indicate how important nine common service failures were to them. They were also asked whether and under what conditions service-recovery techniques were successful in causing them to forgive the failure. Failures included problems such as defects in the core food product, slow service, out-of-stock items, incorrect temperatures, billing errors, and inappropriate server behavior. The study reports that for some service failures, such as inappropriate server behavior, customers were unforgiving regardless of any effort to recover. For technical failures such as delivery of the wrong order or a problem with the food itself, the customers were more forgiving after recovery attempts and were more likely to return. Being successful in service-recovery efforts is critical, because a formerly unhappy guest who leaves happy may tell many others about a terrific experience. An unhappy guest may leave and tell as many others as possible about the terrible experience. A neutralized guest may leave and forget the whole experience and perhaps the organization as well.

In instances of total service catastrophe, neutralizing the unhappy customer may be the best that the organization can hope for. If the surgeon removes the wrong leg, everyone on the cruise gets Legionnaires' disease, or the restaurant meal leads to food poisoning, recovery from the failure is nearly impossible. Even so, most modern hospitality organizations have developed disaster plans to prepare their employees for such situations. Airlines have emergency teams for handling crashes, theme parks have quick-response teams for accidents, and hotels have fire teams for handling evacuations in emergencies. The team's primary responsibility is to handle the emergency situation, such as putting out the fire. The best teams will also provide aid and comfort to the customers affected by the emergency, in part to restore the customer's positive perception of the organization.

The Price of Failure

Ultimately, retaining customers by providing excellent service and avoiding or fixing service failures is essential to organizational success. Frederick F. Reichheld and W. Earl Sasser, Jr., showed that if a company can reduce its rate of customer defections (leaving the organization to go to a competitor) by only 5 percent, it can improve profits by 25 to 85 percent.[8] Since their study, a lot of research effort has been dedicated to determining the lifetime value of a customer. Publicizing this value to employees gives everyone a strong sense of why it is so important to find and fix the service problems that cause customers to switch their support to other companies or use the service less frequently. It costs money to lose a customer.[9]

When the lost revenue of unhappy customers who don't return is added to the lost revenue of customers who don't come because of the negative **word of mouth** from unhappy customers, service failures have created an expensive problem. Over a defecting customer's lifetime, how much potential revenue have you lost? Many companies have sought to make this estimate, and while results differ by the type of product being provided, they invariably show that the price of failure is highly significant for any business.

Consider the following examples. A study of a cruise line showed that the lifetime value of customers ranged from $4,000 to $5,000.[10] Domino's Pizza estimated that over a ten-year period a regular customer spends about $5,000.[11] Mazda Australia estimates that the lifetime value of each customer is over $100,000,[12] while Carl Sewell of Sewell Cadillac in Dallas calculated that each of his customers was worth $332,000 in lifetime sales, service, and referrals.[13] The Ritz-Carlton estimates the lifetime value of its engaged guests at more than $1 million.[14] Thus, fixing service failures is clearly one of an organization's most essential activities. Of course, every business is different, and so every hospitality organization would benefit from taking the time to calculate the value of its long-term satisfied customers. As a case in point, Harrah's Casino and Resorts uses its emphasis on the lifetime value of its customers to refocus its loyalty programs, change how it offers amenities, and improve the way it contacts customers.[15]

Harrah's Casino and Resorts used its estimates of customer value to change the way it provided rewards in its loyalty program.

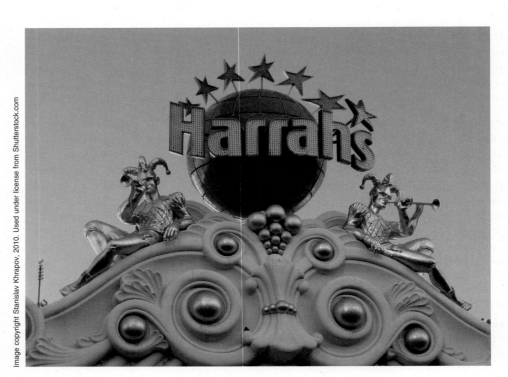

The examples provided earlier reveal that, even for a small business, the lifetime value of a customer may be surprisingly large. To show how a restaurant might come up with numbers like these, assume that the restaurant wows its patrons so much that some come back once a week and others once a month and spend an average of $20 each time they visit. The total value of each wowed customer's business for the next five years would be $5,200 for the weekly customer and $1,200 for the monthly customer. That's a lot of money to throw away by ignoring a complaint about one bad meal. These numbers get even bigger when the number of people that a positive word of mouth guest could bring to your hospitality organization is added in. If our wowed guest tells an average of five others who are also wowed and, in turn, tell five additional people, the multiplier effect is enormous. Over the estimated life of a typical customer, this can add up to many thousands of dollars in potential revenues.

Positive word of mouth has great value, and negative word of mouth is extremely costly. Unhappy customers can be particularly dangerous to a business, as they are approximately twice as likely to spread negative word of mouth as happy ones are to spread positive word of mouth. Research shows that customers who have bad experiences tell approximately eleven people; customers who have good experiences tell approximately six.[16] Multiplying the influence of word of mouth is the Internet. Word of mouth used to be one-to-one. Angry customers used to be limited to writing letters to corporate headquarters or the Better Business Bureau, putting up signs in their yard, or painting "lemon" on the car. Now, anyone with Internet access can write a blog; post comments on a social networking Web site, TripAdvisor, or some similar site; or create a dedicated Web site to tell the world about any offending company. In this day of worldwide communication, a customer can praise or complain over the Internet and instantly reach millions of people. The benefits of avoiding negative word of mouth and turning it positive are obvious.

The Customer's Response to Service Failure

The unhappy or dissatisfied customer is the focus of the **service recovery**. An unhappy customer can do any one or a combination of four actions.

Never Return

First, the customer can leave vowing never to return. Here, the company has lost a stream of potential future revenue. As already noted, lifetime customer values can be substantial, and when guests walk out vowing never to return, it all goes away. One main reason for empowering servers to provide on-the-spot service recovery is to keep dissatisfied customers from leaving that way. Fixing a service problem before the guest leaves your facility is the best thing that you can do to diminish the impact of a failure and prevent the loss of that customer's future business.

Complains

The second action a customer can take is to complain to someone in the organization. A popular book on this subject is *A Complaint Is a Gift*.[17] Good hospitality managers believe that to be true. They encourage guests to complain and thank them when they do. A complaint is a positive opportunity for the organization with several important benefits. For one thing, it gives the company the chance to make an unhappy guest happy; the organization can turn the lemon into lemonade. Unfortunately, only 5 to 10 percent of dissatisfied customers complain.[18] R. L. Day and E. L. Landon found that only 20 to 35 percent of people complained about the most dissatisfying consumer experience they

It may not feel like it at the time, but a customer complaint represents an opportunity to correct a service failure before the guest leaves the establishment.

Image copyright Andre Blais, 2010. Used under license from Shutterstock.com

ever had.[19] To complete the bad news, according to the research of Stephen S. Tax and Stephen W. Brown, most of the relatively few customers who do complain are dissatisfied with how companies resolve their complaints.[20]

If guests can be encouraged to complain, the organization gets valuable information about where problems in the guest experience are located. The customers who return to the counter with uncooked hamburgers, or tell the server about their unhappiness with the slow service, or write letters to the hotel manager describing their dissatisfaction, can all help identify problems in the service product, the delivery system, or the personnel. At the same time, guests give the organization the opportunity to fix the problems before they tell others about their dissatisfaction and before other guests experience the same problem. Unfortunately, according to Tax and Brown, "most firms fail to document and categorize complaints adequately," which makes learning from mistakes more difficult.[21]

Organizations should encourage guests to complain, even teach them how to complain if necessary, and then measure and follow up on complaint resolution. Guests who suffer service failures silently are more apt to leave without returning and to bad-mouth the organization than complaining guests are.[22] British Airways found that of customers experiencing service problems, only 50 percent stayed with the airline if they did not complain to BA personnel. But a full 87 percent of those who did complain stayed and did not defect to a competitor.[23]

Some companies claim even stronger results from successful complaint resolution. They believe that, on average, 70 percent of their guests will stay with the organization if a complaint is resolved in the guest's favor, and that a full 95 percent will do business again if the complaint is resolved favorably on the spot. This is why the benchmark hospitality organizations empower their frontline employees to handle many complaints personally and in the best possible way they can, rather than seeking the manager's authorization first. As former Gaylord Hotels COO John Caparella said, "The only way to meet our mission of 'Flawless Service' is through the commitment and dedication of our front line employees. Our 'STARS' are the ones that are close enough to the customer to recognize and evaluate a problem and make it right for the customer and keep that customer."[24] This has been a point long championed by Hart, Heskett, and Sasser who wrote, "The surest way to recover from service mishaps is for workers on the front line to identify and solve the customer's problem."[25] Just as handling a complaint well can be to the organization's benefit, handling it poorly or not at all can hurt badly. If a dissatisfied customer complains and then finds that the organization can't or won't fix the problem, the organization has now failed that customer twice, and everyone the customer knows will hear about it. A large sticker on the computer screens used by servers at T.G.I. Friday's reads "Every Guest Leaves Happy." Making sure no guest leaves unhappy is obviously to the organization's advantage. The excellent organizations want all of their dissatisfied customers to complain so that they can fix whatever problems might have occurred.

Bad-Mouth the Organization

The third action an unhappy customer can take is to bad-mouth the company, telling everyone who will listen about the terrible experience.[26] If the negative experience was very costly for the customer either financially or personally, the customer is even more likely to spread the bad word. The greater the costs to the customer, the greater the motivation to tell. If someone returns home after spending a lot of time and money flying to the Cayman Islands, staying in a hotel for a week, eating out, and paying admissions to various attractions, friends and neighbors will probably ask, "How was your vacation?" If it was a bad experience, the customer will make every effort to share that information with all who ask, post it on a blog, and add the experience to TripAdvisor. The likelihood that anyone who listened to or read about that person's experience on the Internet will also spend the time and money to go to the Cayman Islands will be substantially diminished. Obviously, the more important the experience is to the customer, the quicker the customer will become unhappy when the experience does not meet expectations. The unhappier a customer is, the more likely that person will complain, leave, and tell people about the experience.

Retaliate

Beyond bad-mouthing the organization, the fourth action an unhappy guest can take is to find a way to retaliate.[27] Getting back at the offending company can take several forms. Some customers get so angry that they conduct public bad-mouthing by taking their concerns to the press or their legislative representative. In rare cases, the retaliation can even be in the form of creating nongovernmental organizations (NGOs) to protest the organization and the practices that have led to the service failure. Airlines are a good example of an industry that has outraged so many people that angry customers have organized into groups to seek new legislation and redress for the airlines' passenger practices and apparent indifference to their guests' needs, wants, expectations and behaviors. As a result airlines face governmental mandates to make higher reimbursement payments for passengers bumped from flights and renewed consideration of Passenger Bill of Rights legislation.[28]

Other retaliatory strategies are available to angry guests who believe that the organization failed them in some way. They can picket organizational facilities, take out ads in newspapers publicizing whatever the organization did to anger them, organize boycotts against the company, or file lawsuits that take company time and money to resolve. Retaliating guests may even take out their frustration on the company's employees.[29] These actions by angry guests all have a cost for the organization. For example, when employees are abused by an angry guest, they themselves are likely to become angry with an employer that makes its customers so angry that employees get unfairly yelled at (or worse) by their customers.

Worst-Case Scenario

If the failure was severe enough, it turns the guest into the angry **avenger** that every organization fears. This is the company's worst-case scenario for a service failure, where the customer leaves vowing never to return, does not complain to the organization, switches to another service provider, bad-mouths the organization, and finds a way to retaliate. The company has not only lost any future business from the angry customer, but it has also lost the business of the many people who will hear and be influenced by the negative word of mouth. This dissatisfied customer has become a true avenger fighting against the organization. A typical dissatisfied customer may tell eight or ten people about the problem. An avenger may create a Web site or a blog and influence millions.

The Value of Positive Publicity: Bad-Mouth versus Wow

On the other hand, the value of a wowed customer can be huge. Picture a family coming back home from a Caribbean island that caters to tourists. They have terrific tales to tell (or twitter) their friends and post on Facebook. Their experience exceeded their expectations. To have these apostles telling everyone they know about their great vacation is very much to the Caribbean island's advantage. This positive word of mouth has great value, not only for influencing others to go to the Caribbean paradise, but also for blunting negative word of mouth. If a potential customer hears strong testimonials or reads the blogs about a guest experience from three trusted friends, disregarding a complaining avenger will be easier.

Credibility

Word of mouth is important for several reasons. People who tell other people tend to be more credible than impersonal or anonymous testimonials.[30] When your friend tells you a restaurant was bad, you no longer believe all the ads on television assuring you that the restaurant is a good place to eat. Not only is the information more credible, but it tends to be more vivid as well. For either good or bad word of mouth, the richness of the detailed personal experience of a friend is more compelling than any commercial advertisement.

Evangelists

Exceeding expectations creates the **evangelists** that every organization hopes to have. Hospitality companies work hard to ensure that their guests have experiences so memorable that they can't wait to get home and tell all their friends and relatives about what a terrific time they had, post on their social network site, or submit a glowing report on TripAdvisor. This positive word of mouth advertising reinforces the company's favorable public image.

Like all companies that seek excellence, the good hospitality organizations work hard to identify and train their people to find and fix the inevitable problems quickly. The best companies plan for failures—by training, using simulations, telling stories to teach how employees have creatively fixed problems in the past, and celebrating employee efforts to find and fix service problems—with the intent of changing a problem into an opportunity to "wow" the guest and perhaps create an evangelist. In *The New Gold Standard: 5 Leadership Principles for Creating a Legendary Customer Experience Courtesy of the Ritz-Carlton Hotel Company*, Michelli reports a Ritz-Carlton example of a problem that was not even the hotel's fault but an employee fixed it anyway. Some Ritz-Carlton hotels operate camps for kids. One guest reported, "My daughter spilled something on her pants soon after arriving there for a day. Our baggage was lost by the airline, and so she didn't have a change of clothes. Not only did the camp counselors have her clothes dry cleaned; they also went to Macy's and bought her a new outfit. I was floored. This is obviously above and beyond anything I would have expected."[31] Guests who get this kind of red-carpet treatment may become evangelists who spread the company word far and wide.

DEALING WITH SERVICE FAILURES

How the Recovery Is Handled

The organization trying to recover from failure can impress the customer positively or negatively.[32] Research shows that for both positive and negative service recoveries, how the recovery is handled can be more important to the customer than the original failure.[33] After a failure, the organization can either end up much better off or much worse off, depending on the customer's reaction to the recovery attempt. A small problem can become a big problem if the recovery effort is halfhearted or misguided. And a big problem can be turned into an example of great service when handled quickly and effectively.

In one study of restaurants, the researchers discovered that the most important determinant of overall customer satisfaction after a service failure was customers' satisfaction with those responsible for dealing with failure: the personnel responsible for the service interaction. The organization's ability to recover from failure also had the largest impact on willingness to return and re-patronize the restaurant.[34] B. R. Lewis and P. McCann asked a sample of hotel guests in a UK hotel to identify any service failures, recovery strategies, and their satisfaction with those recovery strategies. They found that only about half of the guests were satisfied or very satisfied with the hotel's efforts to recover from a service failure. Of those who were satisfied, 77.8 percent said they would stay again compared to only approximately half of the dissatisfied who said they would stay at this hotel again. Lewis and McCann also asked guests to report the occurrence and severity of twenty-six possible causes of failure.[35] A guest had to experience a certain failure more than once for it to be counted. They found a number of interesting results. For example, 61.7 percent of guests reported slow restaurant service. Nearly half reported that the staff was inefficient and the receptionist unfriendly and unhelpful. Since the inefficiency of staff ranked fourth in severity out of the twenty-six possible causes of failure, this hotel obviously needed to focus on this frequent, severe problem. The most serious problems in terms of severity were unclean rooms and billing errors, experienced by nearly one-third of guests reporting. Hotels receiving such ratings will want to consider them seriously if they hope to improve.

Service Recovery: A Message to Employees

Addressing service failure well has one more important outcome: It makes the organization a better place to work. It tells the employees how committed the organization is to customer satisfaction. Employees need to know that this commitment is more than a slogan. How the organization finds and fixes its service errors is a loud message to the employees about what the organization truly does believe in. Let us say that the management of Hotel A is defensive about customer complaints and keeps them secret (though employees will hear about them), resolves complaints as cheaply and quietly as possible, and seeks people to blame for the complaints. The management of Hotel B, on the other hand, aggressively seeks out and fixes service failures. It disseminates findings about complaints and failures to employees, makes quick and generous adjustments for failure, and seeks solutions rather than scapegoats. Which organization's employees will give guests better service?

How the organization handles service recovery will also impact employee morale and satisfaction with the organization. After all, for whom would you rather work—a company that won't let you fix guest problems quickly and fairly, or one that empowers you to tell guests you will find a way to recover from service failures? Most will agree that it is more fun and rewarding to work for a company that wants you to fix guest problems than it is to work for one that doesn't. Research shows that when employees feel a company is committed to providing excellent service, and employees are supported in their efforts and rewarded for doing so, employee job satisfaction is significantly higher.[36]

The Yellow and Black Tags

People on the front line are often the first to notice or be informed of system faults or failures. If they have been properly selected and motivated, they will report the need for system improvement. For example, a British Airways baggage handler at London's Heathrow Airport noticed that passengers waiting for their luggage at the carousel were asking him a strange question: How can I get a yellow and black tag for my bags? The passengers had noticed that bags with those tags arrived first, so they wanted the special tags. The baggage handler realized that because the passengers asking him the question were the first ones to arrive at the carousel, they had to be first-class passengers, who deplaned first. And, yet, they had to wait twenty minutes on average for their bags, while some other passengers were getting first-class luggage service. First-class passengers are highly profitable to airlines, and something was wrong with the service being provided to them.

The baggage handler's inquiries revealed that the passengers perhaps least deserving of "first-class" luggage service, those flying on stand-by, were getting it. Since they were the last to board, their luggage was loaded last and unloaded first. The baggage handler made a simple suggestion: load first-class luggage last. Although the idea was simple and had obvious merit, implementing it meant that BA had to change its luggage-handling procedures in airports all over the world, and that took time. But it was done, and the average time of getting first-class luggage from plane to carousel dropped from twenty minutes to less than ten worldwide, and under seven minutes on some routes.[37]

A dedicated, motivated, observant employee saw a way to improve the system and got it done. He had no idea he would also end up receiving a service award, a cash award of $18,000, and two round-trip first-class tickets to the United States.

Looking for Service Failures

The Complaint as a Monitoring Device

Preventive strategies can reduce the number of problems, but some will inevitably occur, and the organization cannot fix problems it doesn't know about. The research shows clearly that the most important process strategy is to get unhappy guests to complain while they are still in the guest experience. This is a more difficult challenge than one might think. While some guests are all too happy to complain, most are not. They are unwilling to take the time, or they believe that no one cares or will do anything even if they do complain, or they are too angry to say anything and they just leave. Hospitality organizations must let their guests know they and their employees are receptive to complaints. Research on this issue has identified some important ways in which the organization can encourage and recognize customer complaints.

Encouraging Complaints

All service personnel should be trained and encouraged to solicit complaints. Since many service problems involve server errors, getting the servers to solicit complaints about their own performance may be a challenge. If servers see that mistakes are punished more heavily than catching errors is rewarded, it will be difficult to find or fix the errors they make. Most people are less enthusiastic about admitting their mistakes than they are about sharing their successes, and the complaint strategy needs to accommodate this reality of human nature. Furthermore, it is difficult for guests to feel it worthwhile to complain to the very person who just made them angry or offended them.

Body Language as a Complaint

Service personnel can be trained to read body language for clues to an unhappy guest. If a frowning guest walks by a Disney cast member, that person is supposed to inquire as to why "the unhappy face." Taking this initiative can elicit complaints that might otherwise go unmentioned. Food-service workers, hotel front desk agents, and other people who interact directly with guests can also be trained to recognize the signs of unhappy people. Employees must also learn how to be receptive and sympathetic to the complaint once it is elicited. Guests must perceive employees as interested and concerned. If guests do not think anyone cares, they generally won't say anything.

For example, a child visiting the Magic Kingdom at Disney world was excited to see that her favorite character, Captain Hook, was standing next to one of the rides posing for pictures and signing autographs. She too wanted her picture taken with the Captain and to get his autograph. As she got to the front of the line, the cast member in charge suddenly cut off the line and escorted the character off stage for a break. The child was heartbroken, and nothing her parents could say could cheer her up. That night at dinner an alert wait staff member noticed the sadness in the little girl's face and asked her, "How was your day?" After hearing her story and taking the order, the waitress told her shift supervisor the story of the sad little girl. The shift supervisor called the character supervisor to talk about this service failure. While a simple solution would have been to summon Captain Hook to the restaurant to greet the little girl, the two employees agreed that this would be out of character for the ill-mannered Captain. They then hit upon an in-character service-recovery strategy. A plush toy of Peter Pan was taken to the little girl's room and left along with the following note: "Dear Sally: I am sorry that Captain Hook was mean to you today, but he is sometimes mean like that. Next time I see him, I will tell him that he shouldn't be so mean to our guests. (signed) Peter Pan." The little girl was thrilled, and her parents told this story to anyone who would listen to them.[38] Server sensitivity to a little girl's nonverbal communication turned an unfortunate situation around.

Don't Forget to Ask

Although already discussed in Chapter 12, this is a point worth reiterating. The most basic way to find out if there is a service problem is to simply ask the guest "Was everything OK?" though there are a number of more sophisticated options—like comment cards, toll-free 800 numbers, surveys, focus groups, and reports from mystery shoppers. If the guest says no, be prepared to follow-up and try to resolve the service failure.

RECOVERING FROM SERVICE FAILURE

The organization failed. It got the guests in the door, and then it let them down. Now what? Hospitality organizations should train their employees to handle and empower them to creatively resolve the problems when they find them. Scenarios, game playing, video recording, and role playing are good ways to train them on how to respond to an angry guest. Just as umpires can be trained to recognize balls and strikes through watching videos, hospitality personnel can be trained to recognize service errors and taught how to correct the failures they find.

Obviously, the more an organization depends on repeat business, the more critical it is for the organization to acknowledge and act on customer complaints. Some organizations report the results of their complaint investigations back to complaining customers in detail, including information on what people were affected and what systems were changed. In that way the organization shows that it is responsive to the customer's complaint and gives that person a sense of participation in the organization that may positively enhance loyalty and increase repeat visits. If the complaint shows the organization a flaw that can be corrected, and if knowledge of the correction provides the customer with a sense of satisfaction for reporting the complaint, a true win–win situation can result. The key is, if there is a service failure, the company must take action.

Do Something Quickly

The basic recovery principle is to do something and do it quickly. Satisfaction with service-recovery efforts decreases as the amount of time taken to provide a resolution increases.[39] Strive for on-the-spot service recovery. Its many benefits are one major reason why benchmark organizations empower their frontline employees to such a great extent. The one answer a guest does not want to hear is, "I'll have to ask my manager." That's why a standing guideline for empowered employees of the best organizations is: Provide immediate service recovery.

The Ritz-Carlton is famous for empowering its employees to find and fix failures. Here are three of the "Ritz-Carlton Basics" that appear on the Credo Card depicted in Chapter 2, carried by every employee:

- Any employee who receives a customer complaint "owns" the complaint.
- React quickly to correct the problem immediately. Follow up with a telephone call within twenty minutes to verify that the problem has been resolved to the customer's satisfaction. Do everything you possibly can to never lose a guest.
- Every employee is empowered to resolve the problem and to prevent a repeat occurrence.

How the problem came about or who caused it does not matter. Every employee is empowered to resolve it. The $2,000 each employee is authorized to use to recover from a service failure and achieve guest satisfaction backs up that philosophy.

Management must empower employees with the necessary authority, responsibility, and resources to act and act quickly following a failure. The higher the cost of the failure to the guest in terms of money, personal reputation, or safety, the more vital it is for the organization to train the server to recognize and deal with it promptly, sympathetically, and effectively. Of course, empowering employees to recover from failure will not be sufficient if recovery mechanisms are not in place. If the rest of the organizational systems are in chaos, empowering the front line won't do much good.

A necessary further step is that employees should inform their managers about system failures even if they initiate successful recovery procedures. If they don't, the problem may recur elsewhere. In part to help encourage employees to share how they handle service failures, Federal Express created the Golden Falcon Award to recognize employee initiatives in service recovery. Winners not only get a pin to commemorate their success, but they also have an article published in the company newsletter about what they did. In addition, they get a telephone call from the chief operating officer and receive ten shares of the company's stock.[40]

All hospitality personnel should be trained to apologize, ask the guests about the problem, and listen in a way that gives guests the opportunity to blow off steam. Considerable research indicates that having the chance to tell someone in authority about the service failure and the problems it created is very important in retaining the guest's future patronage. This strategy is even more effective when the organization expresses its thanks for the complaint with a tangible reward, even if it is small.[41] Many restaurants will apologize to guests who complain about a longer-than-expected wait and offer a free dessert as a small recognition of their sincere regret for disappointing the guest. Some restaurants do this even if the guest does not complain.

Benefits of Quick Recovery

A quick reaction to service failure has numerous benefits. Solving a problem up front instead of over time reduces the overall expense of retaining guests. It is generally less expensive to fix a problem on the spot than it will be if the guest is further aggravated by the inability of the server to solve the problem without checking with the supervisor. This is where minor annoyance can become true anger and the reason the benchmark hospitality organizations empower their employees to fix the problem on the spot if at all possible. The sooner the guest is satisfied, the more likely the guest will remain with the hospitality organization and the sooner the organization will benefit from the guest's repeat business. Fix their problems and most guests will come back. Fix their problems on the spot and there is a very good chance that they will not only come back but will also likely recommend the organization to their friends. Reward programs and recognition for employees who have done an especially good job of recovering from a service failure offer strong incentives to other employees while providing role models of the organization's commitment to service quality.

How Do Customers Evaluate Recovery Efforts?

A service failure has occurred, and the organization has made an effort to recover from it. Does the guest feel fairly and justly treated? Four dimensions of justice—distributive, procedural, interactive, and informational—need to be considered.[42] According to Tax and Brown, justice dimensions explain 85 percent of the variation in customer satisfaction with how complaints are handled.[43]

Distributive Justice

Distributive justice, or outcome fairness, is an assessment by the customer of the fairness associated with whatever compensation he received to rectify a service failure. What did the organization actually give or distribute to the unhappy customer as compensation for the problem? If the guest complains about a bad meal and gets only a sincere apology because that's all company policy calls for, some guests will feel unfairly treated; sometimes "We're sorry" isn't enough, in the guest's judgment, to compensate for the poor service. Once again, it all comes down to meeting the guest's expectations. The issue is difficult because each guest is different. For many guests, an apology is fair enough compensation for many service failures. For others, nothing is good enough to make up for the problem or difficulty that the service failure created for them. Finding satisfactory compensation may involve methodical trial and error on the organization's part, but the easiest way is to ask the guest. For example, a hotel could offer a disgruntled guest a choice of either a refund or an upgrade.

Procedural Justice

Procedural justice refers to whether the customer believes company procedures for handling service failure are fair and not a procedural hassle full of red tape. Best Buy believes that not giving customers the best value possible is a kind of service failure, so it will pay customers a refund plus 10 percent if they show they were not given the lowest price in the area on a purchased product. Customers feel this is a fair policy. Customers also want an easy process for correcting failures. They feel that if the organization failed them, it is only fair that the organization makes it easy for them to receive a just settlement.

Interactional Justice

Interactional justice refers to the customer's feeling of being treated with respect and courtesy and being given the opportunity to express the complaint fully. If the customer has a complaint and is denied the opportunity to state it to someone because the offending server is rude, indifferent, or uncaring, and the manager cannot be found, the customer will feel unfairly treated. A study of traffic-court offenders by Lind and Tyler revealed that many offenders whose cases were dismissed without a hearing were dissatisfied with the process and angry about the outcome, even though the dismissal was a favorable result for them.[44] Since they were denied their day in court, they were unhappy with the process even though they had won.

Common sense suggests and research shows that a customer who is encouraged to complain–and is then treated with respect, courtesy, and given a fair settlement–is more likely to be satisfied with the experience, spread positive word of mouth, and repatronize the organization than one who was given a fair settlement but only with reluctance and discourtesy.[45]

Informational Justice

Informational justice refers to guests' satisfaction with the adequacy of the information and communication provided by the organization. Were employees of the organization candid with you, or did they not tell you what was going on, hide information, or simply did not communicate to you what the current situation was and what they knew? If a guest is unhappy about a flight delay, it is generally perceived as worse if the airline does not let the guest know the reason for the delay and how long it should realistically take to resolve. Recall from Chapter 11 on waits that, an unexplained wait feels longer than an explained wait. Saying "we're sorry" shows the company is apologetic for the delay, but the guest still wants the service product she originally purchased: the flight from point A to point B. Feeling that the company was honest and forthright with information can go a long way with helping the guest at least understand that there is a legitimate reason for the service failure.

How the Recovery is Managed

Fairness can mean different things in different situations and with different people. A lot of research has been done to see which is more important and when. Studies have found that while all four justice dimensions influence customer satisfaction, procedural justice seems to be most influential.[46] Since this dimension is most closely aligned with the idea of receiving the service you were promised, this conclusion seems reasonable. Some research indicates that customers feel more fairly treated when organizations extend options as compensation for service failure.[47] A separate study of restaurant customers found that interactional justice and procedural justice had a positive effect on customer satisfaction and positive word of mouth but only procedural justice impacts revisit intention. Distributive justice had no impact on any outcomes studied.[48]

More recent studies have found that the impact of justice is more complicated. Wirtz and Mattila found that the recovery outcome (such as compensation or apology), the procedures used to determine that outcome, and the interactional treatment used to deliver that outcome (such as the attitude of the server offering an apology) combine to impact the satisfaction with the recovery.[49] In other words, the research is supporting what common sense would suggest: a compensation that the guest sees as fair for the pain and suffering caused by the failure, delivered in a quick and easy-to-use complaint process by an employee who seems genuinely apologetic for the failure and appreciative of the opportunity to fix it, will seem fair to the guest. Guests who feel fairly treated will likely come back, spread good words about your organization, and be satisfied with the experience.[50]

These effects of justice are well illustrated by the following example, where a customer emerged highly satisfied by what began as a horrendous service failure. Southwest reports a story of how a passenger wrote a letter thanking Southwest for a trip that took twenty-two hours. While most would think this is a cause for a major complaint, the customer saw it differently because of the actions taken by several customer service employees. It seems that weather had caused cancelled flights and closed airports for a traveler trying to get from Salt Lake City to Chicago. The customer service agent, working a seventeen-hour shift to help stranded customers, found a way to book the passenger on actual flights instead of sending him on his way to hope for the best on standby status. Booking a triple connection, the agent got him confirmed seats to his home. At the same time, another agent booked his bags directly to Chicago so they would be there when he finally arrived, and another agent met him at the end of the first leg of his trip and provided him with a snack. In the letter summarizing his experience, the passenger wrote, "Due to your amazing customer service, a flight plan that could have been a nightmare instead became a great story to tell. I received much more attention than expected because your organization truly under-promised and over-delivered."[51]

The important lesson that justice theory teaches is that different people will see failure and recovery through different perceptions of fairness. The extent of dissatisfaction is affected by such factors as the customer involvement in co-production requirements; the length, frequency, closeness, and importance of the relationship to the customer; and the costs of switching to another provider.[52] The stronger guests feel about these factors, the angrier they will be when the organization fails them in some important way. One might then assume that satisfaction with service recovery would only be a function of how much the person gets (i.e., distributive justice) in compensation, but the prior research and the Southwest example shows this not to be the case. Instead, perceptions of service recovery are influenced by the fairness of the process used (procedural justice),

FIGURE **13-1** The Steps of Failure Analysis and Recovery Efforts
© Cengage Learning 2012

the empathy of the employee (interpersonal justice), and the way in which the customer was kept informed (informational justice). The way in which the recovery is managed can thus either help or hinder the guest's future relationship with the organization.

There are a number of key lessons for service recovery that we can learn from the research on fairness: If there is a problem, fix it quickly. If the guest is a long-time loyal customer, fix it quickly and especially well. But solving it quickly and well does not mean just throwing money at a complaint, as that won't make it go away. Find out and care about the problem, be honest when solving the problem, and approach the solution fairly.

Service-Recovery Systems Analysis

Besides the individual tools and techniques discussed in the previous chapters, an overall strategy for failure analysis will serve the guestologist seeking to prevent any guest from being disappointed. Based on a model presented by Gonzalez and his coauthors,[53] Figure 13-1 presents a model that describes how managers should analyze their failures and their efforts at failure recovery. This figure shows that analyzing and correcting service failures has seven steps. The first three steps involve failure analysis, while the last four steps involve the recovery effort.

Specifically, the first step is to identify the failures. The second step is to put them into categories for further analysis. These steps require organizations to be on watch for service failures and to have a system in place to document and track any errors that occur. The third step is to assign reasons for each type of failure, attributing them to who was in charge, how often they happen, and whether those in charge could have controlled what happened. This step is not designed to focus on finding someone to blame or punish, but rather to identify why the problems occurred so that the system can be changed, the employee involved can be trained, or the necessary changes can be made.

The recovery effort begins where the failure analysis ends. The fourth step of the model is to select the appropriate recovery strategy for each type of failure. Strategies can range from a simple apology to some level of compensation to no response at all. During the planning phase, companies must consider the types of failures that might occur and prepare appropriate responses for them. The fifth step is the implementation of the recovery. Its success is grounded in how fair customers perceive it to be, in terms of the justice types we have just discussed. The sixth step is to review the recovery efforts and follow up to see if they were successful. The organization should assess the extent to which the employees involved in attempting recovery performed appropriately and whether the details of the failure have been recorded and retained in the company database for future use and further study of failure causes.

Another critical component of a good failure analysis system is the feedback loop. Information obtained from each part of the process should be shared throughout the organization to help correct problems, prevent similar problems, and help teach other employees how to handle problems. While this feedback should occur throughout the process, in the seventh step the organization should look beyond the specific service failure incident and consider the implications of service failures for the entire service delivery system. For a system to "heal itself" it must be able to learn from its mistakes. The model seen here echoes the point of "the cycle going on" in the planning model presented in Chapter 10.

Characteristics of a Good Recovery Strategy

While the exact mechanisms of a good recovery system will depend on the specific nature of the business and its service product, in general a service-recovery strategy should satisfy several criteria.[54] First, the strategy should ensure that the failure is addressed quickly and fixed in some positive way if possible. Second, recovery strategies must be communicated clearly to the employees charged with responding to customer dissatisfaction. The service people must know that the organization expects them to find and resolve customer problems as part of their jobs. Third, recovery strategies should be easy for the customer to find and use. Finally, they should be flexible enough to accommodate both the different types of failures and the different expectations that customers have of their guest experiences. The service-recovery strategy developed should be based on management understanding that because the customer defines the quality of the service experience, the customer also defines its failures and the adequacy of the recovery strategies.

No Better Makes It Worse

A strategy that does not improve the situation for the complaining customer is worse than useless because the organization makes plain that it can't or won't recover from failure even when informed of it. The work of Hart, Heskett, and Sasser suggests that most recovery strategies are in serious need of improvement. More than half of organizational efforts to respond to consumer complaints actually reinforce negative reactions to the service.[55] In trying to make things better, organizations may make them worse.

Costs of Failure to Guests

One reason that customers view many recovery strategies as inadequate is that they do not really consider all of the costs to the customer. Bad meal? Replace it. Theme park attraction broken? Give a complimentary one-day return pass. Busy signal on the telephone line for airport information? Interject a recorded apology. After such recovery efforts, the organization may think the relationship is back where it started but, for the customer, many other tangible and intangible costs may be associated with failures. The effective organization will try to identify these costs and include some recognition of them in selecting the appropriate service recovery. After all, the customer will think that the fact that the service failed is "not my fault." Why should I have to wait on the side of the road for a long time because the rental car broke down? Why should I have to call back repeatedly to reservations because the airline messed up the original reservation? Why should I have to return ten miles to the restaurant because the drive-through people didn't get the order right?

Making It Right Is Not Enough

Customers clearly think that when a failure occurs, organizations need to do more than simply make it right by replacing it or doing it over again. Of course, organizations should do that, but they should do more. For example, if the failed meal causes the guest to be embarrassed in front of a client or boss, then the recovery strategy must not only include compensation for the meal but some consideration for the guest's other costs and emotional outlays as well. If a dad tells his family about the terrific time they all will have at a famous resort, uses his only week of vacation to go there, and spends all the extra money he has so carefully saved, he has a lot at stake. If the experience fails somehow to meet the family's expectations, the dad loses his time, his money, and his credibility with his family. The outstanding hospitality organization systematically considers how to compensate guests for losses other than financial and makes extra effort to ensure that dissatisfied guests not only have their financial losses addressed in a recovery effort, but the guests have their ego and esteem needs met as well. They want dad to go home a hero to his family.

Being Wrong with Dignity

Even when the guests themselves make mistakes, good hospitality organizations help to correct them with sensitivity. That way guests leave feeling good about their overall experience and appreciating how the organization's personnel helped them redeem themselves. Imagine how depressed you would feel if you came back to the parking lot after a long day at an amusement park to find that you have lost your car keys and are locked out of your car. Then you see the park's "Auto Patrol" coming to your rescue. They even make you a new set of keys for free! Even though such problems are not its fault, the guest-oriented organization believes that the guest needs to be wrong with dignity. It knows that guests who are angry at themselves may transfer some of that anger to the organization. To overcome this very human tendency, guest-centric organizations find ways to fix problems so that angry, frustrated people leave feeling good because a bad experience has not been allowed to overshadow or cancel out all the good. By providing this high level of guest service, the hospitality organization earns the gratitude and future patronage of guests and enhances its reputation when such service successes are circulated to both external and internal customers.

Matching the Recovery Strategy to the Failure

The best recovery efforts match the nature and severity of failure. For example, if a restaurant is out of a certain menu item, compensating the guest with a "rain check" might be appropriate. If the failure is server inattentiveness, an apology by the manager would be a more appropriate response. Sometimes, customers demand more than is reasonable, and a company must respond while finding a way to stay within sensible limitations. For example, a customer claimed that a Starbucks store had sold him two defective coffee makers with a total value of $500, neglected to include a promised free half-pound of coffee, and treated him rudely. The customer was not satisfied by company apologies, replacement and refund offers, and gifts. His suggested recovery strategy was that Starbucks take out a full-page ad of apology in the *Wall Street Journal*, give him a $2,500 coffee maker, and fund a shelter for runaway children.[56] Needless to say, the customer's demands were not met.

Categorizing the severity and causes of service failures is a useful way to show the type of recovery strategy that a hospitality organization might select. In Figure 13-2, the vertical axis represents the severity of the failure ranging from low to high. The horizontal axis divides service failures into those caused by the organization and by the guest. When severity is high and the failure is the organization's fault, the proper response is the red-carpet treatment, as in the case of a sold-out hotel "walking" a guest with reservations to

FIGURE **13-2** Matching the Recovery Strategy to the Failure

© Cengage Learning 2012

a fully paid, upgraded room at another hotel. The organization needs to bend over backwards to fix this guest's problem and should consider trying to provide a wow level of recovery to overcome the negative feeling the guest will have after a severe failure. A less severe problem caused by the organization might be a server bringing to a guest a cold food item that is supposed to be hot. A fitting solution here is to apologize and replace the item quickly. Providing a complimentary dessert might also be appropriate. McDonald's has a policy that anyone bringing a food item back to the counter with the complaint that it is cold is immediately given an apology and a replacement item with no questions asked.

The two general situations in which the guest caused the failure provide terrific opportunities for the organization to make guests feel positive about the experience even when they caused the failure. In a low-severity situation, a sincere apology is sufficient and will make the guest feel that the organization is taking some of the responsibility for a situation that was clearly not its fault. Indeed, some organizations will do even more, if the cost to make a guest feel better is not too high. Many restaurants don't charge their guests for meals or items they don't like or want. Some photo developers have the same policy. The poor pictures may not be the developer's fault, but the customer feels good that the organization won't make customers pay for their own mistakes. The upper-right box represents situations where the problem is relatively severe and the guest or some external force created the problem. These are opportunities for the organization to be a hero and provide an unforgettable experience for the guest.

A Domino's delivery man showed up with pizzas at a house that was still smoldering from a devastating fire. The distraught couple, standing in the front yard of their ruined house looked up at the delivery man with some annoyance, said they hadn't ordered any pizza, and wondered if the delivery person couldn't see that they were overcome by the tragedy. The delivery man responded that he knew; he had passed the house earlier, saw it burning, and had told his manager. The two decided that it would be a kindness to cook up some pizzas and just give them to these people in their hour of sadness. The company became a hero to the couple—customers who didn't even know they were customers.

Learning from Failures

From a guestology view, a failure is an opportunity to improve. If the data collected show that older guests are having problems with reading the signs, then an organizational response would be to increase lettering size. If the data show that the source of customer dissatisfaction is other customers cutting in line, being too loud, or otherwise intruding on guest experiences, then policies and processes can be created to add rope lines, separate guests by a wider space, or institute cautioning measures. If the data show that the loyalty program is making promises on which the organization does not deliver, then the program must be revised to ensure that loyalty awards are easy to obtain, with accessible procedures, as valuable as promised, and actually available when desired. Finally, if the data show that the organization itself has policies, processes, and procedures that cause customer dissatisfaction or service failures, then it has valuable knowledge about what it needs to fix, improve, or change, what employee training to develop, and what innovations to make.

As is true of any data that report failures in any system, guest complaints are valuable and should be collected and analyzed regularly. In an interview with Bruce Laval, retired vice president for planning and operations for the Walt Disney Company, he was asked how he found the things to fix. His response, as the inventor of the term *guestology*, should be a guide to all who wish to create a guest-focused organization: measure what you want to manage and, especially, everything that touches or impacts the guest. In a company like Walt Disney, that includes everything they do.

Service Recovery: Ow! to Wow!

Companies that have invested in the formation and operation of units designed to handle complaints can realize substantial returns on their investment. Putting money and effort into service recovery is good business. A Disney saying is, "Turn tragic moments into magic moments." The best hospitality organizations view a service failure as a great opportunity to create an unforgettable, outrageously positive response. If the guest is upset that the hotel is overbooked and her room is gone by the time she arrives tired and ready for bed, the hotel should not only drive her to a nearby hotel with the price of the room paid but should consider upgrading her room from whatever she had reserved. This guest who was denied her standard room but got a paid-for night in a VIP suite at another hotel might readily forgive the hotel that failed to save her a room. The organization extended its hospitality to a guest, then failed her. It should go the extra mile and then some to repair the damage. The right failure-recovery strategy can turn an irate guest, ready to head for the competition, into a raving evangelist.

Consider the example of how CruiseWest managed a problem that was clearly outside their control, and turned it into a memorable experience. Scott, driving a tour bus with twenty-five guests, was traveling from Fairbanks, Alaska to Denali National Park for CruiseWest, a premium tour company. Suddenly, just outside Nenana, he was forced to stop at the end of a long line of busses from a number of other tour companies making the same journey. They were stopped because of a dangerous fire burning across the road in front of them, and there was no word on when it would be again safe to travel. Scott immediately called back to the supervisor in Fairbanks to report the situation. The supervisor told him to take the guests to a restaurant in Nenana while she sorted this out. While the group was dining, the supervisor called five bush pilots she knew of and arranged for them to fly to Denali. She then called Scott and told him to take the group to the Nenana airport where the bush pilots were now waiting, and who would fly the guests and Scott over the fire (and the fifteen waiting tour busses from the other tour companies). After the short flight, they landed near Denali at Healy where a bus picked them up and took them to their hotel to continue on with their scheduled tour activities. While this creative solution added nearly $10,000 to the operating cost of the tour, it was a far less expensive solution than what the other tour operators faced as they had to both reimburse their angry travelers for the unfulfilled trip experience and give them vouchers

CruiseWest, when faced with a potential service failure caused by circumstances out of its control, used a creative solution to get its guests to the cruise they had purchased and ultimately provide a "wow" experience for its guests.

© CruiseWest

for another trip. This creative and quick solution to what might have otherwise been a complete disaster for CruiseWest guests turned an "ow" into a "wow." In fact, these guests indicated on their comment cards that the flight over the fire was the highlight of the trip and they could hardly wait to tell all their friends what a great cruise experience Cruise-West provided. (As an aside, consider that the bus, and the unanticipated plane trip to Nenana, was really a "wait" for the real service product, the cruise. Because of the way the situation was handled, the guests actually ended up finding the wait for service to be a great moment on the trip!) A motivated and creative employee not only saved the trip and the costs of a major service failure but also created tremendous word of mouth for his company.

Even if you are not responsible for a failure, recovering is an important way to get the guest's attention with impressive service. When no one expects you to fix someone else's mistake and you do it anyway, people are wowed.

Successful Service Recovery

Although beginning a discussion with a definition is customary, we will end with one, by Michel, Bowen, and Johnston: Service recovery is "the integrative actions a company takes to re-establish customer satisfaction and loyalty after a service failure (customer recovery), to ensure that failure incidents encourage learning and process improvement (process recovery) and to train and reward employees for this purpose (employee recovery)."[57] If these recovery actions that the company takes are unsuccessful, then the company has added failure to failure. If the actions restore customer satisfaction and loyalty, then the recovery has succeeded from the customer's point of view, and that is the main thing. But from the company's perception, a truly successful service recovery will be a set of integrative actions that also improve the process and the employees involved. After successful service recovery, the people and the process are all better off.

LESSONS LEARNED

1. If the guest thinks you failed, you failed.

2. Fix their problems and most guests will come back; fix their problems on the spot and they will almost certainly come back.

3. Encourage guests to tell you about problems and failures; a complaint is a gift.

4. Train and empower your employees to find and fix failures.

5. Train your employees to listen with empathy.

6. Don't cause a service-failure problem and then fail to fix it. Don't fail the guest twice.

7. Find a fair solution, and know how guests determine what is fair.

8. Find ways to help guests fix problems they caused.

9. Unhappy guests will tell twice as many people about bad experiences as happy guests will tell about good experiences.

10. Even the best organizations fail a guest occasionally. Be prepared for failure; have a recovery strategy in place.

11. Find out and share with employees how much a dissatisfied guest costs; that will show your staff the importance of recovering from service failure.

12. Service-failure recovery works only if the system works; even an empowered employee can't recover from service failure without support from the system.

13. When you work to solve the service failure, also work to improve the service delivery system.

REVIEW QUESTIONS

1. Recall a service failure during a guest experience of your own.

   A. Describe the failure and your reaction to it.

   B. Describe the organization's response to the failure. Did your reaction to the failure seem to affect the organizational response?

   C. As a result of what happened, how do you feel about this organization now?

   D. If you were not completely satisfied, what could the organization have done to satisfy you and perhaps cause you to be even more loyal to the organization than before?

2. If you ran a hospitality organization, how would you plan to recover from failure?

   A. Would you give employees a list of common failures and their corresponding acceptable recovery strategies, or would you empower employees to use whatever recovery strategies they saw fit? Or both?

   B. Would you try to quick-fix problems immediately or look for longer-term solutions that might prevent future problems?

   C. What would be the characteristics of your service-recovery plan?

   D. One hospitality leader instructs employees to keep offering successively more significant remedies to failure until the guest smiles, then stop. Discuss this strategy.

3. Many service failures occurring during guest experiences at a hotel or at a restaurant can be predicted and fixed. Name two problems that a hotel and a restaurant probably cannot fix. What should the managers do if those failures occur?

4. A guest in your organization starts an argument with another guest who has tried to cut into a waiting line.

   A. Is this a service failure? If so, who or what failed? What should you as a manager do?

   B. If, rather than starting an argument, the first guest punches the second guest, what should you as a manager do?

5. Do you believe that a complaint is "a gift" from the complaining customer to the organization? If you have complained to organizations, has the reaction suggested that they believe you are presenting them with a gift?

6. According to this chapter, some experts suggest that apologizing for failures of which the guest may not even be aware might be a good idea. Do you agree?

ACTIVITIES

1. Have you experienced a recent service failure? If so, write a letter to the establishment's manager complaining about the dissatisfying or failed service experience you have had. (*Do not make up a false complaint!!!*) Describe how the organization responds to your complaint. How does the organization's recovery effort correspond to the suggestions for recovery offered in the chapter?

2. Write a letter to a local hospitality manager complimenting a service experience you have had recently. Send a copy to the company president. Report back on the results. It is okay to mention names in this letter.

3. Be on the lookout for a service failure that others are experiencing. Observe and report how the organization recovers from the failure. Evaluate the recovery strategy based on the material presented in the chapter.

4. Divide into groups. For those who have been employees, describe service failures in which you have been involved. Have you been trained in how to recover from these failures? What recovery steps did you take? Pick the best service recovery and compare with the best of other groups. What lessons can be learned from these successful recoveries?

5. Have a classroom discussion on the topic "Who is more responsible for most service errors: servers or managers?" (Remember that managers plan and implement delivery systems.) Go out to some local restaurants or other hospitality organizations and ask some servers and some managers this question, "What service failures do guests most frequently experience in your place of business, and who is more responsible for most of them: servers or managers?" and report back your results.

ETHICS IN BUSINESS

A certain restaurant has no policy in place about service recovery, and servers have no specific authority to provide any free products to customers. A server in the restaurant sees that an error occurred at her table. In order to keep the customers happy (and to protect her tip), she gives them free drinks without getting permission to do so from her supervisor. A friend who tends bar gives her these drinks when he can do so unobserved. The server feels justified in doing this because her regular salary is low, and she depends on tips from satisfied customers for most of her income. Is her behavior unethical? Does the cost of the free item affect the appropriateness of her actions? Free soft drinks cost the restaurant only pennies. Complimentary drinks from the bar are much more expensive, and alcoholic beverages make up a considerable part of the restaurant's revenue. Does the server's motivation affect your answer—giving the free items because she wants to protect her tips, versus wanting to ensure that her customers have the best possible experience?

A second restaurant does have the policy of ensuring customer satisfaction, and servers have the authority to remove the cost of a meal if a customer is dissatisfied. A patron complains that she did not like her meal, although she did eat it in its entirety, said nothing during the meal, and the server saw no indication of a problem during the meal. The server is suspicious that the customer knows the company's policy and is simply trying to get a free meal, but he has no evidence to support this beyond his gut feeling. What is the right course of action?

CASE STUDIES

Pizza-to-Go

Bob Callahan led a very hectic business life consisting of hard work, long hours, and eating on the run. Bob also liked pizza. It is therefore no surprise that he did a lot of business with his neighborhood Pizza-to-Go outlet. About once a week, just before leaving work, Bob would call PTG; order a medium thin-crust pizza with olives, sausage, and double anchovies; and pick it up on his way home. The PTG people once forgot the sausage and once put pepperoni instead of olives, but Bob forgave them and never mentioned these small slipups. He could do with a little less sausage in his diet, and he liked pepperoni almost as well as olives anyway. Besides, they never got the anchovies wrong, and Bob's favorite part of the entire pizza experience was the overabundance of anchovies swimming in mozzarella cheese.

Last week Bob got home from work and kicked back, ready to enjoy a beer and some pizza fixed "his way." The pizza he took out of the box was fixed somebody else's way; it was covered with olives, sausage, and what looked like a double order of onions. Bob couldn't imagine what kind of person would eat a combination like that. He called PTG immediately. The phone was answered by Vito Cifrese, who had been serving Bob regularly for about two years.

"Very sorry about that, Mr. Callahan. If you could just scrape those onions off this one time, next time you come in I'll comp you your regular order and I'll also throw in a small complimentary pizza with double anchovies for free!" Bob thought that was a pretty fair adjustment. He thanked Vito, scraped off the onions, and

tried to eat the pizza. But the onion flavor remained. Bob couldn't finish the pizza; the combination of olives, sausage, and onion flavor was too much for him.

That all happened on an early Monday evening. On Thursday of the same week, Bob called in and ordered the usual, plus a small pizza with double anchovies. When he got to Pizza-to-Go, Vito was nowhere to be seen. Bob identified himself to the counter server who handed over the two boxes. Bob explained that both items were to be "no charge" because of an error that had been made on a previous order.

The server laughed and said, "I don't think so. Check that sign out there. This is Pizza-to-Go. Pizza-for-Free is up the street."

Bob stayed calm and asked for Vito; he could straighten this out.

"Vito quit Monday night and said he never wanted to see another pizza."

"I've gotten one or two pizzas a week from you people for the past two years. My name's Bobby Callahan. Check under my name in your database and see if Vito left any special instructions."

"What database?" said the server.

Bobby gave up. He'd find another place to do business. "I'll just take the small pizza with double anchovies."

"You don't want the big one?"

"That's right."

"Even though you called in for it? Well, we can warm it up for somebody else, I guess, if anybody else wants a weird combo like olives, sausage, and anchovies."

Bob paid without tipping, left, got home, grabbed a beer, turned on TV, kicked back, opened the box, and took out a small pizza covered with onions.

★ ★ ★

1. Was service recovery called for in this situation?

2. If so, what recovery options would you have considered?

3. What should Bob Callahan do now?

Recovery to the Max

Ben Sharpless, manager of the tackle store at Farney Spa and Fish Camp, had just finished explaining to new sales employee Max Gilley the importance of getting and retaining customers, recovering from service failure, and other basics of serving guests, whether they were fisherfolk who also had spa privileges or spa patrons who wanted to do a little fishing. About an hour later, Ben saw Max talking with regular customer Sally Higgins. He thought he would monitor Max's sales technique, so he moved to a spot where he could hear but not be seen.

Sally Higgins was saying,

"Max, I thought I'd fish down at the bend where you can see them feeding on the bottom."

"Ms. Higgins, you don't want to fish for those little minners. You want to put your bait about 30 feet out, where the big ones are. Here, what about this Orvis reel with the matching graphite rod and tackle box full of lures and other gadgets? I think that'll do the trick. But fishing's even better on the other side of the lake early in the morning. We've also got a fully equipped camping rig here that I can let you use, with the tent, the stove, all the supplies you could ever need. You can camp out, turn in early, and be up and at 'em with the dawn." Ms. Higgins agreed that it was a beautiful rig. Visions of huge trout leaped in her mind. Visions of a big sale leaped in the mind of store manager Ben Sharpless.

"What kind of car do you have, Ms. Higgins? A Mercedes 300-SL, isn't it? This stuff isn't going to fit in there. We just received a special-order Land Rover with matching trailer. You'll look good in that, and you can haul all this camping and fishing equipment in the trailer with room to spare. We could let you use that for a couple of days."

Manager Sharpless was really impressed with Max's results. Max and Sally finished the paperwork, Sally Higgins left, and Sharpless went to Max Gilley to congratulate him on a big sale.

"Gilley, you're quite a salesman. I don't know if I would have loaned her all that fancy camping equipment and the Land Rover, but that Orvis rod and reel plus a fully equipped tackle box is a big sale, maybe several hundred dollars, so I guess it's worth it."

Max looked puzzled. "No, Mr. Sharpless, you got it all wrong. Ms. Higgins was just out for a walk. We started to talk, and she told me the spa was busted. Uh-oh, I say to myself. Service failure. I remembered what you told me: 'It costs several times as much to get a new guest as it does to keep a present guest, Max, so when you see any service failure, spa or fish camp, that service failure becomes yours to correct. You own that service failure until it's fixed, Max. And don't just fix it; go above and beyond. Anything we lose on that transaction will be made up in future business for the spa and fish camp. If we do lose money, what's the worst that can happen? We'll have a satisfied guest.' Wasn't that about it, Mr. Sharpless?"

Sharpless said, "Yes, Max, you learned well, but …"

"So I said to her, 'Since the spa is busted, why don't you go fishing?' Then I gave her the fishing tackle and the tackle box but I only loaned her the rest of the stuff. She seemed right happy, didn't she?"

Manager Sharpless sighed. "Max, if I hadn't been here, I guess you would have given her the whole darn tackle shop."

★ ★ ★

1. What do you think would have been an appropriate adjustment for this service failure? Or should a fish camp employee even be concerned about a spa service failure?

2. How can organizations encourage their employees to take ownership of service failures and try to fix them on the spot, without "giving away the store"?

Letter of Complaint

Consider the following letter of complaint, an actual letter written by the lead author of this book, and tell how you would respond to it if you received it.

⭑ ⭑ ⭑

Mr. P.D. Bacon

Chief Executive Officer

Sun International Limited

27 Fredman Drive

Sandton 2031 Gauteng

Republic of South Africa

Dear Mr. Bacon:

I am writing to tell of an experience I had during my recent visit to one of your resorts, The Zambezi Sun. I want you to know that my experience had good and bad points to it. The good points are largely attributable to two of your employees, Mr. Craig Storkey and Ms. Suzette Venter. The bad points are due to what seems to me to be policies and procedures that did not meet my expectations nor would I expect them to meet those of most American travelers. Thus, please consider this a letter of both compliment and complaint. Let me first detail the situation so you can see the reason for both my compliments and complaints.

In the late morning of June 24, my wife and I were standing in the porte-cochere of the Zambezi Sun in Victoria Falls, Zambia behind our transport to the airport. As I stepped back to avoid the downward closing tailgate of the transport van, a quickly moving jeep clipped my leg with its left side rear tire. Somehow, the tire grabbed my leg to make it stationary while it was wrenched and broken. While we do not know the vehicle number, we were later told it was a Zambian government vehicle. The result was two broken bones in my left leg. At the same time, apparently some hotel employees contacted both the hotel manager and the hotel clinic nurse.

The nurse did a competent job of calmly organizing my care. I was transported back to the hotel clinic (which had no working x-ray machine) and, while I was being interviewed by Zambian police about the accident, she called around to the local medical facilities to find a working x-ray so we could see the extent of damage to my leg. When she finally found one, she then contacted the local ambulance service to transport me. By this time the hotel manager had arrived and was talking to me in the clinic. He was reassuring and concerned. He told us that he would pay the ambulance fee cash requirement and put it on our bill so we could pay by credit card. We were concerned about how much cash we had to pay all that we had to in this cash-driven country. While we were surprised we would pay this fee, we appreciated his help.

The nurse was wonderful. After locating an x-ray and transport, she accompanied us to the Livingstone clinic where the doctor and x-ray were located. She was calm and reassuring throughout this ordeal. That was especially important to me and my wife as we contemplated the challenges of getting medical care in Zambia and then wondered how we would proceed from there to either home or our next medical treatment facility. After getting my leg x-rayed, the Zambian doctor put on a cast and told me I could travel onward. The nurse cautioned me that this might be a problem with a hard cast on an airplane so she persuaded the doctor to put on a cast that could be readily cut to relieve pressure while flying onward.

We then went back to the hotel where the manager had thoughtfully provided a room in the Royal Livingston for us at no charge. The nurse and he had agreed that I needed to stay on the ground that night in case any complications arose that would be harmful to my flying out. The nurse consulted with her supervisors in Johannesburg about what to do with me. They told her to Medivac me and would not approve any other means to transport me out of Zambia. Suzette then consulted with my travel insurance company which would not approve the fee for such transport. They told her that they would only pay for commercial transport and that if I wanted to go out by Medivac, it would be my financial responsibility. This is where the nurse really showed her medical expertise and decision making skills. Since she was able to assess my physical condition and also knew the financial considerations of the options, she patiently and skillfully reviewed what I could do next. After some discussion, we agreed that flying commercially to Johannesburg the next day to seek further treatment was the best choice for me to make.

We found the nurse's handling of my situation remarkable and want to commend her for it. First, her response to my injury was quick, calm, and competent. She made a bad situation tolerable and reduced our level of panic by her calm demeanor and obvious professionalism. She exuded competence. Second, her management of the various steps involved in getting treatment was terrific. She handled it all and made sure we knew what was happening all the time. Third, she helped tremendously in going through the various options we had to carefully consider to decide what to do next. While she had to respect her own leadership's directions as to what to do, she also had to consider our needs and circumstances and we always felt she was considering her patient's needs first. In other words, we were tremendously impressed with her competence, calmness, and professionalism. You are fortunate to have such a terrific employee and you need to know that.

Now, however, I wish to make a complaint about your procedures for handling such situations. Perhaps we in the USA have a distorted picture of what the responsibility of a hotel is in such a situation because of the volume of personal injury litigation we have. I may even be more sensitive to this because I teach, conduct management development seminars, research, and write in the academic field of guest services management. Further, I live in Orlando where the Walt Disney Company has become the world benchmark for guest service excellence. From all these perspectives, I feel your company has much work to do before it matches the standards expected by today's upscale American traveler. For example, no American I know would ever expect to pay for an ambulance to be taken from an injury suffered in the hotel's own porte-cochere. No American would expect to be taken to an upscale hotel clinic that had no working x-ray machine. No American would expect to be asked to pay for emergency medical treatment resulting from an injury on hotel property, and no American would expect the hotel to ask him/her to pay for the meals or telephone calls made while trying to notify all the people that had to be notified to get on to the next destination. While I am certain the manager did all he was authorized to do, I would strongly encourage you to authorize him to do more. In the USA, a hotel manager would typically have picked up all these costs hoping that by doing so he/she could make the guest feel better (and less litigious) about being hit by a car on hotel property. Most of these costs are fairly minimal, especially food costs, and would have made a difference in the feelings that at least this guest had towards the hotel.

As we teach in our classes, this is the type of service failure that every hospitality organization fears. Once it happens, however, the organization should do everything it can to make the failure as tolerable as possible. We call this, in my own textbook on guest services management, the red carpet treatment. While we greatly appreciated your manager's concern with our situation and his helpfulness in making arrangements to get us back to Johannesburg, we teach that a free room upgrade is only one part of the service-recovery effort available to recover from a major service failure like this.

While you may feel that I am overly influenced by what litigation has done to American hotel guest expectations, the point is that those are the expectations that your American guests now have and that you must meet if you wish to satisfy this market. I strongly urge you to revisit your procedures and consider revising them to meet the expectations of your guests no matter where they're from. In my opinion these are becoming the world class standards you must meet if you wish to be considered a world class hotel. There are many things that could have been done to mitigate the anguish I suffered, and world class hotels do the things that make a difference. I would encourage you to hold a simple brainstorming session with your general managers to consider failure scenarios and develop the best way to deal with various service failures like mine. This might help you think through the things that might have been done better here and which, for the most part, have nominal or little cost.

Thank you for the opportunity to share my thoughts with you. You have excellent people trying to do a terrific job in serving their guests, but based on my experience, your own procedures and service-recovery processes leave much to be desired. I hope you find this information useful and that you will publicly recognize the positive contributions that your employees made that made our bad situation less bad. My intent in sharing my complaint is to bring to your attention the need to think through the many other things that you might do to make this dissatisfied guest less dissatisfied. I think that a careful rethinking of some simple procedural changes would allow you to make this type of bad situation less bad for any future guests who suffer the misfortune I did. I urge you to take the time to consider them.

Sincerely,

Robert C. Ford, PhD

Professor of Management

★ ★ ★

1. What did the letter include or not include that a good complaint letter should contain?

2. What response should the hotel's CEO make to this letter?

3. How do you think the company actually responded?

4. Draft a response that you feel represents what the chapter teaches about how a complaint is a gift.

The Hillsbrook Lodge

During the busy times of the year—ski season and the period when the leaves turned—a portion of visitors to New England bed and breakfast establishments sometimes made reservations at two or even three B&Bs. They knew that some B&Bs customarily overbooked, and these guests wanted to be sure they didn't end up after a long drive without a place to stay.

The Hillsbrook Lodge followed the practice of the other bed and breakfast places in its area. During those busy times of the year, the Lodge customarily overbooked by 10 to 15 percent. At first, owners George and Audrey Spain didn't like to overbook; it seemed dishonest somehow. But the other owners were doing it, and the Hillsbrook Lodge couldn't afford to have anything less than 100 percent occupancy during the two periods of the year that enabled them to get sufficiently ahead financially to stay open during the leaner periods. Things usually balanced themselves out; the Hillsbrook Lodge overbooked by about 15 percent, and about 15 percent of the guests usually didn't show up.

The B&B owners in the area had a cooperative service-recovery plan. They networked and kept in touch, so that any owners finding themselves facing guests whose reservations could not be honored could usually make a few phone calls to find another acceptable accommodation for the guests nearby. But supply and demand did not always even out, so occasionally George and Audrey were in the uncomfortable position of telling guests with reservations that not only did they themselves have no room for the guests, but neither did anyone else in the area. Guests did not usually take that news very well. But under the pressures of the next day's activities, the George and Audrey forgot these incidents quickly.

When the prime autumn weekend for viewing the turning of the leaves came, Audrey and George found that they were grossly overbooked. In addition to the 15 percent overbooking that they had reluctantly agreed to, they had each carelessly booked parties without the other's knowledge. So by the middle of Friday afternoon, all ten Hillsbrook rooms were taken, with several parties yet to come.

A fashionably dressed woman and a large man came into the Lodge, announced that they were Bruno and Sophie Tattaglia from New York, and asked to check in.

"Hi, Mr. and Mrs. Tattaglia. Can I call you Sophie and Bruno? Welcome to Hillsbrook Lodge! We've got a little problem. More guests showed up than we thought we were going to get, so since we operate on a first-come, first-served basis, I'm sorry to say we're filled up. But I think I can find accommodations for you at one of the other B&Bs nearby. They're all quite fine."

Sophie Tattaglia protested, "But we had a reservation."

George said, "Well, unfortunately, a reservation doesn't always equal a room on one of the busiest weekends of the year. Let me make some phone calls and see what we can do for you."

George found accommodations for the Tattaglias about twenty miles away. "They don't have quite the view that we do, but it's a nice place," said Audrey. The Tattaglia couple was not smiling but they seemed to accept the situation. After they left, George said to Audrey,

"Well, that wasn't so bad. We recovered pretty well, I thought. I hope these next people coming up the drive are as reasonable."

When Mr. and Mrs. Tattaglia got back to New York, they were still irritated about the Hillsbrook situation. George and Audrey Spain had thought about setting up a page on the World Wide Web to make more people aware of the Hillsbrook Lodge, but they didn't really have the time or the expertise. Mrs. Tattaglia was self-employed as a creator of Web pages. It was easy for her to set up a Web page, available to anyone in the world who had a computer and an Internet connection, describing the Tattaglia experience at the Hillsbrook Lodge, soliciting other stories of negative experiences with the Lodge, and urging potential visitors to New England not to patronize the Hillsbrook.

★ ★ ★

1. Overbooking is common in some parts of the hospitality and travel industry. Can you justify overbooking on ethical grounds?

2. Did the Hillsbrook Lodge have any alternatives to overbooking?

3. Once George and Audrey find out about the Hillsbrook page on the Web, can you think of any service-recovery steps they might take?

Anderson, E. W. 1998. Customer satisfaction and word of mouth. *Journal of Service Research*, 1 (1), 5–17.

Andreassen, T. W. 1999. What drives customer loyalty with complaint resolution? *Journal of Service Research*, 1, 324–332.

Bamford, D., & Zystouri, T. 2005. A case study of service failure and recovery within an international airline. *Managing Service Quality*, 15, 306–322.

Bateson, J. 2002. Are your customers good enough for your service business? *Academy of Management Executive*, 16 (4), 110–120.

Bejou, D., & Palmer, A. 1998. Service failure and loyalty: An exploratory empirical study of airline customers. *Journal of Services Marketing*, 12 (1), 7–22.

Borle, S., Singh, S. S., & Jain, D. C. 2008. Customer lifetime value measurement. *Management Science*, 54, 100–112.

Chebat, J.-C., & Slusarczyk, W. 2005. How emotions mediate the effects of perceived justice on loyalty in service recovery situations: An empirical study. *Journal of Business Research*, 58, 664–673.

Cranage, D. A., & Mattila, A. S. 2005. Service recovery and pre-emptive strategies for service failure: Both lead to customer satisfaction and loyalty, but for different reasons. *Journal of Hospitality and Leisure Marketing*, 13 (3/4), 161–181.

Crie, D. 2003. Consumers' complaint behavior. Taxonomy, typology and determinants: Towards a unified ontology. *Database Marketing & Customer Strategy Management*, 11 (1), 60–79.

Davidow, M. 2003. Organizational responses to customer complaints: What works and what doesn't. *Journal of Service Research*, 5, 225–250.

De Jong, A., & de Ruyter, K. 2004. Adaptive versus proactive behavior in service recovery: The role of self-managing teams. *Decision Sciences*, 35, 457–491.

De Matos, C. A., Henrique, J. L., & Rossi, C. A. V. 2007. Service recovery paradox: A meta-analysis. *Journal of Service Research*, 10, 60–77.

Dong, B., Evans, K. R., & Zou, S. 2008. The effects of customer participation in co-created service recovery. *Journal of the Academy of Marketing Science*, 36, 123–137.

East, R., Hammond, K., & Gendall, P. 2006. Fact and fallacy in retention marketing. *Journal of Marketing Management*, 22, 5–23.

Ekiz, E. H. 2009. Factors influencing organizational responses to guest complaints: Cases of Hong Kong and Northern Cyprus. *Journal of Hospitality Marketing and Management*, 18, 539–573.

Glady, N., Baesens, B., & Croux, C. 2008. Modeling churn using customer lifetime value. *European Journal of Operations Research*, 197, 402–411.

Goodwin, C., & Ross, I. 1990. Consumer evaluations of responses to complaints: What's fair and why. *Journal of Consumer Marketing*, 7 (2), 39–47.

Grewal, D., Roggeveen, A. L., & Tsiros, M. 2008. The effect of compensation on repurchase intentions in service recovery. *Journal of Retailing*, 84, 424–434.

Gupta, S., Hanssens, D., Hardie, B., Kahn, W., Kumar, V., Lin, N., Ravishanker, N., & Sriram, S. 2006. Modeling customer lifetime value. *Journal of Service Research*, 9, 139–155.

Harris, K. E., Grewal, D., Mohr, L. A., & Bernhardt, K. L. 2006. Consumer responses to service recovery strategies: The moderating role of online versus offline environment. *Journal of Business Research*, 59, 425–431.

Helgesen, O. 2006. Are loyal customers profitable? Customer satisfaction, customer (action) loyalty and customer profitability at the individual level. *Journal of Marketing Management*, 22, 245–266.

Hocutt, M. A., Bowers, M. A., & Donavan, D. T. 2006. The art of service recovery: Fact or fiction? *Journal of Services Marketing*, 20, 199–207.

Huang, W. H. 2007. The impact of other-customer failure on service satisfaction. *International Journal of Service Industry Management*, 19, 521–536.

Kumar, V., Lemon, K. N., & Parasuraman, A. 2006. Managing customers for value. *Journal of Service Research*, 9, 87–94.

Lipp, J. 2008. Reward your best guests with simple, easy-to-use loyalty-building programs. *Nation's Restaurants News*, August 11, 22, 34.

Lorenzoni, N., & Lewis B. R. 2004. Service recovery in the airline industry: A cross-cultural comparison of the attitudes and behaviours of British and Italian front-line personnel. *Managing Service Quality*, 14 (1), 11–25.

Mattila, A. 2004. The impact of service failures on customer loyalty. *International Journal of Service Industry Management*, 15, 134–149.

McCole, P. 2004. Dealing with complaints in services. *International Journal of Contemporary Hospitality Management*, 16, 345–354.

Michel, S., Bowen, D., & Johnston, R. 2009. Why service recovery fails: Tensions among customer, employee, and process perspectives. *Journal of Service Management*, 20, 253–273.

Michel, S., & Meuter, M. L. 2008. The service recovery paradox: True but overrated? *International Journal of Service Industry Management*, 19, 441–457.

Moliner, M. A., Sanchez, J., Rodriguez, R. M., & Callarisa, L. 2007. Relationship quality with a travel agency: The influence of the postpurchase perceived value of a tourism package. *Tourism and Hospitality Research*, 7, 194–211.

Nguyen, D., & McColl-Kennedy, J. R. 2003. Diffusing customer anger in service recovery: A conceptual framework. *Australasian Journal of Marketing*, 11 (2), 46–55.

Reynolds, K. L., & Harris, L. C. 2005. When service failure is not service failure: An exploration of the forms and motives of "illegitimate" customer complaining. *Journal of Services Marketing*, 19, 321–335.

Schoefer, K., & Diamantopoulos, A. 2008. A typology of consumers' emotional response styles during service recovery encounters. *British Journal of Management*, 20, 292–308.

Simons, J. V., & Kraus, M. E. 2005. An analytical approach for allocating service recovery efforts to reduce internal failures. *Journal of Service Research*, 7, 277–289.

Stauss, B., Schmidt, M., & Schoeler, A. 2004. Customer frustration in loyalty programs. *International Journal of Service Industry Management*, 16, 229–252.

Tax, S. S., Brown, S. W., & Chandrashekaran, M. 1998. Customer evaluations of service complaint experiences: Implications for relationship marketing. *Journal of Marketing*, 62, 60–76.

Zhu, Z., Sivakumar, K., & Parasuraman, A. 2004. A mathematical model of service failure and recovery strategies. *Decision Sciences*, 35, 493–525.

[1]Stoller, G. 2009. Tarmac ordeal renews push for fliers' rights. *USA Today*, August 11, 3A.

[2]Michales, D. 2009. A Robin Hood for inconvenienced fliers in Europe. *Wall Street Journal*, August 13, p. D1, D4.

[3]Albrecht, A. 1988. *At America's Service: How Your Company Can Join the Customer Service Revolution*. New York: Warner Books, pp. 124–125.

[4]Keaveney, S. M. 1995. Customer switching behavior in service industries: An exploratory study. *Journal of Marketing*, 59, 71–82.

[5]For more research on customers' responses to service failures, see Dutta, K., Venkatesh, U., & Parsa, H. G. 2007. Service failure and recovery strategies in the restaurant sector. *International Journal of Contemporary Hospitality Management*, 19, 351–367; Leong, J. K., & Kim, W. G. 2002. Service recovery efforts in fast food restaurants to enhance repeat patronage. *Journal of Travel & Tourism Marketing*, 12 (2/3), 65–93; Lewis, B. R., & McCann, P. 2004. Service failure and recovery: Evidence from the hotel industry. *International Journal of Contemporary Management*, 16 (1), 6–17; Silber, I., Israeli, A., Bustin, A., & Zvi, O. B. 2009. Recovery strategies for service failures: The case of restaurants. *Journal of Hospitality Marketing & Management*, 18, 730–740.

[6]Berry, L. L. 1995. Relationship marketing of services–Growing interest, emerging perspectives. *Journal of the Academy of Marketing Science*, 23, 236–245; Hess, R. L., Jr., Ganesan, S., & Klein, N. M. 2003. Service failure and recovery: The impact of relationship factors on customer satisfaction. *Academy of Marketing Science Journal*, 31, 127–145.

[7]Silber, I., Israeli, A., Bustin, A., & Zvi, O. B. 2009. Recovery strategies for service failures: The case of restaurants. *Journal of Hospitality Marketing & Management*, 18, 730–740.

[8]Reichheld, R. R., & Sasser, W. E., Jr. 1990. Zero defections: Quality comes to services. *Harvard Business Review*, 68 (5), 105–111.

[9]For more discussion of the lifetime value of a customer and how to measure customers as assets, see the following: Bolton, R. N., Lemon, K. A., & Verhoef, P. C. 2004. The theoretical underpinnings of customer asset management: A framework and propositions for future research. *Journal of the Academy of Marketing Science*, 32, 271–292; Gupta, S., Hanssens, D., Hardie, B., Kahn, W., Kumar, V., Lin, N., Ravishanker, N., & Sriram, S. 2006. Modeling customer lifetime value. *Journal of Service Research*, 9, 139–155; Rust, R. T., Lemon, K. N., & Zeithaml, V. A. 2004. Return on marketing: Using customer equity to focus marketing strategy. *Journal of Marketing*, 68, 109–127; Reinartz, W., & Kumar, V. 2002. The mismanagement of customer loyalty. *Harvard Business Review*, 80 (7), 86–94.

[10]Berger, P. D., Weinberg, B., & Hanna, R. C. 2003. Customer lifetime value and strategic implications for a cruise-ship company. *Database Marketing & Customer Strategy Management*, 11(1), 40–52.

[11]Barlow, J., Møller, C., & Hsieh, T. 2008. *A Complaint Is a Gift: Recovering Customer Loyalty When Things Go Wrong*, 2nd edition. San Francisco: Berrett-Koehler; Crie, D. 2003. Consumers' complaint behavior. Taxonomy, typology and determinants: Towards a unified ontology. *Database Marketing & Customer Strategy Management*, 11 (1), 60–79.

[12]Hailey, L. 2009. *Lifetime Value Pays Small Business Dividends*, Dell.com accessed on line October 10, 2009, at Dell.com.

[13]Sewell, C., & Brown, P. B. 2002. *Customers for Life: How to Turn that One-Time Buyer into a Lifetime Customer*. New York: Pocket Books.

[14]J. A. Michelli, 2008. *The New Gold Standard: 5 Leadership Principles for Creating a Legendary Customer Experience Courtesy of the Ritz-Carlton Hotel Company.* New York: McGraw-Hill, p. 180.

[15]Loveman, G. 2003. Diamonds in the data mine. *Harvard Business Review*, 81 (5), 109–113.

[16]Hart, C. W. L., Heskett, J. L., & Sasser, W. E. 1990. The profitable art of service recovery. *Harvard Business Review*, 68(4), 153.

[17]Barlow, Moller, & Hsieh, 2008.

[18]Chebat, J.-C., Davidow, M., & Codjovi, I. 2005. Silent voices: Why some dissatisfied customers fail to complain. *Journal of Service Research*, 7, 328–342; Voorhees, C. M., Brady, M. K., & Horowitz, D. M. 2006. A voice from the silent masses: An exploratory and comparative analysis of noncomplainers. *Journal of the Academy of Marketing Science*, 34, 514–527.

[19]Kau, A.-K., & Loh, E. W.-Y. 2006. The effects of service recovery on consumer satisfaction: A comparison between complaints and non-complaints. *Journal of Services Marketing*, 20, 101–111.

[20]Tax, S. S., & Brown, S. W. 1998. Recovering and learning from service failure. *Sloan Management Review*, 39 (3), 76.

[21]Ibid., 83.

[22]Chebat, et al., op. cit.

[23]Weiser, C. R. 1995. Championing the customer. *Harvard Business Review*, 73(6), 113.

[24]Ford, R. C., Wilderom, C. P. M., & Capparella, J. 2008. Strategically crafting a customer-focused culture: An inductive case study. *Journal of Strategy and Management*, 1, 143–167.

[25]Hart, et al., 1990.

[26]Wirtz, J., & Mattila, A. S. 2004. Consumer responses to compensation, speed of recovery and apology after a service failure. *International Journal of Service Industry Management*, 14, 150–166; Wangenheim, F. V. 2005. Postswitching negative word of mouth. *Journal of Service Research*, 8, 67–78; Ward, J. C., & Ostrom, A. L. 2006. Complaining to the masses: The role of protest framing in customer-created complaint web sites. *Journal of Consumer Research*, 33, 220–230.

[27]Gregoire, Y., & Fisher, R. J. 2008. Customer betrayal and retaliation: When your best customers become your worst enemies. *Journal of the Academy of Marketing Science*, 36, 247–261.

[28]McCartney, S. 2007. Bumped fliers may get a better deal. *Wall Street Journal*, July 24, D1, D5.

[29]Gregoire & Fisher, 2008.

[30]Wirtz & Mattila, 2004; Wangenheim, 2005; Ward & Ostrom, 2006.

[31]Michelli, J. A. 2008. *The New Gold Standard.* New York: McGraw-Hill, p. 180.

[32]Jones, T. O., & Sasser, W. E., Jr. 1995. Why satisfied customers defect. *Harvard Business Review*, 73 (6), 88–99; La, K. V., & Kandampully, J. 2004. Market Oriented learning and customer value enhancement through service recovery management. *Managing Service Quality*, 14, 390–401; DeWitt, T., Nguyen, D. T., & Marshall, R. 2008. Exploring customer loyalty following service recovery. *Journal of Service Research*, 10, 269–281; O'Neill, J. W., & Mattila, A. S. 2004. Towards the development of a lodging service recovery strategy. *Journal of Hospitality & Leisure Marketing*, 11 (1), 51–64; McCool-Kennedy, J. R., & Sparks, B. A. 2003. Application of fairness theory to service failures and service recovery. *Journal of Service Research*,

5, 251–266; and Dutta, K., Umashankar, V., & Parsa, H. G. 2007. Service failure and recovery strategies in the restaurant sector. *International Journal of Contemporary Hospitality Management*, 19, 351–363.

[33]Silber, et al., op. cit.

[34]Silber, et al., op. cit.; Leong, J. K., & Kim, W. G. 2002. Service recovery efforts in fast food restaurants to enhance repeat patronage. *Journal of Travel & Tourism Marketing*, 12 (2/3), 65–93; Kau & Loh, op. cit.

[35]Lewis, B. R., & McCann, P. 2004. Service failure and recovery: Evidence from the hotel industry. *International Journal of Contemporary Management*, 16 (1), 6–17.

[36]Way, S. A., Sturman, M. C., & Raab, C. 2010. What matters more? Contrasting the effects of job satisfaction and service climate on hotel F&B managers' job performance. *Cornell Hospitality Quarterly*, 51, 379–397.

[37]Robinson, A. G., & Stern, S. 1997. *Corporate Creativity: How Innovation and Improvement Actually Happen*. San Francisco, CA: Berrett-Koehler Publishers, pp. 9–11.

[38]Taylor, K. 2006. When service means everything. *Association News*, November, p. 40

[39]Wirtz & Mattila, 2004.

[40]www.Fedex.com accessed October 10, 2009.

[41]Goodwin, C., & Ross, I. 1992. Consumer responses to service failures: Influence of procedural and interactional fairness perceptions. *Journal of Business Research*, 25 (2), 160. See also Tax & Brown, 79–81.

[42]Liao, H. 2007. Do it right this time: The role of employee service recovery performance in customer-perceived justice and customer loyalty after service failures. *Journal of Applied Psychology*, 92, 475–489.

[43]Tax & Brown, 81.

[44]Lind, E. A., & Tyler, T. 1987. *The Social Psychology of Procedural Justice*. New York: Plenum.

[45]See for example; Mattila, A., & Ro, H. 2008. Customer satisfaction, service failure, and service recovery, in H. Oh (ed.), *Handbook of Hospitality Marketing Management*. Oxford, UK: Butterworth-Heinemann, pp. 296–323; Karatepe, O. M. 2006. Customer complaints and organizational responses: The effects of complainants' perceptions of justice on satisfaction and loyalty. *International Journal of Hospitality Management*, 25, 69–90.

[46]Del Rio-Lanza, A. B., Vazquez-Casielles, R., & Diaz-Martin, A. M. 2009. Satisfaction with service recovery: Perceived justice and emotional responses. *Journal of Business Research*, 62, 775–781.

[47]Chang, C.-C. 2008. Choice, perceived control, and customer satisfaction: The psychology of online service recovery. *CyberPsychology & Behavior*, 11, 321–328.

[48]Ok, C., Back, K.-J., & Shanklin, C. W. 2005. Dimensional roles of justice on post-recovery overall satisfaction and behavioral intentions: Tests of casual dining experiences. *Journal of Foodservice Business Research*, 8 (3), 3–22.

[49]Wirtz & Mattila, 2004.

[50]Liao, 2007.

[51]Laraba, T. 2009. Southwest Servant's Heart. *Spirit Magazine*, September, 16.

[52]See Cranage, D. 2004. Plan to do it right: And plan for recovery. *International Journal of Contemporary Hospitality Management*, 16, 210–219.

[53]Gonzalez, G. R., Hoffman, K. D., & Ingram. T. N. 2005. Improving relationship selling through failure analysis and recovery efforts: A framework and call to action. *Journal of Personal Selling & Sales Management*, 25, 57–65.

[54]Hart, Heskett, and Sasser, 148–156.

[55]Ibid.

[56]Gregoire & Fisher, 2008, op. cit.

[57]Michel, S., Bowen, D., & Johnston, R. 2009. Why service recovery fails: Tensions among customer, employee, and process perspectives. *Journal of Service Management*, 20, 253–273.

CHAPTER 14

Service Excellence: Leading the Way to Wow!

HOSPITALITY PRINCIPLE: LEAD OTHERS TO EXCEL

Leaders think about empowerment, not control.

—Warren Bennis, Leadership scholar and author

If I tell you what to do, then the task is my responsibility, not yours. But if I inspire you to act on your own, the responsibility and results are yours. The difference in dedication is phenomenal.

—Norman Brinker, Former CEO, Chili's Restaurants

LEARNING OBJECTIVES

After reading this chapter, you should understand:

- The overarching framework of the three Ss—strategy, staffing, and systems.
- The difference between competing on service and competing on price.
- Why great future business leaders must also be guestologists.
- The challenges leaders of service firms will face in the future.
- The importance of innovation and managing change.
- The key factors for service leadership.
- The reasons why "it all ends with the guest."

KEY TERMS AND CONCEPTS

basic guest expectations	guest promise	service innovations
"wow" elements	"market niche of one"	transformational leadership

WHAT DOES THE GUEST WANT?

The logic behind guestology is simple. Study the guest, know what that person really wants and expects, and then provide it—plus a little bit more. A guestologist never stops studying the guest, using all the scientific tools available to know what that guest really wants, actually does, and truly values. Since guests change, and because service delivery is invariably a human process, the study is never complete. The service product, the environment, and the delivery system must also change to make sure that each guest is satisfied enough to come back. Leaders of outstanding guest service organizations spend much time and effort studying the guest and using this information to shape their decisions on the three Ss: strategy, staffing, and systems.

We have already covered a lot of ground in this book. We shall conclude by showing how the leader brings it all together and makes it happen both for today's guests and for all future guests.

STRATEGY

In this era when an amazing amount of information about guests and competition in providing services to those guests is available, only organizations that truly understand what guests want will survive and prosper. They first use this information to design a corporate strategy. They discover which of their competencies guests consider core and concentrate on making these core competencies better. They use the wants, needs, expectations, and capabilities of guests to sharpen their marketing strategies, budgeting decisions, organizational and production systems design, and human resource management plans and practices.

Southwest Airlines is an excellent example of a company that has used its understanding of the guest to discover and then provide what its passengers really want. Like most organizations, the airline originally used guest surveys to ask what guests wanted. Southwest learned that guests wanted cheap fares, on-time performance, great meals, comfortable seats, free movies, and more. They quickly recognized that, human nature being what it is, if you ask people what they want—they want everything.

Southwest realized it couldn't give its customers everything because nobody could. Gourmet meals with wine in big comfortable seats and low fares—it can't be done. So Southwest did additional research to dig deeper into guest preferences and learned that customers really wanted low fares and reliable schedules with friendly service. The Southwest service product is now exactly what its target market wanted and, more importantly, wanted enough to pay for and return to again and again. The point is that the guestologist must dig deeper than the simple market survey of guest preferences to understand what preferences actually drive guest behavior. The organization can use the results from this deeper probing to match up the organization's core competencies and mission with what customers want. Even better for Southwest, giving guests what they want provided extra cost savings to Southwest; turning an airplane around between arrival and departure is considerably easier, faster, and cheaper without having to clean up all the mess and clutter caused by unwanted frills like food service.

The Key Drivers

The outstanding guest service organizations have done what Southwest has done. They study their guests extensively to discover what the guests both want and value in the guest service experience and use this information to align all the elements of their corporate strategy with these expectations. On the basis of studying their targeted guest market, these organizations can identify the key drivers of the guest experience. These key drivers all contribute to the impression that the guest takes away from the experience and play a large role in determining whether that guest will return. A trip to a theme park, or a visit to a restaurant or hotel, is a holistic experience to most people; excellent guest service organizations do the research necessary to identify all the separate components of this whole experience. Then, they manage those components.

Drivers: The Basics

In a sense, these key drivers can be divided into two categories. The first group includes those basic things that guests expect the organization to provide if it is to operate in the particular market segment. A resort hotel must have attractively decorated, clean hotel rooms with the expected amenities like flat screen television and good room service. A casual-dining restaurant must have good and reasonably priced food, fair waits, an appropriate number of adequately competent servers, clean rest rooms, and relatively prompt service. Guests expect these characteristics at a minimum. These are **basic guest expectations** that the organization must meet; otherwise the guest will be dissatisfied. If the organization fails habitually to meet these basic expectations, it will fail altogether. The basic characteristics are the necessary *but not sufficient* guest experience aspects that organizations must offer if they seek the reputation that attracts repeat business and leads to long-term success.

Drivers: The Wows

The second group of drivers includes the characteristics and qualities that make the experience memorable. These are the **"wow" elements** that the excellent organizations find ways to provide in some or all parts of the guest experience. These organizations go beyond meeting the basic expectations with which guests arrive when they come in the door or onto the property to have a service need satisfied. They add the wow elements that make the experience memorable. It is the memorable experiences that compel guests to return again and again, and even motivate guests to become evangelists for the company who will tell all their friends about these exceptional organizations.

Disney, Olive Garden, The Ritz-Carlton, and most other guest service organizations continuously survey their guests to find out how well they can provide the basics that guests expect. However, these outstanding organizations go beyond the surveys to dig deeper to identify which key drivers provide guests with a wow experience.

For example, Disney knows that its guests expect transportation to travel from one part of the Walt Disney World Resort complex to another. Disney surveys its guests to make sure that they are satisfied with the transportation system. On the other hand, no one comes to the Walt Disney World Resort to ride a bus, and the transportation system seldom shows up in guest surveys as a source of satisfaction (except for the monorail), nor do guest opinions about the transportation system predict guest intent to revisit Disney. Even when the bus transportation isn't up to the guest's level of expectation, that minor service failure shows no relation to overall satisfaction or with intent to return. Unless the bus service is outrageously poor, dangerous, or grossly unsatisfactory in some other way, it has little or no impact on how guests react to the overall Disney experience. In contrast, the guest's perception of the quality of the rides and attractions, the dazzling nature of the fireworks displays, and the friendliness of cast member interactions with guests are highly correlated with guest satisfaction and intent to return, so they—and not bus service—become the focus of managerial concern: they are the key drivers.

Study, Study, Study

The point is that you don't know what factors in the service product, the environment, and the delivery system are the key drivers of guest satisfaction and intent to return until you carefully study all the possible drivers. Many times, what management learns in such studies is a surprise because what management thought would be keys when it designed the components don't turn out to be so from the guest's point of view. This difference between what the organization delivers and what the guest expects is the service gap that Len Berry identified, and it happens. No matter how much experience an organization has in surveying and studying guests, it will still be surprised occasionally by what guests say is really important to them or what they actually do regardless of what they say.

Accumulating Information

Excellent guest service organizations study their guests extensively and also accumulate the information they have learned about guests, individually and collectively. Computerized databases and sophisticated techniques of database analysis allow the organization to know a great deal about its guests, either as a demographic or psychographic group or as individuals. The best organizations mine these databases to dig up as much as they can about what is important to their guests so they can ensure that what is expected is provided.

A Key Driver: Personalize

The outstanding guest service organizations that attract repeat customers have an added advantage; they can accumulate information on their frequent guests and use this information to further customize the guest experience. In other words, they know that a key driver is to personalize the guest experience (everyone wants to be special and treated like an individual) in ways that make an emotional connection with the guest. Intelligent use of a customer database allows the best to get better at delivering this sort of personalized service. Guests like, feel good about, and want to return to organizations that give them personalized treatment. Customizing each guest's experience to match the guest's unique needs and expectations is becoming increasingly easy.

The Ritz-Carlton is one of the best, but others are finding innovative ways to build a relationship with each customer based on powerful computer analysis of customer information. While personalizing is not easy with a high-volume, mass-produced experience like a theme-park attraction designed to appeal to 20,000 or more guests from all over the world every day, these data-based systems are making it easier for service settings like hotels and even restaurants to provide individualized guest interaction. Epcot's Spaceship Earth, for example, takes a picture of each guest at the beginning of the ride that its technology allows it to use later in an interactive segment of the ride. In that segment, after guests are presented questions by an on-board computer about future life style preferences, the technology finds and superimposes the guests' faces onto characters in an individualized in-car video that offers guests a personalized glimpse into how their chosen lifestyle will look in the future. Making every guest feel special is an important way for an organization to differentiate its guest experience from all others. Finding out what makes that person feel special is one role of a guestologist.

Knowing what makes each guest feel special enables guestologists to add the wow factor that all guest service organizations want to provide to keep their guests coming back time and time again. The wow is the difference that the little bit more than the guest expected can make; it can turn the satisfactory experience into a memorable one and can keep the organization at the top of the customer's mind when thinking about where to go the next time that particular guest service is desired. Wows can be built into the service product, the environment, the service delivery system, or across all parts of the service experience. Based on the knowledge about how guests' likes and dislikes impact their emotions, the designers of the experience can build in those elements they expect will give the wow. They should, however, always follow up to find out if they were successful and, if not, should try to find out where and why they failed.

At Dorney Park

"Wows" don't have to be expensive, complicated, or elaborate, although they may be. Dorney Park in Allentown, Pennsylvania, provides good examples of both a relatively inexpensive and a relatively expensive wow experience. The less expensive illustration is in their "Camp Snoopy" section of the park. While many rides are available for small children, Dorney also provides two simple, yet sizable, play areas. These areas are filled with small stones, so sand doesn't get into children's clothes and shoes. While these areas certainly aren't a major feature of the park, they provide a simple inexpensive experience that appeals to some children. If the children play there long enough, they'll likely have the chance to meet Snoopy, Charlie Brown, or another of the Peanuts characters. This creates a wow experience from a low-tech attraction.

At the other extreme, Dorney Park invests millions in its roller coasters. A recent addition, *Possessed*, hurtles the rider up (and then back down) two vertical spikes each with a 180 degree twist, with speeds reaching 70 mph. The purpose of the attraction is to provide an exhilarating ride, and the screams from the guests indicate that Possessed elicits a wow reaction.

Plan, Plan, Plan

Providing the guest with both the expected basic parts of the guest experience and the wow factors is the result of extensive planning. And as we know, planning starts with knowing the guest. Capacity and location decisions, the design of personnel policies, the selection of production equipment—all must be based on the organization's best estimates of what kind of experience the guests want, need, and expect from the organization as well as their capabilities. For example, if the organization's mission is to provide a theme park experience, then the first issue to resolve is where to build the physical plant and how big to build it. If the organization's mission is to provide a casual-dining restaurant experience, then it must identify what food tastes, portion sizes, price points, locations, exterior appearances, and restaurant size it should have. These decisions can be correctly made only if based on solid and extensive market research, and guestologists use the best data they can find to make them. While many guest service operators still base these decisions on hunches and their own personal preferences, the outstanding ones always start with the guest and make sure that every decision is based on a thorough knowledge and understanding of the guest.

Get Constant Feedback

The best organizations also know that this discovery process is never ending; they constantly seek feedback from their guests about what works and what doesn't. Guest needs, wants, expectations, and capabilities change, and the best organizations respond to their guests' changes with changes of their own. Those organizations that constantly seek to exceed guest expectations build in their own future challenges. Today's wow is tomorrow's standard expectation for the guest who has been there and done that. The outstanding organizations are constantly seeking new ways to wow their guests, and they survey guests constantly to find out what these changing expectations are.

Planet Hollywood, in Orlando, Florida, has two separate floors with their own kitchens, making it an ideal environment for testing different service strategies or menu items.

The Planet Hollywood in Orlando, largest in the chain, has two kitchens—one for each floor. It is therefore a nearly perfect experimental site for testing new menu items, portion sizes, and other service product features. Since the guests are typically tourists who randomly distribute themselves between the two dining levels, different menu strategies and concepts can be tried and compared to see which are best suited for the Planet Hollywood customer. The ability to constantly test and compare new ideas gives the food production people at Planet Hollywood a statistically valid approach to finding new ways to wow their guests.

Culture Fills the Gaps

One last, but critically important issue in the strategy area is the organizational culture. Managers of outstanding hospitality organizations need to remember the importance of the organizational culture in filling in the gaps between what the organization can anticipate and train its people to deal with and the challenges that arise in the daily encounters with a wide variety of guests. There is no way to anticipate the many things guests will do, ask for, and expect from the service provider. The power of the culture to guide and direct employees to do the "right thing" for the guest is critical. Good managers know that the values, beliefs, and norms of behavior that the culture teaches its employees ensure that the frontline employee does what the organization wants done in both planned and unanticipated situations.

The culture must be planned and carefully thought through to ensure that the message sent to all employees is the one the organization really wants to send. An important part of any strategy is to ensure that everything that the organization and its leadership writes, says, and does is consistent with the culture it wishes to define and support. The more intangible the service product, the stronger the cultural values, beliefs, and norms must be to ensure that the guest service employee provides the quality and value of guest experience that the guest expects and the organization wants to deliver.

STAFFING

People Make the Difference

The second S, staffing, has become an increasingly important factor for all guest service organizations as they realize that the most effective way to differentiate themselves from their competitors is on the quality of the service encounters that their customer contact personnel provide. In this day of widespread computerization and standardization, competitors can readily imitate the service product, the physical elements of the environment, and the technical aspects of the delivery system. It does not take long for one service organization to duplicate the successful differentiating factors of another. A chicken fajita wrapped in a soft tortilla that someone can hold while driving a car is an innovation for only as long as it takes competitors to offer one-handed fajitas in their drive-thrus as well. People, not fajitas, usually make the difference.

Getting the Right People for the Job

The challenge is to find, develop, and motivate the server to engage each guest on a personal, individual basis while still maintaining production efficiency and consistent quality in the service delivery process. Roller coasters at any major amusement park operate at a fast pace. The ride attendant greeting the arriving guests has just enough time to check the safety harnesses and tell each guest, "Keep your arms and hands inside the car, sit down, and watch your step when entering the moving sidewalk." This encounter is highly mechanical and too short for the employee to do much more than repeat the scripted and important information before the next guest arrives and needs to be reminded of the same safety precautions. Repeating the same little speech feels to employees very much like working on the assembly-line job of Detroit automakers and Akron tire producers. About every six seconds a new guest, car, or tire arrives; the employee has to do or say something briefly, then the guest, car, or tire disappears down the assembly line to another worker's station. How can this job be made fun, interesting, and important? While the ride attendants at least have the benefit of human contact rather than contact with a tire or an auto, making such jobs fun can be a challenge for both managers and employees.

Finding the right people and putting those people in these routinized jobs suited for them eliminates many of the problems in delivering high-quality guest experiences. People who are just good at and enjoy quickly establishing personal contact with guests can be identified through effective selection techniques. Nevertheless, even with the right types of people in these sorts of roles, these jobs can take an emotional toll on employees as well. Therefore, the best companies know they must find appropriate people who can be trained with the skills necessary for effective service delivery and motivated to perform exceptionally. While many processes are involved in the process of delivering exceptional employee performance, the best hospitality companies know that it begins with hiring the right people.

Server Responsibilities

Recall that servers have three responsibilities in the guest experience: They deliver the service product (or in many cases co-create it on the spot), they manage the quality of the encounters or interactions between the coproducing guest and the organization, and they identify and fix the inevitable problems. Too many organizations train employees only for the first of these responsibilities and neglect the other two. In many instances, receiving the service product is just one element in the guest's determination of the quality and value of the guest experience. Servers must also be trained to deal effectively with the variety of knowledge, skills, abilities, personalities, and emotional states that different guests will bring to the guest experience.

Selection of the right person for the job starts by clearly defining the job requirements. If you want a ticket seller, then you must hire a person with a certain set of skills and a certain temperament. If you want that person to be a vacation planner and also sell tickets to implement these plans, you look for an entirely different person. Any job has knowledge, skills, and ability requirements; the organization's challenge is to find the "ideal employee" who fits these requirements. Such employees can and should be identified so that the employment decision can be made properly. Selecting the right people and placing them in the right jobs is one critical key to ensuring the quality and value of the guest experience.

Training

The second part of the staffing issue is training. The right person in the right job must be trained to perform the job correctly and consistently. Many jobs in the guest service industry are repetitive, simple, or boring. They also require incredible attention to detail and concentration on task performance so that the employee provides the same service experience in the same flawless way for each guest. It is easy for employee Dave Johnson to zone out, daydream, or otherwise lose interest in saying "Thank you for visiting Epcot" to the 20,000th guest. By that time his legs are tired, his attention span is short, and his interest in greeting one more person with a friendly smile and positive eye contact is about zero. Part of Dave's training should include how to cope with the emotional as well as the physical nature of the job. When the encounters are short—as at a fast-food drive-through window, convention check-in, or entry point for a theme-park attraction—the training challenge is particularly difficult.

Satisfaction from Satisfying

Similar jobs exist in the industrial sector, and job rotation, job enlargement, and job enrichment strategies have been tried with varying levels of success. The advantage guest service organizations offer to employees over most industrial settings is the presence of the guest and the positive feedback and stimulation that dealing with guests can bring. Once an employee learns how to derive satisfaction from doing something that makes a guest smile or finding ways to make a child happy, that employee gains a memorable experience. These sorts of experiences give service employees a "something" to remember that increases their enjoyment of the job, as well as stories that they can take home and talk about. Not only did they make wow memories for their guests, but in doing so, made wow memories for themselves. An important contribution to job satisfaction for most hospitality employees is the opportunity to create satisfaction for their guests.

Many hospitality organizations have discovered that some of their best employees are older, retired people. They are often lonely, bored, and are looking for opportunities to develop positive contact with other people. Hospitality jobs are especially good at providing this particular opportunity to them. Some organizations that recruited older people because of labor shortages have found to their pleasant surprise that older people bring an enthusiasm for providing service that makes them great employees.

If you just *process* people, you get discouraged and bored in many hospitality jobs. If you *engage* people, the job becomes interesting. The challenge here is the short-cycle jobs where guest contact is so fleeting that the opportunity to engage guests is nearly nonexistent. As a contrasting example, consider the wait staff in a fine-dining restaurant. With their longer time of contact, employees can use various interpersonal skills to make the job personal, fun, and fulfilling for themselves and their guests. Because they have the time, they can interject their personalities to make the whole service experience a function of their own ability to provide a memorable guest interaction.

Loading a high-volume ride at Six Flags or serving a fast-food customer is a different matter and a far greater challenge for both employees and management. Guests usually don't have time to notice employees and their contributions to the quality of the guest experience. The level of employee engagement and the subsequent satisfaction with providing exceptional customer service are considerably less, and these are the jobs that create the biggest challenges for managers seeking to provide their employees with jobs that are fun, interesting, and important. Their challenge is to find ways to give each employee the opportunity to be unique, recognized, and noticed as an individual by the guest without compromising the speed and efficiency of the production process used to deliver the service product.

Trust the Technology or the People?

Future employees will expect more job challenges and increased opportunities to be responsible for the guest encounter. Future managers will have increasingly efficient mechanized production and delivery systems available to them with which to meet job challenges.

Managers may have to choose between trusting these systems and trusting their employees to provide a high-quality and consistent service experience for their guests. The need to trust the employees will intensify as the competition for talented employees becomes greater. Good employees want to take the responsibility, and successful organizations will find ways to preserve the quality and value of the guest experience while empowering their employees to be responsible for guest satisfaction.

Setting and Reinforcing the Standards

The third part of the staffing issue is the management responsibility to set performance standards and reward employees who meet them. Managers must master the skill of goal setting to define job responsibilities, the standards of performance, and management expectations to employees. These must be clearly spelled out, reinforced, and rewarded by managers every day. Once a manager lets an employee provide service of less than outstanding quality, overlooks poor employee performance, or lets a "bad show" situation continue, the message goes out to everyone that managers don't always really mean what they say about providing high-quality guest service. Just as a guest has many moments of truth during the course of a single hospitality experience, employees have many moments of truth with managers every day. What happens during these moments of truth tells the employees a great deal about what management really believes in. The words and actions of all managers are where the organizational mission statement, corporate culture, and corporate policies about guest focus become real. Just as one employee at one moment of truth can destroy the guest's perception of the entire company, one supervisor who overlooks one violation of quality standards or poor job performance can destroy the way that employees look at the organization's mission. While most organizations have effective selection techniques and appropriate job training, many fall short in their commitment to continuous reinforcement. When they let things slide, they miss the chance both to reinforce the positive and to coach away the negative aspects of employee performance.

The best managers provide regular employee feedback, setting and reinforcing the company's high standards.

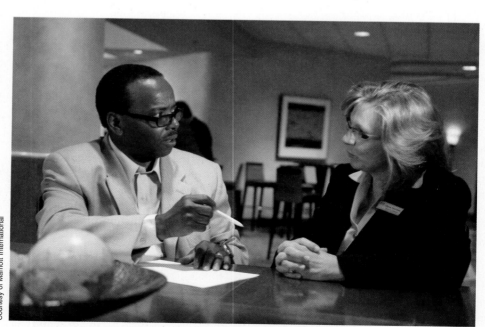

Courtesy of Marriott International

Disney's policy of requiring its managers to spend time in the parks walking the walk and talking the talk is a vital part of how the message is sent to employees that everyone is responsible for guest service, including them. This policy also builds a sense of equality among the employees in that everyone is there to serve the guest.

At Olive Garden

Ron Magruder, former president of Olive Garden, told the story about visiting some of his restaurants in Houston to see how they were doing. He arrived at one restaurant right at the peak of the lunchtime crowd and immediately learned that the store manager was swamped. Two of her cooks had not shown up, and the restaurant was full of hungry and impatient customers. Ron, finding the manager in the kitchen trying to cook as fast as she could to keep up with orders, took off his coat, grabbed an apron, and joined her on the cook line. In the middle of this chaos, a phone call came in for the manager. It was another manager asking her if she had seen Ron yet. She tersely told the other manager not to bother her with such questions while the president of the company was working beside her at the next grill. The story got out rapidly, and there was no doubt in anyone's mind where Ron Magruder stood on customer service or the cultural values of Olive Garden. These kinds of stories do a powerful job of reinforcing the organization's commitment to its guest service mission, and they should be told.

Employ the Guest

Just as organizations can benefit from thinking of their employees as customers or guests, they can also benefit from thinking of their customers as employees. Like employees, guests must be recruited, motivated, sometimes trained, and given the opportunity to "perform." Defining customers as quasi-employees gives the organization a different way of both looking at and thinking about their customers.

While customer performance—purchasing behavior—is what companies fundamentally need from their customers, the guests can serve several other important functions. They can give helpful feedback to the organization regarding their level of satisfaction with the

Darden's Olive Garden has a strong commitment to customer service, reinforced not just by words, but by the actions of their managers.

Courtesy of Darden Restaurants

guest experience. In effect, they can be knowledgeable unpaid consultants. Guests are typically part of the service environment and help create the service experience for other guests. If being surrounded by other guests is an important part of each guest's experience, then how the guests are employed in helping to create each other's experience becomes an important part of the management process.

Most importantly for hospitality organizations, customers almost always have to coproduce hospitality experiences in some way. Knowing when we should or should not allow, encourage, or require the guest to coproduce the service experience is an important management decision. Guests can be required to create the salad they like at the salad bar, encouraged to clean up their own trash at the quick-serve restaurant, or allowed to check themselves out of the hotel. If the service delivery system is properly designed to ensure an excellent guest experience by accommodating varying guest skills and capabilities, these coproduction strategies can benefit both the customer and the hospitality organization. The organization saves on labor costs, and knowledgeable, capable customers are likely to get a greater value from the hospitality experience served "their way" because they helped to produce it. In addition, they don't have to wait for service because they are producing it themselves.

SYSTEMS

The last *S* comprises all the organizational systems that support the guest experience. The best people in the world trained to perfection can't satisfy a guest if they deliver a bad product or deliver a good product late. In a huge, complex system like Walt Disney World Resort or a simple system like Ralph's Restaurant down on the corner, the whole system needs to be carefully managed so the right product is delivered to guests according to their expectations. Guests don't care that the bed sheets are not clean yet because the laundry broke down, that the organization forgot to rotate its stock so the eggs went bad, or that the person responsible for solving their problem is on break. They just want hot, fresh, properly cooked eggs, a clean room and a comfortable bed after a tough day on the road, and someone who will respond promptly to a legitimate concern. If these things don't happen, then the production system, the support system, the information system, or the organizational system has failed, and someone had better fix it fast.

Systems and Guestology

The most highly developed technical applications of guestology can be found in the systems area. Models of guest behavior in many situations can be built and used to understand and predict the ways in which the organization can satisfy the guest's expectations. Simulations are an important technique for achieving this, and with the increasingly user-friendly software packages, simulations will become more available and relevant to all types of hospitality organizations.

Once the planning process has gotten the design right and the measurement systems are in place to solicit guest feedback, the stage is set to use simulations of the entire guest experience to determine whether it all works as a system. By knowing what guests will do, Disney can make sure that the right capacity has been built into the attractions and all other features in the park, from rest rooms to telephones to merchandise outlets, to handle the number of guests expected on the design day. The design-day selection and the parameters used for the design day (such as the fifteen-minute average wait) drive the rest of the capacity decisions to ensure that the "designed" experience can be provided to the guests. Since the Disney design day is set at a high level of attendance, most guests on most days will experience a better-than-design-day experience because the lines will be shorter than designed capacity everywhere, from rest rooms to the best attractions.

The Wait

In many hospitality organizations, the most visible part of the guest experience is the wait for service. The wait system, therefore, requires extra organizational time and attention to ensure that the inevitable waits are tolerable and well within the limits that guests will accept without becoming dissatisfied. Waiting periods are easily modeled and studied with simulation techniques and easy-to-use computer software. Everything from the number of urinals at a football stadium, to the number of front-desk agents at a hotel, to the number of seats on an airline route or a theme park attraction can be simulated based on guest demand data. If you know how many guests are coming to your place of business and can estimate a predictable distribution to represent their arrival patterns and times for service, modeling how the waiting experience can be managed and balanced against capacity is relatively simple.

The management of waiting time is important both from the capacity standpoint and from the psychological standpoint. Since few organizations can build enough capacity to serve peak demand periods, and few hospitality organizations can stockpile their mostly perishable and intangible product, managing the wait is critical for all hospitality organizations. The greater the perceived value of the guest experience, the longer the guest will wait. Again, this area can benefit greatly from empirical research. How long guests will wait for anything before they give up and leave can be studied, measured, and understood. Some guests will wait hours to get into the hottest night-clubs or the trendiest restaurants. In contrast, they won't wait long at restaurants such as McDonald's, so that the organization knows it has to monitor drive-thru times constantly and follow strict procedural standards so that food is delivered quickly. Where virtual waits can be used in place of an actual wait, both guests and organizations will benefit.

The management of strategy, staffing, and systems is the key to guest service excellence. They all count when creating a memorable guest experience, and they are all related. Making any strategic change will necessarily impact the service product, the environment, and the service delivery system. Ultimately, though, it all starts with the guest.

HOSPITALITY AND THE FUTURE

People Making the Difference

The division between those hospitality organizations that figure out how to engage employees and those that use employees only from the neck down will widen. Value added to guest experiences through the skills of employees will become a more important differentiating strategy as the decreasing costs and increasingly available technology make the hospitality product and service delivery system components (except for people) increasingly easy to duplicate and emulate by all competitors. If all burgers taste alike and cost the same, then the "feel-good" part of the burger service experience becomes an increasingly important part of the total. Advertising alone can't provide this difference and, in fact, may be counterproductive if guests don't get what the glowing ads lead them to expect.

Employees make the difference between simply providing a service product and co-creating one that has the emotional connection that produces the memorable wow experience. The quality of employee encounters with guests will determine whether customer experiences are just a disappointment, satisfactory, or the type of exceptional experience that builds the positive word of mouth and repeat business on which everyone in the hospitality industry depends. If your guests are at least 70 percent repeat customers, as is true at the Walt Disney World Resort, you must be doing something right and, if their continued repeat business is vital to your organization's survival, you had better find a way to keep doing it.

Service or Price

Service organizations will increasingly compete on service or on price. A successful group of organizations in every service sector will seek to add value to each guest service experience (like at one of The Ritz-Carlton Hotels) or seek to define value on price alone (like a Red Roof Inn). By making sure that they focus on a particular niche of the market, advertise to that niche, and then ensure that they fulfill what they promise to do, these companies (like RyanAir, JetBlue, or Southwest Airlines) will thrive. The effective use of new technology and techniques in the service delivery system will allow those organizations that seek to focus on a price-conscious market niche to succeed in appealing to and satisfying this market segment. The efficient users of high technology will find ways to offer low prices, provide some unexpected technology-enhanced services to wow their customers, and still make money. The high end of the various service markets will succeed for the same reasons. They too will use technology, but for them technology is only a means to the end of providing the maximum amount of service their guests expect at a reasonable price for the service level. Both types of organizations will rely on technology to deliver the best value to their guests in the most efficient way. They will, consequently, make money through their efficiency where the less efficient competitor will fail. They can increasingly customize the product to each guest's expectations at the price point plus offer a little bit more as they can provide their employees with the necessary information to personalize the service in a prompt, friendly, and efficient way.

The hospitality businesses in the mass market between these two ends of the spectrum will have the most difficult challenge in the future as many are already having today. They will be challenged in offering guest services as personalized as the service-oriented firms in the marketplace have been able to offer and which guests now expect, while providing the low prices which the price-oriented firms in a competitive marketplace have also led guests to expect. This middle group of organizations seeking to serve the mass market may do neither very well. They may find themselves in the position of overpromising and underdelivering, which is not the way to have satisfied, loyal, or repeat guests.

Keeping Promises

The excellent guest service organizations of the future will use every tool at their command to figure out what the guest wants and then provide it in a way that is consistent with the guest expectations of value and quality. If they promise a high-quality experience and friendly service, they had better provide them or the customers will not come back. Most service organizations depend on repeat business, and to fail their guests will cost them dearly in a competitive marketplace. Once you tell your customers what you will do for them, you've made a commitment and a promise. If the **guest promise** is broken or the commitment unrealized, guests will be unhappy and will tell everyone they know how unhappy they are. Few organizations can afford to break their promises, and the more a guest service organization depends upon repeat business, the less chance it can take of violating that trust. Information and opinions about service quality are freely available now and will become even more widespread in the future. If a dissatisfied guest posts a negative comment on the Internet about your service, that

INDEX